Historical Knowledge in Biblical Antiquity

Historical Knowledge
in
Biblical Antiquity

Edited by

Jacob Neusner
Bruce D. Chilton
William Scott Green

BLANDFORD FORUM

Published by Deo Publishing
P.O. Box 6284, Blandford Forum, Dorset DT11 1AQ, UK

www.deopublishing.com

Copyright © 2007 Deo Publishing

All rights reserved. No part of this publication may be reproduced, translated, stored in a retrieval system, or transmitted in any form or by any means, electronic, mechanical, photocopying, recording or otherwise, without prior written permission from the publisher.

British Library Cataloguing-in-Publication data
A catalogue record for this book is available from the British Library

ISBN 1-905679-00-9 / 978-1-905679-00-3

Contents

Preface vii

1. The Task of History for Ancient Israel
   Bruce Chilton 1

2. Does History Matter?
   Meaning-making and the First Two Greek Historians
   Carolyn Dewald 33

3. Are the Dead Sea Scrolls Historical Texts?
   Lawrence H. Schiffman 53

4. History-Writing in, and on the basis of, the Jewish Apocalyptic Literature
   George W.E. Nickelsburg 79

5. Encountering the Past through the Works of Flavius Josephus
   Steve Mason 105

6. The Idea of History in Rabbinic Judaism:
   What Kinds of Questions Did the Ancient Rabbis Answer?
   Jacob Neusner 139

7. Interpreting Legal History in the Mishnaic Division of Agriculture
   Alan J. Avery-Peck 175

8. Archaeology and History: What Archaeology Can Show about Ethnic and Religious Regions in Ancient Galilee
   Mordechai Aviam (with William Scott Green) 196

9. In Search of Jesus: Issues of Character
   Bruce Chilton 216

10. Paul's Thought and Life
    Bruce Chilton 249

11. James, Jesus' Brother, and History
    Bruce Chilton 278

12. Mary Magdalene and History
    Bruce Chilton 302

13. Paul and Gamaliel
    Bruce Chilton and Jacob Neusner 329

14. Historical Questions and Questioning History:
    Can We Write a History of Judaism in Late Antiquity?
    Gary G. Porton 374

15. Different Ways of Looking at Truth
    William Scott Green 405

Index of Authors 416
Index of Scripture and Ancient Writers 422

Preface

Historical knowledge involves two distinct matters, both of which concern us in these pages. They are (1) What do we know about the past, and (2) why is that knowledge important? First come the facts of what we (think we) know about the past and how we know them. In that context historical knowledge is comprised by an account of precisely how things were. Critical challenges to historical sources separate fact from fancy. The second concern is with what we conceive historical knowledge to consist of, the conceptions of history and why the patterns of the past matter. In this other context historical knowledge expresses ideas of history and forms part of the living culture of the community described historically.

We begin with historical conceptions in ancient Israel and Greece. Then, for biblical antiquity, Judaism in its formative age from the fourth century BCE to the seventh century CE, and Christianity in its three centuries, we take up both questions: what was the role of history then, and what is the shape of contemporary, critical historical knowledge of that age today? The former question involves the idea of history in biblical antiquity, the latter, the outcome of historical study of biblical antiquity for present-day culture, with special attention to religion and theology.

A simple example suffices to distinguish the two kinds of historical knowledge treated here. First: What do we know and how do we know it? – the study of the facts of history that contemporary study yields produces critical biography, for instance, the historical Jesus as distinct from the Christ of faith. Second: Of what does historical knowledge consist? The writings of Judaism and Christianity contain conceptions of history and pattern. The study of conceptions of history and biography as Scripture portrays them shows history as a cultural indicator, revealing the character of the community that accounted for its past in one way rather than in another. What do we learn about a religious community from how it accounts for itself over time? These represent the two distinct matters of which historical knowledge is comprised.

Let us now start back with some basic definitions. History, the study of the past aimed at producing a coherent narrative to explain the present, bears a heavy burden. It is asked not only to report on precisely what has happened but to explain and justify why. History is assigned the task of mediating between contending claims on the present. It is expected to justify change or to forestall change. History appeals to the past as a source of right and wrong, good and evil, transforming secular facts into indicators of value and meaning and truth. At stake in evaluating the evidence of the past is identifying the precedents for contemporary reconstruction and reform. Critical transactions of contemporary conflict – issues of politics and culture, the validation of ancient grievances and the resolution of deeply embedded tensions – refer to the patterns of the past.

No wonder, then, that religions too appeal to the language of the past. They offer their accounts of what, among all the diverse things that form the record of historical narrative, settles questions of God's truth. In the monotheist traditions, Judaism, Christianity, and Islam, the resort to history in the form of narratives of state and society, on the one side, and stories of saints and sinners, on the other, takes a central role in theological discourse. Secular facts of history concerning what really happened are adduced to settle theological claims to religious truth. That fact surprises, since history speaks of singular moments in a determinate past, and theology of eternal verities that transcend time and particularities of location. Yet the story of the formation of God's people in Judaism forms a historical narrative from creation to the destruction of the first Temple in 586 BCE, in the biblical books of Genesis through Kings. So too, the account of God incarnate in Jesus Christ in Christianity takes the form of biography in the Gospels. The record of God's revelation to the Prophet ending the age of darkness and marking the age of Islam in the particular setting of the time and place of that revelation takes the form of narratives of one time events. So all three religious traditions derive from the study of the records of the past that use coherent narrative to explain the present that we know as history, encompassing biography.

Historical knowledge finds its place in the religious discourse of the monotheistic faiths, and secular critical considerations intervene. That presents no surprise. The reason is simple. Religious truth appeals to Scripture's historical records of what prophet and people did in response to divine imperatives: the history of God's relationship with holy Israel. So too the imperatives of God incarnate come under secular study in contemporary reading of the Gospels. The study of revelation and tradition takes the language of past-tense history in Islam.

Two distinct realms of thought religious and secular thus intersect. The record of Scripture presents the claim; historical research evaluates it. Criticism based on hard data enters into theological negotiation. Thus Scripture narrates the story of the Exodus of Israel from Egyptian bondage. God intervenes throughout the narrative. But the story concerns things that actually happened – secular facts participate in theological debate. So historians in the service of archaeology go in quest of the detritus of Pharaoh's chariots at the bottom of the Sea of Reeds to which the narrative of the Exodus refers. The Gospels set forth the life and teachings of Jesus Christ. Historical biography undertakes to designate out of the record of the Gospels the words he really said and the deeds he really did. Criticism again intervenes.

The stakes could not be higher. Acutely contemporary issues of politics and theology define what is at stake. Contemporary cases register. In the dispute between the State of Israel and Palestine the historical claims as to secular fact of each party to the conflict to legitimate possession of the Land are supposed to settle questions of right and wrong. History is what is asked to determine the rights of possession from Abraham's response to God's initiative in remote antiquity or from conquest, whether in the eleventh or tenth BCE by Joshua, the seventh century CE by the Arab Muslims, or the twentieth century CE. The contemporary Palestinians and the Israelis frame their contention in terms of historical narrative. Each party tells its tale, which scarcely intersects with that of the other. So history finds itself enlisted in the political struggle, itself framed in theological as much as secular terms. And the same pattern of struggle over facts of the past overspreads Christian theology. The protracted debate between Protestants and Catholics concerning church order comes to expression in appeals to what really happened. Theology asks, but history answers, the questions of the ages. For instance: How many and which sacraments did Jesus himself institute? Did Peter really serve as the founding bishop of Rome? Nor should we neglect the historical narrative that accounts for the primacy of the third Rome in Russian Orthodox Christianity.

It is in the context of contemporary debates in historical and biographical language concerning theological truth that we turn to biblical antiquity, roughly the four centuries BCE and CE that produced Judaism and Christianity. We seek to understand the role of the patterns of the past that validated the competing readings of the common Scriptures, the role of historical thinking in the theological enterprise that yielded the dominant religion of the West, Christianity, and its in-house competition, Judaism.

In those centuries Judaism as it would flourish in the West, formed of Scripture as reshaped by the Rabbinic sages of the Mishnah (c. 200 CE), the two Talmuds (c. 400, 600 CE), and Midrash (c. 200–600 CE), took shape. Christianity, expressed in its orthodox, catholic system by the Bible, the Old Testament and the New Testament, came to realization. Judaism here is defined as the mythic and narrative form of monotheism that appealed to the Hebrew Scriptures of ancient Israel ("the Old Testament") as the record of God's relationship with humanity and the interpretation of those Scriptures by successive generations of Israelites. Christianity is defined as the mythic and narrative biography of Jesus Christ that is contained in the Gospels and other components of the New Testament in dialogue with the Hebrew Scriptures of ancient Israel (the Bible, comprised by the Old Testament and the New Testament).

This brings us back to our starting point, the two foci of historical knowledge in biblical antiquity: what happened, why it matters. We bring to Judaism and Christianity in their formative age a set of fundamental questions concerning history. These take two forms. First, we want to know about the role of historical writing in the Judaic and Christian documents of the formative age: what narratives register and with what consequence for the theology of formative Judaism or Christianity? That is a question concerning the role of historical thinking in religious systems of the West. Second, we ask about the outcome of historical study of the Judaic and Christian documents: what do we really know about the religious systems of Judaism and Christianity in historical context, what sort of historical writing about the formative age – the shape of Judaism in the ancient setting, the story of the historical Jesus and other principals of earliest Christianity – becomes possible for contemporary sensibility? The two registers in which we speak thus treat history-writing as a cultural variable in the literature of formative Judaism and Christianity and history-writing as a critical enterprise in the discourse of contemporary Judaic and Christian scholarship.

We begin with an account of history-writing in the Scriptures of ancient Israel. These are universally and rightly characterized as historical. The Hebrew Scriptures of ancient Israel, all scholarship concurs, set forth Israel's life as history, with a beginning, middle, and end; a purpose and a coherence; a teleological system. All accounts agree that the Israelite Scriptures distinguished past from present, present from future and composed a sustained narrative, made up of one-time, irreversible events. All maintain that, in Scripture's historical portrait, Israel's present condition appealed for explanation to Israel's past, perceived as a coherent sequence of weighty events, each unique, all formed into a great chain of meaning. Professor Chilton's essay portrays the tasks of history in ancient Israel.

The second culture that asked historical writing to bear a heavy burden of thought and analysis – to yield insight for public policy and politics – was the Greek, represented by Herodotus and Thucydides, the former the founder of history in the West, the latter the first great practitioner. Professor Dewald's account of the tasks of history in ancient Greece completes our account of the foundations of historical writing and thinking in pre-Christian and pre-Judaic antiquity.

When we come to ancient Judaism, we take up a number of kindred religious systems, not a single, coherent Judaism. Rather, we deal with a variety of writings that do not intersect and that represent, each on its own, a distinctive viewpoint and sensibility. These distinct collections are four: (1) the Dead Sea Scrolls, (2) the apocalyptic literature attached to the Hebrew Scriptures of ancient Israel, (3) the historian of Judaism and the Jewish War against Rome of 66–73, Josephus, the only important historian in the framework of the formative age of Judaism, and [4] the Rabbinic sages' writings, the Mishnah, Talmuds, and Midrash. Each body of writing has to be read independently of the others, for the four distinct sorts of writing intersect only in Scripture and do not cite one another or acknowledge the presence of the competing groups that produced those writings.

To all these writings we ask the same questions: What is the role of historical inquiry in the canon at hand, and what kind of history becomes possible on the basis of that canon? Professor Schiffman asks our question with precision: Are the Dead Sea Scrolls historical texts? Professor Nickelsburg reviews the way in which the apocalyptic writings attached to the ancient Israelite canon dealt with historical perspectives and facts: How they did history, if they did history? Professor Mason addresses the works of Josephus and describes his program in the context of Scripture and Graeco-Roman historiography alike. This writer turns to Rabbinic Judaism, the religious system that is portrayed by the Mishnah, a philosophical law code concluded in 200 CE, the Talmuds of the Land of Israel, c. 400 CE, and of Babylonia, c. 600 CE, that comment upon the Mishnah, and the Midrash-compilations, collections of comments on selected work of Scripture of the same period. What conception of history governed, if any, and what ideas other than historical ones guided the encounter with the past that sustained Judaism in its normative writings? The conception of history and the competing conception – a theological and philosophical one – do not exhaust the account of history in formative Judaism. It concerns the history of formative Judaism. Professor Avery-Peck undertakes the other half of the project, the writing of history on the foundations of the ancient documents. He specifies as his own the task of comprehending the factors that explain why the law emerged as it did and of identifying the ways in which the evolving law supported the particular social, theological, and political program of those who shaped it. Finally, Professor Green turns our attention from literary to archaeological evidence. He asks that evidence to respond to the same question addressed to the literary record: What kind of history do these sources sustain?

As the senior editor of this project, I decided to assign to a single scholar the entire task of explaining the conception of history in formative Christianity and of describing the kinds of history that can be contemplated. I took as principal the issue of the kinds of history that are possible on the basis of the literary evidence of formative Christianity, with stress on the Gospels and the letters of the apostle Paul. This focus on the oeuvre of one scholar was done with good reason. Because he had produced four distinct approaches to the study of history and biography and theology in formative Christianity I asked Professor Chilton to present four distinct answers to the question: What kind of history, with what outcome, emerges from the New Testament?

Professor Chilton has completed the most original and complex, subtle and nuanced set of answers to that single question that has emerged in the recent past.

He has produced a new model of a life of Jesus in his *Rabbi Jesus: An Intimate Biography* (New York: Doubleday, 2000), sidestepping the established agenda of scholarship on the historical Jesus. His is the biography of the inner life of the man, a profound response to the Gospels' narratives in their Judaic context.

He has produced a new way of pursuing intellectual history, this time an intellectual biography of the apostle Paul, in his *Rabbi Paul* (New York: Doubleday, 2004). What made this work urgent was the systematic correlation of the ideas Paul put forth in his letters and the narrative of the Christian community and the culture of the locations from which, and to which, he wrote those letters.

Third, he gathered the scattered evidence concerning James, the brother of Jesus, and composed the data into an account not only of the life but also of the religious and theological system of James. This he did in *The Brother of Jesus: James the Just and His Mission* (Louisville: Westminster John Knox, 2001).

Finally, he turned to a completely different problem of historical biography in *Mary of Magdala* (New York: Doubleday, 2005). Mary of Magdala yields no sustained biography – the historically useful data are sparse – but serves as a cultural indicator. That is because those who wrote about her use her as an occasion to express their own theological position. What people across time have said about Mary of Magdala tells us about the concerns of those that told stories about her. There is no likelihood of their recording historical facts rather than cultural myths. How to deal with not traditions of Mary of Magdala but traditions about her is worked out in this book. So Professor Chilton addresses four distinct problems of history, biography, the interplay of ideas and the social order (Paul), historical theology and self-revealing culture, and has produced four solutions to those problems. His solutions are diverse, original, and compelling.

The traditions of Judaism and Christianity in the formative age intersect, and how to derive historical data from the one body of writing for the subject of the other body of writing requires a variety of procedures: literary criticism, legal study, interior politics of each community of heirs of the common Scriptures. To show what is required, Professor Chilton and I undertake a technical problem in the study of Paul in the context of the law of the Mishnah. Paul says he studied with Gamaliel, the Pharisaic master of Jerusalem. The house of Gamaliel forms a venue in the Mishnah's account of the law. In our account of the methods of using Rabbinic literature of law for historical purpose, we include our effort critically to correlate the Rabbinic traditions about Gamaliel and his household with the Christian traditions about Paul's Jerusalem years. The upshot is another – a fifth – exercise in showing what kind of history is possible.

When we speak of history as a cultural indicator, we refer to our own times and circumstances first of all. To show what we mean, we turn to the concluding essay, by Professor Porton, which turns outward, to the scholarship of the past fifty years on the history of formative Judaism. He places the specific essays in this book into their larger context. He surveys the debates that have flourished, asking "whether the 'new historians' from the ranks of the post-modernists, deconstructionists, and cultural studies scholars raise questions and employ methods that open up avenues for us to travel to gain new insights into the Jews and Judaism of late antiquity or whether their approaches are irrelevant to us because of the nature of the materials we have available and the types of questions which we must ask."

I invited Professor Green to read the book from start to finish and to reflect on its results in the epilogue. He saw everything whole and complete and placed the parts into a single coherent perspective.

This book came into existence to provide readings for a religion and theology seminar and conference at Bard College on historical knowledge in biblical antiquity, offered by Professors Chilton, Dewald, and myself. We secured the support of the Dean of the College, Michele Dominy, who funded a conference to which we invited the specialists represented in these pages. The students in the seminar Students in the seminar studied the papers reproduced in this book, wrote papers on them, responded to them at the conference, held April 25-27, 2006, at Bard, and, finally, presented their own papers on problems of historical knowledge in ancient Judaism and Christianity.

We could not have carried out this project without the support of Bard College and the active cooperation of our colleagues from other universities: Professors Schiffman, Nickelsburg, Mason, Avery-Peck, Green, and Porton, who took our program of questions seriously and responded to them out of their specialized knowledge, on which we depended. This is one in a series of seminar/conference projects sponsored by Bard's Institute of Advanced Theology, in which we carry forward the College's commitment to active scholarship in undergraduate education.

Jacob Neusner
Research Professor of Theology
Senior Fellow, Institute of Advanced Theology
Bard College
Annandale-on-Hudson, NY 12504-5000, USA
neusner@webjogger.net

1

The Task of History for Ancient Israel

Bruce Chilton

Introduction

Scholars of the Hebrew Bible have recently engaged in intense and sometimes acrimonious debate between "maximalists" and "minimalists." The former group sees a great deal of actual history behind the Scriptural accounts of such formative events for Israel as the exodus, the giving of the Torah to Moses, and the entry into the land of promise. The latter group conceives the apparent history of the Hebrew Bible as a literary construction of a much later period, perhaps as belatedly as the second century BCE.

In their most extreme expressions, neither position appears tenable. Numbers in the Hebrew Bible, for example, are notoriously hyperbolic. The estimate of 603,550 Israelites (apart from Levites; Num 2:32-33) crossing the wilderness around 1300 BCE defies plausibility, in that no ancient source apart from the Pentateuch refers to what would have been a remarkable and wrenching migration. But it is also extremely difficult to imagine a single author, centuries after the time of Abraham (c. 1800 BCE) making up three different stories of his sacrificial covenant with Yahweh (Gen 15; 17; 22), each of which corresponds very well to covenantal practices attested in non-Israelite sources from the ancient Near East.

In remarks soon to be published, Eric Meyers has traced the archaeological dimensions of this dispute:[1]

---

[1] He wrote much of the material in *The Cambridge Companion to the Bible* (H.C. Kee, ed.; Cambridge: Cambridge University Press, 1997); part one, which treats of the Hebrew Bible, represents his work with J.W. Rogerson. I am in the process of preparing a revised edition of the *Companion*, and Professor Meyers wrote these paragraphs (and that cited below) at my request.

The controversy most often referred to as the "maximalist-minimalist debate" originated in the early 1990's, with the publication of a series of books and articles (including Philip Davies' *In Search of Ancient Israel*) that questioned the viability of the Hebrew Bible as a source for the reconstruction of ancient Israel's history. In the course of a few years, scholars from Europe and England also began to question whether even archaeological data could be used to reconstruct Israelite origins prior to the period of the David and Solomon. When viewed from the perspective of the history of scholarship, this debate is a natural outgrowth of the tension that has built for generations between archaeologists working in Israel for many years and biblical scholars since the time of Wellhausen who dated the redaction of the Hebrew Bible during the Exile or later. Most biblical archaeologists during the twentieth century, including Albright, Wright, and Glueck, accepted the historicity of the patriarchs, dating them to the beginning of the second millennium BCE. But by the 1970's scholars not only began to doubt the existence of the patriarchs and matriarchs, but also sought out Israel's origins within the indigenous population of Canaan at the very end of the Late Bronze Age (during the 13th century BCE) and the beginning of the Iron Age (c. 1200 and later).

An Israeli archaeologist named Israel Finkelstein provided an unlikely ally in the deconstruction of the history of early Israel; his surveys and excavations led him to doubt whether there had been an occupation of the central hill country prior to the eleventh century BCE, and whether some key archaeological data used to support the existence of a strongly centralized kingdom (such sites as Beersheba, Dan, Hazor, Gezer, Jerusalem, and Megiddo) had been correctly dated. In lowering the ceramic chronology for dating these sites, he questioned the existence of monumental remains from the tenth and ninth centuries, consequently undermining the case for a strong, urban Jerusalem and key cities prior to the eighth century.

More extreme elements in biblical circles began to suggest that the Persian and even the Hellenistic periods were when Israel's history was composed (not just edited), and that the biblical materials could be used only with the greatest of caution in respect of ancient Israel. The strident tone of some exchanges has created confusion in the field, and while archaeologists are generally in agreement in regard to the existence of a united monarchy under David and Solomon (pace Finkelstein and his few followers), their conceptions of Israelite origins are diverse. Biblical scholarship remains deeply divided concerning the use of relatively late, post-exilic sources to reconstruct pre-exilic history.

The debate between these two schools of thought has illustrated the problem of applying a modern definition of history to ancient sources of most kinds. Those who produced those sources simply did not accept the standards of evidence and proof such as became conventional from the time of the Enlightenment during the eighteenth and nineteenth centuries, which saw the triumph of a positivistic historiography.

The sources

Before one can make any judgment whatever in regard to what events the biblical sources might reflect, one needs to have a clear sense of what those sources are and what their nature is and the purpose they embody. This chart of biblical literature and chronology sketches the development of the documents as commonly understood in scholarship, and the timing of the events implicit within them:[2]

CHART OF ISRAELITE LITERATURE AND CHRONOLOGY
(with approximate dates)

PATRIARCHAL AGE (2000–1300)	oral production of patriarchal stories, cultic legends, and foundation epics
AGES OF MOSES, JOSHUA, JUDGES: Clan period (1300–1000)	early poems (for example Exod 15, Judg 5, Ps 29, Deut 33, Gen 49)
THE UNITED MONARCHY: Saul, David, Solomon (1010–922)	early poems in 1–2 Samuel
	some Davidic psalms
	earliest versions of court history
DIVIDED MONARCHY (922–587/6)	oldest prose of Pentateuch: "J" (920),
10th and 9th centuries	"E" (850)
8th century (Fall of Northern Kingdom, 722/1)	Amos (760–750); Hosea (750–721)
	early prose parts of Former Prophets
	First edition of Isaiah [chs. 1-39] (742–700)
	Micah (740–690)
7th century (Josiah: 640–609)	more psalms produced
	Zephaniah (630–625)
	First edition of the source "D," principally parts of Deuteronomy
	most of Jeremiah (627–582)
	Nahum (612–610)
	Habakkuk (625–598)
EXILIC PERIOD (587–539)	parts of Jeremiah
	early edition of "D" (Deut-Kgs, by 586)
	Ezekiel (593–565)

[2] This chart represents my revision of the *Companion*, collated with the work of Eric Meyers and John Rogerson.

	compilation of Peutateuchal materials, including "P," as well as Proverbs (between 560 and 450)
POST-EXILIC PERIOD (538 BCE–70 CE) Return from exile, 538–516 (Restoration with the beginning of Persian Period)	Second Isaiah [chs. 40-55] (538–522) Haggai (520) First edition of Zechariah [chs. 1-8, and including the earlier prophecy of Haggai] (520–518)
Persian Period (516–332)	Job (5th or 4th cent. BCE) Third Isaiah [chs. 56-66] (500–450) Malachi, Joel, Obadiah (5th cent. BCE) Second edition of Zechariah [chs. 9-14] (5th cent., or later according to many scholars, some of whom locate chs. 12-14 during the Hellenistic Period) Ezra/Nehemiah, Chronicles (450–350) Final shaping of Proverbs (400) Jonah, Ruth, Song of Songs (4th cent. BCE)
Hellenistic Period (332–164)	Former & Latter Prophets collected together as a whole, and canonization of the Pentateuch Esther Ecclesiastes (250) Translation of Pentateuch into Greek (beginning in 250) Translation of Pentateuch into Greek (beginning in 250)
Maccabean period: in 164 BCE Judas Maccabeus sees to the restoration of the cult of Yahweh in the Temple and establishes a dynasty nationally allied with the Romans in 161 BCE which extends the borders of Israel to cover the greatest territory ever by the end of the century.	Daniel (165) Final compilation of Psalter, and canonization with the Prophets, composition of 1 Maccabees (during the 2nd cent. BCE)
Roman Period (63 BCE, when Pompey claimed Jerusalem and Israel for Rome, until the 4th cent. CE)	Close of canon of Hebrew Bible, with continuing shaping of the Psalter, by 200 CE.

Because the dispute between "maximalists" and "minimalists" has typically turned on the interpretation of the Pentateuch (the five books attributed to Moses), that is a good point of access to the issue of Israelite history. A consensus of scholarship – not universal by any means, yet very broad – places the Pentateuch's final composition during the fifth century BCE, with the addition of a specifically Priestly source, which provides direction for the conduct of sacrificial worship. The Pentateuch projects an ideal Israel, according to the regulations of Moses, which became a canonical standard. Torah was now written, and it offered the key for the constitution of Israel.

The materials within the priestly source were, of course, not simply invented during the fifth century. Earlier sources had already been composed. During the tenth century BCE, the Temple constructed by Solomon had become a new center of the understanding of Israel and therefore a focus of the codification of tradition. In addition to the "Court History," an account of David's reign produced shortly after his death (2 Sam 9–1 Kgs 2), the source within the Pentateuch known to scholarship as "J" was produced. "J" (named after its putative author or authors, the "Yahwist" [earlier spelled with a "J" in the Latin or German manner]) first linked, in literary form, the people of the Davidic kingdom with creation, the patriarchs, the exodus and the possession of the land. From the outset, God is known as "Yahweh" in this source.

Earlier, shorter books had been compiled to be recited at cultic centers, so that a treaty, or regulations of purity or ethics, or alleged genealogical connections, or victories and other formative events might be remembered in association with sacrifice at any cultic center. But Jerusalem became the preeminent sacrificial center under the protection of the Davidic dynasty, and that involved the collection of these materials during the tenth century, and an early attempt to present them more coherently, for use in the Temple (and the royal court) during the feasts that were primarily celebrated there.

After Solomon's death, united Israel was divided in 922 BCE into Israel in the north and Judah in the south. 1 Kings lays the blame for that division on Solomon's apostasy (1 Kgs 11:29-40), and there is a thematic link in Scripture between marriage to non-Israelite women and idolatry. But the kings, both north and south, undermined their own authority by their recourse to slavery and their conspicuous consumption, not only their idolatry. The last aspect is nonetheless an especial feature in the careers of the worst kings. During the ninth century BCE, Ahab in the north with his Phoenician wife Jezebel fomented the worship of Baal, and was opposed by the prophet Elijah (1 Kgs 16:29-22:40); in the south during the eighth century, Ahaz renovated the Temple to look like the one in Damascus, and may even have practiced human sacrifice (2 Kgs 16:1-20). It is evident that the alliance of Ahab with Tyre and of Ahaz with Damascus was a formative influence in their respective religious policies.

Prophecy found its voice as a movement in its opposition to the monarchs it regarded as apostate. Prior to the crystallizing impact of that opposition, prophets appear to have been identified as those who spoke for God, often in association with worship in particular sanctuaries. Their prophetic activity might, to a greater or lesser extent, involve unusual states of consciousness and/or atypical behavior, sometimes with the use of music and dance. But first the association with David, and then the antagonism of kings in the north and south made of prophecy a surprisingly coherent movement. The emergence of prophecy as a literary genre is to be dated to the eighth century, and the message of Amos. Fundamentally a prophet of doom against the Northern Kingdom, Amos foretold judgment against Israel's apostate kings, and Hosea vividly generalized that theme to include the nation as a whole. Micah and Isaiah followed them in the south, and an urgent appeal for social justice became a hallmark of prophecy there.

The doom announced against the north by an Amos or a Hosea must have appeared an idle prophecy during periods of prosperity, but when, in 722 BCE, the Assyrians took the capital of the north, climaxing the subjection of Israel to a policy of subjugation and exile, the prophetic message appeared to be vindicated. The works of the northern Prophets were preserved in the south, together with another source of the Pentateuch, known as "E" (for the "Elohist," after the name "God" in Hebrew). That source also tells the story of Israel's beginnings, but with a northern slant.

God is portrayed as revealing his personal name to Moses alone in "E," so that beforehand he was known as "Elohim," God. The mountain of Moses' revelation is known as Horeb, rather than Sinai, and there are alternative versions of stories known in "J," and some new stories; in addition, the conception of God is markedly less anthropomorphic. Clearly, there were those in the north, priests and prophets and scribes, who opposed the royal attempt at syncretism. Nonetheless, the attacks the canonical prophets directed against other, deceitful prophets and against the cultic hypocrisy of some priests is eloquent testimony to the power of the opposition, and its support among both prophetic and priestly groups.

Spurred on by the demise of Israel in the north, whose people were lost to history, the prophets in Judah attempted to purify the life of their people. Isaiah urgently argued against foreign alliances, and insisted that fidelity to God alone would save Jerusalem; Jeremiah ceaselessly denounced faithlessness, and was prosecuted for his trouble; Ezekiel's enactments of coming disaster won him a reputation as a crank. But in the reign of Josiah, a royal reformation backed much of the critique of the prophets (cf. 2 Kgs 22:1-23:30; 2 Chr 34:1-35:27).

Josiah changed worship in the Temple to accord with covenantal norms; he centralized sacrifice, even of the Pesach (Passover), in Jerusalem; he tolerated no foreign incursions. In his program, he was guided by a scroll of the law, which was found in the Temple during the restoration, and scroll which has, since antiquity (and the scholarship of St. Jerome in particular), been associated with the present book of Deuteronomy, which presses an agenda of radical centralization and separation from foreign nations such as impelled Josiah. But in 609, Josiah was killed in battle in an attempt to thwart a military expedition by Pharaoh Necho at the strategic location called Megiddo. The impact of his death may be gauged by the impact of that name upon the apocalyptic tradition, in the form "Armageddon" (Rev 16:16, cf. Zech 12:11).

The end of the kingdom of Judah came fairly quickly after the death of Josiah. Culminating in 587, the Babylonian empire, which had succeeded the Assyrians (cf. the book of Nahum), implemented a policy of exile, subsequent to their siege of Jerusalem and their destruction of the Temple. Had the course of events then followed what happened to Israel in the north, there would today be no Judaism to study. Paradoxically, however, just the forces that must have seemed sure to destroy the religion of the covenant with Yahweh instead assured its survival, and nurtured its international dimension. During the Babylonian exile, the priestly and prophetic movements joined forces to form a united program of restoration that put a form of Israel back on the map within a generation. Even more influentially, they memorialized their vision of that Israel in a book, and made it classic for their successors.

The Josian reforms had already allied some priests with some prophets, and the priests played a central part in the formation of "classic" Israel. Priestly/prophetic scribes redacted "D," the source of the Pentateuch in tune with the message of Deuteronomy, together with "J" and "E." That work, probably completed during the sixth century, was slightly later combined with what is known as the "Deuteronomic History," a relation of events between Moses and the exile that explains success or failure according to the nation's adherence to the program that drove Josiah. The Pentateuch as we know it was completed during the fifth century, with the addition of "P," the specifically priestly source which provides direction for the conduct of sacrificial worship. With the emergence of the Pentateuch, an ideal Israel, attributed to the regulations of Moses, emerged as a truly canonical standard.

The dispossession of Judah to Babylon, then, set up the priestly and prophetic hegemony that made restoration possible. But just as "P" sets out particularly priestly concerns, the prophetic movement also brought a distinctive message to the canon. The prophets generally agreed with their priestly confederates that the land was to be possessed again, and post-exilic additions to the books of Isaiah (40–55), Jeremiah (23:1-8; 31), and Ezekiel (40–48) constitute powerful visions of (and incentives to) return. But the previous abuses of the kings and their sanctuaries made the prophetic movement insist that righteousness was the prior requirement of sacrifice, and that the events of the recent past were a warning.

A Zechariah might be happy to set out the hope of a priestly messiah beside the Davidic king who was to rule (chs. 3 and 4), but even so the predominant emphasis fell upon the crucial necessity of loyalty to the worship of God (see Zech 14). Moreover, eschatology became characteristic of the prophetic movement, both in additions to biblical prophets, such as Isaiah and Ezekiel, and in fresh works, such as Joel and Malachi: the contemporary governance, whether Persian (from 539 BCE), Alexandrine (from 332 BCE), Ptolemaic (from 323 BCE), or Seleucid (from 200 BCE), and the present Temple were provisional, until an anointed king and an anointed priest would rule properly. The image of a priestly orientation redefined by the prophets is projected into the career of Ezra in the books of Ezra and Nehemiah: prophet, priest, and scribe become one in their insistence on the vision of classic Israel, centered upon the restored Temple.

Social history

Obviously, the Pentateuch is deliberately idealized, and might accurately be described as propaganda, in the sense that its concern is more to realize its vision of Israel than to describe Israel as it really was in the past. The perspectives embodied in each of the sources needs to be acknowledged, the sort of literature (poem, psalm, song, epic, narrative, parable, sacrificial manual, prayer, creed) has to be appreciated, and the relationship of a source to the events it refers to all need to be taken into account before judgments can critically be made in regard to what events and persons produced the literature. All biblical history begins with literary history, that is, an assessment of how the literature was generated over time. Necessarily, that involves critical inference, to understand the interplay of sources that led to the documents as we can read them today. Then, to address the events that generated those sources, a second level of inference is required. That second stage of inference should be informed by the literature of cultures surrounding Israel, as well as by archaeology and the insights of social anthropology, but the history that results will always remain at the level of inference (and indeed, inference upon inference) because we simply have no access to "objective" reports or even public records by first-hand observers in the texts as they stand.

Again, Eric Meyers assessment of discussion of the Exodus is illuminating:

> Efforts to demonstrate the historicity of the Exodus narrative have at best made it seem more plausible, rather than achieving any degree of proof. But both conservative and moderate scholars have been quick to point out that the lack of direct evidence – from Canaan, Egypt, and Sinai – does not mean that the Exodus and Sinai (or Horeb) are pure inventions. What is presented as a serious of momentous events, which would spawn religious cultures eventually shaping the experience of millions of people, were in their own time no more than a blip in the shifting movements of peoples in the eastern Mediterranean, unlikely to be noticed by the major powers of the day, and leaving no mark on ancient monuments or in the ruins of desert outposts. But although the specific events, leaders, and masses of people dominating the narrative thread of the first part of the Exodus cannot be verified by history, the overall story line and many of its details are open to verification by archaeology and Egyptology.

An emphasis upon the social construction of history enables us to pursue an Israelite historiography. Judaism in every period is rooted in the notion that Israel is chosen. Indeed, the perennial paradox in the study of Judaism is that the notion of election is more persistent than any definition of what "Israel" might be. We might be thinking of an extended family of Arameans that departed from Mesopotamia in order to settle westwards, of their settlement in Canaan, of the migrant group in Egypt, of those who departed from Egypt, of those who struggled for control of the land of Canaan, of the nation and its eventual monarchy (and civil war), of the dispossessed peoples in Babylonia, of the ideal "Israel" which the Scriptures of the exile project, and/or of those both in the land and in the Diaspora who read those Scriptures as theirs, for whom "Israel" was and is an identification of self. Each of the moments of the development of "Israel" named above (and each of several other stages) has been the object of particular, scholarly attention. But we may, as a convenience, cope with the topic under four stages: (1) the period of pre-history, between the Scriptural Abraham and the Scriptural "judges;" (2) the period of nationalization and monarchy; (3) the period of dispossession and the canonization of Scripture; and (4) the period of radical pluralization (which is widely referred to today as "early Judaism"). Although this scheme will prove useful initially, two further transitional moments will be signaled at the end of this essay.

If the conviction of being divinely elected is a condition *sine qua non* of Judaism, then the traditional notion that Abraham is the father of all Jews is a useful point of departure. After all, he is remembered as being partner to the covenant involving both God's gift of the land, which would be called Israel, and the sign of circumcision (Gen 15:1-21; 17:1-14). But the assumption of Genesis is that Abraham and the patriarchs are semi-nomadic, in the sense that they both migrate and cultivate land. Just that style of living is what brings "Israel," the children of Jacob, who was renamed in a struggle with God (Gen 32:22-32), down to Egypt. The emphasis throughout the patriarchal cycle is upon the actual kinship of the entire group, which may be called Israel.

Moses is particularly associated with the liberation of "Israel" from Egypt, but, just as the quality of the sojourn in that land changed (cf. Exod 1:8-10), so did the constitution of the people. The estimate of more than a half million warriors in Num 1:45, 46 must be hyperbolic, but an increase of population during a period described biblically as of more than four centuries (Exod 12:40) meant that any system of strictly familial lineage was out of the question. In 1207 BCE the pharaoh Merneptah led an expedition whose victory he celebrated in an inscription:[3]

> Canaan is plundered with every evil;
> Ashkelon is taken; Gezer is captured;
> Yanoam is made non-existent;
> Israel lies desolate; his seed is no more.

Although modern historians may flinch at naming "Israel" prior to the tenth century BCE, this pharaoh did not, and shows by his reference that Israel had become substantial enough to attack, and that its

---

[3] Lines 52-55 in the translation of R.J. Williams, *Documents from Old Testament Times* (ed. D. Winton Thomas; New York: Harper & Row, 1961) 139. But I follow Rogerson's dating in *The Cambridge Companion to the Bible*.

extent was not as limited as he thought. Moses was therefore responsible, not simply for the liberation from Egypt, but also for the reconstitution of Israel of an extensive Israel on the basis of his revelation.

The Mosaic constitution would become paradigmatic for every age of Judaism that followed. Clan lineage, on the assumption that the tribes were descended from the sons of Jacob/Israel, replaced familial lineage as the operative definition of the group, and that was an evolution that the weight of numbers alone probably effected. But the "tribal" arrangement by itself was unsystematic, and needed to be balanced by a centripetal impulse, in order for "Israel" to emerge as a functional entity. Moses is the emblem of centralized sacrifice and judgment. His claims upon Pharaoh are predicated upon sacrifice (Exod 3:18), and his relation to Jethro (or "Reuel," in the passage in question), the Midianite priest, makes his cultic interests manifest (Exod 2:15b-22). The notion of "the people" sacrificing creates the notion of the people; apart from some common action, there would be families, extended families, villages, and "stems" (or "staffs," as the tribes are called in the Hebrew Bible), but no organic whole. The drive to sacrifice and the impulse to escape perceived oppression appear to have established just such a unity, short-lived though it sometimes seemed.

The Mosaic constitution established the stem of Levi as the guardians of the sanctuary (cf. Num 4:1-49), and also assured that the conception of Israel's single God would be co-extensive with the conviction of one people: after all, if sacrifice was the charter of liberation, then a declension into multiple gods would return Israel to the division of Egypt (cf. Exod 20:2, 3, 22-26). A corollary of the unity of God and his people is that there should be a single sanctuary, but in the pre-monarchial phase we can speak only of the sporadic pre-eminence of the pan-tribal shrine. At the same time, the tribal stems of Israel were coordinated at the cultic center in a system of judgment (Exod 18:13-26), so that disputes could be regulated, and the appropriate integrity of Israel could be maintained. That Israel should be whole, an integer of divine revelation, becomes the central imperative of the Mosaic covenant.

Sacrifice, within the Mosaic system, is the place of meeting between God and Israel (Exod 24:1-11), such that only what is clean may be involved (cf. Lev 11), and much of it passes to divine ownership (cf. Lev 3:1-17). Not only parts of things offered, but the cultic instruments themselves (Exod 25-31) and the entire tribe of Levi (cf. Num

3:45) are God's. Moreover, the declared aim of entry into the land of promise is to cleanse it of what is not acceptable to God. Everything else, people, beasts, and property, is to be "devoted," that is extirpated (cf. Josh 6; 7). The Pentateuchal emphasis upon that "devotion" (*cherem*) has confused some modern discussion. There has been a tendency to refer to the "Conquest" of Canaan, but much of the language of destruction – which is undoubtedly present – needs to be understood in its sacrificial context.

Joshua and Judges reflect the situation in Canaan much more directly, in their stories of inter-tribal rivalries and wars, accommodations with the indigenous populations, the desire for booty, and the problems inherent in the tendency to erect local shrines. Those glimpses into the turmoil in the midst of which the nation emerged have led to the evolution of distinct, scholarly theories concerning how Canaan was settled by Hebrew-speakers. Martin Noth is associated with the theory of an amphictyony (such as existed in ancient Greece), an association of twelve tribes for cultic purposes. The number twelve is problematic, however. Greek amphictyonies of other numbers are known, and the number within Israel was largely theoretical, perhaps derived from sacrificial practice (cf. Josh 4:9, 20). After all, Levi was left out from the point of view of a geographical inheritance, and "Joseph" in standard lists could be counted three times, as Ephraim and the two "half-tribes" of Manasseh (cf. Josh 17:17, 18; 22:1-6). Unusual lists, such as Judg 1:16-36, have the tribes deviate from the number, names and kinship presupposed ordinarily in the Mosaic covenant. In addition, the point of Levi within Israel is to provide a fixed arrangement of cultic personnel for a moving sanctuary, while in Noth's Greek analogues tribes took turns in providing for a settled sanctuary. But with those crucial allowances, Noth's theory has been remained influential. Crucial changes, however, have been suggested by George Mendenhall and by Norman Gottwald. The former envisages the occupation of the land as an instance of peasants' revolt, while the latter thinks in terms of a union between disenfranchised local elements and migrants from Egypt in opposition to Canaanite hegemony.

The tension between the Pentateuchal picture of a systematic cleansing of the land, to make it fit for divine and human habitation, and the portraits of internecine strife within Joshua and Judges, has generated an understandable skepticism regarding the extent to which the Pentateuch actually reflects anything substantially about the patriarchs, Moses, and the "Conquest." Such skepticism is reinforced by the relatively late date of the emergence of the original sources in the form of actual texts. But it must be borne in mind that while Joshua and Judges in aggregate reflect the tension among and between the people of the "stems," apart from the idea that the stems should be united around a single cult and its covenant, the source of that tension would be difficult to identify. In other words, the vagaries of the "Conquest," while confirming that the "stems" had long since become more social realities than genealogical facts, highlight the importance of the Mosaic constitution. Judges, in particular, demonstrates that "Kenites" had a place in the land (1:16; 4:17-22), and that the Gileadites (12:1-6) and Benjaminites (19-21) were perceived by other "stems" as a threat: the first two groups have no genealogical standing in Israel, while the treatment of the third as a hostile element betrays the shifting loyalties which ultimately gave the structure of "stems" its power. Finally, the memory of Abraham in Canaan and of Moses in Egypt provided a means of access for new elements into the covenant, provided affinity with the chosen people could convincingly be claimed.

The "Israel" which (dis)possessed the land of Canaan, then, was an amalgam of groups which claimed such affinity with Abraham, pursued the worship of God laid down by Moses, and which on that basis sought to rid the land of Canaan of all but its own. Its destruction of other material cultures, particularly urban cultures (as in the case of Jericho, cf. Josh 6), was its hallmark. Leadership consisted in the intervention of "judges," who defended the possession of a given stem or stems, rooted out elements of Canaanite worship, and/or attacked non-Israelite powers. The authority of the judges seems to have resided in their success in pursuing one or more of those aims, which success might be attributed to possession by the spirit of God (cf. Judg 11).

Judges takes a particularly dim view of the institution that obviously would have provided greater stability: the monarchy. The removable "ark of the covenant," which provided the center of Israel's loyalty and devotion, was vulnerable to attack, and the unsystematic convention of "judges," while it might answer to the occasional onslaught of disorganized foes, was no answer to the centralized attack of even a petty kingdom. But the book of Judges casts monarchy as an essentially apostate institution, in that it implicitly involves denying the sovereignty of the LORD (cf. Judg 8:22–29:57).

The prophet Samuel is portrayed as intimately connected with the rise of the monarchy in Israel. He is also closely associated with the ark of the covenant and the priesthood of Eli. Evidently, worship effects the proximity of the LORD, whose will Samuel is then held to interpret (1 Sam 3:1–4:1). Samuel is a fully priestly figure (and a "judge," 7:15–8:2), in that he offers sacrifice himself, and it is notable that he does so in sites other than the "central" shrine (cf. 1 Sam 7; 9:3–10:24; 16). Assertions about the future are involved in his interpretation of God's presence in sacrifice, but interpretation is by no means limited to prediction. Samuel's period of prophecy corresponds to the capture of the ark in war and its removal to Ashdod, a city with a fixed temple for its god, Dagon (1 Sam 4; 5). The ultimate release of the ark, after it was held to cause harm to the inhabitants of any city in which is was held, ends the regular practice of bringing it into battle (7:1, 2, cf. 14:18-22), and a desire for monarchy grows thereafter (8:4-22). Samuel resists, but ultimately gives in, on God's behalf, to popular desire, and anoints Saul (10). Saul is a big man (9:1, 2), in the tradition of the judges, and also a failure. He usurps the function of sacrifice (1 Sam 13:8-15; 14:31-35), fails to "devote" what he should (15), and becomes ambitious for his own family (18-20). God, by means of Samuel, rejects Saul and anoints David (16:1-13).

The Davidic monarchy itself becomes the object of a solemn oath in 2 Samuel 7, where the prophet Nathan promises God's protection of David's progeny. It is notable that David's undertaking to build a temple occasions the promise. The offer itself is accepted, but deferred: it is Solomon who is to accomplish the task (7:13). But the function of the king in protecting, not leading, worship is established, and the role of prophecy as the guide of the king is confirmed. Precisely in those aspects, David differs from Saul, and the promise to David is integrated within the covenant generally.

The centralization of the sacrificial cult in David's city, Jerusalem (2 Sam 6), had both positive and negative effects, from the point of view of faithfulness to the covenant. Positive, because the new center became the focus of codification; the result was "J." But there is also a negative side to the settlement in Jerusalem. With monarchy there came the pressure to trade and compete with other cities: the multiplication of cults – and the *de facto* acceptance of their deities – was a feature of Solomon's otherwise auspicious reign (cf. 1 Kgs 11). Still, he did set in motion the process of Pentateuch formation that has already been described, and established a standard that resulted in the restoration of the Temple.

The Temple as restored was, however, far from ideal. Some who remembered the splendor of Solomon's edifice are reported to have wept when they saw the results of the efforts under Ezra (Ezra 3:10-

13). That imperfect focus nonetheless served to attract a permanent priesthood, and the notion of a canon provided focus to the prophetic movement: now a body of literature, which could be interpreted, was held to provide the guidance which individual prophets formerly gave. Indeed, it is notable that Ezra's own ministry involved guiding Israel on the basis of Scriptural interpretation: the scribe emerges as the dominant, religious personality, as the warrant of true prophecy and the arbiter of priestly conduct (Neh 8–13). But the appearance that scribal leadership was settled is more superficial than representative. Battles concerning the proper conduct of the cult, and the proper personnel of the priesthood, raged during the period of restored Israel, and powerful movements produced literatures outside of scribal control. While the Pentateuch and what are called the Former Prophets (Josh; 2 Kgs) and the Latter Prophets within Judaism may be attributed to the hegemony of priestly and prophet interests which has been described above, the category of "Writings" (the last in the three biblical divisions of traditional Judaism), together with the "Apocrypha" and the "Pseudepigrapha" best characterizes other facets of the religion.

The book of Psalms represents a cultic piety centered on just those aspects Levitical instructions exclude: the music, dance, poetry, prayer, and praise (the term "psalms," *tehillim*, means "songs of praise") that the Temple attracted. They speak more eloquently of the emotional affect of and popular participation in sacrificial worship than any other document in the Bible. Proverbs also represents a non-priestly, non-prophetic focus of piety in restored Israel, defined by prudential wisdom. Job and Ecclesiastes are other examples of that within the canon. Initially, Wisdom is understood to be as aspect of God, which by knowing one can become familiar with God. "Wisdom" is a feminine noun, and came to be personified as a woman; by the time of Ecclesiastics and the Wisdom of Solomon, she is considered a fundamental means of access to God. The Wisdom of Solomon was composed in Greek, but the focus upon Wisdom is by no means unique to what is commonly called Hellenistic Judaism: contacts with Egyptian and Babylonian inquiries into divine wisdom do probably date from the time of the Israelite and Judean kings, as part of their characteristic syncretism. But unlike idolatry and polygyny, wisdom survived and prospered as a suitable and fertile means of communion with God after the notion of the unique covenant with Israel had triumphed. In the case of Philo of Alexandria, whose lifetime straddled the end of the last era and the beginning of our own, the pursuit of wisdom became a philosophical articulation of Judaism; he contributed an awareness of how Judaism and Hellenistic culture – whose contact is already obvious in the "Apocrypha" and "Pseudepigrapha" – might be related. Philo is unusually learned in his representation of a basic development of the Judaism of his period. His simultaneously Greco-Roman and Judaic notion of the *logos* is a case in point (cf. *De opificio mundi*).

The question of the priesthood in the restored Temple, meanwhile, became increasingly fraught. The Persian regime gave way to Alexander the Great: among the dynasties of the generals who succeeded him, first the Egyptian Ptolemies, and then the Syrian Seleucids, largely maintained the enlighten settlement of the Persians. The Seleucid monarch, Antiochus IV (surnamed "Epiphanes") is commonly portrayed as a great exception to the policy, and he did unquestionably occupy Jerusalem and arrange for a foreign cult in the sanctuary, which included the sacrifice of swine (a Hellenistic delicacy; 1 Macc 1:20-64; Josephus, *Ant.* 12.248-256). But Antiochus entered the city as the protector of a high-priestly family, the Tobias, who were then in dispute with the Oniad family (Josephus, *War* 1.31-35). Dispossessed, the latter group moved to Egypt, where a temple was built at Heliopolis, in a form different from the restored Temple in Jerusalem (*War* 1.33; 7.420-432). The cult of Onias appears to have been of limited influence, but the mere existence in the period of restored Israel of an alternative cult, manned by legitimate pretenders to the high priesthood in Jerusalem, is eloquent testimony of deep divisions within the sacerdotal ranks, and within Judaism generally.

"Early Judaism" may conveniently be dated from 167 BCE, with the entry of Antiochus IV into Jerusalem and his desecration of the Temple, but it is evident that the radical pluralization of Judaism prior to Jesus, and of which Jesus was both a symptom and a result, is rooted in the flawed unity of restored Israel during the previous period. But Antiochus's campaign triggered both a fissure of interests and a reconfiguration of those interests, in a way that made pluralism the order of the day. The temple of Onias is only one example, but one which shows that how sacrifice was offered, and by whom, was held by one, familial group to be a better measure of the acceptability of worship than where sacrifice was offered. In Israel, however, there was another group, defined by a desire to remain faithful to sacrifice in Jerusalem by an appropriate priesthood and a resistance to the demands of Antiochus, known as "the faithful" (the famous *chasidim*). Among them was Mattathias; a country priest from Modin, whose son, Judas Maccabeus ("the hammer") introduced the most powerful priestly rule Judaism has ever known, which was known under the name of Hasmoneus,

Mattathias' ancestor (1 Macc 2:1–9:18; and Josephus, *Ant.* 12.265; 16.187; 20.189, 237, 246). Judas, as is well known, turned piety into disciplined revolt, including an alliance with Rome (1 Macc 8) and a willingness to break to Sabbath for military reasons (1 Macc 2:41), which saw the restoration of worship within the covenant in the Temple in 164 BCE (1 Macc 4:36-61). After his death, his brother, Jonathan, was named high priest (10:20), and from that time until the period of Roman rule, the high priesthood was a Hasmonean prerogative

Those events were too rapid for many, and simply unacceptable in the view of some. In strictly familial terms, the Hasmoneans could not claim the high priesthood as a right, and therefore competition with other families of priests was a factor. Moreover, the suspension of the Sabbath for military purposes and the arrogation of the high priesthood and the monarchy by the non-Davidic Hasmoneans seemed particularly vicious to many Jews (cf. Josephus, *War* 1.70), in that Antiochus had sanctioned apostasy, and the regime appeared to be compounding apostasy both in its initial resistance and its consolidation of power. The book of Daniel certainly does not express overt opposition to the Hasmoneans, but it does represent the less activist, apocalyptic stance. The eschatology of the prophets during the period of restored Israel is transformed into a scenario of the end time, in which the Temple would be restored by miraculous means, with the archangel Michael's triumph capped by the resurrection of the just and the unjust (cf. Dan 12). Folk Judaism of the period also anticipated providential interventions (cf. Tobit), but Daniel elevates and specifies that anticipation until it becomes a program of patient attention and fidelity, warranted by both heavenly vision and the pseudepigraphical ascription to the sage of the Babylonian period. In the case of the Essenes, opposition to the Hasmoneans became overt. They pursued their own system of purity, ethics, and initiation, followed their own calendar, and withdrew into their own communities, either within cities or in isolated sites such as Qumran. There they awaited a coming, apocalyptic war, when they, as "the sons of light," would triumph over "the sons of darkness:" not only the Gentiles, but also anyone not of their vision (*The War of the Sons of Light against the Sons of Darkness*; *The Manuel of Discipline*). Their insistence upon a doctrine of two messiahs, one of Israel and one of Aaron, would suggest that it was particularly the Hasmoneans' arrogation of priestly and royal powers which alienated the Essenes.

Most of those who resisted the Seleucids, or who sympathized with the resistance, were neither of priestly families nor of Essene temperament. Nonetheless, the unchecked rule of the Hasmonean priests in the Temple was not entirely acceptable to them. For that large group, the Pharisaic movement held a great attraction. The Pharisees, in their attempt to influence what the Hasmoneans did, rather than to replace them definitively, appear as much more conservative than the Essenes or competing, priestly families. Their focus was upon the issue of purity, as defined principally in their oral tradition, and their interpretation of Scripture, and since issues of purity were bound to be complicated in the Hasmonean combination of secular government and sacrificial worship, disputes were inevitable. Paradoxically, the willingness of the Pharisees to consider the Hasmoneans in their priestly function involved them in the most vocal and bloody disputes of all. Alexander Jannaeus is reported to have executed by crucifixion eight hundred opponents, either Pharisees or those with whom the Pharisees sympathized, and to have slaughtered their families; but his wife came to an accommodation with the Pharisees that guaranteed them considerable influence (*War* 1.96-114). It appears clear that, within the Hasmonean period, purity was a political issue and to some extent a symbol: the acquiescence of one of the dynasty to any Pharisaic stricture implicitly acknowledged that the Hasmonean priesthood was provisional, and the Pharisaic movement probably found its original, political expression in opposition to that priesthood (cf. *Ant.* 13.288-298).

The Pharisees accepted and developed the notion that, with the end of the canon, the age of prophecy in the classical sense had ceased (cf. 1 Macc 4:46). For that reason, they plausibly saw Ezra as their source, and their own, interpretative movement as an extension of his program of restoration (cf. *Aboth* 1:1-18; 2 Esdras 14). But in two, vital respects, the Pharisees need to be distinguished from the reforms of Ezra. First, they identified themselves with no specific, priestly or political figure: their program was its own guide, and was not to be subservient to any particular family or dynasty. Second, Pharisaic interpretation was not limited to the Scriptures, nor was its characteristic focus Scriptural: the principal point of departure was the recollection of earlier teaching of those called "sages." Ultimately, after the period of the New Testament, the ideology of the Rabbis (as the Pharisees came to be) had it that Moses conveyed two Torahs on Sinai, one written and one oral. Even before that understanding, however, the sages treated the teachings of their predecessors in "chains" of tradition as normative. It was not so much that oral tradition was set alongside Scripture, as that oral tradition was Scripture until the canon itself could no longer be ignored as the functional standard of Judaism.

Factionalism among the Hasmoneans, which resulted in rival claims to the high priesthood between Aristobulus and Hyrcanus (the sons of Alexandra), culminated in an appeal by both sides to Pompey, who obliged by taking Jerusalem for Rome and entering the sanctuary (*War* 1.152-154). The *Psalms of Solomon* represents a common, pious expression of horror at the events of 63 BCE, which was probably shared by most Pharisees (whether or not the *Psalms* should be taken as specifically Pharisaic). From that period, and all through the reign of Herod and his relatives, the Pharisees' attitude to the government was ambivalent. Some appear to have engaged in a principled opposition to Roman rule and its representatives as such. Today, that group is known as the "Zealots," but the term is a misnomer. The Zealots were a priestly group of revolutionaries, not rebellious Pharisees, who were associated with Eleazar, son of Simon, during the revolt of 66 – 70 CE (*War* 2.564, 565; 4.224, 225). The rebellious Pharisees are also to be distinguished from the movements of prophetic pretenders, who claimed divine inspiration for their efforts to free the land of the Romans (*War* 2.258-265; 7.437-446). Other Pharisees normally accommodated to the new regime, but resisted – sometimes violently – Herodian excesses, such as the erection of a golden eagle on a gate of the Temple (*War* 1.648-655). Nonetheless, an apparently Pharisaic group is called "the Herodians" (Matt 22:16; Mark 3:6; 12:13), which presumably signals its partisanship of the interests of the royal family as the best support of their teaching of purity. They may be associated with rabbis who enjoyed the protection of Herod and his house; the authorities referred to in Rabbinic literature as the "sons of Bathyra" (cf. *b. Baba Mesia* 85a) may have been such a group. Others still largely cooperated with the Romans, and with the priestly administration of the Temple, although they might fall out regarding such questions as whether the priestly vestments should be kept under Roman or local control (*Ant.* 18.90-95; 20.6-14), or the price of doves for sacrifice (*m. Keritot* 1:7).

The priesthood itself, meanwhile, was fractured further in its response to the fact of Roman governance. Some priests, especially among the privileged families in Jerusalem, were notoriously pro-Roman. The story of sons of the high priest having the surgery called epispasm, in order to restore the appearance of a foreskin (for gymnastic purposes) is well known (cf. 1 Macc 1:14, 15; *Ant.* 12.240, 241).

There is little doubt but that such families, the most prominent of which were the Sadducees and Boethusians, were not highly regarded by most Jews (cf. *b. Pesachim* 57a). They are typically portrayed in a negative light, as not teaching the resurrection of the dead cf. *War* 2.165; Matt 22:23; Mark 12:18; Luke 20:27; Acts 23:8), but the issue may have been one of emphasis: the Torah had stressed the correct worship in the Temple would bring with it material prosperity, and the elite priests attempted to realize that promise. The arrangement gave them such consistent control that they became known as "high priests," although there was in fact only one high priest. But Josephus indulges in the usage, as well as the Gospels, so that it should not be taken as an inaccuracy: the plural is a cultic mistake, but a sociological fact. Caiaphas held an historically long tenure as high priest during the period (*Ant.* 18.35, 95), which reflects the collective nature of the priestly leadership, as well as Roman caution in respect of a post that might have produced a national leader. Herod himself understood the possibilities of the high priesthood in that regard, which is why he had Jonathan and Hyrcanus, potential rivals (albeit relatives by marriage), murdered, and why he married Mariamme (*War* 1.431-437; *Ant.* 20.247-251). His ambition was for a new Hasmonean dynasty, and it appears that only the notorious greed of his sons, combined with his willingness to have them executed, thwarted its realization. As it was, Herod's grandson and namesake, king of Chalcis, did maintain the residual power of selecting the high priest, although as king of Chalcis he had no ordinary authority over Jerusalem (cf. *Ant.* 20.15, 16). Several priests were also prominent in the revolt against Rome, however, and it should not be thought that such priestly nationalists, among whom were Joseph bar Matthias, better known as Flavius Josephus, emerged only at the end of the sixties (*War* 2.562-568). The precedent of the Hasmoneans was there for any priestly family to see as a possible alternative to Roman rule, direct or indirect. Indeed, some priests were not only nationalists, but also revolutionaries, who joined with the Essenes, or with rebellious Pharisees, although any alliance with a prophetic pretender is, perhaps, not a likely supposition.

The Pharisees' mastery of the oral medium made them the most successful – in terms of popularity – of the tendencies within pluralized Judaism. In the period before written communication was standard among the generality of Jews, the use of memorization and recitation was far more prominent. The Pharisees were in a position to communicate guidance in respect of purity, an emerging understanding of Scripture (in the Targumim, whose development they influenced), and their own sense of the authority of the sages, without requiring general literacy. There is no reason to suppose, for example, that rabbis of the first century such as Hillel and Hanina ben Dosa were able to read fluently, although each was a formative member of the Pharisaic, and therefore later of the Rabbinic, movements. The Pharisees willingness to live by craft, rather than by status – the most prominent example being Hillel's menial labor (*b. Yoma* 35b) – also meant that they could move from town to town, promulgating their views. In some respects, their occasional itinerancy was comparable in Israel to that of the Graeco-Roman philosophers of the Mediterranean world (Stoic, Pythagorean, and/or Cynic).

The success of the Pharisees in small towns became all the more pronounced as their power was largely ceded to priestly interests in Jerusalem. Many local scribes, but not all, were likely Pharisees, and the majority would have to account for Pharisaic views. Scribes are, strictly speaking, simply men who can read and write, a skill that in antiquity represented some social and educational attainment. In Israel, given the Roman encouragement of local government, scribes emerged in towns and villages as a focus of judicial and religious power. From the time of the writing of the Torah itself, it was accepted that Moses articulated both aspects of God's rule, the legal and the cultic. The ability of the scribes to read and write made them ideal judges, adjuncts to priests, teachers, and leaders of worship. Indeed, those three functions were probably discharged by an interactive group of scribes, people of priestly lineage, with Pharisees and other elders, in any given village. And it was likely in the same place in a town that cases were settled, purity or impurity declared, lessons given, and the Torah recited from the written form and from memory in Aramaic. There too, disputes would take place among scribes, judges, priests, Pharisees and elders, concerning how the Torah was to be understood and applied. Later Rabbinic literature tends to reduce the disputes of the period to the "houses" of Hillel and Shammai, but that is quite evidently a topos; because they lacked any central leadership in the period before 70 CE, Pharisees differed from movement to movement, town to town, rabbi to rabbi, and even day to day.

The structure of a local council also prevailed under Roman rule in Jerusalem, and the Greek term *sunedrion* was applied to it, and it has become known as "the Sanhedrin," largely as a result of the Mishnah. Mishnah, a document of the second century, cannot be taken as a sure guide of events and institutions during the first century, but it does seem clear, from the Gospels, Josephus, with the Mishnah, that the council in Jerusalem was largely controlled by the high priests, but that elders or aristocrats of the city also participated, among whom were Pharisees (and, of course, some scribes, who may or may not have been priests, elders, or Pharisees). Whether there were actually seventy-one members of the Sanhedrin (as in Rabbinic literature) cannot be known with certainty, and the extent of its capital jurisdiction is not known. But the Romans appear to have given the council the authority to execute (of to demand the execution of) perpetrators of blatant sacrilege (*War* 2.228-231; 5.194; *Ant.* 15.417). The authority of the council of Jerusalem outside of the city followed the prestige of the city itself, and the acknowledged centrality of the Temple. But a ruling of the council there was not automatically binding upon those in the countryside and in other major cities; acceptance of a given teaching, precept by precept, was the path of influence. Pharisees also taught in and around the Temple, the focus of their discussion of purity, and the Pharisees in Jerusalem were the most prestigious in the movement.

References within the Gospels to the groups and movements within Judaism become quite explicable within the social history sketched here. Priests appear locally, in adjudications of purity (Matt 8:1-4; Mark 1:40-45; Luke 5:12-16; cf. Luke 10:31; 17:14, and the exceptional role of Zechariah in 1:5-23), while high priests are essentially limited to Jerusalem, or use Jerusalem as a base of power (cf. Matt 2:4; 16:21; 20:18; 21:15, 23, 45; 26:1-28:11; Mark 8:31; 10:33; 11:18, 27; 14:1-15:31; Luke 3:2; 9:22: 19:47; 20:1-24:20; John 1:19; 7:32, 45; 11:47, 49, 51, 57; 12:10; 18:3-19:21). Jesus enters into disputes with Pharisees (Matt 9:10-13, 14-17; 12:1-8, 9-14; 15:1-26; 16:1-12; 22:15-22; Mark 2:15-17, 18-22, 23-28; 3:1-6; 7:1-23; 8:11-21; 10:2-12; 12:13-17; Luke 5:29-32, 33-39; 6:1-5, 6-11; 11:37-41; 15:1, 2), and finally teaches in the Temple itself and occupies the holy precincts (Matt 21–25; Mark 11–13; Luke 19:28-21:38), where high priests, particularly Sadducees, find him guilty of blasphemy and denounce him to the council of Jerusalem, which makes its recommendation to Pilate (Matt 26:1-27:2; Mark 14:1-15:1; Luke 22:1-23:5). Scribes appear in both in a local context (Matt 5:20; 7:29; 9:3; 12:38; 15:1; 17:10; Mark 1:22; 2:6, 16; 7:5; Luke 5:21, 30; 6:7), even as a part of Jesus' movement (Matt 8:19; 13:52; Mark 12:32, 34; Luke 20:39), and during the final confrontation in Jerusalem (Matt 16:21; 20:18; 21:15; [26:3,] 57; 27:41; Mark 8:31; 10:33; 11:18, 27; 12:35, 38; 14:1, 43, 53; 15:1, 31; Luke 9:22; 19:47; 20:1, 19, 39, 46; 22:2, 66; 23:10) and they are probably to be identified with references to "lawyers" in the Gospels (Matt 22:35; Luke 7:30; 10:25; 11:45, 46, 52; 14:3). The Pharisees engage in vigorous debate with Jesus, because he is also interested in developing teaching in respect of purity, but Jesus himself is to be understood within that movement. He is called "rabbi," has close followers, deliberately promulgates his teaching by travel and sending his disciples to teach, and attempts to influence the conduct of worship in the Temple. The social history of Christianity itself tended to cast scribes, Pharisees, and lawyers into a single category of persecutors and hypocrites, like the "Jews" themselves, and that influence is evident in the present text of the Gospels (cf. Matt 15:1; 23:2, 13, 15, 23, 25, 27, 29; Mark 3:6, 22; 7:1, 5; Luke 6:7; 11:45, 46, 53, 54; 15:2). But the realities of a radically pluralized Judaism in which Jesus was a vigorous participant also shine through the text as it may be read today.

Although an understanding of Israelite history is necessary to any critical understanding of New Testament, the Israelis of the Hebrew Bible continue to have a vitality of their own. In the following schema, generative Israels represented in the Bible are associated with some of the texts that eventuated from them:

Phase One: Incipient Israel

1800 BCE Abraham
1300 BCE the Exodus

Judg 2-3; 4-5; 6-9; 11; 13-16; 17-18; 19-21; Josh 1-8; 9-11; 18; 20; 24; 1 Sam 1-15

The literary basis of the Bible was laid long after 1800 BCE, the time of Abraham, the wandering Aramean who is revered as the primordial patriarch of Israel. Even the exodus from Egypt (c. 1300 BCE) was a distant memory for the clans of people who settled in the land of the Canaanites and claimed common descent from Abraham, Isaac, and Jacob. Their Hebrew was a Semitic language akin to Aramaic with elements of Canaanite grammar and vocabulary added in. Like a young child, Israel's earliest recollection did not directly include their parents or their coming into the world. Those were pictures that were filled out later. What Israel remembered directly, in the earliest sources of the Bible, was the place it first grew up in: the land they called Israel and its earlier inhabitants called Canaan. The story of how the war-god Yahweh helped his twelve clans (or "tribes") of people conquer the land he promised them, and inflicted punishment on anyone who abrogated the basics of his agreement with them (the covenant) is the opening episode in the story of the Bible.

The initial community that produced these texts in Hebrew (developing the Hebrew language as they were settling the land and developing these books) was a confederation of clans that gathered to make war. Stories from the earliest sources in the Bible (detectable in their style of Hebrew, their patterns of thought, and their historical allusions) depict a decentralized social structure. Central leadership was lacking, and clans allied for purposes of war under charismatic military adventurers called "judges." Their policies could be ruthless, a frequently set one clan at war against another. Some judges were also prophets, or at least consulted with prophets: by means of sacrifice, music, and trance, they claimed to speak for Yahweh, the god who linked the clans. But priestly sacrifice was also undertaken by many people from the clan of Levi, who were also known to experiment in the rituals of their surrounding culture. They settled in what we mostly now call the highlands of territorial Israel – Samaria and Galilee. Principally an oral culture, this phase of Israel's existence nonetheless produced the beginnings of a literature, some of which may have been consigned to writing.

Phase Two: The Classic Monarchy

1010–970 BCE King David
970–922 BCE King Solomon

1 Sam 15–31; 2 Sam 1; 3; 6-7; 11–20; 24; 1 Kgs 2–3; 5–11; Gen 2:4b-4; 11:1-9; 12

The war god led his people personally into battle, enthroned on a wheeled box, the ark of the covenant. The text's next stage of development reflects the painful disaster of that ark being captured in the midst of Israel's defeat, and the winding road that brought it back into their possession. Recovering the ark involved developing national institutions: chiefly monarchy and law. The Davidic dynasty brought with it a revised understanding of the divine covenant (including the promise that God would never abandon David's dynasty), and a powerful scribal class. Scribes were now not only the privileged group that happened to be able to write, but also the intellectual branch of the royal propaganda machine: Israel's first historians.

David cleverly legitimated his reign by means of regular consultation with the prophets who had once been oracles, judges, and warlords. They were still in many ways comparable to the mantic sages of Canaan, using their prophetic trance and ecstatic sacrifice to divine the future. Divination became one means by which Israel's foreign, domestic and sacrificial policy was set.

The prophets with their oracular powers emerged literally as kingmakers (and breakers) during this period, but the influence of monarchy was irresistible even for them. The reigns of David (1010-970 BCE) and Solomon (970-922 BCE) saw a period of equilibrium among king, priests, prophets, and scribes. Their alliance produced the Pentateuch (the first five books of the Bible later attributed to Moses), which tells the story of Israel from the creation of the first human couple to Israel's inheritance of the land. This is the source called "J," a work of political theology, poetry, history, and myth that is reflected in many parts of the Pentateuch, an intellectual monument to the extent of the influence of David and Solomon over Israel.

But the Davidic monarchy by no means succeeded in reducing all the prophets of Yahweh to royal chaplains. Tension and conflict remained, and some prophets resisted the claim that Levitical priests were uniquely qualified to offer sacrifice. The prophets themselves persistently engaged in the sacrificial act, by going to local mountaintops to sacrifice to Yahweh. The prophets are charismatic, recognized simply by their infusion with the spirit of God. The priesthood, on the other hand, became an institution in its own right once the Temple emerged. The Levites wrote themselves into their priestly handbook of oral law (the basis of the book of Leviticus), establishing their exclusive sacrificial power on the basis of genealogical descent. While rest of the clans laid claim to specific, territorial possessions within Israel, the Levites enjoyed a much richer inheritance: the wealth of the Temple. And among the Levites only one family, the family friendliest to David, could serve as high priests – the Zadokites.

Phase Three: Division and Prophecy

922 BCE – 722 BCE

1 Kgs 11-12; 14-16; 17:1–2 Kgs 11; Gen 15; 22; 32–33; 37–50; Exod 1–4; 19–20; 24; 32; Num 11; Amos 1–2; 8; Hos 1–2; 8; Mic 3–4; Deut 14–18; Nah; Zeph

The power of the Davidic dynasty and its lust to erect monuments to itself resulted in perhaps the most shameful institution of Israel's history: the enslavement of peoples of the other Israelite clans by the Judeans (David's own clan). The result of that self-indulgent display of arrogance and the suffering slavery involved was revolution, guided for the most part by a loose band of prophets, outlaws, and opportunists. Solomon's son Rehoboam, refusing to relent in the practice of enslaving his own people, was unable to hold Israel together. After the revolution of 922 BCE, the name "Israel" went to the revolutionaries, because all that was left to the house of David was the territory of Judah itself. Bereft of the support and wealth of the north clans, Jerusalem proved easy picking for Pharaohs who pillaged the city, confiscating the ark. Meanwhile, Israel prospered under powerful monarchs who encouraged both trade and religious syncretism with surrounding peoples. Because these kings introduced foreign gods into their country, the prophets increasingly opposed them, and their fundamental message was put into writing for the first time: only complete loyalty to Yahweh could ensure Israel's survival. Any other course, they claimed, would inevitably bring disaster.

The perceived abuses of the Israelite monarchy in the north, then, set in motion the forces that would elevate prophecy into a powerful although marginal institution. During the period of the judges, it had been one of the few centripetal powers in Israel. Eclipsed during David's successful legitimation of his reign, it came to independent voice again after the secession of the north from the south, especially during the reign of Ahab. The prophetic activities of Elijah and Elisha became characteristic of prophecy forever after, involving a dedication to vision and access to the "Chariot" of God's presence, an often strident demand for social justice, overt resistance to the political rule of the house of Ahab and its successors, a violent opposition to idolatry, and a cogent expression of Yahweh's objection to Israelite practice. Part of the literary work of the prophetic movement was a recasting of the entire story of Israel from its beginning. This is the "Elohist" source of the entire Pentateuch, so-called because God is not called "Yahweh" from the beginning, but "*Elohim*" (which in Hebrew means "God[s]," a plural of majesty). For this source, Yahweh only revealed his personal name to Moses, who is portrayed as a prophet comparable to Elijah. One hallmark of this evolving prophetic message was that of the impending doom of the north, taken to be a soon to be exacted vengeance for the prophets as well as just satisfaction for Yahweh's justice.

Phase Four: Destruction and Invention

721 BCE – 539 BCE

2 Kgs 16; 18:1-23; 21:1–23:37; 24-25; Isa 6-8; 36-39; Jer 4; 7; 17-20; 29-31; Isa 40; 42-45; 47; Ezek 1; 4-5; 34-37; 40; Lev 17-19; Hag; Zech 3-5

While Israel prospered, Yahweh's prophets could easily be dismissed as cranks; in any case, monarchs could always consult with other prophets. But in 722 BCE, the powerful northern kingdom was broken by the invasion of the Assyrians, and their policy of cultural genocide: moving conquered peoples from their own lands, and settling strangers in their place. Northern Israel, along with "Galilee of the nations," became a foreign province. In the south, Judah escaped Israel's fate, through a combination of good fortune (the preoccupation of Assyria with greater powers) and its own relative insignificance in Assyrian eyes. That enabled Yahweh's prophets in Judah (some of whom had actually from the north) to draw together the writings of their great predecessors in the north and the south, and the rewrite history according to the principle that Yahweh rewarded loyalty to him with prosperity, and punished rebellion with exile. Ironically, just as that work was completed (chiefly represented by the book of Deuteronomy) and was embraced by King Josiah as a matter of state policy, the surrounding powers closed in on Israel. Josiah himself was killed in 609 BCE at Megiddo (which gave its name to ultimate disaster), and then the new empire of Babylonia besieged and destroyed Jerusalem itself in 587 BCE.

The Babylonians pursued the same policy of dispersing enemies that the Assyrians had. Prominent prophets and priests found themselves with the family in exile in Babylon. Desperation made them cooperate in a way they never had in territorial Israel. The result of that cooperation was the Bible much as we know it: the Pentateuch was completed in exile and the prophetic words compiled with the Pentateuch into a canon. Israel had been lost on the ground, but it had been rediscovered in writing, understood as the word of Yahweh himself.

The Pentateuch or Torah was compiled by editing the sources known as the Yahwist from the Davidic court and the Elohist from the prophetic movement in the north. Both of these provide stories of the patriarchs and the exodus, but they locate the traditions in different places, according to their geographical bias. The mountain of the revelation of the Torah, for example, is the southern Sinai for "J" and the northern Horeb for "E." It should be stressed that there is no way of assigning a book (Genesis, Exodus, Leviticus, Numbers, or Deuteronomy) to one source. Each source is distributed through the books (albeit unevenly). In addition to "J" and "E," the Pentateuch includes the great prophetic work called the Deuteronomist ("D") and a source of the Priesthood ("P"). This complex work, together with the emerging Prophetic canon, gave landless Israel a charter for its existence that survived the exile in Babylon.

Phase Five: Radical Pluralism

539 BCE – 167 BCE

Prov 4–10; Eccl 3–4; Job 19; 41–42; Pss 29; 93; 74; 47; Songs 3–4; Jonah 4; Ruth 3; Esth 7; Hab 2; Joel 2; Obad 1; Isa 56; Zech 14; Ezra–Neh 8

Even with a written Bible, it seems unlikely Israel could have lasted more than a generation or two in exile. Had the Assyrian/Babylonian policy been taken to its usual end, the most we would have known of the Torah and the Prophets would have been a few papyrus fragments from scrolls. And Jerusalem's name and buildings would have been buried under those who came to inhabit the rubble the Babylonians had left behind. But Babylon itself did not last, and Cyrus the Persian developed a radical new policy: toleration. He permitted his subject peoples to return to their own lands and worship their own gods.

When some Israelites did return to Jerusalem in 539 BCE, many covenanted themselves to the prophetic promise and eventually set about rebuilding the Temple (from 520 BCE). But others were quite happy to accept the customs and in some cases the women of the foreigners the Babylonians had settled there. The result was deep conflict between like scribes like Ezra and large numbers of assimilationists. Those who opposed the radical Yahwists especially relied on traditions that made a goddess named Chochma: Wisdom, the consort of Yahweh. She represented all that was best in the prophetic tradition, and could be seen in the patterns of nature and in the best of all human cultures. Yet another group anticipated a final apocalypse, when God himself would bring sense to Israel and all the nations in a final judgment that would include them all. The resettlement of the land, in other words, brought no respite from internal conflict, and the lure of assimilation only grew after Alexander the Great claim territorial Israel in 332 BCE.

The radical Yahwists resisted assimilation, above all in the form of intermarriage, and developed a strict understanding of the purity that was to maintain Israel's integrity in the face of the nations (or Gentiles). They built upon the work of the prophets, but were masters of the written form, and prided themselves on their mastery of Israel's literature. These scribes became all the more important, as the monarchy inevitably wanted in significance. Full power (above all, in foreign affairs) had never been accorded to the house of David by the Persians, and the successors of Alexander had no positive interest in it whatever.

But scribes were also represented in the Diaspora, where the movement for assimilation prospered, as well as within territorial Israel. For this reason, part of our story is the Greek literature that was not included in the canon in Hebrew. The two types of scribes fought over the hearts of the minds of the priests. The side they tilted towards often had as much to do with their judgment of the advantage to be gained by the political regime of the moment as their conviction that one side or another was correct.

One of the most fascinating aspects of Israelite history during this period is the absence of prophecy. Neither the assimilationists nor the Yahwists claimed to speak directly in the name of the God of Israel. A principal reason for that was that the power of the scribes on both sides of the argument had fixed the prophetic voice in writing. Further guidance for Israel was to come from interpretation, rather than from direct inspiration. But that apparent dominance of the scribal mode cannot completely conceal what is evident in the writings which record the folk movements of Israel (such as the Apocrypha and the scrolls from Qumran): the prophetic voice continued, but in a different key. Instead of using the language of direct inspiration, vision became the principal guide into the divine world. A growing dedication to the guidance of seers was about to reshape the theological terrain of Israel.

Phase Six: Final Israels

164 BCE – 100 BCE

Dan; Mal; Tob; Wis; 1 Macc; Mark; John; Acts; Gal; 1 Cor; Rom; Heb; Rev

The last act of biblical formation occurred in an environment of persecution and resistance. One of Alexander's successors, Antiochus Epiphanes, claimed the Temple for Hellenism in 167 BCE by offering swine (a delicacy as far as Zeus was concerned) on the altar. The response was the Maccabean revolt, the most militarily successful movement in the history of Israel. But the Maccabean dynasty proved no less arrogant than their Davidic predecessors did. They attempted to arrogate the powers of kingship and priesthood to themselves, and earned the contempt of many apocalyptists, priests, scribes, and Wisdom teachers. So the victory that might have brought unity in fact resulted in further factionalism. The Essenes of Qumran combined the interests of priests and apocalyptists, while other apocalyptic movements were more purely literary. The Pharisees maintained a loyalty to the Mosaic traditions of Yahweh, but in an oral form (to steer clear of the control of scribes). Meanwhile, die-hard zealots yearned for the days of the Maccabees, and the Wisdom thrived in the Greek speaking Diaspora. In the midst of such conflict, it was easy for the Romans to assert its control of Jerusalem and the entire kingdom of the Maccabees, handing it over to Herod the Great and his family.

After periodic revolts, the national war against Rome was too much for the patience of the Empire, and Titus burned Jerusalem and the Temple in 70 CE. In a single act, he destroyed the power-base of the priests, just as he exterminated the Essenes. Jews in the Diaspora continued to cherish Wisdom, but increasingly they found their loyalties divided between the traditionalism of the Pharisees and the apocalyptic fervor of groups such as the sect called the Christians. Jesus' followers developed – like the Pharisees, their principal competitors in the Diaspora as well as in Israel – their own oral traditions to meet the crisis of the Temple's destruction with the promise of a messiah who would at long last bring the final Israel to earth.

Just as the Pentateuch can only be appreciated by means of a familiarity with its sources, so the different cycles of tradition within the Gospels need to be recognized. They were developed by the most important teachers within earliest Christianity: Peter, James (Jesus' brother), the select group of twelve apostles, and Barnabas (a Levite from Cyprus and Paul's sometime companion). Paul's relation to that considerable establishment of power is also important to assess. Yet all the while those developments are unfolding (until their climax in the Revelation of John), all these Christian teachers were shadow-boxing with their Pharisaic contemporaries, who were shaping Rabbinic Judaism during just the period when the New Testament took shape.

Each of these Israels, crystallized in classic Scriptures, has proved formative in the history of those communities that framed their identities in their acts of biblical interpretation.

Bibliography

E. Auerbach, *Moses* (tr. R.A. Barclay & I.O. Lehman; Detroit: Wayne State University Press, 1975)

J. Bright, *A History of Israel* (Philadelphia: Westminster, 1981)

B.D. Chilton, *The Temple of Jesus. His Sacrificial Program within a Cultural History of Sacrifice* (University Park: The Pennsylvania State University Press, 1992)

P.R. Davies, *In Search of Ancient Israel* (Sheffield: JSOT Press, 1992)

W.D. Davies and L. Finkelstein (eds.), *The Cambridge History of Judaism. Volume One: Introduction; the Persian Period* (London and New York: Cambridge University Press, 1984)

E.R. Goodenough, *An Introduction to Philo Judaeus* (Brown Classics in Judaica; Lanham and London: University Press of America, 1986)

N.K. Gottwald, *The Tribes of Yahweh. A Sociology of the Religion of Liberated Israel 1250–1050 B.C.* (Maryknoll: Orbis, 1979)

H.C. Kee (ed.), *The Cambridge Companion to the Bible* (Cambridge: Cambridge University Press, 1997);

R.A. Kraft and G.W.E. Nickelsburg, *Early Judaism and Its Modern Interpreters* (The Bible and Its Modern Interpreters 2; Atlanta: Scholars Press, 1986)

A.R.C. Leany, *The Jewish and Christian World 200 B.C. to A.D. 200* (Cambridge Commentaries on Writings of the Jewish and Christian World 200 B.C. to A.D. 200, 7; Cambridge and New York: Cambridge University Press, 1984)

N.P. Lemche, *Early Israel. Anthropological and Historical Studies on the Israelite Society before the Monarchy* (Supplements to Vetus Testamentum; Leiden: Brill, 1985)

M. McNamara, *Palestinian Judaism and the New Testament* (Good News Studies 4; Wilmington: Glazier, 1983)

G.E. Mendenhall, "The Hebrew Conquest of Palestine," *The Biblical Archaeologist Reader* 3 (1962) 100-120

J. Neusner, "Josephus' Pharisees: A Complete Repertoire," *Josephus, Judaism, and Christianity* (ed. L.H. Feldman & G. Hata; Wayne State University Press: Detroit, 1987) 274-292

——, *The Pharisees. Rabbinic Perspectives: Studies in Ancient Judaism* (Hoboken: Ktav, 1984)

M. Noth, *The History of Israel* (London: A. & C. Black, 1959)

R.R. Wilson, *Sociological Approaches to the Old Testament* (Philadelphia: Fortress, 1984).

2

Does History Matter? Meaning-making and the First Two Greek Historians

Carolyn Dewald

Herodotus and Thucydides, the first two Greek historians, lived in times as epoch-making and dangerous as our own. They were the first professional western historians, and between them they invented the discipline of historiography, in large part as a passionate and yet reasoned response to the historical events and intellectual movements of their own times.

In Herodotus's father's generation, at the beginning of the fifth century BCE, the East Greeks, living on the coast and the islands west of Anatolia, had already been politically attached to the massive Persian empire to the east of them for several generations. In the late 480s the Persians under Xerxes' leadership began to mount an enormous, well-funded, and well-organized campaign to move against the Greek peninsula itself. A two-year-long war was fought, mostly on Greek soil, between 481 and 479 BCE; when it was over, the Greeks had won, and had even won the Anatolian coastline and islands ("Ionia") back from the Persians, despite the poverty of their resources and the thinness of the ties that bound them together as a cohesive fighting force. Because Persia did not win the Persian Wars but was still a significant threat, the Athenians went on to establish a maritime dominance over the east Aegean that led to the great flowering of Greek culture in the middle fifth century. Because of hostility on the part of many other Greek states, however, this also led directly to the brutal 27-year war between Athens and Sparta that took up roughly the last third of the fifth century, 431-404 BCE.

Herodotus and Thucydides between them chronicled the beginning and the end of this tumultuous period, and in the process also developed the beginnings of historical narrative, at least in its western form.

What they thought they were doing, and why they were doing it, is of course important on its own terms, but it is also relevant to the project of understanding more clearly the point of the field of study they invented, expressed in our own twenty-first century terms. To put it bluntly: why does it matter that like them we look carefully at events of the past and try to understand them, get them right? To state it more provocatively still: sorting out evidence, collecting information in this information-saturated age of ours is both an overwhelming and a tedious task. We now have other social sciences for understanding human beings with: psychology, economics, sociology, anthropology, even biology. We have movies, plays, novels to entertain us with lifelike stories often much more vivid and exciting than the collective accounts of real people from the past. So do we really need history as they defined it – the attempt to tell a true story of human communities – any more? Or is history today, in the era of digital electronics, just part of the lumberroom of the human past, something like the victrola, the typewriter, and the model T, that we can jettison for speedier, more amusing and convenient, or more comfortable post-modern machines of our own? The challenge that Herodotus and Thucydides present is a serious one, to us and to some of our most conveniently held assumptions.

We have the term itself because Herodotus used it. "History" is one of those words that are dangerous precisely because we think we know what they mean. Like other comparable terms – love, or religion, or democracy, for instance – we handle them cheerfully all the time, without thinking very deeply about them. When we look at "history" more closely, however, an interesting ambiguity surfaces. For blended together are often two quite different senses of the word: on the one hand, we understand history to be a complicated series of interlocking events that are lived through in sequence by people in groups. On the other hand (in the English language, at least), history is also the armchair study of that complicated sequence – one might borrow a phrase used of poetry and call it that sequence of events "recollected in tranquillity."

When Herodotus and his successor Thucydides, the two fifth-century Greeks, invented the notion of history in the second sense – the careful, even systematic study of the *realia* of a particular intertwining sequence of events – they did so because they thought it useful precisely for living well through history in the first sense. What they did was intensely original, and we need to appreciate how hard it would have been before they did it to conceive of their accomplishment. For as a discipline that has roots both in the social sciences and the humanities, history is in crisis today. It is often considered irrelevant, anachronistic, or sentimentalizing – perhaps even by its very nature a politically incorrect way of understanding the world. But if we go back to its roots in the fifth century BCE we can see in the nature of Herodotus's and Thucydides' accomplishment why this is not in fact so – why we need right now some of the ways of approaching the world that are implicit in what they taught us to do.[1]

The first historian, often called the father of history, was Herodotus son of Lyxes (c. 480-425 BCE), an East Greek, from Halicarnassus, the modern Turkish city of Bodrum. In the middle years of the fifth century, he began to write down the first history. The first line of his Greek text reads *Herodotou Halikarnesseos histories apodexis hede*, "this is the display/publication (*apodexis* can mean both) of the *historie* of Herodotus of Halicarnassus."

When Herodotus wrote that his big book was the "display of his *historie*," he and his contemporaries did not understand by the word *historie* what we mean when we use the word history – a record of the past, an account in temporal sequence of the causal connections that make things happen as they do, or an analysis of the interplay of sociological and psychological patterning, chance, and human will that we draw on to explain why human beings acting in groups in the past have done one thing rather than another. All of these elements can be found in Herodotus's text (and the fact that they *are* found in his text helps explain why Thucydides was inspired to do what he did some twenty years afterward), but to Herodotus and his Ionian peers in the 450s BCE *historie* meant simply "investigation."

It was a noun formed out of a very old Indo-European stem *vid-* meaning sight, or knowledge gained through sight. We have its cousin words through Germanic Old English in wit, or wisdom, and through Latin, another cousin language, we have vision, and video. In Greek very early, before Homer, the digamma or w-sound was lost, and the stem came in as the verb *idein*, to see, and in its noun of agency, a *(w)istor*, or *histor*, a witness, a man who knows things because he has seen them. In the *Iliad*, a text created three hundred years or so before Herodotus, a *histor* is in one passage a judge of a horse race, waiting at the goalpost to declare the winner, and in another passage he is one of a group of judges gathered to weigh the evidence and determine the

---

[1] Some of the most thoughtful current explorations of these issues are found in Appleby, Hunt, and Jacob, 1994; Berkhofer 1995; Jenkins 1999.

outcome of a manslaughter trial.² What Herodotus did was adopt the old Greek notion of "empirical investigation" – things one can say one knows because one has really seen them – as a way of answering a question that engaged the Greeks of his own day – why was it the Greeks, not the Persians, who won the great war mounted by the Persian empire to take over the Greek peninsula in 481 BCE? Herodotus set out to answer this question about 40 years after the event, when its generation of eyewitnesses and combatant participants was in danger of dying out. To tell the story as he thought it ought properly to be told, he investigated by collecting and critiquing hundreds of stories from all over the Aegean basin; he told first of the almost century-long growth of the Persian empire, and only in the last three books of his nine-book work did he get to his announced subject, the Greek victory of his parents' generation.

We are not sure why or how Herodotus was in a position to ferret out and then arrange the many stories within this gigantic story into a single whole, but we can make some educated guesses. If any of our ancient information is correct, he had been exiled from his own city, Halicarnassus, in the civil wars of his childhood and spent much of his early adulthood as an outsider, a wanderer and a visitor – even, perhaps, a merchant –, observing and understanding the peoples among whom he travelled. When he got to Athens by perhaps the 450s he probably found that he had, by the nature of his own travels and the cosmopolitan nature of his own life, a kind of understanding that few mainlanders from the Greek peninsula proper had. He could understand and tell the whole story of the Persian Wars – why they had happened, how they had turned out as they had – because in his hometown in Asia Minor, other Ionian cities like Samos, and on his travels to Egypt, Babylonia, possibly Scythia and Persia proper, he had collected anecdotes that explained how the four Persian kings of the previous century, Cyrus the Great, Cambyses, Darius, and Xerxes, had embarked on their path of conquest. Because he had travelled among, met and talked with both Persians and many of the peoples the Persians had conquered along the way, he had gathered thousands of stories of many actors in this huge tapestry – rich and poor, female and male, Greek and barbarian. All of this somehow fit into his horizon of interest: the growth of Persian power in the sixth century BCE and its unlooked-for defeat in Greece some eighty years later. Unlike his mainland Greek contemporaries, Herodotus understood the Persians

² *Iliad* 18.497–508, 23.483–87. See Connor 1993.

from an Eastern point of view as well as a Greek one (his own family almost certainly contained Eastern elements), and he thought he knew, better than other Greeks, why the Persians at the end could not succeed in their drive to conquer Greece.

In Herodotus's *Histories*, although the Persians could easily have won, they are brought down by their very blindness about the conditions that really faced them. Insulated by their own wealth and string of imperial successes, the Persians of 480 BCE, led by King Xerxes, did not look closely at the nature of the Greek terrain, or at the love of liberty, the political will, and the nature of the military organization of the Greeks who opposed them. This fact comes fairly clearly through Herodotus's narrative, and one of our current scholarly debates concerns whether it was intended as a theme, perhaps even a message, tacitly directed at the contemporary fifth-century Athenians who were apparently among Herodotus's most enthusiastic audiences. Herodotus understands deeply that no empire lasts forever, because of the nature of the illusions about power that too much power creates in its possessors. Possibly he was warning Athens of some of the weaknesses that they too would display, in the Peloponnesian War that was underway as he was finishing up his monumental piece of writing.

But Herodotus's 800-page work is not a sermon. Our understanding of Xerxes' personal weaknesses as a ruler and the structural weaknesses of powerful empires in general only arises gradually, out of the many stories themselves. The stories are tightly fit together into an intricate mosaic consisting of thousands of individual accounts, all of which are unique and interesting, and which together go into depicting a massive, century-long sweep of Persian imperial growth and then sudden, unlooked-for defeat. The last three books focus on the story of King Xerxes, and how he tried and failed to conquer Greece in 480–479 BCE. But we start about eight generations earlier, with the story of Candaules, the Lydian king who was actually, Herodotus says, in love with his own wife and therefore wanted his bodyguard see her undress, leading indirectly to the loss of the Lydian throne.[3] Herodotus moves from this almost directly to the story of Croesus the phil-Hellene, the distant descendant of that bodyguard, who thought he was the happiest as well as the richest man alive but soon learned otherwise, even if only belatedly he understood what Solon, an Athenian traveler and wise man, had tried to tell him.[4] Croesus was conquered

---

[3] *Histories* 1.8-14.
[4] *Histories* 1.29-44, 85-92.

by Cyrus the Persian, whose grandfather tried to kill him as a baby, but who was saved in a remarkable manner, raised by a village herdsman and his wife, and grew up to conquer the Medes and found the fortunes of the Achaemenid dynasty.[5] Cyrus's son Cambyses conquered Egypt, and this led in turn to the story of Egypt, and within that story, the story of Amasis the king of Egypt (a very postmodern fellow) who melted down a golden urinal-cum-footbath and turned it into a statue to be venerated, to teach his subjects to question appearances.[6] Cambyses himself, though conqueror of Egypt, went mad and shot his vizier's son through the heart to prove that he was not mad or drunk. He also married his own sister and killed his brother, died, and left the royal house in chaos, to be rescued only by a distant Achaemenid relative, Darius. Darius's son was Xerxes, the would-be conqueror of Greece.[7]

Herodotus does not only tell stories of rulers; we are treated along the way to the story of Cyno, the cowherd's wife, who saved the life of baby Cyrus, of Hermotimus the eunuch, the man who lured his former castrator to Asia and then in turn castrated him and all his sons,[8] and of many other people, of both genders and all walks of life. Herodotus blends many anecdotes about them together into a web that is not entirely seamless but does inexorably lead the reader on, because each story plays a part in creating the meaning of the whole. Part of our difficulty in taking his brilliance as a historian seriously lies in the wonderful but distracting gifts as a narrator that Herodotus reveals at every turn along the way. The "red thread" or organizing theme of the *Histories* – the growth of the Persian empire and its unlooked-for defeat in Greece in 481–479 BCE – subtly intertwines itself within the multiple stories, but does not dominate them or emerge to present a clear organizing structure for the whole text.

The mixture of real, lived sixth- and fifth-century history and folktale anecdote, as story follows story, is hard at first for the twenty-first century reader to sort out.[9] It might be illustrative to take one of the more famous sixth-century accounts, almost itself subsumed by the time Herodotus heard it into folktale, to see how his stories (often traditionally labeled "charming") must nonetheless be taken as serious

---

[5] *Histories* 1.95, 108-130.
[6] *Histories* 2.172.
[7] *Histories* 3.27-38, 64-66, 80-88.
[8] *Histories* 1.110-113, 8.104-106.
[9] For a longer discussion of Herodotus's narrative structures, see Dewald 1998, building on Immerwahr 1966.

efforts at early historiography. It concerns Polycrates, tyrant of the Greek island of Samos (c. 540–522 BCE), not one of the most important players in the Greco-Persian conflict that is Herodotus's major theme, but nonetheless a relatively important figure in archaic Greek history. Polycrates was one of the most powerful Greek rulers of his day. He was apparently engaged in trying to resist the growth of the Persian empire, but he did it by rather dubious means. As Herodotus tells us (3.39-43, 120-125), Polycrates had a famous navy, and in fact raised money for himself by capturing ships of other people and selling their contents – calculated acts of piracy. He did this to friend and foe alike and was quoted as saying this was a really good idea, because people would be more grateful to you for returning their goods after you had taken them than for leaving them alone in the first place. This Polycrates was so successful that his good friend, Amasis king of Egypt, began to get worried. It was unnatural, Amasis thought, for anybody to be as continuously fortunate as Polycrates was. So Amasis wrote a letter to Polycrates, and told him he had to do something about his good fortune – that is, he had to take whatever of his possessions was most valuable to him, and voluntarily lose it, throw it away. That way, he would no longer be so dangerously fortunate that bad things would *have* to happen to him as a result.

Polycrates saw the force of Amasis' reasoning, and thought for a long time. His favorite possession, he decided, was a gorgeous gold and emerald seal ring, and so he called his rowers, had himself rowed far out to sea, and threw his ring into the waves. He was devastated, but consoled himself that he had followed Amasis' advice. A few days later, a fisherman appeared at the palace gates. He had, he said, caught an enormous fish, so big that he thought King Polycrates himself deserved it, free of charge. Polycrates was pleased at this and invited the man to dinner. When the fish was cut open, inside was the ring! Polycrates decided that it was hopeless, he was just bound to be happy no matter what he did about it – but he did in fact later end miserably, as Amasis had predicted. After a variety of other fairly unscrupulous doings, Polycrates was lured by a neighboring Persian mainland governor or satrap, Oroetes, to come and visit, seducing him with a pretended desire to revolt from the Persian empire and promising financial benefits. Oroetes showed Polycrates's secretary treasure chests purportedly filled with gold but in reality filled with sand, except for the top layer; Polycrates, who had not investigated carefully enough either the gold or the wicked satrap's motives, took the bait, and was crucified by the satrap, Oroetes, "in a manner not fit to be told."

This story is worth telling in all its folktale glory, because it demonstrates why our world of modern, professional historians for a long time had difficulty taking Herodotus seriously as a historian. Herodotus makes it clear that he was not sure the story about Polycrates and his ring was true in the sense that it had really happened – it was just one of hundreds of stories collected in the process of his investigations about the growth of Persia. But in another and almost equally important sense he believed it *was* a true story, because it was a story that the Samians really had preserved about their famous ruler. Hence, true or not, it pointed to what Samians thought about their sixth-century past and their great tyrant, and thus helps explain who they were as players in the early fifth century Ionian revolt, the prelude in the 490s to Xerxes' war on Greece in the late 480s. We have here evidence of an early Samian maritime ascendancy, the political and military alliances between Egypt and the Greek trading states of the east that attempted to keep the Persian-Phoenician alliance from dominating the East Aegean and the lucrative trade routes to Egypt and the west, and also (very obliquely told) the cessation of the Samian-Egyptian alliance, probably in actuality an alliance that Polycrates called off, rather than Amasis.

The story of Polycrates's downfall was a real one, part of the story Herodotus wants most to tell, about the growth of the Persian empire. It also fits into an emerging pattern that over the course of the *Histories* plays so important a part in explaining the astonishing Persian defeat in 479: how rulers and other exceptionally lucky and important people, sheltered as they are from the difficulties that more ordinary people face, tend to lose their grip on reality, assume that they are in charge of their lives, and make errors of fact and judgment that bring them down. In Polycrates's case, the urgent need for money and his desire somehow to remain independent from Persia obscured from him the dangerous position he was allowing himself to be put in by an unscrupulous satrap. Each different ruler embodies a different version of this problem; a rare few, like Sabacos the Ethiopian (2.139), or perhaps Darius the father of Xerxes and the most successful Persian king of them all, seem largely to escape, but over the course of the *Histories* we see it emerging as one of the most important patterns repeatedly shaping the course of human events – not a pattern because Herodotus as a quasi-novelist has decided it will be a pattern, but one that (according to Herodotus, at least) emerges inductively from the data themselves, the real evidence that these stories from the past contain.

By the time we get to Xerxes in book 7 we understand better, as the story of the Persian offensive unrolls, why Xerxes makes such a poor job of his invasion of Greece. Greece is so small, disunited and poor, Persia so large, wealthy, and powerful, that Xerxes simply cannot imagine the possibility of failure, until it is actually upon him. He has not taken the trouble to learn the facts about Greece – its lack of water, its poor and rocky soil, the fiercely independent political culture of its inhabitants – that would enable him successfully to defeat them.[10] As a result, the terrain, the water, and the freedom-loving Greeks themselves defeat him. Like many other rich and important men in the *Histories*, Xerxes has information sitting right in front of him that he simply cannot hear because he is in the grip of faulty assumptions about the degree of his own control over events. Like Oedipus in the *Oedipus Tyrannus* he does not know what he does not know – but unlike Oedipus, he is not interested in finding out uncomfortable truths.

So, of Herodotus's invention of history we can see the following: Herodotus conceived of the whole human world as a single phenomenon, bound together by story – thousands of stories, multicolored threads, woven together into a single fabric through time and the workings of causal connection. The part of the fabric he chooses to tell is the one connected to the growth of the Persian empire and its check in Greece, though he deviates many times along the way to tell about other things that attracted his attention. The meaning of the story, according to Herodotus, however, is not univocal, and it is not his own. It rather arises out of the patterns formed by the stories themselves. The only caveat he gives as an author is that one cannot listen selectively only to the stories one likes, or those that glorify people or causes one likes or that are convenient to one's own ideological purposes. In Herodotus's version at least, Xerxes could have easily won his war, but only if he had taken the time to try to understand precisely the parts of the story that remained incomprehensible to his imperial assumptions, and the very illusions he held about the extent of his power made it almost impossible for him to do that. *Historie*, investigation, matters: by including us, his readers, in the circle of his investigations, Herodotus seems to think that we share his concern for such things and thus resemble the very small number of intelligent actors within his *Histories*, in that we too are taking the trouble to look closely at the complicated grid of imperial aggression in the Persian

---

[10] See, for instance, Xerxes' conversation with his uncle Artabanus, 7.45-52, or his conversations with Demaratus the Spartan later in book 7 (7.101-104, 209-210).

story.[11] Through that exercise, we too look closely at the world and, unlike Xerxes, collect as much information as possible, information about how the world works; this information will inform our actions, so that we will not be blindsided by things out there that are real but foreign to our assumptions. Herodotus does not state as much explicitly, but if we take Solon's advice to Croesus seriously, Herodotus's challenge to us as readers is one of the highest intellectual order. It reminds us that Herodotus himself was a member of the first great generation of Greek sophists, renouncing traditional customs in favor of "the examined life."

Herodotus, of course, was not the first person in human history to care about the past, but he was the first Greek we have on record as caring about the past in precisely this way. Stories from the past had often been told throughout the ancient world as myth or family glorification, or the assertion of a particular people's power and glory. But Herodotus was apparently the first to see that if one has a question about reality – in his case, why did the Greeks win the Persian Wars? – it is possible, and even necessary, to tell a story with thousands of intertwining foci: to weave together one story that is no one person or family or race's story, but, precisely, the ongoing, evolving story of *everybody* involved – men, women, even children, Greeks, Persians, Medes, Egyptians, Phoenicians, Babylonians, Scythians, Ethiopians, Lydians, Lycians, Thracians, Italians – in short, the whole of the known eastern Mediterranean world. One could ask questions and collect stories, testing them against known facts, and then weave together a story of the whole that was, as much as possible, true, interesting, and useful because it was in some sense everybody's truth, and a truth that could only be understood, really, by narrating it as a series of changes taking place over time (1.5). History in Herodotus's hands was not propaganda for a particular point of view, religion, or race, not wish fulfillment or morality tale, but useful for its readers because it explored the process of change over time, as a serious, critical record of the real doings and thoughts of many real people, ordinary and extraordinary from the lived human past.

That is one half of the story of the invention of historiography in the west. The other half is the story of Herodotus's great and austere successor, Thucydides (c. 460–400 BCE). A generation ago it was an apparently irrefutable truth that, although we generously gave He-

---

[11] Herodotus considers the exercise of clear-sightedness often to be a painful process: 9.16.

rodotus the title "Father of History" it was a courtesy title, given from pious sentiment. The *real* first historian, because the first "scientific" historian, was Thucydides, writing a scant generation later than Herodotus. If we believe what he tells us in the first lines of his *History of the Peloponnesian War*, he began writing right at its beginning, in 431 BCE, about the time Herodotus was laying down his stylus (5.26.5).

To a certain extent, the traditional judgment about Thucydides's superiority as a historian continues to hold some validity. If Herodotus as a historian can be thought of as a hammer and an anvil, beating out for us the huge sheet of the stories of the known world entailed by Persian expansionism, the other inventor of history, Thucydides, is rather a surgical instrument, a brilliantly pointed scalpel. Thucydides took Herodotus's method of careful collection and investigation of stories from the past and adapted it to tell, as his own account, a narrative that he felt was important, holding himself personally responsible to tell it as accurately as possible.[12] What he dissected was the aetiology, the military, psychological and sociological causes, of the course of a vitally important Greek war, one that he had himself participated in as a general.

The 27-year war between Athens and Sparta that we call the Peloponnesian War began in 431 and ended in 404 BCE; the Spartan victory in 404 dashed Athens' hopes for a permanent hegemony through sea power over the Greek communities of the eastern Aegean. (This was very important, because it led to the Macedonians, the Roman empire, medieval Europe, and ultimately the shape of the modern western world that we take for granted). So although the first history, that of Herodotus, was one of Greek victory, the second, written by Thucydides the Athenian, was much darker in tone: it was the story of the defeat of his city, and the death of the vision for Athens that Pericles, Athens' greatest leader, had held.

The transformation Thucydides made in the nascent discipline that Herodotus had bequeathed to him cannot be understood without first saying something more about the intellectual life of the period. Herodotus was finishing his work in 431, as the Peloponnesian War between Athens and Sparta began. An ancient biography has it that about a decade earlier, in the late 440s, the adolescent Thucydides had been in one of Herodotus's audiences, perhaps in Athens, or perhaps at one of the great festivals that periodically took place in the Greek world, at which Herodotus may well have given readings. The 440s

---

[12] Thucydides *History* 1.20-22.

and 430s were the time when a huge intellectual revolution was sweeping Greece, which we call the first sophistic, or the Greek enlightenment. Foreign intellectuals were coming from all over the Greek-speaking world, Sicily and southern Italy to the west and Ionia to the east, drawn by the power and wealth of imperial Athens; they constituted the first known class of professional intellectuals, and what these non-Athenian intellectuals established in the 430s and 420s in Athens was the first professional higher education. The sophists claimed to be able to teach the elite youth of Athens how to argue. Ultimately it is due to their example that we have universities – we owe to them, the fifth-century sophists, the idea of a professionally taught higher education. This essay and the others like it in this volume, are themselves the result of the sophists' efforts; they were the inventors of the notion of a prose that is persuasive because it is organized logically as a piece of coherent argument.

Learning the *techne* or skill of argumentation was necessary in the middle of the fifth century BCE because imperial Athens was a radical democracy, and it was in her law courts and assemblies that decisions were made by a voting majority of the male citizen body. Anyone who wished to be important within the life of the city had to know, first, how to defend himself from legal prosecution by his enemies and, second, how to argue for political positions he thought useful for the city in the democratically constituted Assembly. Thucydides was a pupil of this first great generation of sophists. His family was one of the most important in Athens; he was connected to the Philaids, the family of Miltiades, the victor of the Battle of Marathon. His prose, unlike that of Herodotus, shows in every sentence that he had learned the new rigor of word choice and argument that was the gift of the sophists to the Athenian young. Thucydides is more ambitious in his intellectual aims than Herodotus. He does not only want to retell stories he has investigated, culled from hither and yon and arranged into a single long narrative – on the contrary, he takes Herodotus's idea of a continuous interconnected narrative about the past and systematically applies to it the notion of rigorous standards of argumentation and narrative authority that he learned from the sophists. His history is not a series of interlocking stories but an intensely self-conscious analysis of a terrible war, written by himself, and argumentatively couched in the abstract nouns of social science, that the sophists were busy inventing even as he first began to write.[13]

---

[13] See, for instance, 3.82-85, Thucydides's assessment of the terrible Corcyraean *stasis*.

That is why, despite some basic similarity of aim, the tones of these two great works of history are so different. Herodotus considered himself an outsider, someone who owed his authority to the fact that he was unattached to the particularities of any one city or politics and hence could (often ironically, always genially) tell the stories of everybody. Thucydides was, on the contrary, an insider, passionately embedded in the particularities of Athenian political life. As a member of a famous and wealthy Athenian family, he was expected to play a significant part himself in the political life of the city.

Right from the beginning, his style of presenting himself in his narrative *as* its narrator differs from that of Herodotus. Whereas Herodotus tells us almost nothing of himself, his travels, his family or city, Thucydides in his *History of the Peloponnesian War* firmly if briefly situates himself as a historical actor in his own narrative. He tells us that he had reached an age to understand its significance when the war broke out (5.26), although he was perhaps only in his mid-20s in 431. It is clear from the way his first book begins that he was fully committed to Athens' empire, and to the kind of power that a large and well-trained navy brought to Athens.[14] In fact, as he tells us in books 4 and 5, he was himself at some point in the first ten years of the war entrusted with the naval command of the Athenian fleet in the northwest Aegean, the Thraceward regions of the Chersonese, west of the Hellespont. He had the bad luck to be exercising this command as a young and ambitious general when one of the most astonishing single exploits of the whole 27-year war occurred. In 424, Brasidas, a young and ambitious Spartan general, in personality more like an Athenian than a Spartan himself, took a cadre of 1000 Peloponnesian mercenaries and 700 helots or Spartan serfs on forced marches northwards from the Peloponnese all the way to Amphipolis and the Chersonese, largely through enemy territory. There he unexpectedly brought the subject cities of Athens' empire in the north over to the side of Sparta, persuading them to revolt and promising them Spartan help in doing so.[15] The Athenian demagogues who had controlled political decision-making after Pericles's death from the plague blamed Thucydides for failing to protect the region, and Thucydides spent the rest of the war after 424 in exile, in Corinth, in Italy, or perhaps on some property his family owned on the island of Thasos.[16] We know that Thucydides lived to see the Athenian defeat in 404 (he tells us so in the context of

---

[14] The first narrative in the *History* concerns the growth of sea power, 1.2-15.
[15] *History* 4.78 ff.
[16] *History* 4.104-108, 5.26.5.

a general assessment of Pericles's career in 2.65), but his own narrative stops abruptly in mid-sentence, in a narrative of the year 411, six years before the end of the war proper.

Who knows how Thucydides would have ended the account of the Peloponnesian War? What we do know, because it tacitly infuses almost every page of his narrative of the crucial first ten years of the war, is one compelling reason why he decided to write it up, at the war's end, when he was finally allowed under the general amnesty to return to Athens. Having grown up himself in the exciting years of Pericles's generalship and the power of the Athenian navy, Thucydides clearly remained at least until the end of the war in 404 an unreconstructed partisan of Pericles's vision for Athens. It is a vision that deserves still to be treated with enormous respect, in particular by citizens of the United States, the oldest continuous experiment in constitutional democracy at present. The funeral oration that Thucydides puts in Pericles's mouth early in book 2, honoring the Athenians who died in battle during the first year of the war, remains one of the finest and most succinct statements ever made of some basic democratic ideals.

> Our constitution is called a democracy because power is in the hands not of a minority but of the whole people. When it is a question of settling private disputes, everyone is equal before the law; when it is a question of putting one person before another in positions of public responsibility, what counts is not membership of a particular class, but the actual ability which the man possesses. No one, so long as he has it in him to be of service to the state, is kept in political obscurity because of poverty. And, just as our political life is free and open, so is our day-to-day life in our relations with each other. We do not get into a state with our next-door neighbor if he enjoys himself in his own way, nor do we give him the kind of black looks which, though they do no real harm, still do hurt people's feelings. We are free and tolerant in our private lives; but in public affairs we keep to the law. That is because the law commands our deep respect" (2.37, trans. Warner, with modifications).

We do not know when Thucydides penned these lines – whether they were ever spoken by Pericles, let alone spoken by him on the precise occasion on which Thucydides said they were. What we do know is that Thucydides reproduced these words in his *History* because he intended them to be heard by his Athenian and non-Athenian readers *after* 404, as a reminder of what radical democracy in Athens in the late 430s had really stood for.[17] The Greek world in 404, after the

---

[17] See especially Pericles's last speech, 2.60-64.

defeat of Athens, was quite a different place from what it had been a generation earlier. All of Greece was exhausted by the war. Thucydides was himself a rich intellectual who had been obliged by his exile to sit out the second, much grimmer, half of the war. Ironically, he had in consequence been spared a large part of the corrupting despair and cynicism that affected almost every Athenian citizen in the last, horrible years leading up to 404, the kind of despair and cynicism that led them to the killing of Socrates as a scapegoat in 399.

So Thucydides came home after the war, with his coldly analytical general's mind and his finely honed sophist's tongue, to find a city he did not recognize, a city that was in danger of throwing away its cultural patrimony. They say that history is always written by the victors. But the first great professional history, on the contrary, was written by a loser, doubly so since he had personally been exiled and his city had lost its great war. Thucydides, however, refused to accept that easy assessment, and began instead to take up the tools that Herodotus had bequeathed him, and with a cold and logical passion to chronicle the depth of the loss, the stupidities that had been responsible for Athens' defeat, but also, the greatness of the vision that had inspired Periclean Athens in the first place. For the city had forgotten its own greatness by the war's end. What Thucydides set out to do was remind the Athenians of it – implicitly, to condemn Pericles's successors for the magnitude of the loss they had brought about, and the stupidity they had shown in working not for their city but for their own private, petty, and often venal ambitions. Like Herodotus's Xerxes, the Athenian demagogues who had attempted to direct the war with Sparta after Pericles's death had failed to look carefully at the real circumstances that faced them, and they came to grief in consequence. This is the process that Thucydides chronicles in his history.

In one important way Thucydides was brilliantly successful; today we celebrate fifth-century Athens through the lens that Pericles and Thucydides bequeathed to us. We have trouble remembering what other literary sources of the time tell us: that in 404 BCE Athens was in fact a shattered, superstitious, vindictive state. But what Thucydides set out to do – to recall, after the crushing defeat, what *his* Athens had been like, the Athens that began the war – looked at the time like a very difficult, perhaps even impossible task. It is very likely that his sense of his task's difficulty influenced the voice in which he wrote up his *History*, and goes some significant way to explaining how very different is the impression it makes from that made by Herodotus's genial narrative, and how very strenuous and severe is his authoritative authorial persona. For unlike Herodotus, who had no particular brief beyond narrating the surprising victory of Greeks over Persians, Thucydides had a difficult argument to make with his contemporaries. He insisted that they look back; an important reason for remembering the disastrous war of the near past was, precisely, to take responsibility for the condition in which they found themselves in the present. In order to make this case with conviction, he had to concoct an analytic prose style that would persuade us, his readers, not of his own general alertness or Herodotean catholicity, but rather of his rigorous and impartial authorial integrity both in reporting the facts and in correctly assessing their meaning

At present some scholars mock as intellectual pretension Thucydides' confidence that he had accurately accounted for the Peloponnesian War; it all seems rather old-fashioned. We are much more likely, a la Herodotus, ironically to believe that everyone has his or her own stories and that the point is not to choose among them, but to let them stand in all their unreconstructed diversity of viewpoints. But even if we notice how great the intellectual differences are that distinguish the first two historians in this one respect, we need to notice also the deeper lessons that Thucydides has learned from Herodotus in asserting his new, professional, rigorously accurate historian's authority. For Thucydides too has written a work that is in its own way profoundly dialogic, because it is based on the realities of shared human perceptions about great events lived through. It is a different way of accounting for the numerous voices that must be heard through the narrative of a work of history: where Herodotus tells many stories of the Persian empire's growth and check in Greece, and tells them as the collective story of everyone, Thucydides tells his own story of a war in which all the combatants are at the height of their powers, but he depicts all of the actors in events thinking, speaking, and acting, using those powers as intelligently as possible to achieve their goals.

Even the least attractive actors in Thucydides – I think, for instance, of the notorious demagogue Cleon[18] – speak lucidly and argue intelligently for their own points of view. Right at the war's messy and uninspiring outbreak, in the crisis between Corcyra and Corinth, arguing over which side Athens will take (1.32-43), we are forced as readers to acknowledge the credibility of both sides of the quarrel, and the agonizing difficulties of the various states forced to take sides in consequence. Many real human voices go into the making of the nar-

---

[18] *History* 3.37-40.

ratives of our two historians, and that is ultimately why we trust both Herodotus's Persian Wars and Thucydides's Peloponnesian War as "real" – that is, in some way credible – history, rather than fiction (as Hayden White and some other post-modern historiographers would have it). Herodotus's voices are the voices of the many stories from the past that he retells, while Thucydides's voices are those of the actors in events. But in each case, the historian is listening for the truth of a plot line that is not in its deepest sense his own. He is rather the critical, investigatory intelligence that finds the sources and determines if they are real and serious or not: but his goal is to find out what really happened, as best he can – not to impose his own favorite plot line on events.

One very important topic remains to be addressed: Herodotus's and Thucydides' vision of the role that divinity played in "what really happened." It deserves to be treated explicitly, since this is after all one part of their Greek thought world that remains quite different from that of the Judaeo-Christian history and historiography that forms the principal subject of this volume. Thucydides's attitudes are easy to summarize: he ignores religion as a part of his narrative, and his private religious views, whatever they are, remain entirely absent from the *History*. In book 2, in the description of the terrible Athenian plague, he comments: "equally useless were prayers made in the temples, consultation of oracles, and so forth; indeed, in the end people were so overcome by their sufferings that they paid no further attention to such things" (2.47, trans. Warner). In book 7, he expressly blames Nicias's religious scrupulosity for the Athenian failure to leave Syracuse while there was still time to save the bulk of the fleet. An eclipse of the moon took place, "and Nicias, who was somewhat addicted to divination and practices of that kind, refused from that moment even to take the question of departure into consideration, until they had waited the thrice nine days prescribed by the soothsayers" (7.50, trans. Warner). When one adds Thucydides' silence regarding religion to the general impression left by the sophistic era as a time of freethinking agnosticism (one thinks, for instance, of the critiques of it in Aristophanes's *Clouds*, or Plato's *Apology*), it is easy to assume that personally he was indifferent to the subject altogether. Like the private domestic lives of the actors in the *History*, or indeed, the social and cultural realities of mid-fifth-century life, religion remained largely absent from his intense focus on the course of the war.

Herodotus's relation to religion is very different. In book 2, almost all of which is devoted to the description of Egypt and Egyptian history, he states that he will try to avoid bringing up *ta theia*, "divine matters": "Because I believe that everyone is equal in terms of religious knowledge, I do not see any point in relating anything I was told about the gods, except their names alone. If I refer to such matters, it will be because my account leaves me no choice" (2.3, trans. Waterfield). A little later in the same book, he incorrectly etymologizes the Greek word "god" (*theos*) from the aorist stem of the verb *tithenai*, "to put, to set," "because they had set all things in order and assigned everything its place" (2.52, trans. Waterfield). The individual names of gods he thought came later, as cultural inventions of various peoples. Clearly Herodotus thinks that divine powers exist and direct human affairs. Croesus is sent a dream that his son will die from a weapon; Xerxes has a dream that forces him to continue to go to war; the Delphic oracle's influence is pervasive throughout the *Histories*, directing barbarians and Greeks alike; portents abound as Xerxes begins his march from Asia into Europe.[19] But the trouble with divinity and the signs it sends humanity, at least as the stories of the *Histories* convey it, is that they remain obdurately unpredictable and inscrutable; one only understands by looking back afterward what the gods were saying would happen. It is clear from Herodotus's vantage point in mid-century that the gods did not want one man, Xerxes, to rule the known world, and therefore set out to check his hubris by making a Greek victory possible.[20] But to Herodotus this fact was more or less an obvious tautology: much more interesting to him was the series of very human thoughts, decisions, and actions that brought the Greek victory about. *Ta theia*, the religious aspect of things, he reported only when they played a crucial part of the human record of what happened. So although both Herodotus and Thucydides in practice express reservations about treating religion and the work of divinity as proper topics for historical consideration, they do so in very different ways and for different reasons.

To sum up: significant differences separate the achievements of the first two historians. Herodotus told a story of about seventy-five or eighty years that ended in the generation immediately before his own, and told it by stitching together stories that, he stressed repeatedly, were not his own but had been told him by others. He engaged in *historie*, or investigation of them, knowing their imperfections, but believing

---

[19] Herodotus, *Histories* 1.34; 7.12, 14; 1.48, 7.140, 220, 8.36-39; 7.57.
[20] Herodotus ironically has this sentiment expressed by the trickster Themistocles, 8.109, preemptively laying the groundwork for later claiming favors from Persia.

that even such imperfect witnesses to the past as he had, because they were gathered from everyone involved, would reveal some fairly important truths about how human societies worked – truths that would remain hidden except through the construction of something like the gigantic canvas he was creating: the story of everybody involved first in the growth and then the defeat of the Persian empire in Greece. Moreover, as he said right at the start – because human happiness doesn't remain long in the same place, but big becomes small and small big (1.5) – Herodotus believed that telling everybody's story would save the things for the future that his own generation's vantage point did not yet know were important but, through his efforts to get them all down, were now part of the record that could be consulted. Throughout his *Histories*, divinity plays an inscrutable but active part in shaping the outcome of events.

Thucydides rejected Herodotus's idea of telling others' stories – in fact, he did not believe it was possible to do real history except the history of one's own times, precisely because the stories were too prone to be self-serving and inexact (he criticizes two details found in Herodotus, for just this sort of sloppiness[21]). But he too created a narrative that was profoundly dialogic; the others' voices were not in his case the stories of others, but the thoughts and speeches of multiple contemporaries of his involved in the Peloponnesian War, that he carefully reported: Athenians, Spartans, Syracusans, Boiotians, and even the citizens of tiny Melos – all of those caught, like himself, in the web of the dreadful 27-year war that was decimating Greece. Unlike Herodotus, he chose to ignore the role of the divine, or even religion, almost entirely.

What Thucydides shares with Herodotus is the sense that the past matters, and that coming as close as we can to knowing exactly what happened – who said what to whom, and what happened next – is what will help us make our own decisions wisely, human nature being at base pretty much the same in different places and times (1.22). Both Herodotus and Thucydides wrote out of a profound conviction about the odd ineluctability of facts, and the difficulties that actors in events always have first seeing salient facts clearly and then acting intelligently on them. As we often see in our private lives, and Herodotus and Thucydides in their different ways would be the first to agree, it is no easy matter to discern what is really going on under the complexities of reality and the desires we invest it with. Thucydides believed that

---

[21] *History* 1.20.

the one guarantee we have is that the basic facts that shape our existence will out and cannot merely be imaged, or imagined, away.

This is something we moderns of the west tend to forget, since we live in a world that is increasingly one of mass-produced fantasy, where images can be doctored, voices can be computer generated, numbers through the miracles of the computer can be massaged for self-serving ends. Herodotus believed that there was a basic divine pattern to events, only discernable to most humans after the fact, but valuable and needing to be respected, particularly in its convergence with basic ethical principles. Thucydides was more aggressively secular in his understanding, but at the end it came to much the same thing, even if he referred to *tuche*, chance, interacting with human *gnome* or *xunesis*, intelligence as its patterning principle, rather than a divinely ordered fate. Human beings fare better if they look closely and realistically at the range of facts that confront them, as they begin to decide what to do under pressing events. Ultimately it is their ability to do this, and to hold fast to their most basic and dearly-held values in the process, that determines whether events will brutally overtake them, or whether learning from the past we can also learn to see our presents more clearly, and thus help shape our future. What both men saw clearly, and used the discipline of history to communicate, is that this process requires that the story be an ongoing story of everyone – in Thucydides's case, the Greeks not just of Athens and Sparta, but of Thebes and Plataea, and Corinth, and Amphipolis, and Corcyra, and tiny Melos and Mycalessus; in Herodotus's case, of kings and commoners, knaves and prostitutes, sailors and traders and soldiers and soldiers of fortune from all over the east Mediterranean world.[22]

Bibliography

Appleby, J., L. Hunt, and M. Jacob. 1994. *Telling the Truth about History*. New York and London: W.W. Norton.

Bakker, E., I. de Jong, and H. van Wees. 2002. *Brill's Companion to Herodotus*. Leiden: Brill.

---

[22] An earlier version of this paper was delivered at Vassar College in the spring of 2002, as the college Blegen Lecture. I would like to thank the Classics Department of Vassar College for that initial invitation, and Professors Bruce Chilton and Jacob Neusner for inviting me to rethink it for the Bard College conference and course in the spring of 2006. Some works that further usefully discuss topics found in this paper include Bakker, de Jong, and van Wees 2002; Connor 1984; Dewald and Marincola 2006; Gould 1989; Hornblower 1987; Lateiner 1989; Rood 1998.

Berkhofer, R. 1995. *Beyond the Great Story: History as Text and Discourse*. Cambridge, Mass.: Harvard University Press.

Connor, R. 1984. *Thucydides*. Princeton: Princeton University Press.

_____. 1993. "The Histor in History." In *Nomodeiktes. Greek Studies in Honor of Martin Ostwald*, ed. R. Rosen and J. Farrell. Ann Arbor: University of Michigan Press, 3-15.

Dewald, C. 1998. "Introduction." In *Herodotus. The Histories*, trans. R. Waterfield. Oxford: Oxford University Press, ix-xli.

Dewald, C. and J. Marincola. 2006. *The Cambridge Companion to Herodotus*. Cambridge: Cambridge University Press.

Gould, J. 1989. *Herodotus*. New York: St. Martin's Press.

Hornblower, S. 1987. *Thucydides*. Baltimore: Johns Hopkins University Press.

Immerwahr, H. 1966. *Form and Thought in Herodotus*. Cleveland: APA Philological Monographs 23.

Jenkins, K. 1999. *Why History?* London: Routledge.

Lateiner, D. 1989. *The Historical Method of Herodotus*. Toronto: University of Toronto Press.

Rood, T. 1998. *Thucydides: Narrative and Explanation*. Oxford: Clarendon Press.

3

Are the Dead Sea Scrolls Historical Texts?

Lawrence H. Schiffman

The corpus of manuscripts known as the Dead Sea Scrolls, the term commonly used to refer to the texts found in eleven caves near Qumran along the western shore of the Dead Sea, is often said to have fundamentally revised our sense of the state of the differing approaches to Judaism (or Judaisms) existing the Second Temple period. As such, these texts have turned out to teach us much about the background of Christianity and the development of rabbinic Judaism. No one would ever deny that from the point of view of the history of religions these texts are a goldmine. But can we really call them historical texts? Do they tell us anything about what we normally term history, not the history of religions or the history of ideas?

The Dead Sea Scrolls are a corpus of what in antiquity, before their deterioration, would have constituted some 900 scrolls. This corpus divides up into three roughly equal parts: books known to us as part of the canon of the Hebrew Bible (all are preserved at least in small fragments except Esther); books we term apocryphal, some previously known in the apocrypha or pseudepigrapha and most not; and finally, the sectarian documents representing the particular beliefs and teachings of the group that occupied Qumran, identified by most scholars as Essenes.

We may say at the outset that there are no post-Hebrew Bible historiographical works preserved at Qumran.[1] Rather, we deal with the religious texts of a sect that withdrew from participation in the public life of Judea under Hasmonean rule. The group continued to exist under the Romans and the Herodians. Qumran was occupied from

---

[1] This is true despite the existence of some fragmentary manuscripts termed "Historical Texts" to be discussed below. These texts are too poorly preserved to be certain of their contents and at best may refer to some historical events.

some time after the reign of John Hyrcanus, through to the year 68 CE, when it was destroyed. This was a period of great historical events and developments, and yet there are no historiographical texts in the Qumran collection. 1 Maccabees, composed in Hebrew during this period (c. 100 BCE),[2] was not preserved at Qumran, and we have reason to believe that the sectarians opposed the Hasmoneans. It seems that for the sectarians, and for the groups who authored the various texts gathered at Qumran, the biblical style of historiography had come to an end with the onset of the Hellenistic period – quite a curious development in light of the importance of history writing in the Hellenistic world in general and in Hellenistic Judaism.

In evaluating what constitutes historical writing, we could employ a number of possible definitions. From the point of view of our contemporary understanding, history requires a sense of cause and effect and of human causality. We today do not see a story or a set of facts narrated in chronological order as history. Nonetheless, these tests cannot be applied to ancient Near Eastern historiography or even to Greco-Roman historiography. And in our case, we do not even have annalistic writing, although there are a few exceptions. Essentially the scrolls contain nothing of what we would term history. From this point of view this paper could be obviated with a resounding one word answer to the question we have posed: are the Dead Sea Scrolls historical texts? No!

But there is another way of looking at our question. We can ask if the scrolls supply us with historical information – the kind of information that we would include if we were creating a historical narrative for the period covered by the scrolls collection. Can we find data for the writing of political, social, economic and religious history? Here the Qumran scrolls can and already have provided scholars with the opportunity to reap a rich harvest of historical data, grist for the mill of the modern historian.

Our answer to the question we have posed will in large measure also depend on the way we define the history of religions. The role of the scrolls in allowing us to better reconstruct innumerable aspects of the history of Judaism in late antiquity cannot be exaggerated, if by the

---

[2] 2 Maccabees is an epitome (summary) of Greek work of five parts composed by Jason of Cyrene to which is added some material at the beginning and end by the "author" who completed his work c. 100 CE. There is no reason even to hope for this Greek composition in the Qumran library.

history of Judaism we mean the history of its religious ideas.³ We intend, in this paper, to concentrate on other aspects of the historical enterprise, however.

We should pause here to observe a particular problem related to modern historiography based on the scrolls that will influence our discussion below. This is what I have referred to as the "Christianization" of the scrolls.⁴ Much of the research on the understanding of the scrolls as a source for the history of religions has asked the question of what can be learned about the history of Christianity and has ignored the actual role of the scrolls as a source for the history of Judaism. Let us simply recall that only by understanding the scrolls properly as sources for Jewish history can one appraise their value in the reconstruction of the background of Christianity.

When the scrolls were first discovered, it was assumed that they were of primary interest for Christianity because they seemed to document only a peculiar group of dissidents who, some scholars thought, were parallel to, or even forerunners of, the early Church. The early Qumran scholars missed the point that what the scrolls are best mined for is the evidence they give on the wider Jewish community. Put otherwise, this collection, brought together by a group that had separated itself from other Jewish groups, can be used to understand a tremendous amount about those opposing groups (and some related ones as well), even if this information needs to be taken with a big grain of salt and carefully evaluated. Our question, then, is better widened to: Are the Dead Sea Scrolls historical texts for the history of the Jews and Judaism?

The largest amount of historical data comes from careful analysis of the Pesharim, a group of contemporizing biblical commentaries preserved for parts of Isaiah, the Minor Prophets, and Psalms.⁵ The

---

³ My own synthesis is found in L.H. Schiffman, *Reclaiming the Dead Sea Scrolls: The History of Judaism, the Background of Christianity, the Lost Library of Qumran* (Philadelphia and Jerusalem: Jewish Publication Society, 1994).

⁴ L.H. Schiffman, "Confessionalism and the Study of the Dead Sea Scrolls," *Jewish Studies* 31 (1991) 3-14.

⁵ A good introduction is found in D. Dimant, "Qumran Sectarian Literature," in *Jewish Writings of the Second Temple Period* (ed. M.E. Stone; CRINT II.2; Philadelphia: Fortress, 1984) 503-508, and "Pesharim, Qumran," *ABD* 5.244-51. See also M. Horgan, *Pesharim: Qumran Interpretations of Biblical Books* (CBQMS 8; Washington, DC: Catholic Biblical Association of America, 1979) 229-59; B. Nitzan, *Megillat Pesher Habakkuk: mi-Megillot Midbar Yehudah (1Qp Hab)* (Jerusalem: Bialik Institute, 1986) 29-80; W.H. Brownlee, "Biblical Interpretation among the Sectaries of the Dead Sea Scrolls," *BA* 14 (1951) 54-76; *The Midrash Pesher of Habakkuk* (SBLMS 24 ; Missoula,

Pesharim, together with a few related documents, like the Admonition – the first part of the Damascus Document – provide most of what we know of the sect's internal history and its relations with and attitudes to opposing groups of Jews.[6] But these texts speak in difficult allusions, depending on interpretation of the biblical texts and on a particular set of terms and symbols used by the sect to express its self-image and its view of its opponents.

The material in the *pesharim* covers three primary periods of sectarian history: the early days of the sect; the years immediately preceding, and perhaps following, the Roman conquest in 63 BCE; and the final stages of the End of Days. The last is dealt with primarily in the thematic *pesharim*.

MT: Scholars Press, 1979) 23-36; "The Background of Biblical Interpretation at Qumrân," in *Qumrân: sa piété, sa théologie et son milieu* (ed. M. Delcor; Bibliotheca ephemeridum theologicarum lovaniensium 46; Paris-Gembloux and Leuven: Duculot, Leuven University Press, 1978) 183-93. See also G.J. Brooke, Qumran "Pesher: Toward the Redefinition of a Genre," *RevQ* 10 (1979-80) 483-503 and "The Pesharim and the Origins of the Dead Sea Scrolls," in *Methods of Investigation of the Dead Sea Scrolls and the Khirbet Qumran Site: Present Realities and the Future Prospects* (ed. J.J. Collins, N. Golb, D. Pardee, and M. Wise; Annals of the New York Academy of Sciences; New York: New York Academy of Sciences, 1994) 339-54. Full editions of the pesher texts are available in Horgan, Nitzan and in E. Tov and D. Parry, *The Dead Sea Scrolls Reader* (Leiden: Brill, 2004) 2:2-105.

[6] On the historical relevance of the *pesharim*, see Nitzan, *Megillat Pesher Habakkuk*, 11-28 and 123-45; F.M. Cross, *The Ancient Library of Qumran and Modern Biblical Studies* (Grand Rapids, Mich.: Baker Book House, 1980) 88-120 and "The Early History of the Qumran Community," in *New Directions in Biblical Archaeology* (ed. D.N. Freedman and J.C. Greenfield; Garden City, N.Y.: Doubleday, 1971) 70-89; H. Stegemann, *Die Entstehung der Qumrangemeinde* (Bonn: Rheinische Friedrich-Wilhelms-Universität, 1971); A. Dupont-Sommer, "Lumières nouvelles sur l'arrière-plan historique des écrits de Qumran," *ErIsr* 8 (Sukenik Volume, 1967) 25*-36*; J.D. Amoussine (Amusin), "The Reflection of Historical Events of the First Century B.C. in Qumran Commentaries (4Q161; 4Q169; 4Q166)," *HUCA* 48 (1977) 134-46; J.H. Charlesworth, "The Origin and Subsequent History of the Authors of the Dead Sea Scrolls: Four Transitional Phases among the Qumran Essenes," *RevQ* 10 (1980) 213-34; P.R. Callaway, *The History of the Qumran Community: An Investigation* (JSPSup 3; Sheffield: JSOT Press, 1988) 135-71; F. García Martínez and A.S. van der Woude, "A Groningen Hypothesis of Qumran Origins and Early History," *RevQ* 14 (1990) 521-41; T.H. Lim, "The Wicked Priests of the Groningen Hypothesis," *JBL* 112 (1993) 415-25; H. Eshel, *Megillot Qumran veha-Medinah ha-Ḥasmona'it* (Jerusalem: Ben-Zvi, 2004); J.H. Charlesworth, *The Pesharim and Qumran History: Chaos or Consensus?* with appendix by L. Novakovic (Grand Rapids, MI: Eerdmans, 2002). However, many of the definite identifications proposed by these scholars cannot be sustained by the available evidence.

The Teacher and His Opponents

Considerable historical information is available from the *pesharim*, but often it is obscured by the use of sobriquets or code words for the groups or individuals involved. We first encounter the sect in the *pesharim* under the leadership of the Teacher of Righteousness, whom God has sent to lead the sect. Interpreting Ps 37:24, "for the Lord gives him support," *Pesher Psalms A* states:

> Its interpretation concerns the priest, the Teacher of [Righteousness, wh]om God [ch]ose to arise, f[or] He set him up (or: predestined him) to build for Him [God] a congregation [of His chosen ones in truth]. (pPss A 1–10 III 15–16)

The Teacher is said to have been specifically designated, indeed perhaps predestined, for his role in building the community. In addition, it was he who revealed to the sectarians the meaning of the prophets' words. But he found himself, presumably as a result of his teachings, in conflict with the Man of Lies. A group called the House of Absalom did not support the Teacher in his confrontation with the Man of Lies. The *pesher* explains Hab 1:13, which in the Masoretic text reads, "Why do You countenance treachery, and stand by idly while the evil one devours one who is more righteous than he?" as follows:

> Its interpretation is concerning the House of Absalom and the men of their council who kept silent when the Teacher of Righteousness was rebuked and did not help him against the Man of Lies, who rejected the Torah in the midst of all their con[grega]tion. (1QpHab 5:8–12)

Clearly, the verse has been taken to refer to an episode in the sect's history during which the Teacher was publicly rebuked by the Man of Lies. The House of Absalom was a group the Teacher could have expected to defend him. Some have suggested that the group might be the Pharisees; others believe they were a group within the sect. From the point of view of the community, this event showed that the Man of Lies had effectively rejected the Torah and its laws.

In commenting on Hab 1:5, "Look among the nations and observe well," read by the *pesher* as, "Look O traitors and observe well," the *pesher* states:

> [The interpretation of the matter concerns] those who are traitorous with the Man of Lies, for [they] did not [hearken to the words of] the Teacher of Righteousness from the mouth of God. (1QpHab 2:1–3)

The traitors, apparently led by the Man of Lies, were most probably straying members of the group or a competing group. In any case, this passage shows that the Teacher faced opposition not only from the official priesthood, but from others as well.

The main opponent of the Teacher was the Wicked Priest. It was he who confronted the Teacher and challenged him in the presence of the members of the group. That confrontation is described in an interpretation of Hab 2:5–6, "How much less then shall the defiant go unpunished, the treacherous, arrogant man ... who has harvested all the nations and gathered in all the peoples":

> Its interpretation concerns the Wicked Priest who was called by the name of truth at the beginning when he arose. But when he ruled over Israel, his heart became haughty and he abandoned God, and he rebelled against the laws for the sake of wealth. And he stole and gathered the wealth of the men of violence who had rebelled against God. And he took the wealth of the nations to add to it the guilt of transgression. And he conducted himself according to abom[in]able ways with all impurity. (1QpHab 8:8–13)

The Wicked Priest began his career with the support of the sectarians, but he quickly lost his way and began to transgress in order to increase his wealth. The sectarians regarded this depredation as stealing. The Wicked Priest made war against the other nations and had a conflict with the "men of violence," most likely the Pharisees.

Further, he violated the laws of ritual purity and defiled the sanctuary, as is explained in reference to the extremely difficult Hab 2:17, the end of which says, "For crimes against men and wrongs against lands, against cities and all their inhabitants." To this the text comments:

> Its interpretation: The city is Jerusalem in which the Wicked Priest undertook abominable actions, and he defiled the Temple of God. (1QpHab 12:7–9)

This interpretation must refer to legal rulings and ritual procedures in Temple worship regarded by the sectarians as violations of the Torah. A similar theme recurs in the Damascus Document, 4QMMT, and elsewhere in the sectarian corpus.

The Wicked Priest went so far as to lie in ambush for the Teacher of Righteousness. In interpreting Ps 37:32, "The wicked watches for the righteous, seeking to put him to death," the text states:

> Its interpretation concerns [the] Wicked [Pr]iest who wa[tched out for the Teach]er of Righteous[ness and sought to] put him to death. (pPs A 1–10 IV 8–9)

Although the Wicked Priest sought to kill the Teacher, he did not succeed.[7]

This passage from *Pesher Psalms A* is probably a reference to the very same event described in *Pesher Habakkuk* where we are told about the Wicked Priest that:

> He pursued the Teacher of Righteousness to swallow him up in his intense anger at the place of his (the Teacher's) exile. And at the time of the festival of their abstention from labor he appeared before them to swallow them up and to make them stumble on the day of the fast of the Sabbath of their abstention from labor. (1QpHab 11:5–8)

This account has likewise been interpreted as if it describes the death of the Teacher, but it simply describes a painful confrontation. The "fast of the Sabbath of their abstention from labor" is the Day of Atonement, called in the Bible a "Sabbath" (Lev 23:32) but also a fast. The Wicked Priest confronted the sectarians on this day of their holy Festival, but for him evidently it was not the Day of Atonement. This passage highlights that the sect used a different calendar from that used by the majority of Jews. In the sectarian solar calendar, the Jewish holidays fell on different days.

> ... because of his transgression against the Teacher of Righteousness and the men of his counsel, God gave him over into the hand[s] of his enemies to afflict him with disease so as to destroy (him) with mortal suffering because he had acted wickedly against His chosen one. (1QpHab 9:8–12)

The Wicked Priest's enemies tortured him, which represented divine punishment for his attacks on the Teacher of Righteousness. The sufferings of the Wicked Priest are even more graphically described in another passage:

---

[7] Various theories have sought to identify the Teacher with Jesus, claiming that he was executed by the Wicked Priest. Had that been the case, the text would not have gone on to explain how God took vengeance against the priest by turning him over to the "ruthless ones of the nations" (lines 9–10). And according to this text, the Teacher certainly survived this ambush. Indeed, the entire passage is an interpretation of Psalms where the text continues, "The Lord will not abandon him (the righteous) into his hand (the wicked); He will not let him (the righteous) be condemned in judgment (by the wicked)" (Ps 37:33).

[And all his enemies arose and ab]used him in order [for] his sufferings to be (fit) punishment for his evil. And they inflicted upon him horrible diseases, and acts of vengeance in the flesh of his body. (1QpHab 8:17–9:2)

The one who suffered was the Wicked Priest, not the Teacher of Righteousness. The enemies of the Wicked Priest, the nations against whom he had made war, are said to have tortured him, so that his life ended in mortal disease and affliction.

Hasmonean Historical Context

These scattered references to events in the life of the Teacher of Righteousness and his followers scarcely constitute a historical narrative, but, nonetheless, they can serve as the stuff from which historical accounts can be constructed. Various theories have been suggested to identify the Wicked Priest and to place these events within the context of what we know of Second Temple period history. In many cases, those theories have not been anchored sufficiently in paleography, archaeology, or the general historical sources. However, when these are all taken into consideration, it becomes abundantly clear – and this is unquestionable – that the events described in the texts just surveyed herein must be placed in the early Hasmonean period – in the years soon after the Maccabean Revolt.

Based on the study of 4QMMT, of which we will have much more to say below, it can be established that the sect was founded in this same period. The Teacher of Righteousness must have emerged as the sect's leader some years after the initial break that occurred soon after 152 BCE. The career of the Wicked Priest must be similarly dated. Most scholars now agree that the Wicked Priest is either Jonathan (160–143 BCE) or Simon (142–134 BCE), brothers of Judah the Maccabee, who were the first two rulers of the Hasmonean priestly dynasty.

We have additional information from a text found in Cave 4 (not technically a *pesher*) called *Testimonia*,[8] an anthology of biblical verses. The identical passage occurs also in another apocryphal work, called *Psalms of Joshua*.[9] Here is the text as it appears in *Psalms of Joshua*, with

---

[8] The text was first published by J.M. Allegro, *Qumrân Cave 4.I (4Q158-4Q186)* (DJD 5; Oxford: Clarendon Press, 1968) 57-60 and improved by the corrections of J. Strugnell, "Notes en marge du volume V des 'Discoveries in the Judean Desert of Jordan,'" *RevQ* 7 (1970) 225-29.

[9] C.A. Newsom, "The 'Psalms of Joshua' from Qumran Cave 4," *JJS* 39 (1988) 56-73; H. Eshel, "The Historical Background of the Pesher Interpreting Joshua's Curse on the Rebuilder of Jericho," *RevQ* 15 (Mémorial Jean Starcky, 1992) 409-20; T.H.

the breaks in the manuscript filled in with the help of *Testimonia:*

> Then Joshua finished praising and giving thanks in his psalms, he said, "Cursed be the man who builds this city. He shall lay its foundations at the cost of his firstborn and set up its gates at the cost of his youngest" (cf. Josh 6:26). And behold, a cursed man of Belial who arises to be a fowler's trap to his people and a cause of destruction to all his neighbors. And ... arose [and ruled (?)], so that both of them were instruments of violence. And they rebuilt [th]is [city] and they set up a wall and towers for it to make it a stronghold of evil in Israel and a horror in Ephraim and in Judah ... great [e]vil among the sons of Jacob and they s[pilled blood and com]mitted abomination in the land, and great blasphemy. (They spilled blood) like water on the rampart of the daughter of Zion and within the boundaries of Jerusalem. (PssJosh B 22 II 7–4 = Test 21–30)

Scholars have tried to identify the historical events outlined in this adaptation of Josh 6:26. According to this text, someone tried to rebuild Jericho despite Joshua's curse. In doing so, he lost both of his sons, who themselves had become evildoers, in the view of the author. He himself led his people astray and died, only to be replaced by another ruler, who followed the same course. They were both guilty of shedding the blood of Jews in Jerusalem.

Two theories have been put forward. One holds that this text describes Simon the Hasmonean (brother of Judah the Maccabee). Simon and his two sons (one of whom was probably his eldest and one his youngest) were on a tour of the kingdom and attended a banquet at the newly built fortress of Jericho in 134 BCE. There they were murdered by the local commander, who attempted a coup. Simon's remaining son, John Hyrcanus, was warned and was thus able to escape danger. He then reasserted control and ruled from 134 to 104 BCE.

A second theory places this event after the death of the two Hasmonean scions, Antigonus and Aristobulus I, in 103 BCE. At that time, work on the palaces and fortifications of Jericho was in full swing, as can be shown by recent excavations. The author of the text believed that Joshua's curse was visited on John Hyrcanus when he lost his two sons while rebuilding Jericho. His son Antigonus murdered his own brother Aristobulus I and then died himself shortly afterward. John Hyrcanus would be the accursed man of the text, who led his people astray and paid for his transgressions with the lives of his sons.

Lim, "The 'Psalms of Joshua' (4Q379 fr. 22 col. 2): A Reconsideration of its Text," *JJS* 44 (1993) 309-12.

In the absence of any firm historical evidence, it is not possible to decide to which Hasmonean ruler – Simon or his son John Hyrcanus – this dually preserved text applies. The text shows us that even after the lifetime of the Wicked Priest, the Qumran sectarians continued to be anti-Hasmonean, considering the descendants of the Maccabees as transgressors who led their people astray. This was an underlying view of the Qumran sect and is reflected in quite a number of sectarian texts.

Parallel with Josephus

We next encounter historical information in the *pesharim* in *Pesher Nahum,* which describes a somewhat later period. This material is virtually unique in that it describes actual people known from the pages of history. In this period the ruler is the Lion of Wrath, clearly an allusion to another of the Hasmonean priests who by this time were styled as kings. There we hear of the "interpreters of false laws" (usually translated literally as "seekers after smooth things") and their alliance with:

> [Deme]trius, king of Greece, who sought to enter Jerusalem with the counsel of the interpreters of false laws, [but God had not given Jerusalem over] into the hand of the kings of Greece from Antiochus until the rise of the rulers of the Kittim ... but (later) the city was given into the hand of the rulers of the Kittim. (QpNah 3–4 I 2–4)

This Demetrius, a ruler of the "Greek" empire, tried with the help of the interpreters of false laws to invade Jerusalem but did not succeed. In fact, from the time of Antiochus[10] until the time of the Kittim (a code word for the Romans), no one succeeded in conquering Jerusalem.

The result of the attack of Demetrius is also recorded:

> [... Demetrius who made war] against the Lion of Wrath so that he smote his nobles and the men of his council. (QpNah 3–4 I 5–6)

After the war was over and the Lion of Wrath was victorious, he took his revenge:

---

[10] One text, entitled Acts of a Greek King, has now been decisively understood to refer to Antiochus IV and his invasion of Egypt and ill treatment of Jerusalem. See M. Broshi and E. Eshel, "The Greek King Is Antiochus IV (4QHistorical Text=4Q248)," *JJS* 48/1 (1997) 120-129.

... against the interpreters of false laws in that he hanged men alive [which was never done] in Israel before ... (QpNah 3–4 I 7–8)

Most scholars understand this passage to mean that the Lion of Wrath punished his enemies by crucifying them, a punishment never before practiced by the Jewish people.

The events in this *pesher* text can be thoroughly decoded by drawing upon the evidence provided for the later Hasmonean period in the works of the ancient Jewish historian Josephus. We can identify all the *dramatis personae* in this text. The Kittim are the Romans, a designation common in the scrolls. Demetrius is Demetrius III Eukerus (95–88 BCE). His designation "king of Greece" refers to the Seleucid Empire, often referred to as Greece in Jewish literature. The Antiochus from whose time Jerusalem was never conquered by a foreign king was most probably Antiochus III the Great (223–187 BCE). The Jews voluntarily opened the gates of Jerusalem to him in 198 BCE because of their disenchantment with Ptolemaic rule. The interpreters of false laws are the Pharisees. The Lion of Wrath, ruler of Judea, is the Hasmonean king Alexander Janneus (104–76 BCE), great-grandson of Judah the Maccabee.

The events described here are narrated in greater detail by Josephus (*Ant* 13.372–383). The story begins with public protest over the sacrificial procedures followed by Alexander Janneus. Although Josephus gives no specific information, a Mishnaic parallel (*Sukkah* 4:9) indicates that he followed Sadducean practice, rejecting the water libation required by the Pharisees. A riot ensued as well as objections to his legitimacy as a priest, indeed to that of the entire Hasmonean dynasty. Josephus says that as a result, Janneus killed 6,000 people. After a military setback, he was severely criticized by his subjects, which in turn led him to make war against them. Josephus gives the probably exaggerated figure of 50,000 Jews killed during this conflict with their own king. When he tried to convince the people to make peace, they told him that they wanted him dead. Desperate to throw off the yoke of this cruel ruler, they sent for the Seleucid Demetrius III Eukerus to assist them. He invaded the country. On each side both Jews and Hellenized pagans fought, each appealing to the other to desert. In the ensuing battle, Alexander Janneus was forced to flee. Some Jews came to his aid, and persuaded Demetrius to withdraw, apparently by convincing him that the Jewish people was, in fact, divided in its attitude to Alexander Janneus. The battles continued until Alexander was able to retake Jerusalem and reassert his power. After reestablishing himself, Alexander feasted with his concubines while 800 Jews were crucified and their wives and children slaughtered as they watched. His opponents, numbering 8,000, were forced to flee into exile.

This is exactly the story told in the *Pesher Nahum* from which we learn that Janneus's enemies were the Pharisees. This account agrees with that of the Mishnah,[11] which claims that the trouble began over his following Sadducean legal practices. "His nobles" were the Sadducean leadership with whom Janneus (the Lion of Wrath) closely cooperated. This horrible Jewish civil war is the subject of the historical allusions in *Pesher Nahum*.[12] The account in *Pesher Nahum*, paralleled and supplemented as it is by Josephus, stands out as the one really solid historical account in the *pesher* texts. No such parallels exist for the rest of the material in the *pesharim*.

Other Historical Allusions

It would be helpful to say a few words about a text that is not a *pesher* but is relevant to the historical account derived from the *pesher* texts. After its difficult semicursive writing was deciphered, this curious text was recently identified as a *Prayer for King Jonathan*.[13] Although it is possible that this Jonathan is the brother of Judah the Maccabee, it seems much more likely that it is Alexander Janneus, whose name, "Janneus," is a Greek form of the Hebrew Jonathan ("Yannai" would be shortened from "Yonathan"). If so, we find in the Qumran library a prayer offered for the welfare of this king. The text includes some liturgical poetry, also found in the *Psalms Scroll,* as well as the following prayer:

> Holy One, watch over (or: Arise O Holy One on behalf of) King Jonathan and all the congregation of Your people Israel who are in the four corners of heaven. May peace be on all (of them) and upon Your Kingdom. May Your name be blessed! (Prayer for King Jonathan B1–9)

---

[11] M. Sukkah 4:9.

[12] S. Berrin, *The Pesher Nahum Scroll from Qumran: An Exegetical Study of 4Q169* (Leiden: Brill, 2004) 87-130, 301-306. Some scholars see direct allusions in this text to the end of the Hasmonean dynasty, specifically to the time of Salome Alexandra (76–67 BCE) and her sons, the Hasmonean brothers Hyrcanus II and Aristobulus II (67–63 BCE), but these figures cannot be definitely identified in this text. We do find clear reference, however, to the Roman conquest of Judea in 63 BCE.

[13] The presence of the name Jonathan in this text was deciphered properly by A. Yardeni, and it was subsequently published and analyzed in E. Eshel, H. Eshel, and A. Yardeni, "A Qumran Composition Containing Part of Ps. 154 and a Prayer for the Welfare of King Jonathan and his Kingdom," *IEJ* 42 (1992) 199-229 and "Rare DSS Text Mentions King Jonathan," *BAR* 20 (1994) 75-78.

How can we explain the presence of this prayer in the Qumran corpus? According to *Pesher Nahum*, the sectarians were opposed to Jonathan. Two possible answers may be suggested. First, it is possible that the sectarians initially regarded this king favorably, only later changing their mind as he followed policies they did not accept. Or it is possible that this text simply testifies to the heterogeneous nature of the Qumran collection? It may have happened that a text presenting an opposing view simply ended up there – an exceptional occurrence, but not impossible.

A few other historical personages are also mentioned in the scrolls. These names occur in what are now termed historical texts,[14] but these documents furnish no actual information about these people or their historical context. The name "Shelomzion," the Hebrew name of Queen Salome Alexandra (76–67 BCE), for all intents and purposes the last Hasmonean ruler, appears in *Historical Text* C 1 ii 7 and D 2 4. "Hyrcanus the king," who appears in D 2 6 with Shelomzion, may be either John Hyrcanus (134–104 BCE) or Salome's son Hyrcanus II, who served as high priest from 76 to 40 BCE. On the assumption that it is the latter, the text is restored, "Hyrcanus rebelled [against Aristobulus]." Although he tried to assert himself as Hasmonean king in 67 BCE after the death of his mother, he was defeated by his brother Aristobulus II, who ruled until the Roman conquest in 63 BCE. Yet shortly before the Roman conquest, Hyrcanus II rebelled against his brother, Aristobulus. A text tells us that "Aemillius killed" in *Historical Text* E 1 4. This most likely refers to Aemillius Scaurus, the first Roman governor of Syria (65–62 BCE).[15] We may have here an allusion to a massacre that Scaurus perpetrated. The mention of Scaurus in these texts is most interesting, for he supported the claims of Aristobulus II against those of his brother and rival Hyrcanus II, suggesting that the "Hyrcanus" of our text is indeed Hyrcanus II. Yet the title "king" is more appropriate to John Hyrcanus, who actually reigned over the Hasmonean state. Because of the brief and fragmentary nature of these mentions, they do little to supplement our information on these personages, confirming only the general historical context of the heyday of the sect in the Hasmonean period.

---

[14] S.J. Pfann and P.S. Alexander, et al., *Qumran Cave 4.XXVI: Cryptic Texts and Miscellanea, Part 1* (DJD 36; Oxford: Clarendon Press, 2000) 275-338; cf. M.O. Wise, *Thunder in Gemini and other Essays on the History, Language and Literature of Second Temple Palestine* (JSOTSup 15; Sheffield: Sheffield Academic Press, 1994) 186-221.

[15] Cf. D.R. Schwartz, "Aemilius Scaurus, Marcus," *EDSS* 1:9-10.

Origins and Early History

To understand the schism that gave birth to the Dead Sea sect, we need to frame it against the background of Jewish history and sectarianism in the Hellenistic period. But we now have even more specific information about the particular conflicts, mostly over sacrifices and ritual purity, that led the sectarians to break away and form a distinct group. Indeed, we will see that the origins of the sect are to be traced to the internal priestly turmoil associated with Hellenistic reform, the Maccabean Revolt, and the rise of the Hasmonean dynasty and high priesthood.

A Qumran text, sometimes referred to as a "halakhic letter," demonstrates quite clearly that the root cause that led to the sectarian schism consisted of a series of disagreements about sacrificial law and ritual purity. The full name of this document is *Miqṣat Ma'aśe ha-Torah* (some legal rulings pertaining to the Torah, known as 4QMMT).[16] The writers of its text list more than twenty laws that describe the ways in which their practices differed from those prevailing in the Temple and its sacrificial worship. But even more importantly, the document reveals more precise information about the origins of the sect. This document illustrates how sometimes the most significant historical material can be gleaned from texts that, on the surface, do not speak of what we normally define as historical subjects.

4QMMT begins with a statement about its own intent:

> These are some of our (legal) rulings [regarding Go]d's [Torah] which are [some of the] rulings of [the] laws which w[e hold, and a]ll of them are regarding [sacrifices] and the purity of ... (4QMMT B1–3)

The first sentence announces that what follows are some of "our (legal) rulings" that "we" hold." Throughout the letter the authors refer to themselves in the plural. What then follows is a list of twenty-two halakhic matters over which the sectarians disagree with the addressee of the letter. For most of these, the text includes both the view of the writers as well as that of their opponents. Such phrases as "but you know" and "but we hold," indicate the polemical nature of the text. Examination of the document's specific laws demonstrates unquestionably that this group adhered to the Sadducean trend in Jewish law.[17]

---

[16] E. Qimron, and J. Strugnell, *Qumran Cave 4.V: Miqṣat Ma'aśe ha-Torah* (DJD 10; Oxford: Clarendon Press, 1994).

[17] A discussion of various systems of Jewish law of the Second Temple period as well as in 4QMMT is found in L.H. Schiffman, "The Temple Scroll and the Systems

The second part of the document returns to general principles, presenting the writers' views on the schism now underway. The authors state:

> [You know that] we have separated from the mainstream of the peo[ple and from all their impurities and] from mixing in these matters and from being involved w[ith them] regarding these matters. And you k[now that there cannot be] found in our hands dishonesty, falsehood, or evil. (4QMMT C7-9)

The writers here state that in accepting the aforementioned rulings, they had to withdraw from participation in the rituals of the majority of the people. The purpose of this document was to call on their erstwhile colleagues in Jerusalem and the Hasmonean leader to effect a reconciliation that would allow them to return to their role in the Temple. Needless to say, reconciliation meant accepting the views this document puts forth. Accordingly, the authors make the general statement that the addressees know that the members of this dissident group are reliable and honest, meaning that the list of laws is indeed being strictly observed as stated by the authors.

At this point, the letter plainly explains its purpose:

> [For indeed] we have [written] to you in order that you will investigate the Book of Moses [and] in the book[s of the P]rophets and of Davi[d . . . , in the deeds] of each and every generation. (4QMMT C9-11)

The sectarians have written to the addressee (now for the first time in the singular) in order that "you" will examine the words of the Torah, the Prophets, and David (presumably the biblical accounts of the Davidic monarchy), as well as the history of the generations.

The text then takes up what is to be found in those particular documents, that is, the Scriptures that the sectarians want their opponent to search. The addressee is told (again in the singular) that it has

---

of Jewish Law in the Second Temple Period," in *Temple Scroll Studies* (ed. G.J. Brooke; Sheffield: Sheffield Academic Press, 1989) 239-55; "Qumran and Rabbinic Halakhah," in *Jewish Civilization in the Hellenistic-Roman Period* (ed. S. Talmon; Philadelphia: Trinity Press International, 1991) 138-46; J.M. Baumgarten, "Recent Qumran Discoveries and Halakha in the Hellenistic-Roman Period," in *Civilization in the Hellenistic-Roman Period*, 147-58. See also Y. Sussman, "The History of the Halakha and the Dead Sea Scrolls: Preliminary Talmudic Observations on *Miqṣat Ma'aśe ha-Torah* (4QMMT)," DJD 10: 179-200. The first to realize the Sadducean halakhic tendencies of 4QMMT was J.M. Baumgarten, "The Pharisaic-Sadducean Controversies about Purity and the Qumran Texts," *JJS* 31 (1980) 163-64. A thorough study of the laws of 4QMMT is found in Qimron and Strugnell, DJD 10:123-77.

been foretold that he would turn aside from the path of righteousness and, as a result, suffer misfortune, and that in the End of Days, the ruler will return to God.

The text now returns to the discussion of the kings, recalling the blessings fulfilled during the time of Solomon, son of David, and the curses visited on Israel from the days of Jeroboam, son of Nebat (c. 922–901 BCE, son of Solomon), through the time of Zedekiah (597–586 BCE, last king of Judah). The authors exhort the addressee (singular) to recall the events surrounding the reigns of Israel's kings, to examine their deeds, and to note that those who observed the laws of the Torah were spared misfortune, their transgressions forgiven. Such was the case with David, whom the addressee is asked to remember. The authors then sum up why they sent this text to the addressee:

> And indeed, we have written to you some of the rulings pertaining to the Torah which we considered were good for you and your people, for [we have seen] that you have wisdom and knowledge of the Torah. Understand all these (matters) and seek from Him that He correct your counsel and distance from you evil thoughts and the counsel of Belial, in order that you shall rejoice in the end when you find some of our words correct. And let it be considered right for you, and lead you to do righteousness and good, and may it be for your benefit, and for that of Israel. (4QMMT C26–32)

Here the phrase *miqṣat ma'aśe ha-Torah* (some of the rulings pertaining to the Torah) appears. The authors state that the letter is intended for the benefit of the addressee and the nation. The addressee is credited with being wise and having sufficient knowledge of the Torah to understand the halakhic matters presented in the letter. The writers call on him to mend his ways and renounce all his incorrect views on matters of Jewish law. Doing so will lead him to rejoice at the end of this period (the End of Days), for he will come to realize that the writers of the letter are indeed correct in their views. His repentance will be judged a righteous deed, beneficial both for him and for all Israel.

One of the interesting features of 4QMMT is the way the grammatical number of addressees shifts. In the introductory sentence, the letter is addressed to an individual, but in the list of laws, the authors engage in a dispute with a group ("you," plural). When the text returns to its main argument – at the conclusion of the list of laws – it shifts back to the singular. We will see later that the plural sections are addressed to priests of the Jerusalem Temple, and the singular to the Hasmonean ruler.

It appears that this letter was written to the head of the Jerusalem establishment, the high priest. The comparisons with the kings of Judah and Israel must have been particularly appropriate to someone who saw himself as an almost royal figure. In the letter, the ruler is admonished to take care lest he go the way of the kings of First Temple times. Such a warning could be addressed only to a figure who could identify, because of his own station in life, with the ancient kings of biblical Israel.

4QMMT makes no mention of the Teacher of Righteousness or any other leader or official known from the sectarian documents. Because the sect's own official history, presented in the Damascus Document, claims that their initial separation from the main body of Israel took place some twenty years before the coming of the Teacher (CD 1:10), we can conclude that 4QMMT was written by the collective leadership of the sect in those initial years. This explains why the Teacher does not appear in this text.

Historical Ramifications

4QMMT has wide ramifications for our understanding of Jewish history in the Hasmonean period. In the letter, the views ascribed to the opponents of the emerging sect are the same as those usually attributed in rabbinic literature to the Pharisees or the early Rabbis. When mishnaic texts preserve Pharisee-Sadducee conflicts over the same matters discussed in 4QMMT, the views of the letter's authors match those attributed to the Sadducees.

Only one possible explanation can be offered for this phenomenon: The earliest members of the sect must have been Sadducees unwilling to accept the status quo established in the aftermath of the Maccabean revolt. The Maccabees, by replacing the Zadokite high priesthood with their own, reduced the Zadokites to a subsidiary position for as long as Hasmonean rule lasted. Even after leaving Jerusalem, the Dead Sea sect continued to refer to itself or its leaders as the "Sons of Zadok." Our text makes clear that the designation "Sons of Zadok" is to be taken at face value. The founders of the Qumran sect were indeed Sadducees who protested the imposition of Pharisaic views in the Temple under the Hasmonean priests.

That interpretation explains why the writers of 4QMMT constantly assert that the addressees know the authors' views to be correct. The founders of the sect aimed their halakhic polemics (addressed to a plural opponent) at their Sadducean brethren who continued to serve in the Temple and accepted the new reality. It was these remaining Jerusalem Sadducees who now followed views known to us from

Pharisaic-rabbinic sources and who, in the view of the authors of this letter, knew very well that the old Sadducean practices were otherwise than what they were now observing.

Thus, when Temple worship was entrusted to a usurper – the Hasmonean high priest who acted according to already existing Pharisaic views – some pious Sadducees seceded from participation in the ritual of the Jerusalem Temple. At first the group sought a reconciliation. When that failed, the members experienced disappointment and confusion. The dissonant Zadokite priests increasingly saw themselves as a sectarian group. We can date the true beginnings of the Dead Sea sect to the moment when the Qumran Zadokites' moderate attempts at reform failed, convincing them that Hasmonean succession was not temporary but permanent.

Some have challenged this theory of the sect's Sadducean origins, arguing that it does not explain the group's more sectarian or radical tendencies, especially the animated polemic and xenophobia so often found in later sectarian texts. But those later texts reveal the eventual effects of the earlier schism. After they failed in their initial attempts, exemplified by 4QMMT, to reconcile and win over the Hasmoneans and the remaining Jerusalem Sadducees to their own system of Temple practice, the Qumran Zadokites gradually developed the sectarian mentality of the despised, rejected, and abandoned outcast. Accordingly, they began to look upon themselves as the true Israel, condemning and despising all others.[18]

4QMMT is a sectarian document from the earliest stage in the sect's development, when its members still hoped to return to participation in Temple worship. It is not even certain that the letter postdates the beginning of the self-imposed exile of the sect. In this document we learn of the disagreements about Jewish law that led to the formation of the sect. It was only later that the Teacher of Righteousness and other leaders, most probably priestly,[19] developed the group that was to

---

[18] Another challenge to this theory is the incongruity between some of the beliefs of the sect in its heyday with teachings that Josephus attributes to the Sadducees. However, Sadducean priests were not uniform in their degree of Hellenization nor in all their beliefs. Josephus's descriptions concern only the somewhat Hellenized Sadducees of the Roman period. Moreover, I am not claiming that the Dead Sea sect as we know it is Sadducean, only that its origins and the roots of its halakhic tradition lie in the Sadducean Zadokite priesthood.

[19] The priestly origins of the sect have been noted by Cross, "Early History of the Qumran Community," D.R. Schwartz, "On Two Aspects of a Priestly View of Descent at Qumran," in *Archaeology and History in the Dead Sea Scrolls: The New York University Conference in Memory of Yigael Yadin* (ed. L.H. Schiffman; JSOTSup 8 and

produce the complete corpus of sectarian texts. Another Qumran text – the *Temple Scroll,* essentially a rewritten Torah into which the author has inserted his own views on Jewish law – is also composed of sources deriving from the Sadducean tradition. Indeed, the finds at Qumran are now providing us with insights into this tradition never before available.

The revelations contained in 4QMMT demand that we reevaluate some of the older theories identifying the sect with known Second Temple groups. First, the theories that seek to link the sect and its origins with the Hasidim (pietists) must now be abandoned. Other theories tying the emergence of the sect to some subgroup of the Pharisees are certainly no longer tenable. The dominant Essene hypothesis requires reorientation. Those holding this theory must now argue that the term "Essene" came to designate the originally Sadducean sectarians who had gone through a process of radicalization until they became a distinct sect. Alternatively, they might broaden their understanding of the term to include a wide variety of similar groups, of which the Dead Sea sect might be one.

The notion that the collection of scrolls at Qumran is not representative of a sect but is a balanced collection of general Jewish texts must also be rejected. There is by now too much evidence proving that the community that collected those scrolls emerged out of sectarian conflict, and that that conflict sustained it throughout its existence. 4QMMT characterizes the conflict as a disagreement over points of Jewish law with those in control of the Temple in Hasmonean Jerusalem. Further, the nature of the collection, even if it contains many texts not explicitly sectarian, which might have been acceptable to all Jews in Second Temple times, is still that of a subgroup with definite opposition to the political and religious authorities of the times.

The Exodus to Qumran

When the group who composed 4QMMT decided to move to Qumran, the members took a decisive step in their own evolution. They now defined themselves as a dissenting group struggling against an unsympathetic majority. This was not a sudden step, however. It seems likely that the Qumran center was established after a period of groping that lasted about a generation. Only then did the sect retreat

JSOT/ASOR Monographs 2; Sheffield: Sheffield Academic Press, 1990) 157-79. On the historical relevance of 4QMMT to the founding of the sect, see L.H. Schiffman, "The New *Halakhic Letter* (4QMMT) and the Origins of the Dead Sea Sect," *BA* 53 (1990) 64-73 and Qimron and Strugnell, DJD 10:109-21.

to Qumran. The Teacher of Righteousness, whose leadership had been established sometime after composition of the letter, probably influenced the decision.

How can we determine the nature and date of the exodus to Qumran? Our conclusions must rest on the archaeological finds at Khirbet Qumran, which would suggest late second century CE or around the turn of the century, and on the literary evidence of the sectarian texts. Again here, we face the challenge of trying to extract historical data from decidedly ahistorical texts.

Central to an understanding of the event is the text known as the *Zadokite Fragments*,[20] the first scroll text discovered by Solomon Schechter among the manuscripts of the Cairo *genizah*. Today, we know of at least nine additional manuscripts of this text, which were found at Qumran. Affinities in language and ideology indicate that this document belonged to the Qumran sectarians. Further, other sectarian texts contain excerpts from that text, indicating that it indeed was a document central to the thought of the Qumran sect. Modern scholars refer to this text as the *Damascus Document* or *Damascus Covenant* owing to its symbolic reference to Damascus as the land of the sect's exile.

The text is divided into two parts: the Admonition and the Laws. Our discussion focuses on the Admonition. Although the Qumran manuscripts of this text indicate that there was additional material at the beginning of the *Damascus Document,* they preserve very little significant material from that section, which must at one time have been part of a much longer passage. The text of the *Damascus Document* as preserved in medieval manuscripts begins by declaring that in ancient times, Israel went astray. As a result, God "hid His face" and allowed the destruction of the First Temple (dated in modern scholarly chronology to 586 BCE). Yet a remnant of the defeated people remained, and it was they who ultimately formed the sect. In this narrative, the sectarians regard their way of life and belief as a direct continuation of biblical tradition, claiming to be the tradition's true recipients.

The text presents its understanding of the formation of the sect as follows:

---

[20] The best edition of the *Damascus Document* manuscripts from the Cairo genizah is E. Qimron, "The Text of CDC," in *The Damascus Document Reconsidered* (ed. M. Broshi; Jerusalem: Israel Exploration Society, and the Shrine of the Book, Israel Museum, 1992) 9–49. The Cave 4 Qumran fragments have been published by J.M. Baumgarten, *Qumran Cave 4.XIII: The Damascus Document (4Q266–273)* (DJD 18; Oxford: Clarendon Press, 1996).

> And in the period of wrath, three hundred ninety years after He had handed it (the Temple) over to Nebuchadnezzar king of Babylonia, He remembered them (Israel) and caused to grow from Israel and Aaron the root of a plant (i.e. the sect). (CD 1:5–7)[21]

This official chronology, written by the sectarians themselves, poses a problem for scholars. If we calculate from the modern scholarly dating of the destruction of the First Temple, we arrive at 196 BCE for the founding of the sect. This dating does not square with the archaeological data, however. Further, based on evidence in 4QMMT, the sect must have formally separated itself after the Maccabean Revolt of 168–164 BCE.

Nevertheless, there is evidence that ancient Jews did not have a chronology that matches ours for dating the destruction of the First Temple.[22] Because of a vast gap in the chronology of the Persian period, it is doubtful whether ancient Jews could have made such a calculation with any degree of accuracy. Therefore we can only assume that the *Damascus Document* provides approximate information. We therefore must be content to date the founding of the sect sometime in the second century BCE.

The text of the *Damascus Document* then tells about a period of confusion followed by the rise of the sect's leader, the Teacher of Righteousness:

> Then they understood their transgression and knew that they were guilty. They were like blind (men) groping on the road for twenty years. Then God paid attention to their deeds for they sought Him whole-heartedly, and He set up for them a Teacher of Righteousness to direct them in the way of his (the Teacher's) heart. (CD 1:8–11 = Da 2 I 12–15)

It appears that during an initial period – perhaps of twenty years – the sect was leaderless and perhaps even formless until the Teacher of Righteousness established his leadership over it. Only with the Teacher's emergence and his assumption of control did sectarian teachings and a distinctive way of life take shape.

From what we learned earlier from 4QMMT, we can accept as reliable the account in the *Damascus Document* that describes this initial period between the schism and the emergence of the Teacher's leadership. It was during that period, most probably, that 4QMMT was sent and a reconciliation attempted. After their failure to win over the Jeru-

---

[21] See I. Rabinowitz, "A Reconsideration of 'Damascus' and '390 Years' in the 'Damascus' ('Zadokite') Fragments," *JBL* 73 (1954) 11-35.

[22] *B. Avodah Zarah* 9a.

salem Sadducees and the Hasmonean high priest, the sect became a permanent entity, no longer expecting to rejoin the Jerusalem establishment.

The Teacher of Righteousness assumed leadership of the sect and introduced his teachings; at that time, or shortly thereafter, the sect moved to its site in the wilderness at Qumran. Both the archaeological dating of the site and the literary materials confirm this fact.

The *Damascus Document* has a portion that has become known as the "Well Midrash" (6:3–11),[23] which prominently features Damascus imagery.[24] It is an excellent example of *pesher* interpretation, a form of biblical interpretation that reads biblical verses as prefigurations of contemporary events. Here a verse from Numbers is interpreted: "A well which the officers have dug, which the notables of the people have dug ..." (Num 21:18).

The *Damascus Document* explains:

> The well is the Torah and those who dig it are the returnees (or: penitents) of Israel who leave the land of Judea and who live in the land of Damascus. (CD 6:4–5)

On the face of it, this text seems to refer to an exodus of the sectarians from Judea to Damascus, where they settled, at least for a time. Below this, on the same page, the sectarians are described as: "those who enter the new covenant in the land of Damascus" *(6:19)*. Again this text refers to an exodus to Damascus.

In another *pesher*-type exegesis, the text interprets Amos 5:26–27, "And you shall carry ... the star of your God which you have made for yourselves, and I will exile you beyond Damascus." There we find:

> And the "star" (Amos 5:26) is the interpreter of the law (the sectarian official who interprets Torah for the sect with divine inspiration) who comes to Damascus. (CD 7:18–19)

A literal reading of this passage would suggest that the interpreter of the law left Judea and joined his fellow sectarians at Damascus. Later

---

[23] See G.J. Brooke, "The Amos-Numbers Midrash (CD7^{13b}-8^{1a}) and Messianic Expectations," *ZAW* 92 (1980) 397-404.

[24] N. Wieder, *The Judean Scrolls and Karaism* (London: East and West Library, 1962) 1-52; R. North, "The Damascus of Qumran Geography," *PEQ* 87 (1955) 34-38; S. Iwry, "Was There a Migration to Damascus? The Problem of *Shave Yisra'el*," *ErIsr* 9 (W.F. Albright Volume, 1969) 80-88; C. Milikowsky, "Again: DAMASCUS in *Damascus Document* and in Rabbinic Literature," *RevQ* 11 (1982) 97-106; P.R. Davies, "The Birthplace of the Essenes: Where is 'Damascus'?" *RevQ* 14 (1990) 503-19. Cf. also M.A. Knibb, "Exile in the *Damascus Document*," *JSOT* 99 (1983) 99-117.

on, in describing sectarians who ceased to live according to the ways of the sect, the Damascus Document speaks of:

> those people who had entered the new covenant in the land of Damascus and have turned away and rebelled, and turned aside from the well of living waters. (CD 19:33–34)

The "well of living waters" is God's Torah as correctly interpreted by the sectarians. The Damascus theme is continued further on when the text describes those

> who have despised the covenant and the agreement to which they swore in the land of Damascus, which is the new covenant. (CD 20:11–12)

What then is Damascus? Is it a real place or a metaphorical term? We know that the sectarians, especially in the *Damascus Document*, often spoke in code words. We find all kinds of pseudonyms for actual personages, yet almost never a personal name that would allow a definite identification. The Jewish sects of the day are never mentioned by name even though we see numerous references to them designated with code words in the sectarian texts. Why then should we fall into the trap of taking place names literally? Rather it is more likely that "Damascus" is a code word for Qumran.

The notion is strengthened even more by the use of Damascus as a symbol in other texts of the period. The New Testament pictures Paul receiving a vision of Jesus on the road to Damascus (Acts 9:3–6). It is likely that the symbolic meaning of Damascus as an eschatological stopover would have led to its use here. Indeed, even in Amos 5:27 it is connected with the destruction of syncretist Israelites – those who had mixed worship of the God of Israel with pagan ways – in the End of Days.

In addition, we should mention the suggestion that Damascus was actually at one time the name of the toparchy (administrative district) in which Qumran was situated. This suggestion assumes that Qumran, even though it is located on the western shore of the Dead Sea, was at one time part of the same administrative unit as Damascus and could, therefore, bear its name.

In any case, these possibilities all taken together allow us to regard Damascus as a symbol. Accordingly, we need not seek any specific exodus to Damascus. Rather, we can assume that the desert settlement of Qumran was the Damascus to which the sectarians referred and that it was there that the sect established its settlement at about the same time as the Teacher of Righteousness (perhaps the very same first interpreter of the law) came to the fore.[25]

There is one additional text, *Community Rule*, which must be considered here because it makes the connection between the sectarians' separatism and the desert. This almost intact document lays out the basic theology of the sect as well as its rules of admission and initiation and its code of punishments. At one point, the scroll speaks of the separation of the Qumran sectarians from the main body of Israelites:

> When these form a community in Israel, according to these rules they shall be separated from the midst of the settlement of the people of iniquity to go to the desert, to clear there the road of the Lord, as it is written, "In the desert clear the road of the Lord; straighten in the wilderness a highway for our God" (Isaiah 40:3). This is the interpretation of the Torah [which] He commanded through Moses to observe, according to everything that is revealed from time to time, and as the prophets have revealed by His holy spirit. (1QS 8:12–16)

The passage appears to refer directly to the exodus to the desert. But in fact, this separatism is to be understood symbolically as fulfilling the command of Isa 40:3 to prepare a way through the wilderness as part of the preparations for the End of Days. The passage then goes on to tell us how to interpret that preparation. To prepare the way in the desert means to interpret the Torah, specifically to explain it according to sectarian interpretations.

Despite its mention of the wilderness, the text makes no direct connection between the sect and the desert region. Nonetheless, it is only against the background of the sect's settlement at Qumran that such desert imagery makes sense. In fact, the desert motif is extremely prominent in sectarian literature. The sectarians saw themselves as living a pristine life like that of the Israelites in the period of desert wandering. Further, they saw themselves as having gone into the desert to receive the Torah, just as Israel had in the period of the Exodus. All this is to be expected from a group that had left the more thickly settled areas of Judea to relocate in the wilderness, there to maintain its own standards of sanctity and purity.

---

[25] It is indeed curious that the sectarian texts from Qumran contain no mention of the name of the site; Khirbet Qumran is the Arabic name. Some scholars have theorized that it may be the biblical place Secacah (Josh 15:61), although this is probably an Iron Age site located 4 miles (7 km) southwest of Qumran. In any case, it was to Qumran, not to Damascus, that the sect migrated.

From the date gleaned from two decidedly ahistorical texts, 4QMMT and the *Damascus Document*, we can reconstruct the early history of the sect. The sect came into being, then, after the Hasmoneans had taken over the high priesthood, about 152 BCE. Thereafter, they attempted, as we can see from 4QMMT, to reconcile with their Zadokite-Sadducean brethren who continued to serve in the Jerusalem Temple, as well as with the Hasmonean leaders. When this failed, they still were leaderless until, at some point, the Teacher of Righteousness arose to lead them. It was he who gave the sect shape and direction. Eventually he led the group from its Saducean origins toward its intensely apocalyptic, sectarian mentality and toward the many beliefs that differentiated the sect from the Sadducees. Probably during the early years of the Teacher's career – within a generation or so after the founding of the sect – the members of the group established the sectarian center and library at Qumran.

Conclusion

What emerges from our inquiry is that the discussion of the scrolls as historical texts, like so much about the Dead Sea Scrolls, is complex. When we inquire into the ability of these texts to yield historical information about people, places and events, it is indeed limited, and we have tried here to extract what information is available. These allusions have been filtered by the sectarians through the lens of their own sense of identity and mission. We have to refilter these accounts through our own lenses of modern critical scholarship and historical inquiry in order to be able to make use of it. But from the point of the view of the ancient sectarians, and of other Jews whose works were gathered into the ancient library of Qumran, what they wrote was history, the sacred history of the only true Israel, those who kept the flame burning in the dark years of the Hasmonean dynasty.

So are the Dead Sea Scrolls historical texts? Yes and no! No, because they provide little of what we usually expect historical texts to provide, and tell us so little about actual people and events. What they do tell us requires extensive reconstruction and lacks, for the most part, a wider context. Yes, because they present us with a window into the history of Judaism in Second Temple times that allows us to see, albeit with only a dim light, the events that led to the founding of the sect and some aspects of its own history in the Hasmonean period. And yes because the scrolls allow us to see into the complex world of ideas and movements that constitute the background for the emergence of rabbinic Judaism and the rise of Christianity. In this sense, they may truly be considered historical texts.

4

History-Writing in, and on the Basis of, the Jewish Apocalyptic Literature

George W.E. Nickelsburg

0.1. Introduction

In addressing the topic of this conference, I will pose two questions. (a) How do the writers of the Jewish apocalypses write history? (b) To what extent can we use the apocalypses as the basis for our own writing of the history of the Jews in the Greco-Roman period? Before I address these questions, I will deal with a methodological problem (§1): How do we place these pseudonymous works in their real historical contexts? Then, with the apocalypses set in time, I will pose my first question (§2): how the apocalypticists write their historical summaries and otherwise describe historical events (a). Next I will pose my second question in two parts (§3.1): what bits and pieces of historical information can we extract from their historical summaries (b.1)? Finally (§3.2): looking outside the historical summaries and descriptions, I will cite some examples of the kind of substantial historical information can we glean from the apocalypses (b.2), which are, after all, historical artifacts themselves.

My sources include the major apocalyptic works of the 3rd century BCE to the 1st century CE: parts of *1 Enoch*, Daniel 7–12, the *Testament of Moses*, *4 Ezra*, and *2 Baruch*. I also refer briefly to *Jubilees* and the *Apocalypse of Abraham*.[1]

---

[1] For a definition of the genre apocalypse, see J.J. Collins, "Introduction: Towards the Morphology of a Genre," *Semeia* 14 (1979) 1-10: "'Apocalypse' is a genre of revelatory literature with a narrative framework, in which a revelation is mediated by an otherworldly being to a human recipient, disclosing a transcendent reality which is both temporal, insofar as it envisages eschatological salvation, and spatial insofar as it involves another, supernatural world." The *Testament of Moses* is not an apocalypse strictly speaking, since Moses is not an *otherworldly* mediator of revelation. Nonetheless,

1.1. The Basic Problem: Pseudonymous Ascription

The basic methodological problem in the study of history-writing in the Jewish apocalyptic literature pertains to the pseudepigraphic character of these texts. Their authorship is falsely ascribed to figures of the distant past: Enoch from pre-diluvian times,[2] Moses from the time of the Exodus,[3] Baruch from shortly after Nebuchadnezzar's destruction of Jerusalem,[4] Daniel and Ezra from the Babylonian Exile.[5] The problem has two aspects. First, the spurious attribution masks the time of the real author(s) of a given text. Second, because their real authors set the texts in ancient time, they frequently omit the proper names of the persons (and, to a lesser extent, the places) associated with the events that will take place centuries after the alleged authors.

1.2. Breaking the Pseudepigraphic Code

The pseudonymous ascription of the apocalypses brings with it, however, the seeds of a solution to the problem it creates. In order for the real author to persuade his audience that the message of the ancient prophet pertains to their own time, that author must place on the lips (or rather the pen) of his pseudonymous author identifiable and "accurate" descriptions (allegedly predictions) of that audience's own time and the events that have led up to it. When we, who do not have first-hand familiarity with the events, compare these descriptions with "historical" accounts from antiquity (e.g., 1 and 2 Maccabees, and the writings of Philo and Josephus, Arrian, Dio Cassius, Diodorus Siculus, Strabo, Suetonius, and Tacitus) we are able, with considerable accuracy and probability, to place the pseudepigraphic texts in the real authors' own times.

1.2.1. The Apocalypses in Daniel 7; 8; and 10:1–12:13

These texts can be ascribed to the time of Antiochus IV Epiphanes. The easiest to date is the vision recounted in 10:1-12:13 and dated to the third year of Cyrus (535 BCE) (10:1). An angel appears to Daniel and describes how he has been fighting the angelic prince of Persia and how he will return to finish Persia's prince and take on the angelic prince of Greece (10:2-21). His historical summary of events yet to

---

he is the functional equivalent of such, revealing to Joshua the hidden meaning of his words in the last chapters of Deuteronomy.

[2] *1 Enoch* and *2 Enoch*.
[3] *Jubilees* and the *Testament of Moses*.
[4] *2 Baruch* and perhaps *3 Baruch* if, indeed, it is Jewish.
[5] The canonical book of Daniel and *4 Ezra*.

come begins in 11:2: four kings of Persia will reign, and the last of these will make war against the kingdom of Greece. Within this context, the historical summary that follows parallels extraneous explicit sources about the Hellenistic period. The description begins with the rise of "a mighty king" (Alexander the Great, 11:3) and the division of his kingdom (among the Diadochoi, 11:3). It continues with an account of the wars of "the king[s] of the north" and "the king[s] of the south" (the Seleucids and the Ptolemies, 11:5-45) that climaxes with increasingly detailed descriptions of the reigns of Antiochus III (vv. 15-20) and Antiochus IV (vv. 21-45) and concludes with the death of Antiochus IV in Israel "between the sea and the glorious holy mountain" (v 45). This coded, albeit transparent account of the Hellenistic period allows us to date this historical apocalypse after Antiochus's desecration of the Jerusalem temple (Dec. 167 BCE) and before his death, which occurred not in Israel, as predicted here, but in Babylon (Dec. 164). The conclusion of the vision concurs with this dating. It places the inception of the end time – which begins with Antiochus's death ("at that time," 12:1-3) – three and a half years ("a time, times, and a half") after the desecration of the temple, that is, in the middle of 163.[6] Since the rededication of the temple occurred exactly three years after its desecration, the apocalypse, on this account also, dates from before December 164.

The vision in ch. 7 can be placed at roughly the same time as chs. 10–12. Four beasts represent four kingdoms, the fourth being the worst. The tenth king speaks arrogant words against the Most High and seeks to change the times and the law, and in this he will succeed for a time, times, and a half a time. Here too the details of the vision fit the Hellenistic period and the reign of Antiochus IV.[7] The time stipulation of three and a half years forms the specific point of connection with chs. 10–12. The four kingdoms are Babylon, Media, Persia, and Greece. The blasphemous king is Antiochus IV, who introduced the divine epithet Epiphanes, "(God) Manifest,"[8] and disrupted the cultic calendar and proscribed the Torah.

The vision in ch. 8 depicts the clash of a two-horned ram and a one-horned he-goat, which overthrows it (vv. 1-7). These animals are identified as the kings of Media and Persia and the king of Greece (Alexander the Great) (vv. 20-22). From the great horn a little horn

[6] On the dating of the events described in 11:1-45, see J.J. Collins, *Daniel: A Commentary on the Book of Daniel* (Hermeneia; Minneapolis: Fortress, 1993) 376-90.
[7] Ibid., 294-324.
[8] The full title appears on his coins, *ibid.*, 321.

comes forth that grows great and storms heaven, taking away the daily sacrifice for 2300 evenings and days (that is three years and two months). Like Daniel 7, the dating of this vision coincides roughly with that of chs. 10–12 and focuses on the blasphemous deeds of Antiochus IV and anticipates his destruction within three years and some months.

In short, all three visions depict events in coded but transparent form, which historical sources allow us to locate in the latter years of the reign of Antiochus IV.

1.2.2. *1 Enoch*

The collection known as 1 Enoch is especially difficult to date because it contains only two historical apocalypses with the kind of information that enables us to date them. The first of these, the Animal Vision (chs. 85–90), recounts the history of the world from creation to the eschaton.[9] This account mentions no names or places. It is an allegory about bulls and heifers, stars that descend from heaven and become bulls that mate with the heifers, humanoid figures who descend from heaven and enact judgment, sheep that are preyed upon by wild beasts and birds of prey, and "the Lord of the Sheep." The allegory is transparent, however. The events that it recounts follow the sequence of the Bible from Genesis to Ezra–Nehemiah and beyond into the Maccabean period, which concludes with the divine judgment that initiates the eschaton. The bulls depict the patriarchs through Isaac, who begets a sheep (Jacob) and a wild boar (Esau). Other wild animals began to proliferate after the flood (cf. Gen 11). The stars are "the sons of God" who descended from heaven according to Genesis 6. The sheep, who are the descendants of Jacob, are the Israelites, and the wild beasts and birds are the Gentiles, who prey upon Israel. The humanoid figures are the seven archangels, and the Lord of the sheep is the God of Israel. Given this sequence, we can date the vision to the time of Judas Maccabeus, who is the best candidate to fill the role of a ram with a great horn who does battle with the birds of prey, who represent the Seleucids (90:9b-16). Some duplications in the description of this period may indicate an earlier version of a vision dated from the late third or early second century BCE.[10]

---

[9] For the basis of my treatment of these chapters, see G.W.E. Nickelsburg, *1 Enoch: A Commentary on the Book of 1 Enoch Chapters 1–36; 82–108* (Hermeneia; Minneapolis: Fortress, 2001) 354–408.

[10] *Ibid.*, 360-61, 396-98.

A second historical summary, the Apocalypse of Weeks (93:1-10; 91:11-17) is either a prototype for the Animal vision or a stylized summary of it, which briefly recounts human history and the eschaton in ten periods. Its highly stylized form allows us to date it only at roughly the same time as the Animal Vision.[11]

Taking the Animal Vision as our chronological point of departure, it is possible to provide relative dating for other parts of the Enochic corpus. The prominent role played by the descent of the rebel angels in the episode of the flood and their primordial and final judgment indicate that the Animal Vision is dependent on *1 Enoch* 6–11, and other details reflect the broader account of Enoch's journeys in chs. 12–36.[12] Literary analysis of chs. 1–36 indicates the development of an ongoing tradition that places chs. 6–11 in the early third century or perhaps the late fourth century, with the battle of the giants perhaps depicting the wars of the Diadochoi.[13] The dating of the Book of Parables (chs. 37–71) is disputed.[14] Literary considerations indicate that at least the first, and perhaps the second parable reflect material in chs. 1–36, which indicates the early second century as a *terminus post quem*.[15] The Parables' portrayal of "the son of man" depends on Daniel 7, and this, then, indicates 164 BCE as a *terminus post quem*. Beyond that, the dating of the Parables becomes slippery. In my view, the portrayal of the Son of Man in the Gospels presupposes something very close to that of the son of man in the Parables, and some other elements in Paul's Christology indicate a similar dependence.[16] This would indicate the early first century CE as a *terminus ad quem*. The other major section of *1 Enoch* of importance for this paper is the Epistle of Enoch (chs. 92–105). It is of special interest because of its detailed description of social conditions in the author's time (see below, §3.1.2). Its *terminus post quem* is indicated by its knowledge of the material in chs. 1-36,[17] and its *terminus ad quem* perhaps by a pair of late first-century Qumran manuscripts that may have contained the section.[18] This

---

[11] *Ibid.*, 398-99, 440-441.

[12] *Ibid.*, 359-60.

[13] *Ibid.*, 169-71.

[14] G.W.E. Nickelsburg, *Jewish Literature between the Bible and the Mishnah* (2nd ed.; Minneapolis: Fortress, 2005) 254-55.

[15] *Ibid.*, 250.

[16] G.W.E. Nickelsburg, "Son of Man," *Anchor Bible Dictionary* (6 vols.; Garden City, Doubleday, 1992) 6:142-48.

[17] Nickelsburg, *1 Enoch 1*, 422.

[18] *Ibid.*, 427.

would place it sometime in the second century or the early first century BCE.

1.2.3. The *Testament of Moses*

The *Testament of Moses* purports to recount the last words of Moses and their context.[19] In reality, they are a rewriting of the last chapters of Deuteronomy, whose scheme of history (sin-punishment-repentance-salvation) is used in a double cycle to shape a summary of events (1) before, in and immediately after the Babylonian Exile (chs. 2–4) and (2) in the Hellenistic period (chs. 5–9). A reference to a king who will rule for thirty-four years and his sons who will rule for shorter periods (6:6-7), refers to the reign of Herod the Great and indicates a time of composition before 30 CE, when the reigns of his sons Antipas and Philip were moving toward forty-three and thirty-seven years respectively. The banishment of Archelaus in 6 CE after a reign of ten years may have triggered the notion of shorter reigns. The reference to the death of Herod (6:6), the burning of the temple at the time of Varus, and the incident of the golden eagle, including Varus's crucifixion of some Jewish rebels, indicate 4 BCE as a *terminus post quem*. So we can set the date of the final form of the *Testament* between 4 BCE and 30 CE, and perhaps between 6 and 30 CE.[20]

I say "final form" because, in my view, literary considerations indicate that chs. 6–7 are later additions to a text whose recitation of history climaxed in events that closely correspond to the time of Antiochus IV as we know it from other sources (chs. 8–9) and that are immediately followed by a description of the eschaton. For this reason, I date the Testament perhaps a little earlier than Daniel and a few years before the Animal Vision of *1 Enoch*.[21]

1.2.4. *4 Ezra* and *2 Baruch*

These two apocalypses are set in the aftermath of the Babylonian destruction of Jerusalem, *4 Ezra* thirty years later (3:1), and *2 Baruch* shortly before (chs. 1–8) and in the ten weeks following the destruction (marked by four fasts of seven days [10:1; 12:5; 20:5; 47:2] and a forty-day period of instruction [76:4]). The Babylonian destruction is

---

[19] Nickelsburg, *Jewish Literature*, 74-76

[20] For details see J. Priest, "The Testament of Moses," in J.H. Charlesworth, ed., *The Old Testament Pseudepigrapha* (2 vols.; Garden City: Doubleday, 1983-85) 1:920-21; Nickelsburg, *Jewish Literature*, 247-48, and the studies by A.Yarbro Collins and J.J. Collins, cited in *ibid.*, 299, nn. 32-33.

[21] Nickelsburg, *Jewish Literature*, 76.

uniformly taken to be a prototype for Titus's destruction of Jerusalem in 70 CE.

In the case of *4 Ezra* a date in the neighborhood of 100 CE is confirmed by details in the vision in chs. 11–12. The double vision in chs. 11–12, 13 is a creative interpretation of Daniel 7 (*4 Ezra* 12:10-11). Chapters 11–12 focus on the last of the four beasts, here described as an eagle, and ch. 13 depicts the judicial activity of a man who comes up out of the sea and flies with the clouds. The eagle is a natural symbol for the Roman empire, whose military standards bore the figure of an eagle.[22] The multiplicity of wings and the three heads represent the Roman emperors (12:19-24). This numerology brings us to Domitian, the third of the Flavian emperors and suggests a date in his reign (81–96 CE), with the end being predicted during that reign.[23]

The date of *2 Baruch* is less certain. The many parallels to *4 Ezra* suggest a time of composition in the same, post-destruction period, with *2 Baruch* being, perhaps, a bit later than *4 Ezra*.[24] The details of the text, however, do not help to specify the time of composition more precisely. The book's two visions do not provide the chronological hooks that we find in *4 Ezra* 11–12. The vision in chs. 36–37 and its interpretation in chs. 39–40 briefly describe a sequence of four kingdoms and, like *4 Ezra* 11–12, an end in which the Messiah will confront the last king. The vision in ch. 53 and its extensive interpretation in historical sequence (chs. 54–72), brings Israelite history up to the Babylonian exile (ch. 67) and then briefly describes the post-exilic period (ch. 68) and the present evil times (chs. 69–72), in which the Messiah will triumph and after which the earth will return to its paradisiacal perfection (ch. 73).

1.2.5. Summary

Our discussion has indicated how we are able to date these five apocalypses on the basis of details – especially in their historical summaries – that coincide with information from extraneous historical sources. The apocalypses date to times of severe religious and social crisis in the history of Israel: Daniel, the original form of the Testament of Moses, and the Animal Vision in *1 Enoch* 85–90 to the Antiochan persecution of the Jews; a later form of the *Testament of Moses* to the decade(s) after the death of Herod the Great; and *4 Ezra* and *2 Baruch* to the decades

---

[22] M.E. Stone, *Fourth Ezra: A Commentary on the Book of Fourth Ezra* (Hermeneia; Minneapolis: Fortress, 1990) 348.
[23] *Ibid.*, 10.
[24] Nickelsburg, *Jewish Literature*, 283-85.

after the Roman destruction of Jerusalem. Comparative literary analysis enables us to place other parts of *1 Enoch* both before and after the composition of the Animal Vision, in the early Hellenistic period and in the later Hellenistic period and/or the decades around the turn of the era.

2.0. How the Apocalypticists Wrote History

We turn now to the specific topic of this conference. How did the apocalypticists shape their historical accounts? What principles guided the presentation of their material? How did they understand historical reality?

2.1. The Individual Texts
2.1.1. Daniel 7–12

Several features characterize the writing of history in Daniel 7, 8, 9, and 10–12. First, in all cases, the authors present their material as the product of revelation. Chapters 7 and 8 recount a pair of dream visions whose symbolism is interpreted by an angel (7:1-2; 8:2, 27),[25] while the historical contents of chs. 9 and 10–12 are said to have derived from waking encounters with angels (9:20-23; 10:2-9).[26]

Second, the events of human history are said to be the counterparts of events that take place on the heavenly realm. The demise of the Macedonian kingdom is a function of the session of the heavenly court (7:9-12, 26), and Israel's domination over the nations follows from the exaltation of their heavenly patron, the "one like a son of man" (7:13-14, 27). Antiochus's desecration of the Temple is an assault on the host of heaven (8:9-13). The destruction of both the Persian and the Macedonian kingdoms results from clashes between Israel's angelic patron, "the great prince Michael," and the princes of Persia and Greece (10:13, 20-21; 12:1).

Third, the course of history is divided into periods—the four kingdoms of Assyria, Babylonia, Persia, and Greece in 7:1-8, 17; and seventy weeks of years in 9:24-27—and note is taken of a succession of kings (7:7-8, 24; 11:2-45). In keeping with this, the seers engage in speculation as to the time of the end, placing their calculations in the mouths of their angelic interpreters (7:25; 8:13-14; 9:24-27; 12:11-12).

---

[25] Dan 7:1-2 is explicit. On ch. 8, see F.F. Dailey, *Dreamers, Scribes, and Priests: Jewish Dreams in the Hellenistic and Roman Eras* (JSJSup 2004; Leiden: Brill, 2004) 223-24.
[26] For details, see *ibid.*, 224-27.

Fourth, the recitation of history becomes more detailed as it recounts the most recent events, which lead up to the end-time, thus indicating that the eschaton is near (7:23-25; 8:9-13, 22-25).

Finally, the apocalypticists draw on both Scripture and non-Israelite myth to interpret history. Daniel 9 understands the present crisis in terms of Mosaic covenantal theology,[27] and chs. 10–12 draw on the language of Isaiah and Second Isaiah.[28] Both the enthronement scene in ch. 7 and the description of Antiochus's assault on heaven reflect Canaanite mythology.[29]

2.1.2. *1 Enoch* 85–90 and 93:1-10; 91:11-17

The Animal Vision and the Apocalypse of Weeks are marked by most of characteristics we have seen in Daniel 7–12. Chapters 85–90 are a symbolic dream vision whose patent summary of Genesis through Ezra–Nehemiah requires no angelic interpretation. This summary features throughout an antagonism between Israel and the nations and identifies the oppression by the nations as punishment for Israel's apostasy, described as the blindness and straying of the sheep. As in Daniel, the author posits the interaction of the earthly and heavenly realms. Rebel angels descend to wreak havoc on earth. The archangels descend to execute judgment at the time of the flood and later in the last judgment. The malfeasance of the seventy angelic shepherds creates extraordinary trouble from the time of Manasseh to the time of the end. An angelic scribe records the sins of the shepherds, and both this scribe and Enoch plead for Israel in the heavenly throne-room. History from the time of Manasseh to the end is divided into four periods of twelve, twenty-three, twenty-three, and twelve subdivisions respectively. These calculations, which add up to 490 years (70 weeks of years) appear to be related to the numerology of Daniel 9 (and Dan 7 with its four major divisions).[30]

The Apocalypse of Weeks is also the product of revelation, specifically, Enoch's heavenly vision in which he read the heavenly tablets and listened to their angelic interpretation (93:2). Its summary of human history is much briefer than in the Animal Vision. Although its

---

[27] R.A. Werline, *Penitential Prayer in Second Temple Judaism: The Development of a Religious Institution* (SBLEJL 13; Atlanta: Scholars Press, 1998) 67-81.

[28] R. Clifford, "History and Myth in Daniel 10-1," *BA* 220-21 (1975-76) 25.

[29] Collins, *Daniel*, 286-94; G.W.E. Nickelsburg, *Resurrection, Immortality, and Eternal Life in Intertestamental Judaism and Early Christianity* (expanded ed.; HTS 56; Cambridge, MA: Harvard University Press, 2006) 91-92.

[30] On these calculations, see Nickelsburg, *1 Enoch 1*, 391-93.

periodization is obscure, it is explicit (seven weeks up to the beginning of the eschaton and then three additional weeks) and, to some degree, symmetrical.[31] Important events happen at the end of various weeks. In times of evil, a righteous person is saved. Deceit and violence leads to the flood, as it brings on judgment in the end time. Abraham's election is paralleled by the election of the chosen in the end time. The various sanctuaries are noted in their respective weeks: the tabernacle (93:6); Solomon's temple (93:7-8); eschatological temple (91:13).

2.1.3. The *Testament of Moses*

The history summary in the *Testament of Moses* is revelatory in the sense that the author interprets the last chapters of Deuteronomy with the claim that this interpretation comprises the words of the prophet Moses himself. The author's periodization of history involves the phases of the Deuteronomic historical scheme: sin-punishment-repentance-salvation, which are repeated in a double cycle. As is typical of the apocalypses, the events of most recent history are described in the greatest detail. The function of the Deuteronomic scheme is to identify the present time as the moment in which repentance (the obedience of Taxo and his sons) will bring on the eschaton.

Although I have not discussed the book of *Jubilees* as an apocalypse, it is worth noting that in ch. 23, a similar use of the Deuteronomic scheme places the author at the brink of the end time and indicates that obedience to the Torah as it is expounded in the book will bring on the eschaton.[32]

2.1.4. *4 Ezra* and *2 Baruch*

4 Ezra 11–12 and 13 are this text's two exemplars of the genres I have been discussing. Both are presented as revelation in the form of dream visions. The first is explicitly a reinterpretation of Daniel 7: "The eagle that you saw coming up from the sea is the fourth kingdom that appeared in a vision to your brother Daniel" (12:11). Thus a text that will have been considered scripture by the time *4 Ezra* was written (viz. Daniel) is interpreted through a revelatory medium. Although the imagery is different from Daniel, like Daniel, the author periodizes history, increasing the detail as he approaches the eschaton. Ezra's second dream vision is not a historical review as such, but an additional

---

[31] *Ibid.*, 438-40; J.C. VanderKam, "Studies in the Apocalypse of Weeks (1 Enoch 93:1-10; 91:11-17)," *CBQ* 46 (1984) 518-21.

[32] For *Jubilees* as an apocalypse, see G.W.E. Nickelsburg, "Apocalyptic Judaism," in *Encylopedia of Judaism* (4 vols.; Leiden: Brill, ²2005) I:76-77.

interpretation of Daniel 7, which describes the coming of the Messiah by focusing on the man who rides on the clouds.

2 Baruch contains two symbolic dream visions, which are interpreted by the deity and the angel Remiel respectively (38:1; 39:1; 55:3). In first instance (chs. 36–40), the interpretation adopts the four-kingdom periodizing of Daniel 7, without citing Daniel, and it concludes with the coming of the Messiah. The second dream vision is much broader in scope and, like Enoch's Animal Vision, it tracks key points in the biblical account of human history from Adam to the eschaton (chs. 56–71). Indeed, more than any apocalypse we have discussed, it provides details from biblical history and the proper names of the major characters, specifically the good and evil leaders of Israel and two of their Gentile counterparts. Differently from the other apocalypses, its detailed conclusion does not describe current historical events, but rather a long list of stereotyped characteristics of the end time (chs. 70–71), followed by a detailed description of the paradisiacal conditions that will obtain in the eschaton (ch. 73). The vision's division into periods is explicit in its alternation of black and white waters, which symbolize periods of sin and righteousness.

2.1.5. History – or the lack of it – in the Apocalypses

Our survey of the apocalypses indicates a major characteristic in the "historiography" of the early texts. These authors are not interested in conveying historical information as such. Instead they summarize events that are already well known, either from the biblical accounts or from a general acquaintance with "recent" events. The purpose of these summaries, especially with their more detailed descriptions of the present time, is to place the audience in these sequences and thus to show that they stand on the brink of the end time. Thus, they function to comfort the righteous and to admonish them to stand fast and not capitulate to unfaith or apostasy. Although the two latest apocalypses have a similar function, they differ somewhat from this profile. Fourth Ezra reinterprets Daniel 7 and expands considerably on the activities of the Messiah, whether the Lion of Judah (chs. 11–12) or the Man from the Sea (ch. 13). A similar situation pertains in *2 Baruch*; however, his historical summary (chs. 56–66) reflects a concern about Israelite leaders that mirrors a similar emphasis in the contemporary biblical paraphrase of Pseudo-Philo.[33]

---

[33] See Nickelsburg, *Jewish Literature*, 266.

2.1.6. Summary

The authorial intent to comfort and admonish is also reflected in other characteristics that we have noted in at least some of the apocalypses. The periodizing of history emphasizes the fact that God orders the course of history. By positing the existence of a unseen heavenly or cosmic realm, the authors emphasize that God and God's justice are operative, or imminent, even when the phenomenal world suggests otherwise. Hand-in-hand with this go the claims of the revelation that provides access to this hidden world.[34]

3.0. The Apocalyptic Literature as a Source of Historical Information

Now that we have placed the apocalypses in time and have seen how they shape *their* historical accounts, we can seek to determine what information they provide for *our own* writing of history.

3.1. Extracting Information from the Apocalypses' Historical Accounts

As we have seen, we can identify the time of the apocalypses' composition on the basis of their overlaps with the writings of Jewish and pagan historians (above §§1.2.1-5). So, what information do the apocalypses' historical accounts provide about the events they recount that is *not* available from the accounts of ancient historians? To use a metaphor, let us think of the apocalypses and the historical writings as two superimposed images, in which certain parts of the two images are more or less identical. When we have overlaid those coinciding parts of the images, much is left over that is unique to each layer. In particular, the historical texts describe events in much more detail than the historical summaries in the apocalypses, and they recount many events that are omitted from the apocalypses. But what of the apocalypses? Do they refer to, or describe, events and persons that are omitted in the histories? The answer is "yes," although we learn much less than we might have hoped for.

3.1.1. The Danielic Apocalypses

From the apocalypses in Daniel 7, 8, and 10–12, we learn two things. First, according to 11:14,

---

[34] See my discussion of the apocalyptic construction of reality in *1 Enoch 1*, 37-42.

> ... the violent ones of your people will assert themselves to substantiate the (or a) vision, but they will stumble.[35]

From this obscure passage, we learn that during the reign of Antiochus III, probably in the last decade of the third century, some Jews, informed by a vision, attempted a futile uprising against the Syrian crown. In short, visionary activity was not limited to those who composed the apocalypses in the book of Daniel, and it could lead to a kind of violent activity that Daniel does not countenance.[36]

Secondly, according to 11:33,

> And the wise among the people will make many understand, though they fall by sword and flame, by captivity and plunder (for some) days.

In 12:3, these *maśkîlîm* are identified as "those who cause many to be righteous" (*maṣdîqê hārabbîm*). That is, during the Antiochene persecution, resistance to the king's proscription of the Torah (living the righteous life prescribed by the Torah) was encouraged by the activity of Jewish sages and teachers – presumably the sort who composed the Danielic apocalypses.[37]

3.1.2. *1 Enoch*

Like the Danielic apocalypses, the contemporary Animal Vision (*1 Enoch* 85–90) provides a few bits of information. In its description of the end of the third or the beginning of the second century BCE, the author writes:

> And look, lambs were born of those white sheep, and they began to open their eyes and to see and to cry out to the sheep. But they did not listen to them nor attend to their words, but they were extremely deaf, and their eyes were extremely and excessively blinded (90:6-7).[38]

That is, some of the younger generation of Jews begin to chide their elders for what they claim to be the older generation's apostasy, described as the sheep's blindness and straying from the path. More-

---

[35] Translation draws on Collins, *Daniel*, *ad loc.* and A. Berlin and M.Z. Brettler, eds., *The Jewish Study Bible* (Oxford and New York: Oxford University Press, 2004, *ad loc.*

[36] On the "obscure" character of the passage, see Collins (*Daniel*, 379-80), who recounts the various possibilities of interpretation. On the pacifist ideology of the Danielic authors, see *ibid.*, 66-67.

[37] *Ibid.*, 66.

[38] Translations of *1 Enoch* are taken from G.W.E. Nickelsburg and J.C. VanderKam, *1 Enoch: A New Translation* (Minneapolis: Fortress, 2004). A more detailed exposition of the Enochic texts appears in Nickelsburg, *1 Enoch 1*, *ad loc.*

over, they base their actions on the authority of revelation. Since this claim to revelation takes place within an account of a dream vision, it is possible that, in part, this revelation was also embodied in a vision. A similar take of this period appears in the Apocalypse of Weeks and in other parts of the Epistle that are not parts of a historical summary:

> And at its [the seventh week's] conclusion, the chosen will be chosen,
> > as witnesses of righteousness from the everlasting plant of righteousness,
> > to whom will be given sevenfold wisdom and knowledge.
> And they will uproot the foundations of violence,
> > and the structure of deceit in it
> > to execute judgment. (93:10; 91:11)

Again a group claims to be the recipients of special revelation, here because they are the chosen, and they take a position over against others who are the perpetrators of false religion and violence, as we shall see in a moment. The identity of these recipients of revelation, and presumably of those in the Animal Vision, is clarified at the end of the Epistle:

> ... to the righteous and pious and wise
> > my books will be given for the joy of righteousness and much wisdom.
>
> Indeed, to them the books will be given,
> > and they will believe in them,
> > and in them all the righteous will rejoice and be glad,
> > to learn from them all the paths of truth. (104:12-13)

That is, the righteous, the recipients of revelation, are those who find divine truth *in the books of Enoch*. This division between the pious and enlightened and the sinners, and the religious and social tensions indicated in the Animal Vision and the Apocalypse of Weeks are the subject of further discussion in the Epistle.[39]

> Woe to those who write lying words and words of error
> > and lead many astray with their lies when they hear them ...
> > You yourselves err;
> > you will have no peace but will quickly perish. (98:15)

---

[39] On the religious polemics, see G.W.E. Nickelsburg, "The Epistle of Enoch and the Qumran Literature," *JJS* 33 (1982) = J. Neusner and G. Vermes, eds., *Essays in Honour of Yigael Yadin*, 333-45, reprinted in J. Neusner and A. Avery-Peck, eds., *George W.E. Nickelsburg in Perspective: An Ongoing Dialogue of Learning* (2 vols.; JSJSup 80; Leiden: Brill, 2003) 1:105-18 (hereafter, *GNP*).

> Woe to you who alter the true words
>   and pervert the everlasting covenant
>   and consider themselves to be without sin;
>   they will be swallowed up in the earth ... (99:2)

In short, the Enoch texts indicate that around the turn of the second century BCE, and later in the century, there were sharp religious divisions that the self-proclaimed wise and righteous understood to constitute the difference between the saved and the damned.

Finally, the long strings of woes in the Epistle of Enoch depict actions of the rich and the powerful, who pervert justice and oppress the righteous and the poor in a variety of ways.[40] Of course, one must be careful not to accept uncritically as fact the content of the polemics of one group against the other. In this case, however, granting the possibility of some rhetorical overstatement, I see no reason to write off the content of these woes as simply the delusional complaints of the underdogs. A total disconnect with reality would render these complaints pointless. Thus, the Epistle provides some evidence for social and economic tensions that are not attested in the writings of the Jewish historians.

3.1.3. The *Testament of Moses*

As we have seen, like the Danielic apocalypses, the cycle of the historical summary in the Testament of Moses has numerous parallels with the historians' accounts of the time around the Antiochene persecution, which allow us to date its earliest form to that period. Also like Daniel, the summary adds little to our knowledge of the period, not least because ch. 5 engages primarily in stereotyped polemics. At one point, however, the text agrees with the Enochic texts. Concerning the beginning of this period, it states that "they themselves will be divided as to the truth" (5:2). One could hardly articulate a better, more pithy summary of the texts in the Animal Vision and the Epistle of Enoch cited above. It was a time of religious dispute, when truth and falsehood were major issues.

---

[40] In detail see G.W.E. Nickelsburg, "Riches, the Rich, and God's Judgment in 1 Enoch 92–105 and the Gospel According to Luke," *NTS* 25 (1979) 324-40; and *idem*, "Revisiting the Rich and the Poor in 1 Enoch 92–105 and the Gospel According to Luke," *SBLSP* 37 (1998) 324-44, both reprinted in *GNP* 2:521-85, together with responses by J.S. Kloppenborg and G.W.E. Nickelsburg, *ibid.*, 586-99.

3.1.4. *4 Ezra* and *2 Baruch*
As far as I can see, the historical summaries in these texts provide no significant information about the times that they describe that is not to be found in the Bible and the Jewish historians.

3.1.5. Summary
With the pseudepigraphic apocalypses placed fairly precisely in time, thanks to some close parallels in the Jewish and pagan historians, we have found a few details about Jewish religious and social life that are not mentioned by these historians, principally some indications of religious difference and disputes, as well as attestations of social oppression. While these findings are quantitatively skimpy, we should not minimize their significance. In the first instance, they are indicators early on of a religious pluralism and sectarianism that comes much more to the fore at a slightly later period in the Qumran scrolls. In the second case, we know little enough about social and economic conditions in Palestine in the second century as it was viewed by the underdogs. The Epistle of Enoch presents a view of the rich and riches that is very different from the viewpoint of Joshua ben Sira, the teacher of the aristocratic sons of Jerusalem.[41]

3.2.1. The Apocalypses as Historical Sources
I have suggested that the historical summaries in the apocalyptic literature provide relatively little information about Jewish history that we cannot glean from other sources in much greater detail, and I have argued that, in these sections, the apocalypticists were not really interested in communicating historical information for its own sake. These facts notwithstanding, I will argue in this section that we can, in fact, glean a good deal of important historical information from the apocalypses that is not available elsewhere, or that is available only in bits and pieces. For the fact is that *the apocalypses are themselves pieces of Jewish history*, and careful study of them as historical artifacts sheds important light on the developing multifaceted shape of Jewish religion in its theological, intellectual, institutional, and social aspects.

---

[41] See the discussion by R.A. Horsley, "Social Relations and Social Conflict in the *Epistle of Enoch*," in R.A. Argall, B.A. Bow, and R.A. Werline, eds., *For a Later Generation: The Transformation of Tradition in Israel, Early Judaism, and Early Christianity*, Fs. George W.E. Nickelsburg (Harrisburg: Trinity International, 2000) 100-11.

3.2.1.1. The Centrality of Revelation

First and most obvious, the apocalypses attest the existence in the 3rd century BCE to the 1st century CE of a kind of Jewish religion that attaches central importance to claims of divine revelation.[42] The centrality of revelation in the apocalypses is evident from the fact that these authors embody their message in literary forms that are almost entirely revelatory in nature. Daniel 7–12 consists of dream visions in which the author sees events taking place in the heavenly realm and angelophanies in which the seer learns about the hidden structure and course of history. *1 Enoch* is more complex. It comprises: a prophetic oracle of salvation and damnation (chs. 1–5); a throne-vision and prophetic commissioning (chs. 1–16); journeys through the cosmos and visions of how it operates (chs. 17–19; 20–36; 72–82); another ascent to heaven and a series of journeys through the cosmos (chs. 37–71); two dream visions about the coming judgment and the structure and course of history (83–84; 85–90); a historical summary of information that Enoch read from the heavenly tablets (93:1-10; 91:11-17); forms of woe and encouragement and predictions of the future that echo the prophets, and appeals to earlier revelations of heaven (chs. 94–104).[43] The *Testament of Moses* features a detailed forecast of the future that expounds Moses' prophecy in Deuteronomy 28–32, placing the exposition in the mouth of Moses. Most of *4 Ezra* and *2 Baruch* consists of dream visions about the future and revelatory dialogues with angels and with the deity.

These authors' claims to revelation and to the divine authority that derives from it validate and add persuasive power to the various aspects of their message. The assurance that the eschaton and divine vindication is near offers consolation in times of trouble and provides a rationale for admonitions to stand fast when apostasy or the loss of faith in God's justice are a clear and present danger. In some cases, accounts of journeys through the cosmos to the places where judgment is being prepared or (will be) enacted provides spatial reinforcement for predications of the eschaton.[44] Alternatively such accounts provide assurance that order rather than chaos rules in God's universe. The assertion that "wisdom has been given" to an author or the author's group validates polemics against persons or groups who differ in their interpretation of God's will. In short, what these authors say is the case in matters of existential concern is not simply asserted as

---

[42] Nickelsburg, "Apocalyptic Judaism."
[43] On the literary forms in *1 Enoch*, see Nickelsburg, *1 Enoch 1*, 28-34.
[44] *Ibid.*, 278.

fact, it is presented as God's truth, often when phenomenal "reality" seems to indicate otherwise.

As I have suggested but not emphasized, the apocalypticists often expressed their revelatory claims in forms and rhetoric that are paralleled in the writings of the biblical prophets. This is especially, but not exclusively, true of various sections of *1 Enoch*.[45] This is not to say, however that the apocalypticists were clones of the biblical prophets. I cite two examples from *1 Enoch*. First, in chs. 26–27, the author draws on material in Third Isaiah (Isa 65–66) to describe Jerusalem in the eschaton. But it is not sufficient to quote the prophet; the author presents the material of Isaiah's prophecies in an account of Enoch's cosmic journeys.[46] Second, and more generally, *1 Enoch* exemplifies a fusion of prophetic and sapiential forms, so that, to state it very generally, wisdom is for him revelation, and prophetic material is sapientialized beyond what we find in the prophets.[47] These data indicate a major transition in the theology and intellectual life of Israel. Moreover, the literary data point beyond themselves to the social *realia* that generated them. In what sense is it correct to say that prophecy was dead and prophets were gone by the end of the Persian period? It is a complex problem I cannot address here.[48] What is clear, however, is that there were people in the Hellenistic and early Roman periods who acted and wrote and spoke as if they were prophets of some sort. Thus the apocalypses are both a testimony to and an expression of a major transition in the religious and social history of Israel.

3.2.1.2. Increased Concern about Divine Justice and Speculation about the End Time

By their very nature, Israelite covenantal theologies, psalms of lament, and, to some degree, wisdom speculation concerned themselves with the issue of divine justice. It was axiomatic that God rewards the right-

---

[45] *Ibid.*, 30-31, 34.

[46] Nickelsburg, *1 Enoch 1*, 315-19. On Second and Third Isaiah, see further, *ibid.*, 57-58.

[47] *Ibid.*, 59-60. On the relationship between wisdom and apocalypticism, see the papers in F. García Martínez, ed., *Wisdom and Apocalypticism in the Dead Sea Scrolls and in the Biblical Tradition* (BETL 158; Leuven: Leuven University Press; Peeters, 2003); and in B.G. Wright III and L.M. Wills, eds., *Conflicted Boundaries in Wisdom and Apocalypticism* (Symposium 35. Atlanta: Society of Biblical Literature, 2005).

[48] I touch on this briefly in "The Nature and Function of Revelation in 1 Enoch, Jubilees, and Some Qumranic Documents," E.G. Chazon and M.E. Stone, eds., *Pseudepigraphical Perspectives: The Apocrypha and Pseudepigrapha in Light of the Dead Sea Scrolls, Proceedings of the International Symposium of the Orion Center for the Study of the Dead Sea Scrolls and Associated Literature, 12-14 January, 1997* (STDJ 31; Leiden: Brill,1999) 91-119.

eous and punishes the wicked. But sometimes human experience seemed to falsify the axiom. Times of severe crisis increased the efforts of "the righteous" to deal with this cognitive dissonance. The apocalypses in particular are exercises in theodicy. Early forms of it appear in *1 Enoch* in the prayer in ch. 9 and the lament in ch. 103. Much more developed speculation about God's justice fills the pages of *4 Ezra* and *2 Baruch*, with the former echoing Job's struggle with the Almighty.

The result of these struggles of faith and intellect is usually the assertion that God's justice will come to a full and final resolution in the end time. A concern with what we may meaningfully describe as the end is already evident in the writings of the biblical prophets, preeminently Second and Third Isaiah.[49] Drawing on some of these traditions, the apocalypticists, especially but by no means exclusively, focus on the end as the solution to present problems. The particular characteristics of their "eschatology" include: speculation about the course of history and the events that will occur in the time of the end, not least the great judgment and the resurrection of the dead or its equivalent[50]; usually a spatial dualism that posits a certain correspondence between events in this world and in the heavenly world; and claims of revelation that guarantee the truth of these claims about the heavenly world and the eschatological enactment of God's justice. Since an interest in the end appears in quite a few Jewish works that are not apocalypses, a comparison of these texts with the apocalypses offers another opportunity for us to see where literary historical artifacts overlap, and where they differ from one another.[51]

3.2.1.3. A Range of Attitudes about the Jerusalem Temple

It is axiomatic that the Second Temple was central to the piety of what is often called "Second Temple Judaism." Evidence of the temple's importance is to be seen in the book of Daniel, where Antiochus's pollution of the sanctuary and the cessation of the daily Tamid sacrifice are portrayed as the epitome of his sacrilegious arro-

---

[49] On this issue, see G.W.E. Nickelsburg, "Eschatology (Early Jewish),"*ABD* 2:580-83.

[50] For these variations on the theme, see Nickelsburg, *Resurrection*.

[51] For a sketch of the eschatology of the Jewish writings of the Hellenistic and early Roman periods, see Nickelsburg, "Eschatology," 2:583-93.

gance (8:11-14; 9:27; 11:31; 12:11). The same issue arises in the *Testament of Moses* (8:5).[52]

Several strata of *1 Enoch* paint a different picture however. Most striking is the Animal Vision. According to 89:73-74 the cult of the second temple was polluted from its inception:

> And they began again to build as before and they raised up that tower and it was called the high tower. And they began again to place a table before the tower, but all the bread on it was polluted and not pure. And besides all these things, the eyes of the sheep were blind, and they did not see . . .

The language appears to be drawn from Mal 1:7-8, 12, including perhaps the reference to the blind sheep, which here refers not to sacrificial animals, but to Israel's apostasy. The Enoch text is striking because the blindness of the sheep persists until the author's own time, when some of his own persuasion begin to open their eyes (90:6). The Apocalypse of Weeks is also important in this respect. Although the author mentions the construction of the tabernacle, the construction and destruction of the first temple, and the construction of the eschatological temple (93:6, 7-8; 91:13), he makes no explicit reference to the second temple and describes the post-exilic period as a time of complete perversion (93:9).[53] Yet another possible reference to cultic irregularities occurs in chs. 12–16, where the sin of the rebel watchers is described in language that occurs in explicit polemics against the Jerusalem cult.[54] These polemics in *Pss. Sol.* 8:13 and CD 5:6-7 indicate that *1 Enoch* is not unique in its accusation, but the Enochic texts as a group demonstrate that a criticism of the cult is older than the foundation of the Qumran community and the first-century pietist group that composed the polemics in the *Psalms of Solomon*. The criticism in *1 Enoch* is striking also because according to 26:1, Jerusalem is located at the center of the earth. The place is sacred, but the institution has been perverted.

Other critiques of the second temple occur in texts that were composed in response to the Roman destruction of Jerusalem. For all of

---

[52] J.A. Goldstein, "The Testament of Moses: Its Content, Its Origin, and Its Attestation in Josephus," in G.W.E. Nickelsburg, ed., *Studies in the Testament of Moses* (SBLSCS 3; Cambridge: Society of Biblical Literature, 51-52. See also *T. Moses* 5–6.

[53] His only possible allusion to the temple is in 91:11 (see Nickelsburg, *1 Enoch 1*, 448):
> And they will uproot the foundations of violence,
>   and the structure of deceit in it,
>   to execute judgment.

[54] Nickelsburg, *1 Enoch 1*, 271-72.

his grief over the destruction of the temple and the desolation of Zion, Baruch lays the blame on the priesthood, although the precise reason is not specified:

> But you priests, take the keys of the sanctuary,
>   and hurl them into the heights of heaven.
> And give them to the Lord and say,
>   "Guard your house yourself,
>   for we have been found to be false stewards." (10:18)

In the *Apocalypse of Abraham*, a text from this period that I have not discussed, Manasseh's pollution of the first temple and its consequent destruction are symbolic of the destruction of the second temple and its cause (chs. 25–27).[55]

In short, although some of the prophets criticize the first temple and its priesthood and the cult, and 2 Maccabees, for example, decries the hellenizing excesses of the priests in the years before the Antiochan persecution and defilement of the temple, and the Qumran texts polemicize against a polluted cult, the apocalyptic texts that we have discussed indicate a broader, ongoing critique of temple, priesthood and cult, rooted in the earlier post-exilic period and still evident in the post-70 period.

3.2.1.4. Wisdom – an Intellectual Phenomenon in Transition

Traditional discussions of biblical wisdom literature have focused on Job, to some extent, Psalms, especially Proverbs, and also Qohelet. With the increased study of the non-canonical literature that has followed from the discovery of the Dead Sea Scrolls, the Wisdom of ben Sira, the Wisdom of Solomon, and Baruch have been included as later exemplars of sapiential literature. It is now clear, however, that we must bring the apocalypses into the picture, as well.[56] There is still much that is unclear in this picture, and especially its social settings, but here are a few considerations. "Wisdom" is the self-designation for two or three major parts of *1 Enoch*,[57] a number of the literary forms in *1 Enoch* are at home in the sapiential literature,[58] and significant parts of

---

[55] *Idem, Jewish Literature*, 288.

[56] See above, n. 47. See also J.J. Collins, "Wisdom, Apocalypticism, and Generic Compatibility," in L. Perdue, et al., eds., *In Search of Wisdom: Essays in Memory of John Gammie* (Louisville: Westminster, 1993) 165-85.

[57] See 1:8; 37:1-2; 92:1; 93:10; 104:13; cf. 98:9; 99:10.

[58] Nickelsburg, *1 Enoch 1*, 60.

its contents parallel the contemporary Wisdom of ben Sira (Sirach).[59] The interpretation of dreams and visions is an important element in the book of Daniel, a composition of "the wise" (*maskîlîm*). Sirach 24:23 contains the first explicit identification of wisdom with the Mosaic Torah, and it is followed in this by Baruch 4:1. This identification recurs in *2 Baruch* 51:7; 77:13-16, and the apocalypse is saturated with the vocabulary of intellection,[60] which suggests that we cannot make a clean distinction between sapiential and revelatory literature in this period. *1 Enoch* is striking for the manner in which it ties moral instruction not to the Mosaic Torah, but to the revelations of Enoch, and for its placing the Mosaic Torah on the back burner.[61] That this is not an isolated phenomenon is evident from the Qumran 4QInstruction, which employs typical forms of wisdom instruction, shows little if any interest in the Mosaic Torah, and cites the revelatory *raz nihyeh* (the mystery to be) as the functional equivalent of "wisdom" as we see it, for example, in Sirach.[62]

What we see in these data and many others that could be cited is the existence in the Hellenistic period of a complex set of phenomena that resided in intellectual "circles" that variously claimed the receipt of revelation and practiced the hard-headed search for "wisdom and knowledge" (cf. *1 Enoch* 93:10 for this noun pair) that embraced the heavenly and the earthly and that related to the realm of the sacred and to what we might call the ordinary activities of everyday life. In short, careful study of the apocalyptic literature, as well as related texts from the Qumran caves, considerably muddies the waters as we seek to describe the intellectual life of the Jews in the Hellenistic and early Roman periods and the concrete settings in which it was nourished.

3.2.1.5. Attitudes toward Scripture

The Jewish apocalypses demonstrate some of the variety of ways in which Scripture was used, interpreted, and, indeed, ignored in the Second Temple period. Taken as a whole, the corpus of apocalypses

---

[59] R.A. Argall, 1 Enoch *and Sirach: A Comparative Literary and Conceptual Analysis of the Themes of Revelation, Creation and Judgment* (SBLEJL 8; Atlanta: Society of Biblical Literature, 1995).

[60] Here I am indebted to a graduate seminar paper by Francis Flannery written some years ago at The University of Iowa.

[61] G.W.E. Nickelsburg, "Enochic Wisdom and its Relationship to the Mosaic Torah," in G. Boccaccini, ed., *The Early Enoch Tradition* (JSJSup; Leiden: Brill, 2007, forthcoming).

[62] Nickelsburg, *1 Enoch 1*, 58-59; see also the literature cited in *idem*, *Jewish Literature*, 387, n. 323.

indicates that divine revelation was believed to exist apart from the Tanak. The *Testament of Moses*, on the other hand, posits revelation by rewriting the last chapters of Deuteronomy with specific, detailed, and explicit reference to current events. The authors of the Enochic corpus appear to have known almost all the books of the Tanak,[63] and the author of the Animal Vision recounts the history of humanity by summarizing the content of Genesis through Ezra–Nehemiah. At the same time, these authors' claims to revelation depend on the alleged ancient Enochic authorship of their texts. Moreover, a good part of the corpus as a whole is presented as authoritative scripture,[64] and parts of the parts of the corpus appear to have been considered as authoritative sacred tradition at Qumran. A similar situation pertains to *Jubilees*. It alleges to be the Mosaic transcript of an angelic recitation of heavenly Torah and appears to have been authoritative in the Qumran community. *4 Ezra* accepts the authority of the Tanak and includes his own work in a group of other inspired works intended for the wise (14:37-48). In his messianic chapters, he presents his interpretation of Daniel 7 as the product of a divinely sent dream vision.

In sum, the apocalypses variously: respect the authority of the Tanak, or parts of it; claim to be the inspired interpreters of the Tanak; and claim authoritative revelation apart from it. In Qumran, as our one known example, Daniel, parts of *1 Enoch*, and *Jubilees* were accepted as part of the "corpus" of authoritative sacred writings.

3.2.1.6. The Apocalyptic Writings and non-Israelite Myth

In composing their writings, the early apocalypticists not only drew on Israelite sacred tradition, they also fished in Gentile waters. Daniel 7 and 8 employ Canaanite mythic material to color their vision reports (above §3.2.1.6). In order to explain the origins of violence in his own time, the author of *1 Enoch* 6–11 employed motifs from the Prometheus myth, and other elements from pagan mythology appear in other strata of *1 Enoch*.[65] Thus, the apocalyptic texts provide evidence that in the Greco-Roman period some Jews found it useful to express their Israelite religion by means of non-Israelite symbols. From this we may extrapolate a situation in which they either read pagan texts or inter-

---

[63] Nickelsburg, *1 Enoch 1*, 57-58.

[64] G.W.E. Nickelsburg, "Scripture in 1 Enoch and 1 Enoch as Scripture, in T. Fornberg and D. Hellholm, eds., *Texts and Contexts: Biblical Texts in their Textual and Situational Contexts, Essays in Honor of Lars Hartman* (Oslo: Scandinavian University Press, 1995) 333-54; and in summary, Nickelsburg, *1 Enoch 1*, 57-58.

[65] Nickelsburg, *1 Enoch 1*, 62.

acted with other Jews or with Gentiles who were schooled in these texts. In their use of non-Israelite myth, however, the apocalypticists were not doing a new thing; they were following the precedent of earlier writers of the biblical texts, from the first Genesis creation account to the oracles of Second Isaiah.

3.2.1.7. Sects and Groups

The early apocalypses provide a window into the sociology of early Judaism, in a negative way. There is no reason to believe that Daniel, the *Testament of Moses*, any part of *1 Enoch*, or *Jubilees* was composed by a member of any Jewish sect known to us. Taken along with the Qumran sectarian texts, and earlier quasi-sectarian texts, they attest that a plurality of groups, sects, and perhaps isolated persons of peculiar persuasive dotted the Palestinian landscape between 250 BCE and the turn of the era.[66] To a large degree these groups, sects, and persons appear to have been constituted or theologically and socially shaped by their particular understanding of divine law, but other factors were doubtless at work. Closer scrutiny of these texts may bring this geographic and religious landscape into clearer focus. We may never learn names, but we can get a better view of the religious and social contours.

4.0. Summary

Several conclusions are relevant to the topic of this conference.
1. From a certain perspective, it is difficult to describe history writing in the apocalypses, because the apocalypticists do not seek to convey historical information.
2. Alternatively, they do present historical summaries whose primary purpose is to interpret their present situation and identify their place and the place of their audience with respect to the eschaton.
3. In the process of doing this they assert God's ordering of and control of history.
4. In both respects the claimed source of their history writing is divine revelation.
5. Although the apocalyptic historical summaries do not seek to convey historical information, there are a few tidbits here and

---

[66] G.W.E. Nickelsburg, *Ancient Judaism and Christian Origin: Diversity, Continuity, and Transformation* (Minneapolis: Fortress, 2003) 160-81.

there that help to fill out the pictures created by authors who are self-consciously historians.
6. Perhaps most important for the historian of antiquity, the apocalypses are themselves precious historical data that shed light on aspects of the religious, intellectual, cultural, and social life of the Jews in the Greco-Roman period.

Bibliography of Primary Sources

1 Enoch

G.W.E. Nickelsburg and J.C. VanderKam, *1 Enoch: A New Translation* (Minneapolis: Fortress, 2004). Translation based on the Ethiopic mss., Greek texts, and Aramaic fragments.

M.A. Knibb, *The Ethiopic Book of Enoch* (2 vols.; Oxford: Clarendon, 1978). Vol. 1, reproduction of one Ethiopic ms. with apparatus of others; vol. 2, translation of the one ms., with notes citing the Greek and Aramaic evidence.

idem, "1 Enoch," in H.F.D. Sparks, ed., The Apocryphal Old Testament (Oxford: Clarendon, 1984) 169-319. Translation the same as the previous one.

Daniel

Several translations of the Bible

J.J. Collins, *Daniel: A Commentary on the Book of Daniel* (Hermeneia; Minneapolis: Fortress, 1993). Translation based on a critical text is spread throughout the book.

Testament of Moses

J. Priest, "Testament of Moses," in J.H. Charlesworth, ed., *The Old Testament Pseudepigrapha* (2 vols; Garden City: Doubleday, 1983-1985) 1:919-34.

J.P.M. Sweet and R.H. Charles, "The Assumption of Moses," in H.F.D. Sparks, ed., *The Apocryphal Old Testament* (Oxford: Clarendon, 1984) 601-16.

Jubilees

J.C. VanderKam, *The Book of Jubilees* (Corpus Scriptorum Christianorum Orientalium 511; Scriptores Aethiopici 88; Louvain: Peeters, 1989)

O. Wintermute, "Jubilees," in J.H. Charlesworth, ed., *The Old Testament Pseudepigrapha* (2 vols; Garden City: Doubleday, 1983–1985) 2:142.

C. Rabin and R.H. Charles, "Jubilees," in H.F.D. Sparks, ed., *The Apocryphal Old Testament* (Oxford: Clarendon, 1984) 1-139.

4 Ezra

Found in most editions of the Bible as 2 Esdras

B.M. Metzger, "The Fourth Book of Ezra," in J.H. Charlesworth, ed., *The Old Testament Pseudepigrapha* (2 vols; Garden City: Doubleday, 1983-1985) 1:517-59.

M.E. Stone, *Fourth Ezra: A Commentary on the Book of Fourth Ezra* (Hermeneia; Minneapolis: Fortress, 1990). Translation based on a text is spread throughout the book.

2 Baruch

A.F.J. Klijn, "2 (Syriac Apocalypse of) Baruch," in James H. Charlesworth, ed., *The Old Testament Pseudepigrapha* (2 vols; Garden City: Doubleday, 1983-1985) 1:615-52.

L.H. Brockington and R.H. Charles, "The Syriac Apocalypse of Baruch," in H.F.D. Sparks, ed., *The Apocryphal Old Testament* (Oxford: Clarendon, 1984) 835-95.

Apocalypse of Abraham

R. Rubinkiewicz, "Apocalypse of Abraham," in J.H. Charlesworth, ed., *The Old Testament Pseudepigrapha* (2 vols; Garden City: Doubleday, 1983–1985) 1:681-705.

A. Pennington, "The Apocalypse of Abraham," in H.F.D. Sparks, ed., *The Apocryphal Old Testament* (Oxford: Clarendon, 1984) 393-421.

5

Encountering the Past through the Works of Flavius Josephus

Steve Mason

Julian Barnes's recent novel *Arthur and George* explores the encounter between Sir Arthur Conan Doyle, creator of Sherlock Holmes, and one George Edalji, a thoroughly British man who cannot grasp that his Parsee ancestry might be the cause of sudden legal troubles. One reviewer confides his shock at discovering that the character of George, along with other figures and documents in the novel, are "historical":

> I was initially sorely disappointed. Barnes didn't invent the letters? ... Barnes didn't make up George? But of course he's invented him, or at least raised him from the dead. And using mere kitchen scraps of historical information, has added marrow, muscles, nerves and a pumping heart to a footnote in British legal history, animated long-interred bones in a way no biography ever could.[1]

These observations prompt a number of questions concerning the boundaries between fact and fiction: Does it take a novelist to bring dead characters to life? At what literary threshold does one who writes about such figures cease to be a historian or biographer? What is the relationship, ideal or real, between fact and art in history – or in a novel? Where can we find those "kitchen scraps of historical information," from which to build stories? Are there *simple facts* available somewhere? And what is history, anyway? Such questions are also part and parcel of any investigation of the writings by the first-century priest, soldier, and historian, Flavius Josephus.

Josephus (37–c. 100+ CE) left behind what has always been considered, as it was recopied and reissued in the west until the printing press

---

[1] Z. Gardner, "A Palpable Hit, by George!" (Review of J. Barnes, *Arthur & George* [New York: Random House, 2005], *Globe and Mail*, Saturday Oct. 8 (2005), D-6.

assured its survival, a historical treasure trove. He wrote three works – if we count the short autobiography as an appendix to the *Judean Antiquities* – in thirty Greek volumes. Of these, twenty-eight volumes (viz.: the *Judean War* in seven and the *Antiquities/Life* in twenty-one) are narratives concerning the past, while the two volumes known as *Against Apion* contain an essay-like argument concerning Judean antiquity. Because he set out to write history, some critics of Josephus express the opposite reaction to Barnes's reviewer: the literary art is so pervasive, it is hard to know where the *facts* lie. On the other side of the spectrum, archaeologists digging in modern Israel, using Josephus as their principal guide for Herodian-Roman strata, comment frequently on his accuracy.

Too often these groups of scholars talk past each other, the archaeologists being satisfied that Josephus was basically reliable (and possibly suspecting the text people of pointless ivory-tower word games), while scholars who deal first with the texts become ever more convinced of Josephus's artistry and therefore of the chasm between his accounts and historical reality (perhaps doubting the sophistication of those who declare him reliable). My aim in this essay is – in principle – basic. I want to think with my readers about the problem of "doing history" in relation to the works of Josephus. There is no point attempting this, however, until we reach some preliminary agreement (author-imposed, by necessity) about what we mean by "Josephus" and by "doing history."

Part I. Reference Points: What's in Josephus? What is History?

Before undertaking any critical investigation it is useful to define terms. Much apparent disagreement might turn out to result simply from the different things that scholars have in mind when they speak of "Josephus" or "history." It may be that if we take on board what is actually in Josephus, situate it appropriately in its ancient context, and reason through some basic issues of historical method, we shall already be on our way toward a shared understanding of the possibilities of doing history with Josephus.

A. What is Josephus?

I use the impersonal interrogative "What?" for two reasons. First, we need to resist the powerful tendency to begin with the question, "*Who* was Josephus?" – a question that subordinates the understanding of his narratives to presumed facts about his life and moral character. This is methodologically backwards, since Josephus's writings, which are highly rhetorical and do not easily yield facts, are our only source for his life: it is not something we can know in advance. We should begin, therefore, by trying to understand his writings. Second, even those who have had occasion to read parts of Josephus do not necessarily have a clear picture of what, on closer inspection, is actually there. Having some understanding of the atoms from which Josephus's narratives are constructed seems essential for making judgments about the possibilities of historical use.

The proposition I want to advance here is that Josephus is the creator of his compositions in much the same way that an artist (say, a painter or sculptor) is a creator, even if she uses a model and attempts realistic representation of it. The model is lost to us, and only the art remains. Or if you prefer, Josephus's writing process resembles the combined efforts of screenplay-writer and director in a contemporary film dealing with historical subjects (e.g. *Gladiator, Troy, Elizabeth,* or *The Passion of the Christ*). Although these films have an undeniable basis in "historical reality" – in events that really occurred and lives actually lived – and even though we know this as we watch the films, we realize that we are watching the invention, the *creation* from beginning to end, of a writer and director. Knowing *that* historical realities underlie the work does not immediately help us, in the absence of additional resources, to know *which* parts originated where. Even if we happen to know by other means that Marcus Aurelius was a real man, whereas the general Maximus (as far we know) was not, we could not learn anything from Richard Harris's Marcus in *Gladiator* about that man, since the production as it exists is "pure Hollywood." In a similar way, Josephus has created a master-work, a production combining intricate plot and colorful characters, based largely on real events and people but under his absolute authorial-directorial control.

But we are getting ahead of ourselves. Let me illustrate Josephus's control over his material from three angles: the structure of his works, his use of charged language, and a specific pair of episodes.

Both of Josephus's major works and the autobiography have, interwoven with other structures, a symmetrical or "concentric" literary plan. Josephus alerts us to this when he explains at the beginning of the *Antiquities* (1.7) that he had considered including ancient lore in the *Judean War*, but decided against it because he wished to measure off the beginning against the end. This is the meaning of Greek *symmetreo*, the verb he uses there. *Symmetry* was an essential value of Greek architecture – physical, mental, and literary.

Thus, at the very beginning of *War's* narrative (1.31) Josephus briefly mentions a dissident temple built in Egypt and promises that he will describe it later (1.33). "Later" turns out to be at the very end of the seven-volume work (7.420-436) – a long wait. Other correspondences reinforce the symmetrical plan: the first-century BCE Roman civil war that backgrounds Book 1 is complemented by the Flavian conclusion of the later civil war (68-69 CE) at 7.157; Parthians and "Medes" (a stylized anachronism) dominate the story only in Books 1 and 7; both books feature an "Antiochus" who attempts to end Judean observance, and even an Antiochus Epiphanes (1.31-40; 7.46-53, 219-243). Moving in one step, Books 2 and 6 feature striking parallels in speeches by different characters as well as in story details (e.g. 2.49-50; 6.180-181).

If we fast-forward to the heart of the seven-volume work, to the middle of Book 4, we find clear evidence of literary structuring around this narrative pivot. Josephus is arrested at the end of Book 3 (392-408), but released from chains at the end of Book 4 (622-629). The noisy entrance of the Idumeans into factionalized Jerusalem early in Book 4 (224-235), before they join the Zealots in murdering the nobility, is matched by their exit in alleged disgust after these assassinations, as they realize their mistake (345-354) – except that they continue to turn up in Jerusalem, highlighting the literary artifice of their staged exit. And the central panel of Book 4, therefore of the entire *War*, is in fact the pivotal point in the book: the chief priests Ananus and Jesus, men of character and virtue who have been leading the war effort thus far, are murdered by Zealots and Idumeans (4.314-344; cf. 7.267). Josephus devotes to these men a lengthy joint encomium, which marks this moment as the decisive shift to the tyranny and animal-like behavior (4.326-327, 351, 356) that will spell the end of the city and temple, as God purges the evil.

Each of Josephus's works has this kind of symmetrical plan (which does not preclude other interwoven structures).[2] Such a deliberate effort to structure his compositions has immediate implications for Josephus's historical method: it suggests that he selected, configured, and described events in a way that would suit the plan. This interest becomes particularly obvious in his autobiography, which completely rearranges and also refashions the material about his career that he

---

[2] For the *Antiquities* and *Life*, see my introductory essay in *Flavius Josephus: Translation and Commentary*, vol. IX: *Life of Josephus* (Leiden: Brill, 2001), xxi-xxiv.

already gave in *War* 2-3. Now, the book's only divine revelation (*Life* 208-209) becomes the narrative fulcrum.

An example will illustrate the lengths to which Josephus could go (it seems) for the sake of structure. In *War* 2.614-625 he had described a serious revolt against his generalship in the Galilean city of Tiberias, in the earliest phase of the revolt against Rome. Josephus's arch-rival John takes advantage of a visit to Tiberias's hot baths (ostensibly for health reasons) to foment revolt in the city; Josephus learns of it from his aide Silas, and marches on the city; while he is addressing the citizens in the stadium of Tiberias, John's men arrive and threaten him with swords; he escapes by a hidden route to a boat that takes him to nearby Tarichea; the Galileans are incensed by John's treachery, but Josephus magnanimously calms their anger at his rival. In the *Life*, sitting like massive literary pillars at the one-quarter and three-quarter marks in the narrative are *two* Tiberian revolts against Josephus's leadership (*Life* 85-103, 271-308). But the two stories include some remarkably similar key elements: John's instigation of revolt, Silas's role as Josephus's spy and flight by secret passageway to a boat for Tarichea, and references to Tiberias's stadium and hot baths, as well as to Josephus's clemency.

Did the Tiberians revolt, and did Josephus react, twice in such similar ways? That is hard to believe because of the difficulty of locating two such incidents. In *War*'s version, the single revolt concludes with Josephus rounding up John's followers, threatening them if they do not support him, and consequently welcoming many defectors from his adversary. John's loss of supporters forces him, in turn, to appeal to his powerful friends in Jerusalem, who send a delegation to attempt Josephus's removal. In the *Life*, the earlier of the two revolts closely parallels *War*'s story, as we have seen, but it cannot include the mass defection of John's followers at the end, because it comes too early in the narrative: they must remain to wreak havoc for quite a while. So the *Life* postpones Josephus's threat and welcoming of John's followers until after the second revolt episode (*Life* 369-372), when they are no longer needed. But this disbandment comes *after* a detailed account of the delegation from Jerusalem (*Life* 189-335) whereas in *War* the disbandment of John's group had led him to arrange the delegation.

Whatever the historical realities may have been, it becomes clear that Josephus considered his authorial-directorial freedom nearly absolute – though he still happily referred *Life*'s audience to the *War* for "accurate details" (*Life* 27, 412). The stories in *War* and *Life* – even though they concern his own career, which he knew better than anyone – cannot both be accurate, and given his literary freedom one has every right to ask whether either one is.

In addition to the careful selection, and in some cases wholesale generation, of material that the symmetrical structuring of his works reflects (along with other structural devices too complicated for discussion here), Josephus controls his work also in the sense that the language – diction, sentence structure, emphasis, pitch, and tone – is exclusively his. This is important because it used to be commonly thought that Josephus wrote mainly by collecting stories from others and stitching them together with his own little editorial bridges. His manner of writing has consequences, as we shall see, for the way in which one tries to use his material for historical purposes. To say that he controlled his language does not mean that he left no inconsistencies or loose ends. Anyone who writes books – or reads academic book reviews – knows that such inconsistencies are common even among modern scholars, who possess a desk full of digital tools for checking their consistency, grammar, and spelling. As an editor, I can certify that unedited work by scholars – especially in denser forms of writing such as commentary – often brims with inconsistencies (of spelling, punctuation, transliteration, abbreviation, representation of numbers, etc.), broken sentences, verbatim duplications, spoiled segues, and misspellings. Even the famous directors of the sword-and-sandal epics made mistakes: an "extra" wearing a watch, a white streak across the sky from an airplane's exhaust, actors wearing different clothes in scenes that end up joined together.[3] But just as we do not conclude that these creators merely threw together extraneous pieces from other sources, so also Josephus created his material out of his own language, in spite of the puzzles and inconsistencies one finds throughout his thirty volumes.

In the *War*, the substantial proem (1.1-30) highlights a number of thematic and verbal clusters, aside from the standard declarations about truth in history, precision, lack of partisan favor, and so on. More distinctive elements of Josephus's approach include: the tyrants (*tyrannoi*) and their bandits (*leistai*) who are responsible for Jerusalem's fall; necessity (*anagke*) and fortune (*tyche*); the city's calamities (*symphorai*) and sufferings (*pathe*); emotions (also *pathe*), lament (*olophursis*), and pity (*eleos*); and the paradoxical contrast between benevolent foreigner (*allophylos*) and destructive compatriot (*homophylos*). Crucially, Josephus attributes the ultimate fall of Jerusalem to the civil strife (*stasis*) pursued

---

[3] Cf. http://www.moviemistakes.com.

by the tyrants, and in his prospectus of what is to come, he highlights a lethal triad of political ills that feed upon each other: war (*polemos*), which degenerates into civil strife (*stasis*), which produces famine (*limos*): "But I discriminate among *the sufferings and calamities of the populace*: how much they were afflicted by the *war*, how much by the *civil strife*, and how much by the *famine* before they were taken captive" (1.27).

Now as it happens, this language pervades the following narrative. Very different characters in the story, speaking from different perspectives (i.e. they are not all made to say the same thing), still operate within the same world of discourse, which has been scripted by the author-director. Narrator and characters conspire to shape the audience's questions and interests along converging lines and suspend historical questions. The narrator can explain in his own voice, for example, that alongside *civil strife*, *famine* came about when the *tyrants* and their *bandit* gangs took up residence in Jerusalem and began hoarding supplies, creating "in addition to the *war*, the miseries of *civil strife* and *famine*" (4.137). In case we miss the charged language, when a general fighting loyal to the aristocrats (Niger the Perean) is assassinated, his dying words "called down Roman retribution on them [the Zealots]: *famine* and *plague* on top of *war* and, worst of all, *internecine fighting*..., the most just penalty being that before long they were about to taste the *insanity* of facing each other in *civil strife.*" Did the dying Niger really say those things? That would be extraordinarily convenient for Josephus's narrative.

In *War* 6 Josephus relates a famous account concerning the tragic resort to cannibalism by an upper-class woman named Maria, reduced to desperate straits in besieged Jerusalem, especially because of the *tyrants* and their *bandits* (6.202). Josephus insists that the story is true, though he knows he may be accused of tale-mongering; he claims many witnesses (6.200). So we read that the starving woman takes up her child and addresses it (6.205), "Miserable baby, given this *war and famine and civil strife*, what should I preserve you for?" And not only does she echo Josephus's themes, but when the Roman general Titus hears of her abominable deed he absolves himself of all responsibility by claiming that it was the rebel Judeans who preferred *civil strife, war,* and *famine* to their opposites (2.214). In spite of Josephus's pointed claims about factuality here, can anyone believe that his characters all happened to think and speak in ways that suited his own script?

This passage is also saturated with the tragic themes and language of the prologue (sufferings, calamities, necessity). Maria's assessment that survival among the Romans would inevitably mean *slavery* (6.206) makes little sense as a comment from a mother to the uncomprehending infant she is about to kill, but it gains its significance from the freedom-slavery motif that also pervades the work. It also prepares the audience for the profound recognition by Eleazar at Masada that the tyrants' mad struggles under the banner of "freedom" have brought only slavery and death, whereas prudent submission under honorable terms, though derided by the tyrants as "slavery," would actually have ensured "freedom" (7.324-325, 387).

If we consider further that Josephus views himself as something of a Jeremiah figure (*War* 5.392-393) and shapes other characters in his story to suit Jeremianic themes (6.301-302), and that both the biblical book of Jeremiah and the *Lamentations* attributed to the same author envision women *eating their young in times of siege* (Jer 19:19; Lam 2:20 ["while priests and prophets are killed in the sanctuary" – especially relevant to Josephus's story]; 4:10), we might wonder whether these literary considerations are not sufficient to account for the existence of this story in Josephus. At the very least, anyone who inclines to assume that Maria acted and spoke as Josephus claims she did should think twice, given his literary freedom.

And note: Josephus was outside the city during the siege, with the Romans. He claims that the Romans heard about this case of suffering (*pathos*) "though reports" (6.214). Presumably, then, that is also how *he* heard. But how reliable are rumors about enemy behavior during armed conflict? At any rate, Josephus has written up the story with no visible limitations to his craft.

Although space does not permit a fuller exploration of this question of language, its implications for the historian are obvious. Even scholars often seem to think that, granted that *not everything* in Josephus is historical, we can at least chisel away his "narrative framework" to leave a residue of facts. For now I want merely to expose the problems inherent in that conception, which assumes that Josephus wrote by stringing together pre-existing stories from other sources, so that his "additions" may be removed. He evidently did not write that way, but rather created a virtual reality for his present needs in post-70 Rome. He not only selected and structured, but he also *scripted* his material to suit his ends. The only form in which we have such episodes as Maria's cannibalism is as part of Josephus's ethereal narrative world; it transports us novel-like into the author's constructed cosmos of language and value. The story draws its meaning from the narrative, out of whose verbal atoms it is created, and it has no independent sense if wrenched from that context. Trying to give it independent substance would be something like approaching a cinema screen and reaching out to extract a character from it – a little odd, no matter how compelling or attractive the character.

That Josephus in composing his works drew abundantly from real life is not in doubt. But how *we* may now encounter those historical phenomena, without regard for the surviving production that presents them to us, is not a simple problem to solve.

For a more detailed case study, let us consider the account of Pontius Pilate in the *Judean War*. The Pilate stories commend themselves because: (a) even in the *War* Pilate receives more space than any other early governor (many of the others are not even mentioned), and *Antiquities* offers yet more information; (b) he is mentioned in several other first-century texts besides Josephus – in Pilate's contemporary Philo of Alexandria (*Leg*. 299-305), in Mark (elaborated by Matthew), Luke (in episodes that seem not to be elaborations of Mark but come from other sources), and John; (c) we also have material evidence for Pilate in the form of the famous *tiberieum* inscription from Caesarea (below), in coinage from his period of office, and in aqueduct remains possibly built under his direction; and (d) the narrative seems generally "historical" in tone – that is, there is no *obvious reason to doubt* that the events happened. They contain nothing of the outright miraculous or wondrous, for example. And indeed scholars usually treat these accounts as more or less historical, and take them over into their synthetic accounts of Pilate's career.[4]

Thus Pilate ought to present something of a best-case scenario for historical reconstruction, one that allows us to get past Josephus's narratives by other means. It would require a book to investigate all of this evidence and produce a satisfactory account of Pilate. Here we must limit our scope to considering the Pilate material in Josephus's *War* and its implications for the project of the "historical Pilate." First, here are the contiguous passages in my translation.

> 169. After being sent to Judea *as procurator* by Tiberius, Pilatus introduces into Hierosolyma – by night, *concealed* – the images of Caesar, which are called "*standards.*" 170. After daybreak this stirred up *a huge disturbance* among the Judeans. For those who were close to *the spectacle* were shocked at *their laws' having been trampled* – for they think it proper to

[4] See J.-P. Lémonon, *Pilate et le gouvernement de la Judée: textes et monuments* (Paris: J. Gabalda, 1981); H. K. Bond, *Pontius Pilate in history and interpretation* (Cambridge: Cambridge University Press, 1998); K. Jaros, *In Sachen Pontius Pilatus* (Mainz: von Zabern, 2002).

place no *representation* in the city. And [in addition] to *the indignation* of those in the city, the people from the countryside streamed together *in concert*. 171. They rushed to Pilatus in Caesarea and *kept pleading* for him to take the standards out of Hierosolyma and *to preserve their ancestral [customs]*. But when Pilatus refused, *they fell down around his residence, prone,* and *held out* motionless for five days and nights alike.

172. On the next [day], *Pilatus sat on a tribunal-platform* in the great stadium and, after summoning *the rabble* as though truly intending to answer them, gives the soldiers a signal, according to a scheme, *to encircle the Judeans* with weapons. 173. As the column was positioned around three-deep, the Judeans were speechless at the unexpectedness *of the spectacle*. After saying that he would cut them to pieces *if they would not accept Caesar's images*, Pilatus nodded to the soldiers *to bare their swords*. 174. The Judeans, just *as if by an agreed signal*, fell down *in concert*, bent their necks to the side, and cried out that they were ready to *do away with themselves rather than transgress the law. Pilatus, who was overwhelmed by the purity of their superstition*, directs [his men] immediately to carry *the standards* out of Hierosolyma.

175. After these events he set in motion a different kind of *disturbance* by exhausting the sacred treasury – it is called the *corbonas* – on a water conduit; it conducted [water] from 400 *stadia* away. At this there was *indignation* among the *rabble*, and when Pilatus was present at Hierosolyma *they stood around his tribunal-platform and kept yelling* at [him]. 176. But because he had foreseen their *disturbance* he had mixed in amongst *the rabble* armed soldiers *concealed* in civilian clothes. Having prohibited them from using the sword, but having *enjoined* them instead to strike with sticks *those who had begun shouting*, he gives the *agreed signal* from the *tribunal-platform*. 177. Many Judeans were lost from being hit by the blows, but many others from having been *trampled under* by their very own [people] in the escape. Given the *calamity* of those who had been taken, the beaten down *rabble* became silent.

Let me make four observations.

First, Josephus has thoroughly accommodated the Pilate episodes to *War*'s larger narrative needs and tendencies. Like all the Judean governors in *War* (cf. 2.118), Pilate (member of the lower, equestrian level of the elite) is introduced misleadingly as a "procurator," a less prestigious title than the accurate "prefect," which tends to highlight his unworthy character. (Contrast the legates of Syria, such as Varus and Petronius, who are senators and appear as men of independent character). These two stories emphasize the "disturbances" created by Judea's governors (the term appears 184 times in Josephus, several times with "huge" as qualifier), the "calamities" suffered by the Judeans, and the people's native courage and endurance in the face of physical threats (cf. 1.138) – a fundamental theme of the *War* that challenges the post-war Roman denigration of the Judeans (1.2-3).

The Pilate episodes also prepare *War*'s audience for a much bigger "image of Caesar" problem, when the reviled emperor Gaius Caligula attempts to install his own colossal statue in Jerusalem's temple – and is checked by an aristocratic Syrian governor Petronius (2.184-203). The language crossover from the Pilate stories to the Caligula-Petronius narrative is impressive: again, the people will cling to the second commandment prohibiting images (Exod 20:4-6) in non-violent resistance, ready to die for their laws and ancestral customs (2.195). The threat of violence "if they do not accept [images of Caesar]" appears both here (2.172) and in the later story (2.185). Strikingly, Josephus employs a word for image or representation, *deikelon*, which hardly appears in literature before his time, only here and in the Petronius narrative (2.195). Both Pilate and Petronius express wonder (*thauma*) – an ambiguous bemusement and/or awe – at the "purity of their superstition" (2.174) or their "unmovable devotion [or cult]" (2.198). The Pilate stories are part of the linguistic fabric of the *War*.

Second, the specific diction in the two Pilate episodes is neither neutral nor self-evident, of a kind that would impose itself on any observer such as you or me; it is typical of Josephus's distinctive style and it drives home *his* themes. Examples include "huge disturbance," "set [an event] in motion," calling an event a "spectacle," the colorful phrase "trampling on the laws," "representation [of an image]" already mentioned, having the Judean "rabble" or "masses" move "in close order," the phrase "fall down prone," "hold out," "bare [rather than "draw," for example] their swords," "incline [their necks]," "transgress the law," and "calamity." Many of these terms are unattested or rarely found before Josephus, but they are part of his meaning-charged lexicon.

Although this charged language may be more obvious in Josephus than in some other authors, it is only one instance of the universal problem that all descriptions, even those on the evening news,[5] must use language, and language is not neutral. There may be such a thing as neutral language – in mathematics (2 x 2 meaning the same thing for everyone), possibly in musical notation – and a very small subset of

---

[5] The "news" is of course a highly selective account of perhaps a dozen events from several billions, massaged and interpreted with editorial language. If accompanied by video, that video must begin and end somewhere (excluding context); it can only be from one vantage-point; and it usually requires an interpretative introduction, voice-over, and conclusion.

descriptive categories can approach neutrality: "Age? Height? Weight? Eye Color? Mother's name?" But these neutral categories are just the ones that most ancient writers *avoid* when they describe human characters. And once a writer moves beyond them to the composition of narrative, he or she must make decisions about diction, emphasis, and structure in accord with the work's ethos and aims. Although Josephus's description of certain characters as "tyrants," "bandits," and "insurgents" is obviously far from neutral (not likely, for example, to be shared by the real figures themselves), he had to call these people *something*; there were no neutral terms.

Third (and this point is often missed), the real events behind these two Pilate episodes – supposing for now that there were real events – must have been quite different in kind. The first describes an incident that occurred *during a single night*, whereas the second concerns a popular reaction to a large public works project – aqueduct-building – that must have occurred in several phases over at least a year, probably two or more. A new aqueduct of considerable length (Josephus here makes it 50 miles long) – a mark of prestige and major practical benefit for any city – was notoriously expensive to build. Financing typically required a combination of imperial grants (especially in the case of Rome and its colonies), local community funds, and private donations. This last category was perilous because, as a consequence of death or default, a benefactor's commitment might end up falling to the city treasury.[6] In the provinces, the Roman governor had the decisive role in arranging finances: gathering private donations and community funds (possibly encouraged by a partial rebate of tribute) before seeking the emperor's approval, and possibly requesting additional help from him (cf. Pliny, *Ep.* 10.90).[7]

Such considerations remind us how little Josephus has actually disclosed in his description of Pilate's aqueduct; he had his own literary points to make. But was it indeed *Pilate's* initiative, or that of the Jerusalem leadership, or of a prominent citizen, or a joint effort? Had he or they arranged for private donations, aside from this resort to the temple treasury? (Even if the temple treasury was exhausted, as Josephus says, that does not mean that it covered the entire cost.) Who if anyone mediated Pilate's use of temple funds? (Did he storm the temple? Josephus does not say that, though we might have expected it in such

---

[6] P. Leveau, "Aqueduct Building: Financing and Costs," in D.R. Blackman and A.T. Hodge, eds., *Frontinus' Legacy: Essays on Frontinus' de aquis urbis Romae* (Ann Arbor: University of Michigan Press), 87-88.

[7] Leveau, "Aqueduct Building," 91.

a hostile portrait of Pilate if he had known of such a thing. It seems more likely that some unnamed temple officials helped Pilate, offering support from the treasury, though we cannot know.) Could it be that an intended benefactor died or become insolvent, and the inability to fulfill his commitment forced Pilate to turn to community funds? Was the Roman imperial treasury involved, perhaps indirectly by rebating tribute money or by contributing technicians, surveyors, auxiliary soldiers, or materials such as lead (see below)? Given that these water systems required professional planning, because of the strict technical requirements of elevation and gradient, route, materials, pooling and distribution mechanisms, *who designed and built the aqueduct?* Archaeology reveals that Jerusalem's aqueduct system was fairly complex, from different dates.[8] Which part(s) did Pilate build or rebuild? Most importantly: At what point in this necessarily long process did particular groups become disaffected, and why at that point (Was the aqueduct completed, half-finished, a mere plan?), and which groups? Who constituted the "mob" that confronted Pilate? (In this case Josephus does not have all the Judeans streaming in to protest.) Was it also an internal protest against certain leaders in Jerusalem? On all these rather important questions, about which the historian would need to have some information in order to make a responsible assessment, Josephus is completely silent.

Pondering such open questions and the practical realities of aqueduct-building renders Josephus's manipulation of the story obvious. The parallel story in his later work (*Ant.* 18.60) quietly halves the length of the aqueduct from 400 to 200 *stadia* (from 50 miles to 25). Just as when he retells other stories from the *War*, his freedom seems unbounded. By having Pilate here undertake an aqueduct the size of some of the larger ones that supplied the world capital of Rome and by implying that he unilaterally raided sacred funds for the purpose, Josephus makes the governor appear arrogant and supremely ambitious, confirming the impression of the previous episode. But since we know so little, we must be suspicious about the evidence being suppressed.

Fourth, Josephus works hard to make his audience ignore the qualitative differences between the two episodes, and the historical questions that might arise concerning the second one, by assimilating one episode to the other as two great "disturbances" provoked by this

---

[8] See D. Amit, J. Patrich, and Y. Hirschfeld, *The Aqueducts of Israel* (Portsmouth: Journal of Roman Archaeology, 2002), esp. A. Mazar, "A Survey of the Aqueducts to Jerusalem," 210-42.

unworthy Roman governor. A governor's primary responsibility, everyone knew, was to maintain peace through careful cultivation of the local elite (as Petronius would do – 2.192-203). Although Pilate's tenure was unusually long in historical terms (below), Josephus characterizes it only with these two matching episodes of nastiness. Notice his deliberate parallel structures: both episodes involve life-threatening protests by indignant masses before Pilate and his soldiers, secret plans and signals, "encirclements" involving weapons, a hearing before the governor's tribunal-platform (*bema*), and potentially fatal consequences. Josephus reinforces the parallel by repeating vocabulary from the first episode ("disturbance," "indignation," "rabble," "prone," "tribunal-platform," "surrounding," "concealed," "sword," "agreed signal," "trampled"). In part, this repetition creates dramatic irony: the "concealed" standards anticipate the soldiers' concealed weapons; the "trampling" of the laws leads to the physical trampling of Judeans; and whereas the Roman forces must train hard to remain in "close order," the indignant Judean masses move in close order spontaneously. They instinctively act "as if by an agreed signal," whereas the soldiers need their secret signals to be carefully planned.

Our narrator is by no means merely reporting the facts. He has *fashioned* the two episodes, assimilating the two stories in order to sustain the ominous atmosphere.

This all highlights the problem faced by the historian, though it would be no less of a problem if our author were less skilled. Although Josephus may well have known the answers to the questions we have posed above, it did not suit his interests to record them and so we are left in the dark. We cannot reconstruct them from his highly streamlined episodes, and it is hard to see how any of our speculations, on the basis of Josephus's narrative alone, might achieve historical "probability." If we consider that Pilate may have governed as long as eighteen years (below), it is all the more striking that Josephus can find only these two stories to substantiate his portrayal, and that the second is so awkwardly suited, on close inspection, to the first.

Once again, if we ask what these accounts are made of, the answer is clear: Josephus's creative language. It is not possible to remove this language to reveal a neutral core of historical fact; when his language is removed no residue remains. This observation holds across his writings, from the detailed narratives of Herod's motives and emotions to the speeches at Masada. About one third of his corpus is devoted to what modern scholars identify as the "biblical paraphrase" (*Ant.* 1-11). Intensive research on that long stretch of narrative, where we know his sources in general terms (namely, the Bible), demonstrates his level of control. Even though scholars know he used the Bible, they are unable to agree on the kind of biblical text he used, precisely because he freely rearranged and rewrote the original accounts, omitting and supplementing at will to create something new and internally coherent for his own purposes.[9] Josephus himself does not mark the transition from biblical to post-biblical sources, and we have every reason to think that he freely reinvented from his source material in the same way throughout his narratives.

B. What Ancient Historians Did

It would be a mistake, however, to imagine that Josephus was peculiar in his approach to history-writing, uniquely slippery, deceptive, or untrustworthy. On the contrary, his *Judean War* is a fine example of first-century historical narrative. Its elaborate proem (1.1-30) is arguably the best example of the tropes that were familiar to all historians and would be satirized by Lucian (*How History Should be Written*) a few decades later. The work's literary level – both the writing style and the subtlety of plot and character – is almost uniformly high. We need to recall some of the context of ancient history-writing if we are to appreciate Josephus's work as his first audiences might have done.

1. First, like most forms of writing, composing history was not a professional pursuit. It was a leisure activity, possible only for the elite classes or their retainers – in other words, the tiny male stratum of the population that was alone in a position, through their education (*paideia*) and life experience, to have a larger picture of human affairs. Most of the abler writers, from Thucydides and Polybius to Sallust, Caesar, Cicero, Pliny, Tacitus, and Plutarch (Livy being a notable exception), were men of affairs who wrote after completing a high-profile political career. Josephus, the Jerusalem nobleman of at least respectable ancestry and elite education, of priestly caste, a former diplomat (e.g. emissary to Rome before the war) and military leader, falls into this category – and he is eager to reinforce his aristocratic credentials with his Roman audience.

His writings everywhere express the values and assumptions of the statesman. His own career, generously featured in his writings (*War* 2-3 and *Life*), reflects the assumption that a member of the elite is capa-

---

[9] See the meticulous work of C.T. Begg, (1993). *Josephus' Account of the Early Divided Monarchy (AJ 8,212-420): Rewriting the Bible* (Leuven: Peeters, 1993); Louis H. Feldman, *Josephus's Interpretation of the Bible* (Berkeley, CA: University of California Press, 1998); idem, *Studies in Josephus' Rewritten Bible* (Leiden: Brill, 1998).

ble of handling all aspects of public leadership with equal facility. He is a philosopher, compelling orator, cultic (or "religious") specialist, legal mind and magistrate, wealthy landowner with many clients and "friends" (in the formal ancient sense), civic leader, international diplomat, shrewd and effective military general, administrator and governor, and finally a peerless historian. Whereas in our world any one or two of these would be enough for a career, requiring highly specialized training, in the Roman world the same elite group was educated to handle all of these tasks: that is, to be consummate public servants. Specialization (as teacher, doctor, philosopher) was something for freedmen and lower classes, not for gentlemen. That ideal survived into modern times among the British aristocracy, and may be glimpsed even today in the royal family.

One implication for history-writing was that it was a highly *personal* business, issuing – like all other aspects of social life – from the authority or prestige of the author. The Latin *auctoritas* neatly combines ideas that have become for us quite separate: "authorship" and "authority/prestige/influence." But for the Romans they were still very much two sides of the same coin. Whereas post-Enlightenment thinkers came to believe in the democracy of knowledge and the primacy of neutral "facts" no matter who discovered them, and industrialized societies have since created ample means for qualified experts to pursue and publish knowledge regardless of class or family background (e.g. in the university), Romans generally knew and cared about facts only as a function of their authority-based social system. It was the big men about town who, when it served their interests, put forward cases within their spheres of friendship and influence. Authors "published" their work first of all, and most importantly, by assembling their friends – in ever-expanding circles – to hear them recite. They might share chapters by having the slaves of a friend copy them and read them aloud. History, like all other cultural activity, was grounded in social values and realities of the time. The process was inimical to the discovery and dissemination of new empirical knowledge, for everyone tended to defer to trusted authority – and the older, the better.

2. The governing ethos and norms of all such elite activity were provided by *rhetoric*. Excellence in rhetoric was the increasingly narrow focus of ancient education, as one progressed through its levels.[10] It tells us a great deal about Roman values that rhetoric – the art and

---

[10] See R. Cribiore, *Gymnastics of the Mind: Greek education in Hellenistic and Roman Egypt* (Princeton: Princeton University Press, 2001).

science of making an effective case, as the situation demanded – should have been the glue that held together the diverse facets of the statesman's life. The student was trained to make judicial cases (for or against an accused in court), with the full range of *character* arguments that we find in Cicero's speeches. He should also be able to make convincing "deliberative" speeches before a city council debating future policies, though under the emperors the abilities of cities to make their own decisions was severely constrained; these speeches were mostly developed for artificial performances or literary contexts. It is impossible to tell, in Josephus's deliberative speeches (e.g. *War* 2.345-404; 5.362-419), which are again *his* compositions in their current form, what historical speeches if any they might represent. And every public figure had to know the accepted techniques for extolling or assassinating someone else's character, in *encomium* and *denunciation* – the third function of rhetoric. Note Josephus's opening complaint that other post-war writers have used just such techniques to denigrate the Judeans and flatter the Romans, without caring about the truth (*War* 1.2).

Rhetorical handbooks known as *progymnasmata* reveal the assumption that this training would enable the student to handle every situation in public life (e.g. Aelius Theon, *Prog.* 70; cf. 60), which invariably required a great deal of speech-making to neutralize threats and keep the masses quiet (cf. Plutarch, *Precepts of Statecraft* 801a-804c, 813a-816a). The elite's rhetorical "omni-competence" also meant that they felt able to write in all genres – a point that extends our first observation concerning their lack of professional specialization. Because of their comprehensive rhetorical training and wide practical experience, these men felt equally capable of composing philosophical set-pieces, poetry, geography or ethnography, history, and rhetoric proper – in speeches. Cicero's letters and Tacitus's *Dialogue on Oratory* preserve discussions among members of the elite concerning *which genre* they would next take up (cf. Pliny, *Ep.* 7.17). Tacitus, Pliny, and their friends met to recite poetry, debate philosophy and rhetoric, recite biographies, and discuss history.[11] This meant that each of these genres, and especially historical narrative, were expected to be decorated with elements of the others – "digressions" (lengthy speeches, geographical portraits, ethical portraiture, philosophical asides) that would greatly

---

[11] For a detailed exploration of the interplay between history and geography (and the blurred lines between them) see K.L. Clarke, *Between Geography and History: Hellenistic constructions of the Roman world* (Oxford: Clarendon Press, 1999).

enrich the work by providing interesting variety in content, just as the speaker had constantly to vary tone and pitch.

The rhetoricization of Greco-Roman culture throws much light on Josephus's evident freedom to restructure, reshape, and re-script his material thoroughly. We can watch him doing this when he rewrites *War* 1-3 (composed in the 70s) in the later *Ant.* 12-20 and *Life* (written in the 90s), easily changing *dramatis personae*, roles, motives, outcomes, dates, numbers or amounts – more or less everything. Although scholars have attempted to find serious motives for *some* of these changes in Josephus's putative shifts of outlook or allegiance, they are so pervasive and often trivial that there must be a more basic reason. Apparently, rhetorical values were so ingrained in Josephus's thinking that he considered it more important to convey lessons in political morality than to establish facts for their own sake.

3. The personal and social contexts of Roman-era history-writing and the pervasive influence of rhetoric determined what historians meant when they promised to present "the truth" with "precision" or "accuracy," as Josephus does (*War* 1.3, 6). Given the nature of publication, the nearly irresistible temptation was to flatter those influential friends in the audience who had played a part in the story, their friends and family members. Everyone knew that in its most extreme and obvious forms flattery was tawdry, but Lucian's satirical essay of the mid-second century reveals how common it was in practice. Although the language of "truth" and "precision" *sounds like* a modern-scientific effort to uncover facts in themselves, the apparent connection with Roman historiography is misleading. As we see already in Josephus's elaboration of his claims to truthfulness and precision (*War* 1.2-3, 9), these terms meant essentially the *avoidance of partisan bias*: in Herodotean fashion, one should give all sides of a story and not merely the perspective of the winners or the powerful figures in the audience. This balance might also involve, as it can for Josephus, an attempt at rounded portraiture. Figures such as Herod the Great, Agrippa II, and even rebel leaders and political assassins (*sicarii*), are not simply good or evil in two dimensions. A hated personal rival such as John of Gischala may be forthrightly savaged (*War* 2.585; this will change in the *Life*), but Josephus can find in most others unique combinations of pride, courage, hubris, greed, and cowardice. He is expert at showing how men with understandable motives (right or wrong) found themselves trapped by life's "reversals of fortune."

History-writing was thus a very different thing from its modern counterparts: it was usually one elite statesman's effort to impress his peers with the moral lessons of the past as he chose to construe them, and it was another means of enhancing his own prestige as moral authority and political arbiter.

Josephus's *War* is a highly competent product of this elite culture. It all stems from the author's persona and status (1.1-3), and it attempts to convey his mature assessment of Judean affairs and relations with Rome before and during the great war. The *lumpen* Judean rabble (*to plethos*) are, like their counterparts in Rome and the Greek cities, portrayed as pathetically vulnerable to demagogue-tyrants – if ever Josephus and his aristocratic colleagues should lose their grip, as they regrettably do. Josephus turns his lethal rhetoric against the "tyrants," "bandits," and "insurgents" who engineered this crisis in Judea. But he is entirely capable of weaving richer tapestries, lacing the text with ambiguity, paradox, and irony when he wishes to do so. For the modern historian, this means that merely ascertaining what Josephus meant in telling a story – if indeed he meant any single thing – is far from simple, long before we even think about the events behind the story.

C. What is History (for us)?

Equipped now with some sense of what "Josephus" is made of, which accords well with assumptions about history in his time and place, we conclude the main part of this essay with a consideration of what the discipline of history means for *us*. In our post-modern world there is no perfect meeting of minds on the subject. But we might at least concur that popular use of the term history, like the standard use of "myth" to mean "falsehood," is out of keeping with a disciplined use of language. Popular usage – consider *The History Channel*, the phrase "He/she/it is history!" or the folk maxim, "The past is history; tomorrow is a mystery; today is a gift, which is why it is called the 'present'" – constantly reinforces an equation between history and *the past*. Alas, students required to "learn history" in school emerge, with sobering predictability, under the same illusion: that history is *something given*, recorded somewhere to be memorized by names, dates, and places. It is simply what happened, "historical facts."

A few moments' reflection, however, should be enough to shatter this equation. Obviously, a wide range of disciplines – astronomy, biology, palaeo-zoology, physical and cultural anthropology – deal in the past, though not in history. History must have something to do with the *human* past, then, or perhaps even the civilized human past. Yet settled human life seems to have begun with the Holocene era (9600 BCE), but we call most of that period "pre-historic" – the province of anthropology more than history. Only with the appearance of written scripts, around 3000 BCE, do we begin to enter the "historical" period – suggesting that doing history requires a degree of confidence about what our human ancestors were thinking and feeling. Even still, however, the period before 1000 BCE or even later, for most of the Mediterranean basin (Egypt, Mesopotamia, India, and China are partial exceptions), is largely considered shrouded in mystery and still beyond the reach of history. How can we come to know the human past, and in what senses *can* we know it?

Outside of the university discipline of history, most of us come to know those aspects of the past most relevant to us – concerning our families, towns, states, religious bodies – through what has been handed down from generation to generation: that is, through *tradition*. Of this transmitted knowledge we are expected (as members of the community in question) to be faithful *recipients* and transmitters to the next generation. Tradition is crucial to group formation, identity, and longevity, for groups typically require a story – a "charter myth," which may have many versions, parts, and forms – expressing what defines and unites them. Most of what passes for history in our time is in fact tradition. The two are often confused, as in Henry Ford's famous remark to the *Chicago Tribune* (May 25, 1916), "History is more or less bunk. *It's tradition. We don't want tradition.*" Most of the information about Moses, Jesus, Thomas Jefferson, Winston Churchill, or John Kennedy that has captured the public imagination has been in the nature of *tradition*; also school "history" textbooks typically – in some countries more obviously than in others – contain what the elders want the youth to learn or absorb about the nation's past. This too is tradition.

It is worth noting, incidentally, that virtually all the "historical" narratives we have from the ancient world, including Josephus's, are themselves legacies of tradition and not history. That is: society's leaders, while allowing the vast majority of texts to die a natural death (preservation required the assignment of considerable resources for copying by hand), authorized the regular recopying of only certain texts, or parts of texts, that they found congenial for some reason. In the case of Josephus, it was the Church authorities who baptized his narratives as the most authoritative account of matters relevant to the Gospels, not least because he mentioned Jesus, John the Baptist, and James; he also provided material that could be wrenched out of its context to demonstrate God's judgment on Jerusalem and the Jews – allegedly for rejecting Jesus. Text collections such as the Dead Sea

Scrolls and the Nag Hammadi library may seem to be exceptions to the principle that ancient texts reflect a tradition, since they were found as they were left and not deliberately transmitted through western history. But they are not true exceptions. Given that they too are *copies* of originals, we are simply dealing with ultimately unsuccessful or truncated traditions.

The problem with relying on tradition for knowledge of the past appears immediately, if and when we pose the question: "*How do we know* that X or Y really happened in the way presented by the tradition?" Tradition offers no resources for answering such a question, and does not try to preserve such guarantees. In many cases it does not matter to a tradition whether the founding stories really happened. Many groups are bound by shared values and a certain *esprit de corps*, of which the charter myth may be a convenient expression, but its historical accuracy is not salient. Other traditions, however, or subsets of them, depend upon a shared assumption of historical veracity at the root. (Modern debates among Christian denominations, and to an extent among Jewish denominations, turn on differences of opinion here.) Sometimes the question of historical accuracy forces itself upon members of groups, even if they had not otherwise paid it much attention, when the claims of their tradition clash with those of another. A case in point involves Jewish-Christian relations in western history. Once Jews and Christians found themselves in dialogue as fellow-citizens of a larger polity, it became particularly important to figure out what, especially in Christian tradition (because it said so much about the Jews) *actually happened*. Although this context did not generate the original "quest of the historical Jesus," it certainly energized it through the latter half of the twentieth century.

Here we have stumbled upon the essential characteristic of history. Whatever else it may be – and historians will disagree – history is at bottom the *active, investigator-driven, systematic investigation of the human past*, a kind of yang to tradition's yin. It is no mere coincidence that history burst forth at two moments in western history that were conspicuously characterized by the drive to empirical knowledge in all fields, when thinkers became powerfully dissatisfied with "knowing" the nature of the universe and the past solely through tradition (or "myth" – i.e. story), and insisted rather on personal investigation and testing. First, the quest of Greek philosophers from the presocratics to Aristotle to know things by direct observation produced "the father of history," Herodotus of Halicarnassus – who first applied the Greek word-group for active "research" or "investigation" (*historie, historia;*

verb *historiein*) to the study of the past – and the Athenian Thucydides, who advanced a rigorous program for cross-examining witnesses to the (recent) past. But the promise of that era, in history as in science, was never realized because of the prevailing social structures, discussed above. As long as knowledge remained in the hands of elite authorities, progress was severely limited in scope. And once that elite authority passed to religious leaders, in the fourth and fifth centuries CE, so that knowledge of history became the more tightly bound up with tradition and trust (or faith), it would take the combined force of the Renaissance, Reformation, Age of Reason, and European Enlightenment (16th to 18th centuries) to displace this intellectual juggernaut.

If we can agree on the active nature of historical inquiry, that it is the disciplined investigation of the human past (Herodotus's "Researches"), driven by the investigator's questions and not a given or static "past" to be learned, we have achieved a lot. Even this much is easily forgotten by specialists in Josephus (see the final section below). Much else remains open to debate, of course. Once we set out to explore aspects of the ancient world on our own initiative, how do we go about it? Obviously, investigation begins with a problem that we pose and attempt to solve. But what sorts of questions can be answered with any *probability*? We might like to know Tiberius's mind as he tried to choose a successor, or Nero's motives in dealing with the Greek cities, or what Marcus Aurelius did for entertainment. But our *desire* to know has nothing to do with the *possibility* of knowing. Given the difficulties we have in assessing even a modern political leader's inner life, though the person has massive daily news coverage and "evidence" for the person abounds, can we reasonably hope to know *why* some figure of two millennia ago, the subject of some highly rhetorical writing in one or two different sources (NB: Pilate is close to a best case for diversity of evidence), did what he did? Can we even be sure *what* he did, let alone why? Are there such things as *historical facts* in these cases, and if so, where do they exist? Is the language of "probability" appropriate to ancient-historical study? If so, what makes a historical hypothesis probable?

Or should we give up the hope of recovering actual biographical motives – as a trap set for us by the Roman historians, who liked to write history in biographical (but stylized rhetorical) terms – and focus on general social and economic conditions? These are more amply attested than the actions of individuals and groups, through archaeology as well as incidental notes in the literary texts, and so not dependent on the elusive thoughts or intentions of elite actors. Or again, should we re-conceive historical work in postmodern terms as a matter of engaging texts or narrative worlds from the past, and experiencing each for what it is, without imposing "hegemonic" or hierarchical claims to a single, essential truth?

Such questions may suffice to indicate that even the academic discipline of history can mean many different things to its practitioners. For simplicity's sake, I sketch here five sorts of approaches:

1. History is the effort to pose problems about specific human actions or events in the past, to assemble and evaluate relevant evidence, and where possible to reach solutions to the problems posed: Who did what, and *why* did they do it? Of necessity, the actions in question will mainly be those of elite actors – the only ones for whom we have much evidence. But individuals drive history forward, and so they are of paramount interest. Our object is reconstructing the intentions and outlooks of those who advanced the past, what R.G. Collingwood called the "inside" of events.[12]

2. Although that is not a bad goal in ideal terms, it is infeasible because we rarely (never?) have the resources to permit responsible judgments about such things. A great deal of insight into the past, however, is to be gained simply by getting right Collingwood's "outside" of events. What happened, and who was involved (irrespective of their inner thoughts)? The investigation of individual careers ("prosopography"), for example, offers exciting possibilities for reconstructing the all-important social connections and career possibilities among the elite – or the army. Getting dates correct (e.g. when an official took up or left office in a certain place, when a war began or ended) may throw all kinds of unexpected light on the real world of the past, and that is enough to be going on with.

3. The most important, most reliable, and most useful history is that of governments, institutions, and laws. The aberrations of a Gaius Caligula or Nero are not nearly as important for understanding the world as the general policies and outlooks of the Romans. Political history is valuable for modern societies who would learn from the past and the legacy of the Roman empire. (This kind of history is now decidedly old-fashioned, but it remains a basis for other kinds.)

4. History worthy of the name investigates the general conditions of ancient life for *all* people (women, children, slaves, the poor free, and the elite), rejecting the ancient legacy of personal influence and

---

[12] R.G. Collingwood, *The Idea of History* (Oxford: Oxford University Press, 1976 [1948]), 213.

status. The individual, no matter how brilliant, can only reflect the spirit of the time and the conditions that the period makes possible. What were the conditions of real life for everyone: giving birth, life expectancy and mortality rates, education, social mobility, family life and love, diet, disease, military service, and so on? Even if our elite reporters were not concerned with such issues, the data and analysis honed by the modern social sciences can stimulate fruitful questions and also provide useful models for filling in the blanks left by ancient evidence. (Social and economic history tends to displace the narratives produced by elites in favor of archaeological discoveries: funerary inscriptions, papyrus records from everyday life, household remains, etc.).

5. History is not a social science but, like all disciplines in the *humanities*, properly explores the diverse possibilities of human existence. To search for the (one) truth of the lost past is to pursue a mirage. We have only *stories* or narratives about lives lived: both the ancient accounts transmitted to us and the modern ones constructed by historians. In all these cases we need on the one hand to experience and be challenged by those stories but, on the other hand, to understand their limitations and profound biases. It is naïve to seek out either the intentions of the ancient actors or the one truth about the past.

I am not suggesting that any historian would sign on to one of these configurations, as I have drafted them, but they map out some prominent perspectives in the modern study of history. With such a range of possibilities in view, as we now turn to the efforts to do history with Josephus we may more easily recognize where the various proposals fit (or do not fit) with broader historical programs.

II. The Uses of Josephus in Historical Reconstruction

Before we consider our main problem, which involves doing history with Josephus as our only source, I need to emphasize that the case is qualitatively different when we have two or more independent sources for a person or event, especially where those sources include material remains that were not handed down by tradition but were discovered by active historian-investigators pursuing their inquiries. The existence of more than one direct source means first of all that the figure or event could not have been invented by our first source, Josephus (always a theoretical possibility); second, it allows us to check the biases and rhetoric of Josephus's account. Pilate provides an excellent example of the issue. It seems to me that we *can* reach probable results on at least a couple of issues in Pilate's career, where we have multiple lines of evidence, though the nature of the texts – in Josephus, Philo, and the different Gospels – remains a basic problem for understanding his intentions, outlook, or policies.

A. Doing History with Multiple Sources (including Josephus)

If we pose the historical problem, "What was Pilate's term of office in Judea?" and assemble the relevant evidence, we find conflicting indications. Pilate's dates are customarily given as 26 to 36/37 CE, on the strength of *Ant.* 18.35, which has his predecessor Valerius Gratus in Judea for 11 years (from 15 CE), and *Ant.* 18.89, which gives Pilate 10 years in office.[13] This all seems clear enough, and so one finds it in the textbooks – including those I have written. D.R. Schwartz, however, astutely raises a number of difficulties.[14] (a) *Antiquities* has Valerius Gratus departing Judea after deposing four high priests in rapid succession (after about a year each from 15 CE), leaving Caiaphas as high priest. That should logically put his departure closer to 18 than 26. (b) The very brief account of Gratus's tenure (*Ant.* 18.34-35), who is not even mentioned in *War*, contrasts with the expansive treatment of Pilate's time (18.35-89 and here in *War*), which is odd if they were in office for comparable periods. (c) The remarkably long term of Caiaphas as high priest (18-36 CE) is most easily explained by correspondence with a governor's term. (d) Most important, Pilate's arrival in the *Antiquities* is described along with a series of other events that occurred in 16-19 CE: the founding of Tiberias in Galilee, in about 19 CE (18.36-38), the rule of Orodes as king of Armenia in 16-18 CE (18.52), the death of the Roman Germanicus in 19 CE (18.53-54), and the expulsion of Judeans and Egyptians from Rome in 19 CE (18.65-84; cf. Tacitus, *Ann.* 2.85). If we did not have Josephus's claim about the 10-year term, all this context would imply that Pilate arrived at about the same time as these other events. It is more economical, surely, to doubt the unsupported year counts for Gratus's and Pilate's terms in office than to reject this complex of events in various places.[15]

Schwartz's arguments are supported by K. Lönnquist, on the basis of material remains. His analysis of Judean coins from 6 to 66 CE shows

---

[13] This calculation accounts for Eusebius's (4th-cent.) claim that Pilate began to govern in the twelfth year of Tiberius (= 26 CE; *Hist. eccl.* 1.9).

[14] *Studies in the Jewish Background of Christianity* (Tübingen: Mohr Siebeck, 1992), 182-217.

[15] As Schwartz observes: *Jewish Background*, 184.

that in coins dated between 17/18 and 31/32 CE, the lead content dropped from about 11% to virtually 0% (2000: 465); but after that it returned to its previous levels. Lead was a standard ingredient in Roman aqueduct construction. Although it has not yet been found in the remains of Jerusalem's (badly damaged, often rebuilt) aqueducts, its presence in the contemporary aqueduct system at Banias leads Lönnquist to conclude that it must have been used at least at crucial junctions in the Jerusalem system. The sudden removal of lead from the coinage of 18 to 32 is hard to explain except with reference to the needs of an aqueduct, which would confirm (if the project began under Pilate) that Pilate was in his Judean post by around 18 CE. Incidentally, it would also confirm that he did not simply raid the temple treasury for funds, but also supplied some materials. Moreover, a new type of coin with upright palm, representing good luck, matching a type otherwise reserved for the arrival of new governors, appears in 17/18 CE.[16]

The test of a historical hypothesis lies in its explanatory power: its ability to account for a range (ideally) of independent evidence. That is the situation we have here. If Pilate actually came to Judea in 18 or 19 CE, Josephus's quick movement in *War* from Tiberius's accession in 14 CE to the appointment of Pilate would be more easily intelligible than it is on the customary dating (arrival in 26). His passing over the brief term of Gratus would then match his treatment of the other 2/3-year terms of Coponius (barely mentioned, 2.117), Ambivulus, and Rufus (omitted). He would be focusing on the governor who spent an unparalleled 18 or 19 years in the region, leaving a decisive mark – immediately before Josephus's birth. Such a long term would also match Tiberius's known policy of leaving provincial governors in office as long as possible (*Ant*. 18.170; Tacitus, *Ann*. 1.80; Suetonius, *Tib*. 41) – assuming only that there was some defect with Gratus, Tiberius's first choice. By contrast, the standard date of 26 leaves all these matters as puzzles. Therefore, the former hypothesis is the more probable – though still by no means certain.

Another probable historical hypothesis about Pilate, testable by a range of evidence, is that his title was *praefectus* (prefect) and not *procurator* as Josephus claims in the *War*. The independent evidence includes the *tiberieum* inscription from Caesarea mentioned above (*[Pon]tius Pilatus [Praef]ectus Iuda[ea]e*), the general situation that members of the

---

[16] "Pontius Pilate — An Aqueduct Builder? Recent Findings and New Suggestions," *Klio* 82 (2000), 467-68

"equestrian" appointed to offices were typically called "prefects" of whatever it was they were in charge of, indications that the emperor Claudius changed this practice and called *later* governors (after 53 CE?) "procurators,"[17] and a parallel error of nomenclature made by Josephus's contemporary Tacitus, who also calls Pilate *procurator* (*Ann.* 15.44). Once again, the *praefectus* hypothesis explains the evidence without remainder – Josephus and Tacitus being confused by nomenclature of their own time, and Josephus (even if he knew what was correct) possibly making a deliberate change to diminish the governor's status – , whereas if we posit that the early governors were actually procurators, we cannot explain the evidence as easily.

These are ideal cases, then: varied and independent evidence that can be explained more adequately by one hypothesis than by another. But how far does that get us in understanding Pilate the man: his policies, behavior in office, attitudes, and motives? More or less nowhere, it seems, because here we must fall back on those narrative descriptions, which are all highly rhetorical. One might conclude from his long tenure that Pilate was unusually competent, and this might find support in the fact that Josephus can assemble so little with which to attack him; but Tiberius was preoccupied through much of this period (living from 26 to his death in 37 outside of Rome), and we cannot be sure.

Even where we have multiple sources for items that appear in Josephus, careful attention to what is in each narrative can raise doubts about the validity of long-accepted historical hypotheses. For example, the standard identification of the Dead Sea Scrolls (which do not mention "Essenes") as Essene productions was based in part on the apparent correspondence between items in Josephus's description of the Essenes (chiefly in *War* 2.119-161) and prescriptions for group members in the Scrolls; partly it was based on a statement by Pliny the Elder (*Natural Hist.* 5.73) about the location of the Essenes on the west side of the Dead Sea above En Gedi. More careful examination of Josephus's language when he describes the Essenes, however, shows that it does not match the Scrolls as closely as was thought. More importantly, Josephus's overall configuration of the Essenes for his narrative purposes – as ideal Judean philosophers whose views our Jerusalem aristocrat eagerly endorses – makes it more difficult than scholars have realized to imagine that the group he had in mind were

---

[17] A.N. Sherwin-White, *Roman Society and Roman Law in the New Testament* (Oxford: Clarendon Press, 1963), 6; P.A. Brunt, *Roman Imperial Themes* (Oxford: Oxford University Press, 1990), 163-87.

the dualistic, anti-Jerusalem, and anti-establishment "sons of light" who produced the Scrolls. And careful reading of Pliny suggests that he meant to locate the Essenes not at Qumran, where the Scrolls were found, but in the hills above En Gedi.[18]

B. Doing History with Josephus as our Sole Source

When we turn to the many less than ideal cases, by which I mean those for which Josephus's narratives are our *only source of information*, it seems to me that in principle we are unable to do much by way of historical experimentation and confirmation, at least insofar as we are interested in the events underlying the accounts. In the absence of independent evidence, to begin with, we can never be sure that Josephus did not simply invent characters or events (which he is demonstrably capable of doing). Even if he does not invent them out of whole cloth, we have no reason to believe that his artistic interests have left us any more of the real person than Ridley Scott left of us of the real emperor Commodus in *Gladiator*.

A survey of efforts to exploit Josephus's narrative for historical reconstruction may help to make the point.

The most common approach does not deserve much attention because, though common enough, it obviously lacks credibility. It involves simply excising bits and pieces from Josephus's narrative and wishing or assuming or declaring them to be historically accurate. This approach, often called positivistic (arising from an enthusiasm for "raw data"), characterized the great manuals on ancient Judaism before Lester Grabbe's new approach – as recently as 1992.[19] When Emil Schürer wrote, in his great *History of the Jewish People in the Age of Jesus Christ* (revised and widely used), sentences such as "Antipater was now all-powerful at court and enjoyed his father's absolute confidence. But he was *not satisfied. He wanted total power and could hardly wait* for his father to die,"[20] or "But Sabinus, *whose conscience was uneasy* because of the Temple robberies and *other misdeeds*, made off as quickly as possible,"[21] or when G.A. Williamson described Judea as "torn by *dissension and*

---

[18] See S. Mason, "Essenes and Lurking Spartans in Josephus' *Judean War*: From Story to History," forthcoming in Z. Rodgers, ed., *Making History: Josephus and historical method* (Leiden: Brill, 2006).

[19] L.L. Grabbe, *Judaism from Cyrus to Hadrian*, 2 vols. (Minneapolis: Augsburg Fortress, 1992).

[20] Revised by M. Black, F. Millar, M. Goodman *et al.* (Edinburgh: T. & T. Clark, 1973), 1.324.

[21] Schürer, *History*, 1.332.

bloody strife, and led by *rival self-appointed chieftains lusting for power. . .*,"[22] those scholars were merely dragging Josephus's literary portraits out of their narrative home and restating them as fact, not doing history.

I mentioned in the introduction that some archaeologists are bullish on Josephus's stock as an accurate reporter. Their expressed reasoning is that the correspondence between finds in the ground – e.g. in the south-west corner of Herod's temple mount, at Caesarea, Masada, Herodion, reinforced and breached walls at Gamala and Jotapata – and Josephus's description of the same sites requires us to admit that he is a fairly accurate historian.[23] Here is a case in point of meaning different things by both "Josephus" and "history." As long as we have archaeology, we are not dealing with Josephus alone. If the modern historian's question concerns the design of coastal Caesarea and its harbor (say), then we have independent evidence available through archaeological testing. If our question is about Josephus's narrative, however – say, whether the masses streamed from all over Judea to surround Pilate's residence in Caesarea, remaining motionless for five days and nights – archaeology has nothing to say about the matter. There is little connection, though it is true that evidence of battles in many of these sites gives the broadest kind of confirmation to Josephus's main story. If Josephus had written something akin to a modern historical novel using real settings but *entirely invented characters, plots, and events*, archaeology would need to give much the same positive verdict on his "reliability."

The most far-reaching proposal in recent decades for excavating historical gold from the baser metal of Josephus's narratives hinges on the principle of "contradiction." The logic here is that Josephus wrote to convey certain strong ideas – for example, he allegedly wanted to absolve himself and members of his aristocratic peers from complicity in the war, insisting that it was driven by a mere handful of demagogues, now duly punished. Therefore, any material that contradicts Josephus's aims as identified is likely to be there because it is historical, not part of his literary invention; he would hardly invent material at odds with his purpose. By contrast, he *would* have a reason to include it even if it did not suit his purpose but he knew it to be true – especially if he consid-

---

[22] *The World of Josephus* (Boston: Little, Brown, 1964), 17.

[23] E.g. M. Broshi, "The Credibility of Josephus," *Journal of Jewish Studies* 33 (1982), 379-84; also the essays by D. Syon and M. Aviam in A. Berlin and A. Overman, eds., *The First Jewish Revolt: Archaeology, History, Ideology* (London: Routledge, 2002).

ered it incidental – because of his historian's "conscience."[24] In relation to the war against Rome, scholars have used this principle to forceful effect: they believe that they can learn from Josephus things that he did not mean to say, through a kind of cross-examination of the dead. They can falsify his claims (e.g. that his aristocratic peers wanted nothing to do with the war), on the basis of contrary evidence that he himself provides.[25]

The clearest example that Martin Goodman and Jonathan Price adduce through this method is that of Eleazar, son of the high priest Ananias, who was priestly "commander of the temple" at the time of the revolt. Josephus claims that this young man, supported by many of his youthful contemporaries, halted the customary daily sacrifice on behalf of the Roman rulers and thus laid a foundation for war (*War* 2.408-410). Since these men were part of the aristocratic class (especially Eleazar himself), Josephus is caught trying to conceal what he nevertheless allows to remain visible: the widespread involvement of aristocrats in the war effort.[26]

Two substantial problems with this approach are as follows. First, it reduces Josephus's complex narrative to a sort of slogan (e.g. "the entire aristocracy opposed the war") that cannot be supported from Josephus's work. On the contrary, he features aristocratic involvement in crucial places: the opening sentence (*War* 1.1-3) describing his own role as one who fought the Romans (and "by necessity" [after capture] had to observe from their side), and the central panel of the narrative, the lamentable murders of the distinguished *chief-priestly leaders of the war* in Book 4. Indeed, those aristocrats who deserted their city in its time of dire need, as if "abandoning a sinking ship," receive a sharp send-off (*War* 2.556) – in a passage that introduces Josephus's own proud appointment as theater commander (2.562). Josephus's portrayal of the aristocracy shows them trying to manage the growing conflict with honor and dignity, opposing the demagogues and trying to steer

---

[24] The principle that "incidental" evidence, out of keeping with a source's general aims, is for that reason more valuable, is discussed in Collingwood, *Idea*, 256-82; M. Bloch, *The Historian's Craft*, trans. P. Putnam (New York: Alfred A. Knopf, 1953), p. 61. But these historians observe that such incidental evidence is usually exposed by a second, independent line of evidence.

[25] M. Goodman, *The Ruling Class of Judaea: The Origins of the Jewish Revolt against Rome AD 66–70* (Cambridge: Cambridge University Press, 1987), 20-21; J.J. Price, *Jerusalem under Siege: the Collapse of the Jewish State, 66-70 C.E.* (Leiden: Brill, 1992), 33, 186.

[26] Goodman, *Ruling Class*, 154-60; Price, *Siege*, 31-32.

the nation to a safer course (cf. 2.648-651; 4.320-323); he does not simply present them opposing the war.

Second, the richness of Josephus's narrative makes it unlikely that such an important episode as Eleazar's halting of the sacrifices for foreigners is at odds with his purposes. Josephus, like many ancient authors, gives full play to the theme of inter-generational conflict, especially in the form of youthful "hot-heads" who feel their oats and assert their strength but ignore the wiser counsel of their fathers – and so cause havoc.[27] Eleazar and his young aristocratic friends fit this pattern perfectly; Josephus's very deliberate handling of the Eleazar story (as a foundation of the war) confirms that he wrote it with intent. One way in which he achieves depth and texture is by interweaving many different perspectives among his characters, along with ambiguity even within some of the major players. It is not as simple a matter as figuring out the thesis or position of Josephus's *War*, and then finding things that contradict this position. (Imagine trying to identify the author's position in *Anna Karenina*.) If there is no contradiction, it is all part of Josephus's story, and we have no way to transform it into fact.

The same observation undermines the final strategy that I shall mention for attempting to get past Josephus through his own narrative, namely: source criticism. Although this practice has undergone something of a revival in recent years,[28] its underlying logic stems from an understanding of Josephus (and other ancient writers) that was nearly pervasive in the late nineteenth and early twentieth centuries, as a rather inept compiler of other people's work. No one doubts that Josephus must have relied on written sources and oral traditions for his material. But the source critics thought it possible to reconstruct those sources, therefore to get one step behind Josephus and closer to the events he describes. They proposed that wherever one encountered anything other than a smooth-flowing narrative (which itself might have been stolen from someone else if it seemed beyond Josephus's abilities), one was entitled to ask whether the problem – e.g. repetition of vocabulary or an event, a change of vocabulary for the same object, diction used only once in Josephus, a change of mental or geographical perspective, an abrupt digression or change of subject or scene, sche-

---

[27] *Ant.* 4.14-59; 6.33-34; cf. *War* 1.109, 117; 2.225, 286, 303, 595; 4.128, 133; *Ant.* 8.209; *Life* 12, 36, 80, 126-129; E. Eyben, *Restless Youth in Ancient Rome*, trans. P. Daly (London: Routledge, 1993), pp. 1-66.

[28] D.R. Schwartz, *Agrippa 1: The Last King of Judea* (Tübingen: Mohr, 1990), 2-3; R. Bergmeier, *Die Essener-Berichte des Flavius Josephus: Quellenstudien zu den Essenertexten im Werk des jüdischen Historiographen* (Kampen: Kok Pharos, 1993).

matic summary, reference to an earlier work that we do not possess – did not arise from his borrowing or joining of other sources.

The problem is again the sophistication of Josephus's writing. Close examination of the *War*, the biblical paraphrase of the *Antiquities*, the *War-Antiquities* parallels, the *Life*, and the *Apion* confirms many times over that Josephus generally controlled his material. Old assumptions about his parochial Judean education and inability to write Greek can no longer be sustained (partly because we now have the *Concordance*, completed in 1983, and electronic tools for studying his language). Since a good part of Josephus's art involves changes of narrative voice, complexity of character development, repetition or choosing new words for effect, symmetrical structuring, and so forth, it becomes impossible to devise criteria for extracting his sources from the surviving work of art. This would require a kind of literary Heimlich maneuver, the product of which is not likely to be appealing.

Conclusions

Our journey has led to a conclusion that may seem radical, but is hard to avoid. Josephus is a valuable source for historians investigating the conditions of provincial life in the Roman empire, or for his own elite provincial perspective in that context or, *where we have other sources*, also for particular persons and events. But *where he is our only source,* there is no way to get behind his narrative productions to the underlying events. Where the events, characters, motives, and causal connections that he describes exist exclusively in his formulation, they have no weight or substance of their own. The historian-investigator who wishes to probe their reality has no leverage outside of Josephus, therefore no traction for testing an explanatory hypothesis. The ingredients of his narrative are in this respect like images on a cinema screen, impossible to transmogrify into real people and events.

This conclusion may sound unduly *skeptical* – as some colleagues have suggested. Surely there is no reason to doubt much of Josephus: when he names his sons (*Life* 5), describes his wife's ancestry (*Life* 427), or narrates his trip to Rome with Titus? But these straightforward assertions are part of the same narrative in which he matter-of-factly narrates the two Tiberian revolts (above) and names the leaders of the delegation from Jerusalem (*Life* 197; contrast *War* 2.628), though the earlier account in *War* flatly contradicts these claims.

Scholars often seem to take the position that, whereas a *degree* of skepticism is wise, the principle of moderation requires that we do not take it to an extreme. But with all due respect for those who disagree, it seems to me that such thinking is unhistorical. To frame the problem in terms of degrees of skepticism assumes that our role as historians is to pass verdicts on claims presented to us: we should become passive recipients of the stories handed to us, and accept, accept in part (i.e. be wisely skeptical), or reject them. I hope that I have said enough to indicate why such a procedure has more to do with tradition than with history. The historian is an investigator, not merely a recipient and judge of others' accounts. Like any other kind of scientist (i.e. "knowledge-ist"), the historian can only claim to know, or express probable judgments concerning, objects of systematic inquiry. Until a problem has been subjected to disciplined historical investigation, our only stance (*as* historians) toward the countless claims made by ancient and modern figures can only be one of not knowing (agnosticism).

Comparing the historian to a detective, Collingwood observes that even if someone should tell the investigator "I killed John Doe," the investigator's task is not simply to believe the confession and close the case as if solved, but first to understand and explore further: "This person is telling me that he killed John Doe. *Why* is he telling me that?"[29] The statement might *turn out* to be true, but only after the investigator formulates and tests a hypothesis. Similarly, it would have been pointless to pronounce on whether Josephus was correct about Pilate's ten-year term of office in *Ant.* 18.89 (even if there was no obvious reason to disbelieve him) until we had formulated the question of Pilate's dates as the subject of a comprehensive historical exercise. Our job is not to approve and reject what the narratives propose, but to reconstruct the past according to our own questions. We read what Josephus (or Tacitus or Appian) says and seek to understand why he said it and how it functions in his works. But whether it reflects a particular historical reality is a judgment that must await investigation, *where there is sufficient evidence to render this possible.*

This cannot be overstressed. Since we cannot reasonably take the position that anything *thus far uncontradicted* is to be believed, we must maintain discipline and say that we do not know things about the past, as historians, *unless and until* they have been argued through to probability with evidence of sufficient quality.

I would like to close on a more constructive note. This essay has been about the relationship between Josephus's narratives and the *underlying* facts. My own research, however, has increasingly focused on

---

[29] Collingwood, *Idea*, 275.

the world in which Josephus lived and wrote. That is to say, we happen to have a wide variety of literary and material evidence concerning Flavian Rome in the 70s to 90s, and so we can figure out with some probability the general tenor of official and elite representations of the Judeans following the war with Rome.[30] But this was the world in which Josephus labored to prepare his thirty volumes of artistic narrative, for some Roman audiences he found willing to listen. Whereas Josephus's thirty volumes of artistic production render opaque the underlying realities unless we have other sources, each and every sentence in Josephus is historical evidence *for his engagement with his environment in Flavian Rome*. The question of how a Judean aristocrat captured in the war dealt with his complicated situation in the world capital is of enormous importance for understanding Judeans in the Roman world, also for interpreting his own compositions. What knowledge and attitudes did he assume among his audience? How did he exploit that knowledge and those attitudes to achieve his effects? Did he resort to irony and, if so, how and for what purposes?[31]

The question I am most often asked in discussions following public lectures is this: "How reliable is Josephus?" Now that you have remained with me throughout this essay, dear reader, how would you answer this question?

---

[30] A.J. Boyle and W.J. Dominik, *Flavian Rome: Culture, Image, Text* (Leiden: Brill, 2003), 559-89; J. Edmondson, S. Mason, and J. Rives, eds., *Flavius Josephus and Flavian Rome* (Oxford: Oxford University Press, 2005)

[31] See e.g. S. Mason, "Flavius Josephus in Flavian Rome: Reading on and between the Lines," in Boyle and Dominik, *Flavian Rome*, 559-89; "What a Difference an Audience Makes: Josephus' *Bellum Iudaicum* in its Roman Context," in J. Sievers and G. Lembi, eds., *Josephus between Jerusalem and Rome* (Leiden: Brill, 2005), 70-100; "Figured Speech and Irony in T. Flavius Josephus," in Edmondson, Mason, and Rives, *Flavius Josephus*, 243-88.

6

The Idea of History in Rabbinic Judaism

What Kinds of Questions did the Ancient Rabbis Answer?

Jacob Neusner

> "And the Lord spoke to Moses in the wilderness of Sinai in the first month of the second year after they had come out of the land of Egypt, saying, ['Let the people of Israel keep the Passover at its appointed time. On the fourteenth day of this month, in the evening, you shall keep it at its appointed time; according to all its statutes and all its ordinances you shall keep it.']" (Num 9:1-14):
>
> Scripture teaches you that considerations of temporal order do not apply to the sequence of scriptural stories.
>
> For at the beginning of the present book Scripture states, "The Lord spoke to Moses in the wilderness of Sinai in the tent of meeting on the first day of the second month in the second year after they had come out of the land of Egypt" (Num 1:1).
>
> And here Scripture refers to "the first month,"
>
> so serving to teach you that considerations of temporal order do not apply to the sequence of scriptural stories.
>
> Sifre to Numbers 64.1.1

The ancient Israelite Scripture, or "the Old Testament," is classified as historical because it sets forth a temporal order for organizing and explaining events. Scripture portrays linear history, sustains narrative, and registers the sharp differentiation of present from past.[1] In that context, the statement that considerations of temporal order do not apply jars. Yet it represents the normative rabbinic view of matters.

---

[1] Here I recast some of the findings of my *The Presence of the Past, the Pastness of the Present. History, Time, and Paradigm in Rabbinic Judaism* (Bethesda: CDL Press, 1996); 2nd edition, revised and augmented by six new chapters: *The Idea of History in Rabbinic Judaism* (Leiden: Brill, 2004).

Produced in the first six centuries of the Common Era, rabbinic writing, responding to Scripture, does not encompass sustained historical narratives or biographies and produces the fusion of times past, present, and future into one time. Rabbinic Judaism therefore contributes to this inquiry into the nature of historical knowledge in Graeco-Roman, Christian, and Judaic antiquity the case of a culture that possessed a rich heritage of historical writing and yet ceased to write history. They substituted paradigmatic for historical thinking. Paradigmatic thinking generalizes and treats the past as undifferentiated from the present. The paradigm consists of generalizations concerning the human situation, patterns of conduct and consequence, and the paradigm governs present and past without distinction. That is why it is the opposite of historical.

To state the case simply: the rabbinic sages inherited Scripture, with its sustained and continuous historical narrative from Genesis through Kings. They further possessed in Scripture a definition of time that accorded with conceptions of past, present, and future characteristic of historical time. But discerning patterns in Scripture and in nature, they produced a system of patterns or models, but no history-writing comparable to that which they had inherited. They thought like philosophers, not historians. Their canon encompassed fables and biographical snippets formed into general models, exemplary cases divorced from particular times and places – but no linear history and no continuous biography. And their conception of time totally contradicts that of Scripture.

1. Rabbinic Judaism of Late Antiquity and the Role of Historical Thinking in the Normative Judaism through the Ages

The rabbis of whom I speak, the authors of rabbinic Judaism, flourished in the first six centuries of the Common Era. The system they constructed and the books they wrote defined the norms of Judaism from then to now. In those centuries they transformed the Hebrew Scriptures of ancient Israel into the religious system of theology and law we know as Judaism. This they did by treating the instances of law and theology of Scripture as exemplary and generalizing on the result; so they produced a coherent system out of episodic cases. That approach to Scripture's narratives and laws has a bearing on the issue of what Judaism wishes to learn from history, but in an unanticipated way.

That is because, until modern times, the rabbinic religious system we know as Judaism did not produce historical writing at all, however we define history. Episodic chronicles, which did emerge, did not provoke sustained reflection on the meaning and end of the past. The canonical literature of that Judaism in antiquity was comprised by commentaries on Scripture, law codes and commentaries on those codes, legal opinions, some writings of mystic doctrine, philosophy and theology, and the like. Chronicles were local and episodic. No one thought about history theologically, in the manner of Augustine or even Eusebius, for example. Only rarely before modern times did sustained thinking undertake to link events into sequential narratives and exhibit the patterns of the past, to produce histories. And nothing like critical historical research was even dreamt of.

Not only so, but even when in modern times Jews undertook to write history, the received rabbinic Judaism was not what motivated them. In modern times, from the nineteenth century forward, histories of the Jews did come to be written. But the modern historians of the Jews and of Judaism initially derived their mythopoeic questions from other concerns than those of rabbinic Judaism. Two examples suffice. One major source of history-writing was Reform Judaism, which asked history to validate change and undertook to prove that Reform was not only legitimate but well-precedented. Another important source of history-writing was Zionism, which required and found in history a compelling narrative account of the Jews as a nation, and through archaeology a deed to the Land buried in the sand. That meant possessing a continuous, coherent, linear history, and Zionist historians narrated the history of the Jewish nation as part of their program of demonstrating that the Jews form a people, one people, and establish a state to realize the nationality attested by their unbroken history. No counterpart historical work came out of the declared heirs of rabbinic Judaism in the yeshivah-world.

What makes the neglect of history-writing anomalous for rabbinic Judaism is that the framers possessed but neglected influential models of historical thinking. For instance, they did not have to invent the drawing of theological lessons from narratives of things that were said and done and experienced in the past. These rabbis inherited in Scripture a massive purposeful account of the past, a continuous historical narrative running from Genesis through Kings. They had only to continue the received tale. Not only so, but they themselves lived in interesting times. That ought to have stimulated their interest in presenting to Scripture questions that the record of the past answered through (hi)story-telling. But it failed to do so. Scripture set forth narrative in the carefully delineated past tense of history. So far as history requires narrative, and so far as that narrative has to record what has taken place in a period that has passed and been marked off from our own, a past distinct from the present – and these are the two requirements of historical writing and historical thinking – rabbinic Judaism did not possess an idea of history and did not ask historical questions. Why not?

By any criterion of events antiquity produced plenty of history for the rabbinic Judaic authors to process, to write up and reflect upon. The reason why not is *not* that they did not experience historical events that warranted reflection, study and preservation. The empires that governed them engaged in great wars. They lived on the frontier between the Roman and Iranian empires, which fought for the strategic lands of Mesopotamia and the Holy Land, key to Rome's breadbasket in Egypt. International historical events did not exhaust the historical repertoire.

Consider axiological events that took place in the first six centuries CE and that matched in their historical eventfulness the historical moments highlighted by Scripture. Scripture recorded the possession and the loss of the Land, and current events presented counterparts. Israel had lost the Land of Israel and the Temple had been destroyed. That happened again in the first century CE, but no one among the rabbinic sages produced the counterpart of Scripture's narrative from Genesis through Kings. (Josephus did, Yohanan ben Zakkai, his contemporary, did not.) The Temple of Jerusalem, destroyed in 586 BCE and rebuilt three generations later, which embodied the political autonomy and religious center of the Israelite world, suffered another disaster, this one in 70 CE, when a Jewish rebellion against Roman rule of the Land of Israel led to a siege and the repetition of the event of 586. A Jewish historian, Josephus, wrote massive histories of ancient Israelite antiquities and the war against Rome itself. Some of his stories find their way into the rabbinic literature. But his sustained explanation of what has happened and its meaning finds no counterpart in rabbinic literature. Three generations later, in 132, another war, this one led by a Messianic general, Bar Kokhba, yielded a worse calamity. Now Jerusalem was leveled, the Temple mount ploughed over and dedicated to a Roman temple, and Jews were forbidden from entering Jerusalem altogether. But for a few stories about the repression of the rebellion by Rome, we should know nothing of the event so far as the Rabbis were concerned.

And then there was the not unimportant matter of Christianity, born in the heart of the world of Judaism. The advent of a competing reading of the ancient Scriptures, this one deriving from Christianity, challenged the received understanding of Scripture, finding proof in the ancient prophets for the Messiahship of Jesus. That chronic problem turned acute when the Roman emperor in 312 declared Christianity, long persecuted and proscribed, to be a licit religion. Within a generation Christianity became the state religion of Rome. The Christians pointed to the conversion of Rome to Christianity as evidence that Jesus really was Christ, and that Judaism had been superseded. The Church Father Eusebius wrote a history of the world from creation to Constantine to call attention to history's demonstration of the truth of Christianity. No rabbi responded with a contrary historical narrative. Indeed, a generation later, in 361, another emperor, this one a pagan, to humiliate Christianity decreed that the Jews might rebuild the Temple. But nothing came of it. A bit later the Christian theologian, John Chrysostom, called attention to that marvel of history, the ultimate vindication of Christianity. No rabbi responded. History did not form a stage for debate, for instance, in conflicting narratives. Over the next century, now-Christian Rome nullified the rights of the Jewish community to manage its own affairs and dismantled the ethnic government that the pagan-Roman government had established to administer the ethnic community in the Land of Israel. Surely provoked to reflect on the meaning of events, rabbinic Judaism registered its response with great power – but not in historical writing.

2. The Self-Evidence of Historical Thinking about Scripture

We turn to the standing of self-evidence that the historical reading of the past with special reference to the study of Scripture enjoys. For that purpose I cite a representative example, a statement by G.W. Ramsey.

> A major part of any course in Old Testament is the study of the history of Israel ... the fact that [the history of the Israelite people] constituted the context out of which the Scriptures of the Old Testament emerged gives it special significance... How can we really appreciate the messages of the Old Testament authors unless we are familiar with the situations which produced them and to which they were addressed?
>
> George W. Ramsey[2]

---

[2] G.W. Ramsey, *The Quest for the Historical Israel. Reconstructing Israel's Early History* (London: SCM Press, 1982), xii.

The answer to Ramsey's question given by many centuries of Judaic and Christian exegetes of the Hebrew Scriptures is, "Without the intervention of secular history, we of holy Israel (like our counterparts in the Church of Jesus Christ) appreciate the messages of the Torah very well indeed – just as we have in the millennia since God gave us the Torah, thank you very much!"

Without the slightest familiarity with the situations that produced them and to which they are addressed, we have no difficulty whatsoever in appreciating the messages of Scripture. For in fact Judaic and Christian faithful through the ages take as a premise that it is to the faithful of all times and places that the ancient Israelite Scriptures were and are addressed. Scripture is a letter written this morning to whom it may concern – personally. But contemporary reading of the Hebrew Scriptures not only takes for granted that exegesis begins in history. Statements such as that before us show how contemporary reading also has lost sight of the quite other-than-historical approach to history and to time that governs in all Judaic and much Christian reading of Scripture.

In the rabbinic reading of Scripture no boundary distinguished past from present; time was understood in a completely different way. Within the conception of time that formed consciousness and culture, the past formed a perpetual presence, the present took place on the plane of the past, and no lines of structure or order distinguished the one from the other. That is how, *before* the past two hundred years, Judaism and Christianity ordinarily read Scripture. It is another mode of thought altogether. It was one that replaced history with a different model for the organization of experience: things that happen and their meaning.

This other model I call a pattern, or paradigm, because that model for constructing meaning out of random experience appealed for sense to a pattern or paradigm that imposed order on things that happened. That meaning emerged without regard to temporal and ordinal sequence, without attention to venue or context. Hence paradigmatic modes of thought took the place of historical ones. Thinking through paradigms, with a conception of time that elides past and present and removes all barriers between them, in fact governs the reception of Scripture in Judaism and Christianity until nearly our own day.

At stake, as we shall see, are (1) a conception of time different from the historical one and (2) premises on how to take the measure of time that form a legitimate alternative to those that define the historical way of measuring time. Fully exposed, those alternative premises may prove more logical and compelling than the historical ones. It follows that I mean to regain access to that way of reading and responding to Scripture that, for nearly the whole of the history of Judaism and Christianity, governed the encounter between today and that other time portrayed in the Hebrew Scriptures. The difference is how time is marked and what the marks signify.

3. Thinking through History versus Thinking through Ahistorical Paradigms

We recall in this context the statement of Jacques LeGoff, "The opposition between past and present is fundamental [to historical thinking], since the activity of memory and history is founded on this distinction."[3] Israelite Scripture certainly qualifies as historical. It recognizes both the pastness of the past and also invokes the power of the past to explain the present. Time runs one way, differentiated into past, present, and future, and time is linear. The rabbinic system insists upon the presence of the past and the pastness of the present, instructing the faithful to view themselves, out of the here and now, as living in another time, another place: "Therefore every person must see himself or herself as slave to Pharaoh in Egypt," as the Passover Haggadah-narrative phrases matters. But the same invocation of the present into the past also serves to convey the past into the here and now. That represents an anti-historical mode of thought.

Once a religious obligation imposes the past upon present, shifting the present into a fully realized, contemporary-past, rites of commemoration give way to the reformulation of the ages into a governing paradigm that obliterates barriers of time. Rules of structure and order apply without the differentiation by criteria of time. These rules comprise a paradigm, a pattern of conduct – do this, that will happen – *without regard to temporal circumstance.* An excess of demand over supply will as a rule cause inflation – without regard to time, place, or circumstance. So too mathematically described data register without regard to context or venue, and the episodic order in which facts make their appearance need not explain the facts and rarely does, in economics, for example. Independent of temporal circumstance, the paradigm thus not only imparts sense and order to what happens but also selects out of what happens what counts – and is to be counted.

---

[3] J. LeGoff, *History and Memory* (trans. S. Randall & E. Claman; New York: Columbia University Press, 1992), xii.

That brings us to the fundamental question: how does rabbinic Judaism tell time?

4. Telling Time

History serves as a means of telling time: measuring and evaluating and differentiating within spans of time and the constituents' sequence in passage. But there are other ways of doing so. To identify what is at issue between historical and paradigmatic thinking about events we have, therefore, to identify the premises concerning time and its measurement that define the basis for historical thinking and history-writing, on the one side, and paradigmatic thinking and its systematic reading of Scripture for social rules, on the other.

What, exactly, do we mean by "time"? The word, "time," standing on its own of course baffles us by its abstraction. Time understood in the context of history, or for the purposes of cosmology, or in the setting of geology is readily defined. Utterly different units of time point to variables in context, from nano-seconds to aeons or ages measured in hundreds of millions of solar years. That is to say, in some disciplines of learning, cosmology, for example, time is measured in aggregates so vast as to defy our capacities of imagining. The contrast between units of time found indicative in history, days, months, years, and those treated as consequential in geology, multiples of millions of years, or in astronomy, light-years and beyond, shows what is at stake.

Historical time, by contrast to time required for the natural sciences, appears trivial and inconsequential. That is for an obvious reason. "The ages" for humans, who live perhaps for seventy, perhaps for eighty years, and "the ages" for life on earth scarcely correlate. Not only so, but in other disciplines of learning, time, while measurable, is divided into units with no bearing upon the life of humanity – geology is a good instance. Then let us define time in the setting of humanity and of history. For history takes for its arena of analysis that ephemeral moment out of cosmological or geological time in which humanity's actions take place. But time even in the context of the life of humanity must be defined in both historical and also other than historical terms altogether. History takes as its premise definitions of time and its divisions, that derive from nature. History then further divides these divisions or characterizes them, imposing upon them history's own indicators.

Jacques LeGoff expresses this same conception in a slightly different way when he states:

The basic material of history is time. For a long while, therefore, chronology has played an essential role as the armature and auxiliary of history. The main tool of chronology is the calendar, which goes back far beyond the historian's field, since it is the fundamental temporal framework within which societies function. The calendar shows the effort made by human societies to domesticate "natural" time, the natural movement of the moon or the sun, the cycle of the seasons, the alternation of day and night. But its most effective articulations, the hour and the week, are linked to culture and not to nature.... The past/present opposition is essential to an acquisition of the consciousness of time.[4]

LeGoff underlines the interplay of nature's time and history's time, and that union is precisely what is at stake here.[5] Let me spell out what I mean, beginning with time defined in the context of nature as humanity knows natural time. Nature marks day and night through light and darkness. Then, according to the most common human understanding of things, a set, a unit of light and a unit of darkness, forms one day.[6] That is a convention that commonly serves to define the smallest whole unit of nature's time, the complete cycle of a "day." The solar day is not the sole natural unit of time. Nature moreover marks sets of such units of day and night by the phases in shape and size of the moon. The lunar unit of subunits of light and darkness then measures what we call a month. Here again, we find a complete sequence that is orderly and fixed, from new to full to waning size and

---

[4] J. LeGoff, *History and Memory*, xix, xx.

[5] But LeGoff has no grasp whatsoever of systems of dealing with the past that are not historical and also not cyclical or mythical. He sees an effort "made by human societies to transform the cyclical time of nature and myths, of the eternal return, into a linear time, punctuated by groups of years...centuries, eras, etc. Two important advances are intimately connected with history: the definition of the chronological starting point (the foundation of Rome, the birth of Christ, the Hegira...), and the search for a periodization, the creation of equal, measurable units of time" (p. xx). But we deal with a set of thinkers who inherited out of Scripture linear, historical time and utterly reshaped and recast that conception, and nothing in LeGoff's treatment of matters recognizes those other than historical means of dealing with precisely the same facts as historical thinking that characterized Judaism, and Christianity, for so long a period in the West.

[6] That is not to suggest the ubiquity of the conception of "a day" as a complete cycle of light and darkness. Indeed, even the Talmuds know the *'onah*, which is the smallest whole unit of time and is not equivalent to a solar day, light and darkness, ending with the next light. But it is sufficiently conventional to regard the smallest whole natural unit of time as a solar cycle of light and darkness that we may confidently define matters in that setting. I ignore the conception of "hours," which nature on its own does not yield but form a social convention, all the more so minutes, seconds, and so on. These play no role in my exposition.

shape. These too mark time, which then may be defined as a solar day or a lunar month. That is to say, "time" is the spell marked from one sunset to the next; or "time" is the spell marked from one new moon to the next. That definition hardly is ideal, leaving vague the sense of "spell." But for our purposes (which become transparent in a moment) it suffices.

Matters do not conclude with the solar day and the lunar month. Nature furthermore marks sets of such aggregates of light and darkness as the passage of the moon denotes. This is supplied through observations of the positions of the sun in the southern sky (from the perspective of the northern hemisphere), with the sun at noon high in summer, low in winter; with the shadows long in winter, short in summer; and so on. The solar year then marks off in a natural way still larger aggregates of time. These, then, form the simplest natural boundaries of time: the interplay of light and dark, the fixed sequence of lunar phases or appearances, and the equally fixed sequence of solar ones, further differentiated (in temperate climates) by the passage of the solar seasons (important, but not essential, in this argument). Now nature gives us three spans, units of time, and all three are correlated: the solar day, the lunar month, the solar year. If we wish to ignore the solar year we may claim that a fixed sequence of months denotes a lunar year, but that detail need not detain us, being irrelevant to the argument that is here unfolding.

More to the point about the natural definition of time is a different fact. Nature's time is repeated – cyclical, we should say – since in each solar year, the same events of nature – the seasons – repeat themselves. And the cyclicality of nature's time bears a further consequence. It is reversible, in that *what happens this year happened last year, as much as it will happen next year.* Indicators of time in nature repeat themselves, by definition moving in any direction, forward or backward, equally naturally. Nature's "events" – that is, points of differentiation of otherwise undifferentiated passages – are not unique but gain their signification through their points of commonality; one month by measure, marked time, is the same as the one before and the one to follow, so too the day (unit of light, unit of darkness), so too the year. So much for time as nature defines matters on its own: the interval between sunset and sunset, new moon and new moon, sun at apogee and sun at apogee. The earliest monuments of humanity attest to the widespread definition of these intervals by appeal to solar time (in the Mayan ruins and at Stonehenge, for instance), and lunar time is equally broadly attested as well. So for the purpose and in the context of nature as humanity perceives matters, time finds its definition through the taxonomy of natural phenomena: day, month, year.

Now that simple digression into obvious matters is necessary to permit us to proceed to the question that is urgent here: the conception of time in history, which guides us in differentiating historical from paradigmatic thinking. Precisely what do we mean by "time" in the setting of history, and how does historical time relate to natural time?

We commence with the simple question: How, in history, is time to be defined and measured? History recognizes natural time and imposes its taxic indicators, its points of differentiation, upon it. History knows days, months, years, such as nature defines, but proposes to differentiate among them, treating this day as different from that because on this day, such and such happened, but on that day it did not.[7] So historical time is a way of cutting down to human size the eternities of nature's time. History takes over nature's measures of matters and, making them its own, further marks them in its own way. The heritage of nature's time is clear. Now, history – historical thinking, in its conception of time – takes over nature's time and imposes upon it a second set of indicators or points of differentiation. History takes for granted the facticity of days, months, years, as indicating fixed points in time. *But these spans of time are further differentiated by history, made into something that, in nature, they are not.*

Specifically, the power of history to measure time lies in its capacity to differentiate what in nature is uniform. Nature's time is undifferentiated, history marks unit off from unit; nature's time is repeated and may be reversed; history's events, the indicators of difference, have the power to mark off undifferentiated units of time by the very definitive fact of their uniqueness; and nature's time is reversible, but, for the same reason history's indicators are unique, history's time also is irreversible, moving in only one direction. Nature knows no past that

---

[7] The same description serves for astrology, with its interest in correlating the stars with human events; in that sense, astrology and history compete as modes of explanation of time and change. Appealing to the same kind of logic, linearity and the uniqueness of events, for instance, they propose different bases of explanation spun out of one logic. They differ in history's insistence on the pastness of the past, a matter to which astrology finds itself indifferent. Admittedly, astrology invokes paradigms, but these derive from its alleged observations of natural and historical correlations, while religion's paradigms (those of Christianity and Judaism) derive from God's revelation of them, not humanity's discovery. But astrology as an alternative to history and religion in the definition of time demands no consideration here; we have no astrological scholarship on Scripture, but a great deal of the historical kind.

makes a difference from the present, no present that moves inexorably into the future.

LeGoff's remarks come under view once more. History's time begins with the recognition that what is past is past, but leads to the present; what is present is here and now, separate from the past, also prelude to, but not part of, the future. History's time is linear, marking past, present, future; history's time can conceive of eternity, when time is past altogether. History does its work by recasting nature's time into humanity's dimensions, marking time in such a way that the human understanding can encompass and make sense of matters. History's time forms humanity's perspective on the dimensions of nature, cutting down to human size the enormous dimensions of nature's markings.

How does history's time impose itself upon nature's time? As I have already indicated, history both depends upon and identifies the natural units of time – day, month, year – but further differentiates among them – beyond nature's own points of differentiation – by reference to this-worldly events in the here and now. In such and such a year (however enumerated), in such and such a month (as indicated by its position in the sequence of months within a solar year), on such and such a day (as indicated, for instance, by the position of the moon within the lunar month), something noteworthy happened. That happening then marks the day, the month, the year, differentiating it from all other days and months and years. History's way of marking time, then, is to differentiate among the units of time indicated by nature, and its medium of differentiation is the event that takes place and imparts its distinctive character on one day, month, year, rather than on some other.

History therefore defines and measures time through two intersecting indicators, the meeting of (1) the natural and (2) the human. As is clear in the foregoing remarks, the context in which "time" is now defined is (1) the passage of days, weeks, months, and years, as marked by the movement of the sun and moon and the stars in the heavens and (2) the recognition of noteworthy events that have taken place in specific occasions during the passage of those days and months and years. "Time" then refers to the passage of days, months, years, as marked off by natural phenomena and as differentiated, also, by human activity. For purposes of history, "time" is defined as the making of distinctions between and among days or weeks or months or years, and "history" refers to the utilization, for indicators of the difference between one day and the next or one year and the next, of noteworthy events.[8]

Let me spell out this mode of marking time, since the identification of its premises will lead us deep into the definition of the alternative mode of telling time I wish to set forth. We know that in the course of nature, one season differs from the other by reason of the position of the sun and fixed stars in the firmament, with corresponding changes in the character of the weather on earth, the sun high over the horizon, the heat, or low, the cold, for instance. One form of differentiation of day from day, hence one way of measuring time, then, will derive from events of nature, dry days, wet days, and the like.

But there is another form of differentiation, and that concerns the correlation of the passage of the indicators of the natural world – in Israel's context, the moons in their phases, the sun in the seasons – and chosen indicators of the social world. These, in the Israelite history, are simple enough to identify. King X ruled for so-and-so-many years, and he did such and such, with the specified consequences. In this setting, then, natural time (divisions of, distinctions among days, weeks, months, years) and social time (divisions of, distinctions among days or years) are made to intersect. The advent of a king marks the counting of solar or lunar years; what happens in that sequence of days, weeks, months, years, then is treated as a coherent whole – a reign – and a set of such reigns then may be laid out in sequence.

The sequence of reigns or other social significations of the differentiation of days, weeks, months, years already differentiated by natural indicators (position of the moon, shape of the sun, and the like) then forms the centerpiece of interest. For natural indicators left by themselves yield no sequential narrative, with a beginning, middle, and end, for the simple reason that nature on its own – once more, the sun or the moon in passage through the skies – differentiates days, weeks, months, or years, in only a single way. When we know the position of the sun or the shape of the moon, we know where we stand in the natural sequence of time, but in the nature of things, we also know that last year at this time, or next year at this time, we shall be precisely where we are now. So natural time yields no conception of beginnings, middles, and endings.

---

[8] Barr's discussion in *Biblical Words for Time,* pp. 170-284, provides as ample a survey of opinion on the conception of time as this work requires. The study of words for "time" and the like proves to have no bearing upon the discussion that follows, for reasons that will quickly become obvious.

It is only when the correlation between natural time and the condition of a this-worldly entity, a social group for instance, assumes self-evidence that beginnings, middles, and endings come under consideration. Then, and only then, questions of origins emerge: Who are "we"? When did "we" come into being? Where are "we" heading? By appeal to the analogy of the "I," the individual's birth, life, and death, the social entity made up of individuals is given that same life-course, if not the same life-span. And that is the point at which the social world intervenes in the notation of the passing of the natural indicators of things; time is no longer differentiated, day from day, week from week, month from month, year from year, by appeal to the course of the sun and the moon and the fixed stars. Time now is differentiated by two indicators, not one, the natural in correlation with, in response to, the social. In that lunar cycle, or in that solar cycle (in Israel: month, year, respectively), such and such happened. Then the cycle is indicated not only by reason of the natural difference, with its recurrence, but also of the social difference, with its trait of individuality and even uniqueness.

Concretely, we note the confluence of occasion in the social world – the noteworthy event – and of season (day, week, month, year) in the natural world. And that permits us to define the premises of historical definitions of time:

1. Human events (however defined), viewed as unique happenings, by contrast to the recurrent happenings of natural time, form givens, as much as natural events form givens, in the measurement of time; but these markers differ, being of a quite opposite character from the natural divisions of aggregates of time, the human events being unique, natural events common, human events particular, natural ones, general.
2. And nature's time is cut down to size by history's time. This is done by recasting nature's time, which finds points of differentiation in cyclical events (lunar months, solar seasons), and is therefore marked off by recurrent points of differentiation. Since human events have the power to differentiate one unit of natural time from some other (whether day, month, or year), these events must be viewed as unique, irreversible, irrecoverable, and linear; for if they were not unique, irreversible, irrecoverable, and linear, they would not have the power to differentiate from one another the common, repeated, and cyclical units of measurement that operate in natural time.

3. Consequently, history's premise is that nature's time subordinates itself to history's time; time is itself linear, marked off by unique events, irreversible in direction from past to future, clearly differentiated (for the same reason) into past, present, and future.

Linear history is not the only way of formulating that view of time and its meaning; cyclical history, to which we now turn, bears the same potential of ordering and explaining affairs. Neither linear nor cyclical time takes account of the irregularity of events; both accomplish the goal of demonstrating their regularity. Then neither can accommodate itself to chaos or admit to the unpredictability of things. The logic of history – linearity, division of past from present together with linkage of past to present – and the regularity of cyclical time contradict the disorder of the world and also fail to recognize what is orderly in the world, which, for mathematics, is expressed (for purposes of the present argument only) through fractals, and, for religion, as we shall see, through paradigms.

5. From Historical Time to Cyclical Time and Paradigmatic Time

Let me start with simple definition. Paradigmatic time organizes events in patterns, invokes a model that everywhere pertains. Nature divides time by appeal to not unique events but common ones. Nature marks the aggregates of time by reference to indicators that are reversible, recurrent, and not restricted by considerations of past, present, and future. Is there a way of dividing time that is in accord with dimensions humanity can accommodate, yet also congruent to nature's divisions? That is, are there media for the division of time that humanity may adopt and that are reversible, recurrent, and unrestricted by lines of division between past and present, present and future? The answer is, there are two such ways, one familiar, the other represented here by the rabbinic literature and at the same time unfamiliar *and* absolutely routine in the history of Scripture's reception in Western civilization, Judaic and Christian alike.

History is not the only way of thinking about natural time. History solves the existential problem posed by the enormous disproportion between humanity's experience of time, which is by definition brief (a life-span or five successive life-spans) and ephemeral (here now, gone tomorrow), and natural time, from the perspective of mortal man and transitory society, endless in its farthest limits. But that same problem may be worked out in another way of thinking about time altogether. Time is to be differentiated not only by events, unique, linear, irreversible, deemed to differentiate units of time by imposing their definitive character upon said units. Another way of measuring time within the human ambiance, besides nature's way, may be formulated, in which humanly-sensible aggregates of time may be formulated in their own terms but not made to intersect with natural time at all.

Defining this other way is made easy by finding the answer to a simple question. Can we differentiate nature's time for humanity's purposes by appeal not to indicators that contrast with nature's indicators for dividing time but to indicators that cohere in character with them? Can we find indicators of the division of time that are human but also comparable to the natural ones? If we can find a way of thinking about time that both remains well within the dimensions of humanity's sensibility and intellect (ephemeral, brief, yet encompassing) and also retains the character of consubstantiality with nature's time, then we can answer the question in an affirmative way.

Cyclical Time. One such way, entirely familiar in our context, is the cyclical one. That is the view of time that notes recurrent patterns, or cycles, repeated sequences of specific events that conform to a general pattern. Cyclical time differentiates natural time by marking of sequences of years or months or days marked by a given pattern of events, then further sequences of years or months or days that recapitulate that very same pattern of events. So time is viewed as forming not only natural but also social or historical aggregates, distinct from one another as much as one year is distinct from another, and yet repetitive of a single pattern throughout. The conception of cyclical time takes over from nature that uniformity of day, month, or year, but recasts the terms of uniformity to encompass humanity's, not only nature's, repetitions.

Then history is the discovery of the cycles in an endless sequence. And profound historical thought will require the close study of cycles, with the interest in differentiating cycle from cycle, the discovery, for example, of when the cycles run their course (if they do). All of this intellectual labor is carried on well within the framework of natural differentiation of time. Nature's time and history's time then correspond in that both are differentiated by the appeal to the same recurrent indicators, though the indicators for natural time and those for historical time will differ. So the mode of differentiation is the same, but each set of differentiating indicators conforms to its setting, the human then corresponding to the natural one.

Whence the sense of the cyclicality of time, such as Qohelet (Ecclesiastes) expresses in saying what has been is what will be? An answer drawn from human existence serves. Cyclical time extends to the human condition the observed character of natural time – or reverses the process, assigning to nature the orderly character of human life; the correspondence is what counts. Just as natural time runs through cycles, so humanity marks time through corresponding cycles. For instance, in the aggregates of humanity formed by family, village, or territorial unit ("kingdom," "nation" for example), just as the seasons run from spring through summer to fall to winter, and the human life from youth to middle age to old age to death, so social aggregates prove cyclical.

The territorial unit may be accorded a cycle of time, from birth through maturity, old age, and death, and its "history" may form a chapter in the cyclical patterns of human time, corresponding to natural time. Humanity's mode of differentiating the time marked off by nature, then, accords with the natural indicators of differentiation: the life of the human being forming a metaphor for the life of the social unit. Then humanity's indicators correspond in character to nature's – the cyclicality of the one matching the character of cyclicality revealed by the other. Yet humanity's indicators also prove natural to the human condition, with the life-cycle forming one means (among a variety to be sure) means of differentiating humanly among the divisions of nature's time.

Historical Time. If we revert to the characterization of historical time offered just now, how shall we read the cyclical, as distinct from the historical, mode of formulating a human counterpart to nature's time? Here are the point-by-point correspondences:

1. Human events form givens, as much as natural events form givens, in the measurement of time; but these events correspond in character to those of nature, because, like those in nature, they recur in a fixed and predictable pattern, just as nature's events do; human events, like natural divisions of aggregates of time, are not unique, not particular, not one-time only; they are recurrent and mark off an eternal return of the pattern set forth *ab initio* (whether from creation, whether from the formation of the social order).
2. But the problem of a human formulation of the nature of time is solved as much as it is by history, though in a different way; specifically, nature's time is cut down to human size by cyclical time, but this is done in nature's way. Cyclical time recasts na-

ture's time. As the latter finds points of differentiation in cyclical events (lunar months, solar seasons), so the former – historical time viewed cyclically – is marked off recurrent points of differentiation, but these are, in the nature of things, measured in the dimensions of the human life.

3. Consequently, nature's time does not subordinate itself to history's time; time is itself not linear, not marked off by unique events, reversible in direction from past to future, and not at all clearly differentiated (for the same reason) into past, present, and future.

It follows that nature provides the metaphor for cyclical time. That explains why cyclical time is coherent with nature in a way in which historical time is not. Specifically, nature in humanity is expressed through a cycle of birth, youth, maturity, old age, death. The next step, for cyclical time given the form of historical narrative (for example), is then readily to be predicted. How nature divides the time of a human life then is translated into, or raised to the level of, the social order. Then society (e.g. the territorial unit, the city, the community, the kingdom, the empire) is born, matures, grows old, dies, with a further cycle to follow, onward into time. That is how human time, like nature's time, is deemed to conform to a cycle corresponding to the natural and the individual. The events of the social order viewed as comparable to the natural one are not unique, irreversible, irrecoverable, and linear, but common, recurrent, recoverable, and cyclical.

We see, therefore, two media for the taxonomy of humanity's time, in response to the classification of nature's time, the historical and the cyclical. But there is a third, which I call, the paradigmatic classification of humanity's time; it is not historical, and it also is not cyclical. That is what has now to be defined. Paradigmatic time refers to a pattern, or a model, or a paradigm (the words are interchangeable here) that provides yet another way of defining time in human terms, which is to say, of taking the natural divisions of time and correlating with them aggregates of time that express time in human terms. But paradigmatic time takes a different measure altogether from historical, including cyclical time; and it deems nature's time merely integral to its own. What, precisely, do I mean by "paradigmatic time"?

6. Paradigmatic Time

What is at stake in the conception of time within paradigmatic thinking? By a paradigm, time is marked off by indicators that are utterly free-standing, in no way correlated with natural time at all; a paradigm's time is time defined in units that are framed quite independent of the epiphenomena of time and change as we know them in this life, on the one side, or the cycle of natural events that define and also delineate nature's time, on the other.

Like fractals (in mathematical language) paradigms describe how things are, capturing the shape of time whether large or small, whether here or there, whether today or in a distant past or an unimaginable future. The paradigm identifies the sense and order of things, their sameness, without regard to scale; a few specific patterns, revealed in this and that, hither and yon, isolate points of regularity or recurrence. We know those "fractals" or paradigms because, in Scripture, God has told us what they are; our task is so to receive and study Scripture as to find the paradigms; so to examine and study events as to discern the paradigms; so to correlate Scripture and time – whether present time or past time then matters not at all – as to identify the indicators of order, the patterns that occur and recur and (from God's perspective) impose sense on the nonsense of human events.

In the biblical religions, Judaism and Christianity, it is God who in creation has defined the paradigms – patterns, models – of time, Scripture that conveys those paradigms, and humanity that discovers, in things large and small, those paradigms that inhere in the very nature of creation itself. A paradigm forms a way of keeping time that invokes its own differentiating indicators, its own counterparts to the indicators of nature's time. Nature defines time as that span that is marked off by one spell of night and day; or by one sequence of positions and phases of the moon; or by one cycle of the sun around the earth (in the pre-Copernican paradigm). History further defines nature's time by marking off a solar year by reference to an important human event, for instance, a reign, a battle, a building. So history's time intersects with, and is superimposed upon, nature's time. And cyclical time forms a modification of history's time, appealing for its divisions of the aggregates of time to the analogy, in human life, to nature's time: the natural sequence of events in a human life viewed as counterpart to the natural sequence of events in solar and lunar time.

I cannot overstress the fictive, predetermined character of time as measured in the paradigmatic manner, that is, time as formulated by a free-standing model, not appealing to the course of sun and moon, not concerned with the metaphor of human life and its cyclicality either. Paradigms are set forth by neither nature (by definition) nor natural history (what happens on its own here on earth); by neither the cosmos (sun and moon), or the natural history of humanity (the life cycle and analogies drawn therefrom). In the setting of Judaism and Christianity, paradigms are set forth in revelation; they explain the Creator's sense of order and regularity, which is neither imposed upon, nor derived from, nature's time, nor to be discovered through history's time. And that is why to paradigmatic time, history is wildly incongruous, and considerations of linearity, temporality, and historical order beyond all comprehension. God has set forth the paradigms that measure time by indicators of an other-than natural character: supernatural time, which of course is beyond all conception of time.

So much for a theological formulation of matters. What, in this-worldly language, is to be said about the same conception? Paradigms derive from human invention and human imagination, and are imposed on nature and on history alike. Nature is absorbed, history recast, through paradigmatic time; that is, time invented, not time discovered; time defined for a purpose determined by humanity (the social order, the faithful, for instance), time not discovered by determined and predetermined, time that is not natural or formed in correspondence to nature, or imposed upon nature at specified intersections; but time that is defined completely in terms of the prior pattern or the determined paradigm or fabricated model itself: time wholly invented for the purposes of the social order that invents and recognizes time.

Let me make these abstractions concrete, since I refer, for paradigmatic time, to perfectly familiar ways of thinking about the passage of time, besides the natural (cyclical) and historical ways of thinking. Once I define paradigmatic time *as time invented by humanity for humanity's own purposes,* time framed by a system set forth to make sense of a social order, for example, the examples multiply. The use of BC and AD forms one obvious paradigm: all time is divided into two parts by reference to the advent of Jesus Christ. Islam presents a comparable example in telling time from the moment of the Hegira in 621 CE, when Muhammad made the passage from Mecca to Medina. Another paradigm is marked by the history of humanity set forth in Scripture: Eden, then after Eden; or (as rabbinic paradigms define matters), Adam vs. Israel, Eden vs. the Land; Adam's fall vs. Israel's loss of the Land. The sages will impose a further, critical variable on the pattern of Eden vs. Land of Israel, Adam vs. Israel, and that is, Sinai. A pattern then will recognize the divisions of time between before Sinai and afterward.

7. Paradigmatic Time: An Example in Rabbinic Literature

These general definitions should be made more concrete in the setting of rabbinic Judaism. Let me give a single example of paradigmatic time, in contrast to the conceptions of time that govern in the Hebrew Scriptures. The character of paradigmatic time is captured in the following, which encompasses the entirety of Israel's being (its "history" in conventional language) within the conversation that is portrayed between Boaz and Ruth; I abbreviate the passage to highlight only the critical components:

Ruth Rabbah Parashah Five

40.1.1. A. "And at mealtime Boaz said to her, 'Come here and eat some bread, and dip your morsel in the wine.' So she sat beside the reapers, and he passed to her parched grain; and she ate until she was satisfied, and she had some left over:"

B. R. Yohanan interested the phrase "come here" in six ways:

C. "The first speaks of David.

D. "'Come here': means, to the throne: 'That you have brought me here' (2 Sam 7:18).

E. "'... and eat some bread': the bread of the throne.

F. "'... and dip your morsel in vinegar': this speaks of his sufferings: 'O Lord, do not rebuke me in your anger' (Ps 6:2).

G. "'So she sat beside the reapers': for the throne was taken from him for a time."

I. [Resuming from G:] "'and he passed to her parched grain': he was restored to the throne: 'Now I know that the Lord saves his anointed' (Ps 20:7).

J. "'... and she ate and was satisfied and left some over': this indicates that he would eat in this world, in the days of the messiah, and in the age to come.

2. A. "The second interpretation refers to Solomon: 'Come here': means, to the throne.

B. "'... and eat some bread': this is the bread of the throne: "And Solomon's provision for one day was thirty measures of fine flour and three score measures of meal' (1 Kgs 5:2).

C. "'... and dip your morsel in vinegar': this refers to the dirty of the deeds [that he did].

D. "'So she sat beside the reapers': for the throne was taken from him for a time."

G. [Reverting to D:] "'and he passed to her parched grain': for he was restored to the throne.

H. "'... and she ate and was satisfied and left some over': this indicates that he would eat in this world, in the days of the messiah, and in the age to come.

3. A. "The third interpretation speaks of Hezekiah: 'Come here': means, to the throne.

B. "'... and eat some bread': this is the bread of the throne.

C. "'... and dip your morsel in vinegar': this refers to sufferings [Isa 5:1]: 'And Isaiah said, Let them take a cake of figs' (Isa 38:21).

D. "'So she sat beside the reapers': for the throne was taken from him for a time: 'Thus says Hezekiah, This day is a day of trouble and rebuke' (Isa 37:3).

E. "'... and he passed to her parched grain': for he was restored to the throne: 'So that he was exalted in the sight of all nations from then on' (2 Chr 32:23).

F. "'... and she ate and was satisfied and left some over': this indicates that he would eat in this world, in the days of the messiah, and in the age to come.

4. A. "The fourth interpretation refers to Manasseh: 'Come here': means, to the throne.

B. "'... and eat some bread': this is the bread of the throne.

C. "'... and dip your morsel in vinegar': for his dirty deeds were like vinegar, on account of wicked actions.

D. "'So she sat beside the reapers': for the throne was taken from him for a time: 'And the Lord spoke to Manasseh and to his people, but they did not listen. So the Lord brought them the captains of the host of the king of Assyria, who took Manasseh with hooks' (2 Chr 33:10-11)."

K. [Reverting to D:] "'and he passed to her parched grain': for he was restored to the throne: 'And brought him back to Jerusalem to his kingdom' (2 Chr 33:13).

N. "'... and she ate and was satisfied and left some over': this indicates that he would eat in this world, in the days of the messiah, and in the age to come.

5. A. "The fifth interpretation refers to the Messiah: 'Come here': means, to the throne.

B. "'... and eat some bread': this is the bread of the throne.

C. "'... and dip your morsel in vinegar': this refers to suffering: 'But he was wounded because of our transgressions' (Isa 53:5).

D. "'So she sat beside the reapers': for the throne is destined to be taken from him for a time: For I will gather all nations against Jerusalem to battle and the city shall be taken' (Zech 14:2).

E. "'... and he passed to her parched grain': for he will be restored to the throne: 'And he shall smite the land with the rod of his mouth' (Isa 11:4)."

I. [reverting to G:] "so the last redeemer will be revealed to them and then hidden from them."

The paradigm here may be formed of six units: (1) David's monarchy; (2) Solomon's reign; (3) Hezekiah's reign; (4) Manasseh's reign; (5) the Messiah's reign. So paradigmatic time compresses events to the dimensions of its model. All things happen on a single plane of time. Past, present, future are undifferentiated, and that is why a single action contains within itself an entire account of Israel's social order under the aspect of eternity.

The foundations of the paradigm rest on the fact that David, Solomon, Hezekiah, Manasseh, and therefore also the Messiah, all descend from Ruth's and Boaz's union. Then, within the framework of the paradigm, the event that is described here – "And at mealtime Boaz said to her, 'Come here and eat some bread, and dip your morsel in the wine.' So she sat beside the reapers, and he passed to her parched grain; and she ate until she was satisfied, and she had some left over" – forms not a one-time event but a pattern. The pattern transcends time. More accurately, aggregates of time, the passage of time, the course of events – these are all simply irrelevant to what is in play in Scripture. Rather we have a tableau,[9] joining persons who lived at widely separated moments, linking them all as presences at this simple exchange between Boaz and Ruth; imputing to them all, whenever they came into existence, the shape and structure of that simple moment: the presence of the past, for David, Solomon, Hezekiah, and so on, but the pastness of the present in which David or Solomon – or the Messiah for that matter – lived or would live (it hardly matters, verb tenses prove hopelessly irrelevant to paradigmatic thinking).

Taking account of both the simple example of BC and AD and the complex one involving the Israelite monarchy and the Messiah, we ask ourselves how time has been framed within the paradigmatic mode of thought. The negative is now clear. Paradigmatic time has no relationship whatsoever to nature's time. It is time invented, not discovered; time predetermined in accord with a model or pattern, not time negotiated in the interplay between time as defined by nature and time as differentiated by human cognizance and recognition.

Here the points of differentiation scarcely intersect with either nature's or history's time; time is not sequential, whether in natural or historical terms; it is not made up of unique events, whether in nature or in the social order; it is not differentiated by indicators of a commonplace character. Divisions between past, present, and future lie

---

[9] For the notion of the representation of Israel's existence as an ahistorical tableau, see my *Judaism: The Evidence of the Mishnah* (Chicago: University of Chicago Press, 1981).

beyond all comprehension. Natural time is simply ignored here; years do not count, months do not register; the passage of time marked by the sun, correlated with, or ignored by, the course of human events, plays no role at all. All flows from that model – in the present instance, the model of time divided into chapters of Davidic dynastic rulers, time before the Messiah but tightly bound to the person of the Messiah; the division of time here then can take the form of before Boaz's gesture of offering food to Ruth and afterward; before David and after the Messiah; and the like. A variety of interpretation of the passage may yield a range of paradigms; but the model of paradigmatic time will remain one and the same. Not much imagination is required for the invention of symbols to correspond to BC and AD as a medium for expressing paradigmatic time.

The case now permits us further to generalize. The paradigm takes its measures quite atemporally, in terms of not historical movements or recurrent natural cycles but rather atemporal units of experience, those same aggregates of time, such as nature makes available through the movement of the sun and moon and the passing of the seasons, on the one hand, and through the life of the human being, on the other. A model or pattern or paradigm will set forth an account of the life of the social entity (village, kingdom, people, territory) in terms of differentiated events – wars, reigns, for one example, building a given building and destroying it, for another – yet entirely out of phase with sequences of time.

A paradigm imposed upon time does not call upon the day or month or year to accomplish its task. It will simply set aside nature's time altogether, regarding years and months as bearing a significance other than the temporal one (sequence, span of time, aggregates of time) that history, inclusive of cyclical time's history, posits. Paradigmatic time then views humanity's time as formed into aggregates out of all phase with nature's time, measured in aggregates not coherent with those of the solar year and the lunar month. The aggregates of humanity's time are dictated by humanity's life, as much as the aggregates of nature's time are defined by the course of nature. Nature's time serves not to correlate with humanity's patterns (no longer, humanity's time), but rather to mark off units of time to be correlated with the paradigm's aggregates.

It remains to reconsider those systematic comparisons between history's time and other modes of keeping time that have already served us well. Since the comparison of historical and cyclical time is now in hand, let us turn directly to ask, How shall we read the paradigmatic,

as distinct from the cyclical mode of formulating a human counterpart to nature's time? Here are the point-by-point correspondences:
1. In paradigmatic time, human events do not form givens, any more than natural events form givens, in the measurement of time; while both of those definitions of the eventful correspond in character to the course of nature, paradigmatic events find their definition within the paradigm, within the logic of the system, in accord with the predetermined pattern, and not in response to the givens of the natural world, whether in the heavens or in the life cycle; paradigmatic time also follows a fixed and predictable pattern, but its identification of what is eventful out of what happens in the world at large derives from its own logic and its own perception; nothing is dictated by nature, not nature's time, not history's time, not the linear progress of historical events, not the cyclical progress of historical patterns.
2. Nature's time plays no independent role in paradigmatic time; cut down to human size by cyclical time in nature's way, nature's time in paradigmatic thinking is simply absorbed into the system and treated as neutral – nature's time is marked, celebrated, sanctified, but removed from the entire range of history, which is wholly taken over and defined by the paradigm.
3. Consequently, nature's time plays no role in paradigmatic time; time is neither cyclical nor linear, it is not marked off by unique events, it is simply neutral and inert. Time is inconsequential; the issue is not whether or not time is reversible in direction from past to future, or whether or not time is to be differentiated (for the same reason) into past, present, and future.

The upshot is simply stated. A paradigm predetermines, selects happenings in accord with a pattern possessed of its own logic and meaning, unresponsive to the illogic of happenings, whether chaotic, whether orderly, from the human perspective. A model is just that: there to dictate, there to organize, there to take over, make selections, recognize connections, draw conclusions. To characterize paradigmatic time as atemporal therefore proves accurate but tangential, since atemporality is not a definitive taxic trait, merely a byproduct. Indeed, the very phrase, "paradigmatic time," standing by itself presents an oxymoron. Paradigms admit to time – the spell that intervenes between this and that, the "this" and the "that" beyond defined within the paradigm. In that sense, time pertains, as much as the spell between sunset and sunset or new moon and new moon pertains in nature's time.

But in situating the events in the scale of human time, as history would have matters, to the model of Ruth and Boaz, David, Solomon, and the Messiah, captured in the little gesture, "and he passed to her parched grain; and she ate until she was satisfied, and she had some left over," the matter of time simply does not pertain. For the action was not one-time (even for all-time) nor cyclical, but altogether out of history's and nature's time. Time is contingent, embedded within the model. The paradigm serves to select events; the model, to endow events with order and meaning, structure and familiarity. Rich in time-sequences, the scene is a tableau, full of action but lacking temporality.

8. Paradigmatic Thinking about Past and Future in a Single Tense: The Presence of the Past, the Pastness of the Present

If I maintain that rabbinic Judaism possessed no idea of history because it pursued instead paradigms of human conduct without regard to time, what was the source of those paradigms? Scripture not merely supplied the facts but read in the rabbis' manner laid the foundations for paradigmatic thinking. Before proceeding, let me give a single important case of paradigmatic reading of Scripture: the comparison of Adam and Israel, the loss of Eden and the loss of the Land. For the creation-narrative formed the primary, generative paradigm of the rabbinic theological system. In this paradigmatic reading of Scripture Israel is like Adam, but Israel is the Other, the Last Adam, the opposite of Adam. We shall now systematically compare Adam and Israel, the first man and the last, and show how the story of Adam matches the story of Israel – but with a difference:

Genesis Rabbah 19:9.1-2
2. A. R. Abbahu in the name of R. Yosé bar Haninah: "It is written, 'But they are like a man [Adam], they have transgressed the covenant' (Hos 6:7).

B. "'They are like a man,' specifically, like the first man. [We shall now compare the story of the first man in Eden with the story of Israel in its land.]

Now the composer identifies an action in regard to Adam with a counterpart Action in regard to Israel, in each case matching verse for verse, beginning with Eden and Adam:

C. "'In the case of the first man, I brought him into the garden of Eden, I commanded him, he violated my commandment, I judged him to be sent away and driven out, but I mourned for him, saying "How..."'[which begins the book of Lamentations, hence stands for a lament, but which, as we just saw, also is written with the consonants that also yield, 'Where are you'].

D. "'I brought him into the garden of Eden,' as it is written, 'And the Lord God took the man and put him into the garden of Eden' (Gen 2:15).

E. "'I commanded him,' as it is written, 'And the Lord God commanded...' (Gen 2:16).

F. "'And he violated my commandment,' as it is written, 'Did you eat from the tree concerning which I commanded you' (Gen 3:11).

G. "'I judged him to be sent away,' as it is written, "And the Lord God sent him from the garden of Eden' (Gen 3:23).

H. "'And I judged him to be driven out.' 'And he drove out the man' (Gen 3:24).

I. "'But I mourned for him, saying, "How...".' 'And he said to him, "Where are you"' (Gen 3:9), and the word for 'where are you' is written, 'How....'

Now comes the systematic comparison of Adam and Eden with Israel and the Land of Israel:

J. "'So too in the case of his descendants, [God continues to speak,] I brought them into the Land of Israel, I commanded them, they violated my commandment, I judged them to be sent out and driven away but I mourned for them, saying, "How ..."'

K. "'I brought them into the Land of Israel.' 'And I brought you into the land of Carmel' (Jer. 2:7).

L. "'I commanded them.' 'And you, command the children of Israel' (Exod 27:20). 'Command the children of Israel' (Lev 24:2).

M. "'They violated my commandment.' 'And all Israel have violated your Torah' (Dan 9:11).

N. "'I judged them to be sent out.' 'Send them away, out of my sight and let them go forth' (Jer 15:1).

O. "'... and driven away.' 'From my house I shall drive them' (Hos 9:15).

P. "'But I mourned for them, saying, "How..."' 'How has the city sat solitary, that was full of people' (Lam 1:1)."

Here we end where we began, Israel in exile from the Land, like Adam in exile from Eden.

The case illustrates the mode of thought. The rabbinic sages identified in the written part of the Torah the governing models of Israel's enduring existence, whether past, whether future. And that is precisely why they formed the conception of paradigm, and whence they drew the specificities of theirs. They knew precisely what paradigms imparted order and meaning to everyday events, and their models, equivalent in mathematics to the "philosophy," then selected and explained data and also allowed prognosis to take place. In place of a past that explained the present and predicted the future, sages invoked a paradigm that imposed structure on past and future alike – a very different thing.

9. Paradigmatic Thinking in Contemporary Culture: The Model

I turn to mathematics for help in explaining the alternative to historical thinking represented in rabbinic Judaism's principal exegetical documents. The paradigm forms a medium for the description, analysis, and interpretation of selected data: existence, rightly construed. In this, paradigmatic thinking forms a counterpart to that of the mathematics that produces models. Specifically, mathematicians compose models that, in the language and symbols of mathematics, set forth a structure of knowledge that forms a "surrogate for reality."[10] These models state in quantitative terms the results of controlled observations of data, and among them, the one that generates plausible analytical generalizations will serve. Seeking not so much the regularities of the data as a medium for taking account of a variety of variables among a vast corpus of data, the framer of a model needs more than observations of fact, for instance, regularities or patterns. What is essential is a structure of thought, which mathematicians call "a philosophy:"

> As a philosophy it has a center from which everything flows, and the center is a definition ...[11]

What is needed for a model is not data alone, however voluminous, but some idea of what you are trying to compose: a model of the model:

> Unless you have some good idea of what you are looking for and how to find it, you can approach infinity with nothing more than a mishmash of little things you know about a lot of little things.[12]

---

[10] N. Maclean, *Young Men and Fire* (Chicago: University of Chicago Press, 1992), 257.
[11] Maclean, 261.
[12] Maclean, p. 262.

So, in order to frame a model of explanation, we start with a model in the computer, and then test data to assess the facility of the model; we may test several models, with the same outcome: the formation of a philosophy in the mathematical sense. To understand the relevance of this brief glimpse at model-making in mathematics, let me cite the context in which the matter comes to me, the use of mathematics to give guidance on how to fight forest fires:

> If mathematics can be used to predict the intensity and rate of spread of wildfires of the future (either hypothetical fires or fires actually burning but whose outcome is not yet known), why can't the direction of the analysis be reversed in order to reconstruct the characteristics of important fires of the past? Or why can't the direction be reversed from prophecy to history?[13]

Here the reversibility of events, their paradigmatic character, their capacity to yield a model unlimited by context or considerations of scale, – the principal traits of paradigmatic thinking turn out to enjoy a compelling rationality of their own.

Reading those words, we can immediately grasp what service models or patterns or paradigms served for the rabbinic sages, even though the framing of mathematical models began long after the birth of this writer, and even though the rabbinic sages lived many centuries before the creation of the mathematics that would yield models in that sense in which, sages' paradigms correspond in kind and function to model-explanation in contemporary mathematics. Before us is a mode of thought that is entirely rational and the very opposite of "insubstantial."

What is at stake in the appeal to "paradigm" or "model" to explain how sages answered the same questions that, elsewhere, historical thinking admirably addresses is now clear. To use the term in the precise sense just now stated, philosophy now took the place of history in the examination of the meaning of human events and experience. Forming a philosophical model to hold together such data as made a difference, sages found ready at hand the pattern of the destruction of the Temple, alongside explanations of the event and formulations of how the consequences were to be worked out. And, since the Temple represented the focus and realization of the abstractions of nature – from the movement of sun and moon to the concrete rhythm of the offerings celebrating these events, from the abundance of nature, the

---

[13] Maclean, p. 267.

natural selection, by chance, and presentation of God's share on the altar – nature's time took over, history's time fell away.

Precisely why did the rabbinic sages recast the received historical mode of thinking in such a way as to reread Scripture as a source for not narrative but paradigm? And on what basis did they presume to treat as models what the revealed history of Scripture set forth as a sequence of linear, one-time events? It is time to spell out the result and to explain the facts that characterize the documents as ahistorical, atemporal, and non-linear, but rather as paradigmatic: *history in quest of philosophy*.

10. Concrete Results of the Move from Historical to Paradigmatic Conceptions of Time

The rabbinic sages recognized no barrier between present and past. To them, the present and past formed a single unit of time, encompassing a single span of experience. Why was that so? It is because, to them, times past took place in the present too, on which account, the present not only encompassed the past (which historical thinking concedes) but took place in the same plane of time as the past (which, to repeat, historical thinking rejects). How come? It is because the rabbinic sages experienced the past in the present. What happened that mattered had already happened; an event then was transformed into a series; events themselves defined paradigms, yielded rules. A simple formulation of this mode of thought is as follows:

Mishnah tractate *Taanit* **4:6**

    A. Five events took place for our fathers on the seventeenth of Tammuz, and five on the ninth of Ab.

        B. On the seventeenth of Tammuz

            (1) the tablets [of the Torah] were broken,

            (2) the daily whole offering was cancelled,

            (3) the city wall was breached,

            (4) Apostemos burned the Torah, and

            (5) he set up an idol in the Temple.

        C. On the ninth of Ab

            (1) the decree was made against our forefathers that they should not enter the land,

            (2) the first Temple and

            (3) the second [Temple] were destroyed,

            (4) Betar was taken, and

            (5) the city was ploughed up [after the war of Hadrian].

        D. When Ab comes, rejoicing diminishes.

We mark time by appeal to the phases of the moon; these then may be characterized by traits shared in common – and so the paradigm, from marking time, moves outward to the formation of rules concerning the regularity and order of events.

In the formulation just now given, we see the movement from event to rule. What is important about events is not their singularity but their capacity to generate a pattern, a concrete rule for the here and now. That is the conclusion drawn from the very passage at hand:

Mishnah tractate *Taanit* **4:7**

A. In the week in which the ninth of Ab occurs it is prohibited to get a haircut and to wash one's clothes.

B. But on Thursday of that week these are permitted,

C. because of the honor owing to the Sabbath.

D. On the eve of the ninth of Ab a person should not eat two prepared dishes, nor should one eat meat or drink wine.

E. Rabban Simeon b. Gamaliel says, "He should make some change from ordinary procedures."

F. R. Judah declares people liable to turn over beds.

G. But sages did not concur with him.

Events serve to define paradigms and therefore, also, to yield rules governing the here and now: what we do to recapitulate.

This brings us back to our question: how an event is turned into a series, what has changed what happened once into something that happens. The answer lies in the correspondence (real or imagined) of the two generative events sages found definitive: the destruction of the Temple, the destruction of the Temple. The singular event that framed their consciousness recapitulated what had already occurred. For they confronted a Temple in ruins, and, in the defining event of the age just preceding the composition of most of the documents surveyed here, they found quite plausible the notion that the past was a formidable presence in the contemporary world. And having lived through events that they could plausibly discover in Scripture – Lamentations for one example, Jeremiah another – they also found entirely natural the notion that the past took place in, was recapitulated by, the present as well.

When we speak of the presence of the past, therefore, we raise not generalities or possibilities but the concrete experience that generations actively mourning the Temple endured. When we speak of the pastness of the present, we enter into the consciousness, the dream-world, of people who could open Scripture and find themselves right there, in its record. And that was in not only Lamentations, but also prophecy, and, especially, the books of the Torah, for reasons already instantiated in the parallel of Adam and Israel cited earlier. Here we deal with not the spiritualization of Scripture, but with the acutely contemporary and immediate realization of Scripture: once again, as then; Scripture in the present day, the present day in Scripture. That is why it was possible for sages to formulate out of Scripture a paradigm that imposed structure and order upon the world that they themselves encountered.

Since, then, sages did not see themselves as removed in time and space from the generative events to which they referred the experience of the here and now, they also had no need to make the past contemporary. If the Exodus was irreversible, once for all time event, then, as we see, the rabbinic sages saw matters in a different way altogether. They neither relived nor transformed one-time historical events, for they found another way to overcome the barrier of chronological separation.

Specifically, if history began when the gap between present and past shaped consciousness, then we naturally ask ourselves whether the point at which historical modes of thought concluded and a different mode of thought took over produced an opposite consciousness from the historical one: not cycle but paradigm. For, it seems to me clear, the premise that time and space separated the rabbinic sages from the great events of the past simply did not win attention. The opposite premise defined matters: barriers of space and time in no way separated sages from great events, the great events of the past enduring for all time. How then are we to account for this remarkably different way of encounter, experience, and, consequently, explanation? The answer has already been adumbrated.

Sages assembled in the documents of rabbinic Judaism, from the Mishnah forward, all recognized the destruction of the Second Temple and all took for granted that that event was to be understood by reference to the model of the destruction of the first. A variety of sources reviewed here maintain precisely that position and express it in so many words, e.g., the colloquy between Aqiba and sages about the comfort to be derived from the ephemeral glory of Rome and the temporary ruin of Jerusalem.

Sifre to Deuteronomy 43.3.7

A. Rabban Gamaliel, R. Joshua, R. Eleazar b. Azariah, and R. Aqiba were going toward Rome. They heard the sound of the city's traffic from as far away as Puteoli, a hundred and twenty miles away. They began to cry, while R. Aqiba laughed.

B. They said to him, "Aqiba, why are we crying while you are laughing?"

C. He said to them, "Why are you crying?"

D. They said to him, "Should we not cry, since gentiles, idolaters, sacrifice to their idols and bow down to icons, but dwell securely in prosperity, serenely, while the house of the footstool of our God has been put to the torch and left a lair for beasts of the field?"

E. He said to them, "That is precisely why I was laughing. If this is how he has rewarded those who anger; him, all the more so [will he reward] those who do his will."

8. A. Another time they went up to Jerusalem and go to Mount Scopus. They tore their garments.

B. They came to the mountain of the house [of the temple] and saw a fox go forth from the house of the holy of holies. They began to cry, while R. Aqiba laughed.

C. They said to him, "You are always giving surprises. We are crying when you laugh!"

D. He said to them, "But why are you crying?"

E. They said to him, "Should we not cry over the place concerning which it is written, "And the common person who draws near shall be put to death' (Num. 1:51)? Now lo, a fox comes out of it.

F. "In our connection the following verse of Scripture has been carried out: 'For this our heart is faint, for these things our eyes are dim, for the mountain of Zion which is desolate, the foxes walk upon it' (Lam. 5:17-18)."

G. He said to them, "That is the very reason I have laughed. For lo, it is written, 'And I will take for me faithful witnesses to record, Uriah the priest and Zechariah the son of Jeberechiah' (Is. 8:2).

H. "And what has Uriah got to do with Zechariah? What is it that Uriah said? 'Zion shall be plowed as a field and Jerusalem shall become heaps and the mountain of the Lord's house as the high places of a forest' (Jer. 26:18).

I. "What is it that Zechariah said? 'Thus says the Lord of hosts, "Old men and women shall yet sit in the broad places of Jerusalem"' (Zech. 8:4).

J. "Said the Omnipresent, 'Lo, I have these two witnesses. If the words of Uriah have been carried out, then the words of Zechariah will be carried out. If the words of Uriah are nullified, then the words of Zechariah will be nullified.

K. "'Therefore I was happy that the words of Uriah have been carried out, so that in the end the words of Zechariah will come about.'"

L. In this language they replied to him: "Aqiba, you have given us comfort."

It follows that for the rabbinic sages, the destruction of the Temple in 70 did not mark a break with the past, such as it had for their predecessors some five hundred years earlier, *but rather a recapitulation of the past.* Paradigmatic thinking then began in response to the year 70, in that very event that precipitated thought about history to begin with, the end of the old order. To state the upshot of the matter with heavy emphasis:

But paradigm replaced history because what had taken place the first time as unique and unprecedented took place the second time in precisely the same pattern and therefore formed of an episode a series. Paradigmatic thinking replaced historical when history as an account of one-time, irreversible, unique events, arranged in linear sequence and pointing toward a teleological conclusion, lost all plausibility. If the first time around, history – with the past marked off from the present, events arranged in linear sequence, narrative of a sustained character serving as the medium of thought – provided the medium for making sense of matters, then the second time around, history lost all currency. And what was left but cyclical or paradigmatic thinking. The sages chose the paradigm and defined its structure.

The real choice facing the rabbinic sages was not linear history as against paradigmatic thinking, but rather, paradigm as against cycle. For the conclusion to be drawn from the destruction of the Temple once again, once history, its premises disallowed, yielded no explanation, can have taken the form of a theory of the cyclicality of events. As nature yielded its spring, summer, fall and winter, so the events of humanity or of Israel in particular can have been asked to conform to a cyclical pattern, in line, for example, with Qohelet's view that what has been is what will be. But the rabbinic sages obviously did not take that position at all.

They rejected cyclicality in favor of a different ordering of events altogether. That is because they did not believe the Temple would be rebuilt and destroyed again, rebuilt and destroyed, rebuilt and destroyed, and so on into endless time. That is what is explicit in Aqiba's colloquy of Rome and Jerusalem. The sages stated the very opposite: the Temple would be rebuilt but never again destroyed. And that represented a view of the second destruction that rejected cyclicality altogether. Sages instead opted for patterns of history and against cycles because they retained that notion for the specific and concrete meaning of events that characterized Scripture's history, even while rejecting the historicism of Scripture. What they maintained, as we have seen, is that a pattern governed, and the pattern was not a cyclical one. Here, Scripture itself imposed its structures, its order, its system – its paradigm. And the Official History left no room for the conception of cyclicality. If matters do not repeat themselves but do conform to a pattern, then the pattern itself must be identified. And it was – by rabbinic Judaism.

11. What Kinds of Questions did the Ancient Rabbis Answer?

Paradigmatic thinking formed the alternative to cyclical thinking because Scripture, its history subverted, nonetheless defined how matters were to be understood. Viewed whole, the Official History indeed defined the paradigm of Israel's existence, formed out of the components of Eden and the Land, Adam and Israel, Sinai, then given movement through Israel's responsibility to the covenant and Israel's adherence to, or violation, of God's will, fully exposed in the Torah that marked the covenant of Sinai. Scripture laid matters out, and the rabbinic sages then drew conclusions from that lay-out that conformed to their experience. So the second destruction precipitated thinking about paradigms of Israel's life. And these came to full exposure in the thinking behind the passages that we have surveyed.

The episode made into a series, sages' paradigmatic thinking asked of Scripture different questions from the historical ones of 586 because the rabbinic sages brought to Scripture different premises; drew from Scripture different conclusions. But in point of fact, not a single paradigm set forth by sages can be distinguished in any important detail from the counterpart in Scripture, not Eden and Adam in comparison to the land of Israel and Israel, and not the tale of Israel's experience in the spinning out of the tension between the word of God and the will of Israel.

The contrast between history's time and nature's time shows that history recognizes natural time and imposes its points of differentiation upon it. History knows days, months, years, but proposes to differentiate among them, treating this day as different from that because on this day, such and such happened, but on that day, it did not. History's time takes over nature's time and imposes upon it a second set of indicators or points of differentiation. History therefore defines and measures time through two intersecting indicators, the meeting of (1) the natural and (2) the human. As is clear in the foregoing remarks, the context in which "time" is now defined is (1) the passage of days, weeks, months, and years, as marked by the movement of the sun and the stars in the heavens and (2) the recognition of noteworthy events that have taken place in specific occasions during the passage of those days and months and years. By contrast, paradigmatic time in the context of Judaism tells time through the events of nature, to which are correlated the events of Israel's life: its social structure, its reckoning of time, its disposition of its natural resources, and its history too. That is, through the point at which nature is celebrated, the Temple, there Israel tells time. The upshot is the conception of astral Israel, which comes to its full climax in *Pesiqta deRab Kahana*.

Predictably, therefore, the only history the rabbinic sages deem worth narrating – and not in sustained narrative even then – is the story of the Temple cult through days and months and years, and the history of the Temple and its priesthood and administration through time and into eternity. We now fully understand that fact. It is because, to begin with, the very conception of paradigmatic thinking as against the historical kind took shape in deep reflection on the meaning of events: what happened before has happened again – to the Temple. Ways of telling time before give way, history's premises having lost plausibility here as much as elsewhere. Now Israel will tell time in nature's way, shaping history solely in response to what happens in the cult and to the Temple. There is no other history, because, to begin with, there is no history.

Nature's time is the sole way of marking time, and Israel's paradigm conforms to nature's time and proves enduringly congruent with it. Israel conforming to nature yields not cyclical history but a reality formed by appeal to the paradigm of cult and Temple, just as God had defined that pattern and paradigm to Moses in the Torah. Genesis begins with nature's time and systematically explains how the resources of nature came to Israel's service to God. History's time yielded an Israel against and despite history, nature's time, as the Torah tells it, an Israel fully harmonious with nature – from Eden to the world to come, Eden restored.

7

Interpreting Legal History in the Mishnaic Division of Agriculture

Alan J. Avery-Peck

The Mishnah, a philosophical law code produced by rabbis at the beginning of the second century CE but comprised of statements attributed to authorities who lived over the preceding two hundred or more years, presents historians with two distinct problems. The first concerns the historical development of the law expressed by the Mishnah's authorities. In what ways, we must ask, did later authorities take up and develop ideas expressed by earlier generations? To what extent can we identify a process of legal development and evolution through which the law reached the state in which it emerged in the Mishnah as a whole?

But answering this question is only a first and preliminary step towards understanding the unfolding of the Rabbinic thought represented in this first document of nascent Rabbinic Judaism. Comprehending the stages of Mishnaic legal development provides the foundation for what is surely the more interesting and important task that faces any historian, the task of comprehending the factors that explain why the law emerged as it did and of identifying the ways in which the evolving law supported the particular social, theological, and political program of those who shaped it.

In arguing that the study of Mishnaic law presents the interrelated problems of identifying the evolving legal theories expressed by the rabbis and then of explaining why the rabbis might have adopted these particular approaches, I take up the method of analysis made famous by Max Weber in his study of the rise of capitalism. This approach suggests that developments in legal systems are best explained as responses to the changing social, political, and economic worlds of successive generations of legislators. In this view, the communal infrastructure within which lawyers work and legislate is a primary force in shaping the legal system they create. The task of the legal historian, accordingly, is to ascertain the effect of politics, economics, or religion in determining the shape that a legal system takes in each period.

This approach recognizes that lawyers and legislators react to their environment, creating individual and larger theories of law that respond to and attempt to make sense of the social and political world in which they live. But this approach is not without its problems. While the idea that legislators, like all people, are affected by their environment seems on the surface to be quite reasonable, an historian's focus on that impetus for legal development potentially obscures other factors that may be equally central or even more important in the shaping of legal evolution. Here I refer in particular to the formative power of the antecedent legal tradition. For, as much as legislators are affected by the world in which they live, we cannot discount the influence of their legal heritage. That heritage generally determines the parameters within which legal growth is possible and sets the framework within which all legal thinking takes place. Lawyers and legislators, and this is the case especially for those who understand themselves to work within a tradition of divinely reveal law, thus tend to be conservative, innovating within the narrow confines of the inherited tradition and forcing past modes of behavior to conform to present needs.[1] A second approach to legal history accordingly explains legal evolution by focusing upon the legal tradition itself, seeing the internal dynamics of the existing legal system as an important factor, perhaps the most important factor, in producing legal change.

The problem in the following is to see what we discover when each of these two approaches is applied in the interpretation of a specific legal system, in this case, that of the Mishnah. What do we learn from each of the approaches? How secure is that knowledge? And what happens when these two methods are used alone or in juxtaposition? Overall, what can we expect to know not only about how the law contained in the Mishnah evolved but about why it evolved, about the power of antecedent tradition or the Mishnaic legislators' own historical circumstance in shaping their legal thinking?

I state my general conclusions at the outset. What we might call the cognitive-developmental approach, which focuses upon the inherited legal system, explains the internal logic of the evolving law, locating

---

[1] These first paragraphs draw upon the introductory observations of Shael Herman in a review of Alan Watson, *The Making of the Civil Law,"* Israel Law Review 18/3-4 (1983) 490-503. Herman makes this particular point on p. 491.

the source of specific legal themes and explicating the theoretical stance that accounts for legislation on particular topics. It tells us from where legislators may have gotten certain ideas and it accounts for the power of those ideas within their legal system. Accordingly, this approach helps us paint a picture of the cognitive world of the legislators, describing their foundational legal philosophy and indicating how that philosophy came to be expressed through their legal corpus as a whole. Insofar as this approach focuses upon the concrete details of the legal system, it tends to be epistemologically strong, serving as a foundation for all subsequent analysis. In the case at hand, for instance, the cognitive-developmental approach accounts for many of the details of what the Mishnah's rabbis propose, for their larger choice of topics, and to a great extent for what they have to say about those topics.

At the same time, the limits of this explanatory model should be clear. The cognitive-developmental approach focuses on, but does not intend to go beyond, an explanation of the evolutionary potential of the inherited legal system. The problem is that, within that potential reside any number of possible paths – choices among a range of legitimate interpretations of the tradition – to be taken by the legislators of each age. Insofar as the developmental approach leaves open the question of why those who stand behind the legal system chose one path and not another, this approach falls short of addressing what historians rightly see as their most interesting question, the question of why a legal system evolved along one specific course and not another. Why, to refer to the case at hand, did rabbis – real people living in specific historical settings – choose one particular course of legal development legitimated by the scriptural heritage and not some other? Especially to the extent that, within the evolution of Mishnaic law, a quite striking shift in approaches to legal decision-making occurs in a period of extreme historical upheaval, the question seems particularly pressing.

What we might refer to as a historical-functional approach, which explains legal development by associating emerging ideologies with the human setting of the legislators, accordingly becomes an important historical methodology, a method that suggests the societal motivations likely to stand behind the evolving legal system. By focusing upon economic, political, and religious context, this approach probes the particular significance to a group of legislators of the legal and philosophical system they create. How, this is to say, are they responding not just to the broader set of traditions within which they were raised but to the particular historical setting in which they now live? These are the questions that reveal the human dimension of all legislative activity and that therefore most directly address what those who developed the law hoped, consciously or unconsciously, to accomplish.

As we shall see, however, while this historical approach's results may be intellectually interesting, they tend to be epistemologically weak. Like much of historical argument, they stand or fall upon an argument of plausibility but are not subject to proof or refutation. Legislators rarely make explicit, and, as just noted, are not even necessarily conscious of, the philosophical or social statement their legislation makes within the historical circumstances of their own day. Still, to abandon the historical-functional approach would be to leave historians largely with the very limited job of describing cultural phenomena while eliminating the possibility of determining those phenomena's human significance. While the historical method's limitations must be taken seriously, so that it not be used to explain too much too soon, it still offers a great potential for helping us comprehend the meaning evolving legal systems had within the worlds in which they were created. While the cognitive-developmental approach must be the initial and perhaps primary focus of scholarly interest, the historical method ultimately provides a level of understanding that has the potential truly to make sense of the historical data.

1. Historical-Functional and Cognitive-Developmental Approaches to Legal History

In the past decades, interpretation of the Mishnah has focused upon that document viewed as a whole, on the theology it expresses and on the meaning it had for those who, in the early third century CE, formulated and redacted its laws. This scholarship thus has moved to the heart of the human issue, of how people in a particular time period conceived and made sense of their world and of how and why they preserved their perceptions in one literary form and not another. Yet as in the study of all legal systems, the methodological problem – how to determine why those responsible for formulating and interpreting law thought and wrote as they did – has been brought dramatically to the surface. This methodological question is particularly pressing in the case of the Mishnah, which is compiled of materials collected over a period of centuries and which is formulated expressly to conceal all evidence of social, political, or theological context and motivation. How to move from the Mishnah's laws to their significance for the individuals who produced them accordingly presents a central problem for contemporary scholarship.

The most familiar current approach emerges from the work of Jacob Neusner,[2] who, beginning some three decades ago, began to argue that the legal thinking of the Mishnah's rabbis was directly affected by the political environment of their own day. Accordingly Neusner and those who have taken up his approach have related Mishnaic laws, and the system they comprise, to the presumed psychological needs and emotions of the Mishnah's creators. As in all historical reconstructions, this is done by drawing conclusions about the point of the document in question and about the period in which it was created and by finding an explanation that seems plausibly to relate the two. As we shall see below, the result for the case at hand is a reading of the Mishnah as a program of social and theological reconstruction responding to the destruction of the Second Temple and the failed Bar Kokhba revolt.

Two methodological problems plague this historical interpretation. First, insofar as the Mishnah's authorities consciously hid all signs of outside influence or historical relevance, this approach depends here, even more than in other instances of its application,[3] upon the historian's judgment of "plausibility." Even if based upon a law-by-law analysis of the content and legal ideology of the Mishnah, such a historical reconstruction can neither be finally proven nor, for that matter, falsified.

Second, this approach depends upon the underlying assumption that developments in the Mishnah's legal thinking should be understood *first and foremost* as reactions to the evolving life situation of the Mishnaic lawyers. Scholars writing about other periods have been conscious that, in Shael Herman's words, "the true causes of legal evolution" can often be discovered more easily "in the legal tradition itself than in the broader (and more remote) social and economic context in which a legal system evolves."[4] The opposite view, perhaps most famous from Weber's study of the rise of capitalism, continues rightly to have important proponents.[5] Yet, as Herman notes, the argument that

---

[2] His initial statement of the results of his massive study of the Mishnah are found in his *Judaism: The Evidence of the Mishnah* (Chicago: University of Chicago Press, 1981). Professor Neusner's more recent statement of the relationship of Rabbinic Judaism to the specific events of the early rabbis' day is discussed below.

[3] See by contrast the example below in section IV, concerning the theological function of the Deuteronomic history. In that case, as in the instance of Roman lease law (below, n. 5), a range of historical evidence as well as the clearer content of the documents in question provide firmer warrants than are possible in the case of the Mishnah.

[4] Herman, *op. cit.*, 490.

[5] This approach is exemplified, for instance, by B.W. Frier, *Landlords and Tenants in Imperial Rome* (Princeton, 1980), *passim* and in particular 196-219. As Frier states, the

"intrinsic legal forces are more powerful than [for instance] economic conditions in shaping law" was already "implicit in Weber's inability to explain why England achieved capitalistic supremacy without a 'calculable, logically formal legal system.'"[6] In short, the evidence from other legal systems does not uniformly support the premise that legal thinking reflects first and foremost the social, political, or religious climate of its day.[7] While societal influence certainly is present in all legal systems, employing such influence as one's *primary* hermeneutic in explaining specific systems, such as that of early Rabbinic Judaism, is prone to serious difficulty.

In light of the problematic nature of the historical-functional approach, students of the Mishnah have employed as well a developmental approach, explaining the Mishnaic legal system by referring to the inner logic of the antecedent legal tradition, beginning in Scripture. This approach envisions the Mishnah's laws as a legal tradition that evolved along lines explained by the dynamics of human legal thinking in general and according to the internal needs of the tradition itself. It accordingly leaves open the question of the relationship between the Mishnah's rabbis and the outside world.

This approach shows the extent to which the Mishnaic framers' choice of ideologies flows logically from the legal tradition within which they worked. Yet, since it does not, as we shall see, explain the specifics of the rabbis' legal ideology or the choices they made, it is essentially incomplete, a mode of description that stops short of explanation. The larger point accordingly is that despite their hermeneutical weakness, historical reconstructions attentive to the outside world comprise a central aspect of the interpretive task. But like any hermeneutical method, such interpretations must be used carefully, based on

---

ability convincingly to relate legal developments to social context depends upon the extent of our knowledge of the jurists' role in society, our understanding of their social and political ideals and, of course, our comprehension of the working of the courts in which their laws were employed. Frier argues that sufficient evidence is available for the case of Roman lease law, despite the fact that Roman juristic writing (like the Mishnah!) "for the most part simply declares the law, offering no intellectually sufficient explanation or justification" and that arguments "seem to conceal more than they disclose about the foundation of juristic decisions" (197). The point in the following is that the character of the Mishnah makes historical explanation of its law considerably trickier.

[6] Herman, *op. cit.*, citing J.M. Trubeck, "Max Weber on Law and the Rise of Capitalism," *University of Wisconsin Law Review* (1972), 720.

[7] Below I report in detail on legal evolution in the medieval period, which points in this same direction.

an initial exegesis attentive to the internal characteristics of the legal tradition being analyzed.

In the following, I examine the results of the application to the Mishnah of the two hermeneutical approaches I have outlined. But before turning to these analyses, we must understand the underlying themes and legal perspectives of the particular section of the Mishnah chosen for evaluation, the Division of Agriculture. We start by outlining the Division's topical interests and the specific legal evolution it reveals.

2. The Mishnaic Theory of Agriculture

The Division of Agriculture details the proper modes through which Israelites are to plant, harvest, process, and eat the crops they grow for sustenance upon the land of Israel. For the Mishnah these matters concern, first, how Israelites are to pay from the produce the agricultural tithes that support the poor and contribute to the maintenance of the priests and Levites who served in the Temple in Jerusalem.[8] Beyond this, the law considers the other Scriptural rules that dictate the Israelites' proper use of their land. The crops, for instance, must be arranged in the field in ways that prevent different species from growing together. Other rules preclude the consumption of fruit from a tree's first three years of growth and prohibit the planting and harvesting of crops in the seventh year of the sabbatical cycle.[9] The division as a whole thus takes up the wide range of concerns that revolve around the production and consumption of food in the Israelite world.

For the Mishnah's rabbis, these agricultural laws comprise a theological system detailing how Israelites are to maintain and use a land that ultimately is the special possession of God. The Mishnah's rabbis, that is, do not understand the payment of tithes simply to be a method of maintaining the Temple-cult or of supporting the needy of their community. Nor do they understand the other regulations that control use of the land to fulfill only general agricultural, social, or economic

---

[8] In addition to describing each of the major tithes and providing rules for their separation (Tractates *Peah*, *Maaser Sheni*, *Bikkurim* and parts of *Terumot* and *Hallah*), the Mishnah's authorities discuss how the tithes are to be prepared for consumption (Tractate *Terumot*) and detail how Israelites are to make certain that they do not eat produce from which these tithes have not been separated at all (Tractate *Demai*). Tractate *Maaserot* and parts of *Hallah* describe when Israelites are required to tithe.

[9] The concerns listed here are taken up in Tractates *Kilaim*, *Orlah* and *Shebiit*, respectively.

functions (e.g., the possible agricultural value of allowing all land to lie fallow once every seven years; the economic function of legislating that certain produce, or its value, be brought to Jerusalem). The Mishnah's authorities, rather, see in these regulations descriptions of how Israelites are to use their land in accordance with the specific nature of God's creation of the universe and in keeping with God's special relationship with the people and land of Israel.[10]

Since the Mishnah's themes and much of what the rabbis have to say about them are predictable on the basis of Scripture, what is significant for interpretation of the division must be narrowly defined. First is the very fact that the Mishnah's framers chose to take up in a systematic way topics that Scripture refers to in only a smattering of verses[11] and discusses with no consistent theological agendum.[12] Second, the Mishnah's framers became intensely concerned about agricultural offerings destined for priest, Levite, and Temple in a period in which the cult had been destroyed and priests and Levites accordingly had ceased to have a concrete function in the consecration

---

[10] In creating the world, God rested on the seventh day. The land of Israel, God's special possession, therefore must rest each seventh year. In creating the world, God distinguished discrete species of plants. In planting their fields, too, Israelites must not mix together different kinds. Finally, since crops that grow upon the land of Israel partake of the bounty of God's property, they are bonded to God and may not be eaten until God's interest in them has been satisfied, through payment of agricultural offerings.

[11] A total of sixty-eight verses are scattered in nineteen passages, the majority of which contain only one or two lines. The overall number of verses is raised considerably by the long passage at Deut 26:1-15, which discusses the liturgy for the presentation of the firstfruits and for Scripture's "year of tithing."

[12] The unsystematic nature of Scripture's tithing laws has prevented scholars from reaching a consensus concerning their significance. The problem arises with the attempt to locate in Scripture a unitary system of agricultural offerings (see e.g. Aharon Oppenheimer, "Terumot and Ma'aserot," in *Encyclopedia Judaica*, XV, 1025-1028). This approach leads to claims of a dual focus of the tithing system, upon piety, on the one hand, and taxation, on the other (see H. Guthrie, "Tithe," in *Interpreters Dictionary of the Bible*, III, 654-655 and J. MacCulloch, "Tithes," in *Encyclopedia of Religion and Ethics*, XII, 346-350). As R. Sarason, *A History of The Mishnaic Law of Agriculture: A Study of Tractate Demai* (Leiden, 1979), 3-10, points out, in contrast to the unitary perspective of the Mishnah, the Deuteronomic and Priestly sources contain two distinct theories of tithing. The former holds that the separation of tithes acknowledges God's ownership of the land of Israel and expresses gratitude for the land's fertility. The latter holds that the tithes go to the Levites and Aaronide priests as their pay for serving in the Temple. Mishnaic authorities take Scripture's diverse statements and in part conflicting definitions and derive from them a unitary and focused set of laws concerned with the sanctification of Israelite life.

7. AVERY-PECK *Legal History in the Mishnaic Division of Agriculture* 183

of Israelite life. Third, and most notably, the Mishnah's rabbis bring to this topic a distinctive interest in the processes of sanctification – that is, in how, by growing and processing food, Israelites cause holiness to come into being.[13] This issue is absent from Scripture, which, for its part, is primarily concerned that the priest and Levite receive their designated share but which, unlike the Mishnah, does not question how, in the hands of non-priests, produce becomes sanctified as that share.[14]

Having isolated the specific themes of the Division of Agriculture, let us focus as well upon the legal ideology expressed through those topics. Most interestingly, we find that, over the period of the emergence of the laws now codified in the Mishnah, these themes received varied treatment. A development occurred in the rabbis' approach to the law, such that the legislation deriving from each of the two major period in the Mishnah's evolution reflects that period's distinctive legal interests and sense of how one determines right and wrong.[15] Let me elaborate.

The earliest Rabbinic authorities, those living before the destruction of the Jerusalem Temple in 70 CE and in the period from the destruction until the Bar Kokhba Revolt in 132-135 CE, are concerned primarily with matters of definition and with basic laws facilitating observance of rules that are only sketched in Scripture.[16] A single theory of law stands behind these materials. The rabbis of the academy at Yavneh consistently exclude attention to the motivations or perceptions of the Israelite whose deeds are under scrutiny. The personal reasons or perceptions that led an individual to act, that is to say, have

---

[13] This specific interest presumably accounts for the failure of the Mishnah's rabbis to speak systematically about first tithe, which is not consecrated. See my *Mishnah's Division of Agriculture: A History and Theology of Seder Zeraim* (reprint: Leiden, 2005), 386 n. 5.

[14] The Division of Agriculture has little to say about the actual transfer of agricultural offerings to the priests and Levites. It thus ignores Scripture's central interest in favor of its own primary concern, the role of the non-priest in the processes of sanctification.

[15] The following conclusions are based upon chapters two through eleven in my *Mishnah's Division of Agriculture*. There I systematically organize the rules of the tractates on agriculture so as to ascertain which ideas derive from each of the major periods of Mishnaic legislation.

[16] These rabbis, for instance, (1) give concrete measurements that define a field, (2) delineate what field labors may or may not be performed in the Sabbatical year, (3) outline the quantity of produce to be taken as each tithe and agricultural offering and (4) indicate specifically how the offering is to be set aside.

no bearing upon the permissibility of that behavior. The status of a deed, rather, depends solely upon the nature of the actions through which it was carried out. It thus does not matter to Yavneans why an Israelite collected stones in his field during the seventh year, a period during which Scripture forbids cultivation of the land of Israel. The fact is that, by gathering stones, he facilitated farming. His actions therefore are culpable as a violation of the law. This is the case even if he simply desired to build a stone fence, which is permitted, and had no intention to engage in agricultural acts at all.[17]

These ideas reveal the Yavneans' comprehension of the existence of an objective standard that demarcates right and wrong, permissible and impermissible. That standard takes into account what an individual physically does and in no way considers the person's intentions or purposes. In this approach, correct acts are those that conform completely to preset norms of behavior. Actions, not intentions or perceptions, count. The result of one's deeds, not their underlying motivation, is determinative.

The later generation of authorities, those active in the academy at Usha in the period following the Bar Kokhba revolt, developed this ideal in a consistent pattern. Unlike the earlier generation of Rabbinic masters, the Ushan authorities always analyzed actions in light of the intentions of the individual who performed them and on the basis of the perceptions of those who witnessed them. To continue with our example of the Sabbatical year, Ushans thus understood the permissibility of field labor in the seventh year to depend upon the Israelite's intentions in carrying it out. They deemed an action permitted so long as the individual who performed it did not intend to break the rules of the seventh year and so long as he worked in a manner that prevented others from assuming that he proposed to break the law.[18] Unlike Yavneans, Ushans thus seem to recognize no order or meaning in the world other than that imposed by Israelites. In the Ushan view, an action has no inherent significance but can be explained and inter-

---

[17] Along these same lines, Yavneans define physical entities in light of their shape and form, without regard to the use to which Israelites intend to put them. They deem a field, for instance, to be demarcated by geographical boundaries, by hills, streams or trees that set off one area of land from adjacent lots. The farmer's own actions in choosing to treat one area as autonomous are considered immaterial.

[18] In the same way, the efficacy of the individual's separation of agricultural offerings depends upon the intention with which the separation is carried out, not upon the physical actions by which the deed is accomplished. In this view, finally, Israelites' own perceptions define which crops are orderly and distinct or disorderly and mixed together, so as to be permitted or forbidden to be planted together in a field.

preted only in light of the intentions of those who carry it out and the perceptions of those who witness it. Insofar as, in this view, there is no objective way of determining the culpability or permissibility of any action, Israelites largely live in a world of their own making. Through their intentions and perceptions, they give meaning to their activities in planting, tilling, and harvesting produce on the land of Israel.

This description of the legal perspectives found in the two main layers of law in the Division of Agriculture represent a first stage in explaining the history of Rabbinic law and provides the foundation for an interpretation of this Mishnaic division. What happened in the emergence of the law now is clear: an earlier legal philosophy that did not consider an actor's intentions gave way to a later view in which intentions and perceptions were central. With this picture in hand, the problem is to explain that particular development. This means asking, first, why, in the period after the destruction of the Temple and loss of Israelite sovereignty over the land of Israel, did the Mishnah's framers focus upon topics so closely connected to the maintenance of the Temple cult[19] and God's sovereignty over the land. And it means questioning, second, the reason for the shift from the Yavnean inattention to an individual's intentions and objectives to the Ushan theory in which actions have no intrinsic meaning at all.

3. The Evolution of Mishnaic Law:
A Cognitive-Developmental Approach

The cognitive-developmental approach referred to above focuses upon facts internal to the Mishnah. It explains the Mishnah' legal themes and ideologies (1) as determined by factors internal to the legal tradition and (2) as reflections of the sorts of thinking found in human society in general. Beginning with the former aspect of the Rabbinic agendum, we must recall the extent to which the Mishnah's authorities take up and develop Scripture's own topics. While the orientation towards Temple and priest might strike us as unrealistic for the period in question, still, we must recognize that the rabbis' choice of legal concerns follows the established framework of Judaic thinking. The rabbis thus insisted upon the people of Israel's obligation to abide by the covenant by following the rules introduced in Scripture. This recognition is particularly important for the case of the Division of Agriculture, many

---

[19] This fact of course is not unique to the Mishnaic Division of Agriculture but pertains as well to three of the five other divisions, which also focus upon the Temple, its offerings and Temple-purity.

laws of which could be followed even in the aftermath of the destruction of the Temple. Even though there are topics within the division – the rules for first fruits, for instance – that clearly were no longer applicable, we should not be too shocked at the rabbis' taking up of legal categories that for millennia had defined the relationship of the people of Israel to God.

The two different types of legal ideology found in the Mishnah likewise reflect approaches found in Scripture itself. The Yavnean realism represents the perspective portrayed, for instance, in the priestly creation story at Gen. 1:1-2:4. Here God creates a complete and perfected world. God creates each thing "according to its kind," so as to leave humans an already ordered world, in which they would not need to apply their own powers of categorization. Seeing the completed world, God also takes responsibility for its sanctification, the final divine gift that creates the Sabbath. Thus Yavnean authorities leave no room for the human perspective in determining the legal implications of any human action. What humans think or want is irrelevant, for they confront an already well-ordered and completed world.[20]

Yet the relativistic approach espoused by Ushan authorities also figures in Scripture. It appears explicitly in Leviticus's laws of holiness, which distinguish between Israelites' intentional and unwitting consumption of holy things. Beyond this specific parallel, the idea of a human role in organizing, and so imparting meaning to, the world, is clear in the second creation story, beginning at Gen 2:4, which describes God's assigning to Adam the task of naming the animals and so completing God's acts of creation.[21] We see then that the Mishnah's topical interests as well as both the Yavnean and Ushan legal approaches have close antecedents in Scripture.

The fact that the content of and ideologies expressed in Mishnaic law emerged directly from Scripture suggests that the rabbis may have worked independently of any contemporary historical motivations. Additional support for this thinking is in the fact that the evolution of

---

[20] A biblical parallel to the Yavnean approach is the story at 2 Sam 6:6-8, where Uzzah is struck down by God for reaching out to steady the ark of the covenant as it is being brought to Jerusalem. The ark's holiness, and so its power, is intrinsic and operates without regard to Uzzah's intentions in touching it. This is a quite different view from what appears in the later layers of Mishnaic law, both in the Division of Agriculture and, notably, in Ushan treatments of the Temple altar, which they assert has an impact only upon items that, in the first place, are pertinent to it.

[21] See on this H. Eilberg-Schwartz, *The Human Will in Judaism: The Mishnah's Philosophy of Intention* (Atlanta, 1986), ch. 5.

the Division of Agriculture's law follows a pattern of development familiar from other legal systems. It is a kind of growth, that is to say, that occurs independently of any specific historical context. Such growth occurs, for instance, in medieval law,[22] in which an early period's inattention to motive and circumstances gives way, in the development of the legal system, to laws that take carefully into account the human motivations that stand behind specific actions. Thus, prior to the twelfth century, within Church law, piety was understood to demand only a precise daily routine and, even in Anglo-Saxon criminal codes, no distinction was made, for instance, between intentional slayings and deaths caused by negligence. What counted was not what one intended but what actually happened. But, as in the Mishnah, in subsequent centuries, these attitudes were increasingly rejected: thus, around 1100, the widespread custom of oblation, in which young children, unable to commit themselves to life as monks, were in all events turned over to be raised in monasteries, was discontinued, and, in general, in matters of criminal and social law, the purposes and intentions of individuals were increasingly taken into account.

The development of attitudes towards culpability in medieval law exhibits the same pattern of growth found in the Division of Agriculture. In both legal systems an early view that ignores motivation gives way to a later understanding that views the human element as central. The example of oblation shows how closely this shift resembles the development in Mishnaic law. Since oblates had not, of their own accord, chosen to become monks, "high standards of asceticism or spirituality was hardly possible in their case" (Radding, 578), and later medieval law rejected the formalism inherent in such individuals' performance of their liturgical responsibilities. Priestly ministrations performed without proper intention now were viewed as invalid. This is strikingly similar to Ushan authorities' – but not Yavneans' – insistence that, to be valid, a designation of heave-offering, for instance, must be carried out by an individual who has formulated the intention to consecrate that which he separates as the priest's share. Later Mishnaic law and later medieval legal thinking thus both came to consider as invalid any actions performed without proper intention.

In light of the parallel from medieval law, interpretation of the Mishnah's legal development becomes a problem of explaining in general terms the reasons for growth of such similar character in obviously

---

[22] A complete list of sources is found in the bibliography of C.M. Radding, "Evolution of Medieval Mentalities," in *The American Historical Review* 83:3 (June, 1978) 557-597. On the following, see in particular 578-579.

unrelated cultural, religious, and political environments.[23] Charles Radding states the interpretive problem clearly, beginning by setting out the interpretative problem faced by the many historians who, he argues, have failed adequately to explain this developmental pattern:

> Sometimes the matter has simply been sidestepped by indefinite references to "social and economic change." Another approach has related the new ideas in law and religion to an intellectual renaissance of the eleventh and twelfth centuries, on the theory that the innovations were connected with the wider use of reason in human affairs. But more intellectual activity does not necessarily mean different thoughts. Equally plausible is the argument that dissatisfaction with old attitudes stimulated the growth of scholarly debate. The changes also have been attributed to the new institutions of the twelfth century... (579-580).

The problem as Radding sees it is the impossibility of proving a connection between a shift in mental attitudes and changes in social, political, and intellectual environments that could, after all, lead to a variety of different legal or philosophical responses. Radding therefore does not search for specific factors within the milieu of the eleventh and twelfth centuries that would explain the legal growth of that period. Instead, he turns to the work of cognitive psychologists to show the extent to which both the earlier and later attitudes found in these legal systems represent stages in the growth of human thinking. The point is not that, in all societies, a lack of interest in intention gives way to a concern for the human attitudes that inform action. He shows, rather, that both types of thinking are usual for people in general, such that we should not be surprised to find them alone or in historical juxtaposition. Thus he notes, following Piaget, that the "lack of interest in intention exhibited in primitive law resembles the attitude toward rules – called 'moral realism' – that is typical of children in all societies" (Radding, 582)[24] and that this notion, which holds that authority and doctrine are exterior to the individual's mind, begins to change when children reach the age of about ten. Then, to use the

---

[23] This fact poses the greatest challenge to the attempt to explain legal evolution through reference to external forces. See Herman, *op. cit.*, p. 492.

[24] Radding states: "According to Piaget, moral realism has at least three features: (1) the belief that any act that shows obedience to a rule is good and that any act that does not conform is bad; (2) the rule is not to be taken as something to be judged and interpreted but as something that is given, already made and external to the mind, so that the letter and not the spirit of the rule is obeyed; and (3) acts are evaluated in terms of their conformity with the rule and not according to the motive that prompted them" (582).

example of their attitudes towards play, children begin to see rules not as "sacred and untouchable" but as validated by agreement of all players. Now, a "less rigid attitude toward rules is founded on an increased ability to understand the other person and to cooperate on the basis of mutual development of subjective responsibility...so that taking intentions into account presupposes cooperation and mutual respect" (583).

The two stages Piaget points out in attitudes towards law and authority resemble the stages in the development of the law of the Division of Agriculture. The Yavnean perspective, which views Scripture's restrictions as preset and unaffected by circumstance, corresponds to the attitude of younger children, who judge matters in terms of the letter of the law and the concrete effects of action. The Ushan perspective resembles that of older children and adults, who look for the intent of the law and who determine the morality of an action in light of the actor's desire to conform with that intent.

The question is what we, as historians, are to make of the parallel between the evolution of culture and society and the growth of thought in individual human beings. The point, let me be clear, cannot be that phylogeny recapitulates ontogeny, since psychological theory applies to individual people but not to societies as wholes (see Radding, 595). Indeed, the notion that the growth of cultures necessarily parallels that of individual human beings is disproved by the fact that in many instances of growing legal and cultural systems, the development found in Mishnaic law and medieval society is lacking. Radding notes, for instance, that "the history of late Roman culture might show a reverse trend – from communitarian to authoritarian conceptions of morality" (595). We already have seen that the Hebrew Bible, which both early and later rabbis read closely, contains both ideas, making no effort to distinguish between them.

If the parallel between medieval legal developments and what we have seen in the Mishnah cannot be construed to claim a normative evolution, then the lesson it teaches must be narrowly defined. It teaches first and foremost that both the Yavnean and the Ushan approaches to the law are natural within individual human beings and therefore are expected within the conglomerates of individuals that comprise societies. Finding first at Yavneh and then at Usha a predominance of a certain mode of thought points to the shared mentalities of individuals who live in a common social, cultural, and political environment. Their shared perspectives on law indicate the extent to which rabbis, first at Yavneh and then at Usha, developed a communal intellect and common ethical perspective. This in itself may at least in part account for the development of the moral relativism of the later period, which, as Piaget noted, "presupposes cooperation and mutual respect" (cited in Radding, 583).

At the same time it is important to recognize the rarity – and therefore significance – of quick, large scale shifts in group mentality. As Radding puts it: "Usually, of course, one generation, through its interactions with the next educates it into the same ways of thinking, just as the intellectuals and leaders of the twelfth century – by the institutions they created and the questions they posed, and the students they taught – assured that their concerns would be those of subsequent generations" (595). Since, in an extremely short period of time, the Mishnah's masters shifted entirely from one pattern of legal thinking to a quite different one, the quest for a reason seems particularly urgent.

4. The Evolution of Mishnaic Law: The Historical-Functional Approach

The identification of a historical document's central theme leads, as a matter of course, to a reconstruction that relates that theme to the political and social environment of its creators. This standard approach to the writing of history is illustrated, for instance, within the field of biblical scholarship, which commonly faces the problem of a document written in one period yet claiming to derive from and speak about a different time. Frank M. Cross's description of Noth's understanding of the Deuteronomist is illustrative:[25]

> The theme running through the framework of the Deuteronomistic history, according to Noth, is a proclamation of unrelieved and irreversible doom.... The Deuteronomistic author, according to Noth, thus addressed his work to the exiles. His theology of history, revealed in the framework of his great work, justified God's wrath and explained the exile's plight.

This brief citation cannot do justice to Noth's argument; but it does illustrate the common method of historical reconstruction, which looks for a plausible relationship between theological or legal themes and the period in which they developed. Thus the specifics of Noth's description of the theology of the Deuteronomist were modified, for instance, by Von Rad[26] and by Cross himself. The basic approach to

---

[25] *Canaanite Myth and Hebrew Epic* (Cambridge, 1973), 275.
[26] See his *Studies in Deuteronomy*.

understanding the Deuteronomic documents, however, to this day remains unchallenged. Scholars seek the most plausible way to understand the relationship between a particular philosophy or theology and the period in which it develops.

In this way, recognition of the central themes of the Division of Agriculture and, indeed, of the Mishnah as a whole has led to interpretations that relate these themes to the political context in which the Mishnah's rabbis worked. In particular, these interpretations point out a possible connection between the destruction of the Temple in 70 CE, the failed Bar Kokhba revolt of 132-135, and the formulation within the Mishnah of a system of law that, while insisting on the enforcement of Scripture's rules, does so by focusing upon the centrality of individual Israelites, of non-priests, in the determination of what is right and wrong. My own comments concerning Tractate *Terumot*[27] illustrate this approach to the interpretation of the Mishnah:[28]

> To make the claim of God's continuing presence, the tractate...focuses upon the actions and responsibilities of the Israelite who sets aside and protects the priestly due. By describing these actions and responsibilities, it makes the powerful point that even with the Temple gone, cultic sanctification remains. This means that God himself still rules over the people and land of Israel. He moves in response to the intentions and perceptions of Israelites who separate the offering he mandated. This message is poignant. For as is clear, with the Temple destroyed and the Land defiled, these intentions and perceptions were all that remained to deny the events of history and affirm God's Lordship.

The evidence for the evolution of the legal theories found in the Mishnah leads to a refining of the theory just summarized. In the period immediately following the war in 70, Israelites expected the imminent rebuilding of the Temple and the return of the sacrificial cult. Life was expected soon to return to exactly as it had been before the destruction. This may explain the apparent insistence of Yavneans that there exists a preset and hierarchical order in the universe, as was represented by the presence, in their midst, of the Temple and the God-ordained cult practiced in it. Only with the Bar Kokhba revolt,

---

[27] *The Priestly Gift in Mishnah* (Chico, 1981), p. 7.

[28] For comparable interpretations of other tractates in the Division of Agriculture, see Martin Jaffee, *Mishnah's Theology of Tithing: A Study of Tractate Maaserot* (Chico, 1981), 3-6, Mandelbaum, *op. cit.*, 3-4, Roger Brooks, *Support for the Poor in the Mishnaic Law of Agriculture: Tractate Peah* (Chico, 1983), 35-36 and Newman, *op. cit.*, 17-20. All of these volumes are now reprinted: Leiden, 2005-2006. For one of the original statements of this thesis, see Jacob Neusner, *Judaism*, 271.

the point at which the expectation that the Temple would be quickly rebuilt could no longer be maintained, did the circumstances ripen for new legal developments. These placed common Israelites at the center of Israelite theology by claiming that, through their own perceptions and intentions, they impose meaning upon a world otherwise seen to be in a state of chaos. Israelites, that is, were given the power themselves to recreate a world out of the ashes.

In this reading, viewed as a whole, the Mishnah's law reaffirmed the validity of the covenant described in Scripture. In many of its details, accordingly, it indicated how Israelites were to carry out their obligations in that covenant, for instance, by properly planting and harvesting crops. In making their statement, however, the Mishnaic rabbis articulated a theology that uniquely symbolized their own historical, political, and religious situation. This theology replaced the lost cult and its priesthood with new centers of focus, the rabbis themselves, viewed as the bearers of revelation, and the common Israelites, whose thoughts and deeds were made primary to the creation of a perfected world.

The strength of this reconstruction is its focus upon central aspects of the Mishnah and on the period in which that document was formulated. 1. The rabbis' evolving legal ideologies and their choice to develop areas of law that, in their own day, largely could not be observed[29] represent the primary keys to explaining their larger purpose and perspective. 2. The significance of the destruction of the Temple and the Bar Kokhba revolt for Jews in the land of Israel in the first centuries seems undeniable. In its broadest parameters, the interpretation at hand thus does what good historical reconstructions must do. It takes up the most prominent historical facts and relates them to each other in a way that explains each on the basis of the others. Most important, by doing this, it answers the question that stands at the heart of historical inquiry and that is left open by the cognitive-developmental approach, the question of why, in their own particular period, the Mishnah's rabbis chose to deal with the topics they did in the particular way it did. Insofar as we have seen that the rabbis made choices in their selection as well as in their treatment of topics, the simply fact of the existence of biblical antecedents is an insufficient explanation for what they did.

---

[29] Even the agricultural law, large parts of which could be observed, is striking in this regard. The Division of Agriculture legislates the support of Temple personnel who no longer have a concrete role in Israelite cultic life.

At the same time, as I already have stated, this approach depends upon what is, in the end, an unprovable assumption, that external events, the war of 70 CE and the disastrous Bar Kokhba revolt, explain the character and content of the Mishnah and, beyond it, of Rabbinic Judaism in general. The problem is that, as Jacob Neusner has recently shown in detail, neither the destruction of the Second Temple nor the Bar Kokhba revolt are treated explicitly within Rabbinic texts as events of legal or theological significance. Rabbinic Judaism's overarching theological precepts, rather, are completely familiar from and in line with past Israelite responses to the vicissitudes of history. Neusner describes the shared theological response of the prophets to the destruction of the First Temple and of the rabbis to the destruction of the Second Temple and failed Bar Kokhba Revolt as follows:[30]

> That theology posed the choice: keep the Torah and prosper, rebel against the Torah, which embodies the covenant, and face God's wrath. A single embodiment of the thesis offered here suffices. Had Jeremiah witnessed Yohanan ben Zakkai's response to the siege of Jerusalem, he would have found in the Rabbinic sage a kindred soul – and so throughout. To state matters more historically: the figure of Yohanan ben Zakkai is shaped in the model of Jeremiah. Rabbinic Judaism formed its response to the disasters of the age, 70 and 132-135, out of the paramount theology of Scripture and should be characterized as *prophetic-Rabbinic* Judaism, the necessary continuation of Scripture's paramount system. The negative side of that affirmative proposition is, the destruction of the Second Temple merely reinforced the received theological system, and the defeat of Bar Kokhba formed a footnote to an ancient theological text.

Neusner's conclusion emerges from his careful study of all the Rabbinic texts that reflect upon the destructions of the First and Second Temples and the Bar Kokhba Revolt. And his result puts into perspective any attempt, such as is reviewed here, to argue that, in Neusner's words, "the catastrophe of 70 brought about a revolution in the symbolic system and mythic construction – the law and theology – constituted by Rabbinic Judaism." For Neusner finds, to the contrary, that "the Rabbinic response to 70 and 132-135 represents a close recapitulation of the prophetic response to 586. Concomitantly, nothing that characterized Rabbinic Judaism after 70 requires us to form an explanation based solely on the destruction of the Second Temple in particular" (290). Neusner develops his argument as follows:

---

[30] *How Important Was the Destruction of the Second Temple in the Formation of Rabbinic Judaism* (Lanham, 2006, xxiii).

> What might we have anticipated had 70 denoted a decisive turning? An obvious candidate is an account of the life and affairs of the synagogue, supposedly the surrogate for the ruined Temple, its rites replacing, for the interim, the altar's offerings. For one striking instance, the Halakhah in the Mishnah's category-formations never provides for rites to replace those of the Temple during the interim of the Temple's ruin. Prayer is supposed to be the surrogate, but that is a generic judgment, not made specifically in the context of a particular prayer corresponding to a particular offering. True, the canon contains sayings that the study of the laws of sacrifice yields the same result as if one had actually made the offering. But when it comes to practice, these allegations yield nothing. Study of the Torah is not characterized by any Halakhic category-formation as the substitution for the Temple offerings (295).

Neusner thus argues that the Mishnah's concentration on Temple and priesthood proves that, for its authorship, the Temple's destruction was not a theological or even social turning point. Had the Temple's destruction entered the Rabbinic system as a significant event, the rabbis would have per force needed to cease focusing upon it, its cult, and its rules They would have needed to turn instead to exactly those topics that are almost completely absent from the Mishnah as it stands before us, to the institutions and rituals that would demarcate post-destruction Judaism, the synagogue and its liturgy.

Neusner's evaluation highlights the explanatory power of an approach to the Mishnah that details the ways in which its authors took up and recapitulated approaches to Judaic theology and social construction that were deeply embedded in Israelite history, approaches that shaped the rabbis' own cognitive world. And yet, we should be clear, if, in the overall theology they presented the rabbis simply reiterated what prophetic Judaism had long asserted, in the specifics of how they articulated that message, they expressed interests and ideals that were uniquely their own. The question that the historical-functional approach attempts to answer therefore remains. For, some two generations beyond the Bar Kokhba revolt, the Mishnah's framers made the rather improbable decision to focus on Temple and priesthood rather than upon synagogue and liturgy. This decision is as notable a choice as was their determination, in the Division of Agriculture, to legislate specifically on the farmer's role in the system of tithes, to focus upon intention in the determination of culpability, and to omit reference to the actual payment of agricultural gifts to priests and Levites.

This means that, alongside the rabbis' firm location within the cognitive world of biblical Judaism, we find conscious and distinctive choices that they made, choices to focus upon one aspect of the law and not another, and choices to take a position vis à vis the law that would change over the course of their own legal deliberations. We can, through reference to the Judaism out of which they emerged, understand much about the rabbis' legal interests and theological ideologies. And, yet, recourse to the cognitive world of ancient Judaism leaves open the ultimate question of how that inherited ideology found particular meaning and focus within the specifics of Rabbinic law and within the actual society that in the third century received that law.

5. Conclusion: Law and the Cognitive World of the Rabbis

The Mishnah reflects the cognitive world of ancient Israelite thinking that was shaped in response to the destruction of the First Temple in 586 BCE. This means that the first and primary step in comprehending the Mishnah is to place its message within the rabbis' own theological and legal context, to understand the rabbis' interests and laws as playing out themes that emerged through their reflection upon texts and ideas they understood as divine and that continued to speak to their own contemporary circumstance in the aftermath of the destruction of the Second Temple and the failed Bar Kokhba revolt.

And, yet, the Mishnah's framers took up and re-articulated Scripture's theology through modes of thinking and literary expression that were uniquely theirs. They made choices of what specifically to talk about within the larger topics controlled by Scripture and, over time, they elected what legal theories they would express through those topics. These choices reveal the extent to which the rabbis operated in a world the boundaries of which were much broader than those demarcated by the inherited biblical legacy. This means that, even as they worked within the cognitive world shaped by that legacy, their thinking was informed by other forces as well. The cognitive-developmental approach provides a foundation for comprehending the thought world out of which Rabbinic Judaism emerged. But the historical-functional approach, while epistemologically weaker, offers the historian an opportunity to get at the specifics of the decisions and choices that expressed the rabbis' distinctive ingenuity, the choices through which they created a system of thinking that re-articulated the inherited Judaism in ways that allowed it to continue to have meaning and power within the much changed world within which they and their descendants would live.

8

Archaeology and History: What Archaeology Can Show about Ethnic and Religious Regions in Ancient Galilee

Mordechai Aviam (with William Scott Green)

Archaeology is the study of excavated material from the past. Its objects are uncovered or unearthed, rather than preserved and restored for transmission by and reception from one generation to another. Archaeology is indispensable to history. The range of items discovered by archaeology is extensive. It includes texts, inscriptions, monuments, lamps, coins, buildings and their elements, tools, utensils, weapons, clothing, and works of art and crafts.

The credibility and probity of archaeology depends less on what is found than on how it is found. In fieldwork, method and discipline are everything. Careless or crude excavating, sloppy recording of data, imprecise or inconsistent measurement, and comparable flaws undermine the quality of the evidence. The field is not different from a laboratory, and fieldwork discipline is as important as laboratory procedure.

Archaeology is both comparative and multidisciplinary. The results of a single site acquire significance as they are placed in the context of other sites from the same time, place, and culture. Thus, an archaeological survey can be an effective tool to discover and analyze ancient cultures and their remains. Archaeology is arguably the most comprehensive of the humanities. The full description of its material discoveries necessarily draws on many fields of learning, particularly biology, geology, geography, architecture, hydrology, and engineering, to say nothing of expertise in transmitted ancient texts.

Because the findings of archaeology are uncovered and discovered, scholars may regard them as "innocent" evidence, more neutral than texts handed on and received. To some degree, this is a reasonable assumption. In particular, the non-textual remains of ancient cultures studied by archaeologists can help determine such components of those societies as, for example: estimates of population, economic status, intercultural relationships, domestic living conditions, and architectural styles. The relationship between the world the ancients wrote about and the world they left behind is an important datum in the writing of history.

The goal of this article is to illustrate the general observations above with a set of concrete materials from ancient Galilee. Its aim is to demonstrate how material remains from ancient Galilee can help us identify and define the geographical boundaries between various ethnic and religious groups. This kind of work is gaining ground in the world of archaeology and history (Meyers, 1993; Chancey). Many archaeological finds from ancient Galilee were common to both Jews and non-Jews: types of common pottery, coins, types of tombs, clay and stone sarcophagi, working and agricultural tools, etc. However, there also are some types of finds that indicate a very sharp line of division between ethnic and religious regions or zones. A distribution map of quantities of Nabatean pottery in the south of Israel and Jordan, for instance, can indicate centers of the Nabatean ethnos as well as the scope of Nabatean influence.

This article maps the locations of archaeological finds from the Hellenistic, Roman, and Byzantine periods and illustrates how the distribution of the finds can help identify their place of origin and thereby define ethnic and religion zones in ancient Galilee.

The article also compares the distribution of the archaeological data with the claims of and references in the writings of Josephus and rabbinic sources. The discussion of each artifact is accompanied by a distribution map. The conclusion of the article attempts to correlate the maps with the claims of key texts and offers a brief case study of how this method can help in the writing of history.

Galilean Coarse Ware

Frankel *et al.* (61-62) and I (Aviam: 46) have discussed the identification of a type of pottery, which I named Galilean Coarse Ware (GCW), as a type of clay vessel produced in the Hellenistic Galilee by the local pagan population. This identification was based at the beginning on survey finds only (pottery, coins and figurines from Beer Sheba of the Galilee) and later was reinforced by the important excavation at the temple of Mizpe HaYamim as well as those at Yodefat (Adan-Bayewitz and Aviam), Qedesh (Herbert and Berlin), Kh. esh-Shuhara (Aviam and Amitai) and Qeren Naftali (Aviam: 59-88). The distribution of this type of pottery, which is associated with non-Jews, mainly in Upper Galilee and its edges in northern Lower Galilee, suggests that the Jewish area of Galilee, before the Hasmoneans, was in the southern Lower region, since it has revealed no presence of GCW. This geographic distinction also is reflected, or at least suggested, in the books of Maccabees, Judith, and the writings of Flavius Josephus. Some of the GCW sites were completely abandoned at the end of the second century BCE, probably as a result of the Hasmonean conquest. Other sites continued to exist, but without GCW and, as we shall see, with the addition of Hasmonean coins.

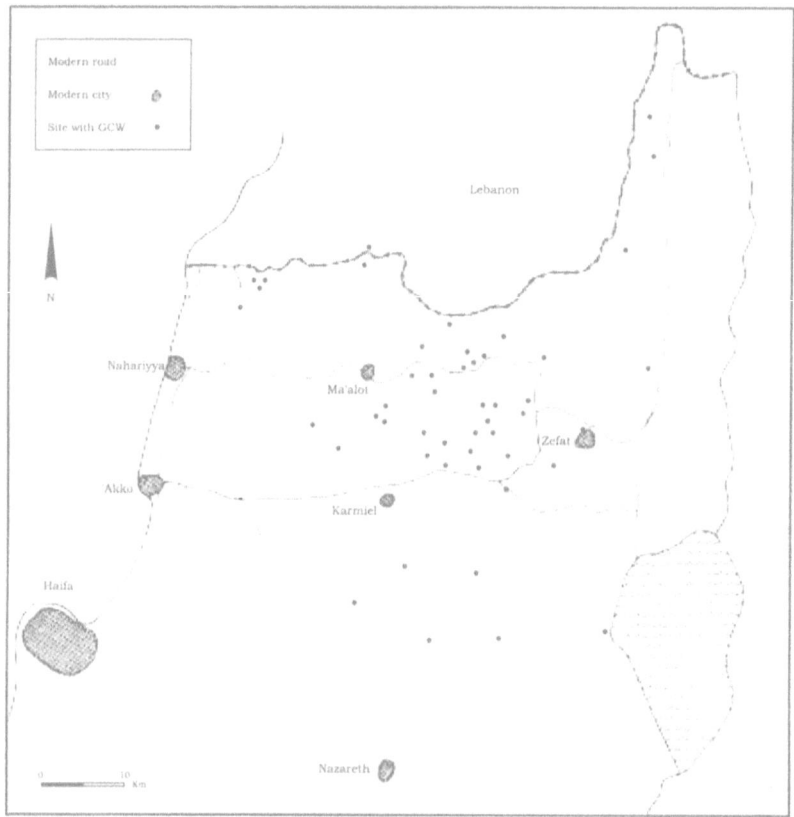

Map 1. Distribution of GCW sites

Hasmonean Coins

An analysis of the distribution of Hasmonean coins (based on Syon) shows a very clear picture. Western Upper and Lower Galilee have a very small amount of Hasmonean coins. Out of the thousand coins from second-century BCE Akko, for instance, only a few are Jewish.

The Hasmonean coins form the majority in some fortresses surrounding Akko, such as sites no. 78 (Tefen fortress) and 120 (Rushemiya fortress). Sites nos. 52, 54, 87, 88, 104, Yodefat no. 123, and some others were once sites with GCW.

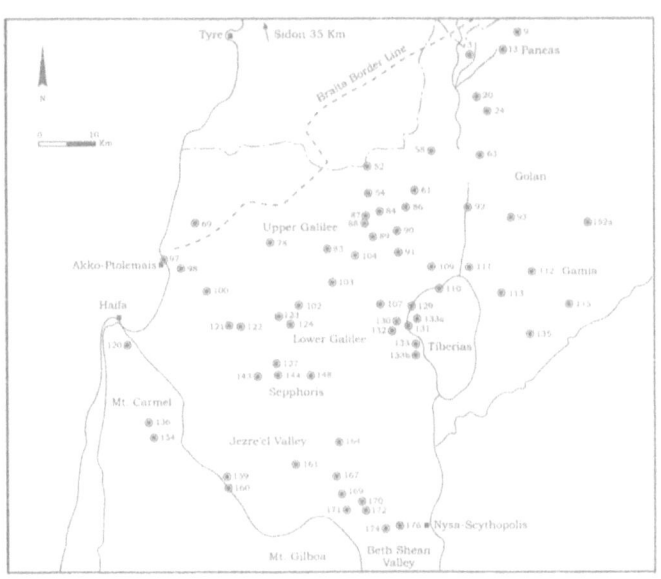

3 – Hagoshrim	89 – Sammuiya	115 – Hispin	144 – Sepporis
9 – H. Snaaim	*90 – Zefat	120 – Rusmiya	148 – Kafr Canna
13 – Paneas	91 – Akhbara	121 – Ibilin	152a – Golan (Hoard)
20 – Tel Anafa	92 – Ateret	122 – Tel Mador	154 – Umm El Zinat
24 – Tel Yardinon	93 – Qasrin	123 – Yodefat	159 – Meggido
52 – Kh. El Shuhara	97 – Akko-ptolemais	124 – H. Qana	160 – Legio
*54 – Gush Halav	98 – En Hamifraz	127 – Shihin	161 – Merhavya
58 – Qeren Naftali	100 – Tel Keisan	129 – Ginosar (Boat)	164 – H. Zafzafot
61 – Merot	103 – H. Zalmon	130 – Aebel Caves	167 – Givat Boler
63 – Darbashiya	104 – H. Beer Sheva	132 – Arbel	169 – Givat Qumi
69 – Kh. Muslim	107 – Huquq	133 – Tiberias	170 – Shatta
78 – H. Tefen	109 – Korazim	133a– kinneret (Hoard)	171 – Tel Slawim
83 – Rama	110 – Kepernahum	133b– bet Maon	172 – H. Shamot
84 – H. Qiyyuma	111 – Besaida	135 – El Al	174 – Tel Basul
87 – Meron	*112 – Gamla	136 – Sumaqa	176 – Hanot Bet Shean
88 – H. Shema	113 – H. Kanaf	143 – H. Shimshit	

Map 2. Hasmonean Coins (according to Syon 2004) and the "Baraita of the Boundaries" Border Line

Miqva'ot

Most scholars agree today that the plastered, stepped, installations, in different sizes but of similar shape, are ritual baths (Meyers, 2000). This type of installation was found only in Jewish sites that date from the Hasmonean to the late Byzantine period. They are rare in the north during the Hasmonean period and so far have been found only in three sites, since only a few Hasmonean layers have been uncovered in the Galilee: Qeren Naftali (Aviam: 69-70), Sepphoris [see short description and bibliography in Chancey: 71] and Gamla [Gutman, 1993: 463; 1994: 118-119). During the Roman period, the appearance of *miqva'ot* increases significantly; it decreases again in the Byzantine period. The distribution map of *miqva'ot* in the Galilee shows that they entirely cover areas identified in other sources as Jewish.

Map 3. *Miqva'ot* (Hellenistic to Byzantine Periods)

Stone Vessels

There is virtually no scholarly doubt about the correlation of chalk vessels with Jewish communities. Magen's monumental book supplies a comprehensive picture. More evidence on Jewish stone vessels in Galilee has emerged since: for instance, the discovery of a workshop cave between Reina and Nazareth, excavated by D. Amit,[1] and Shaked's

---

[1] I am grateful for his permission to use this information here.

survey in the Hulla Valley (Shaked and Avshalom-Gorni). More than twenty-five sites have yielded stone vessels. Most of the types are known from Judea, but there are probably some "Galilean" types as well.

Map 4. Distribution of Stone Vessels

Synagogues and Pagan Temples

There is no doubt at this point that synagogues are the best indication of a Jewish community. The Galilee has more ancient synagogue remains than any other area in Israel. There are approximately eighty sites with evidence of synagogues, and roughly 20 of them have been completely or partially excavated. The earliest sites date to the second and third centuries CE (Gamla, in the Golan, is dated to the first century CE), and some of them survived to the Early Arab period. After a century of field survey and research, the area of distribution of the synagogues in the Upper Galilee is clear. It stretches from Yisod HaMa'ala in the east to Sasa in the west, and it extends from Baqa (Peqi'in) in the northwest to Rama in the south. In the Lower Galilee, the territory widens from Tiveon and Bet She'arim in the west down to Bet Alfa in the Jezreel Valley and along the Sea of Galilee in the east.

The distribution of pagan temples – Jabel Bilat, ed-Duweir, Qedesh, Qeren Naftali, Omrit, Paneas, and Hippos – is a mirror image of the distribution of synagogues and demonstrates little geographical overlap in Galilee between Jewish and pagan religious institutions.

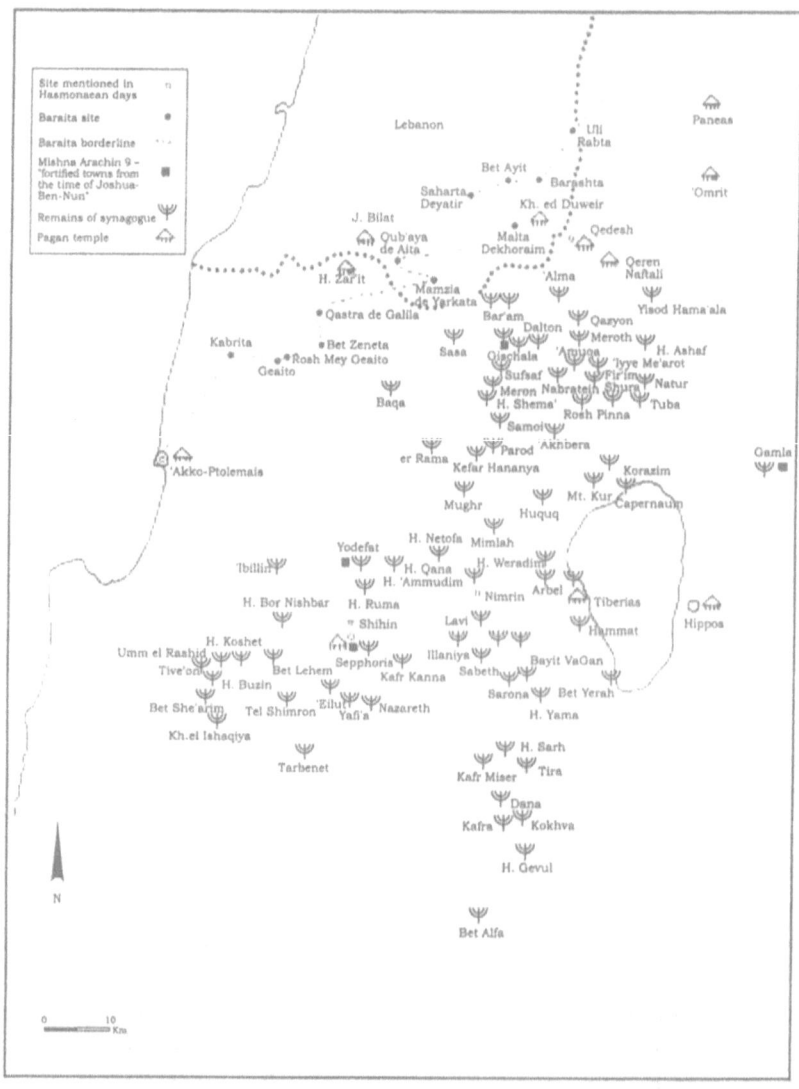

Map 5. Pagan Temples and Synagogues

Christian Churches and Monasteries

In the Byzantine period, the Upper Galilee continued to display the same distribution pattern between Jewish and non-Jewish religious institutions, but Christian churches took over the sites of pagan temples. In a century of surveys and excavations, no church has been identified in eastern Upper Galilee. The most southerly church remains are those of a small monastery at Kh. Battia, north of Yesod HaMa'ala, excavated by H. Abu Uqsa.

The situation in Lower Galilee is completely different. Churches and monasteries were erected near, around, and sometimes within Jewish villages, such as the sites of Rama, Capernaum, and Nazareth. This is probably the result of the Christian sanctification of some sites and regions in Lower Galilee – such as Kefar Cana, Mt. Tabor, Nazareth, and the Sea of Galilee – which became not only places of worship but also important pilgrimage destinations.

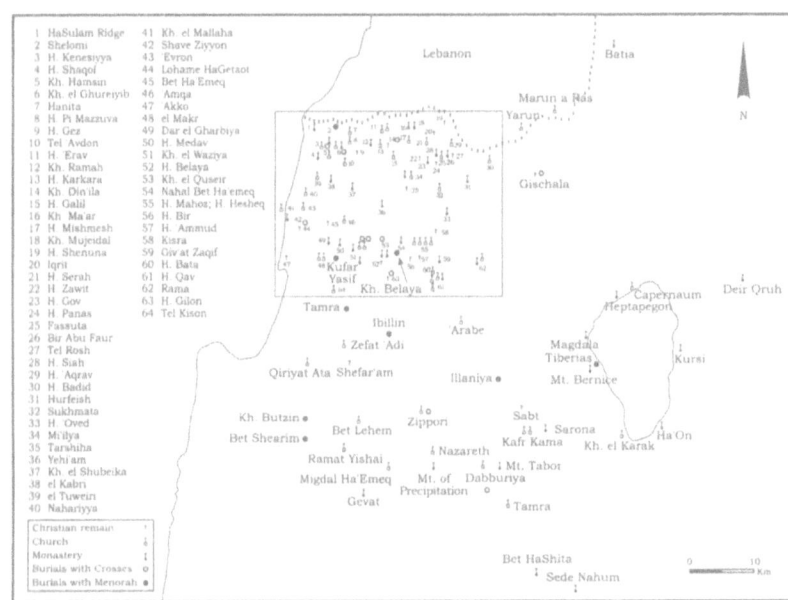

Map 6. Churches and Monasteries. Tombs with Crosses and Tombs with Menorahs

Clay Vessels

In the field of pottery, one of the best demonstrations of the importance of distribution maps is the comparison between two types of vessels in Upper Galilee (already discussed by Frankel *et al.*). The first is the so called "Kefar Hananya"1 C-E type, known in the past years as the "Galilean bowl". As it was produced at Kefar Hananya, and perhaps in other Jewish villages as well, it was commonly used by Jews, probably for religious or nationalist reasons. The second is the "Roman Phoenician" jar, which was mainly used by the non-Jewish population in the western Galilee. They were both current in the second to third centuries CE. The map supplies an excellent illustration of the "mirror image" of distribution that was evident above. The regional boundary line is the same as in the former examples. The distribution pattern demonstrates the phenomenon of Jewish religious avoidance of certain types of pottery (Ariel and Strikovsky).

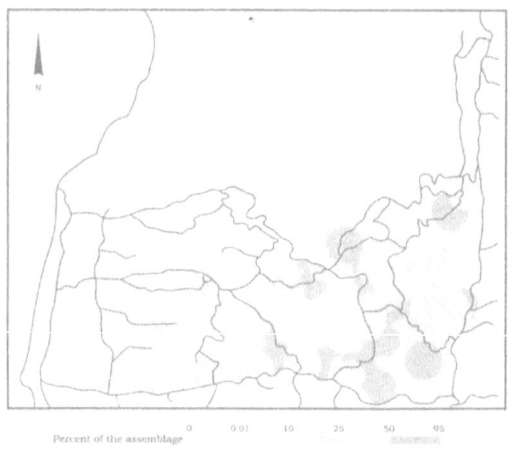

"Kfar Hananya Type 1B" – Roman Period

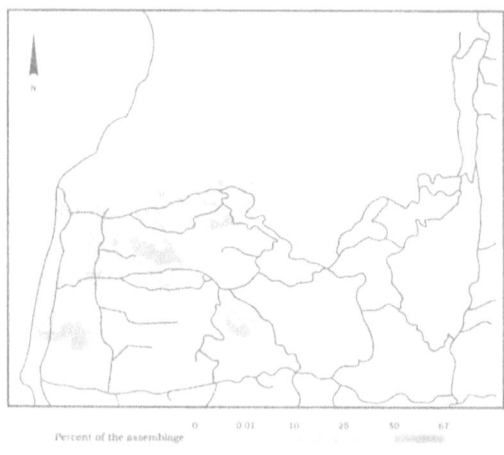

"Phoenician" Jar – Roman Period

Map 7. Distribution of Clay Pottery in Upper Galilee
(according to Frankel, Getzov, Aviam and Degani, 2001)

Statuary

Other archaeological items that can clearly illustrate ethnic and cultural differences are the remains of statuary. A large group of Roman pagan statues was excavated and published at Paneas (Friedland), and a few statues and fragments were found at the nearby temple of Omrit[2] and Dan (Biran). Bases for statues and other fragments were found at Hippos (Segal *et al.* 2003, 2004), Akko, Qedesh (Fischer, Ovadiah, and Roll), Shave Ziyyon, Gabae (Issac), Hamat Gader (Ben Arieh), and Dor (Stewart). These sites encircle the Galilee in a large ring.

Map 8. Human Statuary

Ossuaries

Secondary burial in ossuaries is widely recognized as a typical Jewish burial custom. Our research on Galilean ossilegium described about thirty sites with ossuaries (Aviam and Syon). It seems likely that this custom did not reach the Galilee before mid-second century CE be-

---

[2] I am grateful to A. Overman for sharing this information with me.

cause no "clean" first-century Jewish tomb with ossuaries has ever been found there. The ossuaries in the Galilee differ from those of Jerusalem and Judea in the first century CE. They are much cruder, mostly not decorated, and there is a group of clay – as opposed to stone – ossuaries. The distribution is very clear and matches the other data surveyed above.

Map 9. "Non-Figurative" Jewish Sarcophagi and Ossuaries

Secret Hideaways

Kloner and Tepper have studied the appearance of secret hideaways in Judea and suggest that they are primarily associated with the Second Revolt. Dating issues aside, it is clear that the hideaways are limited to Jewish sites. In my recent study in the Galilee, I surveyed twenty-two sites where such complexes were identified (Aviam: 123-132). Their distribution is similar to the other Jewish remnants mentioned above.

Map 10. Secret Hideaways

Correlating Text and Artifact on the Borders of Ancient Galilee

We have reviewed ten different sets of archaeological remains and their distribution in ancient Galilee. How do the distributions of these remnants correlate with textual descriptions of Galilee's borders in rabbinic sources and Josephus? A comparison of these the artifactual and textual data demonstrates one way in which archaeology can assist in the writing of history.

Rabbinic Descriptions of Borders

Let us turn first to what is perhaps the classic rabbinic statement on the borders of ancient Galilee, the so-called "baraita of the boundaries," Tosefta *Shevi'it* 4:11. It reads in part:

> The region of the Land of Israel [includes the following areas]:
> The crossing of Ashkelon, the Tower of Sher, the Cliff of Dor, the fortification wall of Caesarea and the fortification wall of Acco, the source of

the waters of Gaton, Gaton itself, and Kabritha, and Kaznita, Fort of the Galilee, Hollows of Aitha, Fort of Khur and Great Khuray, Tanfnith, S'nofta, the cave region of Yattir, Memtsi of Abhata, and the source of the waters of Marhesheth, and the river of Yiftsael and 'Ulshatha, Avlas, and the Tower of Harub, the Hollow of 'Iyon, Mesha, Tukrath, the towns of Bar Sannigora, Tarnegola above Caesarea, Kenath, Petra, Trachona in the area of Bozrah, Yegar Sahadutha, Nimrin, Melah of Zarvai, Yubka, Heshbon, and the brook of Zered, Raphia, Hungra, Ammon, Moab, and Rekam Geah, and the Gardens of Ashkelon, and the great road that leads to the desert (trans. Newman).

This text is the earliest description of "ethnic" borderline in Galilee because it marks the largest Galilean territory that is mentioned in any source as Jewish. Moreover, the sites it mentions in Galilee correlate with the distribution of Hasmonean coins (Map 2), *Miqva'ot* (Map 3), and the fortress of Qeren Naftali (see below). They also reflect the boundary between Jewish and pagan regions suggested by the distribution of synagogues and pagan temples in Map 4.

A second text that describes boundaries in Galilee occurs at Mishnah *'Arakhin* 9:6. It reads:

And what is a *dwelling house in a walled city* (Lev 25:29)?
A city in which there are not less than three courtyards, each with two houses, surrounded by a wall from the time of Joshua ben Nun, such as the old castle of Sepphoris, the fortress of Gush-Halav, old Yodefat, Gamla, Gedor, Hadid, Ono, Jerusalem, and the like (trans. Neusner, 823).

This text lists the "Accra" or fortress of Gush-Halav in Upper Galilee, "old" Yodefat and the "Qastra" or castle of Sepphoris in Lower Galilee, as well as Gamla in the Golan. Following Richard Horsley (26), I suggest identifying these sites as Hasmonean strongholds in the region newly conquered by the Hasmoneans. Although there are only four places mentioned, they are in central Lower Galilee, eastern Upper Galilee and the Golan.

Josephus's Description of Borders
In the latter half of the first century CE, Josephus described the borders of Jewish Galilee in his account of the war with Rome. His borders are narrower than those given in Tosefta *Shevi'it* 4:11. The size of the region of Galilee controlled by Jews diminished in the late first half of the first century CE, probably after the exile of Herod Antipas. Josephus's detailed description of the border supplies exact points, on the ground, that demarcate the Jewish region: from Thella in the

northeast to Baca in the northwest, from Khabul in the west to Tiberias in the east, and as far south as Xaloth. Around them are

> the Carmel, a mountain once belonging to Galilee and now to Tyre ... Gaba, the city of cavalry ... on the south the country is bounded by Samaria and the territory of Scythopolis ... on the east the territory of Hyppos, Gadara ... on the north Tyre and its dependent ... the village of Baca, the frontier of Tyrian territory (*War* 3, 35-40).

Map 11. Fortified settlements from the time of Joshua Ben-Nun (*m. Arakhin* 92)

Josephus classifies the Tyrians and the residents of all the other cities as "foreign nations," that is, as peoples living on the other side of the border. Another border line is created by Josephus's list of fortified sites (*War* 2, 572-576); it includes the entire Lower Galilee and eastern Upper Galilee.

Map 12. Josephus's Fortifications and Border Settlements

There are two other pieces of textual evidence that correlate with the material evidence displayed on the distribution maps: the priestly courses and the home villages of rabbis.

Priestly Courses
The ethnic zones of Josephus also are reflected in the list of twenty-four priestly courses that is known both from the Jewish sources, especially the *piyyutim,* and from archaeological finds, such as fragments of inscriptions from Caesarea and Nazareth and a complete one from Yemen. According to rabbinic tradition, the priestly groups that fled from Jerusalem settled in Galilean villages; their names and locations are preserved in some hymns (Safrai: 261-264). All of these villages are within Josephus's borders.

Map 13. Priestly Courses in Galilean Villages

Rabbinic Home Villages

The distribution map of the home villages of rabbis cited in the rabbinic literature offers a superb example of congruence between the textual and artifactual records of ancient Galilee. To be sure, there were rabbis who lived and taught in non-Jewish cities, such as Akko-Ptolemais or Akhziv, but all the other villages mentioned in rabbinic sources fall within the borders of Jewish Galilee. Indeed, there is a complete overlap between the two sets of data. The rabbinic home villages, Josephus's list of settlements and fortifications, and the priestly courses, occupy the same regions in which synagogues, *miqva'ot*, stone vessels, secret hideaways, and ossuaries were found.

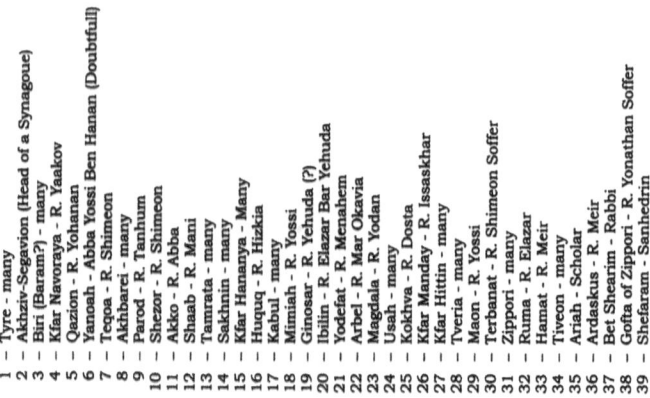

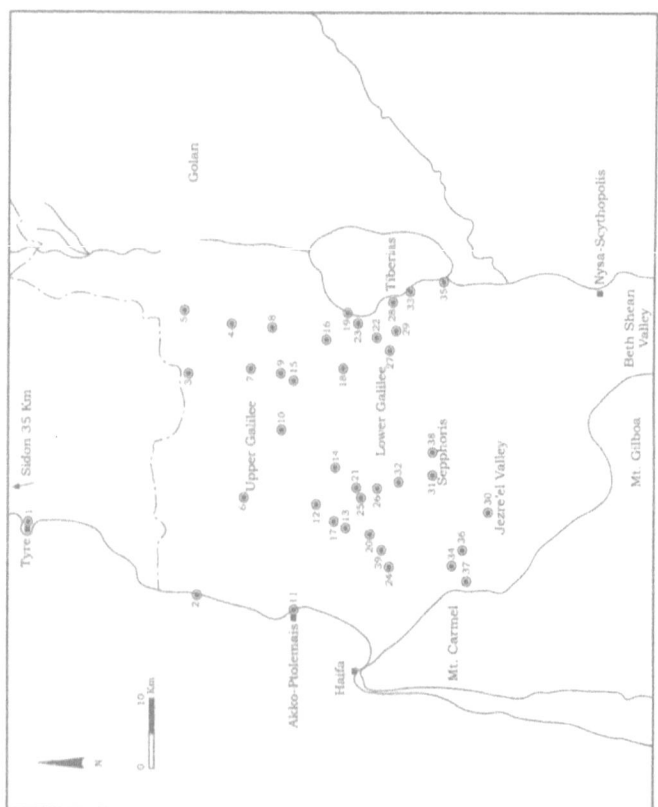

Map 14. Rabbinic Home Villages

Archaeology and History: The Case of Qeren Naftali

An excellent case study that combines archaeological evidence and literary sources is the survey and the excavations at the fortress of Qeren Naftali (Aviam: 59-88). The site is located just south of the suggested border line of the "baraita of the boundaries," in northern Upper Galilee. The survey and excavations conducted at the site revealed a well-preserved fortress on a high peak above the Hula Valley, above the main road. The site controls the largest spring in the valley and is in eye contact with Qedesh, the local administration center of Southern Phoenicia in the Hellenistic period (Herbert and Berlin). In its first stage, Qeren Naftali was a Hellenistic fortress, and it probably belonged to the local authorities of Tyre and its branch at Qedesh. At the end of the second century BCE, the fortress was conquered by the Hasmoneans. The Hasmonean coins found at the site, and the large, typically Hasmonean *miqve* that was planted inside the basement of an earlier Hellenistic room, justify this suggestion. In the next stage of the life of the place, the *miqve* went out of use. It was filled with ashes that included a substantial amount of Eastern Terra Sigillata pottery – which is rare in Jewish settlements in the Galilee – figurative oil lamps, and animal bones that included non-kosher and hunted species. The date of the fill is the second half of the first century BCE. On the basis of these facts, together with the remains of circumvolution wall that surrounds the fortress and the suggested siege camps on the saddle to the west, I identify Qeren Naftali as a Hasmonean fortress that was besieged by the Herodian alien armies in Herod's campaign against the Galilean and the Hasmonean garrisons in the Galilee in 38 BCE, as described by Josephus.

The fortress went out of use during the first century CE and was north of the Jewish Galilee according to the border description of Josephus. This is the likely reason it was not used in Josephus's fortification operation. In the second and third centuries CE, a pagan village that included a temple was built. This is reflected by two Greek inscriptions that were found there, as well as architectural fragment uncovered in our excavations.

The interpretation of the finds at Qeren Naftali requires many of the elements cited above to identify ethnicity and ethnic changes in the Galilee: a fortress with GCW shards; a Hasmonean, Jewish *miqve*; Hasmonean coins; Roman-pagan figurative oil lamps; pagan temple remains; and correlation with written records.

Conclusion

The method employed here can be used in any region for which there is both material and textual evidence. Human material culture, especially the elements that concern religion, can be surveyed and mapped, and the results will yield borders and zones. The Galilee from the end of the second century BCE to the fourth century CE was populated mainly by Jewish villages, towns and cities. The Jews constituted the majority well into the Byzantine period, although there was a growing number of Christians in the two capitals of Galilee – Tiberias and Sepphoris as well as in new Christian villages and monasteries. The correlation of archaeological remains and textual testimony consistently points not only to a vast majority of Jews but also to a clear isolation of Jewish villages in the Jewish region and Gentile villages around it. On the basis of these facts, accurate history can be written.

Bibliography
Adan Bayewitz, D. and Aviam, M.
    1997   "Iotapata, Josephus, and the Siege of 67: Preliminary Report on the 1992-94 Seasons," *JRA* 10. 131-165.

Ariel, D.T. and Strikovsky, A.
    1990   Appendix, in D.T. Ariel (ed.). *Excavations at the City of David 1978-1985*. Vol. II. 25-28.

Aviam, M.
    2004   *Jews, Pagan and Christians in the Galilee*. Rochester.

Aviam M and Amitai A.
    2002   "Excavations at Khirbet esh-Shuhara." in Z. Gal (ed.) *Eretz Zafon*. Jerusalem. 119-133.

Aviam M. and Syon D.
    2002   "Jewish Ossilegium in Galilee," in V. Rutgers (ed.). *What Athens has to do with Jerusalem*. Leuven. 151-187.

Ben Arieh, R.
    1997   "The Marble Statues from Hammat Gader," in Y. Hirschfeld, *The Roman Baths of Hammat Gader*. Jerusalem. 456-462.

Biran, A.
    1992   *Dan*. Jerusalem. (Hebrew).

Chancey, M.A.
    2002   *The Myth of a Gentile Galilee*. Cambridge.

Fischer, M., Ovadiah, A. and Roll, I.
    1986-7   "The Epigraphic Finds from the Roman temple at Kedesh in the Upper Galilee," *Tel Aviv* 13-14. 60-66.

Frankel R., Getzov N., Aviam M. and Degani A.
    2001   *Settlement Dynamics and Regional Diversity in Ancient Upper Galilee*. (IAA Reports 14), Jerusalem.

Friedland, E.
    1999   "Graeco-Roman Sculpture in the Levant: the Marbles from the Sanctuary of Pan at Caesarea Philippi (Banias)", in J.H. Humphrey (ed.). *The Roman and Byzantine Near East*. Portsmouth and Rhode Island. 7-22.

Gutman, S.
  1993 "Gamla," in E. Stern (ed.). *The New Encyclopedia of Archaeological Excavations in the Holy Land.* Jerusalem. 459-463.
  1994 *Gamla – A City in Rebellion.* Tel Aviv.
Herbert, S.C. and Berlin, A.M.
  2003 "A New Administrative Center for Persian and Hellenistic Galilee: Preliminary Report of the University of Michigan/University of Minnesota Excavations at Kedesh," *BASOR* 329. 13-59.
Horsley, R.A.
  1996 *Archaeology, History and society in Galilee.* Valley Forge.
Issac, B.
  1988 "Two Greek Inscriptions from Tell Abu-Shusha." In B. Mazar (ed.) *Geva.* Jerusalem. 224-225. (Hebrew).
Kloner, A. and Tepper, Y.
  1987 *The Hiding Complexes in the Judean Shephelah.* Tel Aviv.
Magen, Y.
  2000 *The Stone Vessels Industry in the Second Temple Period.* Jerusalem.
Meyers, E.M.
  1993 "Identifying Religion and Ethnic Groups through Archaeology," in: A. Biran and J. Aviram (eds.). *Biblical Archaeology Today.* Jerusalem. 738-745.
  2000 "Yes, They Are" *BAR* 26:4. 46-49, 90.
Safrai, Z.
  1981 *The Galilee in the Time of Mishna and Talmud.* Maalot. (Hebrew).
Segal, A., Mlynarczyk, J., Burdajewicz, M. and Eisenberg, M.
  2003 *Hippos-Sussita.* Haifa.
Segal A., Mlynarczyk. J., Burdajewicz. M., Schuler. M., and Eisenberg M.
  2004 *Hippos-Sussita.* Haifa.
Shaked, I. and Avshalom-Gorni, D.
  2004 "Jewish Settlement in the Southern Hula Valley in the First Century CE," in D.R. Edwards (ed.). *Religion and Society in Roman Palestine.* New York and London. 28-36.
Stewart, A.
  1995 "Marble Sculpture," in E. Stern (ed.). *Excavations at Dor.* Vol. I B. Jerusalem. 457-459.
Syon, D.
  2004 "Tyre and Gamla," Ph.D. Dissertation. Hebrew University. Jerusalem.

9

In Search of Jesus: Issues of Character

Bruce Chilton

Summary

From the point of view of critical definition, Jesus is not a datum within the Gospels, but a point of departure for the communities that produced the Gospels. Part I, "Aim," shows how Jesus is a figure of critical history to the extent, and only to the extent, that he permits us to explain how these texts arose in their mutual relations. Part II, "A Generative Exegesis," argues in the case of the Eucharist that a definable practice, with its own initial senses, was introduced into fresh environments of people who in turn took up the practice as they understood it and produced their own meanings. The initial meaning therefore did not determine subsequent meanings. Part III, "Sources of Meaning," shows that we are presented in our principal sources (the Gospels of the New Testament and *Thomas*) with ways of seeing Jesus within the communities for which each document was intended. Identifying the view of Jesus each one takes, we can infer how Jesus must have acted to produce that view of him, together with the distinct views of him that pre-documentary sources take. Part IV, "Material and Social Contexts of Jesus," describes Jesus' environment within the context of Galilee, so that we can place him within the unfolding of the sources together with his unique religious vision. Part V, "The Kabbalah of Rabbi Jesus," specifies the content of that vision, so that Jesus emerges as a reading of all the available evidence that permits us to explain, in religious terms, the emergence of Christianity out of Second Temple Judaism.

I. Aim

Confusion has inhibited critical understanding of Jesus.

Within the study of the New Testament reference to Jesus is unavoidable; the effort of Neo-Orthodoxy to rely on the "Christ of faith" trumping "the historical Jesus" has failed.[1] The only decision to be made is how reference to Jesus is to be developed, not whether it can be avoided.

Since the Enlightenment it has been evident that the Jesus of the canonical texts is not identical with the Jesus of Christian doctrine, although some scholars still try to square history with the circle of faith.[2]

Familiarity with Judaism is rudimentary within New Testament research; some scholars still assert that any similarity with a Rabbinic institution must be attributed to Jesus, rather than his followers (who – it is supposed – were non-Judaic Hellenists[3]). Yet figures in history are generally of significance owing to their distinctiveness among their contemporaries. If Jesus were indistinguishable from other rabbis of his period, it seems unlikely he would be an object of study, much less of worship.

Still less defensibly, some scholars persist in assuming that any similarity between Jesus and Judaism must be a late import, ignoring the depth of the analogies between Judaic sources and Christian writings of all periods and all stages of their composition.[4] The teachers we call rabbis were masters (in varying degrees) of parable and exposition and judgment and ethics and purity and health and healing and other aspects of covenantal wisdom. It has long been commonplace in the field to acknowledge that the formalism of a rabbinate, including a concern for succession and a notion of a syllabus to be mastered by

---

[1] For discussion, see *Redeeming Time. The Wisdom of Ancient Jewish and Christian Festal Calendars* (Peabody: Hendrickson, 2002) 1-20. (For the purpose of this article, authorship is attributed to the present writer unless otherwise indicated.) As ever in scholarship, there are attempts to revive eclipsed fashions; see Luke Timothy Johnson, *Living Jesus. Learning the Heart of the Gospel* (San Francisco: HarperSanFrancisco, 1999).

[2] See L.E. Keck, *Who is Jesus? History in Perfect Tense*. Minneapolis: Fortress, 2001 and the review in *TJT* 19 (2003) 80-82; B.D. Chilton & C.A. Evans (eds.), *Studying the Historical Jesus. Evaluations of the State of Current Research* (NTTS 19; Leiden: Brill, 1994, repr. 1998).

[3] See G. Vermes, *Jesus in his Jewish Context* (Minneapolis: Fortress, 2003) and the review in *Int* 58.2 (2004) 210. For a survey of similar attempts and efforts to correct them, see "Jesus and Judaism," *New Blackfriars* (1982) 237-244 and "Jesus within Judaism," *Judaism in Late Antiquity. Part Two, Historical Syntheses* (HO 17; ed. J. Neusner; Leiden: Brill, 1995) 262-284.

[4] See J.D. Crossan, *The Historical Jesus: The Life of a Mediterranean Jewish Peasant* (Edinburgh: T. & T. Clark; San Francisco: HarperCollins, 1991). His book may be read as an extended attempt to construct a portrait of Jesus without reference to Judaism. "Jesus within Judaism" criticizes this approach.

disciples, only prevailed with the emergence of rabbis as the basis of systemic redefinition of Judaism in the period after 70 CE.[5]

It is therefore not surprising that there are analogies between the Gospels and Judaic literature, including literature of the Rabbinic period, and that Jesus is called "rabbi" more than any other name in the Gospels.[6] The dating of all the sources, and the relationships among the documents naturally needs to be taken into account, but the fact of comparable materials remains.

Comparison has been thwarted, however, by a positivist approach to literary sources that is in its way as crude as a positivist approach to Jesus. Attention has been limited to the issue of whether the Gospels borrow from Judaic literature. That limitation is further obscured by referring to this concern as a search for "parallels," although the very definition of parallel lines is that they do not meet at all. Our discipline's continuing affliction with obscurantist language reveals its difficulty in coming to terms with Judaism.

In fact, borrowings between Christianity and Judaism go both ways insofar as the written evidence attests.[7] Whether borrowings occur from document to document is usually not provable, since the proportion of writings that has survived is small, and the relationship of written sources to substantial interaction among teachers (Christian, Judaic, and others) is unknown. In any case, the adjudication between what is "borrowed" and what is "original" has proven susceptible to apologetics.

---

[5] Cf. H. Lapin, "Rabbi," *ABD* 5.600-602. As a matter of interest, we might note that the earlier article of P. Parker ("Rabbi, Rabbouni," *IDB* 4.3) comes to much the same conclusion. See also *A Galilean Rabbi and His Bible. Jesus' Use of the Interpreted Scripture of His Time* (Wilmington: Glazier, 1984) also published with the subtitle, *Jesus' Own Interpretation of Isaiah* (London: SPCK, 1984) 34-35; J.P. Meier, *A Marginal Jew: Rethinking the Historical Jesus* (ABRL 3; New York: Doubleday, 1991).

[6] See "Judaism," 398-405; "Rabbinic Traditions and Writings," 651-660; "Targums," 800-804; *Dictionary of Jesus and the Gospels* (ed. J.B. Green, S. McKnight & I.H. Howard; Downers Grove: InterVarsity, 1992); *Rabbi Jesus. An Intimate Biography* (New York: Doubleday, 2000); "Jesus, A Galilean Rabbi," *Who was Jesus? A Jewish-Christian Dialogue* (ed. P. Copan and C.A. Evans; Louisville: Westminster John Knox, 2001) 154-161.

[7] B.D. Chilton & P.R. Davies, "The Aqedah: A Revised Tradition History," *CBQ* 40 (1978) 514-546; B.D. Chilton, "Isaac and the Second Night: A Consideration," *Bib* 61 (1980) 78-88; "Irenaeus on Isaac," in: E.A. Livingstone (ed.), *Studia Patristica* XXIII (Oxford: Pergamon, 1982) 643-647; "John xii 34 and Targum Isaiah lii 13," *NT* 22 (1980) and *Targumic Approaches to the Gospels. Essays in the Mutual Definition of Judaism and Christianity* (Studies in Judaism; Lanham and London: University Press of America, 1986) 81-84.

What we can ascertain is that there are analogies between the Gospels and Judaic literature. These analogies might be matters of comparable thought or expression, of common cultural reference (for instance, to the Temple), of mutual exegesis (of Isaiah, say), or of joint usage of a tradition that links them (the proverbial truth that you are measured with the measure you measure with, for example).[8] However analogies are characterized, no finding for or against what is usually called the historicity of the Gospels can be buttressed by observing them, but the simple fact of a relationship with Judaic literature has been well established.

The Gospels refer back to Jesus as their source, but there is no "historical Jesus" in the sense of a person whose deeds and character are accessible by means of verifiable public evidence. Expectations of that positivist kind have been disappointed for more than a century, but for the most part history is no longer defined in that reductionist way in any case.[9]

Only the literarily historical Jesus is a fact of reading. We cannot understand the documents unless we identify the Jesus they believe they are referring to. That Jesus, of course, is an object of their belief. He becomes historical for us in the literary sense when we discover that we must suppose facts about Jesus (for example, his teaching of the kingdom with an eschatological meaning[10]) in order to explain the generation of a given text. *For that reason, Jesus is a figure of critical history to the extent, and only to the extent, that he permits us to explain how certain texts arose in their mutual relations and in their literary and cultural milieus.*

---

[8] See "Targumic Transmission and Dominical Tradition," *Gospel Perspectives* 1 (1980) 21-45; "A Comparative Study of Synoptic Development: The Dispute between Cain and Abel in the Palestinian Targums and the Beelzebul Controversy in the Gospels," *JBL* 101 (1982) 553-562; "Sennacherib: A Synoptic Relationship among Targumim of Isaiah," *Targumic Approaches to the Gospels*, 163-177 and *Society of Biblical Literature 1986 Seminar Papers* (ed. K.H. Richards; Atlanta: Scholars Press, 1986) 544-554; "Reference to the Targumim in the Exegesis of the New Testament," *Society of Biblical Literature: 1995 Seminar Papers* (ed. L.H. Lovering; Atlanta: Scholars, 1995) 77-82; "Four Types of Comparison between the Targumim and the New Testament," *JAB* 2 (2000) 163-188.

[9] See "Biblical Authority, Canonical Criticism, and Generative Exegesis," *The Quest for Context and Meaning. Studies in Biblical Intertextuality in Honor of James A. Sanders* (Biblical Interpretation Series 28; Leiden: Brill, 1997) 343-355. An exception of this general rule is the program of "The Jesus Seminar;" see *The Five Gospels. The Search for the Authentic Words of Jesus* (ed. R.W. Funk and R.W. Hoover; San Francisco: HarperSanFrancisco, 1993). The volume's dedication to Thomas Jefferson makes its Enlightenment perspective evident.

[10] See *Pure Kingdom. Jesus' Vision of God* (Studying the Historical Jesus 1; Grand Rapids: Eerdmans; and London: SPCK, 1996).

Literary comparison of the New Testament with other sources (Jewish, Hellenistic, Ugaritic, Egyptian, or Persian) by itself does not solve "the problem of the historical Jesus," but it can proceed in a way which does not exacerbate it, and which may be productive for further analysis. Finally, the "historical Jesus" is a variable in the overall equation of how the New Testament arose; for that reason, comparative study with other sources may be expected to provide that variable with more specific value than is possible in positivistic assertions about Jesus. That next stage of comparison, historical rather than literary, involves inference on the basis of the sources that refer to Jesus.

II. A Generative Exegesis

A generative exegesis maintains a particular focus among the many critical questions that arise in the course of reading. The issue of generation is: in association with what practices and in which communities did a text arise, so as to attest those practices, their emotional valences, and the meanings attributed to them? That issue is cognate with the task of sorting out the purposes, development, and dating of ancient Judaic literature, and the analogies offered can prove helpful.[11]

---

[11] See "Varieties and Tendencies of Midrash: Rabbinic Interpretations of Isaiah 24:23," *Gospel Perspectives* 3 (1983) 9-32; *The Glory of Israel. The Theology and Provenience of the Isaiah Targum:* JSOTS 23 (Sheffield: JSOT, 1982); *The Isaiah Targum. Introduction, Translation, Apparatus, and Notes* (AB 11; Wilmington: Glazier; and Edinburgh: T&T Clark, 1987); "Shebna, Eliakim, and the Promise to Peter," *The Social World of Formative Christianity and Judaism* (ed. J. Neusner, P. Borgen, E.S. Frerichs, R. Horsley; Philadelphia: Fortress, 1989) 311-326; "Commenting on the Old Testament (with particular reference to the pesharim, Philo, and the Mekhilta," *It is Written: Scripture Citing Scripture, Essays in Honour of Barnabas* Lindars (ed. D.A. Carson and H.G.M. Williamson; Cambridge: CUP (1988), 122-140; "Recent and Prospective Discussion of *bar enash,"* *From Ancient Israel to Modern Judaism: Intellect in Quest of Understanding. Essays in Honor of Marvin Fox:* Brown Judaic Studies 173 (ed. J. Neusner, E.S. Frerichs, N.S. Sarna; Atlanta: Scholars, 1989) 119-137; "A Coin of Three Realms: Matthew 17:24-27," *The Bible in Three Dimensions. Essays in Celebration of Forty Years of Biblical Studies in the University of Sheffield* (JSOTS 87; ed. D.J.A. Clines, S.E. Fowl & S.E. Porter; Sheffield: JSOT, 1990) 269-282; "[hos] phragellion ek skhoinion [John 2:15]," *Templum Amicitiae. Essays on the Second Temple presented to Ernst Bammel* (ed. W. Horbury; Sheffield: Sheffield Academic Press, 1991) 330-344; "The Son of Man: Human and Heavenly," *The Four Gospels: 1992. Festschrift Frans Neirynck* (ed. F. van Segbroeck, C.M. Tuckett, G. van Belle & J. Verheyden; BETL 100: Leuven, 1992) 203-218, also published in *Approaches to Ancient Judaism. Religious and Theological Studies* (South Florida Studies in the History of Judaism 81; ed. J. Neusner; Atlanta: Scholars, 1993) 97-114; "Typologies of Memra and the Fourth Gospel," *Targum*

In the case of the Eucharistic texts of the New Testament, the diversity of extant witnesses alerts us to the possibility that a variety of practices and communities might be reflected. The breadth and depth of the textual distribution invite us to take up the case of Eucharistic praxis here.

For over a decade, I have developed an account of the development of Eucharistic praxis within primitive Christianity, beginning with the contributions of Jesus as a conscious practitioner of Judaism. I engaged initially with the work of anthropologists of sacrifice, in order to assess Jesus' position in relation to the sacrificial cult in Jerusalem.[12] My prin-

---

Studies 1 (1992) 89-100; "Jesus and the Question of Anti-Semitism," *Anti-Semitism and Early Christianity. Issues of Polemic and Faith* (ed. C.A. Evans and D.A. Hagner; Minneapolis: Fortress, 1993) 39-52; "God as 'Father' in the Targumim, in Non-Canonical Literatures of Early Judaism and Primitive Christianity, and in Matthew," *The Pseudepigrapha and the Early Biblical Interpretation* (JSPSS 14; ed. J.H. Charlesworth and C.A. Evans; Sheffield: JSOT, 1993) 151-169; "Reference to the Targumim in the Exegesis of the New Testament"; "Salvific Exile in the Isaiah Targum," *Exile: Old Testament, Jewish, and Christian Conceptions* (JSJS 56; ed. J.M. Scott; Leiden: Brill, 1997) 239-247; "Two in One: Renderings of the Book of Isaiah in Targum Jonathan," *Writing and Reading the Scroll of Isaiah. Studies of an Interpretive Tradition 2* (VTS 70.2; ed. C.C. Broyles and C.A. Evans; Leiden: Brill, 1997) 547-562; "Prophecy in the Targumim," *Mediators of the Divine. Horizons of Prophecy, Divination, Dreams and Theurgy in Mediterranean Antiquity* (South Florida Studies in the History of Judaism 163; ed. R.M. Berchman; Atlanta: Scholars, 1998) 185-201; "The Brother of Jesus and the Interpretation of Scripture," *The Use of Sacred Books in the Ancient World* (ed. L.V. Rutgers. P.W. van der Horst, H.W. Havelaar, L. Teugels; Leuven: Peeters, 1998) 29-48; "Yochanan the Purifier and His Immersion," *TJT* 14.2 (1998) 197-212; "The Targumim and Judaism of the First Century," *Judaism in Late Antiquity. Part Three, Where We Stand: Issues and Debates in Ancient Judaism* (vol. II) (HO 41; ed. J. Neusner and A.J. Avery-Peck; Brill: Leiden, 1999) 15-150; "Jesus und die Frage des Antisemitismus," *Studien zu einer neutestamentlichen Hermeneutik nach Auschwitz* (SBAB.NT 27; ed. P. Fiedler and G. Dautenberg; Stuttgart, 1999) 31-52; "Temple Restored, Temple in Heaven: Isaiah and the Prophets in the Targumim," *Restoration. Old Testament, Jewish, and Christian Perspectives* (ed. J.M. Scott; Leiden: Brill, 2001) 335-362; "John the Purifier: His Immersion and his Death," *Teologiese Studies* 57.1-2 (2001) 247-267; "Theodicy in the Targumim," *Theodicy in the World of the Bible* (ed. A. Laato and J.C. de Moor; Leiden: Brill, 2003) 728-752.

[12] *The Temple of Jesus. His Sacrificial Program within a Cultural History of Sacrifice* (University Park: The Pennsylvania State University Press, 1992). See also "The Purity of the Kingdom as Conveyed in Jesus' Meals," *Society of Biblical Literature. 1992 Seminar Papers* (ed. E.H. Lovering; Atlanta: Scholars, 1992) 473-488; "A Generative Exegesis of Mark 7:1-23," *The Journal of Higher Criticism* 3.1 (1996) 18-37; "Jesus' Dispute in the Temple and the Origin of the Eucharist," *Dialogue* 29.4 (1996) 17-28; *Jesus in Context. Temple, Purity and Restoration* (AGAJU 39; with C.A. Evans; Leiden: Brill, 1997); "Jesus, Levitical Purity, and the Development of Primitive Christianity," *The*

cipal concern was to evaluate Jesus' attitudes toward and his actions within the Temple itself. But in the course of the work, I saw the direct connection between Jesus' last meals with his followers and his action in the Temple. The Eucharist emerged as a surrogate of sacrifice. Encouraged by several scholars, notably Bernhard Lang, I then undertook an exegetical study[13] in order to detail the evolution of the texts within the typical practices of the first Christians.

Here I wish briefly to explain the six types of Eucharist attested within the New Testament that I have identified on exegetical grounds. These types characterize the particular groups that produced them. The types attest fluidity in ritual acts, different constituent communities, and distinctive accounts of meaning. Even Jesus, on my reading, developed not one but two types of Eucharist during his life.

Six Types of Eucharist in the New Testament

The Mishnah, in an effort to conceive of a heinous defect on the part of a priest involved in slaughtering the red heifer, pictures him as intending to eat the flesh or drink the blood (*m. Para* 4:3). If Jesus' words are taken with their traditional, autobiographical meaning, his Last Supper can only be understood as a deliberate break from Judaism. Either Jesus himself promulgated a new religion, or his followers did so in his name, and invented "the Last Supper" themselves. Both those alternatives find adherents today among scholars, and the debate between those who see the Gospels as literally true reports and those who see them as literary fictions shows little sign of making progress. But in either case, the nagging question remains: if the generative act was indeed anti-sacrificial (whether that act was literal or literary), how did the cycles of traditions and the texts as they stand come to their present, sacrificial constructions?

The Gospels are composite products of the various social groups that were part of Jesus' movement. When we place Eucharistic practices within the social constituencies that made the Gospels into the

---

Book of Leviticus. Composition and Reception (VTS 93; ed. R. Rendtorff and R. Kugler, with S.S. Bartel; Leiden: Brill, 2003) 358-382.

[13] *A Feast of Meanings. Eucharistic Theologies from Jesus through Johannine Circles* (NovTS 72; Leiden: Brill, 1994). Lang himself has taken up my theory and extended it into an analysis of later practices and theologies in *Sacred Games. A History of Christian Worship* (New Haven: Yale University Press, 1997). Professor Lang and I have both contributed to the recent volume edited by A. Baumgarten, *Sacrifice in Religious Experience* (Numen Book Series 93; Leiden: Brill, 2002).

texts we can read today, we can understand the original meaning Jesus gave to the Last Supper, and how his meaning generated others.

The Last Supper was not the only supper, just the last one. In fact, "the Last Supper" would have had no meaning apart from Jesus' well-established custom of eating with people socially. There was nothing unusual about a rabbi making social eating an instrument of his instruction, and it was part of Jesus' method from the first days of his movement in Galilee.

Many sorts of meals are attested in the literature of early Judaism. From Qumran we learn of banquets at which the community convened in order of hierarchy; Pharisees took meals within fellowships at which like-minded fellows would share the foods and the company they considered pure. Ordinary households might welcome the coming of the Sabbath with a prayer of sanctification over a cup of wine, or open a family occasion with a blessing over bread and wine.

For Jesus, eating socially with others in Israel was an enacted parable of the feast in the kingdom that was to come. The idea that God would offer festivity for all peoples on his holy mountain (see Isa 2:2-4) was a key feature in the fervent expectations of Judaism during the first century, and Jesus shared that hope, as may be seen in a saying from the source of his teaching conventionally known as "Q" (see Matt 8:11 = Luke 13:28, 29[14]):

> Many shall come from east and west,
> and feast with Abraham, Isaac, and Jacob
> in the kingdom of God.

Eating was a way of enacting the kingdom of God, of practicing that rule. As a result, Jesus accepted as companions people such as tax agents and others of suspect purity, and received sinners at his meals. Meals for him were signs of the kingdom of God, and all the people of God, assuming they sought forgiveness, were to have access to them.

Jesus' practice coincided to some extent with the Pharisees', although his construal of purity was unusual. Given the prominence accorded wine in his meals,[15] we might describe the first type of his meals – the practice of purity in anticipation of the kingdom – as a

---

[14] Because my interest here is in the traditional form of the saying, prior to changes introduced in Matthew and Luke, I give a reconstructed form; see *God in Strength: Jesus' Announcement of the Kingdom* (SNTU 1; Freistadt: Plöchl, 1979; repr. Biblical Seminar 8; Sheffield: JSOT Press, 1987) 179-201; *Pure Kingdom*, 12-14.

[15] See the order of wine followed by bread in 1 Cor 10:16; Luke 22:19-20; *Did.* 9:1-5, and the particular significance accorded the wine in Mark 14:25; Matt 26:29; Luke 22:18.

meal of sanctification, a *kiddush* of the kingdom. Indeed, there is practically no meal of Judaism with which Jesus' meals do not offer some sort of analogy, because the meal was a seal and an occasion of purity, and Jesus was concerned with what was pure. Both the nature of his concern and the character of his meals were distinctive: Israel as forgiven and willing to provide of its own produce was for him the occasion of the kingdom. That was the first type in the development of the Eucharist.

Jesus also brought his teaching into the Temple, where he insisted on his own teaching of purity. The incident that reflects the resulting dispute is usually called the "Cleansing of the Temple" (Matt 21:12-13 = Mark 11:15-17 = Luke 19:45-46 = John 2:13-17). From the point of view of the authorities there, what Jesus was after was the opposite of purification. He objected to the presence of merchants who had been given permission to sell sacrificial animals in the vast, outer court of the Temple. His objection was based on his own view of purity, grounded in a commitment to realize prophetic predictions such as Zechariah 14: Israel should offer, not priest's produce for which they bartered, but sacrifices that they brought into the Temple. He and his followers drove the animals and the sellers out of the great court with the use of force.

Jesus could not simply be dispatched as a cultic criminal. He was not attempting an onslaught upon the Temple as such; his dispute with the authorities concerned purity within the Temple. Other rabbis of his period also engaged in physical demonstrations of the purity they required in the conduct of worship. One of them, for example, is said to have driven thousands of sheep into the Temple, so that people could offer sacrifice in the manner he approved of (see *b. Besah* 20a-b). Jesus' action was extreme, but not totally without precedent, even in the use of force.

The trigger of Jesus' arrest by the authorities of the Temple was not only his raid in the great court, but also the new meaning he imputed to his meals after that incident. He continued to celebrate meals as a foretaste of the kingdom, just as he had before. But his bid to change Temple praxis having failed, Jesus said of the wine, "This is my blood," and of the bread, "This is my flesh" (Matt 26:26, 28 = Mark 14:22, 24 = Luke 22:19-20 = 1 Cor 11:24-25 = Justin, *1 Apology* 66.3).

In Jesus' context, the context of his confrontation with the authorities of the Temple, his principal point was that, in the absence of a Temple that permitted his view of purity to be practiced, wine was his blood of sacrifice, and bread was his flesh of sacrifice. This meaning of "the Last Supper," then, actually evolved over a series of meals after Jesus' occupation of the Temple. During that period, Jesus claimed that wine and bread were a better sacrifice than what was offered in the Temple: at least wine and bread were Israel's own, not tokens of priestly dominance.

In essence, Jesus made his meals into a rival altar, and we may call such a reading of his words a ritual or cultic interpretation. This second type of Eucharist offered wine and bread as a mimetic surrogate of sacrifice. The cultic interpretation has two advantages over the traditional, autobiographical interpretation as the meaning Jesus attributed to his own final meals. The first advantage is contextual: the cultic interpretation places Jesus firmly within the Judaism of his period and the final dispute of his life, and at the same time accounts for the opposition of the authorities to him. The second advantage is the explanatory power of this reading: the cultic interpretation enables us to explain sequentially four subsequent developments in the understanding of Eucharist within earliest Christianity.

The third type is that of Petrine Christianity, when the blessing of bread at home, the *berakhah* of Judaism, became a principal model of Eucharist. A practical result of that development was that bread came to have precedence over wine, and Acts refers to the ritual as the "breaking" of bread (see Acts 2:42-47). The circle of Peter conceived of Jesus as a new Moses, who gave commands as Moses did on Sinai, and who also expected his followers to worship on Mount Zion in memory of the covenant.

As compared to Jesus' practice (in its first and second stages), Petrine practice represents a double domestication. Adherents of the movement congregated in the homes of their colleagues, rather than seeking the hospitality of others. Further, the validity of sacrifice in the Temple was acknowledged. Both forms of domestication grew out of the new circumstances of the movement in Jerusalem and fresh opportunities for worship in the Temple; they changed the nature of the meal and the memory of what Jesus had said at the "Last Supper" to include reference to the "covenant."

The fourth type of Eucharist, which I associate with the circle of James (the brother of Jesus), pursued the tendency of domestication further. The Eucharist was seen as a Seder, in terms of meaning and chronology (see Mark 14:12-16, and the contradictory timing indicated in vv. 1-2). So understood, only Jews in a state of purity could participate fully in Eucharist, which could be truly recollected only once a year, at Passover in Jerusalem among the circumcised (see Exod

12:48). The Quartodeciman controversy (concerning the timing of Easter) of a later period, fierce though it appears, was but a shadow cast by much a more serious contention concerning the nature of Christianity. The Jacobean program was to integrate Jesus' movement comprehensively within the liturgical institutions of Judaism, to insist upon the Judaic identity of the movement and upon Jerusalem as its governing center. Nonetheless the Jacobean "Last Supper" does not supplant the other types of Eucharist in the New Testament.

Paul and the Synoptic Gospels represent the fifth type of Eucharist. Paul vehemently resists Jacobean claims, by insisting Jesus' last meal occurred on the night in which he was betrayed (1 Cor 11:23), not on Passover. He emphasizes the link between Jesus' death and the Eucharist, and he accepts the Hellenistic refinement of the Petrine type that presented the Eucharist as a sacrifice for sin associated with the Temple (see e.g. Rom 3:25).

In the Synoptic Gospels the heroism of Jesus is such that the meal is an occasion to join in the solidarity of martyrdom.[16] The Synoptics insist by various wordings that Jesus' blood is shed in the interests of the communities for which those Gospels were composed, for the "many" in Damascus (Matt 26:28) and Rome (Mark 14:24), on behalf of "you" in Antioch (Luke 22:20). The Synoptic strategy is not to oppose the Jacobean program directly; in fact, the Passover chronology is incorporated (producing internal contradictions). But any limitation of the benefits of Eucharist to circumcised Israelites is superseded by the imperative to join Jesus' martyrdom and its sacrificial benefits.

The feeding of the five thousand – understood as occurring at Passover – is taken up in John 6 in a fully Paschal sense. Jesus identifies himself as the *manna*, miraculous food bestowed by God upon his people. Paul had articulated the motif (1 Cor 10:1-4, an analogy that trumps the claims of the Jacobean circle), but John develops it to construe the Eucharist as a Mystery,[17] in which Jesus offers his own flesh and blood (carefully defined to avoid a crude misunderstanding; John 6:30-58). That autobiographical reading of Jesus' words – as giving his personal body and blood in Eucharist – had no doubt already occurred to Hellenistic Christians who followed Synoptic practice and appreciated its sacrificial overtones.

---

[16] I would not deny that a sense of impending martyrdom suffused Jesus' last meals with his disciples; see *Rabbi Jesus*, 253-268. The elevation of that sense to the predominant meaning, however, appears to me a later development.

[17] See Dennis E. Smith, *From Symposium to Eucharist. The Banquet in the Early Christian World* (Minneapolis: Fortress, 2003) 78-79, 167-168.

The Johannine practice made that meaning as explicit as the break with Judaism is in the fourth Gospel. The sixth type of Eucharist can only be understood as a consciously non-Judaic and Hellenistic development. It involves participants in joining by oath (*sacramentum* in Latin, corresponding to *musterion* within the Greek vocabulary of primitive Christianity; John 6:60-71) in the sacrifice of the Mysterious hero himself, separating themselves from others. Eucharist has become sacramental, and involves a knowing conflict with the ordinary understanding of what Judaism might and might not include.[18]

"The Last Supper" is neither simply Jesus' "real" Seder nor simply a symposium of Hellenists to which the name of Jesus happens to have been attached. Such reductionist regimens, which will have the Gospels be only historical or only fictive, starve the reader of the meanings that generated the texts to hand. The engines of those meanings were diverse practices, whose discovery permits us to appreciate the richness of tradition. A generative exegesis of Eucharistic texts may not conclude with a single meaning that is alleged to have occasioned all the others. One of the principal findings of such an approach is rather that meaning itself is to some extent epiphenomenal, a consequence of a definable practice with its own initial sense being introduced into a fresh environment of people who in turn take up the practice as they understand it and produce their own meanings. The sense with which a practice is mediated to a community is therefore one measure of what that community will finally produce as its practice, but the initial meaning does not determine the final meaning.

Eucharist was not simply handed on as a static tradition. Eucharistic traditions were rather the catalyst that permitted communities to crystallize their own practices in oral or textual form. What they crystallized was a function of the practice that had been learned, palpable gestures with specified objects and previous meanings, along with the meanings and the emotional responses that the community discovered in Eucharist. There is no history of the tradition apart from a history of meaning, a history of affective response, a history of practice: the practical result of a generative exegesis of Eucharistic texts is that practice itself is an appropriate focus in understanding the New Testament.

---

[18] In this regard, see R. Bieringer, D. Pollefeyt, F. Vandecasteele-Vanneuville (eds.), *Anti-Judaism and the Fourth Gospel* (Deo; Louisville: Westminster John Knox, 2001), reviewed in *Shofar* 22.3 (2004) 150-152.

III. Sources of Meaning

A generative exegesis naturally focuses on issues of meaning, but the corollary concerns of cultural milieu and the agency of sources cannot be avoided. Consequently, circles of meaning have already been characterized: dominical, Petrine, Jacobean, Synoptic and Pauline, Johannine. By means of inference, it is possible to consider the periods in which their traditions emerged, how they interacted, and (in most cases) who the likely tradents were.

The Eucharistic teachings of Jesus did not, it goes almost without saying, exert a direct influence upon the text of the Gospels. They were already incorporated, and given a new meaning, within a cycle of narrative catechesis associated with Peter and his fellow "pillars." The Petrine cycle must have been available in Aramaic by c. 35 CE, in time for Paul to be informed of it at the time of his visit to Jerusalem (Gal 1:18). But the very name "Peter" attests early translation into Greek, in association with the wide field of activity that apostle ploughed. The Petrine cycle substantially included the initial call of the first disciples, the healing of Jairus's daughter, the confession at Caesarea Philippi, the Transfiguration, the Eucharist, and the struggle in Gethsemane. By design and in fact, the Petrine usage of narrative for the purpose of catechesis established a paradigm in the primitive Church; the Synoptic Gospels are a monument to that narrative strategy.

The purpose of the Petrine teaching of the Eucharist is indicated by the sense of "covenant" in Matt 26:28; Mark 14:24. "New covenant" in Luke 22:20; 1 Cor 11:25 represents a Hellenistic phase of the Petrine cycle. The reference to the covenant represents the meal as under the type of Moses' covenantal sacrifice of sharings (Exod 24), so that Jesus is accorded foundational importance, but any perception of competition with the Temple is avoided. Towards the same end, the "memorial" in Luke 22:19; 1 Cor 11:24, 25 links Jesus action to what is immolated on the altar for the purpose of a sacrifice such as Moses offered.

Passover became the principal association with Eucharist in the circle of James. However emphatic the association (Matt 26:17-20; Mark 14:12-17; Luke 22:7-14), it is also artificial (see Matt 26:1-5; Mark 14:1, 2; Luke 22:1, 2, 15, 16), an example of interpretation by addendum. In a stroke, the meal was more tightly linked to the liturgical year than it ever had been before, and its only possible occasion was in Jerusalem. The dominical and Petrine meals were repeatable anywhere and frequently. The Jacobean transformation of what is now a last Passover could only truly be enacted "between the evenings" of 14 and 15 Nisan, and in the vicinity of the Temple, where the paschal lambs were slain.

What was produced within James's circle was not an independent cycle, but substantial recastings of the Petrine cycle and the source of sayings known as "Q." Both the Petrine cycle and the Jacobean revision of that cycle were known in Antioch prior to the council in Jerusalem that took place c. 46 CE (see Gal 2). The Jacobean revision itself may be dated c. 40 CE, since it went through some development before Paul became acquainted with it in Antioch, although he was not apprised of it at the time of his visit with Peter c. 35 CE.

The source of Jesus' sayings known as "Q" has contributed little to the Eucharistic texts as they may be read today. But Jesus' wistful statement that he had greatly desired to eat the Passover (but could not), attested only in Luke 22:15-17, manifests no incorporation within the Jacobean program. In its earliest phase, "Q" was a collection of sayings in the nature of a mishnah which a rabbi's disciples might learn, virtually contemporaneous with the Petrine cycle. In the present case, the mishnaic source confirms that, prior to the Petrine cycle, Jesus was understood to refer to the wine before he referred to the bread. From its origins in Jesus' movement as instruction of the Twelve, the source known as "Q" developed in the environment of Syria in a markedly apocalyptic direction.

The Jacobean revision of the Petrine cycle was promulgated in Greek by Joseph Barsabbas and Silas in Antioch (see Acts 15:22-33). After 70 CE, "the little apocalypse," a Syrian addition to the Jacobean revision, was composed; it is a response to James' martyrdom and the Temple's destruction. The compiler may have been Silas, who under a more current form of his name (Silvanus) was involved in several sorts of apocalyptic speculation (cf. 1 Thess 1:1; 2 Thess 1:1; 1 Pet 5:12). In any case, the Jacobean revision of the Petrine cycle would have included (prior to any apocalyptic addendum) the insistence that the Twelve alone could provide the sense of the parables, a collection of such parables, a note of Jesus' rejection by his own neighbors, a commissioning of the Twelve, and the paschal interpretation of the Eucharist within a more anecdotal story of the passion than the Petrine cycle had offered.

The primitive cycles or revisions of tradition (Petrine, Jacobean, instructional ["Q"], and apocalyptic) were amalgamated into the Hellenistic catechesis reflected in the Synoptic Gospels, probably first of all in Antioch. The most likely exponent of the unified catechesis is Barnabas. His standing is consistent with the wide acceptance of the

Synoptic tradition, and the greater accommodation to Jacobean influence in the Synoptics as compared to Paul would be characteristic of Barnabas. But the Synoptic Eucharist addresses the needs of its overwhelmingly Hellenistic constituency, in presenting the Last Supper as a well-ordered symposium, a sacrifice for sin that offered its benefits to all who joined themselves to the heroic martyr's witness.

The Synoptic catechesis was a paradigm that was then developed and published in Rome (Mark, c. 73 CE), Damascus (Matthew, c. 80 CE), and Antioch itself (Luke, c. 90 CE). The spine of each Gospel is the narrative catechesis of the Petrine cycle, supplemented by Jacobean revision of that catechesis, the apocalyptic addendum of Joseph Barsabbas and Silas, and the instruction of the Twelve with its addenda ("Q"). Their similarities and differences are best understood as functions of the particular sort of catechesis (preparation of catechumens) that was current in each community. No Gospel is simply a copy of another; rather, each represents the choices among varying traditions, written and/or oral, and the development of those traditions that had taken place in a given locality.

Thomas (from Edessa, during the second century) represents a different ordering principle, based upon the mishnaic genre of the instruction of the Twelve, rather than the Petrine catechesis. The same cannot quite be said of John. Although there is formally no counterpart of the Last Supper, the substance and theology of the Synoptic tradition (if not of the Synoptic Gospels themselves) are reflected in John. Neither John nor *Thomas* represents a single source of Jesus' teaching, but both documents show that the genre of instruction proved to be a useful vehicle of theological reflection.

The identification, tracing, and dating of documents and sources is evidently a matter of inference. The procedure of reading, from text through its levels of generation, differs from the historical logic of starting at the beginning. But a generative exegesis uses the ordinary criteria of redaction criticism – diction, syntax, and meaning – in order to sort out one string of tradition from another.[19] The result looks more like strings than the beads or atoms of an earlier, form critical orientation, because no assumption is made that we know what the shape of tradition was before we encounter it in its written form.[20] Within the assessment of their relationships, reference to Jesus is only appropriate sporadically, within the generative patterns discerned. That

---

[19] See *Profiles of a Rabbi. Synoptic Opportunities in Reading about Jesus* (BJS 177; Atlanta: Scholars, 1989).

[20] See *God in Strength*, 11-23.

reference may be sharpened with reference to Jesus' cultural environment.

We are presented in our principal sources (the Gospels of the New Testament and Thomas) with ways of seeing Jesus within the communities that each Gospel was intended for. Identifying the view of Jesus each one takes, we can infer how Jesus must have acted to produce that view of him, together with the distinct views of him the other sources take. We are dealing, not only with four or five documents, Matthew, Mark, Luke, John, and *Thomas*, but with the groups of followers of Jesus that produces materials for those documents.

Use of the so-called "criteria of authenticity" represents an obstacle to knowledge, because they are not criteria, and they do not measure authenticity as far as Jesus is concerned. They are refugees from the time when the existence of precise "forms" of tradition was taken as established in some schools of thought.[21] Remove that assumption, and it is obvious that (1) we have no categorical assurance of how traditions developed (so: the "criteria" are not criteria), and further that (2) the relationship among traditions measures their development, not historical data concerning Jesus (so: "authenticity" is not measured).

The issue of how Jesus stands in relation to the Gospels cannot be resolved by merely imagining Jesus on one hand, and four or five authors composing documents on the other hand. Between Jesus and the texts there were groups of teachers, each of which generated its own view of Jesus. We need to address the generative question – how did the texts emerge? – by attending to how Jesus must have acted and how communities much have reacted to their memory of him and their own circumstances in bringing their Gospels to voice. The unfolding of the sources themselves is a fascinating question, but our concern here is a step beyond that and at the same time a narrowing of the generative concern: what we must infer of Jesus within his Jewish environment to explain how the texts emerged in their variety and in their agreement?

IV. Material and Social Contexts of Jesus

Until recently Jewish Galilee has been as mysterious as Jesus himself. A largely oral culture, as resistant to change as it was to the Romans who

---

[21] For treatments of this and related questions, see *Authenticating the Words of Jesus* (NTTS 78.1; ed. with C.A. Evans; Leiden: Brill, 1999) and *Authenticating the Activities of Jesus* (NTTS 78.2 (ed. with C.A. Evans; Leiden: Brill, 1999).

occupied it, Jewish Galilee condemned itself to silence from the point of view of history.

In 1997, a book appeared that conveys the range of excavations that have been conducted recently in Galilee.[22] That evidence underscores the relative isolation of rural Galilee within Hellenistic urban culture, and attests the cultural integrity of Galilean Judaism. This characterization complements much literary evidence.[23]

Galilean villages persistently attest a great concern for purity, the definition of who belongs to Israel and of how contact with those outside Israel should be regulated. Stone vessels for purificatory washing are typically found. They are characteristic of Jewish practice, and quite unlike vessels for cooking or the large cisterns used to store water for drinking. They are more persistent in Galilee than the *miqveh*, the stepped bathing pool, or the synagogue, but all of them have been found, and they lead to the conclusion that Jewish Galilee had established institutions and practices that question any supposed assimilation within Greco-Roman culture.

All these finds have shattered the myth of a purely Hellenistic Jesus living in an urbanized Galilee.[24] Until a synagogue was found in Galilean Gamla, it was routinely claimed that synagogues were only a post-Christian institution.[25] Before *miqvaoth* were discovered in several towns, bathing was often dismissed as purely the elitist practice of aristocrats and Pharisees in Judea. Indeed, it was often said that Jesus spoke Greek, rather than Aramaic, but the discovery of the Dead Sea Scrolls shows that Aramaic was used during the first century and earlier, and the discovery of scrolls near Qumran establishes that the usage of Aramaic persisted until the second century CE.

---

[22] D.R. Edwards and C.T. McCollough (eds.), *Archaeology and the Galilee. Texts and Contexts in the Graeco-Roman and Byzantine Periods* (South Florida Studies in the History of Judaism 143; Atlanta: Scholars, 1997).

[23] See R.A. Horsley, *Archaeology, History, and Society in Galilee. The Social Context of Jesus and the Rabbis* (Valley Forge, PA: Trinity Press International, 1996) 67-70.

[24] As is very forcefully shown, for example, by R.A. Horsley in *Archaeology, History, and Society in Galilee*. More recently, the same point has been made by J.L. Reed, *Archaeology and the Galilean Jesus. A Re-examination of the Evidence* (Harrisburg: Trinity Press International, 2000). This is a much more critical work than J.D. Crossan and J.L. Reed, *Excavating Jesus. Beneath the Stones, Behind the Texts* (San Francisco: Harper-SanFrancisco, 2001). See "Review Essay: Archaeology and Rabbi Jesus," *BBR* 12.2 (2002) 273-280.

[25] For what archaeology has now taught us about synagogues and *miqvaoth*, see *Ancient Synagogues. Historical Analysis and Archaeological Discovery* (SPB; ed. D. Urman and P.V.M. Flesher; Leiden: Brill, 1995).

The archaeological Galilee is a Jewish Galilee, as far as Jesus and his movement are concerned; philo-Roman urban enclaves such as Sepphoris are notable for their absence from Jesus' itinerary in the Gospels. Archaeological and textual scholarship has revolutionized how we should think about Galilee and about Judaism, and that means the once fashionable (and in some circles, still fashionable) picture of Jesus as an Athenian in Jewish dress must change.

Various forms of Judaism vied with one another, both in Israel and the Diaspora, and in their competition they shared a kindred hope: the hope that God would personally and actively intervene on behalf of his people. That was just the hope that Jesus articulated when he announced, in the Galilean dialect of Judaism, the kingdom of God. His dialect of Judaism was one among many, and they were to varying degrees Hellenistic (as well as Egyptian and Ethiopian and Latin and Libyan and Persian, among other cultural influences). Judaism was an international religion during the first century, and it is impossible to reduce it to a single cultural form.

Galilee produced Jesus, not just in the happenstance of his life, but at the center of his religious identity. Once we have understood his environment within the context of Galilee, we can place him within the unfolding of his unique religious vision. By properly evaluating that, we will see him in his distinctiveness, and at the same time appreciate the fundamental commonality of Judaism and Christianity.

Jesus was Jewish not only in the circumstances of his life, but in his dedication to that identity. Confronted with the increasing certainty that he was to die for his beliefs, Jesus taught his followers a carefully crafted teaching (a *kabbalah*) of suffering. *Kabbalah* refers particularly to a discipline of the vision of God that can be passed on from one person to another, and Jesus' characteristic *kabbalah* made human hardship into a crucible for experiencing the divine. His development of that *kabbalah* made the Gospels possible, and perhaps made Christianity inevitable.

V. The Kabbalah of Rabbi Jesus

Development is the proper perspective of biography. In the case of Jesus, his religious impact will never be understood until we can identity what the pivots of transition were in his unlikely journey from a Galilean boy accused of irregular birth[26] to a popular rabbi who chal-

---

[26] See "Jésus, le *mamzer* (Mt 1.18)," NTS 46 (2001) 222-227.

lenged the operation of the Temple in Jerusalem, directly confronting both the high priest of the time and the representative of Rome's power in the process. How was that possible, and why should the shameful result of that confrontation, Jesus' crucifixion, have resulted in the conviction that God had raised him from the dead?

Development is key to addressing all such questions. The focus cannot be just what is usually called "the life and teaching of Jesus." Typically, scholarly studies deal only with the public side of his activity in the year or two prior to his death. This has been justified on the basis of the foreshortened perspective of time in the Gospels, but that is a function of their catechetical purposes, not a concern for history. The result is that Jesus becomes a two-dimensional icon: there is the height of his teaching and the breadth of his action, but no depth of character. Now that we know more about Judaism and about Galilee, we no longer have to accept that situation. Rather, we can understand how he emerged as the figure he did, how he developed and changed over time, and how his activity set in motion the generation of the relevant sources.

But why speak of *kabbalah*, and then link that to Jesus? The "Kabbalah," as that term in commonly used, refers to a movement of Jewish mysticism from the twelfth century through the Renaissance (in its classic flowering).[27] Its focus was on the mystical union with God, in a way analogous to the paths advocated by Christian mystics such as Julian of Norwich and Johannes Eckhart. Its character included an intellectual discipline, literary focus on the precise wording of the Torah, and even an academic rigor in the description of the divine spheres into which the initiate was to enter with great care. What relation might that have to a rabbi of the first century from Galilee, whose attainments did not include the ability even to write, and whose own references to the Hebrew Bible were so imprecise as to indicate he was illiterate?

Although Kabbalah indeed can be used with a restrictive meaning, its underlying orientation is nothing other than the approach of God's *Merkabah*, the heavenly chariot throne from which divine power and wisdom emanated for the ordering of all creation. The conception of

---

[27] See Gershom Scholem, "Kabbalah," *EJ* (Jerusalem: Keter, 1972) 10.489-653 and the fine introduction of J. Dan in *The Early Kabbalah:* The Classics of Western Spirituality (New York: Paulist, 1986) 1-41. Among many more recent works, reference should be made to M. Idel, *Kabbalah. New Perspectives* (New Haven and London: Yale University Press, 1988) and E.R. Wolfson, *Through a Speculum that Shines. Vision and Imagination in Medieval Jewish Mysticism* (Princeton: Princeton University Press, 1994).

that *Merkabah* is much more ancient, profoundly rooted in the theology of Israel, than the development of kabbalistic techniques during the Middle Ages and later. Indeed, the ascent to the divine throne is older than Israel itself.

From Mesopotamia, from the twenty-third century BCE and the fifteen-century CE, stories are told of kings and courtiers entering into the palace of heaven and receiving visions and empowerment there.[28] Israel learned these royal traditions from Babylonia and converted them into prophetic authorization, especially during the time of Ezekiel (in the sixth century CE). Ezekiel himself related his classic vision of the throne of God as a chariot, a *Merkabah*, and what is usually called *Merkabah* mysticism derives from his vision (in Ezekiel 1). After Ezekiel, the book of Daniel (ch. 7) detailed this vision further (during the second century BCE). And by the time of Jesus, the Book of Enoch (*1 Enoch*), found in fragments in Aramaic at Qumran, took that tradition further.

The book of Genesis says of Enoch only that "he walked with God, and he was not" (Gen 5:22). This disappearance is taken in *1 Enoch* as a sign that Enoch enjoyed a vision by ascent into the multiple heavens above the earth, and was authorized to relate that wisdom to Israel, indeed to act as an intermediary to the angels who had disobeyed God. From Ezekiel, through Daniel and Enoch and on to John and Jesus, there is a growing tradition, a *kabbalah* (something received), which reflects a deep commitment to the disciplined practice of the vision of God's throne. The fragments of *Enoch* at Qumran are found in Aramaic, which suggests that the book was used, not just by the Essenes (who tended to guard their sectarian documents in Hebrew), but by a wider audience, which included the Essenes.[29] In fact, *1 Enoch* is also quoted at a later stage in the New Testament, so that there can be no doubt of its widespread use. Another work found in Hebrew at Qumran and widely attested elsewhere, the book of *Jubilees*, also presents Enoch as a figure of revelation: he himself knows the Torah later communicated to Moses by angelic communication.

The development of these traditions is obviously not independent: there is a successive building and borrowing from one to the other. The ascent to the divine throne was an aspiration that was "received" or "taken," one source from others. To "receive" or to "take" in both

---

[28] See B. Lang, "Die grosse Jenseitsfahrt," *Paragana* 7.2 (1998) 24-42, 32; S. Dalley, *Myths from Mesopotamia* (Oxford: Oxford University Press, 2000) 182-187 and J.D. Tabor, "Heaven, Ascent to," *ABD* 3.91-94.

[29] For an introduction and translation, see E. Isaac, "1 Enoch," *OTP* I.5-89.

Aramaic and Hebrew is expressed by the verb *qabal*, from which the noun *qabbalah* is derived, and the noun is used in both Mishnah and Talmud to refer to ancient tradition, including the Prophets and the Writings within the Bible of Israel (as distinct from the Torah).[30] What is *qabal*ed might be any sort of authoritative tradition, but it is tradition concerning the *Merkabah* that is our concern here. When Paul wishes to underline that authority of his teaching concerning the Eucharist, he says, "For I received from the Lord what I also delivered over to you," and he goes on to speak of both Jesus' last meal with his followers *and* its significance and correct observance (1 Cor 11:23-33). The sources of Paul's authority include what he learned from primitive Christians (especially Peter, see Gal 1:18), but more importantly what he calls the *apokalypsis*, the uncovering, of Christ Jesus (Gal 1:12). That disclosure occurred in a supernatural realm, the third heaven, the paradise to which Paul says he was once snatched up, where he was told unutterable wisdoms (2 Cor 12:1-4).[31]

The confidence of Paul that this ascent was a self-evident aspect of his authorization that his readers would appreciate invites us to look back, to seek traces of the *Merkabah* in the Gospels. As in the case of treating generative exegesis, only couple of examples can be cited here, which emerge from my long-standing collaboration with Jacob Neusner and from my narrative treatment of Jesus.[32]

Traces of the *Merkabah* are perhaps plainest in Jesus' baptism, and in what that reception of the Holy Spirit produced in him. That takes us back to Jesus' association with John called the "immerser" (the *baptistes* in Greek). From the writings of Josephus, we know that John was not the only such figure; Josephus refers to his own study with another immerser, named Bannus.[33] Pilgrims' local *miqvaoth* (immersion pools, if they even had access to one) might not correspond to the Pharisaic design, and would be much less luxurious than those of the Sadducees, less elaborate than those of the Essenes. But John offered them purification in God's own water, and the assurance that this was the science

---

[30] See the article by Cecil Roth appended to Scholem's, *EJ* (Jerusalem: Keter, 1972) 10.653-654.

[31] See V.P. Furnish, *II Corinthians* (AB; Garden City: Doubleday, 1984) 542-54, and *Rabbi Paul. An Intellectual Biography* (New York: Doubleday, 2004).

[32] See *Comparing Spiritualities. Formative Christianity and Judaism on Finding Life and Meeting Death* (with J. Neusner; Harrisburg: Trinity Press International, 2000) and *Rabbi Jesus*.

[33] See Josephus, *Life* 11. For a discussion of John, Bannus, and their methods of purification as related to Jesus, see *Jesus' Baptism and Jesus' Healing. His Personal Practice of Spirituality* (Trinity Press International, 1998).

of Israel's true purity. Then what they faced in Jerusalem was less daunting; the claims and counter-claims of various factions would be put into perspective by the confidence that one had already been purified by God's own living waters.

Immersion, for John, was no once-for-all act, as in later Christian baptism. In the practice of the primitive Church, after the resurrection, believers felt that they received the Spirit of God when they were immersed in the name of Jesus. That conviction was only possible after the resurrection, because it stemmed from the belief that Jesus was alive and at the right hand of God, so as to be able to dispense divine spirit. In Peter's speech at Pentecost (the Magna Carta of baptismal theology), Jesus, having been exalted to the right hand of God, receives the promise of the Holy Spirit from the father and pours it out on his followers (Acts 2:33). Once received by a Christian, that Spirit did not come and go. Subsequent immersion could not top up a lack of spirit. A Christian lived in the power of God's Spirit; its influence might increase or decrease, but the fact of its presence was irrevocable. But in John's practice, as in Judaism as a whole, purification was a routine requirement, and people might return to John many times, and they naturally engaged in many forms of purification other than John's, whether in their villages or at the Temple. Impurity was a fact of life, and therefore so was purification. But John was there in the wilderness to attest that the natural, living water provided by God would achieve acceptability before God, provided that immersion was accompanied by repentance.[34]

But for the *talmidim* of John, this continual immersion – as well as the immersion of others – was more than a matter of simple repentance. Within that activity, there was an esoteric meaning. John conveyed a definite understanding of the final significance that his purification for Israel offered. The sources are plain: for John, immersion brought one to the point that one could understand what God was about to do with Israel. As John himself expressed it, immersing oneself in water prepared one to receive the Spirit of God himself, which was to drench all Israel with its sanctification. The key to John's preparation for God himself lies in the wording attributed to him, "I immerse you in water, but he himself will immerse you in Holy Spirit" (Mark 1:8; see Matt 3:11; Luke 3:16). Within the context of Christianity after the resurrection, those words are fulfilled by what the

---

[34] See J. Taylor, *The Immerser. John the Baptist within Second Temple Judaism* (Studying the Historical Jesus; Grand Rapids: Eerdmans, 1997).

risen Jesus endows the believer with; but that assumes Jesus' identification with God at that point, because only God himself can give of his own Spirit. Within the context of John the immerser, however, what is at issue is the purification that prepares the way for divine Spirit. The link between purification with water and the vindicating presence of God's Spirit is explicitly made in the book of Ezekiel, the same book that is the *locus classicus* of the *Merkabah* (Ezek 36:22-27):

> Therefore, say to the house of Israel: So says the Lord, the LORD: Not for your sake am I acting, house of Israel, but for my holy name, which you have profaned among the peoples you came to. I will sanctify my great name, although profaned among the peoples among whom you have profaned it, and the peoples will know that I am the LORD, says the Lord, the LORD, when I am sanctified among you before their eyes. I will take you from the peoples, and gather you from all the lands, and bring you to your land. I will sprinkle on you clean waters and cleanse you from all your uncleannesses and from all your idols I will cleanse you. I will give you a new heart and a new spirit I will put in your midst, and remove the heart of stone from your flesh and give you a heart of flesh. My Spirit I shall put in your midst and I will make you walk according to my statutes and keep my judgments and do them.

The close and causal connection between water and Spirit here has led to the insight that we have here an important Scriptural precedent of John's immersion.[35]

John practiced a *kabbalah* of envisioning the throne of God, which backed up his practice of immersion. He and his *talmidim* saw the Spirit of God before the *Merkabah*, ready to drench Israel, just as Israel was drenched in the waters of purification. The careful discipline of these *talmidim*, their repetitive, committed practice, their sometimes inadequate diet and exposure to the elements all contributed to the vividness of their visions of God's throne. John Allegro suggested some years ago that the ingestion of psychotropic mushrooms was a part of this discipline.[36] While the influence of herbs and grasses, as well as

---

[35] See O. Böcher, "Johannes der Täufer," *Theologische Realenzyklopädie* 17 (1988) 172-181, 175. This insight, suggested to me by B. Lang, is worked out more fully in *Jesus' Baptism and Jesus' Healing*.

[36] *The Sacred Mushroom and the Cross. A Study of the Nature and Origins of Christianity within the Fertility Cults of the Ancient Near East* (Garden City: Doubleday, 1970). His suggestion that "Jesus" was simply a name for a mushroom assured Allegro a frosty reception, and his attempt to see Jesus as entirely mythical (indeed, hallucinatory) reads as a desperate attempt not to place him within historical context. Nonetheless, his approach still finds a hearing; see C.A.P. Ruck, B.D. Staples & C. Heinrich, *The*

mushrooms, on people's psychological states cannot be discounted, the greater influence of these visions was the *kabbalah* itself, its intentional recollection and envisioning of the throne of God. A fragment from Qumran praises God as the apex of a heavenly panoply:

> He is God of gods of all the heads of the heights and king of kings for all eternal councils.[37]

The foundation of *kabbalah* is putting the intent of the mind into envisaging the heavenly throne. Jesus' skill in this vision made him one of John's most prominent *talmidim*, but it also led to Jesus' break with John. The Gospels all relate the baptism of Jesus in a way that adumbrates baptism in early Christianity. But they also refer to the particular vision of Jesus, which not every baptized Christian could or did claim (Matt 3:13-17; Mark 1:9-13 Luke 3: 21-22).

As Jesus was immersed for purification, he came to have an increasingly vivid vision, of the heavens splitting open, and God's Spirit coming upon him. And a voice: "you are my son, beloved; in you I take pleasure." Each of these elements is resonant with the Israelite *kabbalah* of the divine throne.

The heavens are viewed as multiple, hard shells above the earth, so that any real disclosure of the divine must represent a rending of those firmaments. But once opened, Jesus' vision is not of ascending through the heavens, as in the case of Enoch, but of the Spirit, as a dove, hovering over him and descending. That image is a vivid realization that the Spirit of God at creation once hovered over the face of the primeval waters (Gen 1:2), as a bird. The bird was identified as a dove in Rabbinic tradition, and a fragment from Qumran supports the association.[38] The Spirit, which would one day come to Israel, in Jesus' vision was already upon him, and God took pleasure in him as a "son."

Jesus' vivid experience within his practice of John's immersion, a persistent vision occurring many times, may be contrasted with a story about Hillel, an older contemporary of Jesus'. Hillel was held in such high esteem that he was thought worthy to receive the Holy Spirit. That estimate appears all the more exalted, but also strangely wistful,

---

Apples of Apollo. Pagan and Christian Mysteries of the Eucharist (Durham, NC: Carolina Academic Press, 2001) and the review in *The Classical Bulletin* 78.2 (2002) 261-263.

[37] The fragment was found in the fourth cave from near Qumran (its designation is 4 Q403 frg. li). E. Glicker Chazon of the Hebrew University in Jerusalem showed me a copy.

[38] See D.C. Allison, "The Baptism of Jesus and a New Dead Sea Scroll," *BAR* 18.2 (1992) 58-60.

when it is borne in mind that the rabbis held that the Spirit had been withdrawn since the time of the last prophets of Scripture. These motifs are drawn together in a Rabbinic story:[39]

> Until the dead live, namely Haggai, Zechariah, and Malachi, the latter prophets, the Holy Spirit has ceased from Israel. Yet even so, they made them hear *bath qol*. An example: the sages gathered at the house of Guria in Jericho, and they heard a *bath qol* saying, There is here a man who is predestined for the Holy Spirit, except that his generation is not righteous for such. And they put their eyes on Hillel the elder, and when he died, they said of him, Woe the meek man, Woe, the faithful disciple of Ezra.

With the withdrawal of Spirit until the prophets live again, God's favor is made known by an angelic echo, a *bath qol* ("daughter of a voice"). But the poignancy of this story is that, for all Hillel's merit, the Spirit itself is withheld. Jesus' approach to the *Merkabah* by means of John's *kabbalah* had opened the prospect that the gates of heaven were open again for the Spirit to descend upon Israel.

Another case where stories concerning divine voices find resonance in the New Testament is the Transfiguration (Matt 16:28-17:8; Mark 9:2-8; Luke 9:27-36). The narrative structure is reminiscent of Moses' ascent of Sinai in Exodus 24. At the close of that story, Moses is said to ascend the mountain, where God's glory, as a cloud, covered it (v. 15). The covering lasted six days (v. 16), which is the amount of time between the Transfiguration and the previous discourse in both Matthew (17:1) and Mark (9:2). After that time, the LORD calls to Moses from the cloud (Exod 24:16b), and Moses entered the glory of the cloud, which is like a devouring fire (vv. 17-18). Earlier in the chapter, Moses is commanded to select three worshippers (Aaron, Nadab, and Abihu) together with seventy elders, in order to confirm the covenant (vv. 1-8). The result is that just these people (v. 9) see the God of Israel in his court (v. 10) and celebrate their vision with a meal. The motifs of master, three disciples, mountain, cloud, vision and audition recur in the Transfiguration.

Other details in the presentation of the story cohere with Exodus 24. Matthew 17:2 uniquely refers to Jesus' face shining like the sun, like Moses' aspect in Exod 34:29-35. In more general terms, Mark's reference to the whiteness of Jesus' garments also establishes a heavenly context. A variation in Luke is more specific and more interesting. Luke puts a distance of eight days, rather than six, between the previ-

---

[39] Tosefta *Sotah* 13:3. For a discussion, see *Profiles of a Rabbi*, 77-89.

ous discourse and the Transfiguration. Although that has baffled commentators, in Rabbinic interpretation that variation is meaningful. In the Targum Pseudo-Jonathan (Exod 24:10-11), Nadab and Abihu are struck by God, because their vision contradicts the principle that "man will not see God and live" (Exod 33:30). But their punishment (narrated in Num 3:2-4) is delayed until the *eighth* day.

In this heavenly vision two figures of Rabbinic tradition who were understood not to have tasted death, Moses and Elijah, also make their appearance. Elijah, of course, is the primordial prophet of the *Merkabah*. Elijah's *talmid*, Elisha, sees Elijah taken up into the heavens with God's "chariot of fire and horses of fire" (2 Kgs 2:11; the term for "chariot" here is *rekhev*, simply the masculine form of the feminine *Merkabah*). At least from the time of Josephus, Moses was also held to have been taken up alive into the heavenly court.[40] Taken together, then, Elijah and Moses are indices of Jesus' access to the heavenly court. Peter's apparently inept suggestion to his rabbi, of building "lodges," also corresponds to the enclosure for God's glory on earth which Moses is commanded to build in the chapters of Exodus after chapter 24. Taken as a whole, the Transfiguration at its generative moment attests Jesus' introduction of his *talmidim* to a vision of the divine throne comparable to his own at his baptism.

Jesus' conscious framing of a *kabbalah*, an approach to the divine *Merkabah* for himself and for his own *talmidim*, naturally includes an understanding of his own identity. All three Synoptic Gospels have Jesus propelled by the Spirit into the wilderness, in order to be pressed to the limit by Satan (Matt 4:1; Mark 1:12; Luke 4:1), and Matthew and Luke both include three itemized temptations at this point (Matt 4:1-11; Luke 4:1-13). In all three, the sense is conveyed that one's possession of the Spirit of God in baptism brings one into conflict with the primordial source of resistance to that Spirit. That catechetical logic is at odds with the simple observation that Jesus can only be tested with these particular temptations near the end of his life, by which time he had actually experienced power in various idioms.

After the story of his temptations,[41] Luke alone has Jesus return "in the power of the Spirit into Galilee" (Luke 4:14). There can be no question, then, but that at this paradigmatic moment, as Jesus com-

---

[40] See *Antiquities* 4.326. For further discussion, see "The Transfiguration: Dominical Assurance and Apostolic Vision," *NTS* 27 (1980) 115-124; "Transfiguration," *ABD* 6.640-642.

[41] The story of itemized temptations is the contribution of the source called "Q;" for an account of the contents of "Q," cf. *Pure Kingdom*, 107-110.

mences his public activity, the issue of the Spirit is uppermost in the reference to Jesus' divine identity within Luke. The inauguration of this activity takes place – only in Luke – by means of an appearance in a synagogue in Nazareth, where his citation of the book of Isaiah is pivotal (Luke 4:14-30).

The utility of this passage within the overall structure of Luke-Acts had led to the finding that it has been synthesized by the editorial work that went into those two documents. And the utility of the passage within Luke-Acts cannot reasonably be denied. The entire pericope, from v. 14 until v. 30 in Luke 4, sets up a model – of reading Scripture in a synagogue, enjoying some success but then violent rejection, a rejection that leads to a turning to non-Jews – which corresponds to the pattern of presentation of Paul and Barnabas in the book of Acts, especially at Pisidian Antioch in Acts 13:13-52.[42] Together, Luke 4 and Acts 13 set out a pattern for the Church of Luke-Acts. The name "Antioch" is a key to the importance of the latter passage, just as the verb "to anoint" in the former passage is profoundly evocative. The two are as if violins in an orchestra set at a quaver distance, at which one instrument causes the other to resonate. For Luke-Acts, Paul and Barnabas resonate with the purpose, program and authorization of Jesus himself.

The words cited from Isaiah begin, "The Lord's Spirit is upon me, forasmuch as he anointed me." Here, then, is the specification of how the Spirit has been with Jesus since the moment of his baptism. The Spirit is his anointing. Jesus is Messiah because the Spirit is upon him, and the text from Isaiah becomes an itinerary of his activity.

Just here, however, the *dissonance* between Jesus' own typical activity and the text of Isaiah 61, cited by Luke, becomes evident. The simple facts are that Isa 61:1, 2 refers to things Jesus never did, such as releasing prisoners from jail, and that Jesus did things the text makes no mention of, such as declaring people free of impurity (see Matt 8:2-4; Mark 1:40-45; Luke 5:12-16). This dissonance cannot be a Lukan creation, because the pattern of the Gospel is to make the correspondence to the Septuagint in biblical citations as close as possible. As the text stands, moreover, a change from any known form of the biblical text results in a lost opportunity to relate directly to the activity of Jesus, as well as introducing an element of greater dissonance. The phrase "to bind the broken of heart" is omitted from the citation, and

---

[42] I have worked out this correspondence in some detail in *God in Strength*, 123-156.

wording similar to Isa 58:6, a reference to setting the oppressed at liberty, has been inserted.

Although Luke's Gospel presents the wording – evidently inspired from Isaiah – as a routine reading in a synagogue, it evidently was not so in the tradition prior to Luke. Jesus' "citation" is no citation at all, but a freer version of the biblical book than could have been read. The wording of the passage in the Old Syriac Gospels (in a language closely related to Jesus' indigenous Aramaic) is freer still:

The Spirit of the Lord is upon *you*,
  on account of which he has anointed *you* to message triumph to the poor;
And he has sent me to preach to the captives release, and to the blind sight
  – and *I* will free the broken with release –
  and to preach the acceptable year of the Lord.

The oddities Luke preserves are present, together with what has been homogenized in Luke: the radical change in pronouns.[43] By speaking these words, Jesus portrays himself as responding to a divine charge: "The Spirit of the Lord is upon you, on account of which he was anointed you to message triumph to the poor." Then he emphatically accepts that charge: "And he has sent me to preach to the captives release, and to the blind sight – and I will free the broken with release – and to preach the acceptable year of the Lord." Both the charge and the emphatic acceptance are produced by the signal changes in pronouns, which are italicized above. They are part and parcel of a conscious alteration of the language taken from the book of Isaiah, an alteration that voices the text in a way that makes it akin to the baptismal *bath qol* and the *bath qol* at the Transfiguration.

The alteration is typical of Jesus' style of employing Scripture, especially the book of Isaiah (and especially in a targumic form).[44] His aim was to use the Scripture as a lens of his own activity of behalf of God, such that the wording focused on how God was active in what he said and did, without suggesting a complete fit between the text and what Jesus referred to. The Scripture was a guide to the experience of God in the present, but that experience was more important than the text, and could be used to refashion the text.

Clearly, the association of Jesus as Messiah with the Spirit gained currency after and as a consequence of the resurrection, as we have already seen. But its currency is very difficult to explain, as Marinus de

---

[43] For a full discussion, see *God in Strength*, 157-177.
[44] See *A Galilean Rabbi and His Bible*, 148-198.

Jonge points out, if "Jesus himself avoided this designation and discouraged his followers from using it."[45] *Some* consistent usage of messianic language would likely have been in the background of Jesus' teaching for the term to emerge as the primary designation of Jesus. In that Luke's Gospel was composed in Antioch around 90 CE in a community in which both Greek and Aramaic were spoken, it is the most likely source among the Synoptics to have indicated what this background might have been. The tight connection between the Spirit of God and the verb "anoint," as in Jesus' reference to Isaiah 61 in Luke 4, provides us with just the indication that fills out the picture of the development of early Christian usage. Anointed by the Spirit of God, Jesus' viewed himself as enacting and articulating the claims of God's sovereignty ("the kingdom of God"). His teaching indeed does not spell out the content of being "Messiah" by means of a precise program drawn from biblical or pseudepigraphic literature, but it does relate the Spirit to his own activity, and in Luke 4 that relationship involved explicitly messianic language.

The Lukan presentation is precisely what makes the form of the "citation" of Isaiah 61 all the more surprising. As a Lukan invention, the reference would have accorded with the Septuagint. Indeed, the Old Syriac Gospels provide an insight into the shape of the reference to Isaiah 61 by Jesus before it was partially accommodated to the Septuagint within the Lukan presentation. The fractured reference to Isaiah 61 focuses Jesus' messianic identity on the issue of the Spirit, and that was the point of departure for the development of primitive Christology.

Luke provides us with a centered view of Jesus' Christology, focused on the Spirit of God. Within the recent study of Jesus, two discarded pictures of his Christology have emerged again, and I would suggest in closing that they are likely to be discarded again. The first stresses the undoubted importance of the political challenge to the identity of Israel within the first century. Jesus then becomes the "Davidic messiah," a ruling figure who sets up his throne in association with the Temple.[46] This, despite the portrayal of Jesus in the Temptations as rejecting a picture of such rule, and despite his own rhetorical question, "How do the scribes say the messiah is David's son?" (Mark 12:35, together with Matt 22:42; Luke 20:41). That question assumes a tradition of identifying the Messiah and the ben David, but it also –

---

[45] *Early Christology and Jesus' Own View of His Mission* (Studying the Historical Jesus; Grand Rapids: Eerdmans, 1998) 101.

[46] For a sophisticated argument to this effect, see R.A. Horsley, *Sociology and the Jesus Movement* (New York: Crossroad, 1989) 105-145.

and obviously – refutes it.[47] Any messianic theology inherently involved a political dimension, but to make that dimension the only index of meaning runs against the grain of Jesus' contention that Davidic and messianic claims were not simply identifiable. Another view, derived ultimately from the Albert Schweitzer's picture of Jesus as a failed apocalyptist, imagines Jesus as personally taking on himself all the conditions of the covenant with Israel, in a desperate attempt to get God to fulfill the covenantal promises.[48] This, despite the fact that the term "covenant" within sayings of Jesus only appears in a single case, in what seems to be a liturgical addition to the meaning of the cup of wine in the context of his last meals in Jerusalem. Peter and Paul were undoubtedly theologians of this covenant, because they had directly to face the issues of who was and was not of the people of God. Jesus, however, does not appear to have confronted that question in covenantal terms.

But once Jesus' approach to the *Merkabah*, on the basis of his endowment with Spirit, is seen to be the pivot of his experience and his program of activity, his care in defining how he was and how he was not messiah acquires its sense. His messianic identity was a function of his self-consciousness and the awareness of his *talmidim* that his *kabbalah* offers the vision of God in his glory because divine Spirit makes that vision possible. The historical Jesus is a reading of all the available evidence that permits us to explain, in religious terms, the emergence of Christianity out of Second Temple Judaism.

Appendix: A Chronology for Jesus
(with pages numbers referring to discussion in *Rabbi Jesus*)

40-4 BCE The reign of Herod the Great as a client king of Rome.

31 BCE The empire of Augustus becomes secure, following the assassination of Julius Caesar in 44 BCE.

4 BCE The death of Herod results in the division of his kingdom: his son Archelaus takes Judah, Herod Antipas inherits Galilee and Perea; Herod Philip rules Trachonitis.

2-16 CE The birth of Jesus in Galilean Bethlehem, his childhood in Nazareth.

---

[47] See "Jesus ben David: Reflections on the *Davidssohnfrage*," *JSNT* 14 (1982) 88-112.
[48] For this neo-orthodox re-reading of Schweitzer, see N.T. Wright, *Jesus and the Victory of God* (Minneapolis: Fortress, 1993).

In early spring of 2 CE, Joseph and Mary meet, marry, and conceive Jesus in Nazareth prior to establishing a common residence there (6-8).

Jesus' birth in Bethlehem of Galilee, Joseph's residence, in late autumn (6, 8-9). [By October 23, for example. Mars had traveled to the west, and was in alignment with Saturn.]

Eight days later, his circumcision in accordance with the Torah at Bethlehem (3-5, 9-15).

The family moves in with Mary's family in Nazareth before the end of the year (13-14).

Jesus begins his local travel with Joseph as a journeyman just after turning ten in 12 CE (20).

Joseph dies in 15 CE (20-22).

A year later, Mary takes her family to Jerusalem for the feast of Sukkot in the autumn of 16 CE, staying with Mary and Martha of Bethany (23-32).

16-21 CE His apprenticeship with John the Baptist.

Turning fourteen, Jesus remains in Jerusalem after his family returns from the celebration of Sukkot in 16 CE (32-37)

Jesus seeks out and meets John the Baptist early in 17 CE (37-43).

During the course of immersions following John's practice, Jesus increasingly experiences divine Spirit, and by 19 CE John begins to call him "the lamb of God" (55-58).

Jesus' new view of purity, derived from his experience of divine Spirit, puts him in conflict with his rabbi during 20 CE (58-60).

21 CE The death of John.

Herod Antipas orders the execution in 21 CE, on a critical reading of Josephus (60-63).

21-24 CE The return of Jesus to Nazareth at the age of 18, and his excursions outward as journey worker and rabbi until his expulsion from Nazareth.

Jesus returns home to a festive reception through Samaria in order to avoid capture in 21 CE, but his conversation with the Samaritan woman has alienated some of John's former disciples (62-71).

Beginning in 22 CE, Jesus' journeywork from the base of Mary's house in Nazareth takes on the character of holy feasts that involves him and his family in increasingly heavy debts of honor (74-78).

By 23 CE Jesus' has come into contact with Capernaum and Magdala, denouncing their wealth (78-82).

Jesus' conviction that purity is a power released within people leads him to practice exorcisms that are unusually direct and abrupt (83-93).

The strain on his family exerted by his debts of honor and his embarrassing exorcisms (93-95) leads to a break, and he makes his way to Capernaum in 24 CE.

24-27 CE Using Capernaum as a base, Jesus' itinerancy makes him a major figure in Galilee by his 25th year.
- His reputation in Capernaum is established by an exorcism in the synagogue in 24 CE (96-97). But his fame there leads Jesus to confront the elders in Nazareth with his claim that he has been anointed by God's Spirit, and he is nearly killed by stoning late in the summer (97-106), leading to a brief retreat to Jerusalem to enjoy the hospitality of some of John's former disciples and Barnabas.
- At the pool of Bethesda, he heals a person for the first time, leading to his contact with Barnabas during Sukkot and with Nicodemus during the feast of the Chanukah. But increasing opposition from priestly and Pharisaic authorities pushes him back to Capernaum the following year (106-123).
- From 25 CE, Capernaum becomes Jesus' base of support, and until 27 CE a stable haven where he enjoys his holy feasts, travels less than previously, and accepts disciples, exorcizes and heals (124-148).
- During the fifteenth year of Tiberius, in 27 CE, Jesus has become such a renowned figure that Herod Antipas seeks to end his life, just as he had executed John the Baptist, so that Jesus is forced to flee Capernaum (148-149).

27-31 CE Herod Antipas's threat forces Jesus to skirt and crisscross Galilean territory, and gather his followers in Syria
- Stilling of the storm in 27 CE occurs during a transit eastwards, to Bethsaida, formerly the home of Peter and Andrew (153-161).
- His sojourn in Bethsaida follows Jesus' contact with a centurion, 27-28 CE, which draws attention (161-168).
- Sojourn on the eastern side of the Sea of Galilee, ending with the destruction of the pigs, 28-29 CE [winter] (168-171)
- Dispatch of delegates, 29 CE (174-178)
- Revival of Jairus's daughter, 29 CE (178-179)
- Encounter with the Syro-Phoenician woman, 30 (181-182)
- Wedding at Kana, 30 CE (182-185)
- The sign of feeding in Gaulanitis, 30 CE (186-188)
- The Transfiguration, 30 CE [Sukkot], followed by the Temptations (190-197)
- Walking on the water, 31 CE (197), with Mark 7:31-37 and 8:22-26 prior (Mary Magdalene, 62).

31-32 CE Jesus' last year in Jerusalem, aged 30.
- Final drive through Galilee (with Shabbat and tax issues), 31 CE (197-203)
- Entry into Jerusalem and raid in the Temple, 31 CE [Sukkot] (225-230).
- The death of Sejanus in Rome on 18 October 31 CE (239-242).
- Jesus' execution prior to Passover in 32 CE, and visions of him risen from the dead during the spring and summer (254-268, 269-289).

35 CE The meeting of Peter and James and Paul in Jerusalem, and the availability of the earliest sources of the Gospels: Peter's instruction for apostles such as Paul, and the mishnah of Jesus' teaching known to modern scholarship as "Q."

37 CE The removal of Pontius Pilate and Caiaphas from power.

40 CE The adaptation of Peter's Gospel by James, the brother of Jesus, in Jerusalem.

45 CE In Antioch, outside of Palestine, followers of Jesus are for the first time called "Christians."

53-57 CE Paul writes his major letters, Galatians, 1 & 2 Corinthians, and Romans.

62 CE The death of James by stoning in Jerusalem, at the instigation of the high priest.

64 CE The death of Paul and Peter in Rome.

70-73 CE The burning of the Temple by the Roman troops under Titus; the composition of Mark's Gospel in Rome; the end of the revolt against Rome in Palestine.

75 CE Josephus publishes his *Jewish War*.

80 CE The composition of Matthew's Gospel, in Damascus.

90 CE The composition of Luke's Gospel, in Antioch.

93 CE Josephus publishes his *Antiquities of the Jews*.

100 CE The composition of John's Gospel, in Ephesus.

10

Paul's Thought and Life

Bruce Chilton

Introduction

Paul was a visionary thinker who combined Stoicism, Judaism, and nascent Christian theology, transforming all of them in the mix. He is one of the most frustrating and tantalizing figures in our intellectual tradition, because he tried to change every group he joined, every idea he embraced. He wove his thoughts from his complex background and his volatile temperament, and produced a new way of thinking and feeling about what it means to be human. He emerged as an innovator and a radical ideologue by synthesizing the popular philosophy of the Greco-Roman world and his passionate Judaism into a new hybrid.

The first synthetic thinkers of Christianity – "the Fathers of the Church" – considered Paul their premier theologian, and referred to him simply as "the Apostle." To this day he is widely considered responsible for separating Christianity from Judaism by teaching that God did not require people to obey him, but only to love him. Paul made Jesus the center of a new religion, the Christ who offered a special relationship with God despite any human fault or failing, and with or without the Torah. That established Paul as the principal architect of the Church, the thinker who gave Christianity its doctrine and form.

Paul's influence over the Church has only grown with time. The Protestant Reformation pinned its hopes for a comprehensive program of reform on Paul and considered him the only theologically correct thinker. For all the vehemence of its stand against Protestantism, Roman Catholic Christianity since the Second Vatican Council has increasingly emphasized Paul's teaching that God's favor cannot be earned by obedience to convention, and Orthodox Christianity has always venerated "the Apostle."

Meanwhile revisionist theologians and critics – ancient and modern – have pilloried Paul, making him responsible for whatever is wrong with Christianity. They have portrayed Paul as anti-feminist, homophobic and doctrinaire – while Fundamentalist Christians often embrace such attitudes as part of their Pauline inheritance. Paul's own letters do give support to this picture. He wrote that women in Corinth should shut up in church; he despised homosexual prostitution, and he fussed endlessly in an effort to get the congregations he addressed in his letters to behave decently and think coherently – according to his standards.

When you consider the number of letters written by Paul in the New Testament, the number of letters attributed to him, and the space devoted to his activities in the Acts of the Apostles, it is easy to come to think of him as the real founder of Christianity. There is no shortage of works that make Paul into Jesus' evil twin: Jesus preached love, Paul set up an organization. Or: Jesus told simple stories, Paul insisted upon complicated dogma; or: Jesus was a loyal rabbi of Judaism, Paul wanted a new religion. Or: all of the above. Paul is the preferred target when intellectuals wish to attack Christianity, because he can be portrayed as the manager and ideologue and entrepreneur of the movement, while Jesus, it is commonly (and wrongly) supposed, was not concerned with practical issues or radical changes in religion.

These images of Paul have their merits, but they inevitably distort "the Apostle" because they do not trace the sources of his ideas, explain why he combined them the way he did, or account for how he changed, often chameleon-like, to impress his vision on the different communities that he proselytized. They do not convey the passion of a man who lived his ideas.

How can we get at the truth about Paul as a human being and appreciate his thought? It takes more to encounter Paul than reading an ancient text or two. The New Testament gives us Paul's life and thought in fragments, sometimes through second-hand sources.[1] His letters are the earliest documents in the New Testament, when they are genuine. But some are spurious, and one of the most important of the authentic letters (2 Corinthians) is pasted together from separate pieces of correspondence. Even when we have whole and genuine letters, we are in the position of an eavesdropper who can hear only one side of a conversation, since we do not have letters written back

---

[1] He does not even give us his full name. He just signs himself "Paul" in his letters – two names short of the classical Roman style of *praenomen*, *nomen*, and *cognomen*.

to Paul. We need to parse his words to access the issues he is addressing and his perspective, and we have to gather the settings and milieus that he addressed from what he says about them. We can do that by examining the historical and archaeological evidence of the cities and towns in which Paul taught while keeping his own writings at the forefront.

Paul helped make Christianity in a way no other person did, and we can see that happen in his letters, written just as this new faith emerged. That is why his letters are priceless to anyone interested in religion, for any reason. But his letters are also as limited as Paul was. He did not write one line about his physical environment during the thousands of miles he traveled by foot, caravan, and ship. He mentioned many people by name, sometimes with tenderness and sometimes with anger, but only for what they did or did not do in the service of his message and its announcement. Paul, in his own mind, was simply a herald of the only truth that mattered. His emotional restraint was always at war with his unreserved passion for Christ.

What Paul does not say makes the book of the Acts of the Apostles an extremely valuable resource in any attempt at biography. A broad consensus of scholars puts the date of Acts around 90 CE (if not later), some thirty years after Paul had stopped writing. But the writer of Acts clearly incorporated earlier material in his narrative: the travel notes of one of Paul's companions, for example.[2] The likely author of those notes was Timothy, in my judgment.

Many details in Acts correspond to historical and archaeological evidence. That obviously does not make Acts more reliable than Paul's letters, but it does mean that what Acts says should be assessed, not simply rejected.[3] Sometimes there is good reason to infer that Paul keeps a self-interested silence that Acts breaks, while sometimes Acts' mythic convictions – of peace and unanimity in the early church, for example – are simply implausible.

---

[2] For a sober and representative treatment of this question and others, see Raymond E. Brown, *An Introduction to the New Testament* (Anchor Bible Reference Library; New York: Doubleday) 225-332.

[3] A.J. Malherbe has in my opinion struck the right balance in coordinating Acts with Paul's letters: *The Letters to the Thessalonians* (Anchor Bible 32B; New York: Doubleday, 2000) 55-78. J. Knox argued that Paul's letters should be privileged in relation to Acts: *Chapters in a Life of Paul* (New York: Abingdon, 1950). Even W. Ramsay's *St. Paul the Traveller and the Roman Citizen* (New York: Putnam's, 1896), still revered as an icon of scholarship among conservative Evangelicals, acknowledges that Acts shapes the story it relates. Where we contradict Acts with Paul (or vice versa), I think we need to state our reasons.

Perpetually restless, reckless with his own life and the lives of others, Paul careened around the Mediterranean – Asia Minor, Judea, Syria, Greece, and Italy – wrecking the tranquility of synagogues, forums, and fledgling churches, making friends and breaking friendships with the compulsive abandon of a man possessed. In detailing that itinerary and its punctuation with visits to Jerusalem, the place of inference is comparable to the approach I take in the study of Jesus,[4] although the sources involved are as different as Paul is from Jesus. I consciously acknowledge that historians *infer* from evidence, and do not really "prove" anything in a scientific or mathematical sense. That is a well-established principle in the study of history, although some students of the New Testament cling to the nineteenth-century myth of historical "objectivity." Paul is inexplicable apart from the environment of apocalyptic zeal, intense mysticism, and incipient violence that characterized first-century Judaism. Never an armchair theologian, Paul was nothing like as pious or serene as his reputation among dogmatists and hagiographers.

Paul is the most complex, brilliant, troubled figure in the New Testament. He speaks for himself – inviting us to trace his turbulent, dramatic life through the evolution of his vastly influential theology. The more we delve into the man and his thinking, the closer we approach the inner flame that once ignited a new religion.

Method as developed in recent approaches

Recent treatments of Paul fed my own approach, by illustrating the incomplete pictures that can result from attempts to reconstruct his thought on the basis of archaeological reconstruction alone or by theological synthesis alone. These works represent the best of current thinking in regard to Paul, and yet also point to the necessity for a revision of critical method.

All three of the books I would like to discuss manage for the most part to avoid common stereotypes about Paul. The authors realize, for example, that Paul's network of relationships fell short of being an organization, that his theological reflections did not amount to a system, and that his object and hope was not for a new religion, but – as he said himself – that "all Israel shall be saved" (Rom 11:26). There is a dark side to the mystery of Paul: a passionate intellectual, the entire direction of his efforts is often distorted by Christianity's intellectual critics. Except for one work to be considered here, that distortion does

---

[4] See *Rabbi Jesus. An Intimate Biography* (New York: Doubleday, 2000) xx-xxii.

not find champions here, and even A.N. Wilson – who sets himself up as a kind of anti-Paul[5] – realizes that the old picture of Paul the bureaucrat will not stand up to critical attention.

The most sweeping of these books is by A.N. Wilson. He concerns himself with Paul's "mind" on the grandest of scales – and with good reason. The actual content of Paul's thought has proven to be one of the most seminal influences in the way we in the West think about humanity. That is the case whether we reflect at the level of the individual or at the level of society. "For I do not do the good that I will, but I perform the evil that I do not will" – a single sentence within an eloquent analysis (Rom 7:19) brings home the truth of living with a divided being and a torn self-consciousness. If Paul did not spell out the significance of that statement, Augustine did (in his *Confessions*), while Dostoyevsky and Freud explored its implications nearly two millennia after Paul's death.

The same Augustine also took up the social critique that Paul pioneered. Paul wrote that people in society tend to falsify what they perceive of God, and to turn worship into a service of self. And they have to live with the result, which Paul incomparably described: "God gave them over in the desires of their hearts to uncleanness, so that they dishonored their bodies among themselves" (Rom 1:24). Human experience develops in the tension between a people's perception of God and their devotion to their own selfish ends. As Augustine put it in his comprehensive account of global history (*On the City of God*), the city defined by the love of God is ever opposed to the city defined by the love of self, until God will emerge as victorious at the end. The conviction that history is instructive, and will vindicate the force that ultimately shapes it, remains with us. It is perhaps most obvious in the analysis of Karl Marx, but it is also what animates the (perhaps, as the past decade has shown, overly optimistic) claim in the West that the American victory in the Cold War signals the triumph of free enterprise capitalism.

Paul's profound and disturbing contributions to human thought, his analysis of what corrupts us individually and socially, have proven difficult to make peace with. Just as there are periodic rediscoveries of Paul (most notably, during the Reformation), so rebellion against his insights has become a regular feature of discourse in the West. Wouldn't it be easier to make our way in life if we were not con-

---

[5] A.N. Wilson, *Paul. The Mind of the Apostle* (New York and London: Norton, 1977).

flicted within ourselves, and if we did not need to live with the consequences of our own history? In his book, Wilson even makes the claim that the Cold War was an example of Pauline thought at odds with itself: the West represented Paul's individualism, while the Soviet Union represented his historicism.[6]

That sweeping generalization is by no means incidental, because Wilson holds that it is part of our Post-Christian faith that we no longer accept Pauline breaches within ourselves, between the good and our ability to achieve it, and outside ourselves, between history and our aspirations for change. As he himself puts his position:[7]

> The majority of good people in the world, and the majority of religious people, have always been Stoics and Pharisees... It is our function to follow the precepts of chastity, generosity towards those less fortunate to ourselves and piety. That is the whole requirement of the Torah.

Part of Wilson's effort is to argue for this rational understanding of religion against Paul's paradoxical version of religious truth.

When Wilson claims Paul is "the first romantic poet in history,"[8] that represents no compliment. Wilson is appreciative of Paul's eloquence, especially in Romans;[9] he rightly attacks those who see Paul as a misogynist, and even makes him out as a feminist – relatively speaking, of course.[10] In the latter regard, Wilson actually corrects (and in my view over-corrects) the argument of his earlier book on Jesus, and claims that Paul's activity, rather than Jesus' influence, brought women into the movement and therefore – by the projection of the primitive Christian ethos onto Jesus – into the Gospels. But Wilson feels free to put aside all the trivial attacks that have been directed against Paul because his own complaint is far more fundamental. Paul's idea that the tortured figure on the cross should represent the divine vocation and hope for humanity at the end of time seems to Wilson "bizarre enough within the context of Jewish hopes," and "simply gibberish" outside that context.[11]

Paul's expectation of the actual end of things seems noble to Wilson in its inclusion of outsiders, but also appears "a completely literal" conception. Wilson's observation at this point is perhaps the most

---

[6] Wilson, *Paul. The Mind*, 190.
[7] Wilson, *Paul. The Mind*, 123-125, 154-158, 124.
[8] Wilson, *Paul. The Mind*, 221.
[9] Wilson, *Paul. The Mind*, 194.
[10] Wilson, *Paul. The Mind*, 142-145.
[11] Wilson, *Paul. The Mind*, 177.

revealing in his book:[12]

> It disturbs us that a sublime religious genius could entertain such primitive and limited ideas, but that is our man.

It is interesting (and not a little ironic) that, of the three books in question, Wilson's is the keenest to invoke historical objectivity as its standard, because in the end, it is the one that most clearly represents the challenge of Paul's ideas in theological terms. Wilson's ambitious project tries to replace Paul's faith with his own.

Paul's ability to start an argument has never been in much dispute. What *is* intriguing is this: Why did Paul come to say what he did? Where did his convictions and ideas derive from, and how did they become influential within Christianity (and beyond Christianity)? These three books all contribute answers to those questions. What they have to say is not always complementary, and there are some direct disagreements to be observed, but each in its own way points the way ahead to an appreciation of Paul, as I hope I will shown by the end of this essay.

a. Jerome Murphy-O'Connor

Pride of place among the three books belongs in my view to Jerome Murphy-O'Connor's study,[13] which is at once refreshing and comprehensive. No teacher can afford not to consider its treatment carefully, as the author (Professor of New Testament at the École Biblique in Jerusalem), wends his way through the major questions and issues of Pauline scholarship with persistent reference to both primary sources and critical literature. This is no doubt the most demanding, but also the most rewarding, of the three books. It provides you with both Murphy-O'Connor's own views (some of which are original and daring) and a good sense of what the (enormous) field of Pauline studies looks like at the moment.

Murphy-O'Connor's prose is lucid and lively, even when he is discussing scholarship that is less so. He understands that we should begin our study of Paul with the letters he himself wrote, and use Acts as an ancillary resource. This principle was applied stringently by John

---

[12] Wilson, *Paul. The Mind*, 177, 178.

[13] J. Murphy-O'Connor, *Paul. A Critical Life* (New York and Oxford: Clarendon, 1996).

Knox,[14] but Murphy-O'Connor is rightly more accommodating of Acts in his biography. He agrees with Acts that Paul was a Roman citizen, born in Tarsus, who was also called Saul, although he is more skeptical about Paul having relatives in Jerusalem (a disagreement in which I have taken the side of Acts against Murphy-O'Connor).[15] Yet at times Murphy-O'Connor is perhaps a little credulous in his embrace of Acts' reconstruction. Knox may have been too zealous in denying that Paul had lived in Jerusalem, but moved directly from Tarsus to Damascus, yet Murphy-O'Connor himself stretches Paul's stay in Jerusalem as a Pharisee to a period of some fifteen years, during which time he studied under Gamaliel (so Acts 22:3).[16] Although the influence of Gamaliel upon Paul may be traced, the assertion that Paul was Gamaliel's disciple appears hyperbolic to me.[17]

Murphy-O'Connor's chronology puts a well-connected Paul in Jerusalem in 30 CE, the year of the crucifixion, but Murphy-O'Connor points out that "Hassidic students in Jerusalem today manage to maintain their principle of avoiding knowledge of secular events; it is even reported that they were completely unaware of Anwar Sadat's peace visit to Israel, which brought the whole of Jerusalem into the streets."[18] Still, the young Paul was not painfully isolated, since in Murphy-O'Connor's reconstruction he also had a wife and children. They perished in an earthquake or an epidemic, which fed Paul's desire to persecute Christians:[19]

> A well-known psychological mechanism switches anger from unacceptable to acceptable channels of expression. As a Pharisee, Paul believed God had a hand in all that happened in history ... one part of his theology would lead him logically to ascribe blame to God, but this was forbidden by another part of his religious perspective, which prescribed complete submission to God's will. If his pain and anger could not be directed against God, it had to find another target. An outlet for his pent-up desire for vengeance had to be rationalized.

Murphy-O'Connor is happy with this explanation, because it accounts both for Paul's zeal in persecution and for his silence regarding his wife and family.

---

[14] J. Knox, *Chapters in a Life of Paul* (New York: Abingdon, 1950).
[15] Murphy-O'Connor, *Paul. A Critical Life*, 35-46, cf. Chilton, *Rabbi Paul*, 18-19.
[16] Murphy-O'Connor, *Paul. A Critical Life*, 54-55, 59.
[17] Chilton and J. Neusner, "Paul and Gamaliel," *The Bulletin of Biblical Research* 14.1 (2004) and *Review of Rabbinic Judaism* 8.1 (2005) 113-162; Chilton, *Rabbi Paul* 28-47.
[18] Murphy-O'Connor, *Paul. A Critical Life*, 61-62.
[19] Murphy-O'Connor, *Paul. A Critical Life*, 62-65

One of the features of Murphy-O'Connor's work (here and elsewhere) that makes it outstanding is that he directly confronts and responds to critical questions. He does not hide behind the academic dodge (commonly called being "judicious") of weighing up other people's answers until the original question seems to disappear. And what he says about Paul the Pharisee, complete with wife and children, is not out of line with other controversial stands that he takes in this book. He is willing, for example, to accept the hypothesis of Paul's imprisonment in Ephesus, several years before his final arrest, despite the description in Acts of a generally peaceful (but certainly not "entirely peaceful," as Murphy-O'Connor states[20]) ministry there. Moreover, he assigns Colossians, Philemon, and Philippians to this early period, before Corinthians and Romans, and just after Galatians (pp. 158-184). Then, too, he returns to an interesting idea he has floated before, that when Acts 18:25 refers to Apollos as "familiar with only the baptism of John," that does not imply he was a disciple of John the Baptist. Rather, the reference is to baptism "as administered by Jesus when he was preaching John's baptism."[21] There is real strength in this vigorous assertion of new possibilities in the address of persistent questions.

Still, the speculation in regard to Paul's wife and children goes well beyond the usual resort to inference in scholarship, although it may be a necessary corollary to imagining Paul as a resident in Jerusalem during fifteen years of professional Pharisaism. (During this period, Murphy-O'Connor also assumes that Paul practiced no trade and did not work manually.[22] How he would then have broken into the highly controlled profession of tent-making remains unexplained.) There is nothing inherently implausible in imagining Paul as widowed or divorced. Paul's argument for remaining single in 1 Corinthians includes the wish that people might follow his example (1 Cor 7:7, 8). That is the sort of advice that a currently married man obviously should not give, and would not likely get away with giving. Although it is just possible that a widowed or divorced person might offer such counsel, it seems more likely to me that Paul's personal status would be offered in imitation on the understanding that he had *remained* unmarried (in this regard, see also 1 Cor 9:5, 6). Discussion of this issue shows no sign of abating; Murphy-O'Connor has assured that it will become

---

[20] Murphy-O'Connor, 175.

[21] Murphy-O'Connor, 172-173. I have developed implications of this insight in *Rabbi Jesus*, 41-63 and *Rabbi Paul*, 175-181.

[22] Murphy-O'Connor. 86.

even more heated and it certainly cannot be settled here. Still, if we are not in a position to resolve so basic an issue, can we say that anyone is capable of writing a "critical life" of Paul by following Murphy-O'Connor's lead?

What is even more interesting here is the use Murphy-O'Connor makes of his own speculative finding about Paul's marriage. Paul's persecution of Christians is not taken to be an activity authorized by the high priest (as Acts says), but is characterized as the behavior of "an immature religious bigot working out his personal problems."[23] His conversion made a huge difference: he ended his life of scholarly leisure and began to earn his living as a tent-maker, and identified his purpose from the outset as preaching the gospel to the Gentiles, of all people.[24] Although Murphy-O'Connor acknowledges that the Pharisaic community in Jerusalem must have offered Paul considerable support, as he sees it, Paul's conversion involved framing his life in a new way in conscious relationship to others:[25]

> The conviction that led him to a new life had nothing to do with rational evidence. It was a leap of faith rooted in an unknowable impulse. Yet he would not have been human had he not felt the need for some justification. This he found in those whose lives exhibited, not only the fruits of the effort he was making (and perhaps considered inadequate), but the pattern of behaviour appropriate to the new mode of existence.

Although the range of its detail might be the most obvious feature of Murphy-O'Connor's study, this insight (based, in turn, upon Abraham J. Malherbe's exegesis of 1 Thessalonians) is a profoundly important help in understanding Paul. Whether or not Murphy-O'Connor's speculations in regard to Paul's early life are convincing, what emerges from the pages of Paul's own letters is a deep commitment to working out who the people of God are on the basis of the faith shared by being joined by Christ in baptism.

b. A.N. Wilson and Tom Wright

Although Murphy-O'Connor's book is wonderfully lucid, few studies of Paul can compete with Wilson's for the pleasure of reading. He is a skilled writer, and his imaginative powers are considerable. Sometimes, his imagination gets the better of critical common sense. So: the fire in

---

[23] Murphy-O'Connor, *Paul. A Critical Life*, 69.
[24] Murphy-O'Connor, *Paul. A Critical Life*, 85-95.
[25] Murphy-O'Connor, *Paul. A Critical Life*, 120.

Rome that Nero blamed on the Christians might have been their fault after all, "Who knows? An accidental fire might well have started in the hutment of some early Christian zealot baking bread or sizzling kebabs."[26] Speculation is fine, but Wilson's does nothing to explain the rumor (attested by Tacitus) that the fire was started by order, nor does it accord with what one would expect to be available by way of food and cooking facilities in an underclass Roman "hutment," as Wilson calls what every other historian refers to as a tenement. The comment just seems to be a way of trying to make Nero somehow more palatable and Christians more clueless.

More to the point, Wilson paints an implausible picture of Paul's career in Jerusalem. He inverts the principle that Paul's letters should be given preference to Acts, and denies that Paul was truly a Pharisee. Instead, Wilson exaggerates Acts to make Paul an actual member of the police of the Temple, and he argues that his interest was financial:[27]

> And one can only assume that in a city when 20,000 sheep were slaughtered in a single day there was a lively trade in sheepskin and other leathers. A useful place if you happened to make your money converting animals hides into tents. If one were also a tentmaker with a religious obsession, where better to spend some years of your youth than Jerusalem?

Had Wilson spent a little more time with ancient descriptions of tent-making (which involved working with felt, not only leather) and the operation of the Temple (which strictly controlled its markets), that rhetorical question would have been cut. Murphy-O'Connor may easily be consulted on both points for clarification. Unlike Murphy-O'Connor, Wilson does not fight shy of the implication that Paul may have been aware of the arrest and execution of Jesus; indeed, Wilson even concludes that Paul took an active part in those events.[28]

Precisely because Paul was partially responsible for the crucifixion of Jesus, he came to see Jesus and the Torah as two principles in opposition. Wilson can only understand that Pauline opposition in psychological terms.[29] As he then goes on to explain:[30]

> The great blessing in the life of a Jew, the Divinely-given Teaching (Torah) becomes in Paul's vision a Law which is a curse. The accursed thing, the Roman torture, becomes a blessing in which he "glories."

---

[26] Wilson, *Paul. The Mind*, p. 4.
[27] Wilson, *Paul. The Mind*, 51-52.
[28] Wilson, *Paul. The Mind*, 55.
[29] Wilson, *Paul. The Mind*, 57.
[30] Wilson, *Paul. The Mind*, 72.

This reading of Gal 3:13, 14 (to which Wilson returns on several occasions) is compelling, and it identifies the conflict Paul referred to again and again, between the promise of the covenant and the attempt – the failed attempt in Paul's mind – to guard the covenant by means of legal obedience. When Wilson mines the book of Acts for Paul's position, it is in order to discover the same conflict, resolved by the salvation offered in Christ alone.[31]

But the portrait of Paul as a policeman of the Temple, and the suggestion that the Temple wielded the kind of jurisdiction Acts attributes to it, are really quite implausible. The embellishment of Paul's active trade in sacred animal skins is fanciful. These weaknesses need to be acknowledged, but they should not distract the careful reader from the underlying strength of much of what Wilson says. The dialectical tension between the promise of the covenant and the obligations of the Torah *is* precisely the starting point of Paul's thought (at least, after his baptism), and the fulcrum of his religious experience. But in Wilson's case, as in Murphy-O'Connor's, we need to keep in mind that we know of these tensions as a result of Paul's intellectual development, attested in his letters, not from any psychological case study of Paul's personality. The situation is similar to that of Jesus, where the development of his teaching and experience as he moved from place to place is palpable, although his personal psychology remains a matter of surmise.

Scholars will no doubt delight in citing Wilson's mistakes and missteps, but the reason for the basic good sense of some of what he says also needs to be considered. Of the three books reviewed here, his is the only one that takes serious account of Paul's background and experience in the Diaspora. Although Murphy-O'Connor is more precise in evoking Tarsus, Wilson makes the connection to the religious milieu of the city, and makes a comparison between Paul and Philo of Alexandria. Because he is aware of the variety possible within early Judaism, he can imagine Paul converting his experience of the cross of Jesus into a Mystery similar to the death and rising to life of Herakles:[32]

> In the mind of the Romanised Jew, the tormented Pharisee, the temple guard and tentmaker for the legions, it was Paul himself who was nailed to that instrument of torture, Paul who died, Paul who suffered, Paul who rose.

---

[31] So, for example, in Acts 13:38-39, on p. 122.
[32] Wilson, *Paul. The Mind*, 24-29, 38-39, 60.

If we take away the psychological speculation, what we have here is a sure-footed attempt to find new terrain for Paul, to locate his intellectual center in the Diaspora, rather than in Palestine.

Many books have been written on the topic of Paul and the religion of the territorial Israel of his time (usually referred to as "Palestinian Judaism" in the secondary literature). But the Hellenistic Diaspora, not "Palestine," was the seedbed of Paul's life and thought. Asia Minor's Judaism had its own flavor and character, venerating the memory of Noah, for example, whose ark was said to have landed locally, on Mount Ararat. Jews in Tarsus even claimed their town was identical with the primeval city mentioned in connection with Noah called Tarshish (Gen 10:4, connected to Tarsus by Josephus, *Antiquities* 1.127). Legends of this kind express the religious sensibility of the Diaspora during the first century, where the vast majority of Jews lived.

Classicists are familiar with the oracle called the Sibyl – -the premiere prophetess of Greco-Roman culture. She was such a pivotal figure of prophecy that Judaism claimed her as its own. The *Sibylline Oracles* (3:809-829), a popular Diaspora book written in Greek and never included in the Bible (whether in Hebrew or Greek), present the Sibyl as Noah's daughter-in-law! Sometimes obviously made-up history is the most accurate measure of an ancient people's faith, because it shows us what they wanted to believe was true.

For Israelites in the Diaspora, the most noble of non-Jewish people (such as the mantic Sibyl), even if they did not fully embrace Judaism by circumcising their males, could acknowledge the God of Israel by following the commandments of Noah: refraining from idolatry, from consuming blood, and from promiscuous sexuality. Such people were known as worshippers of God or God-fearers, who – like their Jewish contemporaries – held themselves aloof from some of the civic religions of Tarsus. Precisely this group offered Paul an introduction to his mission to the Gentiles after his conversion, as Wilson's study alone among the three reviewed here makes clear.

Tom Wright closes his study of Paul with a comprehensive critique of Wilson's position.[33] He is most scathing of Wilson's attempt to place Paul in the context of the Diaspora. Enough has been quoted from Wilson's prose to make it plain that his tone, when it concerns Christianity and Judaism, is mostly patronizing, but it is *not* quite true to say

---

[33] N.T. Wright, *What Saint Paul Really Said. Was Paul of Tarsus the Real Founder of Christianity?* (Grand Rapids: Eerdmans, 1997) 167-178.

that he "assumes, throughout, that Judaism was a local, almost tribal religion."[34] In fact, Wilson is prepared to describe the Pharisees in remarkably universalistic terms:[35]

> They taught that the Teaching (Torah) which came from Almighty God – while itself being holy and unchangeable – was of universal application. It was addressed to all mankind, to Gentiles as well as to Jews, and it was therefore necessary in every age and in every place to interpret the Torah for those willing or able to listen to it.

Although there is much to criticize in Wilson's book, its attempt to balance the Judaism and the Hellenism implicit in Paul's thought makes it both worthwhile and intriguing. What is less understandable is how Wilson (and Wright, for that matter) can have so excluded the issue of purity from a discussion of Pharisaism. That omission is fortunately made up for by Murphy-O'Connor.

Wright slips into the pattern of more conventional recent scholarship by seeking to place Paul in a pre-defined Judaic niche. Where Murphy-O'Connor looks to the Pharisaism of Hillel (derived from Gamaliel), Wright tries to make the young Paul into a follower of Shammai. He does so on the ground that Paul described himself as zealous for the traditions of his fathers (Gal 1:14), that "zeal" was a characteristic of revolutionary aspirations, and that the followers of Shammai were especially revolutionary in that sense.[36]

All of those assertions are problematic. Rabbinic literature presents a stereotype of opposition between Hillel and Shammai; what each of them actually taught is a matter of debate, and no responsible scholar would claim to know the attitudes of either of them. Given the state of the evidence, it would take more than simple assertion to show that Shammai was actually on the side of revolution. (As Wright knows, Acts in any case puts Paul in the circle of Gamaliel.) "Zeal," of course, can be what animates "Zealots" (as Josephus named one group during the period of the revolt against Rome), but one might also be zealous for spiritual gifts, which is just what Paul tells his readers to be in 1 Cor 14:1. Paul describes himself in terms of his zeal to persecute the Church in Phil 3:6, but he does not portray "zeal" for revolution as the center of his former life.

That center is rather occupied by the Torah (or law [nomos], as Paul says in his Greek idiom). When Paul calls himself a Pharisee in Phil

---

[34] So Wright, *What Saint Paul Really Said*, 171.
[35] Wilson, *Paul. The Mind*, 121.
[36] Wright, *What Saint Paul Really Said*, 25-35.

3:5, he does not identify himself with any particular group, but he says he was "as to law, a Pharisee." That is an interesting qualification. It may suggest that Paul was more a Pharisee in his own mind than he was in public affiliation – hardly an unusual position for a recent arrival to Jerusalem to be in. In its description of Stephen's preaching, and eventual stoning, Acts refers to his dispute in Jerusalem with several groups of Jews from the Diaspora (6:9). Some of the people involved came from Cilicia, whose principal city was Tarsus. This section of Acts, of course, is where Paul is introduced, as the young Saul, at whose feet the witnesses against Stephen deposited their clothing (Acts 7:58). In its implicit characterization of Saul/Paul as a zealous outsider, Acts may be more accurate than the three recent studies reviewed here.

The real point of Wright's study is not its speculation regarding Paul's early life, but its engagement with the issue of Paul's theology. In centering that theology on the cross, he insists that Paul "means that the entire scriptural story, the great drama of God's dealings with Israel, came together when the young Jew from Nazareth was nailed up by the Romans and left to die."[37] That realization carried with it two profound implications, which are the focus of Wright's lucid discussion. First, the great victory Israel anticipated was not purely in the future, but had already occurred. Second, faith in what God had done in Christ, rather than the Torah, now became the marker of the people of God.[38]

That shift in the definition of Judaism, a shift that Wright persistently (and correctly) describes as *within* Judaism, involves attributing divinity to Jesus. Wright devotes a chapter to this theme, and shows that "Paul saw the human Jesus as the revelation of the one God."[39] So profound was Paul's conviction and experience, that he came to contend "that at the heart of Jewish monotheism – within the oneness of the one God – lay a plurality, a reciprocal relationship." The connection between how God is revealed and how God is understood to be within the divine nature is crucial for an understanding of Paul's conception of God and of Jesus.

c. Assessment

What remains after all the theories about Paul, of course, is the mys-

---

[37] Wright, *What Saint Paul Really Said*, 49.
[38] See especially Wright, *What Saint Paul Really Said*, 93-94.
[39] Wright, *What Saint Paul Really Said*, 63-75, 72.

tery of Paul. All three of the books we have considered have a great deal to teach us, about Paul in his historical circumstances (Murphy-O'Connor), about Paul in his religious and intellectual milieu (Wilson), about Paul as a Judaic theologian (Wright). But turn back to our original question: how did Paul manage to make his extraordinary contribution to the way we think about ourselves individually and in human society?

In a way, all of our authors deepen our sense of the mystery, because they demonstrate clearly, beyond any reasonable doubt, that Paul was not in any position to speak as a commanding philosopher of the Greco-Roman world. Trying to convince a few dozen congregations of primitive Christians about the nature of God, he nonetheless wound up giving a lesson about human being that would endure for at least two millennia.

The tendency to psychologize Paul is understandable, because it is natural to look for some sort of psychic irregularity in any great figure. But it simply does not illuminate the mystery of Paul to say he was a bigot who found love (so Murphy-O'Connor) or a greedy zealot who found guilt (so Wilson) or a violent revolutionary who learned to experience and seek peace (so Wright). Those pictures are excessively speculative, not based on critically reliable arguments, and they do not get at Paul's real originality.

In his letter to the Galatians (above all, in chs. 3–4), Paul spells out how he pursues the truth of God in a way that distinguished him from other Christian teachers of his time. For him, the covenant with Abraham was a promise God made to all people, when he said, "In you all the nations shall be blessed" (Gal 3:8). That promise was kept on hold when God gave the Torah, but in the end that functioned as Law, and proved to be an obstacle to the promise. Finally, however, in the case of Christ Jesus, Paul was convinced, we all have a focus of faith which makes us the inheritors of the promise, God's own children and Abraham's, and God pours Spirit upon us just as he did upon Jesus.

That is the original argument of Paul, spelled out in various ways in his letters. We can read how Paul found his insight (Galatians), how he fought for it in controversy (1 and 2 Corinthians) and how he framed it on cooler reflection (Romans), how he felt about it (Philippians). What was original about his argument was not that Jesus was the Son of God or that non-Jews might receive baptism. Those were matters of broad consensus. James, Peter, Barnabas and others all agreed that circumcision was not to be required of all Christians.[40] (There were teachers who insisted upon circumcision, but – contrary to what Wilson seems to believe – the New Testament shows us they were not in a predominant position.) Then again, it is just silly to argue that Paul invented the Eucharist;[41] the variety of texts in the New Testament attests that there were a variety of practices, and Paul was never in a position during his lifetime to determine the practice of the church as a whole.[42]

All the arguments that portray Paul as the great "originator" of Christianity miss the point. (Wilson gets the closest to making this argument, but even he does not actually subscribe to it, despite the impression given on the jacket of his book.) There were Christians before Paul, and after Paul there were Christians who disagreed with him. During his active career, Paul was quite aware that every other major teacher in Christianity (including his colleague Barnabas) disagreed with him (see Gal 2 above all). So it just will not do to pretend that Paul was the heroic founder of the religious movement known by the name Christian before he became a major figure within it (see Acts 11:19-26).

Paul's genius was that he saw that movement, which had a history by the time of his conversion that went back to the Galilean ministry of Jesus, as the fulfillment of the covenant with Abraham. Wright clearly understands the covenantal center of Paul's thought, but unfortunately he attributes a similar theology to Jesus himself.[43] Curiously, he is the only writer of the three who diminishes Paul's creativity. In effect, he sees Jesus as the fulfillment of the covenant *in Jesus' own messianic understanding* (a generalization few scholars would agree with), so that all Paul needs to do is then offer that fulfillment beyond the borders of Israel, among the Gentiles. But all you need do is consult a concordance of the New Testament to see that Paul, not Jesus, provided Christianity with an original theology of the covenant with Abraham.

Paul's teaching of the hidden covenant, promised to us and yet not part of our natural awareness, is precisely what brings us to the two great influences of his thought. Because if God has indeed called you,

---

[40] See Chilton and J. Neusner, *Judaism in the New Testament. Practices and Beliefs* (London and New York: Routledge, 1995).

[41] Wilson, *Paul. The Mind*, 165.

[42] See Chilton, *A Feast of Meanings. Eucharistic Theologies from Jesus through Johannine Circles* (NovTSup 72; Leiden: Brill, 1994).

[43] Wright, *What Saint Paul Really Said*, 178-183.

and wills you to have the divine Spirit within you, you have to wonder what it is within yourself that can resist such love. And alongside that flaw within us, Paul's teaching raises the question: how can the life of a society, inhibited by self-interest and legalism, come to reflect the glory of God? The perception of both those deep conflicts, the division within and the tension without, derive from Paul's vision that our humanity is rooted in a single covenant, promised to Abraham and sealed in Christ. That vision proved finally not to be compatible with the centrality of the unchanging Torah, which emerged as the supreme axiom of Rabbinic Judaism, but it was a generation before Christianity discovered, in the Epistle to the Hebrews, that its faith had made Christ the formal replacement of every major institution of Judaism. Once that had occurred, Christianity could emerge with its Pauline profile, against all that people might have expected during the time of Paul himself. The whole of Paul's life must be traced developmentally in order to appreciate the emergence of Christianity as an autonomous religion, distinct from Judaism. Within my analysis of that development, I have crafted a chronological account of pivotal moments with my biography of Paul:[44]

52-50 BCE: Cicero serves from Tarsus as governor of Cilicia.

47 BCE: Tarsans rename their city Juliopolis in honor of a visit from Julius Caesar.

42 BCE: on behalf of the Triumvirate, Mark Anthony confirms Tarsus' civic status and grants it exemption from duties.

15 BCE: Athenodorus, the tutor and adviser of Augustus, retires to Tarsus.

7 CE: Paul is born in Tarsus in Asia Minor into a proudly Jewish family, prospering in the profession of making tents.

28 CE, summer: Paul departs Tarsus for Jerusalem, taking the Aramaic name of Saul, to train as a Pharisee.

32 CE, between Passover and Pentecost: The Gospels attest a sequence of resurrection appearances, and the book of Acts indicates there were a series of visions during that summer. After the stoning of Stephen, and therefore during the summer, Paul's vision of the risen Jesus takes place

---

[44] See *Rabbi Paul. An Intellectual Biography* (New York: Doubleday, 2004), to which the pages numbers cited refer.

(Gal 1:15-17). He does not return to Jerusalem at that time, but goes to Arabia for three years, and returns to Damascus. At the end of this period of activity he has to escape from Damascus from Aretas IV, king of Nabatea, in a basket (2 Cor 11:32-33), probably after his first public flogging in a synagogue.

35: Three years after his conversion, Paul meets with Peter and James, Jesus' brother, in Jerusalem. During a period of fifteen days, he learns what Peter regularly teaches those baptized in Jesus' name (Gal 1:18-20). This is followed by a return to his native land probably after his second public flogging (Gal 1:21-24; pp. 84-85),

36: Defeat by Herod Antipas's army by Aretas IV (*Ant* 18.109-119).

37: The removal of Pontius Pilate and Caiaphas from office by the Roman legate Vitellius (*Ant* 18.88-95). Paul pioneers his sense of the Eucharist in Tarsus (pp. 92-93).

40: Paul joins Barnabas in Antioch, following Peter's vision (pp. 87, 99, 105).

42 (spring, pp. 113-116), or fourteen years before his correspondence with Corinth (2 Cor 12:2-4): Paul says he was taken up into the third heaven. This vision corresponds to his commission in Antioch under Barnabas's leadership to take his work among Gentiles into new areas (Acts 13:1-3). Striking across Cyprus first, Paul and Barnabas accepts the benefaction of Sergius Paulus, and travel into Asia Minor.

43: Paul's expulsion from Antioch in Asia Minor, probably along with his third flogging (p. 120); the threat of stoning at Iconium, perhaps with a fourth flogging? (p. 121), and the actual stoning at Lystra (pp. 122-123).

44: Paul's recovery in Derbe (pp. 124-130); the death of Herod Agrippa in Israel.

45 Paul returns to Antioch (p. 131), where followers of Jesus are for the first time called "Christians."

46, or fourteen years after the commission (p. 133): Paul again goes to Jerusalem with Barnabas and Titus (Gal 2:1-10). In addition to determining that circumcision should not be required of Gentile believers, spheres of apostolic influence are a principal concern (pp. 141-146). Peter's is the territory historically associated with circumcision, while Paul's is traditionally Gentile lands (v. 8). At the same time, Paul agrees to meet the needs of the community around in James in Jerusalem, which has been afflicted by the famine that has plagued Judea.

47: The circumcision of Timothy (pp. 148-149).

48: Paul, Silvanus, and Timothy visit Philippi (pp. 151-154), and Paul first encounters the lictor's rods before moving on to Thessalonica (pp. 154-157).

49: Claudius's expulsion of many Jews from Rome, while Paul is in Berea (pp. 157-158) – where the Jewish opponents from Thessalonica may have engineered the fifth flogging – and Athens (pp. 158-161).

50: Paul meets Priscilla and Aquila in Corinth (Acts 18:2, 1 Cor 16:19). From Corinth, Paul writes with Silas and Timothy to the Thessalonians (pp. 161-170) during the tenure of Gallio (July 1, 51– July 1, 52: Acts 18:12). Violence, probably including a second beating with rods (p. 167), ends a successful period.
In Paul's absence, a meeting in Jerusalem – sealed by a decree from James – stipulates requirements of purity for Gentile believers. Later in 52, the penultimate journey of Paul to Jerusalem (Acts 18:22).

53: The confrontation at Antioch, occasioned by the decree of James (Gal 2:11-21; Acts 15:19-24; pp. 169-170).

53-56: Paul's period in Ephesus (with a retreat to Macedonia and Troas at the end, after Paul's third beating with rods); the composition of Galatians, 1 Corinthians, and 2 Corinthians (pp. 173-221).

57: Letter to the Romans, written from Miletus, off the coast from Ephesus, and final arrangements for the Sacrifice of the Nations. Paul's arrest in Jerusalem and detention in Caesarea; the composition of Philemon the following year (pp. 222-242).

59-62: Festus's tenure, overlapping with the end of that of the high priest, Ananias (Acts 25–26). Paul's appeal to the Philippians for help in his letter to that city, written with Timothy from Myra in 60 (p. 242) and later expanded by Timothy (pp. 242-245).

62: The death of James, and Paul's release, his final period in Rome, and the composition of poetry later incorporated by Timothy in the letter to the Colossians (pp. 246-250).

64: Paul's death in Rome under Nero (pp. 250-253). Paul's followers, Timothy most prominently, begin to collect and edit his works in Ephesus, Troas, and Miletus.

66: The refusal of the Emperor's offerings in Jerusalem, signaling the national scale of revolt against Rome.

70: The burning of the Temple by the Roman troops under Titus.

73: The composition of Mark's Gospel in Rome; the end of the revolt against Rome in Palestine.

75: Josephus publishes his *Jewish War*.

80: The composition of Matthew's Gospel, in Damascus.

90: The composition of Luke's Gospel and Acts, in Antioch. Timothy's release of letters written by Paul with his help, together with the Epistle to the Ephesians (pp. 254-255). The Pastoral Epistles are composed later in the same decade (pp. 255-260).

93: Josephus publishes his *Antiquities of the Jews*.

95: The Epistle to the Hebrews (pp. 261-262).

100: The composition of John's Gospel, in Ephesus.

Although no moment in this development is marginal to Paul's intellectual biography and to the emergence of Christianity, his conversion clearly serves as the common point of reference, and will serve as our paradigmatic case in framing an approach to Paul.

Paul's Conversion
Twenty years after the fact, Paul explained the meaning of his own conversion (Gal 1:15-17):

> When it pleased the one who separated me from my mother's belly and called me through his grace to uncover his Son in me so that I should announce him triumphant among the Gentiles, I did not confer with flesh and blood. Neither did I go up to Jerusalem to those who were apostles before me; but I departed to Arabia, and again I returned to Damascus.

This revelation was prophetic – like a prophet Paul felt he had been predestined to this moment from his "mother's belly" (Jer 1:5; Isa 49:1-6). The unveiling of God's Son within took priority over any human contact or circumstance.

He puts the deep content of this experience so economically you might miss its pivotal reference: God determined "to uncover his Son in" Paul. Conventional translations have stood in the way of what he clearly said here. The term "uncover" (*apokalupsai*) in Greek is typically rendered "reveal" in English versions of the Bible. By the same token, the noun *apokalupsis*, our "apocalypse," becomes "revelation." These translations make readers think in terms of external stimuli coming to the seer like ordinary sense perceptions. The basic meaning of this language, however, is that a heavenly mystery has its cover (its -*kalupsis*) taken off (*apo*): the veil of circumstance is momentarily stripped from spiritual reality. Here the cover is removed from God's Son, who is "in" (Greek: *en*) Paul, within his consciousness in an experience uniquely his.

Paul's experience was not of an objective event that other people witnessed with him. He alone was converted that day. His brief reference in Galatians relates to a personal moment of disclosure, an unveiling of the divine. He conceived of his mystical breakthrough in ways rooted in his mixed background, pagan and Jewish. Part of its significance for him was that the risen Jesus represented the fusion of his Tarsan heritage and his Judaic faith.

Many Stoics in Tarsus were taken up with the possibility of people moving beyond knowledge of the divine – and becoming divine themselves. Cicero – the Stoic philosopher who briefly governed Cilicia and was familiar with the teaching of Athenodorus of Tarsus – voiced this hope for exaltation to the status of the gods. Cicero related the Stoic theme of *apotheosis* in his classic composition, the "Dream of Scipio," his friend.

In the dream, Scipio is taken into heaven, reminded of its superiority to the earth by an angelic guide, and then told he is not limited by his own mortality (*Republic* 6.24):

> Know, then, that you are a god, which lives, feels, remembers, and foresees, indeed rules, governs, and moves the body over which it is set, just as the supreme god does with the universe. And just as this eternal god moves the imperfectly mortal universe, so an everlasting spirit moves a frail body.

Stoics promised immortality, *apotheosis* forever, and foretastes of that in this world. Knowledge of one's true self mirrored the power of the supreme god of heaven.

The popular source of early Judaism called *1 Enoch* reflected a similar longing, and shows how the God of Israel could fulfill Stoic aspirations.[45] Precisely because it was a popular, composite work, there were many add-ons through the centuries, but among the most ancient of its visions has Enoch describe his mystical journey into heaven (*1 Enoch* 14:8-12):

> And behold I saw the clouds: And they were calling me in a vision; and the fogs were calling me; and the course of the stars and the lightnings were rushing me and causing me to desire; and in the vision, the winds were causing me to fly and rushing me high up into heaven. And I kept coming until I approached a wall which was built of white marble and surrounded by tongues of fire; and it began to frighten me. And I came into the tongues of fire and drew near to a great house which was built of white marble, and the inner walls were like tessallated sheets of white marble, the floor of crystal, the ceiling like the path of the stars and lightnings between which stood fiery cherubim and their heaven of water; and flaming fire surrounded the wall, and its gates were burning with fire.

In this classic from ancient Judaic visions, Enoch then proceeds to the very Throne of God that Moses, Isaiah, Ezekiel and Daniel had also seen.

Enoch relates a vision, while Scipio experiences a dream, but they share a common focus: ascent beyond astral forces into the very presence of God. Paul's vision showed him neither his personal immortality, as in Scipio's case, nor the heavenly court Enoch had described. Rather, in his words the "Son" of God was disclosed inside him.

Two thousand years of Christianity makes us think instantly of Jesus when we hear of the "Son of God." But the phrase had a life of its own before it was applied to Jesus, referring to angels (Gen 6:2), the whole people called Israel (Hos 11:1), and the king in David's line (Ps 2:7). Direct revelation extends God's favor to people and angels; each is "the Son," "the beloved," as Jesus became[46] in his vision at his baptism.

When Paul felt the divine "Son" uncovered within himself, he encountered the revelation he had known as a Pharisee in the Temple,

---

[45] There is good evidence that *1 Enoch* circulated in Greek in the Diaspora as well as in Aramaic in Judea and Galilee (where it influenced both John the Baptist and Jesus). See E. Isaac, "1 (Ethiopic Apocalypse of) Enoch," The *Old Testament Pseudepigrapha* (New York: Doubleday, 1983) 1.5-12.

[46] See Mark 1:11 and *Rabbi Jesus*, 41-63.

but now it was raging inside him. As angels had once guided Scipio and Enoch, a supernatural guide, a "Son" representing the divine Father, brought Paul to the heaven within himself. That is why the answer to his question, "Who are you, Lord?" came as the most terrifying thing he ever heard. "I am Jesus, whom you persecute!" (Acts 26:15). No response could have agonized him more. Profound loyalty to the Temple, not malice, had led Paul to serve Caiaphas, to resist the malcontents from Galilee and the Diaspora who claimed their dead rabbi's authority trumped the high priest's. Yet now this angelic Son of God identified himself as Jesus, risen from the dead.

Obeying the apocalyptic voice meant that Paul had to be baptized in Jesus' name. This practice had been introduced among Jesus' followers in Jerusalem to signal that, just as John had once immersed people in water, so the risen Jesus now drenched believers in the Holy Spirit (Acts 1:5). Among Jesus' first followers, this immersion in Spirit was the indispensable ritual of faith.

Paul never named the man who baptized him. For him baptism was a supernatural event, so its human agency did not matter. From first to last, he was a man of ideas, virtually without interest in circumstantial details. Occasionally, he lets some historical information slip while making an argument, but that is usually inadvertent. It is as if Paul begrudged the curiosity of later historians.

He even says that he "did not confer with flesh and blood" after the uncovering of God's Son within (Gal 1:16) – but departed to Arabia. Grammatically that *could* mean he had absolutely no contact with anyone. But that makes no sense: someone must have baptized him, brought him to the moment when – as he said happens to everyone who believes in Jesus (Gal 4:6; Rom 8:14-15) – the Spirit of God's Son entered his heart, and he called upon God as his own *Abba*, his divine Father.

When Paul says he did not confer with flesh and blood at this point, he must mean he did not have any human encounter that was important to him. His mind was totally occupied with the vision of Christ that baptism brought to completion. He says nothing about who actually did the baptizing and where. Nonetheless, he later states that, after his baptism and a three-year sojourn in Arabia, he "returned to Damascus" (Gal 1:17). So we have got him: he admits he had been in Damascus before, which is just where the book of Acts puts Paul's baptism. Pinning Paul down is difficult, but by cross-examining his letters, paying attention to Acts, and keeping his historical setting in mind, we can pick up the track of Christianity's most mercurial apostle.

This is a case where the classic problem of the relationship between Galatians and Acts cannot be escaped. In two of its three tellings of Paul's vision, Acts names Ananias as the disciple who – acting under divine guidance – baptized Paul (9:10-19 and 22:12-16). There is no reason to doubt that, following the crucifixion and resurrection, Jesus' Galilean followers found their old haunts uncongenial, and would gravitate to cities such as Damascus. Ananias knew the city, familiar with "the Way called Straight" between two of the city's famous seven gates (Acts 9:11) – where Paul stayed with a disciple named Judas just after his vision.

What happened to Paul next suggests that Ananias was a merchant, with contacts in Galilee, Judea, and Jerusalem, as well as in Syria and Nabatea.[47] There were hundreds, perhaps thousands of his kind three years after Jesus' resurrection: people convinced that visions of Jesus alive and elevated to his Father's Throne fulfilled God's promises to Israel. They didn't think of themselves as "Christians" yet. That word had not even been coined. They persistently called the teaching of their resurrected rabbi "the way" (*hodos* in Greek; Acts 9:2; 19:9, 23; 22:4; 24:14, 22), the equivalent of the Rabbinic term *halakhah*. In this time before there was any formal division between Judaism and Christianity, when Jesus' followers saw their master as the fulfillment of Israel's destiny, most of them worked out their peculiar vision in peace with their Jewish neighbors.

Paul's conversion also cut short the prospect of any sojourn in Damascus. Judas and Ananias cared for him, and he recovered at least some of his sight after something like a week (Acts 9:9, 19). He unwisely started right away to announce in synagogues that Jesus was the divine Son, prompting the inevitable skepticism. People knew about the stoning of Stephen, and knew this budding Pharisee from the Diaspora had traveled to their city to denounce those baptized in Jesus' name. That is what prompted their taunt (Acts 9:21): "Is he not the one who laid waste in Jerusalem to those calling upon this name, and came here for this purpose?" Why should they accept the word of an interloper who remade himself so readily – into a Jerusalem Pharisee one day, a follower of "the way" another day?

Just where Ananias succeeded, Paul could only fail. Most faithful Israelites who believed in Jesus continued to live in Damascus and other cities, as well as towns and villages, with little problem. As long as they

---

[47] Josephus speaks of a different Ananias, a pious merchant whose contacts as far as Adiabene resulted in attracting King Izates to Judaism (*Ant.* 20.34-48). Ananias convinced him not to circumcise for reasons of state, but to remain a God-fearer.

were not involved with the conflict in Jerusalem between Caiaphas and Jesus' movement, there was no particular occasion for friction with other Israelites. Men like Ananias achieved what Paul never could: a peaceable association between believers in Jesus and other Jews. No wonder Paul never mentioned Ananias in his letters. The contrast was painful, because Paul's past as a persecutor of "the way," coupled with his sudden conversion, made his character seem dubious and the movement itself appear unstable.

When Jesus and his followers claimed that the Temple was to be ruled by Zechariah's prophecy rather than the high priestly party, who could expect the high priests to cheer? But there was little reason, except in extreme cases, for opposition to this new movement outside of Jerusalem. The problem was that Paul *was* an extreme case – and remained so all his life, whether as Pharisee or apostle. Once converted, Caiaphas's supporters could only see him as a traitor, and Paul's visionary flip-flop made it easy for them to spread distrust in him personally.

Jesus' followers were wary, too. Paul remembered people shaking their heads in wonder, saying, "The one who once persecuted us now announces the faith that he once laid waste" (Gal 1:23). He tried to put a positive spin on that, but it did not enhance his reputation for integrity. In the full flow of his rhetoric at a much later stage in his life, Paul bragged that he had become all things to all people (1 Cor 9:22). At this stage Paul wasn't anything to anybody.

Remaining in Damascus would have produced only increased animosity. A return to Jerusalem at this stage was out of the question although Acts naively does have him go back there at this stage (9:26), reflecting a programmatic interest in Jerusalem as the first center of Christianity. Even commentators who argue for the general reliability of Acts do not believe that.[48] It would take years before he could enter Jerusalem again, as Paul unequivocally indicates in his letter to the Galatians. He specifically says he did not go to Jerusalem, but departed for "Arabia," only returning to Jerusalem via Damascus *three years* later (Gal 1:17-18). The Arabian peninsula – the country southeast of Israel, politically at that time the kingdom of the Nabateans[49]– is where Paul

---

[48] See C.K. Barrett, *A Critical and Exegetical Commentary on the Acts of the Apostles* (International Critical Commentary; Edinburgh: T&T Clark, 1994) I.467-468; J. Jervell, *Die Apostelgeschichte übersetzt und erklärt: Kritisch-exegetischer Kommentar über das Neue Testament* (Göttingen: Vandenhoeck & Ruprecht, 1998) 286-287.

[49] In this case Acts seems to me willfully silent, much as Paul managed to avoid naming Ananias. Jerusalem for the book of Acts is the center of operations, so "Ara-

worked out the implications of his vision for himself during three years of self-imposed exile from all the people he knew, whether in Jerusalem or Tarsus.

Nabatea at first seems an unlikely destination for Paul at this time. Although Aramaic was spoken there, it was a different dialect from what he learned in Tarsus or had adapted to in Jerusalem. The religion of the Nabateans consisted of the worship of tribal totems and the veneration of their ambitious kings among Arabian peoples who, like the Jews, practiced circumcision.[50] What pushed Paul into this hive of ancient Semitic idolatry, unalloyed with the healthy influence of Greek philosophy?

When it came to departing from Damascus and avoiding Jerusalem, he did not have a great deal of choice. And it is quite in character that he did not return to Tarsus at this juncture, although his native city would have provided a cosmopolitan, philosophically freewheeling environment. Paul was an ambitious young man. He had already been advanced in his knowledge of Judaism when he was back in Tarsus, and he had left home to achieve the status of an expert in the oral Torah of the Pharisees: to walk in Gamaliel's footsteps, not just sit at his feet. Until he could claim real advance in *something*, there was little chance of his returning to Tarsus. To go back as a beginner in any new philosophy meant showing up home as a failure.

In any case, "the way" of Jesus scarcely had the status of a philosophy at this stage. It was only a rustic, apocalyptic version of Judaism with bizarre claims about its teacher having survived death in some manner. The odds of making anything of such a teaching within Tarsus' free market of ideas were very long indeed.

With the self-confidence of hindsight, Paul later said, "Those things that were gain to me I counted forfeit for Christ" (Phil 3:7). He was proud of that exchange – paradoxically, since he claimed the transaction gave him humility. But he could only boast of his sacrifice once he had publicly advanced in the way of the Christians. In the early

---

bia" – that is, the kingdom of the Nabateans – is an inauspicious place for the newly minted apostle to start preaching. Moreover, there is no indication of any successful Christian proselytizing in Nabatea in Acts although successes in Syria, Egypt and north Africa, Ethiopia, Asia Minor, Greece and Rome are proudly recorded in Acts. Not mentioning Arabia would be sensible, however, if an apostle dear to Acts had tried to convert people there, and had gotten nowhere.

[50] See M. Hengel, "Paul in Arabia," *Bulletin for Biblical Research* 12.1 (2002) 47-66. He speculates (p. 54) that the Nabatean city Hagra should be associated with Hagar, following the suggestion of H. Gese. A more secure finding is that a massive project of irrigation was one source of King Aretas's great power and success (p. 49).

days and years after his conversion, he avoided public scrutiny, and eked out an existence with the only trade he knew: making tents. Ananias and Judas must have provided the contacts for Paul to make his way, but he took a big step down the ladder of status. As the boss's son and something of a grandee in Tarsus, and later as the high priest's Pharisaic recruit in Jerusalem, Paul never worked with his hands. This truly was a loss. It meant doing work for hours that he was familiar with, but not as a worker. The calluses on his hands were hard come by – and welcome, because working a needle pushed hard with the heel of the hand is painful work, especially for anyone with bad vision.

Another, more profound force moved him to "Arabia" – a pull rather than a push. The letter to the Galatians provides this clue to Paul's experience and provides his religious motivation for traveling to the kingdom of the Nabateans. Talking about the mount of vision, where Moses was given the Torah, he says that Sinai is "in Arabia" (Gal 4:25). During the modern period, Sinai has been located on the Sinai peninsula (hence the name), but in antiquity people venerated Nabatea as the place of Moses' vision. Paul went to Arabia, to the mountain of vision, because it was only there that he could resolve the deepest conflict he ever faced, a conflict that left a permanent mark on his thinking and on the character of Christianity.

From this juncture Paul made his way, always a minority way in his lifetime, but gradually the main line of Christianity. It was a way resonant within the philosophical and religious thought of the West because, as Wilson suggests, Paul was a hybrid of some of the most basic impulses of Stoicism as well as Judaism, which had already begun their fusion in the Diaspora. But attempts such as Wilson's (and Murphy-O'Connor's) to psychologize Paul mistake the critical difference between tracing development and diagnosing mental conditions. As Murphy-O'Connor correctly maintains, archaeology has a role to play in analyzing Paul, but against Murphy-O'Connor, two cautions have emerged: (1) archaeology must be distinguished from the simple imagination of physical circumstances (such as the earthquake that allegedly killed Paul's alleged wife and children), and (2) the influence of the surrounding cultures must be related to the cities from which and to which Paul wrote, as identified both in his letters and in Acts. Finally, I can only agree with Wright in regard to the theological focus of Paul's entire development, while insisting that his thought is a matter of development, rather than that of a fixed system, and I have to disagree with Wright's attempt to make Jesus into Christianity's premier philosopher of the covenant. That really is Paul's place, and we can never appreciate the covenantal divide between Christianity and Judaism[51] until we have properly assessed the thought of Paul.

---

[51] See Chilton, "The Covenantal Divide," *The National Jewish Post & Opinion* 71.48 (17 August 2005) 8-15.

11

James, Jesus' Brother, and History

Bruce Chilton

Introduction

Interest in Jesus' brother Ya'aqov, Anglicized as "James," is flourishing. Among recent contributions, one might mention a presentation of texts and analysis by Wilhelm Pratscher,[1] a semi-popular treatment by Pierre-Antoine Bernheim,[2] and a careful, innovative contribution from Richard Bauckham.[3] These books represent vigorous attempts to recover a critical portrait of James. They all respond, directly and indirectly, to the controversial thesis of Robert H. Eisenman, who has argued over a number of years that James is to be identified with the righteous teacher of Qumran.[4] Among the many and vehement responses to that thesis, perhaps the most mature and effective is that of John Painter.[5]

Recovery of interest in James is a useful corrective in both historical and theological terms, in that his place within primitive Christianity had been all but eclipsed by the influence of Paulinism in its many forms. The vehemence of response to Eisenman's thesis, quite apart from the specific questions it raises (exegetical, historical, and even archaeological), might best be explained on theological grounds. A

---

[1] W. Pratscher, *Der Herrenbruder Jakobus und die Jakobustraditionen* (FRLANT 139; Göttingen: Vandenhoeck & Ruprecht, 1987).

[2] A. Bernheim, *James, Brother of Jesus* (tr. J. Bowden; London: SCM, 1997); cf. *Jacques, Frère de Jésus* (Paris: Nôesis, 1996).

[3] R. Bauckham, *James: Wisdom of James, Disciple of Jesus the Sage* (New Testament Readings; London and New York: Routledge, 1999).

[4] Among his many publications, see especially R.H. Eisenman, *James the Brother of Jesus. The Key to Unlocking the Secrets of Early Christianity and the Dead Sea Scrolls* (New York: Viking, 1996).

[5] J. Painter, *Just James. The Brother of Jesus in History and Tradition* (Columbia: University of South Carolina Press, 1997).

silent James is, after all, more easily accommodated to the picture of a smooth transition between Jesus and Paul than is a James who (as in Eisenman's reconstruction) substantially contradicts both Paul *and* Jesus.

Within this debate, a well-defined set of issues has been perennially in play:[6]

- Was James really Jesus' brother?
- Was James sympathetic to Jesus prior to the resurrection?
- Did James require circumcision of males along with baptism by way of initiation into the movement of Jesus?
- Was there any substantial place for non-Jews within James' understanding of the covenant with Abraham, Isaac, and Jacob?
- Did James oppose a Pauline teaching of salvation by grace with an insistence upon obedience to the Torah?
- Was James the most prominent person in Jesus' movement between the resurrection and his own death?

None of the treatments cited above fails to take a stand on each of these issues, and for the most part each issue is also responsibly engaged in those and other discussions. Of the six questions here cited, only one is easily dismissed on the basis of the evidence to hand. But even that, the third question – and the old *canard* that James required circumcision of all believers – continues to exert so great an influence in popular and even scholarly discussion that it should be addressed here.

In what follows, we will work through the six questions to a conclusion, reviewing major primary sources as we proceed, and articulating what I take to be coherent assessments of the secondary literature in the positions that they staked out. The basis of my evaluation has largely been developed during meetings of "the Consultation on James," which I have chaired on behalf of the Institute of Advanced Theology. But the Consultation itself speaks through its own publications,[7] and often expresses ranges of agreement and disagreement, rather than attempting to forward set conclusions (in the manner, say of "the Jesus Seminar"), so that judgments expressed here are not attributable to other members of the Consultation.

---

[6] For a typical presentation, see the table of contents of Bernheim's book.

[7] See B.D. Chilton and C.A. Evans (eds.), *James the Just and Christian Origins* (NovTSup 98; Leiden: Brill, 1999), where I first posed these questions without answering them (p. 4); B.D. Chilton and J. Neusner (eds.), *The Brother of Jesus* (Louisville: Westminster John Knox, 2001); B.D. Chilton and C.A. Evans (eds.), *The Missions of James, Peter, and Paul. Tensions in Early Christianity* (NovTSup 115; Leiden: Brill, 2005).

None of the primary documents at issue is claimed by most scholars to have come directly from James himself. His views are attested even more indirectly than his brother's are. But the case of Jesus sheds light by way of analogy on James: for all that a Jesus of history is not "in" our sources, there is no doubt but that there is a Jesus of literary history behind them, and that approach may be applied to James.

That is, the Gospels (as well as other documents) refer back to Jesus as their point of generation, and we may infer what practices Jesus engaged in, what beliefs he adhered to, what teachings he promulgated, so as to produce the accounts concerning him in the communities of followers that produced the documents. The framing world of those practices and beliefs in the formative period of the New Testament (whether in the case of Jesus, James or their followers) was Judaism. Practices and beliefs are attested in the documents manifestly, whether or not their attribution to Jesus is accepted, and that is a suitable point of departure for the genuinely critical question of Jesus. That question cannot critically be formulated as, What did Jesus really say and really do? The critical issue is rather, What role did Jesus play in the evolution of practices and beliefs in his name?[8]

That generative question may be broadened, of course, to apply not only to Jesus and the Gospels, but also to primitive Christianity and the New Testament.[9] In the present case, that involves specifying the practices and beliefs that attach to James within the sources, and seeking to understand his place within them. Not every practice, not every belief may be assumed to be correctly attributed to James, but the various streams of tradition the documents represent do come together to constitute stable associations of practices and beliefs with James. The nodal issues of practices and beliefs, not "facts," represent our point of departure.

Was James really Jesus' brother?

The point of departure for considering this question is Mark 6:3 (cf. Matt 13:55-56), where James is actually named as Jesus' brother, along with four other men; at least two sisters – unnamed and unenumerated

---

[8] For my development of this perspective, see Chilton, *The Temple of Jesus. His Sacrificial Program within a Cultural History of Sacrifice* (University Park: The Pennsylvania State University Press, 1992) and *Pure Kingdom. Jesus' Vision of God* (Studying the Historical Jesus 1; Grand Rapids: Eerdmans and London: SPCK, 1996); *Rabbi Jesus. An Intimate Biography* (New York: Doubleday, 2000).

[9] See B.D. Chilton and J. Neusner, *Judaism in the New Testament. Practices and Beliefs* (London and New York: Routledge, 1995).

– are also mentioned. Until recently, Roman Catholic opinion has been dominated by the position of St. Jerome (in his controversial work, *Against Helvidius*), who argued that although "brothers" and "sisters" are the terms used in Greek, the reference is actually to cousins. Dispute has focused on the issue of whether that view can be sustained linguistically, and on the whole the finding has been negative. Before Jerome, Helvidius himself had maintained during the fourth century that the brothers and sisters were just what their name implies – siblings of Jesus: although Jesus had been born of a virgin, Jesus' brothers' and sisters' father was Joseph and their mother was Mary. That view clearly played havoc with the emerging doctrine of Mary's virginity after Jesus' birth, and that issue occupied the center of attention. In a recent work by a prominent Roman Catholic scholar that received the Imprimatur, John P. Meier has endorsed the Helvidian theory, to some extent on the basis of support from second-century Fathers.[10] During that century, a group referred to as the Ebionites even denied Jesus' virgin birth in the technical sense; his "brothers" and "sisters" were implicitly that in the full sense of those words (see Irenaeus, *Against Heresies* 1.26.1-2).

Richard Bauckham has given new currency to the view of Jesus' relationship to James developed by Epiphanius during the fourth century (*Panarion* 1.29.3-4; 2.66.19; 3.78.7, 9, 13), and supported by the second-century *Protoevangelium of James* 9.2 and perhaps the *Gospel of Peter* (according to Origen's *Commentary on Matthew* 10:17).[11] On this view, Mary was Jesus' mother, not James's, since Joseph had a wife prior to his marriage to Mary. Joseph's relatively advanced age is traditionally held to account for his early departure from the narrative scene of the Gospels, and that reasonable inference lends support to this theory, while James's emphasis on the Davidic identity of the Church (see Acts 15:16) is easily accommodated on this view. James's seniority relative to Jesus might be reflected in the parable of the prodigal (Luke 15:11-32). The story of those with Jesus seizing him in the midst of exorcism (Mark 3:21; cf. 3:31-35) reflects the kind of almost parental concern an older brother might feel for a younger brother.

Another, more pragmatic consideration provides support for

---

[10] J.P. Meier, *A Marginal Jew: Rethinking the Historical Jesus* I (New York: Doubleday, 1991) 332.

[11] See R. Bauckham, "The Brothers and Sisters of Jesus: An Epiphanian Response to John P. Meier," *CBQ* 56 (1994) 686-700.

Epiphanius's theory,[12] although in a modified form. As mentioned, Joseph disappears from the scene of the Gospels from when Jesus was in early puberty.[13] Joseph's death at that time has been the traditional surmise, and such a chronology has implications for understanding Jesus' relationships with his siblings. On the Helvidian view, Mary must have given birth to *at least* seven children in twelve years (Jesus, his brothers, and two or more sisters). Assuming that not every child she gave birth to survived infancy, more than seven labors would be required during that period, all this within a culture that confined women after childbirth and prohibited intercourse with a woman with a flow of blood, and despite the acknowledged prophylactic effect of lactation and Joseph's age.

Although the consideration of a likely rate of fertility provides some support to the Epiphanian theory, in its unadulterated form and in its own way it also strains credulity. A widower with at least six children already in tow is not perhaps the best candidate for marriage with a young bride. A modified form of the theory (a hybrid with Helvidius's suggestion) would make James and Joses the products of Joseph's previous marriage, and Jesus, Simon and Judah the sons of Joseph with Mary.[14] The latter three sons have names notably associated with a zealous regard for the honor of Israel, and may reflect the taste of a common mother. Absent their names, or even a count of how many were involved, no such assignment of marriages can be attempted for Jesus' sisters.

On the Helvidian view, James was Jesus' younger and full brother, in a family quickly produced whose siblings were close in age. On the Epiphanian view, James was older, and Jesus' half brother; it seems to me that, suitably modified, Epiphanius provides the more plausible finding.

---

[12] Discussion of this issue has typically adjudicated among the Helvidian, Epiphanian, and Hieronymian theories, as a result of the typology of J.B. Lightfoot, *Saint Paul's Epistle to the Galatians* (London: Macmillan, 1865). I am not convinced that this nomenclature has clarified discussion.

[13] For study of the issue of doubtful paternity in Judaism during this period and later, see M. Bar Ilan, "The Attitude toward *mamzerim* in Jewish Society in Late Antiquity," *Jewish History* 14 (2000) 125-170; Chilton, *Rabbi Jesus*, 3-22; S.D. Cohen, "Some Thoughts on 'The Attitude toward *mamzerim* in Jewish Society in Late Antiquity,'" *Jewish History* 14.2 (2000) 171-174; M. Sawicki, *Crossing Galilee*, 171-173; A. van Aarde, *Fatherless in Galilee: Jesus as Child of God* (Harrisburg: Trinity Press International 2001); Chilton, "Jésus, le *mamzer* (Mt 1.18)," *New Testament Studies* 46 (2001) 222-227; "The *mamzer* Jesus and His Birth," *The Bible and Interpretation* 2005; "Recovering Jesus' Mamzerut," *Ancient Israel, Judaism, and Christianity in Contemporary Perspective: Essays in Memory of Karl-Johan Illman* (ed. J. Neusner: Lanham: University Press of America, 2005).

[14] See *Rabbi Jesus*, 14, 23, 72, 78.

Was James sympathetic to Jesus prior to the resurrection?

The Gospels, when they refer to James at all, do so with no great sympathy.[15] He is listed at the head of Jesus' brothers in the Synoptic Gospels, but in a statement of a crowd in Nazareth that rejects the proposition that one whose family they know can be responsible for wonders (Mark 6:1-6; Matt 13:53-58). In John, he is presumably included among the unnamed brothers who argued with Jesus about his refusal to go to Jerusalem for a feast (John 7:2-10),[16] and James is also referred to anonymously in the Synoptics as among the brothers whom, even with his mother, Jesus refused to interrupt his teaching in order to greet (Mark 3:31-35; Matt 12:46-50; Luke 8:19-21).[17] The most plausible inference would be that Jesus and James were somehow at odds during this period, but personal animosity is scarcely provable. The real breaking point came when the population at Nazareth came to the attempted stoning there (Luke 4:16-30),[18] which seems to have made Jesus negative about his own family.

On the other hand, James is recognized within the earliest list of those to whom the risen Jesus appeared (1 Cor 15:7), and – closely associated with the Temple – he quickly emerged as the dominant figure in the Jesus movement.[19] Taken together, that would suggest that, by the end of Jesus' life, during his last pilgrimage to Jerusalem, James and his brother had been reconciled. Aside from Paul's reference to James in his list of witnesses to the resurrection, the New Testament does not record an actual appearance to James, but the non-canonical *Gospel of the Hebrews* does. There, Jesus assures his brother that "the Son of Man has been raised from among those who sleep" (cited by Jerome, *Liber de Viris Illustribus* 2). This vision occurs after James had fasted in consequence of his brother's death. The authority of James, it seems, was a key force in the complete identification between Jesus and the figure of one like a son of man in Daniel 7 (see also Hegesippus, as cited by Eusebius in his *History* 2.23.1-18) – an angelic figure in the heavenly court – after the resurrection.

---

[15] This is a point of departure for R.H. Eisenman, *James the Just in the Habakkuk Pesher* (Studia Post-Biblica 35; Leiden: Brill, 1986).
[16] See *Rabbi Jesus*, 97-102.
[17] See *Rabbi Jesus*, 166-168.
[18] See *Rabbi Jesus*, 97-102.
[19] In contrast to Eisenman, this is the point of departure for E. Stauffer, "The Caliphate of James," *Journal of Higher Criticism* 4 (1997, from his 1952 German article) 120-143. The original appeared in the *Zeitschrift für Religions- und Geistesgeschichte* 4 (1952) 193-214. I pursued this insight in *Rabbi Jesus*, 200-202.

Did James require circumcision of males along with baptism by way of initiation into the movement of Jesus?

Acts attributes to James (and to James alone) the power to decide whether non-Jewish male converts in Antioch needed to be circumcised. He determines that they do *not*.[20] Under the influence of the thesis of F.C. Bauer, it is sometimes assumed that James required circumcision of all such converts,[21] but that requirement is attributed to Christian Pharisees in Acts (15:5), not to James. Nonetheless, James does proceed to command non-Jewish Christians to observe certain requirements of purity (so Acts 15:1-35). That explains why emissaries from James make their appearance as villains in Paul's description of a major controversy at Antioch.[22] They insisted on a separate meal-fellowship of Jews and non-Jews, while Paul with more than equal insistence (but with little or no success) argued for the unity of Jewish and non-Jewish fellowship within the church (Galatians 1:18–2:21). How precisely James came to such a position of prominence is not explained in Acts; his apostolic status was no doubt assured by the risen Jesus' appearance to him.

Like Josephus (*Ant.* 20.197-203), Hegesippus (in concert with Clement, Eusebius reports) portrays James as killed by Ananus at the Temple. In addition, Hegesippus describes James in terms that emphasize his purity in such a way that, as in Acts, his association with the Nazirite vow is evident (cf. Acts 21:17-36). James's capacity to win the reverence of many Jews in Jerusalem (not only his brother's followers) derives from this practice and his encouragement of others in the practice, even with Gentile funding. The fact is frequently overlooked, but needs to be emphasized, that the Mishnah envisages the Nazirite practice of slaves, as well as Israelites, both male and female (see *Nazir* 9:1).[23] James's focus was purity in the Temple under the aegis of his risen brother, the Son of Man, but there is no trace of his requiring circumcision of Gentiles. It needs to be kept in mind that Jesus himself

---

[20] See R. Bauckham, "James and the Jerusalem Church," *The Book of Acts in its Palestinian Setting* (ed. R. Bauckham; Grand Rapids: Eerdmans, 1995) 415-480.

[21] On the influence of "the Tübingen school," see E. Haenchen, *The Acts of the Apostles* (tr. B. Noble, G. Shinn, H. Anderson, R. McL. Wilson; Philadelphia: Westminster, 1971) 15-24. In view of Professor Hengel's association with Tübingen during the intervening period, we may have to think again about this designation! (Cf. n. 27 below.)

[22] See *Rabbi Paul*, 168-170.

[23] For the roots of the practice, see E. Diamond, "An Israelite Self-Offering in the Priestly code: A New Perspective on the Nazirite," *The Jewish Quarterly Review* 88.1-2 (1997) 1-18.

had expelled traders from the Temple, not as some indiscriminate protest about commercialism, but as part of Zechariah's prophecy (see Zech 14) of a day when all the peoples of the earth would be able to offer sacrifice to the LORD without the intervention of middlemen.[24] James' Nazirite practice realized that prophecy in his brother's name.

Josephus indicates that James was killed in the Temple in 62 CE at the instigation of the high priest Ananus during the interregnum of the Roman governors Festus and Albinus (*Ant.* 20.197-203). Hegesippus gives a more circumstantial, less politically informed, account of the martyrdom. James is set up on a parapet of the Temple, being known and addressed by his opponents by the titles "Righteous and *Oblias*," Hegesippus reports. The second title has caused understandable puzzlement (especially when Hegesippus's rendering of the term as "bulwark" is accepted[25]), but it is easily related to the Aramaic term *'abal*, which means, "to mourn." Recent finds in the vicinity of the Dead Sea (not only near Qumran) have greatly enhanced our understanding of Aramaic as spoken in the time of Jesus and his followers. The use of the term is attested there.[26] James was probably known as "mourner."

A minor tractate of the Talmud lays down the rule that a mourner (*'aval*) "is under the prohibition to bathe, anoint [the body], put on sandals and cohabit" (*Semachoth* 4:1). This largely corresponds to the requirements of a Nazirite vow and to Hegesippus's description of James's practice; for Jesus himself to have called his brother "mourner" would fit in with his giving his followers nicknames. A tight association with the Temple on James's part is attested throughout and from an early period, but not a universal requirement of circumcision.

Was there any substantial place for non-Jews within James' understanding of the covenant with Abraham, Isaac, and Jacob?
Hegesippus's account of James's prominence is confirmed by Clement, who portrays James as the first elected bishop in Jerusalem (also cited by Eusebius, *History* 2.1.1-6), and by the pseudo-Clementine *Recognitions*, which makes James into an almost papal figure, who provides the correct paradigm of preaching to Gentiles. Paul is so much the butt of this presentation that *Recognitions* (I.43-71) even relates that, prior to his conversion to Christianity, Saul physically assaulted James in the

---

[24] See *Rabbi Jesus*, 213-230.

[25] As a matter of fact, Hegesippus accepts that this signification is Greek; James seems to be so named here because after his death the siege of Jerusalem was successful.

[26] See J.A. Fitzmyer and D.J. Harrington, *A Manual of Palestinian Aramaic Texts* (Biblica et Orientalia 34; Rome: Biblical Institute Press, 1978).

Temple. Martin Hengel refers to this presentation as an apostolic novel (*Apostelroman*), deeply influenced by the perspective of the Ebionites, and probably to be dated within the third and fourth centuries.[27]

Yet even in Acts 15, the use of Scripture attributed to James, like the argument itself, is quite unlike Paul's. James claims that Peter's baptism of non-Jews is to be accepted because "the words of the prophets agree, just as it is written" (Acts 15:15), and he goes on to cite from the book of Amos. The passage cited will concern us in a moment; the form of James's interpretation is an immediate indication of a substantial difference from Paul. As James has it, there is actual agreement between Symeon and the words of the prophets, as two people might agree: the use of the verb *sumphoneo* is used nowhere else in the New Testament in respect of Scripture. The continuity of Christian experience with Scripture is marked as a greater concern than within Paul's interpretation, and James expects that continuity to be verbal, a matter of agreement with the prophets' words, not merely with possible ways of looking at what they mean.

The citation from Amos (9:11-12, from the version of the Septuagint, which was the Bible of Luke–Acts) comports well with James's concern that the position of the Church agree with the principal vocabulary of the prophets (Acts 15:16-17):

> After this I will come back and restore the tent of David which has fallen, and rebuild its ruins and set it up anew, that the rest of men may seek the Lord, and all the Gentiles upon whom my name is called....

In the argument of James as represented here, what the belief of Gentiles achieves is, not the redefinition of Israel (as in Paul's thought), but the restoration of the house of David, with Gentile recognition of the Torah as it impinged upon them.[28] The argument is possible be-

---

[27] See "Jakobus der Herrenbruder – der erste "Papst"?' *Glaube und Eschatologie. Festschrift für Werner Georg Kümmel zum 80. Geburtstag* (ed. E. Grässer and O. Merk; Tübingen: Mohr, 1985) 71-104, 81. The ordering of Peter under James is clearly a part of that perspective, as Hengel shows, and much earlier J.B. Lightfoot found that the alleged correspondence between Clement and James was a later addition to the Pseudo-Clementine corpus (see J.B. Lightfoot, *The Apostolic Fathers* 1 [London: Macmillan, 1890] 414-420). But even if the Pseudo-Clementines are taken at face value, they undermine Eisenman's view (or the view of the "Tübingen school," as Hengel [p. 92] points out is the source of such contentions): they portray James as the standard for how Hellenistic Christians are to teach (see *Recognitions* 11.35.3).

[28] See M. Bockmuehl, "The Noachide Commandments and New Testament Ethics," *Jewish Law in Gentile Churches. Halakhah and the Beginning of Christian Public Ethics* (Edinburgh: T&T Clark, 2000) 145-173.

cause a Davidic genealogy of Jesus – and, therefore, of his brother James – is assumed.[29]

Did James oppose a Pauline teaching of salvation by grace with an insistence upon obedience to the Torah?

It is true that the Epistle of James sets out an elaborate argument – including a reading of Genesis 22 which seems to contradict Paul's – to the effect that faith without works is dead (see Jas 2:14-26 and Rom 4). But the Epistle does not set out Paul's position in anything like detail; as Peter Davids has remarked, "There is no sense of the Pauline tension between faith and Torah piety, for James' community is in a different context."[30] Paul is without doubt the most prominent explorer of that tension, but his position is subtler than what is refuted in the Epistle of James.[31] That is no surprise, since Paul himself had to correct antinomian readings of his own views among those sympathetic to him (see 1 Cor 5-6). The Pastoral Epistles and 2 Pet 3:15-16 suggest this difficulty only grew over time.

The dating of the Epistle of James, and particularly the question whether it was written before or after the destruction of the Temple in 70 CE, continues to cause controversy.[32] But the sense of social crisis reflected in the Epistle is unmistakable, as well as its urgent expectation of Jesus' parousia (Jas 5:7-8, cf. 2 Pet 3:4, 12). But if we think back to Hegesippus's description of James's ethos, that is not surprising. With the threat to the very possibility of sacrificial worship in the Temple (whether after its destruction or — as seems less likely to me – in the turbulent conditions which preceded that trauma), a fundamental aspect of James's position was compromised, an aspect with which Paul himself could agree (as Acts 21:16-36 and Rom 15:16 suggest). What remained was Jesus' identity as the Son of Man, and the challenge to James's theology (before or – more probably – after his own death) was to maintain and even enhance that identity, as worship in the Temple became increasingly problematic. In that context, whether

---

[29] See E. Stauffer, *Jesus and His Story* (tr. R. and C. Winston; New York: Knopf, 1960) 13-15.

[30] See "James' Message: the Literary Record," *The Brother of Jesus* (ed. B.D. Chilton and J. Neusner; Louisville: Westminster John Knox, 2001).

[31] In this regard, see G.B. Caird, *New Testament Theology* (ed. L.D. Hurst; Oxford: Clarendon, 1994) 190.

[32] See W. Popkes, *Der Brief des Jakobus* (Theologischer Handkommentar zum Neuen Testament 14; Leipzig: Evangelischer Verlagsanstalt, 2001).

James happened to have agreed with Paul in a doctrine that Paul had articulated in quite a different context appears a secondary concern.

Was James the most prominent person in Jesus' movement between the resurrection and his own death?

It is telling that, in his attempt to draw together the material relating to James, Jerome cites the Gospel according to the Hebrews alongside the New Testament, Hegesippus, and Josephus. The conflation attests the fragmentary nature of the references, as well as the appearance they give of having been spun out of one another, or out of cognate traditions. For all that use of these sources is unavoidable, as the necessary point of departure for any discussion of James, they all make James into an image that comports with their own programs. The Gospels' James is kept at bay so as not to deflect attention from Jesus until the resurrection, when James implicitly or explicitly (in the case of Paul and the Gospel according to the Hebrews) becomes an important witness; the James of Acts reconciles the Church within a stance which leads on to the position of Paul; Paul's James divides the Church; Josephus relates James's death to illustrate the bloody-mindedness of Ananus, the high priest; Hegesippus does so to illustrate the righteousness of James and his community; Clement makes James the transitional figure of the apostolic tradition, and the *Recognitions* use and enhance that standing in order to attack the figure of Paul.

Right the way through, James is deployed in these sources to assert what is held to be an authoritative construction of Jesus' movement.[33] Accordingly, he is marginalized (in the Gospels), appealed to as an authoritative witness (in Acts and Paul), criticized (in Paul[34]), portrayed as a victim (by Josephus) or a hero (by Hegesippus), hailed as both a source of unity (by Clement and in the tradition of Acts) and the trump card to use against Paul (in the *Recognitions*). Everything that makes the figure of "the historical Jesus" in a historicist understanding problematic makes "the historical James" in that sense out of the question.

James's devotion to the Temple and to his brother as the Danielic Son of Man after the resurrection made him the most prominent Christian leader in Jerusalem. The practice of the Nazirite vow was his distinguishing feature, and his belief in his brother as the gate of

---

[33] See K.L. Carroll, "The Place of James in the Early Church," *Bulletin of the John Rylands Library* 44 (1961) 49-67.

[34] See W. Schmithals, *Paulus und Jakobus* (Göttingen: Vandenhoeck & Ruprecht, 1963).

heaven, the heavenly portal above the Temple, made him a figure to be revered and reviled in Judaism, depending upon one's evaluation of Jesus. Among Christians, he promulgated his understanding of the establishment of the house of David by means of an interpretation reminiscent of the Essenes, although he insisted that baptized, uncircumcised non-Jews had an ancillary role. As the bishop or overseer (*mebaqqer*, in the Dead Sea Scrolls) of his community, he exercised a function which entered the Greek language as *episkopos*, and the influence of his circle is attested in the New Testament and later literature (including the *Gospel according to Thomas*, the *Apocryphon of James*, the *Protoevangelium of James*, the *First* and *Second Apocalypse of James*, the *Gospel of Peter*, the *Apocalypse of Peter*, the *Kerygma Petrou*, the *Kerygmata Petrou*, the *Acts of Peter*, the *Letter of Peter to Philip*, and the *Act of Peter*.

Once James's distinctive importance has been recognized, it is natural to ask, How great was his influence upon the earliest phase of primitive Christian and early Christian literature? It has been argued, for example, that passages within the Synoptic Gospels might well bear the stamp of James's perspective. Within the narrative of Jesus' passion in the Synoptics, only one passage makes the Last Supper correspond to Passover (Matt 26:17-20; Mark 14:12-17; Luke 22:7-14), and that presentation conflicts with the Johannine and Pauline presentations. That would limit participation in the meal and in its commemoration to those circumcised, in the case of males (see Ex 12:48), a move that would accord with James's Israelite construction of the Christian leadership.[35] Similarly, the teaching attributed to Jesus in regard to vowing property as *qorbana*, a gift to the Temple, manifests an interest in and a familiarity with cultic institutions, as well as a style of exegesis associated with the *pesharim* of Qumran, which better accords with James than with Jesus (Matt 15:1-20; Mark 7:1-23).[36] Lastly, the story of the demons and the swine of Gergesa, with its emphasis on the impurity of non-Jews (Romans especially; Matt 8:28-34; Mark 5:1-20; Luke 8:26-39) has been linked with a Jacobean cycle of tradition, and the secret knowledge of the demons that Jesus was *Nazarenos*, a Nazirite, is

---

[35] See Chilton, *A Feast of Meanings. Eucharistic Theologies from Jesus through Johannine Circles* (NovTSup 72; Leiden: Brill, 1994) 93-108.

[36] See Chilton, "A Generative Exegesis of Mark 7:1-23," *The Journal of Higher Criticism* 3.1 (1996) 18-37.

plausibly linked to the same cycle.[37] That link, however, raises questions of the state of the available sources and whether James may be constructed historically at all, an issue that will concern us at the close of the Conclusion.

Conclusion

Within the terms of reference of early Judaism and primitive Christianity, no single issue can compare in importance to that of the Temple. The Nazirite practice attributed to James and those in contact with him provides a highly focused degree of devotion to the Temple. As usually discussed, of course, the social history of primitive Christianity and early Christianity has been Hellenistic in orientation. That is perfectly natural, given the actual provenience and language of the New Testament and the bulk of the corpus of Christianity in late antiquity. Still, social histories such as those of Wayne Meeks,[38] Abraham Malherbe,[39] and Dennis Smith and Hal Taussig[40] have tended not to engage the sources of Judaism, and especially the Judaism of Aramaic and Hebrew sources, with the same vigor that has been applied to the Hellenistic dimension of analysis. That is perfectly understandable, given the particular documents they have dealt with, and the specific questions that they applied to those documents. But a figure such as James will simply remain a cipher, and in all probability a cipher for some form of Paulinism or another, as long as he is not located within the milieu which not only produced him, but which was embraced as a consciously chosen locus of devotion and activity. Many teachers associated with the movement of Jesus managed at least partially to avoid the Temple; James is found virtually only there after the resurrection.

The specificity of that location raises the issue of James's relation to other forms of Christianity, to other forms of Judaism, and especially to those responsible for the operation of the Temple. Here the analysis of James in socially historical terms comes closest to classic history, in its specificity.

---

[37] See *The Body of Faith. Israel and the Church*: Christianity and Judaism – The Formative Categories 2 (with J. Neusner; Valley Forge: Trinity Press International, 1996) 98-101.

[38] See W. Meeks, *The First Urban Christians: The Social World of the Apostle Paul* (New Haven: Yale University Press, 1983).

[39] See A.J. Malherbe, *Social Aspects of Early Christianity* (Philadelphia: Fortress, 1983).

[40] See H. Taussig, *Many Tables: the Eucharist in the New Testament and Liturgy Today* (Philadelphia: Trinity Press International and London: SCM, 1990).

Whether in the key of an emphasis on the "social" or the "historical" within socially historical analysis, what emerges from our consideration is a distinctive, cultic focus upon the validation of the covenant with Israel which blesses all nations on the authority of Jesus, understood in his resurrection to be identifiable with the "one like a son of man" of Daniel 7.

The Interplay of Sources and the Assessment of James

Within the portrayal of the status of being a Nazirite within the New Testament, there is a strong difference between a direct and stringently practical depiction, and an evidently metaphorical characterization. This distinction makes the linkage of sources to James, and the understanding of what that linkage means, problematic, but also points the way forward for the recovery of James's significance.

a. The Practical Nazirite

In Acts 18:18, Paul is said to shave his head in Cenchraea, because he had a vow.[41] The reference to the cutting of hair naturally associates Paul's practice with the Nazirite vow, because a Nazirite was held to have completed his vow at the time he shaved his hair and offered it at the altar (see Num 6:18). As set out in Numbers 6, a Nazirite was to let his hair and (if at issue) beard grow for the time of his vow, abstain completely from grapes, and avoid approaching any dead body. At the close of the period of the vow, he was to shave his head, and offer his hair in proximity to the altar (so Num 6:18). The end of this time of being holy, the LORD's property, is marked by enabling the Nazirite to drink wine again (6:20).

Although the identification of the vow may seem straightforward, such a simple reading is immediately complicated by any attempt to read Acts 18 within the terms of reference of Numbers 6. After all, Num 6:18 is quite specific that the Nazirite is to shave his head at the opening of the tent of appointment and put the hair on the fire under the sacrifice of sharings. The text would seem to suggest that the vow could only be fulfilled by shaving one's head at the threshold of the sanctuary and by placing one's hair on the fire in the sanctuary. That has caused commentators to be cautious about equating Paul's vow and Nazirite practice.

The text of Numbers itself, however, invites further consideration.

---

[41] For the situation of this vow within Paul's biography, see *Rabbi Paul*, 237-240.

Numbers 6:2 opens with the explicit statement that the vow might be undertaken by a man or a woman. Evidently, therefore, the Nazirite practice would not always have included their admission into the sanctuary, where the presence of women was regularly prohibited and the presence of men was not infrequently prohibited, so that the presentation of the hair in the that place must have been by means of a surrogate.

Indeed, the Mishnah conceives of Nazirite vows as being undertaken by slaves, as well as Israelites, so that a strict association with the sanctuary would have been untenable (Nazir 9:1). Such vows in regard to hair alone were held in Mishnah to equate to a Nazirite vow (*Nazir* 1:1); the opening of the tractate is also emphatic that a precise pronunciation of the term nazir was not necessary to engage the full requirements of the vow. So whatever Paul or Acts thought of his vow from his own perspective, many would have seen him as falling in with the program of what is referred to in the Mishnah, and some would have seen him as obligated by the prevailing custom.

In his careful evaluation of Paul's practice, Maas Boertien has crafted a skillful association between Acts 18:18 and 21:23-26, where Paul is convinced to undertake the expenses of four Nazirites.[42] The reference to their shaving their heads makes the association with Numbers 6 evident, especially since the context within the Temple makes the identification with a Nazirite vow straightforward. Boertien's overall argument is that Paul had his hair shorn in Cenchraea to fulfill the temporal requirements of his vow, and then took part in an offering in the Temple to fulfill the sacrificial requirements of his vow. To make out that case, Boertien must show that the moment of cutting of the hair and the moment of sacrifice could in fact be dissociated from one another.

Particularly, in regard to hair, he must answer the question: if Paul's vow is as a Nazirite, what would he have done with the hair he had cut? After all, one was holy, to the LORD, all the days that one vowed (Num 6:5, 13), by virtue of that uncut hair. Two institutions enable Boertien to reply to that question.

First, within the terms of reference of Numbers 6 itself, the problem of what we might call the missing hair is addressed in the Mishnah. When a Nazirite's head is rendered impure by the sudden death of one near to him, he shaves on the seventh day, the day of

---

[42] The discussion appears in M. Boertien, *Nazir (Nasiräer). Text, Übersetzung und Erklärung nebst einem textkritischen Anhang* (Die Mischna; Berlin: de Gruyter, 1971) 28-29, 71-72, 90-95.

purification (Num 6:9), and then he offers at the opening of the tent of appointment on the eighth day (Numbers 6:10). The priest takes these offerings as a sacrifice for sin and a whole sacrifice, and makes appeasement; the Nazirite's head is consecrated again (Num 6:11), and the vow starts all over again (Num 6:12). Numbers accounts for everything but the hair that has been cut in view of impurity. Temurah 7:4 provides the answer: such hair is buried, in an evident analogy to the blood of a slaughtered animal, which is poured into the ground when it is not poured out in sacrifice.

But cutting hair in view of purity is obviously different from cutting one's hair to fulfill the vow, which is what Paul is portrayed as doing in Acts 18:18. That is why the second institution is crucial to Boertien's analysis. *Nazir* 3:6 attributes to beth Shammai the regulation of those who undertake Nazirite vows outside of Israel: when they fulfill the requirement of time abroad, they are to serve out an additional thirty days in the land of Israel. Implicitly, the hair is cut outside Israel, and the offering is accomplished in the Temple.[43] The only question left open by Mishnah is whether an additional thirty days is really necessary. The fact of the temporal fulfillment of Nazirite vows abroad is taken for granted.

The case of hair shorn abroad in fulfillment of the vow is analogous to hair shorn in view of contamination. In both cases, shearing is performed under conditions of impurity. *Nazir* 6:8 stipulates that the sacrificial offering of the hair by the Nazirite is to be carried out, even when he has been shorn outside of Jerusalem, but that the "shearing of impurity" is not to be offered.[44] But that still leaves the Nazirite from abroad with the problem of missing hair: what is he to offer? Beth Shammai solves the problem by providing for an additional month to grow some more. But what of those who proceed directly to the sacrificial moment specified by Numbers 6?

Boertien addresses that question by referring to the practice of association within a Nazirite offering. *Nazir* 2:5 sets out an at first sight complicated arrangement, which addresses what to do when a Nazirite pledges himself to bring both his own hair offering and the hair offering of another Nazirite. Under those circumstances, the recommenddation is to make this offering with a fellow, to economize on the costs involved. After all, each Nazirite was to offer three animals and grain with oil and the accompanying wine (so Num 6:14-15): the

---

[43] See Boertien, *Nazir*, pp. 90-91.
[44] See Boertien, *Nazir*, 93.

expense involved was considerable. So one could make a commitment to double one's pledge, while paying only as if for oneself. In this way, even a person of relatively modest means — by taking on the expenses of Nazirites — could imitate the prosperous piety of Agrippa I (*Ant.* 19.293f.).

Boertien brings all of these elements together in order to account for Paul's practice as narrated in Acts. Paul first completed his Nazirite vow outside Israel (Acts 18:18) and then, after his arrival in Jerusalem, offered the sacrifices of dedication in association with other Nazirites (Acts 21:23-26).[45] In this regard, Boertien calls particular attention to Acts 21:26, where Paul observes a period of seven days of purification before he completes the offering. That corresponds to the seven days stipulated in Numbers (6:9-10) for cases in which a Nazirite has encountered impurity. In effect, residence outside of Israel was itself treated as an instance of impurity.[46]

The question of Paul's vow in Acts 18:18 has been dogged by the problem that, although some relationship to Numbers 6 seems to be implicit, Paul is not near enough to the Temple to accord with the requirements of the Nazirite vow. Boertien resolved that problem, by showing that the issue of Nazirites outside of Israel was addressed in the Mishnah. He was aware that Mishnah could not be assumed to be contemporaneous with the New Testament, and in fact attributed this section of the tractate *Nazir* to Yudah ben Ilai, the Tanna of the second century. Whether or not that association is fully tenable, the assumption within the tractate that such vows can be effectuated, much as in the case of the vow of *Qorbana*.[47]

Beyond that, however, Boertien seems to press Acts into the mold of the Mishnah. *Nazir* 2:5 assumes that, at the time one pledged, one might agree to take on the expenses of someone else. Acts clearly separates Paul's own vow (18:18) from the suggestion of James and the elders, that Paul should — as a public display of piety — demonstrate his fidelity to the Torah (Acts 21:24). Paul and his companions arrive in Jerusalem and are confronted by James and the elders' report to them that Paul's reputation in Jerusalem is that he is telling Jews in the Diaspora to forsake Moses, and especially to stop circumcising their children (Acts 21:17-21). Paul is then told to take on the expense of four men who had taken a vow, entering the Temple with them to

---

[45] Boertien, *Nazir*, 72.

[46] So Boertien, *Nazir*, 92 (citing *Nazir* 7:3).

[47] Mishnah envisages a man saying, "Qorban be any benefit my wife gets from me, for she stole my purse" (*Nedarim* 3:2).

offer sacrifice (Acts 21:22-26). The indications of time in Acts simply do not allow for Paul to accord with the halakhah of beth Shammai; he delays one week, not one month. Further, James's attempt to have Paul correspond to the halakhah on a more liberal understanding is a failure according to the narrative in Acts: once in Jerusalem, Acts portrays Paul as received joyfully (21:17), and then as proceeding to follow the advice given him the following day (21:26). That advice, of course, had disastrous consequences. Paul's entry into the Temple caused a riot, because it was supposed he was bringing Greeks in. As a result, he was arrested by a Roman officer (Acts 21:27–28:21), and so began the long, legal contention that resulted ultimately in his death. Even Acts has to admit that there was some substance in the accusation of the "Jews from Asia": they had seen Paul in the city, not with a quartet of Nazirites, but with a Greek from Ephesus (Acts 21:27-29). And when Paul defends himself before Felix, his own protestation of innocence is not framed in terms of his own or others' Nazirite vow, but in terms of his bringing alms and offerings, the occasion of his having purified himself (Acts 24:17-19).

Acts, in other words, agrees substantially with Paul's own statement of his program in regard to the Temple: the priestly service of preaching the gospel is to lead to the presentation of the offering of the Gentiles (Rom 15:16). The tangible generosity of congregations in Greece is a matter of pride for Paul, and he boasts that, "having sealed this fruit," he will return "with the fullness of Christ's blessing" (Rom 15:25-29). Openly boastful though he is at this stage (so Rom 15:17), Paul is also cautious: he urges his Roman supporters to pray that he might escape the unpersuaded in Judah, and that his service for the saints in Jerusalem might be an acceptable offering (15:30-33).

And then, having mentioned both his sacrificial offering in Jerusalem and his fear of some in Judah, Paul goes on in the present text of Romans to recommend Phoebe to the Romans, the servant of the congregation among the Cenchraeans, whom Paul describes as an aid of many, including himself (Rom 16:1). The Romans are asked to accept her, and to aid her "in whatever matter in which she has need of you." Chapter 16 of Romans opens with a famously long list of Paul's associates and helpers, but Phoebe is the only person who is commended in this way. She is called a servant (*diakonos*, the same term used of Christ in 15:8) just after Paul has referred to his own collection as service (*diakonia*, in Rom 15:31), and has referred to his own activity as serving (Rom 15:25).

The importance of these links is attenuated, of course, if one follows the argument that ch. 16 is an addition to the original letter, perhaps initially destined for Ephesus. Pierre Benoit has nonetheless come to the conclusion that Phoebe is the bearer of the letter, and that the salutations are designed to underscore Paul's familiarity with those known to the congregation(s) in Rome.[48] If the reference to Phoebe and the congregation in Cenchraea is Pauline, then we can correlate the itinerary of Acts with Paul's implicit itinerary. If, on the other hand, the chapter is an appendix, then it reflects a later correlation of the two itineraries. Either way, Cenchraea turns up as a linking moment between Paul's activity among the Gentiles and what is about to happen in Jerusalem.

The Cenchraean moment is a time when Paul is well aware of enmity in Judah, and when he is disquieted by it. His response is to align himself as best he can with the most powerful Christian group in Jerusalem, the one associated with James. That, indeed, is the best explanation for Paul's willingness to take on a Nazirite vow, and to take on the expenses of other Nazirites. As cited by Eusebius (see *History* 2.23.1-18), Hegesippus characterizes James, Jesus' brother, as the person who exercised immediate control of the church in Jerusalem. Although Peter had initially gathered a group of Jesus' followers in Jerusalem, his interests and activities further afield left the way open for James to become the natural head of the community there. That change, and political changes in Jerusalem itself made the Temple the effective center of the local community of Jesus' followers. James practiced a careful and idiosyncratic purity in the interests of worship in the Temple. He abstained from wine and animal flesh, did not cut his hair or beard, and forsook oil and frequent bathing. According to Hegesippus, those special practices gave him access even to the sanctuary. These practices of holiness are for the most part consistent with the requirements made of those undertaking a Nazirite vow. The additional notice, that James avoided oil, is consistent with the especial concern for purity among Nazirites. They were to avoid any contact with death (Num 6:6-12), and the avoidance of all uncleanness – which is incompatible with sanctity – follows naturally. The avoidance of oil is also attributed by Josephus to the Essenes (*Jewish War* 2.123), and the reason seems plain: oil, as a fluid pressed from fruit, was considered to absorb impurity to such an extent that extreme care in its preparation was vital.[49] In the absence of complete assurance, absti-

---

[48] See *La Bible de Jérusalem* (Paris: Les éditions du Cerf, 1977) 619-1620.

[49] See Josephus, *War* 2.590-594; *m. Menahoth* 8:3-5 and the whole of *Makhshirin*. The point of departure for the concern is Lev 11:34.

nence was a wise policy. James's vegetarianism also comports with a concern to avoid contact with any kind of corpse. Finally, although Hegesippus's assertion that James could actually enter the sanctuary seems exaggerated, his acceptance of a Nazirite regime, such as Acts 21 explicitly associates him with, would account for such a remembrance of him, in that Nazirites were to be presented in the vicinity of the sanctuary.

b. The Metaphorical Nazirite

Alongside the stringent reflection of Nazirite practice, another source within the New Testament is willing to call Jesus a Nazirite, when he does not engage in any such vow, and regularly engages in practices contrary to the requirements of Numbers 6. The existence of this source evidently complicates the analysis of James and his influence.

The first exorcism story in Mark's Gospel represents this alternative source. The demon "speaks," but the people in the synagogue hear only inarticulate shrieks. Jesus alone understands the meaning of the sounds. The demon identifies itself with all unclean demons of the spirit world in a fascinating switch of pronouns in the text (here italicized; Mark 1:24): "*We* have nothing for you, Nazarene Jesus! Have you come to destroy *us*? *I* know who you are – the holy one of God!"

The slip back and forth between plural and singular surprises any reader of Mark's text.[50] Multiple demons – like Mary Magdalene's seven (Luke 8:2) and the demon that found seven colleagues to repossess a person in Jesus' saying (Luke 11:24-26; Matt 12:43-45) – signaled the resistance of the demonic world as a whole. Like a military commander who claims that acts by insurgents only prove they are desperate, Jesus viewed the violence of demons as part of the impending defeat of their regime. In addition to its identification with unclean spirits as a whole, the demon in the synagogue also specifies the purpose of Jesus' exorcisms: not simple banishment, but their definitive removal from power. That is what the demon fears on behalf of the whole realm of unclean spirits: regime change instigated by Jesus as the agent of God's kingdom, the kind of demonic retreat Mary Magdalene had experienced.

Fearing destruction, the unclean spirits act before Jesus speaks, initiating a preemptive strike by naming him. The term "exorcise" (*exorkizo* in Mark's Greek) appears explicitly here, and means "to bind

---

[50] See Chilton, "Exorcism and History: Mark 1:21-28," *Gospel Perspectives* 6 (1986) 253-271.

with an oath" (which is the point of an exorcism). The oath was a formula that exorcists usually used to invoke divine power and force demons to obey their commands. Such spells were more effective when they identified a demon by name. In this case, however, the demon jumps in with a spell and a naming of its own. In effect, it is exorcising the exorcist, a notable departure from the well-documented form of exorcism stories in the ancient world.

Mary's source describes this as a very noisy event. The demon "cried out" (Mark 1:23). Jesus shouted back in the rough language of the street, "Shut up, and get out from him!" (v. 25). The demon's obedience comes under protest; it "convulsed" its nameless victim and departed with a scream (v. 26).

These acute observations all point toward a storyteller with keen knowledge of the deep combat with evil that Jesus' exorcisms involved, their raucous quality, and the danger that the exorcist would be defeated. Moreover, the storyteller knows how Jesus interpreted the demons' wordless shout (Mark 1:34). Whoever conveyed this story had to know both what went on and what Jesus thought about it. Mary Magdalene best fits the description of that storyteller.

Hand in hand with that identification, calling Jesus "Nazarene" finds its purpose. Jesus "the Nazarene" (*Nazarenos* in Greek) is the grammatical equivalent of "Magdalene" (*Magdalene*), allowing for a change of gender. (In Aramaic, which both Jesus and Mary spoke, the antecedents would have been the equally resonant terms.) English pronunciation conceals a rhyme that would have caught the ear of any Greek or Aramaic speaker who heard these names spoken aloud: the texts reverberate with an implicit connection between Jesus and Mary.

To call Jesus "the Nazarene" naturally evokes Nazareth as his native village,[51] just as "Magdalene" evokes Magdala on the Sea of Galilee. The verbal echo between the names reflects the geographical proximity between the two villages and their contacts with one another. Mark's Gospel, the earliest of the Gospel's and the closest to the Aramaic idioms of Jesus' movement, preserves the resonance between

---

[51] This geographical meaning is also expressed in the Gospels by another term, "Nazorean" (*Nazoraios* in Greek), which does not rhyme with "Magdalene." "Nazorean" predominates in the Gospels according to Matthew, Luke, and John, while Mark uses only "Nazarene." See the still worthwhile article by H.H. Schader in *Theological Dictionary of the New Testament* (ed. G. Kittel; tr. G.W. Bromiley; Grand Rapids: Eerdmans, 1978) 874-879. In the Talmud and other Rabbinic sources, Jesus is called the *Notsri*, an evident play on *Nazaraya* and *Nazoraya*. The term *Notsri* means some one who keeps or hinders: Jesus and his followers keep their own traditions, and therefore hinder other Israelites.

Rabbi Jesus' nickname and Mary's.

The form "Nazarene" also resonates with the traditional word "Nazarite" (*nazir* in Hebrew), which means "consecrated." The name "Nazarene", paired with the designation "the holy one of God," evokes Jesus' consecration and reinforces his spiritual threat to the world of the demons in the dramatic opening exorcism in Mark's Gospel (Mark 1:23-27). Just as Jesus' contemporaries are "astounded" when the demons in Capernaum shudder in the presence of his purity, the Magdalene and her companions are "completely astounded" by a vision of a young man who tells them Jesus "the Nazarene" has risen from the dead (Mark 16:1-8). Here too, revelation troubles those it comes to, and that disturbance echoes through the names "Nazarene" and "Magdalene."

To Jesus' mind, Mary was "the Magdalene," the woman who had embodied the impurity to which Herod had subjected Magdala. To Mary, Jesus was "the Nazarene," the force of Galilean rural purity that could vanquish her demons. "Nazarene" and "Magdalene" together invoke the way Jesus and Mary became joined, the enduring link between them, and the disturbing thought that the force of the holy cannot be contained by the ordinary conventions of this world.

This comes to expression also in the story of the man with the legion of demons, set in the Decapolis, just on the other side of the Sea of Galilee from Magdala. There Jesus confronts a horde of demons that have taken up residence in a man who inhabits a cemetery (Mark 5:1-17; Luke 8:26-37; Matthew 8:28-34). When Jesus demands to know the demons' names (a standard feature in exorcisms of the time) they say they are "legion," the designation for a 6,000-man Roman military unit. The story is related in the same simple, vigorous, abrupt voice of the Capernaum exorcism (Mark 5:1-13):

> And they came to the opposite side of the Sea, into the area of the Gerasenes. He got out from the boat, and at once there met him from the tombs a person with an unclean spirit. He had the habitation among the tombs, and no one was any longer able – even with a chain – to bind him. (For many times he had been bound with fetters and chains, and the chains were torn apart by him, and the fetters smashed, and no one was capable of subduing him. And all night and day he was among the tombs and in the hills, shouting and wounding himself with stones.) He saw Jesus from a distance, and ran and worshipped him, and shouting with a big sound he says, I have nothing for you, Jesus Son of the highest God! I adjure you by God, do not torment me! Because he had been saying to him, Unclean spirit, get out from the person! And he interrogated him, What is your name? And it says to him, Legion is my name, because we

are many. And they summoned him a lot, so that he would not dispatch them outside of the area. Yet there was there by the hill a big herd of pigs grazing. They summoned him and said, Send us into the pigs, so that we may enter into them. And he permitted them. The unclean spirits got out and entered into the pigs, and the herd rushed over the cliff into the sea, about two thousand, and they were choked in the sea.

By several stark images (the victim's habitation in a cemetery, his habit of wounding himself, his residence in Gentile territory), this exorcism targets uncleanness as the evil Jesus addressed in all his exorcisms. The possessed man embodies impurity and is named "legion" just in case a hearer or reader might miss the point of where the contagion came from. When Rabbi Jesus drove demons out of people, he acted on behalf of those possessed, but we can clearly see that he was also acting against the source of impurity – Rome and Rome's collaborator, Herod Antipas. Mary Magdalene, whose town lay adjacent to Antipas' new capital, knew the reality of this uncleanness. With equal clarity, the narrative drives home the theme of the struggle involved in this exorcism. The demons were numerous, talked back to Jesus, and did not obey a direct command.

It was unusual in the ancient world to insist that the demons formed a violent, coordinated front of impurity, and bizarre to depict them as dictating how an exorcist should handle them. The legion story deliberately engages in exaggeration, to the point that no commentator[52] has been able to draw the line between the story's symbolic meaning and the literal event it depicts. Still, the symbolic meaning remains clear no matter how literally we take the details: as the divine kingdom takes root, Rome will be dislodged. Roman demons were no more threatening than panicked pigs; they will neutralize themselves in God's encompassing purity, which is as deep as the sea.

It is startling, however, that in this case, Jesus is not called "Nazarene" at all, as he is in the first exorcism story in Mark (which comes from the Magdalene source[53]). Just as the impurity in the story has been exaggerated, so any association with Nazirite practice is avoided. This attests the influence of James, for here the practical meaning of

---

[52] See Chilton, "Friends and Enemies," *The Cambridge Companion to Jesus* (ed. M. Bockmuehl; Cambridge: Cambridge University Press, 2001) 72-86 and *Rabbi Jesus*, 168-173, where the context of the events in the deadly threat to Jesus from Herod Antipas explains the political symbolism of this exorcism. The sequel to the exorcism (Mark 5:14-17) is also discussed in those pages of *Rabbi Jesus*.

[53] For the recovery of this source, see Chilton, *Mary Magdalene: A Biography* (New York: Doubleday, 2005) 33-46, 203-206.

the Nazirite vow superseded the metaphorical vision of Nazirite practice championed by Mary Magdalene.

Prospect

The association of the Nazirite vow with James is well established, and has long been acknowledged. But alongside that practical institution, language and imagery derived from Numbers 6 is also applied to Jesus in the New Testament in a metaphorical way, most notably in the Magdalene source. James's position should not be confused with the stance of Jesus, as if Jesus himself were a conscious Nazirite,[54] or as if James's stance can be applied to all the circles of belief and practice that contributed to the New Testament. Rather, prospects for the study of James are at their most promising when it is acknowledged that he contributed a distinctive perspective to his brother's movement. At the end of the day neither history nor biography may be practiced in respect of the New Testament, except in the analysis of the meaning of sources and their interactions, whether complementary or contradictory.

---

[54] This is the position of Marcus Bockmuehl, given at the meeting of the Studiorum Novi Testamenti Societas in Birmingham in 1997. Of all the arguments adduced, the most attractive is that Jesus' statement concerning wine and the kingdom involves his accepting Nazirite vows. See P. Lebeau, *Le vin nouveau du Royaume. Etude exégétique et patristique sur la Parole eschatologique de Jésus à la Cène* (Paris: Desclée, 1966); M. Wojciechowski, "Le naziréat et la Passion (Mc 14,25a; 15:23)," *Biblica* 65 (1984) 94-96. But the form of Jesus' statement has not been rightly understood, owing to its Semitic syntax. He is not promising never to drink wine, but only to drink wine in association with his celebration of the kingdom. See Chilton, *A Feast of Meanings: Eucharistic Theologies from Jesus through Johannine Circles* (NovTSup 72; Leiden: Brill, 1994) 169-171.

12

Mary Magdalene and History

Bruce Chilton

Two factors have impeded a clear and critical understanding of Mary Magdalene: (1) evidence from the first century regarding her is limited to the Gospels, and even then is scant, and (2) legends concerning Mary Magdalene that developed after the first century (continuously, and now into the twenty-first century) have proven explosive. Both from the point of view of the *transmission* of material and from the point of view of the *reception* of evidence, the issue of her identity has proved fraught. Either factor, taken alone, might be taken to make the attempt to understand Mary Magdalene impossible.

One possible response to this situation is to deny that any historical portrait of Mary is recoverable. That has been the suggestion of Bart Ehrman, as well as other professional scholars of the New Testament, in his reaction to a fictional work, *The DaVinci Code* by Dan Brown.[1] This perspective is understandable, but I want to begin by explaining why I think it is also harmful to the critical study of religion.

Although the evidence regarding Mary is slim while legends about her abound, the earliest sources – that is the Gospels – categorically insist that she was a vital figure, most prominently in developing the conviction that Jesus was raised from the dead after his crucifixion. By refusing to investigate Mary's history, we leave that vital moment in the emergence of Christianity unexplained and unexplored. Moreover, the legends in regard to Mary have proven so powerful (the very latest of them sometimes exerting the most influence) that refusing to deal historically with Mary simply paves the way for fiction of one sort or another to triumph.

---

[1] B. Ehrman, *Truth and Fiction in* The Da Vinci Code. *A Historian Reveals What We Really Know about Jesus, Mary Magdalene, and Constantine* (New York: Oxford University Press, 2005)

The attempt to say that we cannot know anything historically about Mary is as outmoded as that same claim is in regard to Jesus. Fifty years ago, Rudolf Bultmann ruled the field of New Testament studies with his dictum that Jesus cannot be known as a figure of history, because there are no public records about him. To Bultmann and those who followed him, the reader of the Gospels was only called upon to decide existentially for or against Jesus and his way of life; information about him was irrelevant.[2] Occasionally that fossilized view of history is dusted off and exhibited proudly by literary critics who attempt for their own reasons to deny an historical dimension in the New Testament; Harold Bloom, whose recent work we will consider in the conclusion of this paper,[3] exemplifies such an evangelical agnosticism.

Whether championed by a Bultmann or a Bloom, this view of history, which demands public archives to prove or disprove a given fact, has long been recognized as too limited. History *is* sometimes a matter of deductive argument, especially when issues of forgery and authentication are in play. Scholars of history have recognized for more than half a century that their task concerns the *explanation* of evidence, not just proving or disproving whether one event or another happened. The whole spectrum of related meanings – including texts and events and contextual issues and archaeological, sociological, economical and/or political analysis – needs to be assessed historically, so as to explain patterns of evidence. That involves including drawing inferences concerning the most vital generative moments, at the beginning of a pattern as well as along the line, which produced a given movement in history. Fact remains the point of departure in any history, but fact in the service of meaning.[4] Deploying mechanical views of history ignores the meaning of the term *historia* in Greek, which is "inquiry." Scholars who make their business that of disproving what Dan Brown says give his novel more attention than it merits, cheapen their own view of history, and probably wind up advertising *The DaVinci Code* more than they discredit it.

Here I suggest that a critical awareness of the historical task leads to a clear apprehension of Mary Magdalene and of her importance within

---

[2] I have discussed the intellectual environment that fomented this attitude in *Redeeming Time. The Wisdom of Ancient Jewish and Christian Festal Calendars* (Peabody: Hendrickson, 2002).

[3] H. Bloom, *Jesus and Yahweh. The Names Divine* (New York: Riverhead, 2005).

[4] See Chilton, "Biblical Authority, Canonical Criticism, and Generative Exegesis," *The Quest for Context and Meaning. Studies in Biblical Intertextuality in Honor of James A. Sanders* (Biblical Interpretation Series 28; Leiden: Brill, 1997) 343-355.

Jesus' movement from the earliest stages. If we will see history as the exploration of patterns of evidence, including inferences of what people in the past said or did to initiate these patterns of meaning, then Mary Magdalene is recoverable from the whole spectrum of text, artifact, and legend, much as Jesus and Paul and James are recoverable. The difference is that the scantiness of the earliest evidence and the explosion of legend are so extreme, distorting both the material to be explained and the attitudes people bring to the study of Mary, that it is necessary to keep the historical task firmly in mind as we face the challenge of knowing Mary Magdalene. The same factors that make her a problem in knowing her historically also demand conceptual clarity in the historical task, a clarity also needed for the study of Jesus and Paul and James, but all too rarely achieved.

The Scarcity of Early Evidence

Mary Magdalene was the disciple who best appreciated Jesus' visionary teaching of resurrection, and, without her, Christianity would have been entirely different. It is not even clear that its core faith in Jesus' victory over the grave could have emerged without Mary. That is why she has been known as "the apostle to the apostles" since the second century:[5] It was from her that the apostles first learned that Jesus had been raised from the dead.

By the time the Gospels were written, more than forty years after Jesus' death, Christianity had developed an increasingly physical or material view of the resurrection. This, however, was not Jesus' view, because he compared people raised from the dead to angels (Mark 12:25). This spiritual perspective on resurrection set him apart from other Jewish teachers of his time, many of whom saw the afterlife in a materialistic way.

Mary Magdalene's experience of Jesus as risen from the dead accorded with Jesus' own teaching. For that very reason, it was "corrected" over time to agree with the emerging orthodoxy of a physical resurrection. When Mary and her companions lifted their eyes at the mouth of Jesus' tomb in Mark (the earliest of the Gospels), they "perceived that the stone had been rolled off" (Mark 16:4; see the full text of passages related to Mary under "Contexts and Sources" below). The verb "perceive" represents a precise choice of words. *Theoreo* in Greek (from which our English term "theory," the equivalent of the

---

[5] The broadest survey available is by S. Haskins, *Mary Magdalen: Myth and Metaphor* (New York: Harcourt Brace, 1993).

noun *theoria*, is derived) refers to the women's deliberate perception, filled with both anxiety and hope. The women had just posed the desolate question, "Who will roll the stone away from the door of the memorial for us?" (Mark 16:3) A bleak description of the rock follows, "it was exceedingly big" (Mark 16:4). Caught between their own despair and the size of the rock, they lifted their eyes and "perceived." This moment of extraordinary perception opened them to the announcement of Jesus' resurrection, and their vision became the vessel of Christian hope in life after death.

Precisely because it represents the core of Christianity's message, the resurrection of Jesus continues to touch off controversy and misunderstanding. What the texts say about the events concerned is persistently distorted — as much by the projection of those who impose their own wishes for afterlife onto Jesus as by the denial of those who resent the influence of Christianity in the modern world. Either way, modern presuppositions torment the meanings of ancient texts to the point that even scholars find it difficult to specify what the documents say. In no other question have modern dogmas, both ecclesiastical and secularist, so obscured ancient history.

Mary's experience in Mark's Gospel gives us access to her encounter with the risen Jesus apart from modern presuppositions, whether pious or skeptical. Since the time before there was any religion called Christianity to believe in or not believe, before there was any question of influencing theological opinion, the faith that people adhere to, or their views on life after death, Mary's vision and voice have awaited a hearing in their own terms.

The distortion of Mary's vision — sometimes willful, sometimes inadvertent — has plagued the interpretation of the New Testament. In fact, as I have shown in a recent book, her witness to the resurrection was progressively marginalized even in the Gospels that came after Mark.[6] Her experience conflicts with many conceptions widely assumed to be part and parcel of Christianity. Because her experience came first, those who came after her manipulated what she said to accord with their own views. In this case as in others, when a teacher sets in motion a powerful idea or tradition — which the resurrection of Jesus undoubtedly is — the price of this primacy is often paid in the form of the misinterpretations that come later.

By the word choice of *theoreo* rather than *horao* (the verb for physical seeing) the women's visionary discernment literally becomes a matter

---

[6] *Mary Magdalene: A Biography* (New York: Doubleday, 2005).

of deep perception rather than ordinary vision. Mark's awareness that the women's insight was supernatural shines through the meaning of several elements in the account of what happened at the tomb. The women's apprehension of heaven was so important to them that physical circumstance no longer mattered. Mark says that they move in the direction of Jesus' corpse. But do they advance "to" the tomb or "toward" the tomb? Or might it be "up to" the tomb or "into" the tomb? The preposition *eis*, the term chosen in Mark's Greek, might bear any of those meanings, because it refers to direction without exactly specifying extent (Mark 16:5). An author who wanted to specify the physical proximity of the women to the exact place where Jesus' corpse had been deposited would have to say more, as actually happens in the other Gospels. Instead, Mark chooses succinct ambiguity.

Mark places the women at the mouth of the tomb when their vision transfixes them. The Gospel does not concern itself with telling us how far the women got into the tomb. It does not say whether the giant rock they "perceived" to have been rolled away had been literally removed or not. We might want to know whether these visionary events corresponded to what happened in the material world, but for Mark exterior facts of that sort did not matter. Rather, the women's experience pivots on their apprehension of the angel who speaks to them (Mark 16:5): "a young man sitting on the right appareled in a white robe ..." The women leave the corporeal realm when Mark says, "they were utterly astounded."

What causes their astonishment? It is not, as is alleged by a tiresome and inaccurate convention, "the empty tomb."[7] "The empty tomb" is a bad heading for this passage, although it is the designation frequently

---

[7] In her recent book, *The Resurrection of Mary Magdalene. Legends, Apocrypha, and the Christian Testament* (New York: Continuum, 2002), Jane Schaberg talks of the experience of Mary Magdalene as necessitating the "empty tomb" as the jolt (pp. 282-291) that it took to make her vision happen. In my opinion, that vastly underestimates the force of meditative practice, and reduces varied texts to a single, simplistic meaning. Because part of the argument of her book is against the "conflation" of passages and of people, Schaberg's own harmonization is glaring. She goes on to say (p. 284), "But I do not think this commits me to the belief that the resurrection must be thought of as the resuscitation of a corpse; rather, it is compatible with a lost or stolen corpse, and compatible with exaltation/ascent, and compatible with the mystery of the unknown fate of the corpse, and compatible with the destruction of the corpse." She apparently agrees with me that "When the women turned from the tomb of Jesus, directed away from any search for Jesus' corpse by their vision of the white-robed youth, the question of what became of his physical body was left open for ever" (*Rabbi Jesus*, 273). Had Professor Schaberg observed that they make no search in Mark's text, so that the "empty tomb" is moot there, she would have saved herself complication.

provided in printed English Bibles. For the simplest of reasons, we have to let that heading go: in Mark's Gospel, the women do not actually enter or inspect the tomb. They do so in later Gospels (which also reduce Mary's importance), but not here. At the tomb's mouth, Mary Magdalene and her companions see an angelic "young man." *That* is what astonishes them.

In their astonishment, they do not say (and might very well not have known) whether they were in the door, beside it, or inside the tomb. Visions often occluded a sense of ordinary circumstances. Once, Saint Paul referred to a visionary experience when he was "taken up into the third heaven." He said he could not even tell whether he was "in the body or outside the body," a phrase that derives from Jewish mystical practice.[8] So it was with Mary and her women companions: the force of vision was upon them, and they do not say whether they went into the tomb or searched for Jesus' corpse.

Although Jesus' resurrection represents the most emphatic connection with Mary Magdalene, and at the same time the progressive denigration of Mary's influence in later Gospels, the rituals of exorcism and anointing represent other examples of the same pattern. Mary is intimately associated with them, but as the New Testament developed these rituals were increasingly assigned to men, and as a consequence these stories about Mary retreated to the margins of text and memory. By the time of John's Gospel (written around 100 CE), not a single story of exorcism or of Mary's anointing survived marginalization.

The case of exorcism is startling, because Luke's Gospel names Mary as the woman "from whom seven demons had gone out" (Luke 8:3). That fact has been well noted in the secondary literature and in legend for more than a thousand years, but another fact has been ignored: Mary Magdalene is the only named recipient of Jesus' exorcism in the New Testament. Moreover, the way in which she is referred to here intimates repeated exorcism, and every detailed story involving Jesus and unclean spirits bears associations with Mary (geographical, in their proximity to Magdala, and literary, in their reference to Jesus as "the Nazarene" in a way that in Greek and Aramaic echoes Mary's surname, "the Magdalene").

Mary's association with anointing is taken as a matter of course in the story of the visit to the tomb, and for that reason she is the likely woman involved in the extended, pivotal story of the anointing of

---

[8] 2 Cor 12:2-4; *Rabbi Paul. An Intellectual Biography* (New York: Doubleday, 2004) 114-116, 119, 203, 228.

Jesus prior to his death in Mark 14:3-9, although her name is repressed there. Why should that have been the case? Elsewhere in the New Testament, it is assumed that male elders and apostles will anoint (Jas 5:14; Mark 6:13), not women, just as exorcism is claimed as a male, apostolic prerogative (again, see Mark 6:13, although that by no means exhausts the references). With the allegation of the "natural" authority of men over women in the post-Pauline period,[9] an increasingly male clergy tightly controlled exorcism and anointing just as a materialistic view of resurrection began to prevail. It is not surprising that after her death Mary Magdalene was nearly written out of the record of Christian memory.

The Gospels relate that she was called "Magdalene," telling us where she came from, and that until Jesus healed her, she had been possessed by seven demons. She followed Jesus in Galilee and helped to support him (Luke 8:2-3). She participated in Jesus' burial in Jerusalem, and on the way to anoint his corpse, she and her companions were the first to learn of his resurrection (Mark 15:42-16:8). All four Gospels agree about her role in Jesus' interment and her experience that he was raised from the dead, but each goes its own way in depicting those scenes. That is all the Gospels have to say directly about Mary Magdalene by name, although she is implicated in several other passages, as well. Had Jesus not insisted, "wherever the message is proclaimed in the whole world, what she did will also be spoken of in memory of her" (Mark 14:9), this effacement might well have been complete.

The Explosion of Legend
The force of legend concerning Mary is such that the initial questions posed by journalists today are likely to be: (a) Was she a prostitute? (b) Did she become Jesus' lover (and perhaps bear his child or children)? and, (c) Was she truly "The Apostle to the Apostles?" It will serve to illustrate my approach to the challenge of studying Mary that I resist saying whether or not she was "a" or "b" or "c". Making that judgment before evidence is assessed and patterns are investigated is an example of the immature history I believe we need to outgrow. (To this extent, the fact-checking of Ehrman invites the factoid-making of Brown, and *vice versa*.) In order to get at the question of pattern, it serves us better to ask when and why she was portrayed as harlot, as

---

[9] See 1 Tim 2:13-15, "Because Adam was first fashioned, then Eve." For the post-Pauline dating of this letter and this passage, see *Rabbi Paul*, 255-262.

Jesus' concubine, and as "The Apostle to the Apostles." Those questions can be answered, and answering them elucidates the figure of Mary. These are by no means all of the threads taken up in the rich medieval tapestry of Magdalene legends that still contribute to popular opinion about Mary, but I regard them as being principal portraits within the history of her legends.

In 594 CE, almost five and a half centuries after her death, Mary Magdalene became a prostitute. She did not do so because she needed the money; by then she was commonly portrayed as living a rich and luxurious life. But Pope Gregory the Great wanted to warn against the lure of wealth, and to urge his congregation of monks to refine their corrupt desires until they became pure, holy passion. Toward that end, he developed a compelling analogy between the male monk and the female lover in the biblical Song of Songs. Then he further extended his image by identifying Solomon's beloved Shulamit with Mary Magdalene, and went on to identify her with a completely different woman described as sinful in Luke's Gospel (7:36-50). The result is as seamless as it is powerful:

> Mary Magdalene, who had been a sinner in the city, loved the Truth, and so washed away with her tears the stains of wickedness. Thus was fulfilled the voice of the Truth who said, Her many sins have been forgiven her, because she loved much. She had abandoned her wicked ways, and washed away the stains of heart and body with her tears, and touched the feet of her Redeemer.

This flourish of Gregory's is frequently mentioned in the secondary literature to imply that Gregory had been hopelessly confused. In fact he engaged his texts, not as a historian, but as a contemplative theologian, and knew very well he was dealing with analogy (the usual method of Christian mysticism), rather than literal description. But one of the reasons the medieval period has been called the Dark Ages is that mystical insight was frequently confounded with literal truth, and Mary's prostitution consequently became a virtual dogma.

It took Mary longer still to become Jesus' sexual partner. By the thirteenth century, a late form of Gnosticism flourished in the West, chiefly in the South of France and in the Rhineland of Germany.[10]

---

[10] See M. Lambert, *The Cathars* (Oxford: Blackwell, 1998); R. Weis, *The Yellow Cross: The Story of the Last Cathars' Rebellion against the Inquisition, 1290-1329* (New York: Vintage, 2002); R. Nelli, *Écritures Cathares* (ed. A. Brenon; Monaco: Rocher, 1995); M. Barber, *The Cathars: Dualistic Heretics in Languedoc in the High Middle Ages: The Medieval World* (Harlow: Longman, 2000); R. van den Broek, "The Cathars:

Known as the "Alibigensians" (after the city of Albi in France) or the Cathars (perhaps from the Greek term *katharos*, "pure"), they insisted upon a strict separation between this world and the realm of Spirit. That led to their notion that sins of the flesh, while regrettable and to be outgrown before one's death, were only to be expected. Even Jesus as a person of flesh had to be distinguished from the spiritual Christ. But of what sin could Jesus have been guilty?

Mary Magdalene came ready-made as a sinner, given the legends regarding her trade as a prostitute that had by then circulated and expanded for centuries. From there it was a short step to make her into Jesus' concubine. Their relationship symbolized human weakness, and gave Jesus a sin that did not involve him in violence. Pope Innocent III was outraged, although his vehemence may have had more to do with the Cathars' denial of papal authority (as part of the structure of this world) and their refusal to pay tithe to the Church than with their peculiar teaching about Jesus and Mary. Innocent declared a crusade against the Cathars, and the result has been called the first European genocide.

The city of Béziers in the south of France took in some fleeing Cathars, and refused to give them up to the Catholic Crusaders. But on the feast day of Mary Magdalene in 1209, 22 July, the siege was over, and the Crusaders killed some fifteen thousand people. One contemporary chronicler, Pierre des Vaux-de-Cernay, conveys the impulse that led to the atrocity:

> These disgusting dogs were taken and massacred during the feast of the one that they had insulted.[11]

Mary's designation as "The Apostle to the Apostles" appears to have been well established by the second century. Feminine ministry in its complexity and breadth, authorized by the memory of Magdalene, surfaces in even the most dogmatic texts of Catholic Christianity during the ancient period. A famously conservative priest of third-century Rome named Hippolytus designated Mary as the *ur*-apostle. His conservatism is what has led to the judgment by Elaine Pagels and others that the designation itself came from the previous century, and it is interesting that he develops his ideas, as did Gregory the Great centu-

---

Medieval Gnostics?" *Studies in Gnosticism and Alexandrian Christianity* (Nag Hammadi and Manichaean Studies 39; Leiden: Brill, 1996) 157-177.

[11] P. des Vaux-de-Cernay, *The History of the Albigensian Crusade. Peter of les Vaux-de-Cerny's Historia Albigensis* (tr. W.A. and M.D. Sibly; Woodbridge: Boydell, 1998) 51 (para. 91).

ries later, in a commentary on the Song of Songs.[12] In Hippolytus's case, the point is not the purification of the passions, but the clarity and power of Mary's insight that Jesus had been raised from the dead, making her the leading figure in promulgating belief in his resurrection.

Hippolytus also features Mary's role of anointing. Mary Magdalene, the Holy Spirit, and the practice of anointing all converged in ancient Christian practice. An order of church worship and regulation called the *Didascalia of the Twelve Apostles* – compiled in Syria during the third century on the basis of earlier traditions – explicitly commands, "You shall revere the deaconess in the place of the Holy Spirit" (9.26.6).[13] Women in the ordained role of deaconess actually represented the Spirit in divine worship as far as the ancient Syriac community that produced the *Didascalia* was concerned. The primordial Semitic association between the Spirit of creation and divine Wisdom, both feminine, survived and flourished where Jesus' own patterns of thought and practice were remembered.

Holy Scripture mandated the role of deaconesses according to the *Didaskalia*, and Mary Magdalene provided the premier example (*Didascalia* 16.12.4, referring to Matt 27:55-56): "We have said that the service of a woman deaconess is above all obligatory and necessary, because our Lord and Savior was served by women deaconesses, who are: Mary Magdalene, Mary the daughter of James, and the mother of Joses, and the mother of the sons of Zebedee with other women."

While Catholic sources of the third century emphasize Mary's example in the field of ritual, Gnostic documents of the same period stress her insight in regard to resurrection. In 1896, a manuscript was discovered in Egypt, entitled *The Gospel according to Mary*. That document has forever changed our understanding of Mary.

The Gospel according to Mary dates from early third-century Egypt, a text used among the prosperous landowners who sustained Gnosticism throughout the ancient period. The "Mary" of the title refers to the

---

[12] See A.G. Brock, *Mary Magdalene, The First Apostle. The Struggle for Authority* (Harvard Theological Studies 51; Cambridge: Harvard University Press, 2003) 2, 15; Pagels, "Ritual in the *Gospel of Philip*," *The Nag Hammadi Library after Fifty Years. Proceedings of the 1995 Society of Biblical Literature Commemoration* (Nag Hammadi and Manichaean Studies 44; ed. J.D. Turner and A. McGuire; Leiden: Brill, 1997) 280-291.

[13] See F. Nau, *La Didascalie des Douze Apotres*: Ancienne Littérature Canonique Syriaque 1 (Paris: Lethielleux, 1912); R.H. Connolly, *Didascalia Apostolorum* (Oxford: Clarendon, 1929). For a succinct description of the relationship among the various orders of the ancient church, see W. Jardine Grisbrooke, *The Liturgical Portions of the Apostolic Constitutions: A Text for Students* (Brancote: Grove, 1990).

Magdalene,[14] and the Coptic text reflects the Gnostic Christianity that thrived in the Egyptian hinterland seventeen hundred years ago.

The Coptic language itself is key to Gnosticism's success in Egypt. The hieroglyphics of ancient Egypt were difficult to write and read, but Coptic put that language into the phonetic system of the Greek alphabet (with four extra characters). That innovation enabled people with leisure in rural Egypt to read and hear recitations of the world's wisdom in their own tongue. They became avid for philosophy, religion, and esoteric knowledge, and Gnosticism packaged them all in a way that assured its advance on Egyptian soil. Mary's centrality for these seekers has attracted considerable attention from feminist theologians and textual scholars alike.

Following a Gnostic trope, Jesus appears to his disciples after his death for an extensive period of time in *The Gospel according to Mary*. His risen persona does not provide reassurance, as he usually does in Gnostic literature. Instead, Jesus' appearance produces anguish. The disciples do not despair because they are bereft. They have the opposite problem. Jesus is all too present, and – as in life – all too demanding. He insists that his followers act in ways that seem unnatural and perilous to them, commanding them to bring his message to the Gentiles. He does the same thing in the Gospel according to Matthew and the book of Acts, but in *The Gospel according to Mary* the disciples respond more fearfully than they do in the New Testament. Jesus' disciples know that it was the Romans who killed him and they realize all too clearly that if they obey him they court a similar fate. "If they did not spare him," they moan, "how will they spare us?" (*Gos.*

---

[14] In fact a couple of recent scholars have inserted "Magdalene" – or (worse still) the Aramaic "Magdala" – into the title of this Coptic work, apparently trying to capitalize on the spike in modern interest in the Magdalene. Occasionally such ploys are part of a fashion to date *The Gospel according to Mary* much earlier than scholarship has established, and to treat it as if it were somehow a primitive Aramaic source, although remains have been found only in Coptic and Greek. Among many useful treatments, see J-Y. LeLoup, *The Gospel of Mary Magdalene* (tr. Joseph Rowe; Rochester VT, 2002); K.L. King, *The Gospel of Mary of Magdala. Jesus and the First Woman Apostle* (Santa Rosa: Polebridge, 2003), and A. Pasquier, *L'Évangile selon Marie. Texte établi et présenté* (Bibliothèque Copte de Nag Hammadi; Québec: Université Laval, 1983), a book that merits an edition in English. Although the insertion of "Magdalene" or "Magdala" into the title of this Gospel is inaccurate and perhaps opportunistic, it is more a minor annoyance than a serious deception. After all, in this Gospel "Mary" engages her risen teacher on the precise topic of how the vision of him raised from the dead is possible, so it is pretty obvious that she must be the same pivotal figure of all the resurrection accounts in the canonical Gospels – Mary Magdalene. That inference is sound, even though it does not warrant changing the ancient title of the Gospel.

Mary 9.10). By the time this Gospel was written, its audience knew that the move to proselytize non-Israelites, although crucial to the emergence of Christianity, had also proved to be a deadly gambit for many of Jesus' closest followers.

Peter is a key figure in *The Gospel according to Mary*, as he is in the book of Acts; in both cases, contact with non-Jews is Peter's central concern.[15] This source – for historical reasons or theological reasons, or some blend of the two – presents a view of how the message of Jesus reached non-Israelites that contradicts the book of Acts, making Mary rather than Peter the pivotal disciple who prompted that religious revolution. *The Gospel according to Mary* goes its own way in portraying Peter as bewildered by Christ's command to approach people outside Israel. He needs to ask for Mary's advice, because he cannot understand why Jesus would tell him to court mortal danger. Mary does understand, so Peter turns to a woman's authority, despite his male antipathy towards doing so.

While Peter and his colleagues grieve at the prospect of the suffering that awaits them at Gentile hands, Mary intervenes, "greeting them all" and cajoling them to rely on God who "has prepared us and made us into men" (*Gos. Mary* 9.19-20). The Magdalene emerges as an androgynous hero who strengthens the males in the apostolic company by means of the manhood, the visionary commitment to remain loyal to Jesus despite the risk of martyrdom, that she herself has received from Jesus. To be a "man" in this Gospel is to live in the realm of Spirit despite the threat of danger in the world of flesh.

Mary kisses her colleagues, "greeting them all." In Coptic as in Greek, the verb *aspazomai* implies a mouth-to-mouth embrace of fel-

---

[15] To that extent *Mary* and *Acts* agree, and their common portrayal of Peter – not Paul – as the true starting point of a deliberate extension of Jesus' message to Gentiles is historically accurate. See Acts 10:9-48, 11:5-17, 15:7-11; *Rabbi Paul*, 94-99.

In Acts Peter's reluctance to consort with Gentiles comes from his concern for purity. When he is offered unclean food in a vision, Peter responds that nothing unclean has ever entered his mouth (Acts 10:14). In *The Gospel according to Mary* simple, personal fear motivates Peter; he shares the anguish of the apostles as a whole that the Gentiles will treat them no better than they did Jesus.

These two sources disagree even more profoundly over the degree of Peter's competence in the domain of vision. His personal apparition in Acts resolves the issue of how he (and the consensus of all believers, according to Acts) should behave toward non-Israelites. As he sees unclean animals lowered from heaven in a linen sheet of cosmic dimensions, a voice tells him that what God has purified he should not treat as unclean. Consequently he agrees to visit the house of a Gentile, the Roman centurion named Cornelius. In *The Gospel according to Mary* Peter is bereft of personal vision; it apparently assumes that Peter's vision in Joppa came later.

lowship. This gesture of trust among men and women signaled familial intimacy throughout the Mediterranean world. Men kissed men, women kissed women, women kissed men and vice versa. The "holy kiss" became a key Christian ritual, featured centrally in both Catholic and Gnostic sources.

But the fact that the verb *aspazomai* is used here should not be misconstrued: it does *not* make Mary an especially sexual figure. Sadly, some modern translators have Mary "kissing" her colleagues, while elsewhere her male counterparts are portrayed as "greeting" each other, although exactly the same term is used. Loose, opportunistic translations of this kind perpetuate the Magdalene's caricature as modern Christianity's favorite vixen.

Peter is at a loss in *The Gospel according to Mary* without Mary's guidance and strengthening, her special manhood. He and the apostles have given her a hearing because she is among the select company who experienced the resurrected Jesus. Her kiss is the seal that she belongs in this company, not an invitation to sex. When she speaks of her own revelation, her discourse forms the core of *The Gospel according to Mary* and its content authorizes the apostolic commission to Gentiles in Jesus' name, marking Christianity's emergence in the ancient world.

She speaks very briefly in the text as it stands, because several pages containing her discourse have been physically removed. Yet even in its truncated form, her address offers the clearest evidence we have of how ancient Christianity and Gnosticism conceived of visionary experience. Her words vibrate with a simple grandeur and elegance (*Gos. Mary* 10.6-20):

> I saw the Lord in a vision and I said to him, Lord I saw you today in a vision. He answered and said to me, You are privileged, because you did not waver at the sight of me. For where the mind is, there is the treasure. I said to him, Lord now does he who sees the vision see it through the soul or through the spirit? The Savior answered and said, He sees neither through the soul nor through the spirit, but the mind which is between the two – that is what sees the vision and is –

Then the document breaks off for several pages. That excision, apparently inflicted on the text in antiquity, forms yet another scar over the memory of Mary.

Whatever Mary goes on to say in the missing part of the document, Peter and Andrew together rebuke Mary after her speech. Their anger – summed up in a rhetorical question – stems both from what she says and from what their paternalism considers her inferior gender (*Gos. Mary* 17.9–19.1): "Has he revealed these things to a woman and not to us?" Mary's articulate insight and her gender upset Peter and his cohort. A woman had had a visionary breakthrough that permitted her to see Jesus' purpose in reaching out to Gentiles before Peter himself did.[16] *The Gospel according to Mary* also understands that, in portraying the resurrection in trenchantly visionary terms (as the perception of the "mind," not of physical eyes or ears or hands), Mary directly contradicted a growing fashion in Christianity that conceived of Jesus in the flesh resuscitated from the grave.

This Gospel reflects not only Mary's theory of vision as she had articulated it from the first century, but also the controversies of later periods, using the characters of Peter and Andrew to portray the reaction against Mary within the Catholic Church during the second and third centuries of the Common Era. As theologians became increasingly materialistic in their conception of how Jesus rose from the dead and how all believers were to be resurrected,[17] Mary's vision fell into disfavor.

Contexts and Sources

Just as the changing contexts of Christianity militated against the continuing influence of the most ancient traditions and practices of Mary Magdalene, so by recovering the first-century contexts of Judaism, her setting and power may be understood afresh. Each of the three areas of

---

[16] Yet by the time Peter himself later had a vision in the city of Joppa – the vision Acts relates, of all the four-footed beasts of the planet, the reptiles of the earth and the birds of the air in a surreal image, derived from the book of Ezekiel (Acts 10:12-14) – he had learned from Mary that he was seeing with his mind, not his eyes. He knew the vision did not concern literal animals, but contact with people who were non-Israelites. That pivotal moment, when Peter authorized contact with Gentiles, was the culmination of a visionary path Mary Magdalene had set him on. The same woman who helped Peter see the risen Jesus in the first place guided him to the visualization of what this resurrection meant in terms of letting it be known to non-Israelites. *The Gospel according to Mary* is of deep historical value in permitting us to see that Peter's vision was not spontaneous, as Acts implies, but arose as a result of apostolic controversy over contact with Gentiles and Mary Magdalene's guidance.

[17] During this period Irenaeus, bishop of Lyons (in today's France) – having inherited the millenarian theology of his teachers in Asia Minor – preached a physical resurrection of the flesh; cf. *Against Heresies* 2.29; 4.18; 5.7-16, 36. Despite what Paul had clearly said in 1 Cor 15, Irenaeus called anyone who did not go along with this millenarian literalism a heretic. The Catholic Church of this period largely defined itself by its opposition to Gnosticism, and therefore by a stubborn assertion of the value of the flesh, even if that meant contradicting Saint Paul.

her influence as attested in the Gospels, exorcism, anointing, and vision, is attested as women's practice in ancient Judaism.

The ancient world agreed that *daimonia* could do harm, invading people, animals, and objects, inhabiting and possessing them.[18] While *daimonia* are in some ways comparable to psychological complexes, they are also analogous to our bacteria, viruses, and microbes. People protected themselves from invisible *daimonia* with the care we devote to hygiene, and ancient experts listed them the way we catalogue diseases and their alleged causes. Such lists have survived on fragments of papyrus that record the ancient craft of exorcism.[19] The fact that these experts disagreed did not undermine belief in *daimonia* any more than changing health advice today makes people skeptical of science.

Some rabbis charged women in general with magic, a term which included the practice of exorcism. Why did the Law of Moses say that you shall not permit a *"witch"* to live (Ex 22:18), rather than any sorcerer, whether male or female? The answer to that question was obvious enough (*y. Sanh.* 7:13), "Torah has taught you how things really are, for the vast majority who practice sorcery are women."

One reason for this association is that women also featured prominently among practitioners of anointing in ancient Judaism.[20] They ran

---

[18] C.B. Ubieta (tr. L.F. Llorente), "Mary Magdalene and the Seven Demons in Social-Scientific Perspective," *Transformative Encounters: Jesus and Women Re-viewed* (ed. I. Rosa Kitzberger; Biblical Interpretation Series 43; Leiden: Brill, 2000) 203-223. Should we see the exorcism of Mary's seven demons as a series of events or a single, explosive rout? Luke's spare reference does not answer this question. The demons are simply described as having "gone out" (*exeleluthei*) of Mary. If a Greek speaker wanted to imply that on a single, spectacular occasion Jesus expelled them all, it would have been more natural just to say that he cast them out (using the verb *ekballo*), as happens at other points in the Gospels (see Mark 5:1-20; Luke 8:26-39; Matt 8:28-34). The use of the verb *exeleluthei* and the absence of any reference to any dramatic expulsion of the demons make it seem likely that Mary's demons balked when Jesus commanded them to depart. A later version of Luke's description, which was pasted on to the Gospel according to Mark (16:9), changed the wording, to describe the demons as having been "cast out" (*ekbeblekei*). This pastiche ending of Mark is much later than the Gospel itself. In the way of many summary references in the Gospels, it irons out the troubling feature of demonic contention with Jesus.

[19] H.D. Betz, *The Greek Magical Papyri in Translation, Including the Demotic Spells* (Chicago: University of Chicago Press, 1992).

[20] See T. Ilan, "In the Footsteps of Jesus: Jewish Women in a Jewish Movement," *Transformative Encounters: Jesus and Women Re-viewed* (ed. I. Rosa Kitzberger; Biblical Interpretation Series 43; Leiden: Brill, 2000) 115-136 and *Mine & Yours are Hers. Retrieving Women's History from Rabbinic Literature* (Arbeiten zur Geschichte des Antiken Judentums und des Urchristentums 41; Leiden: Brill, 1997) 105, 230-232. M. Morgen-

their households, and their domestic arts included unction as a medium of healing. Experienced healers recited therapeutic formulae as they applied oil to relatives or friends. The Talmud of Jerusalem, a Rabbinic commentary on the Mishnah finalized during the fourth century CE, is an especially rich source for appreciating these traditional practices. The cases involved were sometimes life-threatening, but anointing also dealt with benign conditions. A person with pain in the lower body (*y. Shab.* 14:3, 4) could have the ache treated with oil without fear of breaking the prohibition against work on the Sabbath.

The Talmud of Jerusalem also speaks of anointing with spit with the intention to heal. Women were typical practitioners of this type of healing. In one case, the woman applies her unction of saliva seven times,[21] much as Jesus had to act several times to clear up the blind man's sight (Mark 8:22-26). Matthew and Luke repressed these stories of healing with spit not only because they involved more magic than they were comfortable with, but because Jesus was following a practice of women's household sorcery that he had learned, in all probability, from his most prominent female disciple – Mary Magdalene.

It was customary, as well as a commandment of the Torah, that Israelites attended to the corpses of relatives and friends, even victims of crucifixion. A first-century ossuary, discovered outside Jerusalem in 1968, contains the bones of a young man named Yochanan. An iron spike with an attached piece of wood is embedded in his right heel.[22] Properly tending to the dead was incumbent on every Israelite, and any prefect would court rebellion by deliberately flouting that imperative. The Roman prefect must have released Yochanan's broken body for burial: his ossuary indicates that the Romans honored Israelite concerns.

Following ancient practice, those who received Yochanan's crucified corpse bathed and anointed it, wrapping the body in linen and placing it in a funeral cave. According to usual burial practice, they deposited the bones in a limestone box after a year,[23] and carved Yochanan's name on the ossuary's side.

---

stern has recently published an Aramaic text of exorcism that involves anointing; "Notes on a Recently Published Magic Bowl," *Aramaic Studies* 2.2 (2004) 207-222.

[21] See *Sotah* 1:4, 16d and – more generally – *Shab.* 14:4.

[22] C.A. Evans, *Jesus and the Ossuaries* (Waco: Baylor University Press, 2003) 98-103. The nail had been driven into a hard knot of olive wood, and could not be removed as the others evidently were.

[23] See R. Hachlili, "Burials, Ancient Jewish," *Anchor Bible Dictionary* (ed. D.N. Freedman, G.A. Herion, D.F. Graf, J.D. Pleins, A.B. Beck; New York: Doubleday, 1992) I:798-994.

This discovery directly contradicts the claim, fashionable for more than a century in revisionist circles, that Jesus' body was tossed to the dogs after his execution.[24] Foundational texts of Judaism give precise instructions for dealing with corpses from crucifixion (see Deut 21:22-23; the document from the Dead Sea called 11Q64:11-13; Josephus, *Life* 421; *m. Sanh.* 6:5-6); a dead body that was exposed was a source of impurity and offended God. Mary and her companions returned to Jesus' tomb in order to fulfill the Torah's commandment, having waited until sundown on the Sabbath so that they could buy materials for anointing Jesus' corpse. Modern readers often express disgust and incredulity at the thought of returning to a corpse that had already been interred for some 36 hours. But mourners in antiquity were not squeamish: death had not yet been banished to the mortician's ghetto. Death's impurity had to be dealt with, and people accepted the temporary uncleanness of handling the corpse in order to assure the purity of the land and the community of Israel.

Mary's vision at Jesus' tomb, as well as her journey there for the purpose of anointing, is also precedented as a women's experience within Judaism of the first century. A work called *The Testament of Job* enhances the portrait of the biblical Job and designates his daughters as heirs of his mystical practice. He becomes a model of patience (rather than of the kind of complainer he seems in the Bible) and an expert in the practice of the mystical Chariot of God,[25] the *Merkavah* that con-

---

[24] J.D. Crossan has propagated this picture recently in "The Dogs Beneath the Cross," *Jesus. A Revolutionary Biography* (San Francisco: HarperSanFrancisco, 1994) 123-158, but it comes from the century-old work of Alfred Loisy. Loisy's scholarship could not have taken into account Yochanan's ossuary, and he typified foibles of his time in ignoring Judaic evidence for the burial of crucified people. Crossan tries to talk away this evidence in his liking for a sensationalist image. The post-modern period, in its enthusiasm for theory, has allowed of too much explaining away, instead of accounting for the data at hand. I have detailed this problem in *Rabbi Jesus*, 270-272, 308. Evans (p. 101) also contradicts Crossan, as does J. Schaberg, *The Resurrection of Mary Magdalene: Legends, Apocrypha, and the Christian Testament* (New York: Continuum, 2002). 239-240. On pp. 280-281, Professor Schaberg agrees with my reconstruction of the basic elements of Jesus' interment, although she does not discuss the location I have suggested on the basis of the discovery of the ossuary of Caiaphas (*Rabbi Jesus*, 214-215, 270-272).

[25] In referring to Job's "patience" (Jas 5:11), the New Testament appears to have the *Testament of Job* in mind, rather than the biblical book. Like Elijah (*T. Job* 52:8-12), this Job is even taken up in the divine Chariot that represents God's presence at the end of his life. *Merkavah* mysticism is introduced in *Rabbi Jesus* with reference to critical discussion, 41-63, 157, 161-165, 190-196, 269-289, 306-307.

veyed the swirling energy of divine presence to those who meditated on this master symbol of Judaic mysticism.

Prior to his death in the *Testament of Job*, Job is taken up to heaven in his vision and given three sashes that shimmer with the light of the sun. Each of them has a title that corresponds to the wisdom it accesses when a person wears the sash: the "Spirit," the "Creation of the Heavens," and the "The Paternal Splendor" (*T. Job* 46:1–51:4).[26] Job gives these sashes to his three daughters as an inheritance, enabling them to speak in the language of angels. They became the authors of *Merkavah* hymns, much as Enoch is named as a seer of the *Merkavah* in the book named after him. The *Testament of Job* completely overturns the modern assumption concerning women's roles in Judaism, especially in the context of mysticism. Finally, we come to an intriguing association with Mary: Job's three daughters are said in Rabbinic literature[27] to have settled and eventually to have died in Magdala.

Ancient Jewish literature permits us to see that women pioneered popular practice of the *Merkavah*, and that Magdala was an important center of that tradition. Along with her vessel for unction, Mary Magdalene carried with her a mystical teaching of the Spirit that her anointing art conveyed, and her association with anointing and exorcisms also locates her firmly within her cultural context.

Recent years have seen an increased awareness that major teachers in the New Testament – Paul, Barnabas, Peter, James, and the other apostles – were not just empty vessels filled with Jesus' message, but powerful sages in their own right. Their teachings shaped the Gospels and crafted the practices and beliefs that made Christianity into a world religion. Mary Magdalene belongs on this list of the creators of Christianity, and a better awareness of her cultural context – especially in view of the stylistic peculiarity of narratives of exorcism, anointing, and Mary's vision – reinforces the evidence of her influence already clearly attested within the Gospels. Mary provided the source of the Gospels' detailed stories of exorcism and influenced much of what early Christians believed about how to treat demonic possession. For

---

[26] See R.P. Spittler, "Testament of Job (First Century B.C. – First Century A.D.): A New Translation and Introduction," *The Old Testament Pseudepigrapha* (ed. J.H. Charlesworth; Garden City: Doubleday, 1983) I:829-868. The actual texts of this document are quite late, and no one would want to take everything about the *Testament of Job* literally, but the fact of mystical legends about women cannot be refuted.

[27] See H.C. Kee, "Satan, Magic, and Salvation in the Testament of Job," *Society of Biblical Literature Seminar Papers* (Missoula: Society of Biblical Literature, 1974) I:53-76 and Schaberg, 312, citing *Pes. de R. Kahanah* 7; *Exod. Rab.* 17:4; *Ruth Rab.* 1:5.

that reason she should be recognized as one of the principal shapers of Christianity's wisdom for dealing with the world of spirits.

Mary's method of exorcism was intimately linked to the ancient Judaic practice of anointing, and she emerges in the Gospels as a model of that practice as well. Oil served to consecrate people for ritual purposes, to signal celebration, and as a medium for communing with the divine. Exorcism and anointing involved mastering the ebb and flow of spiritual energy – and, in this arena, Mary must have been one of Jesus' most gifted adepts.

Her mastery included a profound understanding of what it means for a person to be raised from the dead. Jesus himself bluntly denied that resurrection involved a simple continuation of physical life on this earth. This view set him apart from other Jewish teachers of his time, many of whom saw the afterlife in a materialistic way, but it corresponds to the Magdalene source.

What follows is a direct translation from Luke and Mark, isolating passages where Mary's source appears to lie behind the text as it stands:

> And there were some women who had been healed from evil spirits and ailments – Mary who was called Magdalene, from whom seven demons had gone out, and Joanna, Khuza's wife (Herod's commissioner), and Susanna and many others who provided for them from their belongings. (Luke 8:2-3)

> And they proceed into Capernaum. At once on the Sabbaths he entered into the synagogue and taught. And they were overwhelmed at his teaching, because he taught them as having authority, and not as the letterers. And at once there was in their synagogue a person with an unclean spirit. He cried out and said, We have nothing for you, Nazarene Jesus! Have you come to destroy us? I know who you are – the holy one of God! Jesus scolded it and said: Shut up, and get out from him! The unclean spirit convulsed him, sounded with a big sound, and got out from him. And all were astounded. Result: they argued together, saying, What is this? A new teaching with authority? Even the unclean spirits he directs, and they obey him. And his fame went out at once everywhere, into all the surrounding land of Galilee. (Mark 1:21-28)

> And they came to the opposite side of the Sea, into the area of the Gerasenes. He got out from the boat, and at once there met him from the tombs a person with an unclean spirit. He had the habitation among the tombs, and no one was any longer able – even with a chain – to bind him. (For many times he had been bound with fetters and chains, and the chains were torn apart by him, and the fetters smashed, and no one was capable of subduing him.) And all night and day he was among the

tombs and in the hills, shouting and wounding himself with stones. He saw Jesus from a distance, and ran and worshipped him, and shouting with a big sound he says, I have nothing for you, Son of the highest God, Jesus! I adjure you by God, do not torment me! Because he had been saying to him, Unclean spirit, get out from the person! And he interrogated him, What is your name? And it says to him, Legion is my name, because we are many. And they summoned him a lot, so that he would not dispatch them outside of the area. Yet there was there by the hill a big herd of pigs grazing. They summoned him and said, Send us into the pigs, so that we may enter into them. And he permitted them. The unclean spirits got out and entered into the pigs, and the herd rushed over the cliff into the sea, about two thousand, and they were choked in the sea. (Mark 5:1-13)

And a woman who had a flow of blood twelve years (having suffered a lot from many physicians and spending everything that was hers and not improving, but rather getting worse) had heard things concerning Jesus. She came in the crowd from behind, touched his garment. Because she was saying that: If I touch even his garments, I shall be saved. And at once the fountain of her blood dried up, and she knew in the body that she was cured from her scourge. Jesus at once recognized in himself the power gone out from him and turned back in the crowd; he was saying, Who touched my garments? And his students were saying to him, Look at the crowd pressing you around, and you say, Who touched me? And he glared around to see the woman who had done this. But the woman was afraid and trembling, knowing what had happened to her; she came and fell before him and said all the truth to him. But he said to her, Daughter, your faith has saved you; depart in peace and be healthy from your scourge. (Mark 5:25-34)

He again went out from the regions of Tyre and came through Sidon to the Sea of Galilee in the middle of the regions of Ten Cities. And they carry to him a deaf and mute person and they summon him so that he might lay the hand on him. He took him away from the crowd privately and put his fingers into his ears, spat and touched his tongue. He looked up into heaven and sighed and said to him, Ephatha (that is, Be opened up). And his hearings were opened, and the bond of his tongue was loosed, and he spoke clearly. He ordered them strictly so that they would speak to no one, but as much as he ordered them, they announced rather all the more. And they were overwhelmed beyond all measure, saying, He has done everything well: he even makes the deaf hear and the dumb speak. (Mark 7:31-37)

And they come into Bethsaida, and they carry to him a blind person and summon him, so that he would touch him. He took hold of the blind person's hand and carried him away outside the village; he spat into his eyeballs, laid hands on him and interrogated him, You looking at anything? He looked up and was saying, I am looking at people, because I see them as walking trees. Then he laid hands on his eyes again; and he directed his gaze and was restored and perceived everything clearly. And he delegated him into his house, saying, Do not even enter the village. (Mark 8:22-26)

They came to the students and saw a big crowd around them and letterers arguing with them. At once all the crowd saw him and were completely astounded; they ran and greeted him. And he interrogated them, What are you arguing about with them? One from the crowd answered him, Teacher, I brought my son to you, who has a dumb spirit. And wherever it seizes him, it tosses him down, and he foams and gnashes his teeth and shrivels. And I talked to your students, so they would throw it out, and they were not capable. He answered them and says, Faithless generation, how long will I be for you? How long will I endure you? Bring him to me! And they brought him to him. The spirit saw him and at once convulsed him up; he fell upon the ground and rolled, foaming. And he interrogated his father, For how much time has it happened like this to him? But he said, From infancy, and often it throws him into even both fire and water, to destroy him. But if you can, help us – feeling for us! But Jesus said to him, "If you can" – everything is possible to one who believes! At once the father of the child shouted and was saying, I believe: help my unbelief! But Jesus saw that a crowd was running together, and scolded the unclean spirit, saying to it, Dumb and deaf spirit, I direct you, get out of him and no longer enter into him. It shouted and convulsed a lot, and got out; and he became as if dead. Result: many said that he had died. But Jesus held his hand fast and raised him, and he arose. He entered into a house and his students interrogated him privately, Why were we not able to throw it out? And he said to them, This sort can go out by nothing except by prayer. (Mark 9:14-29)

He was in Bethany in the home of Simon the scabby, recumbent, and there came a woman who had an alabaster of genuine, expensive nard balm. Smashing the alabaster, she poured it over his head. But there were some angry among themselves, Why has this waste of the balm happened? Because this balm could have been sold for more than three hundred denarii and given to the poor! And they were upbraiding her. But Jesus said, Leave her: why are you making problems for her? She has done a fine deed with me. Because you always have the poor with yourselves, and whenever you want, you can do them good, but me you do not always have. She acted with what she had; she undertook to oil my body for burial. Amen I say to you, wherever the message is proclaimed in the whole world, what she did will also be spoken of in memory of her. (Mark 14:3-9)

It already became evening, and since it was preparation (that is before Sabbath), Joseph from Arimathea – a pious councilor who himself expected the kingdom of God – came and dared to go into Pilate, and implored the body of Jesus. But Pilate was surprised that he had already died, and summoning the centurion, interrogated him, Has he already died? He knew from the centurion and granted the corpse to Joseph. He purchased linen, took him down, wrapped him in the linen and placed him in a tomb which was carved from rock and rolled a stone upon the opening of the tomb. Yet Mary the Magdalene and Mary of Joses perceived where he was placed. (Mark 15:42-47)

And when sabbath elapsed, Mary the Magdalene and Mary of James and Salome purchased spices so they could go anoint him. And very early on the first of the sabbaths they come upon the tomb when the sun dawned. And they were saying to one another, Who will roll the stone away from the opening of the tomb for us? They looked up and perceived that the stone had been rolled off (because it was exceedingly big). They went towards the tomb and saw a young man sitting on the right appareled in a white robe, and they were completely astounded. But he says to them, Do not be astounded completely. You seek Jesus the crucified Nazarene. He is raised; he is not here. Look – the place where they laid him. But depart, tell his students and Peter that he goes before you into Galilee; you will see him there, just as he said to you. They went out and fled from the tomb, because trembling and frenzy had them. And they said nothing to any one; they were afraid, because – (Mark 16:1-8)

The Historical Mary Magdalene and the Magdalene Chronology

The question naturally emerges, How are contexts and sources to be assessed in association with literary evidence across a very long period of time to identify Mary Magdalene and her influence? What view of history might prove fruitful? In his recent book, *Jesus and Yahweh*, Harold Bloom deploys two different approaches to history. Considering them helps us, in closing, to position ourselves critically in relation to Mary Magdalene.

In regard to Jesus Bloom observes, in a throw-back to Bultmann's position, that there are "no verifiable facts about Jesus of Nazareth," thereby sidelining him for the rest of the book.[28] When he deals with

---

[28] *Jesus and Yahweh*, 17. Instead Bloom deals with "Christ," constructed as a philosophical cipher, rather than a person.

Yahweh, however, Bloom discovers a historical "psychology," "A breathless, hard-breathing Yahweh, perpetually contracting and withdrawing into Elohim, retains his dynamism and his ill-temper."[29] He does so working back from the Pentateuch to the source called "J," a source about which he earlier wrote a book with David Rosenberg.[30] From the inference of "J," Bloom moves back through another level of inference to what Yahweh did and said to produce the source. The overall result, of course, produces a nice irony: a mythical Jesus and an historical Yahweh.

But for all that Bloom's irony is enjoyable, it is only possible by switching the view of history that is applied to the two figures, and by ignoring how the two are referred to by their own literatures. (The only reviewer to have spotted this conceptual incoherence so far has been Jacob Neusner.[31]) The Gospels, and come to that contemporaneous Jewish and pagan literature, only know Jesus as a person, while the Pentateuch and its sources, together with Persian and Hellenistic and Roman and (later) Christian literature, all identify Yahweh as a transhistorical god. For that reason, Yahweh cannot be known in history, although the *experience* of Yahweh is palpably historical, and might be identified through any of the people associated with the Yahwist source or the Pentateuch more generally.

Just this method is being deployed by David Rosenberg, in his biography of Abraham.[32] He is applying to Abraham the approach advocated in this volume for Jesus, Paul, James, and Mary, and developed in the publications that have been mentioned. This is a more serious way forward than Bloom's to an understanding of Jesus and his disciples including Mary Magdalene, and of Yahweh for that matter (that is, as experienced by known people). The inferential history that Bloom mistakenly applies to Yahweh has served and/or will serve for Abraham and Jesus, Moses and Paul, Aaron and James, Miriam and Mary, but not for Yahweh and Sophia.

It is crucial in the study of history to distinguish between any inference which might possibly be drawn from a text and those inferences which, arranged in a generative pattern, explain the texts and events and artifacts which form the web of human meaning from the past. By means of this approach, as we have seen, it is possible to coordinate findings in respect of Jesus and James and Paul insofar as they intersect

---

[29] *Jesus and Yahweh*, 227-228.
[30] H. Bloom and D. Rosenberg, *The Book of J* (New York: Grove, 1990).
[31] See *Reviews in Religion and Theology* 13.3 (2006) 279-281.
[32] See D. Rosenberg, *Abraham: The First Historical Biography* (New York: Basic, 2006).

with one another. Owing to her close relationship with Jesus, this feature of intersection is stronger in the case of Mary Magdalene. That is why Jesus' chronology offers a bridge to the chronology of Mary Magdalene, and of the development of Magdalene legends.

The Magdalene Chronology for Jesus
(page number refer to discussion in *Mary Magdalene*)

63 BCE In the midst of an internecine strife among the Maccabees, Pompey enters Jerusalem and the Temple, claiming them for Rome.

47 BCE Julius Caesar arranges for the governance of what became Syria Palestina, the Philistine region of Syria, including Israel.

4 BCE The death of Herod results in the division of his kingdom: his son Archelaus takes Judah, Herod Antipas inherits Galilee and Perea; Herod Philip rules Trachonitis.

1 BCE–13 CE The birth of Mary in the fishing town of Magdala and her childhood there (p. 3).

2-16 CE The birth of Jesus in Galilean Bethlehem, his childhood in Nazareth.

16-21 CE Jesus' apprenticeship with John the Baptist in Judea.

19 Herod Antipas's construction of Tiberias near Magdala (pp. 21-22).

21 The death of John the Baptist and the return of Jesus to Nazareth at the age of 18.

24-27 Using Capernaum as a base, Jesus becomes a well-known teacher in Galilee by his twenty-fifth year. Near the beginning of this period, during the year 25 (p. 1), Mary Magdalene meets Jesus for the first time, seeking exorcism, and starting to craft her source of Jesus' exorcisms (Mark 1:21-28, pp. 35-37).

27-31 Herod Antipas's threat forces Jesus to skirt and crisscross Galilean territory, and gather his followers in Syria; Mary returns to Magdala and tells the story of the man with a legion of demons (Mark 5:1-17, pp. 37-39) and (after Jesus' return to Galilee in 29, p. 39), his meeting the woman with a flow of blood, p. 61, the Transfiguration (in 30 CE, pp. 77-78), and the story of the epileptic boy (Mark 9:14-29, pp. 40-41, 46-47). The healings of the deaf mute and the blind man come from the year 31 (p. 62).

31-32 Jesus' last year in Jerusalem, accompanied by Mary Magdalene and other disciples as well as the Twelve (pp. 46-48). This leads up to the anointing in the house of Simon (pp. 48-52), and Mary's vision at Jesus' tomb (pp. 59-60, 70-79, 81-86)

35 The meeting of Peter and James and Paul in Jerusalem, and the availability of the earliest sources of the Gospels: Peter's instruction for apostles such as Paul, and the mishnah of Jesus' teaching known to modern scholarship as "Q."

37 The removal of Pontius Pilate and Caiaphas from power.

40 The adaptation of Peter's Gospel by James, the brother of Jesus, in Jerusalem.

45 In Antioch, outside of Palestine, followers of Jesus are for the first time called "Christians."

53-57 Paul writes his major letters: Galatians, Corinthians, and Romans.

62 The death of James by stoning in Jerusalem, at the instigation of the high priest.

64 The death of Paul and Peter in Rome.

66 The insurrection against Rome is supported by the authorities in the Temple, and Josephus is dispatched to Galilee, where he organizes resistance in Magdala and elsewhere.

67 Titus defeats Magdala and the Jewish fleet off the shore. Thousands are slaughtered systematically at the order of Vespasian. This is the likely date of Mary Magdalene's death in her native land (pp. 89-91).

70-73 The siege and capture of Jerusalem by the Romans, the burning of the Temple under Titus; the end of the revolt in Palestine; the composition of Mark's Gospel in Rome (p. 33).

75 Josephus publishes his *Jewish War*.

80 The composition of Matthew's Gospel, in Damascus (pp. 102-105).

90 The composition of Luke's Gospel, in Antioch (pp. 105-109).

93 Josephus publishes his *Antiquities of the Jews*.

100 The composition of John's Gospel, in Ephesus (pp. 129f.).

During the second century: Mary's link with Song of Songs and her designation as ur-apostle are established (see Hippolytus, p. 114, who writes during the third century, but reflects an earlier association); *The Gospel According to Thomas* (pp. 132-137); *Fractio Panis*, p. 112.

During the third century: in the *Didascalia of the Twelve Apostles*, Mary is designated as the principal deaconess, and as such the representative of the

Holy Spirit (pp. 114-116); *The Gospel According to Mary* (pp. 122-128); *The Gospel According to Philip* (pp. 139-144).

During the fourth century: *Pistis Sophia*, "You are she whose heart is more directed to the kingdom of heaven than all the others" (pp. 145f.). This is also when Ephesus claims the remains of Mary Magdalene.

594 Sermon of Gregory the Great – Mary becomes lover, prostitute (by means of Luke 7, pp. 6, 58, 147), and the sister of Martha. The legend of Mary of Egypt (an allegedly fourth-century personage) circulates during the same century (pp. 7-8), as well as Mary and the egg which changed color during her discussion with Tiberius (p. 2).

During the ninth century: transfer of Mary's alleged remains from Ephesus to Constantinople.

During the eleventh century: Vézelay legend well established, although it claims to rest on the exploits of Badilus, who took the remains from under the Saracens' noses in Provence in 749 (pp. 13-14).

1146 Bernard preaches the Second Crusade from Vézelay (p. 154).

During the twelfth century: Honorius Augustodunensis asserts that "Mary of the Castle" had been wealthy, but became "a common and filthy prostitute." But he also saw that her companionship with Jesus was natural within Judaism. Hence the statement of Pierre Celle, "Out of a prostitute, Christ made an apostle" (pp. 29, 116, 165, 171). Cf. the city planning of leper ghetto, Jewish ghetto, and houses for prostitutes (pp. 131-132)

During the thirteenth century: *The Golden Legend* of Jacobus de Voragine has Mary travel to France with Martha and Lazarus, founding the church of Marseille, and going to La Sainte-Baume from Saint-Maximin (pp. 8, 24, 27, 138-139, 154). Beforehand, she had squandered the wealth that came from owning Magdala and Bethany, and became a prostitute.

1204 Constantinople sacked during the Fourth Crusade.

22 July 1209 Béziers is destroyed, and its inhabitants burned for the assertion, according to Pierre des Vaux–de-Cernay, that Mary had been Christ's concubine (pp. 15-16, 147-149). Yet Franciscan sermons from the end of the century identify her with the woman taken in adultery, p. 149.

December 1279 Charles of Salerno excavates at Saint-Maximin (pp. 14-15, 151-152).

1375 Banner of Mary Magdalene for a fraternity of flagellants (p. 7)

1517 Jacques Lefèvre d'Etaples, author of a study entitled *De Maria Magdalene et triduo Christi disceptatio*, banned and declared a heretic by the University of Paris in 1523 (pp. 58-59). By this time, *The Dominican Legend* was going the opposite way in the support of Saint-Maximin (pp. 154-155).

1532 Martin Luther opines that Jesus and Mary had an adulterous affair (p. 148).

1884 *Baraheen Ahmadiyya*, by Mirza Ghulam Ahmad, leads to the identification of Jesus tomb in Srinagar.

1911 Bérenger Saunière (curé of Rennes le Chateau since 1885) found guilty of trafficking in masses. The Vatican in 1915 found him disobedient and guilty of financial irregularities. It seems clear he sold materials he found during repairs to his church. He resisted condemnation to the end, but died in 1917, a massive program of building still in progress, all inherited by Marie Dénarnaud.

1935 Identification by Kiyomaro Takeuchi of record of Jesus' burial in Herai (presently Shingo).

1962 *Les Templiers son parmis nous*, by Gérard de Sede.

1967 *L'Or de Rennes* published by Pierre Plantard, P. de Chérisey and G. de Sède, including faked parchments by de Chérisey.

1969 Separation of the two Marys in the Roman Catholic calendar (p. 153).

1982 *Holy Blood, Holy Grail*, by M. Baigent, H. Leigh, and H. Lincoln (p. 16).

1997 *The Templar Revelation*, by C. Thomas and L. Picknett.

2003 *The DaVinci Code*, by Dan Brown (pp. 86-87).

13

Paul and Gamaliel

Bruce Chilton and Jacob Neusner

I. Did Paul Learn from Gamaliel? The Problem

Acts 22:3 claims on Paul's behalf that, as a Pharisee, he studied "at the feet of Gamaliel," that is, with the patriarch of the Pharisaic party of the Land of Israel in the succession from Hillel, thence, via the chain of tradition, from Sinai. What can he have learned from Gamaliel? Here we identify a program of topics that Paul can have taken up in his discipleship or indeed any association or familiarity with Gamaliel, specifically, subjects and in some cases even Halakhic principles important in certain formal constructions of the Mishnah plausibly identified with the patriarchate in general, with Gamaliel (or at least a Gamaliel) in particular.[1] We propose to outline subjects treated in such construc-

---

[1] Which Gamaliel is meant by Acts and which by the counterpart rabbinic sayings attributed to a Gamaliel? Two Gamaliels flourished in the first century, the one, Hillel's heir, the other, the grandson of Hillel's heir. The chain of tradition set forth in tractate *Abot* ch. 1 knows from Shammai and Hillel forward, the following:
1:16 A. Rabban Gamaliel says,
1:17 A. Simeon his son says,
1:18 A. Rabban Simeon b. Gamaliel says
It is generally assumed that "Simeon his son" is duplicated by "Rabban Simeon b. Gamaliel." Thus Gamaliel I is represented as Hillel's successor in the chain of tradition, followed by Simeon b. Gamaliel I. Elsewhere, a statement attributed to Judah the Patriarch claims Hillel as Judah's ancestor. The patriarchal links are explicit. There is, moreover, a second Gamaliel in the first century, who flourished after the destruction of the Second Temple. And that Gamaliel II produced a second Simeon b. Gamaliel, the one who flourished in the second century and fathered Judah the Patriarch, sponsor of the Mishnah. The two Gamaliels and the two Simeon b. Gamaliels, continuing the Hillelite line, are further identified as patriarchs in their generation, a convention of the documents that will play a role presently. How does this fit together with Paul's having studied with (a) Gamaliel? The first Gamaliel was Hillel's son, so would have flourished in the first third of the first century, when Paul was getting his education.

tions that are covered, also, in Paul's letters – a limited proposal but one that, in context, carries implications at once historical and theological.

Formulating the problem in a minimalist framework conveys our critical judgment that we cannot immediately reconstruct the teachings of its named authorities, including Gamaliel, from the Mishnah. Why should we not take whatever the rabbinic sources – early, late, and medieval – attribute to (a) Gamaliel at face value? The answer to that question hardly requires elaborate statement, but perhaps it does bears repeating in outline. No critical scholar today expects to open a rabbinic document, whether the Mishnah of c. 200 CE or the Talmud of Babylonia (*Bavli*) of c. 600 CE, and to find there what particular sages on a determinate occasion really said or did. Such an expectation is credulous.[2] There is a second problem, separate from the critical one. Even if we were to accept at face value everything Gamaliel is supposed to have said and done, we should still not have anything remotely yielding a coherent biography, or a cogent theology, or even a legendary narrative of more than a generic and sparse order. We have only episodic and anecdotal data, bits and pieces of this and that, which scarcely cohere to form a recognizable whole.

Then Simeon b. Gamaliel ("Simeon, his son...Rabban Simeon b. Gamaliel...") would figure in the second third of the century, active in the time of the First War against Rome. Now, since Josephus claims him as worthy adversary (*Life* 191f.), Simeon b. Gamaliel would have thrived down to the destruction. Then comes his son, Gamaliel (II), after 70. What of the Gamaliels of whom the Mishnah speaks? It must follow that the Mishnah's Gamaliel can be either the first, with whom Paul in Acts is alleged to have studied, or his grandson. When a Gamaliel is mentioned in the company of Eliezer, Joshua, and Aqiba, that is the second. So the problem of the historical Gamaliel proves complicated by the question, which Gamaliel, and to whom do otherwise-indeterminate Gamaliel-sayings and stories belong? And the answer we give is, a particular corpus of Gamaliel-sayings represent the patriarchate, But which ones? We answer that question in detail.

[2] A choice example of false premises within a scholarly program is supplied by S.J.D. Cohen, "The Significance of Yavneh: Pharisees, Rabbis, and the End of Jewish Sectarianism," *Hebrew Union College Annual* 55, 1984, pp. 27-53. To formulate and prove his theory, he has exhibited that gullibility that characterizes some scholarship even now in the encounter with the rabbinic sources for historical purposes. Except for arbitrary reasons of his own, Cohen consistently takes at face value the historical allegation of a source that a given rabbi made the statement attributed to him. That is his starting point throughout. This critique is spelled out in J. Neusner, *Reading and Believing: Ancient Judaism and Contemporary Gullibility* (Atlanta: Scholars Press for Brown Judaic Studies, 1986). The argument there is that only on the premises of believing pretty much everything as historical fact can a variety of scholars have built their constructions.

Although the person of Gamaliel is not accessible, we do have a corpus of compositions that portray convictions characteristic of the institution of which in his time he was head,[3] and which is represented by passages in the Mishnah that exhibit a distinctive form and *Sitz im Leben*. We refer to what became the patriarchate. Gamaliel, as we shall see, is identified as part of the patriarchal chain of tradition that begins at Sinai and culminates in the Mishnah. What became the patriarchate is embodied in Hillel, Gamaliel I, Simeon his son, Gamaliel II (after 70), Simeon b. Gamaliel II (of the mid-second century), and the Mishnah's own sponsor, Judah the Patriarch (c. 170-210). Whatever its standing and form prior to 70, its theological tradition is situated by tractate *Abot* chs. 1–2 squarely within that traditional continuum. Form-analysis of traditions formally particular to Gamaliel and Simeon b. Gamaliel affords episodic access to a number of theological convictions and topics important to the continuing tradition of the patriarchate preserved, on its own terms, in the Mishnah. These, then, in our view will suggest the topical program and perspective to which Paul would have been exposed in any association with the patriarch, Gamaliel – a program characteristic of the patriarchate throughout its history, as we shall show.[4]

---

[3] We hasten to add: this "institution" in the pre-70 period was most unlike the political-religious authority of the early third-century patriarchate, with its Roman sponsorship. Clearly, the transformation of a sect, the Pharisees, into the administrative arm of the Roman government in the Land of Israel (meaning: for the ethnic community of the Jews), such as unfolded in the later first through the early third century, deserves study in its own terms. What is important is that the fully-articulated patriarchate, represented by Judah the Patriarch, sponsor of the Mishnah, traced itself back to Hillel via Gamaliel I and II and Simeon b. Gamaliel I and II, and, as we shall show, in the Mishnah preserved their traditions in a privileged literary formation, the domestic *Ma'aseh*, as distinct in its formal traits from the juridical *Ma'aseh*. The former reports personal practice as exemplary virtue, the latter reports court rulings not validated by the person of the sage who made the ruling, but by the consensus of sages. We maintain, then, that the topical program characteristic of the domestic *Ma'aseh* forms an ongoing tradition, preserved in its own literary construction, by the family represented in the tradition as Hillel–Gamaliel–Simeon b. Gamaliel–Gamaliel–Simeon b. Gamaliel–Judah the Patriarch (see n. 1).

[4] Obviously, we claim no more than that. We do not allege that it was only from the patriarchate (or its earlier, Pharisaic formation of the pre-70 age) that Paul could have derived that portion of his topical program represented in this study.

II. The Patriarchate and the Collegium of Sages

Our account of the theologies of the patriarchate and sages' collegium begins not with the Mishnah but with Abot, its first apologia, which reached closure c. 250 CE, a generation or so after the completion of the Mishnah. There we begin, as the passage cited indicates, with a chain of tradition extending from Sinai to Hillel – and which links the figures of the Patriarchal house, Gamaliel, Simeon, Gamaliel, Simeon, and Judah, to Sinai through Hillel. An abbreviated citation suffices:

M. Abot 1:1-18
    1:1 A. Moses received Torah at Sinai and handed it on to Joshua, Joshua to elders, and elders to prophets.
    B. And prophets handed it on to the men of the great assembly.
    1:2 A. Simeon the Righteous was one of the last survivors of the great assembly.
    1:3 A. Antigonos of Sokho received [the Torah] from Simeon the Righteous.
    1:4 A. Yosé b. Yoezer of Seredah and Yosé b. Yohanan of Jerusalem received [it] from them.
    1:6 A. Joshua b. Perahiah and Nittai the Arbelite received [it] from them.
    1:8 A. Judah b. Tabbai and Simeon b. Shatah received [it] from them.
    1:10 A. Shemaiah and Abtalion received [it] from them.
    1:12 A. Hillel and Shammai received [it] from them.
    1:16 A. Rabban Gamaliel says,
    1:17 A. Simeon his son says,
    1:18 A. Rabban Simeon b. Gamaliel says ...

The following chapter carries the list forward with the names of Judah the Patriarch, sponsor of the Mishnah, and his sons; then breaks off and reverts to Yohanan ben Zakkai – as heir of Hillel and Shammai.

The pivotal names here are:

    2:1 A. Rabbi
    2:2 A. Rabban Gamaliel, son of R. Judah the Patriarch
    2:4 C. Hillel

The stem of the tradition of Sinai that encompasses sages (not the patriarchate) begins with the explicit intrusion of an authority who received the tradition not from Simeon b. Gamaliel via Gamaliel but directly from Hillel and Shammai, a stunning shift possible only as part of an accommodation of the authority of the sages with that of the patriarchate: both derive from Sinai, both pass through Hillel.

    2:8 A. Rabban Yohanan b. Zakkai received [it] from Hillel and Shammai.
    C. He had five disciples, and these are they: R. Eliezer b. Hyrcanus, R. Joshua b. Hananiah, R. Yosé the priest, R. Simeon b. Netanel, and R. Eleazar b. Arakh.
    2:15 A. R. Tarfon says ...

What is important is, the chain of tradition is picked up by Rabbi [=Judah the Patriarch] and his two sons, named for the first-century figures, Gamaliel and Hillel. Then, as we said, comes a new and comparable institutional continuator to receive the Torah from Hillel and Shammai, namely, the sages' collegium. That is embodied in the figure of the founder of the Yavnean academy after 68 CE, Yohanan b. Zakkai, and his disciples, including the two principal masters of the generation of Yavneh, Joshua and Eliezer, masters of Aqiba.

The critical language therefore presents itself in the duplicated genealogy of the dual Torah: Hillel to Gamaliel and Simeon his son, Hillel and Shammai to Yohanan b. Zakkai and his disciples, principals of the period after 70. The Mishnah, sponsored by the Patriarchate, and embodying the normative law of the rabbinic sages, joins two distinct institutional partners. The upshot may be simply stated: (1) the chain of tradition runs from Sinai to the masters of the Mishnah through the patriarchate – Hillel, Shammai, and Hillel's heirs and successors, Gamaliel, Simeon, Gamaliel, Simeon – and (2) it is also taken up by the collegium of the sages, represented by Yohanan b. Zakkai and his disciples.

The pertinence of that fact to our problem will become clear when we ask, how do the two foci of authority, patriarch and sage, relate? In the portrait of the Mishnah, the following anecdote, famous in the study of Rabbinic Judaism, captures the conflict and how it is resolved, that is, the conflict between institutional authority vested in the patriarch, here, Gamaliel, and the juridical authority vested in qualified sages. This is how the sages, who dominated in the formation of the Mishnah, represent matters, with the obvious acquiescence of the patriarchate.

M. Rosh Hashanah 2:7
>2:7 C. Whether it appears in the expected time or does not appear in the expected time, they sanctify it.
>D. R. Eleazar b. R. Sadoq says, "If it did not appear in its expected time, they do not sanctify it, for Heaven has already declared it sanctified."

M. Rosh Hashanah 2:8-9
>2:8 A. A picture of the shapes of the moon did Rabban Gamaliel have on a tablet and on the wall of his upper room, which he would show ordinary folk, saying, "Did you see it like this or like that?"
>B. *M'SH* S: Two witnesses came and said, "We saw it at dawn on the morning of the twenty-ninth] in the east and at eve in the west."
>C. Said R. Yohanan b. Nuri, "They are false witnesses."

D. Now when they came to Yabneh, Rabban Gamaliel accepted their testimony [assuming they erred at dawn].
E. And furthermore two came along and said, "We saw it at its proper time, but on the night of the added day it did not appear [to the court]."
F. Then Rabban Gamaliel accepted their testimony.
G. Said R. Dosa b. Harkinas, "They are false witnesses.
H. "How can they testify that a woman has given birth, when, on the very next day, her stomach is still up there between her teeth [for there was no new moon!]?"
I. Said to him [Dosa] R. Joshua, "I can see your position [and affirm it over Gamaliel's]."
2:9 A. Said to him [Joshua] Rabban Gamaliel, "I decree that you come to me with your staff and purse on the Day of Atonement which is determined in accord with your reckoning [so publicly renouncing his ruling in favor of Gamaliel's]."
B. R. Aqiba went and found him [Joshua] troubled.
C. He said to him, "I can provide grounds for showing that everything that Rabban Gamaliel has done is validly done, since it says, 'These are the set feasts of the Lord, even holy convocations, which you shall proclaim' (Lev 23:4). Whether they are in their proper time or not in their proper time, I have no set feasts but these [which' you shall proclaim'] [vs. m. 2:7D]."
D. He came along to R. Dosa b. Harkinas.
E. He [Dosa] said to him, "Now if we're going to take issue with the court of Rabban Gamaliel, we have to take issue with every single court which has come into being from the time of Moses to the present day, since it says, 'Then went up Moses and Aaron, Nadab and Abihu, and seventy of the elders of Israel' (Ex 24:9). Now why have the names of the elders not been given? To teach that every group of three [elders] who came into being as a court of Israel—lo, they are equivalent to the court of Moses himself."
F. [Joshua] took his staff with his purse in his hand and went along to Yabneh, to Rabban Gamaliel, on the Day of Atonement that is determined in accord with his [Gamaliel's] reckoning.
G. Rabban Gamaliel stood up and kissed him on his head and said to him, "Come in peace, my master and my disciple – My master in wisdom, and my disciple in accepting my rulings."

The key language is, "My master in wisdom," which concedes to the collegium of sages superior knowledge of the Torah. But the patriarchate gets its share too: "My disciple in accepting my rulings." The obvious bias in favor of the sages' claim need not detain us. How the patriarchate will have represented matters institutionally remains to be seen. The Gamaliel-stories we shall consider signal the answer to that question.

Aqiba holds that the action of the sages' court in sanctifying the new month is decisive, Eleazar b. R. Sadoq maintains that the decision is settled in Heaven, whatever the state of sightings of the new moon on earth. Aqiba supports Gamaliel's ruling – not because it is the patriarchal decision but because it is the decision of the Torah-authorities on earth (including the patriarch to be sure). Dosa still more strongly invokes the authority of sages in support of the patriarch. So both affirm Gamaliel's authority, by reason of his acting in behalf of the sages' collegium. That theme recurs in the Mishnah, which both acknowledges the patriarchal authority and insists on its subordination to that of the collegium of sages: the normative Halakhah defined by them. How the contrary position, that of the patriarchate, is represented remains to be seen.

What reliable historical information do we claim to derive from this story? It concerns not the historical patriarch, Gamaliel II, nor the historical Joshua, Aqiba, and Dosa; and we do not allege that we know what happened in determining the advent of Tishré and the date of the Day of Atonement in some specific year after 70. What we claim is that the institutional arrangements upon which the Mishnah rests come to the surface in the narrative at hand. There the sages' perspective on matters governs: the patriarchate has the power, but the sages have the learning, and he concedes that fact in so many words.

Within that perspective, we may ask how representations of incidents involving Gamaliel yield an account of a man within the institutional framework. The answer now is clear: what we allege to define is a reliable picture of enduring attitudes and institutionally supported teachings of, if not a particular patriarch, then the patriarchate over time, including the earlier times – from the third century back to the first. But then the formally distinct composites and compositions concerning an individual patriarch, Gamaliel, embedded within the Mishnah but distinct from its normal media of discourse, will lead us from the institutional figure to the representations of a particular individual within the institution. So everything rests on the identification of individuated compositions and composites: formally-distinct writings that in form and content stand for a particular patriarch within the larger patriarchal view of matters.

III. The Patriarchal Authority as Portrayed by the Collegium of Sages

The governing criterion for identifying stories and sayings that portray Gamaliel within the patriarchal framework requires definition. First comes a negative indicator. The sages' ideology of the patriarchate, paramount in the Mishnah and explicit in the famous story of Gamaliel and Joshua cited earlier, represents the patriarch as subject to the same principles of legitimacy as govern all (other) sages, but as possessed of authority by reason of position: "My master in wisdom, and my disciple in accepting my rulings." A story at *y. Horayot* 3:1 fills in the obvious gap: Why, apart from the patriarch's superior power represented as Roman in origin (inclusive of a platoon of Gothic troops assigned to his service), should sages submit to him? In the translation, bold face represents the Mishnah, italics, the use of Aramaic, and plain type, the use of Hebrew; indentations signal secondary developments of the primary composition:

Y. Horayot 3:1

[A] **An anointed [high] priest who sinned and afterward passed from his office as anointed high priest,**

[B] **and so too, a ruler who sinned and afterward passed from his position of greatness —**

[C] **the anointed [high] priest brings a bullock,**

[D] **and the patriarch brings a goat [M. 2:6].**

[E] **An anointed [high] priest who passed from his office as anointed high priest and then sinned,**

[F] **and so a ruler who passed from his position of greatness and then sinned –**

[G] **a high priest brings a bullock.**

[H] **But a ruler is like any ordinary person.**

[I:1.A] Said R. Eleazar, "A high priest who sinned – they administer lashes to him, but they do not remove him from his high office."

[B] Said R. Mana, "It is written, 'For the consecration of the anointing oil of his God is upon him: I am the Lord' (Lev 21:12).

[C] "That is as if to say: 'Just as I [stand firm] in my high office, so Aaron [stands firm] in his high office.'"

[D] Said R. Abun, "'He shall be holy to you [for I the Lord who sanctify you am holy]' (Lev 21:8). [E] "That is as if to say: 'Just as I [stand firm] in my consecration, so Aaron [stands firm] in his consecration.'"

[E] R. Haninah Ketobah, R. Aha in the name of R. Simeon b. Laqish: "An anointed priest who sinned – they administer lashes to him by the judgment of a court of three judges.

[F] "*If you rule that* it is by the decision of a court of twenty-three judges [that the lashes are administered], it turns out that his ascension [to high office] is descent [to public humiliation, since if he sins, he is publicly humiliated by a sizable court]."

[G] R. Simeon b. Laqish said, "A ruler who sinned – they administer lashes to him by the decision of a court of three judges."

[H] What is the law as to restoring him to office?

[I] *Said R. Haggai, "By Moses! If we put him back into office, he will kill us!"*

[J] R. Judah the Patriarch heard this ruling [of Simeon b. Laqish's] and was outraged. *He sent a troop of Goths to arrest R. Simeon b. Laqish. [R. Simeon b. Laqish] fled to the Tower, and some say, it was to Kefar Hittayya.*
[K] The next day R. Yohanan went up to the meeting house, and R. Judah the Patriarch went up to the meeting house. He said to him, "Why does my master not state a teaching of Torah?"
[L] *[Yohanan] began to clap with one hand [only].*
[M] *[Judah the Patriarch] said to him,* "Now do people clap with only one hand?"
[N] He said to him, "No, nor is Ben Laqish here *[and just as one cannot clap with one hand only, so I cannot teach Torah if my colleague, Simeon b. Laqish, is absent].*"
[O] *[Judah] said to him,* "Then where is he hidden?"
[P] He said to him, "In the Tower."
[Q] He said to him, "You and I shall go out to greet him."
[R] R. Yohanan sent word to R. Simeon b. Laqish, "Get a teaching of Torah ready, because the patriarch is coming over to see you."
[S] *[Simeon b. Laqish] came forth to receive them and said,* "The example that you *[Judah]* set is to be compared to the paradigm of your Creator. For when the All-Merciful came forth to redeem Israel from Egypt, he did not send a messenger or an angel, but the Holy One, blessed be he, himself came forth, as it is said, 'For I will pass through the land of Egypt that night' (Ex 12:12) – *and not only so, but he and his entire retinue.*
[T] "[What other people on earth is like thy people Israel, whom God went to redeem to be his people (2 Sam 7:23).] 'Whom God went' [sing.] is not written here, but 'Whom God went' [plural – meaning, he and all his retinue]."
[U] *[Judah the Patriarch] said to him,* "Now why in the world did you see fit to teach this particular statement *[that a ruler who sinned is subject to lashes]?*"
[V] He said to him, "Now did you really think that because I was afraid of you, I would hold back the teaching of the All-Merciful? [And lo, citing 1 Sam 2:23F.,] R. Samuel b. R. Isaac said, '[Why do you do such things? For I hear of your evil dealings from all the people.] No, my sons, it is no good report that I hear the people of the Lord spreading abroad. [If a man sins against a man, God will mediate for him; but if a man sins against the Lord, who can intercede for him? But they would not listen to the voice of their father, for it was the will of the Lord to slay them' (1 Sam 2:23-25).] [When] the people of the Lord spread about [an evil report about a man], they remove him [even though he is the patriarch]."

When the sage stands up to the patriarch, both parties subject to the same Torah, it is the sage that knows its meaning – that construction conveys the sages' view of matters. The patriarch is given no counterpart statement. But in due course we shall see elements of one. The ideology of this Talmudic account of the patriarch's authority does not greatly differ from that of the story at *m. R.H.* 3:8-9. So much for the negative account supplied by the collegium of sages. What positive evidence do we find in the Mishnah to afford access to the theological and legal agenda of the patriarchate?

IV. The Gamaliel-Corpus in the Mishnah's *Ma'asim:* Form-Analysis

We find within the Mishnah a distinct strand of materials particular to the patriarchate in a Mishnah-form that is linked in particular to the patriarchate via the names of two patriarchs, Gamaliel and Simeon b. Gamaliel. To understand this strand, we need to recall that, in addition to its apodictic statements of law, the Mishnah occasionally sets forth a kind of narrative that it marks with the label, *Ma'aseh,* which stands for a case or a precedent.

Usually the Mishnah's *Ma'aseh* follows a simple, fixed form: statement of a situation in court or school-session or a transaction, a sage's ruling, thus:

M. Sukkah 3:8
> A. "They bind up the lulab [now: palm branch, willow branch, and myrtle branch] only with [strands of] its own species," the words of R. Judah.
> B. R. Meir says, "Even with a rope [it is permitted to bind up the lulab]."
> C. Said R. Meir, "*M'SH B:* The townsfolk of Jerusalem bound up their palm branches with gold threads."
> D. They said to him, "But underneath they [in fact had] tied it up with [strands of] its own species."

The precedent that is adduced is rejected in the transaction, the *Sitz im Leben* of which clearly is the court or school-session. The Mishnah contains numerous such cases or precedents, all situated in the same life-situation, and these include Gamaliel in the status of a sage among sages.

But there is another kind of *Ma'aseh,* the domestic *Ma'aseh,* characteristic only of patriarchal figures, Gamaliel and Simeon b. Gamaliel, exceedingly rare for prominent sages. We now turn to the complete Gamaliel-corpus among the Mishnah's *Ma'asim.* Through the use of differing margins, broad for the narrative, indented for the context, we preserve the narrative in its larger Halakhic setting while signaling its particular limits. We cannot point to any narrative that stands autonomous of its context. We present in detail the *Ma'asim* that speak of Gamaliel or other patriarchal figures (Simeon b. Gamaliel, occasionally,

Hillel). To place the Gamaliel-*Ma'asim* into their larger form-analytical context, the entire corpus of *Ma'asim*, division by division, is summarized at the end of the presentation of each division of the Mishnah's six divisions.

A. Seder *Zeraim*
M. Berakhot 1:1
   A. From what time do they recite the Shema' in the evening?
   B. From the hour that the priests [who had immersed after uncleanness and awaited sunset to complete the process of purification] enter [a state of cleanness, the sun having set, so as] to eat their heave offering –
   C. "until the end of the first watch," the words of R. Eliezer.
   D. And sages say, "Until midnight."
   E. Rabban Gamaliel says, "Until the rise of dawn."
   F. *Ma'aseh*: His sons came from the banquet hall.
   G. They said to him, "We have not recited the Shema'."
   H. He said to them, "If the morning star has not yet risen, you are obligated to recite [the Shema']."
   I. And not only [in] this [case], rather, all [commandments] which sages said [may be performed] until midnight, their religious duty to do them applies until the rise of the morning star.
   J. [For example], as to the offering of the fats and entrails – the religious duty to do them applies until the rise of the morning star.
   K. All [sacrifices] which are eaten for one day, their religious duty to do them applies until the rise of the morning star.
   L. If so why did sages say [that these actions may be performed only] until midnight?
   M. In order to keep a man far from sin.

This ruling concerns the household, not the court, and treats Gamaliel's conduct as exemplary. Gamaliel's domestic rulings are then treated as normative law. The narrative, *m. Ber.* 1:1F-H, consists of an incident, (1) the sons came home late and (2) consulted their father on whether it is still appropriate to recite the Shema', and (3) his ruling that it is. The ruling repeats his abstract opinion, E, that the time for reciting the Shema' extends to dawn. The case is free-standing. The narrative is ignored at I-M, which carries forward the ruling of Gamaliel at E and at the end bears a mediating explanation of the positions of sages and Gamaliel.

The form of the Mishnah's *Ma'aseh* is captured here: (1) statement of the case and (2) the sage's ruling, unadorned and stripped down to its simplest elements. Rarely do we find analysis of the problem, secondary development of the ruling, or other marks of revision in context. But, as we shall see, focus on domestic conduct is characteristic of Gamaliel's and the Patriarchs' *Ma'asim*. That bears an implication: the patriarchs' household represents the model for normative conduct within the community of Israel, and his rulings in private bear public, Halakhic weight. What is important, as we shall see in due course, is that domestic rulings in the *Ma'aseh* form are common for the patriarchal names and rare for other names.

M. Berakhot 2:5

> 2:5 A. A bridegroom is exempt from the recitation of the Shema' on the first night
> [after the wedding] until after the Sabbath [following the wedding],
> B. if he did not consummate [the marriage].
> C. *Ma'aseh* S: Rabban Gamaliel recited [the Shema'] on the first night of his marriage.
> D. Said to him [his students], "Did our master not teach us that a bridegroom is exempt from the recitation of the Shema' on the first night?"
> E. He said to them, "I cannot heed you to suspend from myself the kingdom of heaven [even] for one hour."
> 2:6 A. [Gamaliel] washed on the first night after the death of his wife.
> B. Said to him [his students], "Did not [our master] teach us that it is forbidden for a mourner to wash?"
> C. He said to them, "I am not like other men, I am frail."
> 2:7 A. And when Tabi, his servant, died, [Gamaliel] received condolences on his account.
> B. Said to him [his students], "Did not [our master] teach us that one does not receive condolences for [the loss of] slaves?"
> C. He said to them, "Tabi my slave was not like other slaves. He was exacting."

The formal pattern, repeated three times, involves a report of what Gamaliel did, *m.* 2:5C, *m.* 2:6A, and *m.* 2:7A, the question raised by the disciples, and his response thereto. The set involves diverse classifications of the Halakhah – reciting the Shema', washing in the mourning period, receiving condolences for a slave – and what holds the stories together as a composite are the formal pattern, including the name of Gamaliel. In each case, the point of the narrative is reached only at the end: Tabi is different. That answers the question of the students and explains the data of the case. Without the climax of 2:5C/2:6C/2:7C, the three cases have no context, and the students' question, at B, only articulates the context and focuses attention on what is to come. The patriarch is represented as unique and still exemplary.

The Halakhic context serves only *m.* 2:5A-B, but *m.* 2:6, 2:7 encompass the Halakhic context within the narrative discourse, using formulaic language portrayed as the master's own words. The topical principle of category-formation dominant in the Mishnah is set aside in favor of the selection of teachings about the named patriarch, whose household is regarded as at the one time exemplary and unique. He is a model of piety, unwilling to relinquish the performance of religious obligations even beyond the measure of the law; so too, his slave was exceptional; and he was frail, a mark of piety within the rabbinic framework:

Lamentations Rabbah 74.12
- A. A member of the household in the establishment of Rabban Gamaliel had the habit of taking a basket carrying forty *seahs* of grain and bringing it to the baker.
- B. He said to him, "All this wonderful strength is in you, and you are not engaged in the Torah?"
- C. When he got involved in the Torah, he would begin to take thirty, then twenty, then twelve, then eight *seahs,* and when he had completed a book, even a basket of only a single *seah* he could not carry.
- D. And some say that he could not even carry his own hat, but others had to take it off him, for he could not do it.
- E. That is in line with this verse: "encrusted with sapphires." [For study of the Torah drains the strength of people].

Stories such as the foregoing attest to the attitude that finds virtue in physical weakness, a mark of prowess in Torah-learning.

M. Peah 2:5-6
- 2:5 A. One who sows his field with [only] one type [of seed], even if he harvests [the produce] in two lots
- B. designates one [portion of produce as] peah [from the entire crop].
- C. If he sowed [his field] with two types [of seeds], even if he harvests [the produce] in only one lot,
- D. he designates two [separate portions of produce as] peah, [one from each type of produce].
- E. He who sows his field with two types of wheat –
- F [if] he harvests [the wheat] in one lot, [he] designates one [portion of produce as] peah.
- G. [But if he harvests the wheat in] two lots, [he] designates two [portions of produce as] peah.
- 2:6 A. *Ma'aseh*: R. Simeon of Mispah sowed [his field with two types of wheat].
- B. [The matter came] before Rabban Gamaliel. So they went up to the Chamber of Hewn Stone, and asked [about the law regarding sowing two types of wheat in one field].
    - C. Said Nahum the Scribe, "I have received [the following ruling] from R. Miasha, who received [it] from his father, who received [it] from the Pairs, who received [it] from the Prophets, [who received] the law [given] to Moses on Sinai, regarding one who sows his field with two types of wheat:
    - D. "If he harvests [the wheat] in one lot, he designates one [portion of produce as] peah.

E. "If he harvests [the wheat] in two lots, he designates two [portions of produce as] peah."

A–B serve C–E. Without A–B, C–E stand on their own. Read as a unitary construction, the narrative is, (1) Case, (2) Gamaliel was asked to rule and referred it to the higher court. Referring cases to the higher court is rare among the *Ma'asim* of the Mishnah.

Let us now consider the Gamaliel-compositions with the other *Ma'asim* of Mishnah Seder *Zeraim*. These follow the same form in that they uniformly describe a situation and specify the Halakhic ruling that governs.

1. *M. Ber.* 2:5: Gamaliel/bride groom/Shema'
2. *M. Ber.* 2:6: Gamaliel/mourning/washing
3. *M. Ber.* 2:7: Gamaliel/mourning/condolences for slave
4. *M. Ber.* 5:5: Hanina b. Dosa/how he knows when prayer will be answered
5. *M. Shebi'it* 10:3: Hillel/access to loans/prosbol
6. *M. Hal.* 4:10-11: priests' decision in cases of priestly gifts, dough-offering, firstfruits, firstborn, from wrong place or at wrong time

The narratives of Mishnah Seder *Zeraim* are few, uniform, and subordinate to the purposes of the Mishnah-composition in which they are situated. That is, the Halakhic context frames the narratives, and in most instances is required to make sense of them. The sages' Halakhic *Ma'asim* follow a single form, *described incident + ruling*. The exposition of the described incident is simple and never complex; the presentation is one-dimensional, limited to a laconic, economical account of the action a person took that requires classification or the situation that requires resolution. There is no character-differentiation, let alone development, no consideration of motive, no picture of details that amplify the incident or action, no sequence of action and response, only the stripped-down sequence: X did so and so with the following consequence. The context supplies the remainder of the information required for comprehension, meaning: the rules of narrative respond to and take for granted the documentary setting. Outside that setting none of the Halakhic narratives is fully comprehensible; none exemplifies much beyond itself. So the narratives of the *Ma'aseh*-classification take for granted the Mishnaic-Halakhic context as much as the expository prose that defines their setting.

The Patriarchal names, Gamaliel and Hillel, are represented as Halakhic models, and in the narratives and pseudo-narratives no one sage corresponds. The Patriarchate can have represented its principals as

Halakhic models and sources, through their very deeds, of authoritative law. But that explanation for the phenomenon competes with others. We do not know what to make of the omission of the signal, *Ma'aseh*, from the priests' cases, which otherwise conform to the precedent-form. Provisionally, we may conceive that *Ma'aseh* signals a sage's precedent only.

At no point do we leave the limits of the Halakhic setting in which the narrative is situated. The principal purpose of the narrative is to show how an anomaly is resolved, or to illustrate how the Halakhah functions in everyday life, or to provide a precedent for a ruling. None of these entries carries us to some viewpoint outside of the Halakhic framework. In the narratives as authentic stories that we meet at *m. R.H.* 2:8-9 (and *m. Ta.* 3:9-10, not cited here), we see how a narrative finds its focus outside the limits of the Halakhic context altogether.

B. Seder *Moed*

M. Shabbat 16:8

> 16:8 A. A gentile who lit a candle –
> B. an Israelite may make use of its light.
> C. But [if he did so] for an Israelite, it is prohibited [to do so on the Sabbath].
> D. [If a gentile] drew water to give water to his beast, an Israelite gives water to his beast after him.
> E. But [if he did so] for an Israelite, it is prohibited [to use it on the Sabbath].
> E [If] a gentile made a gangway by which to come down from a ship, an Israelite goes down after him.
> G. But [if he did so] for an Israelite, it is prohibited [to use it on the Sabbath].
> H. *Ma'aseh* B: Rabban Gamaliel and elders were traveling by boat, and a gentile made a gangway by which to come down off the ship, and Rabban Gamaliel and sages went down by it.

The incident, H, forms a precedent and an illustration of the law, not a narrative in which the order of events or sequence of actions registers. The action of the patriarch is deemed authoritative for "elders," and they are not represented as ruling in concurrence, only as replicating his action and accepting his ruling. The sages clearly acknowledge his authority and subordinate themselves to it.

M. Erubin 4:1-2

> 4:1 A. He whom gentiles took forth [beyond the Sabbath limit],
> B. or an evil spirit,
> C. has only four cubits [in which to move about].
> D. [If] they brought him back, it is as if he never went out.
> E. [If] they carried him to another town,
> F. or put him into a cattle pen or a cattle-fold,

G. Rabban Gamaliel and R. Eleazar b. Azariah say, "He may walk about the entire area."

H. R. Joshua and R. Aqiba say, "He has only four cubits [in which to move about]."

I. *Ma'aseh* S: They came from Brindisi [Brundisium] and their ship was sailing at sea.

J. Rabban Gamaliel and R. Eleazar b. Azariah walked about the whole ship.

K. R. Joshua and R. Aqiba did not move beyond four cubits.

L. For they wanted to impose a strict ruling on themselves.

4:2 A. On one occasion [*P'M 'HT*] they did not enter the harbor until it had gotten dark [on Friday night] —

B. They said to Rabban Gamaliel, "Is it all right for us to disembark?"

C. He said to them, "It is all right, for beforehand I was watching, and we were within the Sabbath limit before it got dark."

The two *Ma'asim*, each in sequence bearing its conventional marker ([1] *Ma'aseh*, [2] *P'M 'HT*), hardly qualify as narratives. The first of the two, *m.* 4:1I-L, illustrates the rulings of *m.* 4:1G, H; there is no progression toward a conclusion that makes the rest cohere. *M.* 4:1E-H and 4:1I-L are out of context. The second of the two, *m.* 4:2, is tacked on and does not connect to the abstract Halakhah of *m.* 4:1A-H. Here is no domestic *Ma'aseh*, rather, the patriarch is deemed no more authoritative than any other sage.

M. Erubin 6:1-2

M. 6:1 A. "He who dwells in the same courtyard with a gentile,

B. "or with [an Israelite] who does not concede the validity of the fictive fusion meal —

C. "lo, this one [the gentile or nonbeliever] restricts him [from using the courtyard]," the words of R. Meir.

D. R. Eliezer b. Jacob says, "Under no circumstances does anyone prohibit [the believer in the fictive fusion meal to make use of the courtyard] unless two Israelites prohibit one another."

M. 6:2 A. Said Rabban Gamaliel, *Ma'aseh* B: "A Saducean lived with us in the same alleyway in Jerusalem.

B. "And father said to us, 'Make haste and bring all sorts of utensils into the alleyway before he brings out his and prohibits you [from carrying about in it].'"

Once more, the function of the *Ma'aseh* is to provide a setting for the ruling. Without the ruling, *m.* 6:1, *m.* 6:2 is wholly out of context. Of greater interest here: the ruling involves the domestic practice of the patriarch's household, not the public decision of a sages' court.

M. Erubin 10:10

A. A bolt with a knob on its end —

B. R. Eleazar prohibits.

C. And R. Yose permits.

D. Said R. Eleazar, *Ma'aseh* B: "In the synagogue in Tiberias they permitted [using it on the Sabbath],

E. "until Rabban Gamaliel and elders came and prohibited it for them."
E R. Yosé says, "They treated it as prohibited. Rabban Gamaliel and the elders came and permitted it for them."

A situation is described, with the sages' decision recorded, following the pattern of the *Ma'aseh* as precedent. This remains wholly within the Halakhic framework. The form persists in singling out Gamaliel from the collegium of elders.

M. Pesahim 7:2
A. They do not roast the Passover offering either on a [metal] spit or on a grill.
B. Said R. Sadoq, "Rabban Gamaliel said to Tabi his servant, 'Go and roast the Passover offering for us on a grill.'"
C. [If] it touched the earthenware part of an oven, one should scale off that place [which has been roasted by the heat of the oven side].
D. [If] some of its gravy dripped on the earthenware and went back onto it, he must take some [of the meat] away from that place [and burn it].
E. [If] some of its gravy dripped on the flour, he must take a handful away from that place.

Gamaliel's action is recorded in a domestic framework. His action is treated as equivalent to an abstract ruling. It is not "They do not roast ... and R. Sadoq said Rabban Gamaliel said, They do roast ..." Rather, the formal ruling is set aside and left implicit in the exemplary, authoritative deed of the patriarch in instructing his slave.

M. Sukkah 2:1
A. He who sleeps under a bed in a Sukkah has not fulfilled his obligation.
B. Said R. Judah, "We had the practice of sleeping under the bed before the elders, and they said nothing at all to us."
C. Said R. Simeon, "*Ma'aseh* B: Tabi, Rabban Gamaliel's slave, slept under the bed.
D. "And Rabban Gamaliel said to the elders, 'Do you see Tabi, my slave – he is a disciple of a sage, so he knows that slaves are exempt from keeping the commandment of dwelling in the Sukkah. That is why he is sleeping under the bed [rather than directly beneath the Sukkah-covering, which is what defines the Sukkah and renders it effective in fulfilling the commandment of dwelling in the Sukkah, that is, under its shade, during the festival].'
E. "Thus we learned that he who sleeps under bed has not fulfilled his obligation."

As in the triplet of cases in *m. Berakhot* 2:5-7, what marks the *Ma'aseh* as a narrative is E, which imparts cogency and significance to the record of action and speech of C–D. The conflict is between Halakhic rulings, A vs. B. Then the *Ma'aseh*, C–D, realizes the same conflict in the narrative, which is resolved at E. The narrative qualifies as a Halakhic precedent, pure and simple. What is required to fulfil the formal requirement is a report of an action and a comment on that action. The correspondence of *m.* 2:1A and E underscores that the domestic arrangement of the patriarch qualifies as valid ruling, no different in standing from an explicit Halakhic ruling of a sage or of sages as a collegium.

M. Sukkah 2:4-5
> 2:4 A. He who makes his Sukkah among trees, and the trees are its sides – it is valid.
> B. Agents engaged in a religious duty are exempt from the requirement of dwelling in a Sukkah.
> C. Sick folk and those who serve them are exempt from the requirement of dwelling in a Sukkah.
> D. [People] eat and drink in a random manner outside of a Sukkah.
> 2:5 A. *Ma'aseh* W: They brought Rabban Yohanan b. Zakkai some cooked food to taste, and to Rabban Gamaliel two dates and a dipper of water.
> B. And they said, "Bring them up to the Sukkah."
> C. And when they gave to R. Sadoq food less than an egg's bulk, he took it in a cloth and ate it outside of the Sukkah and said no blessing after it.

The Halakhic ruling, *m.* 2:4D, is illustrated by *m.* 2:5A-B vs. C. That is, eating in a random manner outside of a Sukkah during the Festival is illustrated by Sadoq, who consumed less than the amount of food required to constitute a meal, while Yohanan b. Zakkai and Gamaliel reject the rule of *m.* 2:4D and eat even a random meal in the Sukkah. The described action does not rise to the status of a narrative, because there is no point at which the logic of teleology imposes coherence on the components. What illustrates the Halakhah does not qualify. That point distinguishes *m.* 2:4-5 from *m.* 2:1.

The *Ma'aseh, m.* 2:8C, takes on meaning only in the Halakhic context. There is no teleological logic that holds the details together otherwise.

M. Besah 3:2
> 3:2 A. Nets for trapping a wild beast, fowl, or fish, which one set on the eve of the festival day –
> B. one should not take [what is caught therein] out of them on the festival day,
> C. unless one knows for sure that [creatures caught in them] were trapped on the eve of the festival day.
> D. Ma'aseh B: A gentile brought fish to Rabban Gamaliel, and he said, "They are permitted. But I do not want to accept them from him."

The *Ma'aseh* supplies an illustrative case in the Halakhic framework. Here again the patriarch shows himself distinguished in piety, not taking advantage of lenient rulings that are commonly accepted.

M. Rosh Hashanah 1:5-6

    1:5 A. Whether [the new moon] appeared clearly or did not appear clearly,
       B. they violate the [prohibitions of] the Sabbath on its account.
       C. R. Yose says, "If it appeared clearly, they do not violate the prohibitions of the Sabbath on its account."
    1:6 A. *Ma'aseh* S: More than forty pairs of witnesses came forward.
       B. But R. Aqiba kept them back at Lud.
       C. Rabban Gamaliel said to him, "If you keep back the people, you will turn out to make them err in the future."

The *Ma'aseh* coheres only in line with *m.* 1:5, with the conflicting positions, *m.* 1:5A vs. B, C, replicated at *m.* 1:6C vs. 1:6A-B. This is another Halakhic illustration, lacking the indicative qualities of a narrative.

The foregoing corpus of *Ma'asim* in Mishnah Seder *Moed* are part of the larger population as follows:

1. *M. Shabbat* 1:4 These are some of the laws which they stated in the upper room of Hananiah b. Hezekiah b. Gurion when they went up to visit him. They took a vote, and the House of Shammai outnumbered the House of Hillel.
2. *M. Shabbat* 3:3-4 The people of Tiberias brought a pipe of cold water through a spring of hot water.
3. *M. Shabbat* 16:8 Rabban Gamaliel and elders were traveling by boat, and a gentile made a gangway by which to come down off the ship, and Rabban Gamaliel and sages went down by it.
4. *M. Shabbat* 24:5 In the time of the father of R. Sadoq and of Abba Saul b.Botnit, they stopped up the light hole with a pitcher and tied a pot with reed grass [to a stick] to know whether or not there was in the roofing an opening of a handbreadth square.
5. *M. Erubin* 4:1-2 They came from Brindisi [Brundisium] and their ship was sailing at sea. Rabban Gamaliel and R. Eleazar b. Azariah walked about the whole ship R. Joshua and R. Aqiba did not move beyond four cubits.
6. *M. Erubin* 6:1-2 Said Rabban Gamaliel, *Ma'aseh* B: "A Sadducean lived with us in the same alleyway in Jerusalem. And father said to us, 'Make haste and bring all sorts of utensils into the alleyway before he brings out his and prohibits you [from carrying about in it].'"
7. *M. Erubin* 8:7 From the water channel of Abel did they draw water at the instruction of the elders on the Sabbath.
8. *M. Erubin* 10:9 In the poulterers' market in Jerusalem they used to shut up their shops and leave the key in the window above the door."
9. *M. Erubin* 10:10 In the synagogue in Tiberias they permitted [using it on the Sabbath], until Rabban Gamaliel and elders came and prohibited it for them.
10. *M. Pesahim* 7:2 "Rabban Gamaliel said to Tabi his servant, 'Go and roast the Passover offering for us on a grill.'"
11. *M. Yoma* 6:3 Arsela led it out, and he was an Israelite."
12. *M. Sukkah* 2:4-5 They brought Rabban Yohanan b. Zakkai some cooked food to taste, and to Rabban Gamaliel two dates and a dipper of water. And they said, "Bring them up to the Sukkah."

13. *M. Sukkah* 2:7 Was not the precedent so, that the elders of the House of Shammai and the elders of the House of Hillel went along to pay a sick call on R. Yohanan b. Hahorani, and they found him sitting with his head and the greater part of his body in the Sukkah, and his table in the house, and they said nothing at all to him
14. *M. Sukkah* 2:8 Shammai the Elder's daughter-in-law gave birth, and he broke away some of the plaster and covered the hole with Sukkah roofing over her bed, on account of the infant
15. *M. Sukkah* 3:8 The townsfolk of Jerusalem bound up their palm branches with gold threads
16. *M. Besah* 3:2 A gentile brought fish to Rabban Gamaliel, and he said, "They are permitted. But I do not want to accept them from him."
17. *M. Besah* 3:8 Abba Saul b. Botnit would fill up his measuring cups on the eve of a festival and hand them over to purchasers on the festival itself.
18. *M. Rosh Hashanah* 1:5-6 More than forty pairs of witnesses came forward. But R. Aqiba kept them back at Lud.
19. *M. Rosh Hashanah* 1:7 Tobiah, the physician, saw the new moon in Jerusalem – he, his son, and his freed slave. And the priests accepted him and his son [as witnesses to the new moon], but they invalidated the testimony of his slave.
20. *M. Ta'anit* 2:5 In the time of R. Halapta and R. Hananiah b. Teradion someone passed before the ark and completed the entire blessing, and they did not answer after him "Amen."

This list shows the singularity of the items in which Gamaliel figures; the domestic *Ma'asim* in which he is principal have few counterparts or parallels. We cannot ignore the special interest of *m. R.H.* 2:8-9, concerning Gamaliel and Joshua, cited above, and the famous story of Honi the Circle-Drawer and Simeon b. Shatah, *m. Ta'anit* 3:8-9, which in this context requires no discussion. The complex stories of Gamaliel and the sages, on the one side, and Honi and the sages, concern the power-relationships within the institutional frameworks of rabbis in relationship to others, the patriarch, and the wonder-worker, respectively. But they attest to the rabbinic viewpoint on Honi, and we are inclined to think, on Gamaliel as well, whose authority prevails even though his decision errs. In both cases the message is, greater force prevails, sometimes, over rabbinic wisdom and learning. In both cases it is Heaven's right to override sages' knowledge. So the remarkable narratives of *m. R.H.* 2:8-9 and *m. Ta.* 3:9-10, about Honi and the sages, Gamaliel and the sages, respectively, set forth the perspective of the rabbinic narrator and his politics. They attest to rabbinic thought, which has coalesced and been realized in an other-than-conventional way.

C. Seder *Nashim*

We find no domestic case-reports. Here is the repertoire of *Ma'asim* in this division:

1. *M. Yebamot* 16:4 A certain person fell into a large cistern, and came up [alive] after three days. A blind man went down to immerse in a cave, and his guide went down after him, and they stayed [in the water] long enough to drown. A certain man in Asya was let down by a rope into the sea, and they drew back up only his leg.
2. *M. Yebamot* 16:6 A certain person stood on top of a mountain and said, "Mr. So-and-so, the son of So-and-so, of such-and-such a place, has died." And they went but did not find anyone there. And they [nonetheless] permitted his wife to remarry. In Salmon, a certain person said, "I am Mr. So-and-so, the son of Mr. So-and-so. A snake has bitten me, and lo, I am dying." And they went, and while they did not recognize him, they permitted his wife to remarry.
3. *M. Yebamot* 16:7 Said R. Aqiba, "When I went down to Nehardea to intercalate the year, Nehemiah of Bet Deli came upon me. He said to me, 'I heard that only R. Judah b. Baba permits a wife in the Land of Israel to remarry on the evidence of a single witness [to her husband's death].' The Levites went to Soar, the date town, and one of them got sick on the road, and they left him in an inn. And upon their return, they said to the inn hostess, 'Where is our good buddy?'" She said to them, 'He died, and I buried him.' And they permitted his wife to remarry [on the strength of her evidence]."
4. *M. Ketubot* 1:10 Said R. Yose, *M'SH B*: "A girl went down to draw water from the well and was raped.
5. *M. Ketubot* 7:10 In Sidon there was a tanner who died, and he had a brother who was a tanner Sages ruled, "She can claim, 'Your brother I could take, but I can't take you [as my levir]."
6. *M. Nedarim* 6:6 R. Tarfon prohibited me from eating eggs which were roasted with it [meat]."
7. *M. Nazir* 2:3 A woman was drunk, and they filled a cup for her, and she said, "Lo, I am a Nazirite from it. Sages ruled, "She intended only to say, 'Lo, it is unto me as a Qorban.'"
8. *M. Nazir* 3:6 Helene the Queen – her son went off to war, and she said, "If my son comes home from war whole and in one piece, I shall be a Nazir for seven years." Indeed her son did come home from war, and she was a Nazir for seven years.
9. *M. Nazir* 6:11 In behalf of Miriam of Tadmor [Palmyra] one of the drops of blood was properly tossed, and they came and told her that her daughter was dying, and she found her dead.
10. *M. Gittin* 1:5 They brought before Rabban Gamaliel in Kepar Otenai the writ of divorce of a woman, and the witnesses thereon were Samaritan witnesses, and he did declare it valid
11. *M. Gittin* 4:7 In Sidon a man said to his wife, 'Qonam if I do not divorce you,' and he divorced her. But sages permitted him to take her back, for the good order of the world."
12. *M. Gittin* 6:6 A healthy man said, "Write a writ of divorce for my wife," and then went up to the rooftop and fell over and died —

13. M. *Gittin* 7:5 In Sidon there was a man who said to his wife, 'Lo, this is your writ of divorce, on condition that you give me my cloak,' but the cloak got lost. Sages ruled, 'Let her pay him its value.'"
14. M. *Qiddushin* 2:7 Five women, including two sisters, and one gathered figs, and they were theirs, but it was Seventh-Year produce. And [someone] said, "Lo, all of you are betrothed to me in virtue of this basket of fruit," and one of them accepted the proposal in behalf of all of them

We do not see how these items qualify as a narrative focused on conduct in the household as halakhically exemplary.

D. Seder *Neziqin*
M. *Eduyyot* 7:7
- A. They gave testimony concerning the boards of bakers, that they are susceptible to uncleanness.
- B. For R. Eliezer declares [them] insusceptible.
- C. They gave testimony concerning an oven which one cut up into rings, between each ring of which one put sand,
- D. that it is susceptible to receive uncleanness.
- E. For R. Eliezer declares it insusceptible.
- F. They gave testimony that they intercalate the year at any time in Adar.
- G. For they had said, "Only up to Purim."
- H. They gave testimony that they intercalate the year conditionally.
- I. *Ma'aseh* B: Rabban Gamaliel went to ask for permission from the government in Syria and he did not come back right away, so they intercalated the year on the condition that Rabban Gamaliel concur.
- J. And when he came back, he said, "I concur."
- K. So the year turned out to be deemed to have been intercalated.

The sages' explicit subordination to the Patriarch's ruling is illustrated, but this is clearly not a domestic *Ma'aseh*.

M. *Abodah Zarah* 3:4
- A. Peroqlos b. Pelosepos asked Rabban Gamaliel in Akko, when he was washing in Aphrodite's bathhouse, saying to him, "It is written in your Torah, And there shall cleave nothing of a devoted thing to your hand (Deut 13:18). How is it that you're taking a bath in Aphrodite's bathhouse?"
- B. He said to him, "They do not give answers in a bathhouse."
- C. When he went out, he said to him, "I never came into her domain. She came into mine. They don't say, 'Let's make a bathhouse as an ornament for Aphrodite.' But they say, 'Let's make Aphrodite as an ornament for the bathhouse.'
- D. "Another matter: Even if someone gave you a lot of money, you would never walk into your temple of idolatry naked or suffering a flux, nor would you piss in its presence.
- E. "Yet this thing is standing there at the head of the gutter and everybody pisses right in front of her."
- F. It is said only, "... their gods" (Deut 12:3) – that which one treats as a god is prohibited, but that which one treats not as a god is permitted.

Not correctly labeled as a *Ma'aseh*, this composition establishes a narrative setting to dramatize the exchange of opinions; it does not fall into the Halakhic framework at all, and Gamaliel is not represented as a singular authority in the Halakhah.

These are the only items that include Gamaliel within a composition bearing the marker, *Ma'aseh*. The pertinent *Ma'asim* of Seder *Neziqin* are as follows:

1. *M. Baba Mesia* 7:1: *Ma'aseh* B: R. Yohanan b. Matya said to his son, "Go, hire workers for us."
2. *M. Baba Mesia* 8:8: In Sepphoris a person hired a bathhouse from his fellow for twelve golden [denars] per year, at the rate of one golden denar per month [and the year was intercalated].
3. *M. Baba Batra* 9:7: The mother of the sons of Rokhel was sick and said, 'Give my veil to my daughter,' and it was worth twelve maneh. And she died, and they carried out her statement.
4. *M. Sanhedrin* 5:2: Ben Zakkai examined a witness as to the character of the stems of figs [under which the incident took place].
5. *M. Sanhedrin* 7:2: The daughter of a priest committed adultery. And they put bundles of twigs around her and burned her.
6. M. *Eduyyot* 5:7K: Karkemit, a freed slave girl, was in Jerusalem, and Shemaiah and Abtalion administered the bitter water to her."
7. *M. Eduyyot* 7:7: Rabban Gamaliel went to ask for permission from the government in Syria and he did not come back right away, so they intercalated the year on the condition that Rabban Gamaliel concur.
8. *M. Abodah Zarah* 3:7: In Sidon there was a tree which people worshipped, and they found a pile of stones underneath it. Said to them R. Simeon, "Investigate the character of this pile of stones."
9. *M. Abodah Zarah* 5:2: Boethus b. Zonen brought dried figs by ship, and a jar of libation wine broke open and dripped on them, and he asked sages, who permitted [the figs, once they had been rinsed].
10. *M. Abodah Zarah* 3:4: Peroqlos b. Pelosepos asked Rabban Gamaliel in Akko, when he was washing in Aphrodite's bathhouse, saying to him, "It is written in your Torah, And there shall cleave nothing of a devoted thing to your hand (Deut 13:18). How is it that you're taking a bath in Aphrodite's bathhouse?"

Nos. 1 and 3 enter the category of a domestic Ma'aseh. They do not conform to the domestic Ma'aseh form, containing no ruling, just an anecdote from which a ruling may be adduced.

E. Seder *Qodoshim*
M. Keritot 1:7

    A. The woman who is subject to a doubt concerning [the appearance of] five fluxes,
    B. or the one who is subject to a doubt concerning five miscarriages
    C. brings a single offering.
    D. And she [then is deemed clean so that she] eats animal sacrifices.
    E. And the remainder [of the offerings, A, B] are not an obligation for her

F. [If she is subject to] five confirmed miscarriages,
G. or five confirmed fluxes,
H. she brings a single offering.
I. And she eats animal sacrifices.
J. But the rest [of the offerings, the other four] remain as an obligation for her [to bring at some later time] –
K. *Ma'aseh* S: A pair of birds in Jerusalem went up in price to a golden denar
L. Said Rabban Simeon b. Gamaliel, "By this sanctuary! I shall not rest tonight until they shall be at [silver] denars."
M. He entered the court and taught [the following law]:
N. "The woman who is subject to five confirmed miscarriages [or] five confirmed fluxes brings a single offering.
O. "And she eats animal sacrifices.
P. "And the rest [of the offerings] do not remain as an obligation for her."
Q. And pairs of birds stood on that very day at a quarter-denar each [one one-hundredth of the former price].

While not a domestic *Ma'aseh*, this item belongs among *Ma'asim* because the patriarch's ruling is represented as absolute. The *Ma'aseh* at K would ordinarily carry in its wake a description of sages' response, e.g., "sages' ruled" + N-Q, and that would serve the purpose.

All the *Ma'asim* of the fifth division are Halakhic, some of them formally more conventional than others.

1. *M. Menahot* 10:2 *Ma'aseh* S: It was brought from Gaggot Serifin, and [the grain for] the two loaves [Lev 23:17] from the valley of En Sokher.
2. *M. Bekhorot* 4:4 The womb of a cow was removed. And R. Tarfon had it [the cow] fed to the dogs. The case came before sages, and they declared it permitted.
3. *M. Bekhorot* 5:3 An old ram, with its hair dangling – quaestor saw it He said, "What sort of thing is this?" They said to him, "It is a firstling. And it is slaughtered only if there is a blemish on it." He took a dagger and slit its ear. And the case came before sages, and they declared it permitted.
4. *M. Bekhorot* 6:6 One squeezed and it did not descend. And it was slaughtered. And it [the testicle] was found cleaving to the groin.
5. *M. Bekhorot* 6:9 *Ma'aseh* S: The lower jaw stretched beyond the upper one.
6. *M. Arakhin* 5:1 *Ma'aseh* B: The mother of Yirmatyah said, "The weight of my daughter is incumbent on me." And she went up to Jerusalem, and weighed her [Yirmatyah], and paid her weight in gold.
7. *M. Arakhin* 8:1 *Ma'aseh* B: One man sanctified his field because of its poor quality. They said to him, "You declare first." He said, "Lo, it is mine for an issar." They said to him, "It's yours!"
8. *M. Keritot* 1:7 A pair of birds in Jerusalem went up in price to a golden denar. Said Rabban Simeon b. Gamaliel, "By this sanctuary! I shall not rest tonight until they shall be at [silver] denars." He entered the court and taught [the following law]..."

We see no domestic *Ma'aseh* comparable to those involving Gamaliel.

F. Seder *Tohorot*
M. *Kelim* 5:4
- A. An oven which was heated from its outer sides, or which was heated without his [the owner's] knowledge, or which was heated in the craftsman's house, is susceptible to uncleanness.
- B. *Ma'aseh* S: Fire broke out among the ovens of Kefar Signa, and the matter came to Yavneh, and Rabban Gamaliel declared them unclean.

This is a standard *Ma'aseh*, following the established form. It does not qualify as domestic, and the deed of the patriarch is not represented as authoritative, only his ruling in the manner of the sages. We do not log it in to the list of authoritative rulings based on narratives of domestic arrangements of the patriarch.

M. *Yadayim* 3:1
- A. He who pokes his hands into a house afflicted with a Nega –
- B. "his hands are in the first remove of uncleanness," the words of R. Aqiba.
- C. And sages say, "His hands are in the second remove of uncleanness."
- D. Whoever imparts uncleanness to clothing, when in contact [with them], imparts uncleanness to the hands –
- E. "So that they are in the first remove of uncleanness, the words of R. Aqiba.
- F. And sages say, "So that they are in the second remove of uncleanness."
- G. Said they to R. Aqiba, "When do we find that the hands are in the first remove of uncleanness under any circumstances whatsoever?"
- H. He said to them, "And how is it possible for them to be in the first remove of uncleanness without his body's [being] made unclean, outside of the present case?"
- I. "Food and utensils which have been made unclean by liquids impart uncleanness to the hands so that they are in the second remove of uncleanness," the words of R. Joshua.
- J. And sages say, "That which is made unclean by a Father of Uncleanness imparts uncleanness to the hands. [That which has been made unclean] by an Offspring of Uncleanness does not impart uncleanness to the hands."
- K. Said Rabban Simeon b. Gamaliel, "*Ma'aseh* B: A certain woman came before Father.
- L. "She said to him, 'My hands entered the contained airspace of a clay utensil.'
- M. "He said to her, 'My daughter, By what had it been made unclean?' [He thus wished to ascertain the remove of uncleanness that had affected the contained airspace of the clay utensil.]
- N. "But I did not hear what she said to him."
- O. Said sages, "The matter is clear. That which has been made unclean by a Father of Uncleanness imparts uncleanness to the hands. [That which has been made unclean] by an Offspring of Uncleanness does not impart uncleanness to the hands."

Here is a standard *Ma'aseh,* not based on the domestic arrangements of the patriarch or sage. But the patriarch, Gamaliel, is represented as a legal authority certainly as learned as any other, contrary to the claim of *m. R.H.* 3:8-9.

The *Ma'asim* are as follows:

1. *M. Kelim* 5:4 *Ma'aseh* S: Fire broke out among the ovens of Kefar Signa, and the matter came to Yavneh, and Rabban Gamaliel declared them unclean.
2. *M. Ohalot* 17:5 Letters were coming from abroad to the sons of the high priests, and there was on them a seah or two seahs of seals, and sages were not scrupulous about them on account of uncleanness
3. *M. Miqvaot* 4:5 *Ma'aseh* B: "A trough of Jehu was in Jerusalem, and it was perforated with a hole as large as the spout of a water-skin.
4. *M. Niddah* 8:2 One woman came before R. Aqiba. She said to him, "I have seen a bloodstain."
5. *M. Makhshirin* 1:6 People in Jerusalem hid away their fig cakes in water because of the usurpers.
6. *M. Makhshirin* 3:4 The people of Mahoz were dampening [wheat] in sand.
7. *M. Yadayim* 3:1 Said Rabban Simeon b. Gamaliel, "*Ma'aseh* B: A certain woman came before Father. She said to him, 'My hands entered the contained airspace of a clay utensil.' He said to her, 'My daughter, By what had it been made unclean?'

G. Domestic precedents in the Mishnah:
Practice in the household of a named authority, by authority

One can make a case for a *Sitz im Leben* in the Patriarchal setting (inclusive of Hillel). The domestic conduct of the named authority in a specific incident is represented as equivalent to a sage's ruling in the following cases involving *household practice,* not in a sages' court, as a precedent or exemplary case:

Domestic Ma'asim *assigned to Patriarchs, Gamaliel, Simeon*
Gamaliel/Simeon b. Gamaliel: *M. Ber.* 1:1, 2:5, 6, 7 (triplet focused on Gamaliel's unique actions); *m. Peah* 2:5-6; *m. Shab.* 16:8 (Gamaliel's action is deemed ample precedent, sages concur and follow suit); *m. Er.* 4:1-2 (Gamaliel rules for Joshua, Aqiba, Eleazar b. Azariah); *m. Er.* 6:2 (Gamaliel reports his father's ruling); *m. Pes.* 7:2; *m. Suk.* 2:1 (Gamaliel/Tabi); *m. Suk.* 2:5; *m. Bes.* 3:2; *m. Yad.* 3:1 (ruling attributed to Gamaliel I)

13

Domestic Ma'asim *assigned to members of the Collegium of Sages*

Abba Saul b. Botnit: *M. Bes.* 3:8	– 1
Aqiba	–
Daughter of Shammai the Elder: *M. Suk.* 2:8:	– 1
Eleazar b. Azariah	–
Eliezer	–
Hillel	–

Ishmael	–
Joshua	–
Judah	–
Meir	–
Sadoq: *M. Suk.* 2	– 1
Shammai	–
Simeon	–
Tarfon: *M. Ned.* 6:6	– 1
Yohanan b. Zakkai: *M. Suk.* 2:5	– 1
Yohanan b. Matya: *M. B.M.* 7:1	– 1
Yohanan Hahorani: *M. Suk.* 2:7	– 1
Yosé	

By our estimate the Mishnah contains 20 domestic *Ma'asim*, and 65% of them involve patriarchal names. While in the corpus of Gamaliel (father and son) the domestic precedent plays a considerable role, no other authority is represented as setting forth his Halakhic rulings on the foundations of domestic arrangements and conduct. What is characteristic of the presentation of the rulings of patriarchs is rare in the report of sages, and even there, at least occasionally (Yohanan b. Zakkai) sages' domestic conduct is reported along with that of the patriarch. What the sages could do only in the context of the collegium of sages, the patriarchal figures could do within their households. And the form of the domestic *Ma'aseh* should register: a deed described, not a ruling set forth in abstract terms. The specific actions of the patriarchal figure weighed as heavily as the general ruling of a sages' court. The patriarchal theology implicit in that contrast, its bearing on the definition and standing of the Torah of Sinai in its acutely contemporary realization – these matters are now blatant and hardly require comment.[5]

VII. The Institutional Perspective in the Gamaliel-*Ma'aseh* Corpus

What do we think we learn about the historical Gamaliel, whichever Gamaliel we contemplate? Nothing at all. What we learn about the institution of the patriarchate and its theology, by contrast, is considerable.

---

[5] Whom Paul would have identified as the counterpart, the patriarch or *nasi* is of Christian counterpart to the Pharisees, is not at issue at this point. But he clearly conceived of a hierarchical church order, and, outside of the genealogy of Jesus (unlike James) and not possessed of living traditions received in the lifetime of Jesus (unlike Simon Peter), he will have had to frame a useful theory of authority on other grounds than the conventional ones.

1. *Logic of Coherent Discourse and Organization:* We learn that the patriarchate, represented by the Mishnah's domestic *Ma'aseh*, had its own theory of how the Mishnah should be composed. It preferred organizing data by the name of an authority, rather than by a topic, as shown in the Gamaliel-stories that cross topical boundaries. The very name of the patriarchal authority on its own imposed coherence on data that, organized topically, would not cohere.

2. *Rhetorical Preference:* The patriarchate rejected the notion of preserving disputes but focused on the rulings of a single unchallenged authority, as shown in the utter absence of contrary opinions in the domestic *Ma'asim*. Disputes represented exchanges between equals, and the special standing accorded to the patriarch in the Halakhic exposition could not be conveyed if his opinion were balanced against other equally authoritative rulings.

3. *Topical Preference and propositions:* Above all, the patriarchate regarded the record of the patriarch's deeds as sufficient to illustrate the normative law. Not only so, but the patriarchate did not concede the characterization of the patriarch as less in knowledge of the Torah than the body of sages, let alone as bereft of moral authority and dependent on Gothic troops. On the contrary, the patriarch demanded of himself a more rigorous observance of the law than applied to ordinary people, and claimed for himself the markers of mastery of the Torah, physical weakness commensurate with his intellectual power. The patriarch need not apologize for his mastery of the Torah, but he distinguishes himself from other masters of the Torah by reason of his ancestry, and with that, the ancestry of the Torah in Israel: a chain of oral tradition from Sinai, in which the patriarchs form the links of the chain.

What was at stake for the patriarchate clearly concerns who carries forward the tradition of Sinai embodied in the Torah. These components of a theological system sustaining the authority and centrality of the patriarchate in the disposition of the Torah's power point to the heart of the matter, which defined our starting point. At issue is the theology of the patriarchate: the patriarch, deriving from Judah the Patriarch back to Hillel, in his own right possesses the Torah of Sinai and stands in a chain of tradition to Sinai. Then tractate *Abot* forms the patriarchal apologia for the Mishnah, as much as the patriarchal institutional theology. The Mishnah stands on the integrity of the claim of its sponsor, the patriarchate, to possess a free-standing oral tradition of Sinai.

A further formal peculiarity of the Mishnah underscores the specificity of that claim. In the aggregate, the Mishnah only occasionally adduces proof-texts in behalf of its legal rulings. The contrary view – "whence this ruling...as it is said..." – embodies the apologia for the Mishnah that would represent the sages, possessed, as they constantly allege, of superior knowledge of the Torah, with special reference to its exegesis. The Tosefta frequently, and the two Talmuds very commonly, adduce scriptural foundations for laws that the Mishnah sets forth without proof-texts, rather, as free-standing traditions. In that context, Hillel's confrontation with the sons of Beterah on the matter of the Paschal lamb and the Sabbath, *t. Pisha* 4:13ff., resolves itself precisely where the patriarchate would have wished. After logical arguments by analogy, by arguments based on shared language, and by arguments a fortiori, Hillel triumphs, at *t.* 4:14C, with the argument that the Patriarchate deemed decisive: "And furthermore: I have received a tradition from my masters that the Passover-sacrifice overrides [the prohibitions of the Sabbath] – and not [solely] the first Passover but the second Passover-sacrifice, and not [solely] the Passover-sacrifice of the community but the Passover-sacrifice of an individual." Then, and only then, the opposition gave way.

The claim of tradition governs, and the chain of tradition continues from Sinai to Judah the Patriarch through Hillel, Gamaliel, Simeon b. Gamaliel, Gamaliel, and Simeon b. Gamaliel, father of Rabbi. Domestic doings then form links in that chain, and the successive patriarchs embody the Torah in exemplary realizations through their household activities. No wonder then that, in re-presenting the Mishnah, the two Talmuds' sages would preserve domestic *Ma'asim* about sages' and not only patriarchs' or exilarchs' deeds in the household. But that is another story. But the story that we cannot recover at the end we should recall: the biography of the historical Gamaliel.

These are topics on which traditions reliably assigned to patriarchal authorities ruled:

1. *M. Ber.* 2:5 Gamaliel/bride groom/Shema'
2. *M. Ber.* 2:6 Gamaliel/mourning/washing
3. *M. Ber.* 2:7 Gamaliel/mourning/condolences for slave
4. *M. Shabbat* 16:8 Rabban Gamaliel and elders were traveling by boat, and a gentile made a gangway by which to come down off the ship, and Rabban Gamaliel and sages went down by it.
5. *M. Erubin* 4:1-2 They came from Brindisi [Brundisium] and their ship was sailing at sea. Rabban Gamaliel and R. Eleazar b. Azariah walked about the whole ship. R. Joshua and R. Aqiba did not move beyond four cubits.
6. M. *Erubin* 6:1-2 Said Rabban Gamaliel, *Ma'aseh* B: "A Sadducean lived with us in the same alleyway in Jerusalem. And father said to us, 'Make haste and bring all sorts of utensils into the alleyway before he brings out his and prohibits you [from carrying about in it].'"

7. *M. Erubin* 10:10 In the synagogue in Tiberias they permitted [using it on the Sabbath], until Rabban Gamaliel and elders came and prohibited it for them.
8. *M. Pesahim* 7:2 "Rabban Gamaliel said to Tabi his servant, 'Go and roast the Passover offering for us on a grill.'"
9. *M. Besah* 3:2 A gentile brought fish to Rabban Gamaliel, and he said, "They are permitted. But I do not want to accept them from him."
10. *M. Eduyyot* 7:7 Rabban Gamaliel went to ask for permission from the government in Syria and he did not come back right away, so they intercalated the year on the condition that Rabban Gamaliel concur.
11. *M. Yadayim* 3:1 Said Rabban Simeon b. Gamaliel, "*Ma'aseh* B: A certain woman came before Father. She said to him, 'My hands entered the contained airspace of a clay utensil.' He said to her, 'My daughter, By what had it been made unclean?'

If we had to construct components of the curriculum of studies that Paul would have followed at the feet of Gamaliel, that is, under the auspices of the patriarch, it would include questions of liturgy, mourning, treatment of slaves, observance of the Sabbath (travel on the Sabbath, carrying objects from one domain to another on that day), preparation of the Passover offering, preparation of food on the festival, intercalation of the calendar, matters of uncleanness – nearly the whole of the Pharisaic program involving Sabbath and festival observance and cultic cleanness that is well-attested to first-century venue. Working our way forward from the topical program that Paul can have followed in his studies with Gamaliel to the topics important in Paul's corpus begins, then, with these highly likely areas of Halakhic learning. But it cannot end there.

VIII. Paul: The Narrative of Acts

Those who programmatically maintain the historicity of Acts express confidence about Paul's study with Gamaliel,[6] but caution is appropriate.[7] Paul himself proudly asserts he was a Pharisee (Phil 3:5) but nowhere identifies his principal teacher. A recent school of thought holds that Paul remained a Pharisee during this activity as an apostle of Jesus Christ (both in Acts and in his own mind).[8] But for all that his

---

[6] For an informative defense of this view, see B. Rapske, *The Book of Acts and Paul in Roman Custody* (The Book of Acts in its First Century Setting 3; Grand Rapids: Eerdmans, 1994) 94-99.

[7] See the strictures of D.H. Akenson, *Saint Saul. A Skeleton Key to the Historical Jesus* (Oxford: Oxford University Press, 2000) 246-247.

[8] See J. Jervell, *The Unknown Paul. Essays on Luke-Acts and Early Christian History* (Minneapolis: Augsburg, 1984) 71, who characterizes "the Pharisee Paul who remains a Pharisee after his conversion and never becomes an ex-Pharisee." The characteriza-

Pharisaic status prior to his conversion is evident, and that his standing as such in some regards is conceivable, his own letters never mention Gamaliel in any connection.

Acts may be said to be apologetic in purpose, but Paul's silence in this regard is also tendentious: his theme when he speaks of his conversion in Galatians is that his gospel came from heaven by apocalypse and that human contacts in that connection are beside the point (Gal 1:11-12). Who actually immersed Paul in Jesus' name? Acts might be wrong in saying it was Ananias (Acts 9:17-18; 22:12-16), but someone evidently did (so Gal 4:3-7), despite Paul's reticence to say whom. Where was he baptized? Galatians 1:16-17 gives the appearance of an immediate departure for "Arabia" after God "uncovered his Son in" Paul, but he admits in the same breath that after an Arabian sojourn of three years, he "returned" to Damascus. In this case, he lets a circumstantial detail slip, rather than giving anything out. Although Paul speaks of his mastery of patriarchal tradition in Galatians (1:14), the only source of the Torah he studied that he mentions is Moses and the angels (Gal 3:19). Even that mention is ultimately designed to show that he, Paul, confronts the divine glory more directly than Moses ever did (2 Cor 3:12-18). (How such assertions can be squared with the thesis that Paul remained a Pharisee after his conversion is beyond the scope of this consideration.) Paul wrote in the bold strokes of an eternal paradigm, where the details that mattered were how salvation could be won and sanctification effected; the little matter of his Pharisaic and Christian teachers was lost in the shuffle of his conversion from Moses' covenant to Jesus' fulfillment of the covenant with Abraham.

The principle of John Knox, that Paul's letters are to be accorded precedence over Acts in writing about Paul, has been broadly accept in the present phase of Pauline scholarship, although it has also been refined, to allow for the place of Acts as a resource for the study of earliest Christianity.[9] But absent confirmation from Paul's letters, the reference to Gamaliel in Acts is often dismissed as a legend. When accepted, it is usually on the *a priori* grounds of Acts' alleged reliability.

It has been asserted that the debate must be resolved on the basis of such global considerations as the balance between legend and reliability in the book of Acts. Jerome Murphy-O'Connor has observed that

---

tion is taken up by Rapske, *The Book of Acts and Paul*, 94. A similar analysis is arrived at independently by Akenson, *Saint Paul*, 248-253, 251, who describes Jesus and Paul as Pharisees "of a slightly off-brand sort."

[9] For a fine consideration, see J. Murphy-O'Connor, *Paul. A Critical Life* (Oxford: Clarendon, 1996) v-vii.

"The details of Gamaliel's teaching are not relevant" to this consideration. Yet in the same study, he does cite Gamaliel's teaching in regard to the two Torahs in a relatively late source (*Sifre* 351),[10] in order to support the contention of Acts that Gamaliel was a prominent Pharisee.[11] We wish to demur both from excluding reference to Gamaliel's teaching in relation to Paul's thought and from adducing the position of Gamaliel on the basis of its latest attested forms.

Although the identity of Paul's teacher can not be established on purely literary grounds, we will suggest in our "Analysis" below that there are affinities between Paul's teaching in his letters to views of Gamaliel as articulated in the Mishnah, the Tosefta, and Talmud. These affinities are the only interest here; in that sense, the concern is literary. The "historical" Paul and Gamaliel are not the issue, but the textual figures that the New Testament and rabbinic documents refer to as such. In the case of Paul, letters sometimes called "authentic," whose priority to the others has been well established, are privileged, because they set the standard within any literary comparison. For Gamaliel, we will make a start with passages of the form-critical category of the *ma'aseh* – the "deed" form – because they have been shown to constitute a genre that was established prior to the redaction of the Mishnah c. 200 CE. Other passages will be cited in their increasing distance from the Mishnah. In this way, we do not compare historical figures, but Paul and Gamaliel as literary references at key moments within the evolution of the relevant literature. One might take a further step of inference from literary history to history as such, but that is a separate project.

Following our "Analysis," we infer that within some topics Paul's argumentation was analogous to Gamaliel's; we leave open the identity of the Pharisee who personally instructed Paul.

IX. Analysis: Patriarchal Narratives of Gamaliel and the Pauline Corpus

In that the present purpose is comparison with the Pauline corpus, the material attributed to Gamaliel will be reviewed heuristically, by topic: (a) calendar, travel and contact with idols in the Diaspora, (b) keeping house, marriage, work, and slaves, and (c) rules for festivals and the

---

[10] Cf. Neusner, *The Rabbinic Traditions about the Pharisees before 70* (South Florida Studies in the History of Judaism; Atlanta: Scholars, 1999) I:343.

[11] Murphy-O'Connor, *Paul*, 54-56: 56.

Temple. These are appropriate rubrics in line with our findings on the domestic and non-domestic *Ma'asim,* their topics and their tendency. Once the topic registers, we are able to take up other details besides those covered by the domestic *Ma'aseh.* At some few points we recapitulate sources already set forth. Unless otherwise signified, all passages derive from the Mishnah.

a. Calendar, travel and contact with idols in the Diaspora
Gamaliel's authority in establishing the calendar, his contacts with the government, and his influence in the Diaspora are attested in what has been shown to be an early form of tradition in the Mishnah, called the *ma'aseh*. In this form, what a sage did is shown to establish *halakhah* (*Eduyyot* 7:7):

> Rabban Gamaliel went to ask for permission from the government in Syria and he did not come back right away, so they intercalated the year on the condition that Rabban Gamaliel concurred. And when he came back, he said, I concur. So the year turned out to be deemed to have been intercalated.

What kind of permission did Gamaliel seek in Damascus (the seat of government in all Syria, and therefore the center of government for Jerusalem and Judea as well)? The Mishnah provides no direct answer. The sages who produced that work were much more interested in getting the year right than in the politics of the Empire.

Rome nonetheless had an interest in when great feasts were held and arrangements for security during those feasts. Festal celebrations could and sometimes did tip into riot or revolt, and the governor in Damascus and the prefect in Judea jealously guarded the Emperor's arrangement to have the sacrifices he provided offered by Israelite priests in the Temple.[12] This vignette reflects a time when Gamaliel was a go-between who negotiated the interests of the Temple with the government, demonstrating his role in international Judaism as well as in Jerusalem proper.

As in the case of Christian texts, Roman histories, Greek philosophical discourses and Gnostic speculations, the Mishnah and other rabbinic sources sometimes speak from the context of a cultural environment and people that we can identify. In the case of Gamaliel, the form of *ma'aseh* is often used in a way that refers clearly to the period

---

[12] See Chilton, *The Temple of Jesus. His Sacrificial Program within a Cultural History of Sacrifice* (University Park: The Pennsylvania State University Press, 1992) 69-111.

prior to the destruction of the Temple. Guided by his observation of that form, we can discern Gamaliel's location in the society of Jerusalem.

The Tosefta (*Sanhedrin* 2:6)[13] depicts Rabban Gamaliel and elders writing by means of a scribe named Yohanan to Galilee and the Diaspora:

A. *M'SH B*: Rabban Gamaliel and sages were in session on the steps to the Temple.
B. And Yohanan the scribe was before them.
C. He said to him, "Write:
D. "[In Aramaic]: 'To our brethren, residents of Upper Galilee and residents of Lower Galilee, May your peace increase! I inform you that the time for the removal has come, to separate the tithes from the olive vats.'
E. "'To our brethren, residents of the Upper South and residents of the Lower South, may your peace increase! We inform you that the time for the removal has come, to separate the tithes from the sheaves of grain.'
F. "'To our brethren, residents of the Exile of Babylonia, and residents of the Exile of Media, and of all the other Exiles of Israel, may your peace increase! We inform you that the pigeons are still tender, the lambs are thin, and the spring-tide has not yet come. So it is proper in my view and in the view of my colleagues, and we have added thirty days to this year.'"

Setting the calendar – in this case by introducing an intercalated month to coordinate Passover with springtime – obviously impinged directly on the cycle of sacrifice in the Temple, and this tradition no doubt makes Gamaliel more autonomous in relation to the priesthood than he really was. Still, Gamaliel clearly emerges from the sources as a force to be reckoned with in Jerusalem and beyond, although that influence is also something of a puzzle.

The "brothers" are most unlikely to be Pharisaic colleagues, since the evidence for Pharisees in the Diaspora is thin at best. But it does seem reasonable that the Pharisees would attempt to influence practices such as tithing far outside their own immediate circle (see the charge in Matt 23:15).[14] For this reason, the existence of "some sort of archive for the preservation and transmission of written materials" has plausibly been suggested.[15]

Gamaliel's influence in this field was such that his son Simeon also was involved in such correspondence according to a later source,

---

[13] See *The Rabbinic Traditions* I:356-357, 360-361, 368, 372-373 (cf. *y. Ma'aser Sheni* 5.4 and *Sanh.* 1.2; *Sanh.* 11b).

[14] Cf. S. McKnight, *A Light among the Gentiles: Jewish Missionary Activity in the Second Temple Period* (Minneapolis: Fortress, 1991).

[15] *The Rabbinic Tradition*, I:358.

Midrash *Tannaim* to Deut 26:13.[16] The issue here, of course, is not the fact of that correspondence, but Simeon's repute for engaging in such correspondence. That reputation is consistent with the Mishnaic statement that people appealed to him to adjudicate how to charge rent during a year in which there was an extra month (*Baba Mesia* 8:8). The case concerned derives from Sepphoris, so the presence of Pharisees or Pharisaic sympathizers is presupposed. The recent evidence concerning first-century buildings suitable for synagogues and *Miqvaot* in Galilee would tend to provide context for that finding.[17]

The memory of Gamaliel's contacts with the Diaspora is persistent. The Talmud recollects that he had five hundred young men in his "house" (meaning his quarter of the city) who studied Torah and five hundred who studied Greek wisdom (*b. Baba Qamma* 83a). Even allowing for hyperbole, that attests an influence far beyond Jerusalem proper. In fact, the text goes on to relate that Gamaliel was exceptional because he had close contacts with the Roman administration.

Contacts with the Diaspora, we have seen, are said to be both physical (in the case of the Syrian journey) and textual (in the case of the encyclical letter). Gamaliel's practices when at sea also became legal precedents, because he defined how to maintain the prohibitions of work and extensive travel on the seventh day under those conditions (*Shabbat* 16:8[18]):

> Rabban Gamaliel and elders were traveling by boat, and a gentile made a gangway by which to come down off the ship, and Rabban Gamaliel and sages went down by it.

He exemplified a practice in which an Israelite can avail himself of the results of what a Gentile does, although such work would be prohibited to an Israelite. Still, this was a permissive teaching, not a requirement. When a Gentile brought fish to Rabban Gamaliel under similar circumstances, he said, "They are permitted. But I do not want to accept them from him" (*Besah* 3:2). Another deed-story (*Erubin* 4:2) portrays Gamaliel as permitting his colleagues to disembark from a ship on the Sabbath, because he observed that before the Sabbath had begun at sundown, their boat was so near to port it did not go beyond the limit permitted as a Sabbath-journey.

---

[16] *The Rabbinic Traditions*, I:378-379]).

[17] See J.L. Reed, *Archaeology and the Galilean Jesus: A Re-examination of the Evidence* (Harrisburg: Trinity Press International, 2000).

[18] There is another Gamaliel at sea story in *Erubin* 4:1, but that seems to refer to a later member of Gamaliel's family, judging by the other Rabbis named.

Living among Gentiles as he often did, Gamaliel could be called upon to justify his behavior. An elaborate story (not a simple *ma'aseh* albeit still in the Mishnah) conveys that kind of defense (*Abodah Zarah* 3:4):

> Peroqlos b. Pelosepos asked Rabban Gamaliel in Akko, when he was washing in Aphrodite's bathhouse, saying to him, It is written in your Torah, And there shall cleave nothing of a devoted thing to your hand (Deut 13:18). How is it that you're taking a bath in Aphrodite's bathhouse? He said to him, They do not give answers in a bathhouse. When he went out, he said to him, I never came into her domain. She came into mine. They don't say, Let's make a bathhouse as an ornament for Aphrodite. But they say, Let's make Aphrodite as an ornament for the bathhouse. Another matter: Even if someone gave you a lot of money, you would never walk into your temple of idolatry naked or suffering a flux, nor would you piss in its presence. Yet this thing is standing there at the head of the gutter and everybody pisses right in front of her...that which one treats as a god is prohibited, but that which one treats not as a god is permitted.

Gamaliel's principle is simple, and its application would permit any Jew to pass as a participant in Greco-Roman culture: provided an Israelite realizes that what is treated as a god is no such thing, the little matter of an idol in a bathhouse was neither here nor there.

The assumption of this story, of course, is that it is pleasant to bathe, and that was a feeling Gamaliel shared with his predecessor (according to *Abot* 1:18, cf. 13-16; 2:5), Hillel. Hillel once remarked (according to a late tradition in *Lev. Rab.* 34:3 which nonetheless accords with the perspective of Gamaliel in the Mishnah) that, if idolaters think it an honor to wash the images of their gods, so an Israelite should embraces the honor of bathing his body, which is made in the image of God.

b. Keeping house, marriage, work, and slaves

Erubin 6:2 is embedded in a consideration of what to do when there is objection to the construction of an *erub*. Gamaliel taught his family that if they had to share an alleyway with priests, they should awaken early to put any vessels outside the house. That way the priests would have no opportunity to set out their own vessels and insist that only their receptacles could be in the alleyway that day. Staking a claim to an *erub* may have been the point of the teaching prior to its incorporation here, but it is notable that there is no direct reference to the *erub* in what Simeon reports in his father Gamaliel's name. The issue might initially have been a more routine question of how to deal with nearby

Sadducean families who claimed that the presence of their vessels in an alleyway precluded others, on grounds of priestly purity. In either case, however, the assumption of this story is that, while there was a Sadducean neighborhood in proximity to a Pharisaic neighborhood (in Jerusalem, presumably), and that they disputed about who could use the alleyway. That supports the assertion that the father in the story is Gamaliel, and the plausibility of the attribution to Simeon ben Gamaliel.[19]

The extent of Gamaliel's influence is shown by his capacity to establish that a single witness could establish a man's death, and therefore the freedom for the wife to marry again (*Yebamot* 16:7).[20] That discussion unfolds in a consideration of the calendar, because the Israelite calendar also involved the taking of testimony (in relation to phases of the moon, especially). Just as the application of Gamaliel's principle allowed the testimony of slaves and female slaves in the case of a man's death, Samaritans could witness a writ of divorce in his view (*Gittin* 1:5). Indeed, the testimony of a man who commanded a writ of divorce and then committed suicide was in Simeon ben Gamaliel's opinion to be accepted (*Gittin* 6:6). He was familiar with cases as far away as Sidon (*Gittin* 7:5). But although the influence of Gamaliel's house was felt widely, there was no question of its exerting central authority. In the matter of conditions of work, for example (*Baba Mesia* 7:1), Simeon ben Gamaliel insisted that "the practice of the province" should be honored.

Gamaliel was so attached to Tabi, his slave, he allegedly broke his own rule that a man should not receive condolences for the death of a slave (*Berakhot* 2:7). His justification? "Tabi my slave was not like other slaves. He was exacting." By contrast, when his wife died, Gamaliel washed on the first night after the death of his wife (*Berakhot* 2:6). His disciples remonstrated; Did not our master teach us that it is forbidden for a mourner to wash? He said to them, "I am not like other men, I am frail."

c. Rules for festivals and the Temple

Influence such as Gamaliel's did not come just from acting wisely and speaking to the point. His house could also, by means of devoted *disciples*, enforce his teachings, even in the Temple. A deed-story in the Mishnah tractate *Sheqalim* (3:3) demonstrates that. When he gave in the annual Shekel tax, he had a member of his household throw it

---

[19] *The Rabbinic Traditions*, I:379-380.
[20] *The Rabbinic Traditions*, I:348-350.

right in from of the collector, to make sure his money went for public sacrifices. If the collector needed prompting, a little gang of Pharisees gathered, yelling out, "Take up the offering, take up the offering." Gamaliel's crowd was learned, but also resourceful. The result was that they defended their own way of determining when an animal should be excluded from sacrifice (Bekhorot 6:9), cooking the lamb of Passover (Pesahim 7:2), sleeping in a Sukkah (Sukkah 2:1), determining how much of a field should be left unharvested for the poor to glean in (Peah 2:5-6), and adjudicating when an unclean oven might convey impurity to a woman's hand (Yadayim 3:1). In the cases of Passover preparation and bedtime in a Sukkah, Gamaliel's Gentile slave Tabi features prominently.

Simeon ben Gamaliel's resourcefulness and influence in Temple praxis is implicit in a case in which he was angered by how much a pair of sacrificial birds cost for any woman who wished to purify herself after a miscarriage or an irregular period (Keritot 1:7). He reacted by teaching that a woman in that position could wait until five such cases had passed, before bringing the birds. The priests and the merchants they authorized to sell on the Mount of Olives got the message, and the price of birds in Jerusalem plummeted.

Ad hoc interventions are instanced in several deed stories. When his sons returned late from a banquet with the embarrassing news that they had failed to recite the Shema' that evening, Gamaliel ruled that they could do so until the appearance of Venus, the morning star (Berakhot 1:1). But this attitude was not simply one of leniency. He himself agreed (Berakhot 2:5) that a bridegroom is exempt from the recitation of the Shema' on the first night of his marriage. But his disciples heard him recite it on his own wedding night. When they reminded him of his teaching next morning he said, "I cannot heed you to suspend from myself the kingdom of heaven [even] for one hour."

Gamaliel, finally, is associated with particular devotion to the remembered place of the ark in the Temple (Sheqalim 6:1-2):

- A. (1) Thirteen shofar chests, (2) thirteen tables, [and] (3) thirteen acts of prostration were in the sanctuary.
- B. The members of the household of Rabban Gamaliel and the members of the household of R. Hananiah, Prefect of the Priests, would do fourteen prostrations.
- C. And where was the additional one?
- D. Toward the woodshed,
- E. for so did they have a tradition from their forebears that there the ark was stored away.

6:2 A. *M'SH B*: A priest was going about his business and saw that a block of the pavement was slightly different from the rest.
B. He came and told his fellow.
C. He did not finish telling [him] before he dropped dead.
D. Then they knew without doubt that there the ark had been stored away.

B–E clearly establishes Gamaliel's association with Hananiah, which is consistent with our analysis of the traditions regarding the calendar. Moreover, 6:2 A–D underscores their common practice as having an esoteric and potentially dangerous dimension. Perhaps we should associate with this aspect of Gamaliel's teaching the claim that he "saw directly by the holy spirit" (*t. Pesahim* 1:27[21]) and preserved his separateness (*Sotah* 9:15) and that his son deliberately guarded his silence (*Abot* 1:17).

X. Inference

Placing Gamaliel in Jerusalem in the period 20 to 50 CE[22] makes his overlap with Paul possible and his influence in the Diaspora enhances any such overlap. The Temple oriented material in several of the stories attributed to Gamaliel makes Acts 5:34 seem more plausible than might otherwise be the case.[23]

But for all those incidental considerations, what stands out unmistakably is that there is nothing like a quotation from Paul of Gamaliel's teaching (or *vice versa*), nor a common reference to a specific exegetical tradition, nor a comparable stance to an institution (for example, the Temple). These three types of analogy, which have been instanced in the study of the Gospels in relation to rabbinic literature,[24] simply do not apply to the case of Gamaliel and Paul.

But a fourth type of analogy does apply: an analogy of logic or argumentation. If we review Paul's concerns through the lens of Gamaliel's *halakhah*, we discover a resonance between the two which, at the level of thought, is as striking as the shared traditions which the Gospels sometimes evince with rabbinic documents.

---

[21] See W.D. Davies, *Paul and Rabbinic Judaism. Some Rabbinic Elements in Pauline Theology* (London: SPCK, 1958) 331.
[22] *The Rabbinic Traditions*, I:294; III:306.
[23] *The Rabbinic Traditions*, III:314.
[24] See Chilton, "Reference to the Targumim in the Exegesis of the New Testament," *Society of Biblical Literature: 1995 Seminar Papers* (ed. L.H. Lovering; Atlanta: Scholars, 1995) 77-82.

a. Calendar, travel and contact with idols in the Diaspora

Paul's upset with his readership in Galatia includes the complaint that they observe days and months and seasons and years (Gal 4:10); it makes him despair that he had labored for nothing (Gal 4:11). In that Paul had called his readers from the planetary worship of the local elementary substances, the abuse he has in mind is likely of Galatian (that is, Celtic) origin. Yet at the same time, he makes a transition through the section in which he elaborates on his despair (vv. 12-20) to speak in the most derogatory terms he ever uses of the law and covenant given on Sinai (vv. 21-31): the correspondence he posits with Hagar, rather than Sarah, and slavery as distinct from freedom would make him – if he were still a Pharisee – the oddest member of the class imaginable.

Here contrast with Gamaliel totally dominates any glimmer of similarity. In the same letter, Paul does evince interest in a "season" (*kairos*), but of a different sort: the eschatological harvest (Gal 6:9). This trumping of calendrical time with the eschatological moment is also instances in the effective sarcasm of 1 Thessalonians, where Paul, Silvanus and Timothy remark that they have no need of writing concerning times and season, because their readers know accurately that "The Lord's day comes as a thief in the night" (1 Thess 5:1-2). In the foreshortened time in which Paul lived, feasting and fasting were as irrelevant as mourning the rejoicing, because the very structure of this world was passing away (1 Cor 7:29-31).

Where contrast with Gamaliel is blatant in the case of calendar the instrument of the divergent teaching is interesting: in Paul's case, the use of letters as means to influence communities is manifest. Indeed, he even attempts to convene a court of judgment in a Corinth at a distance, demanding that the Corinthians gather with his own spirit and the power of Jesus to condemn a case of fornication (1 Cor 5:1-13), and he insists that such courts should be routine in the settlement of less drastic cases (1 Cor 6:1-11).

The issues of travel and Sabbath do not consume Paul's attention, but that of fellowship at meals does. The events of Galatians 2 need not be rehearsed here,[25] but it is worth noting that they are crucial events in Paul's recitation. That is, Paul uses Peter's *deeds* to contradict his behavior. Because Peter once ate together with Gentiles, and then withdrew when people from James arrived, Paul accuses him of hy-

---

[25] See B.D. Chilton and C.A. Evans (eds.), *James the Just and Christian Origins* (NovTSup 98; Leiden: Brill, 1999).

pocrisy (Gal 2:11-21). The form of *ma'aseh* is here used to devastating effect. But that does not prevent him from specifying elsewhere the people one is not to eat with (so 1 Cor 5:11), and foods to be avoided when eating them might promote idolatry (1 Cor 8:1-13; Rom 14:13-23).

The issue of idolatry brings us to an argumentative analogy between Gamaliel and Paul, rather than a contrast. Paul's principle is simple: "We know that there is no idol in the world and that there is no God but one" (1 Cor 8:4). So the notional sacrifice of food to idols (contrary to the position of James as cited in Acts 15:19-21) must be beside the point. Yet if the freedom of action this principle implies were to lead a brother to falter, he says he would prefer not to eat meat at all (v. 13, cf. Rom 14:13, 20).

As Paul's statement of the principle is much less colorful than Gamaliel's vivid depreciation of Aphrodite, his application is also more cautious. After all, he is dealing with some people who had actively served idols. For all that, it is striking that Paul simply asserts the view that idols are nonentities, as if a position along the lines of Gamaliel's had been widely accepted.

b. Keeping house, marriage, work, and slaves

Paul's conception of an eschatologically foreshortened time did not prevent him from setting out famous advice in regard to marrying and not marrying, divorcing and virginity in the same discussion in which he speaks of time's shortness (1 Cor 7). A particular point where he and Gamaliel agree was that death freed a wife from the bonds of marriage so as to marry without any suspicion of adultery (see Rom 7:1-3).

Although he does not address the issue of purity in a household as such, Paul does in two ways speak of domestic matters in terms of the related issue of sanctification. First, he turns out in 1 Corinthians to be much less sanguine about idols than 1 Cor 8 alone might suggest. In the run-up to his discussion of Eucharistic practice, he sets out a very tough analysis in the course of demanding his readers flee idolatry (10:14-22). Referring to food sacrificed to idols, he says "what they sacrifice, they sacrifice to demons and not God: I do not want you to become partners with demons" (v. 19). Further, he insists that "You cannot drink the Lord's cup and the demons' cup; you cannot take part in the Lord's table and the demons' table" (v. 21). These demons and their offerings might be nothing (as he repeats in v. 19), but they are to be avoided absolutely, because the sacred meal of Christ is directly compared with the sacrifices in the Temple (vv. 16-18). That sanctification in Eucharistic practice obliges a complete removal of idolatry at home.

Second, this same principle of sanctification adheres to the physical bodies of those baptized into Christ. The idea of the body of Christ is fully worked out in 1 Cor 12:12-31, but already here, in ch. 10, Paul refers to baptism (vv. 1-13) as well as Eucharist, and speaks of belonging to a single body (v. 17). Just as body of the faithful forms the body of Christ, so individual believers form the body of the faithful. The individual, too, is "a temple of Holy Spirit, of which you have from God" (1 Cor 6:19). This sanctification cuts two ways: *against* making your flesh one with that of a prostitute (1 Cor 6:15-20), and *for* the corollary that a man or a woman "sanctifies" an unbelieving spouse, so that their children are "clean" (1 Cor 7:14).

The issue of work as such does not appear to have disturbed Paul, except as a necessity (see 1 Thess 2:9; 1 Cor 4:12; 9:19; 2 Cor 11:7). But just as he argued for remaining married if one were married, and remaining single if that were one's state, he also – and in this same discussion – advised against epispasm as well as circumcision, against seeking manumission as well as against putting oneself into artificial submission (1 Cor 7:17-24).

But if this is intended as a global imperative, the letter to Philemon is a startling exception. There Paul pleads the case of Onesimus: as a servant he was taken from Philemon for a while, but Philemon should now accept him back as a "brother" (v. 16). Like Tabi before him, Onesimus could hope for a better deal than most in his station.

c. Rules for festivals and the Temple

Given our findings under section "a," we might expect this section to be extremely thin. Once the body of a believer has been made into the Temple, and the Eucharist is the altar of sacrifice, interest in the Jerusalem Temple would seem to be precluded. But famously that is not the case. Even omitting Acts from consideration, which mentions Paul's vow (18:18) and his underwriting Nazirites' offerings in the Temple (21:17-26), Paul manifests a cultic interest.

Paul was unquestionably capable of using cultic language as metaphor. Romans 12:1 provides the example of the addressees being called to present their bodies as "a living sacrifice, holy and acceptable to God." Indeed, Romans 15:16 itself can only refer to Paul's priestly service metaphorically, as the means by which the offering of the nations might be completed. But is "the offering of the nations" itself to be taken only as a metaphor? Two standard commentaries suggest that should be the understanding as matter of course. C.E.B. Cranfield reads the metaphor explicitly within the context of a cultic theology of the significance of Jesus' death:[26]

> The sacrifice offered to God by Christ, which Paul has here in mind, consists of the Gentile Christians who have been sanctified by the gift of the Holy Spirit...

Otto Michel links the passage more strictly with 12:1, and takes it that, in both cases, the cult is transcended eschatologically:[27]

> Das Besondere an dieser Bildsprache des Paulus besteht darin, dass der Begriff auf den eschatologischen Vollzug der Heilsgeschichte hinweist. *Was der Kultus besagen will, erfüllt sich in der Endgeschichte.*

Both of these exegeses rely upon the invocation of contexts which may indeed be recovered from Paul's theology, but which are not explicit here. It is, of course, impossible to exclude the meanings that Cranfield and Michel suggest, but it is striking that neither commentator considers the possibility that Paul might speak of an actual offering, provided by Gentile Christians for sacrifice in Jerusalem. That meaning should not be excluded, unless the straightforward sense of the words is found to be implausible.[28]

In that Paul refers to the collection just ten verses after he speaks of the offering of the nations (cf. Rom 15:16, 26), it seems only prudent to associate the two. In 1 Cor 16:8, Paul even refers to his decision to stay where he is until the feast of Pentecost: it has been suggested that he intends at that time to take the collection he refers to in 16:1, 2.[29] Whether or not that is the case, Paul clearly keeps the calendar of Judaism in his own mind (even though he did not commend it to Gentile Christians, as we have seen) when the issue of the collection is in play.

A final contrast with Gamaliel completes this picture. While Gamaliel's prostrations suppose knowledge of where the ark had been in the Temple, Paul refers to Christ as a *hilasterion*. Because sacrifice in the

---

[26] See *Epistle to the Romans* (The International Critical Commentary; Edinburgh: T&T Clark, 1986) II:757.

[27] *Die Brief an die Römer* (Kritisch-exegetischer Kommentar über das Neue Testament; Göttingen: Vandenhoeck & Ruprecht, 1966) 458.

[28] For a further defense of this point of view, see Chilton, *A Feast of Meanings: Eucharistic Theologies from Jesus through Johannine Circles* (NovTSup 72; Leiden: Brill, 1994) 182-193.

[29] See H. Conzelmann (tr. J.P. Leitch), *1 Corinthians: A Commentary on the First Epistle to the Corinthians* (Hermeneia; Philadelphia: Fortress, 1975) 294-297.

Temple still proceeds, Paul's assertion in Rom 3:25 is not to be understood as positing a formal replacement of the cult by Jesus' death. The standard references to similar usages in 2 Maccabees (3:33) and *4 Maccabees* (6:28, 29; 17:20-22) ought long ago to have warned commentators against any reading that involves such notions, whether in the key of Hebrews (as in Cranfield's reading) or in the key of a transcendent eschatology (as in Michel's reading).

2 Maccabees 3:33, after all, simply speaks of a high priest "making appeasement" by cultic means. That usage is an extension of the Septuagintal language of *hilasmos*, where the emphasis falls on the divine affect involved in forgiveness. Even *4 Maccabees*, which is probably too late a composition to be used as representing the milieu which was the matrix of Paul's letters, maintains a distinction between God's pleasure in sacrifice, and the means of that sacrifice. In 6:28, 29, God is asked to be pleased (*hileos*) with his people by Eleazar, and to make his blood their purification and his life their ransom. The plea is that heroic martyrdom be accepted in an unusual way in the light of a radical challenge to the usual means of sacrifice. *4 Maccabees* envisages the restoration of cultic sacrifice in the Temple as a result of the sort of heroic sacrifice that is praised.

The usage of the Septuagint, and particularly of 2 Maccabees and *4 Maccabees*, militates against the conflation of *hilasterion* in Rom 3:25 with the "mercy seat" of Leviticus 16, as – of course – does the absence of the definite article in Paul's usage. There is a natural relationship between the two, because the *hilasterion* of Leviticus 16 (vv. 2, 13, 14, 15) is where the high priest makes appeasement (*exilasetai*, v. 16, cf. vv. 17, 18, 20). Jesus for Paul is a *hilasterion* because he provides the occasion on which God may be appeased, and for that reason an opportunity for the correct offering of sacrifice in Jerusalem.

XI. Conclusion

What we have shown are points of congruence, intersections of topics set forth in the two traditions, Paul's and the Mishnah's for the patriarchate. Our intent has been not only to move from the particular, Gamaliel, to the general, the patriarchate, to the global, the topical program, and back via the global and the topical and the general to the particular, Paul, as we have done. It is also to identify the fundamental principles that animated the theological systems of Paul and of the patriarchate. The particulars and the consequent topical interests attain cogency precisely where, in Judaism, they should, which is, in the theology of the Torah and its contemporary realization that animated the Mishnah and that in the counterpart to the Torah, Christ, formed the foundation of Paul's system as well.

14

Historical Questions and Questioning History: Can We Write a History of Judaism in Late Antiquity?

Gary G. Porton

I

This essay investigates several issues under discussion among scholars of Judaism in late antiquity, as well as within the broader scholarly community. In general terms, we shall consider whether the "new historians" from the ranks of the post-modernists, deconstructionists, and cultural studies scholars raise questions and employ methods that open up avenues for us to travel to gain new insights into the Jews and Judaism of late antiquity or whether their approaches are irrelevant to us because of the nature of the materials we have available and the types of questions which we must ask. We shall approach our topic from two perspectives. We shall examine the validity of the objections the new historians raise against the methods and conclusions of the "traditional historians," and we shall investigate the problems one faces when attempting to apply the methods of the new historians to studying Judaism in late antiquity.[1]

We shall follow Bowersock, Brown, and Grabar in defining "late antiquity" as 250-800 CE.[2] At the beginning of the period Jews lived in Syria-Palestine from Punon south of the Dead Sea to Antioch and Aleppo in the North. Jews resided in Rome, in scattered settlements throughout the Roman Empire, multiple areas in North Africa, and in small settlements in modern Iraq. By the end of the period, Jews lived in Iraq from Basra near the Persian Gulf to Sarari, Argiza and as far as

---

[1] I wish to thank my colleagues Alan Avery-Peck, Bruce Rosenstock, and James R. Barrett for reading earlier drafts of this essay and for their comments.

[2] G.W. Bowersock, P. Brown, and O. Grabar, *Late Antiquity: A Guide to the Post-classical World* (Cambridge and London: 1999), vii-xiii.

Kurdistan, in the North. In North Africa Jews were spread from Sale, Tingus and Abyla in the west, to Daphane and Pelusium in the east. Jews were in Spain, France, Italy, Greece, and Germany. In short, while the "centers" of rabbinic Judaism were in northern Palestine until the fifth century and in Iraq until the tenth century, Jews were in numerous other locations, even before the rise of Islam. Those scholars who focus on "rabbinic Judaism" need to keep this Jewish dispersion in mind. There were a large variety of Jewish communities that may have been totally unaffected or just marginally affected by the rabbis, their views, and their texts. While the rabbinic documents produced in late antiquity, especially the Babylonian Talmud, shape all subsequent forms of Judaism, that process perhaps begins at the end of period, but more likely after the tenth century. The vast materials from the Cairo geniza beginning at that time offer us some of the types of information we crave when dealing with Judaism and Jews in late antiquity, such as court dispositions, marriage contracts, bills of divorce, wills, deathbed declarations, deeds of manumission of slaves, letters of attorney, deeds of sales and gifts, and personal correspondences.[3]

Although there are some important material artifacts from the period, such as the synagogues in Syria-Palestine[4] and the incantations on the bowls from Nippur,[5] and there are references to Jews in non-Jewish texts, especially among the Christian writers and the Byzantine rulers and jurists,[6] the vast majority of the material dealing with Jews and Judaism we have comes from the corpus of rabbinic texts.[7] There are few literary and non-literary artifacts which directly confirm, contradict, or supplement the information in the rabbinic corpus,

---

[3] S.D. Goitein, *A Mediterranean Society: The Jewish Communities of the World as Portrayed in the Documents of the Cairo Geniza* (6 vols.; Berkeley, Los Angeles, and London, 1999).

[4] The scholarship on the synagogues is vast and somewhat contentious. However, the most convenient study of the material is L.I. Levine, *The Ancient Synagogue: The First Thousand Years* (New Haven and London, 2000).

[5] There is a website which contains a good bibliography on the topic: faculty.washington.ed/snoegel/aramaicincantationbowls.htm.

[6] The scholarship on the Christian references to Jews is massive; however, two good introductions to the material remain M. Simon, *Verus Israel: A Study of the Relations between Christians and Jews in the Roman Empire (135-425)* (tr. H. McKeating; Oxford, 1986) and R.R. Ruether, *Faith and Fratricide: The Theological Roots of Anti-Semitism* (New York, 1974). For the Jews in the legal materials see A. Linder, *The Jews in the Legal Sources of the Early Middle Ages* (Detroit, 1997).

[7] J. Neusner, *Introduction to Rabbinic Literature* (New York, London, Toronto, Sydney, and Aukland, 1994); H.L. Strack and G. Stemberger, *Introduction to the Talmud and Midrash* (tr. M. Bockmuehl; Edinburgh,1991).

especially with regard to the Jews in Babylonia, modern-day Iraq. For the most part, historians have one type of data in their possession, and these documents come from an elite scholarly class of men whose views shaped everything they said and taught.

When employing these texts as historical sources, one faces numerous difficulties. All of these texts are collections of materials amassed over at least two hundred years in the case of Mishnah and the early midrashim, to over six hundred years in the case of the Babylonian Talmud. In no instance do we have first-hand knowledge of the actual collector(s)/editor(s) of the documents or the "editorial principles" they followed. We simply have no reliable information from where the editor(s)/collector(s) derived their information, how faithfully they transmitted it to us, how they altered it, what they discarded, or why they selected to transmit what they in fact chose. In brief, we have no way to ascertain the reliability or accuracy of the records before us. We cannot easily or accurately separate "reliable" first-hand accounts and information, if they exist, from information created centuries after the events they describe or the people they discuss. Is it possible, then, to construct a history of Judaism in late antiquity?

II

For most of the nineteenth and twentieth centuries, historians believed that they could uncover "the Truth." Ranke, his students, and his colleagues were obsessed with discovering what really happened (or "how" it really was), *wie es eigentlich gewesen*.[8] These authorities argued that professional historians should and could be totally objective and that there was a "Truth" waiting for the "scientific" scholar to discover and to transform into a narrative. History should be based on documents, and because the vast majority of these documents and "first-hand" accounts came from the upper classes of past societies, traditional historians focused on politics and the great men who controlled the governments and institutions of the world. These historians believed that "great men" controlled the course of human events, so that history was a picture from above drawn from the words and deeds of kings, ministers, generals, and even churchmen.[9]

---

[8] Cited in E. Breisach, *Historiography: Ancient, Medieval and Modern* (Chicago, ²1994), 233.

[9] P. Burke, *New Perspectives on Historical Writing* (University Park, ²2001), 3-6.

14. PORTON *Can We Write a History of Judaism in Late Antiquity?* 377

Although historical study developed along many paths and employed a variety of new social scientific methods during the twentieth century, for the most part historians still believed that they could find out what really had happened in the past, and many continued to direct their attention to political leaders, believing that history "was made" by great men. By the middle of the twentieth century, however, many non-historians as well as historians began to challenge the older paradigm. Because of new social, philosophical, and intellectual movements, such as feminism, decolonization, ecological concerns, orientalism, globalization, cultural relativism, deconstructionism, and the like,[10] many historians began to doubt that they could accomplish the goals which Ranke set forth. Much of "new history" either no longer focused on politics and political structures or studied them in entirely new ways, asking different questions from the previous generations of scholars. A mark of the "new historians" was that many began to investigate all facets of human activity, all classes and elements of human society, and all artifacts of human activity. Finally, the "new historians" seriously doubted that they or anyone could compose "objective" or unbiased accounts of anything, even the past.[11]

In the study of Judaism in late antiquity, the shift to a contemporary style of historical writing has been slow. The theological importance of the rabbinic texts and their claim that their contents were part of the oral torah which God transmitted to Moses on Mount Sinai have prevented many from applying the new historical methods to the documents, or from even engaging in the enterprise of the traditional historians. However, at least since the nineteenth century traditional historians have dominated the study of Judaism and Jews in late antiquity; one could subject the rabbinic texts to careful scrutiny, but one could not really argue that they were not reliable historical sources.[12]

---

[10] See Burke, *New Perspectives*, M. Bentley, *Modern Historiography: An Introduction* (London and New York, 1999), A. Green and K. Troup, *The Houses of History: A Critical Reader in Twentieth-Century History and Theory* (New York, 1999), and J. Appleby, L. Hunt, and M. Jacob, *Telling the Truth About History* (New York and London, 1994) for discussions of how and why the writing of history has changed.

[11] Burke, *New Perspectives*, 3-6.

[12] The Jewish historians who engaged in what we now call "traditional historical writing" date to the 16th century (cf. M.A. Meyer, *The Ideas of Jewish History* [New York, 1974], 17-21; A. Funkenstein, *Perceptions of Jewish History* [Berkeley, Los Angeles, and Oxford, 1993], 25; Y.H. Yerushalmi, *Zakhor: Jewish History and Jewish Memory* [Seattle and London, 1982], 7-74). Among the "traditional" historians of the period and of Jewish history we should mention W. Bacher, *Tradition und Tradenten in den Schulen Palaestinas und Babyloniens* (Leipzig, 1914); A. Büchler, *The Economic Conditions*

Among twentieth and twenty-first century "historians," pride of place goes to Jacob Neusner. While Neusner has moved well past his early historical work, those studies remain paradigmatic examples for those who believe that one can construct traditional history primarily on the basis of the rabbinic documents. The work is based on a detailed and careful reading of the original texts, engagement with generations of scholars, recourse to whatever archaeological materials were relevant, and an analysis of the pertinent non-Jewish sources.[13] Among other important scholars one should consult the work of David Goodblatt,[14] Isaiah Gafni,[15] Ze'ev Safrai,[16] Shaye J.D. Cohen,[17] Lawrence H. Schiffman,[18] Michael Avi-Yonah,[19] Gedaliah Alon,[20] Martin Goodman,[21] and Seth Schwartz[22] to see what "traditional historians" are producing today. These are only some of the authors who have written "traditional" histories of the Jews in late antiquity, and the notes contain references only to their most easily accessible works in English.

of Judaea after the Destruction of the Second Temple (London, 1912); Das Synedrion in Jerusalem und das grosse Beth Din in der Quaderkammer des Jerusalemischen Temples (Vienna, 1902); J. Derenbourg, Essai sur l'Histoire et la Géographie de la Palestine d'après les Thalmuds et les autres sources rabbiniques (Paris, 1867); J.M. Jost, Geschichte des Judenthums und seiner Sekten (Leipzig, 1857); J. Juster, Les Juifs dans L'Empire Romain, leur condition juridique, économique, sociale (2 vols.; Paris, 1914); J.H. Weiss, Dor Dor veDorshav (5 vols.; Vilna, 1904).

[13] A Life of Rabban Yohanan ben Zakkai, ca. 1-80 C. E. (Leiden, 1962); A History of the Jewish of Babylonia (5 vols.; Leiden, 1965-1970).

[14] Rabbinic Instruction in Sasanian Babylonia (Leiden, 1974); The Monarchic Principle: Studies in Jewish Self-government in Antiquity (Tübingen, 1994); D. Goodblatt, A. Pinnick, D.R. Schwartz, Historical Perspectives: From the Hasmoneans to Bar Kokhba in Light of the Dead Sea Scrolls (Leiden, 2001).

[15] The Jews of Babylonia in the Talmudic Era: A Social and Cultural History (Jerusalem, 1990), "Babylonian Rabbinic Culture," in D. Biale, Cultures of the Jews: A New History (New York, 2002).

[16] The Economy of Roman Palestine (London and New York, 1994).

[17] The Beginnings of Jewishness: Boundaries, Varieties, Uncertainties (Berkeley, Los Angeles, and London, 2000); From the Maccabees to the Mishnah (Philadelphia, 1987).

[18] From Text to Tradition: A History of Second Temple and Rabbinic Judaism (Hoboken, 1991).

[19] The Jews of Palestine: A Political History from the Bar Kokhba War to the Arab Conquest (New York, 1976).

[20] The Jews in Their Land in the Talmudic Age (tr. Gershon Levi; 2 vols.; Cambridge and London, 1989).

[21] The Ruling Class of Judaea: The Origins of the Jewish Revolt against Rome, A.D. 66-70 (Cambridge, 1987); Mission and Conversion: Proselytizing in the Religious History of the Roman Empire (Oxford, 1994).

[22] Imperialism and Jewish Society: 200 B.C.E. to 640 C.E. (Princeton and Oxford, 2001).

One could add numerous other scholars writing in Hebrew, French, German, and English.[23]

For the most part, these authors follow the scholarly agenda set by Ranke. Their work focuses on the men who created and the institutions which appear in the rabbinic sources. They carefully weigh the sources, set the rabbinic information into the contexts of whatever Roman, Persian, and Byzantine materials are available, and describe reality from the rabbinic point of view, limiting the questions they ask and the categories they investigate to those set forth in the Jewish texts. Although scrutinized following the best "traditional historical techniques," the data in these rabbinic and other documents are accepted more or less at face value. Some may dismiss particular accounts as fanciful, exaggerations, or miraculous, but for the most part the historical details and depictions of Jewish life are considered to be reliable. The belief that even fanciful accounts contain a "kernel of historical truth" pervades many of these studies.[24]

The "new historians" have raised serious challenges to the work of the traditional historians. Because the majority of scholars who study Judaism in late antiquity follow the agenda of the traditional historians, we must consider whether their objections are relevant to us and our work.

III

More than anything else the internet symbolizes the connectivity of the world human population of the twenty-first century as individuals as well as social, political, and economic communities. The current "buzz word" is globalization, shorthand for "we are all in this to-

---

[23] While not without their faults, see S.J.D. Cohen and E.L. Greenstein, *The State of Jewish Studies* (Detroit, 1990), 55-112; M. Goodman, *The Oxford Handbook of Jewish Studies* (Oxford, 2002), 79-140.

[24] These scholarly endeavors should not be rejected out of hand. They are the products of careful scholars, and they often accurately present what the documents describe and how they describe those phenomena. Even when the several rabbinic collections are conflated into one continuous narrative, the information in these studies often offers us an accurate perspective of exactly the view of history and reality that the texts and the "rabbinic tradition" wanted to construct and transmit. Thus, while these studies fail to tell us "what really happened," they often do expose the deep contours of rabbinic mythology. They tell us what the rabbis wanted us to know, and they offer us windows into the rabbis' theological, philosophical, and legal systems and priorities, at least those "they put down on paper."

gether."[25] Because we are focusing more on the connections among the world's populations, we also understand that nothing comes into existence spontaneously. Nothing is created *de novo*. Nor does anything exist in and of itself. While we may not always understand or recognize the causes for current phenomena, actions, or activities, we do know that "things don't just happen." If everything is connected to everything else, this interrelationship is true not only at any current moment, but also in the past as well.

However, we err if we imagine that globalization is a new reality which occurred only at the end of the twentieth century. Any glimpse into the past will reveal that the discrete entities on the globe have always been interconnected – people, plants, animals, civilizations have always moved, migrated, traveled, and interacted. Among our first western "histories" is Herodotus's narrative about the war between the Persians and the Greeks. His account is almost a travelogue of "exotic" places. The earliest Sumerian, Assyrian, Egyptian, and biblical records recount the interactions, movements, and struggles among peoples, as individuals and as collectivities. Alexander's travels eastward and Caesar's conquest of Gaul reflect the same phenomenon to which globalization points. In brief, historians have always known that their subject matter does not exist in isolation. They have always recognized that connections among peoples, institutions, and communities exist and must be explicated.

Not only are phenomena connected synchronically, they are also related diachronically. While any discrete object may not have a future, each does have a present and a past, and that present and past are interconnected to the presents and the pasts of multiple other discrete elements. Some of these relationships are more easily observed or discovered than others, but they exist whether or not we fully realize that they do. Objects and relationships may change over time, but they are not altered randomly or haphazardly. Each datum and each relationship has an inherent set of limits and boundaries which prevent its metamorphous into *any other possible or imagined* object or reality. We may not always be able to predict how something will change in the future or discover how it has become what it is today, but there are intrinsic limitations which prevent an apple from becoming a donkey, or a parrot's having descended from a lion. Mountain peoples do not borrow symbols from coastal peoples without good reason and with-

---

[25] The publications on globalization are vast; however, on might consult Beyer for a study of globalization and religion: P. Beyer, *Religion and Globalization* (London, Thousand Oaks, and New Delhi, 1994).

out drastically altering their interpretations; borrowing among such disparate cultures is not random or haphazard.

Given the complex interrelationships which exist among discrete entities, both in the present and throughout time, some have argued that we simply cannot "know" anything significant about the present or the past. One cannot amass enough information to identify and then unpack all of the "causes" of any "effect." Any analysis will of necessity be incomplete and inaccurate because no one can know all of the elements that stand behind any datum in human life or in the realms of human collectivities.

There is of course truth to this claim: no single scholar, or even group of scholars, can know all of the elements that stand behind any historical datum, yet the reasons for this truth vary, depending, in general terms, on the period one examines. For example, in the "modern" world we often have too much information to gain a firm grasp of *all* of the "relevant" data needed, for instance, to analyze the course of America's engagement in Vietnam. Even if one could gain access to all of the American government's documents, meetings, and private conversions which related in any way to the war, given the relationship of American foreign and economic policies to the workings of other nations, this point of view demands that we also investigate the materials from all the other countries/nations which affected how the American politicians and military leaders thought about, designed, and implemented their Vietnam policy. Exactly how far back in the twentieth or perhaps even nineteenth century one would have to go to gather "all of the relevant documents and comments" is not even certain. If, however, one *could* amass all of the material, how would anyone or any group successfully study and analyze it in any meaningful fashion? The amount of material would be overwhelming. At least for most of the modern period – without even attempting to define "modern" – there is simply too much material.

With regard to the ancient world, the problem is just the opposite: there is not enough data. For example, we know that the Jerusalem Temple was destroyed in 70 CE during the Roman siege of the city. However, we only have Josephus's account of that event – granted, in two versions, which complicates the interpretation even further. We do not have any records from the Roman forces or the Roman government, much less from the Jewish side of the conflict, Josephus notwithstanding. In addition, we do not have the type of economic, political, and social data that would allow us to "explain" the actions of *either* the Romans or the Jews, much less both. If we cannot gain an accurate picture of the Temple's destruction, how can we pretend to understand the Revolt itself? We know virtually nothing about the political or social realities of the Jews other than Josephus's accounts, little more about the Egyptians, and perhaps a little more about the Romans. But we do not have adequate information about any of these larger national entities, much less the various "factions" within each of them. We lack, with few rare exceptions, first-hand accounts from members of the governments, the military, the economic classes, or the social classes in general that could help us understand the war. How can we even begin to claim that we can understand why the Jews and Romans engaged in the war, the course of the war, or why the Temple was destroyed? All we can know is what our scant written records and material artifacts tell us about the events, and that information is hardly sufficient for us to comprehend what occurred.

Thus, there is some truth to the claim that it is impossible to gather *all* of the information one would need to explain any human event fully. The peoples and communities in the world are so interconnected that it is impossible to construct an accurate historical narrative of any one entity without taking into account many other entities. It is also correct that we can never know "everything" we might need to know about an event. But that does not mean that we should not attempt to understand individual events. We do not need to know "everything" to understand an individual entity, action, or event.

With the exception of a few post-Enlightenment classics[26] and lost Hellenistic texts,[27] few writers ever believed they were explaining or analyzing all the interconnections of world (in the unfortunate sense of western) history in the way that these critics address, and even fewer, if any, are attempting to write "complete" histories now. At most we have multivolume collections by an array of authors on a variety of topics. They tend to be collections of disparate articles whose only connection is a vague, extensive chronological period. These are not sustained studies of periods or problems. And, in the examples we now

---

[26] One thinks of A.J. Toynbee's *A Study of History* (12 vols., 1934-61); W. and A. Durant's *The Story of Civilization* (11 vols., 1935-1975); O. Spengler's *Der Untergang des Abendlandes* (2 vols.; 1918-1923; ET: *The Decline of the West*). Among the historians who focused on Jewish History one thinks of I.M. Jost's *Geschichte der Jude seit der Zeit der Maccabäer bis auf unsere Tage* (12 vols, 1820-47), H. Graetz's *Geschichte der Juden* (11 vols., 1853-1876), and A. Baron's incomplete *Social and Religious History of the Jews* (18 vols.; 1952-1983).

[27] On the "universal" historians of the Hellenistic period see M. Hadas, *Hellenistic Culture: Fusion and Diffusion* (New York, 1959), 115-119; W.W. Tarn, *Hellenistic Civilisation* (rev. G.T. Griffith; Cleveland and New York, 1961), 281-287.

have, they suffer from the deficiencies of being "traditional" historical essays. In effect, they recount what the documents want to tell us, and that is all we learn from them.[28] They do not move much past the information they claim to be analyzing; they most often simply repeat it, either completely or with some "scholarly" modifications.

While it is fallacious to argue that because a historian cannot know everything about an event she should not attempt to explain it or analyze it from the data at hand, it is also simplistic to believe that one has written all that can be written on any specific historical datum. We must be as "complete" as we can be. We should choose those topics which we can study effectively. And we should not attempt to investigate those issues for which we have no evidence or only inadequate information. We need to frame our topics of study carefully, but even then, we need to realize that we will never know everything or be able to explain anything fully.

In a sense, the "traditional historians" understood this problem, for they limited themselves to what they had, the rabbinic documents and some contemporaneous information from the Persian, Greek, Roman and Byzantine empires. They asked the questions that they believed their documents could answer. They believed that their documents were accurate and authentic accounts of the rabbinic period. They wrote as if the rabbinic corpus contained virtually all of the relevant information they needed to write their historical narratives. They wrote under the assumption that the rabbis "made history," and to understand them – their statements and their institutions – was to gain a total comprehension of Judaism and Jews in late antiquity. Thus, even though they limited their source material to the rabbinic texts, they thought they were explaining all of Judaism in late antiquity, and for some, all of Judaism until the modern era.

The response to the traditional historians of Judaism in late antiquity, however, is not to limit our investigations to ever smaller topics or to continue to study the rabbinic documents in their cultural isolation.[29]

---

[28] One thinks of M. de Jonge and S. Safrai, *Compendia Rerum Iudaicarum ad Novum Testamentum* (5 vols.; Philadelphia, 1976-1988) and W.D. Davies and L. Finkelstein, *The Cambridge History of Judaism* (3 vols.; Cambridge, 1984-1999). The former set appears to have stopped "in the middle," or even "near the beginning." They might continue, but one suspects that they will never achieve their original goals. The latter is moving at a "snail's pace."

[29] A number of recent works have demonstrated the importance of using the rabbinic or other Jewish data as information for explicating other cultures or issues. See, for example, J. Neusner, *Take Judaism for Example* (Chicago and London, 1983); M.

One of the more interesting challenges to those who wish to concentrate on the smaller details of the human past comes from the *annales* –school of history.[30] These historians attempted to place human activity/history into its larger contexts – geographical, geological, climatological, etc. In a response to those who focused their historical studies on limited topics, such as the politicians, rulers, or upper classes, the *annalistes* argued for looking at all elements of society, focusing often on the rural/lower classes, and frequently moving from politics to economics. In addition, they turned their attention to more extensive periods of time than the mere reign of a monarch. These scholars wanted to understand the overarching structures of time, society, and geography. For example, Braudel,[31] one of the later representatives of this way of writing history, pointed to three layers of historical time. The first, which focused on humanity's relationship to the environment, moved in cycles of hundreds of years. The second, which encompassed economic cycles and population changes, occurred in ten to fifty-year cycles. The third, composed of political and diplomatic history, was short-lived. This was the "ephemera of history" which can be compared to the "crests of foam that the tides of history carry on their backs."[32] The *annalistes* draw our attention to the physical environment as a setting in which human activity occurs, remind us that social, political, and economic activity are interrelated, so that as historians we must take all three into consideration, point to the importance of the lower/rural classes, and suggest that change within a human system occurs at variable rates and that each datum must be placed in a variety of "time lines" to be fully understood.

The *annalistes* remind us that as historians of the ancient world, we need to be more attuned to the geological, geographical, and climatological sciences. In addition, we should pay more attention to those cultural artifacts which stand outside of the world of the authors of our texts. We need to move past the view that their world views predominated and that all the non-literary data we amass must be interpreted in light of their documents. We must place the information

Bunzl, *Symptoms of Modernity: Jews and Queers in Late-Twentieth Century Vienna* (Berkeley, Los Angeles, and London, 2004); D. Biale, M. Galchinsky, and S. Heschel, *Insider/Outsider: American Jews and Multiculturalism* (Berkeley, Los Angeles, and London, 1998).

[30] For critical appraisal of this type of history see M. Bentley, *Modern Historiography*, 103-115.

[31] See his classic work, F. Braudel, *The Mediterranean and the Mediterranean World in the Age of Philip II* (tr. S. Reynolds; 2 vols.; London, 1949, repr. 1975).

[32] Quoted in A. Green and K. Troup, *The Houses of History*, 89.

in the documents we have into their larger contexts, and we must remember that written and non-literary evidence may complement and supplement each other, as well as represent different world views.[33]

We possess a number of traditional studies of the ancient world which could theoretically help us understand the realia of the rabbinic texts. There are several studies of the geography of Palestine in late antiquity[34] and several investigations of the realia of day-to-day life.[35] We also have several works about agriculture at that time.[36] We have some parallel investigations relevant to the Babylonian Jews of late antiquity.[37] Although in theory these studies could follow the plan set forth by the *annalistes*, in fact they follow the pattern of the "traditionalists." All of the work has been done within the confines of the two Talmuds and the other rabbinic sources. The chronological and geographical boundaries are set by the rabbinic texts as is the intellectual agenda. In effect, these studies rely on the texts not only to set out the questions they pursued, but also the limits of the answers to the questions. These studies are little more than extended commentaries to the documents; they are not precursors of the types of studies the *annalistes* suggest we should undertake. Basically, the latter want us to place the information in the rabbinic documents into larger contexts, contexts which expand far beyond the limited range of the rabbinic collections. The *annalistes* want us to move from outside the texts into them instead of from the texts to the environment, geography, and physical realia.

Whether one accepts the need to investigate discrete historical data or moves in the directions of the *annalistes*, many recent writers have claimed that because historians suffer from the intellectual fault of subjectivity, they cannot possibly discover "what really happened." This indictment of traditional historians has two major aspects. The first is that historians are guided by their individual points of views, biases, and prejudices. When we write history, we are imposing ourselves and

---

[33] For illustrations of the importance of this point see R.S. Kraemer, "Jewish Women in the Diaspora World of Late Antiquity," in J.R. Baskin, *Jewish Women in Historical Perspective* (Detroit, ²1998), 46-72 and M. Aviam and W.S. Green, "The Ancient Synagogue: Public Space in Judaism."

[34] See B.M. Bokser, "An Annotated Bibliographical Guide to the Study of the Palestinian Talmud," in H. Temporini and W. Haase, *Aufstieg und Niedergang der römischen Welt*, II.19.2 (Berlin and New York, 1979), 211.

[35] Bokser, "Annotated Bibliographical Guide," 212.

[36] Bokser, "Annotated Bibliographical Guide," 214.

[37] D. Goodblatt, "The Babylonian Talmud," in Temporini and Haase, *ANRW* II.19.2, 330.

our ideas onto the past.[38] No one is truly objective, because no one *can* be objective. Therefore, historical studies tell us virtually nothing about the past, but a good deal about the person writing on the subject of the past. The critics would claim that the problem with the traditional historians of Judaism in late antiquity is that they believed in a theological sense that the rabbis were faithfully transmitting everything they heard from their teachers exactly as they heard it. The Talmud was part of the oral torah, revealed to Moses on Mount Sinai, so its contents had to be accurate. Those who rejected these theological points engaged in different types of historical enquiries, but they merely reflected their own theological biases, not necessarily the contents of the documents they investigated. The second aspect of this objection develops out of the first. Given that historical narratives tell us most about the people who composed them, all historical reconstructions are equally valid because everyone has a right to express his or her own views of the past. This last point is amply illustrated by the various, often contradictory and sometimes mutually exclusive, historical narratives we encounter about the same historical data. Those who believed in the theology behind the concept of the Oral Torah would accept the information in the documents at face value, while those who did not accept that theological position would be less inclined to accept the information at face value.[39]

The claim that a work of history teaches us only about the historian and not the past she claims to be writing about is common among many current critiques of the traditional historical enterprise.[40] Also, it is common to hear that because we cannot write objective history, all historical writing is flawed, biased, and merely a matter of someone's opinion. In actuality, however, the goal of writing objective, neutral history is recent. Before the 19th century, historians found many reasons for examining the past besides discovering what really happened. The contemporary critics' arguments that Ranke's goals cannot be reached are valid, but his goals are not the only reasons historians have engaged in their craft.

---

[38] Green and Troup, quoting E.H. Carr: "our first concern should not be with the facts which it [a historical work] contains but with the historian who wrote it" (Green and Troup, *The Houses of History*, 7).

[39] For an example of radically differing interpretations of the same small amount of data see the articles in R.A. Kraft and G.W.E. Nickelsburg, *Early Judaism and Its Modern Interpreters* (Atlanta, 1986) and E.J. Epp and G.W. MacRae, S.J, *The New Testament and Its Modern Interpreters* (Atlanta, 1989).

[40] For example, Green and Troup, *The Houses of History*, 206, 300; Appleby, Hunt, and Jacob, *Telling the Truth*, 7, 201-212.

Thucydides undertook his task as perhaps the first "self-conscious" historian, setting himself apart from others who had recorded and transmitted the deeds of generations long past. He writes that unlike the poets whose creations demand that they exaggerate or the chroniclers who "are attractive at truth's expense," he has relied upon the clearest data, so that he could reach "conclusions as exact as can be expected in matters of such antiquity." He has done this despite "the known disposition of the actors in a struggle to overrate its importance."[41] The narrative of the events, he claims, "rests partly on what I saw myself, partly on what others saw for me," and he evaluated the results he gleaned from his evidence, "by the most severe and detailed tests possible." Despite his concern for accuracy, Thucydides tells us that "my habit has been to make the speakers say what was in my opinion demanded of them by the various occasions, of course adhering as closely as possible to the general sense of what they really said."[42]

Isocrates (436-338 BCE) argued that history was an art, not a science, in the Aristotelian senses of those terms. The historian should employ all of the rhetorical devices of melodrama to capture the readers' attention, even by arousing his audience's pity or fear.[43] Asclepiades of Myrlea (first century BCE) divided narrative prose into three categories: true history, false history, and history as it may likely have happened. Hadas writes, "the first category includes unadorned chronicles; the second such fantasies as Lucian's *True History*, of which the author himself says it contains no truth, and the third must be based on truth but admits of elaborations provided they have verisimilitude and are edifying."[44] From the first century onward history written in the West was designed to make a point. If written by Christians the texts demonstrated the truth of Christianity; if composed by Jews, they demonstrated God's plan in the world which vindicated, or would vindicate, the claims of Judaism.[45] History was written to make a point, to teach. History was most often "true" in a theological sense, in that it validated the message of either Judaism or Christianity. Almost all historical studies were interior, in that they were less

---

[41] M.I. Finley, *The Portable Greek Historians: The Essence of Herodotus, Thucydides, Xenophon, Polybius* (New York: 1959), 230.
[42] Finley, *The Portable Greek Historians*, 231.
[43] Hadas, *Hellenistic Culture*, 117.
[44] Hadas, *Hellenistic Culture*, 121.
[45] See Meyer, *The Ideas of Jewish History*; A. Funkenstein, *Perceptions of Jewish History*; Y.H. Yerushalmi, *Zakhor: Jewish History and Jewish Memory*.

interested in the outside world than in maintaining the community's interior beliefs and integrity.

There is no doubt that each historian approaches her material from his own point of view, including her own likes/dislikes, prejudices, and presuppositions. The data of the past do not speak for themselves. Nor, in fact, do the events of the past exist in the present. While the consequences of past events may live on in our present, the events themselves are forever gone. While discrete data may remain which are a result of past realities, one of the historian's tasks is to put that data together in order to discover from what/where they originated. The historians create the picture of the past from the data they encounter and the ways in which they assemble the data into a coherent account. Above all, this task is a mental process accomplished by individuals who have been nurtured in particular intellectual and cultural environments. Historical studies only answer the questions which the historians pose, and those questions are shaped by the historians' personalities, with all of their strengths and weaknesses, which reflect their cultural environments. Despite these realities, historical inquiries can be carefully executed. Historians can approach their material fully aware of their limitations, biases, and prejudices, and if they are not, others in the profession will point them out to them. Being objective does not require that we all undertake our work as empty slates upon which the historical data impresses itself. If this were the expectation, history would never be written. Rather, objectivity points us towards "a commitment to honest investigation, open processes of search, and engaged public discussions of the meaning of historical facts."[46] In brief, while the historian cannot empty her mind of all of his "biases," she can engage in an honest investigation of her material which is then vetted in the public arena. The consequences of this understanding of objectivity are that the historians must realize that the historical data needs to be investigated over and over again, by various historians throughout numerous periods of time. We, as historians, must accept that there is never *one definitive* historical study or interpretation. Instead, we gain historical knowledge by integrating a number of perspectives over a period of time.[47] We learn about a historical datum by approaching it from as many perspectives as possible – not only from the perspectives of different methods, but also from the perspec-

---

[46] Appleby, Hunt, and Jacob, *Telling the Truth*, 10.
[47] See Appleby, Hunt, and Jacob, *Telling the Truth*, 241-270, for the implications of the above definition of "objectivity."

tives of different individual historians.[48] While all historians write from an individual point of view, carefully executed studies can most likely provide us with information which is valuable and ultimately useful in our own understanding of the past. We are dependent on one another's work, especially because none of us has the required expertise to pursue all of the relevant issues with the necessary acumen. By drawing on different studies of a topic, all of which reflect a different point of view or perhaps a different intellectual approach, we can begin to see the data from different perspectives. From this new vantage point we can achieve a more nuanced insight into the various facets of the data we wish to understand.

The discussion above assumes, of course, that there are historical data and that we as working historians today can access those data in significant ways. However, some suggest that the nature of human language itself prevents our entrée into the past. These arguments are often based on the work of the great Swiss linguist Ferdinand de Saussure. Saussure argued that there was no inherent connection between a word and the thing to which the word pointed. He maintained that language does not proceed from a person's experiencing something real "out there" and then attempting to describe or name it. Rather, the word comes after we develop a mental concept. Thus, the word points to a mental construction and not to an objective reality. If this is true, our language, including our historical narratives, does not point to anything real, anything out there. If we accept this theory of language and this analysis, we are forced to conclude that all we can learn from a historical study is what the historians have created in their minds.[49] Claiming to know anything about Judaism in late antiquity from the works discussed above would be pointless. And, in fact, many modern relativists make this claim.

The language issues are complex. Many who argue for cultural and historical relativism[50] rely on Saussure's ideas. However, Saussure's thought is much more complex than most scholars who use him realize. His major work was collected from notes and published after his death. He developed his ideas over time, and refined, expanded, or changed some of his thoughts found in his early lectures in his later

---

[48] For an interesting discussion of the problem of relativism see M. Bunge, *Social Science under Debate: A Philosophical Perspective* (Toronto, Buffalo, and London, 1999), 237-239.

[49] See Appleby, Hunt, and Jacob, *Telling the Truth*, 214.

[50] Saussure's most important work was a collection of his lectures/notes published posthumously under the title *Cours de linguistique general* (Lausanne and Paris, 1916).

ones.[51] Saussure argued that language is a system of signs, against those who focused on words. Signs reflect "the union of a concept . . . and an acoustic image." The points upon which many relativists focus are Saussure's claim that there is no inherent relationship between the mental concept and the acoustic image ("word" to us), that the acoustic image points back to a person's mind and not to an object in the world, and that the acoustic images change through time. The only significance of a particular concept and its acoustic image is that they are different from all other signifiers and signifieds,[52] not any relationship they may have to real things in the world. This argument seems to suggest that language is an arbitrary mental system which points to no reality outside of the system itself. If this is true, words cannot help us understand the realities of the past, or, for that matter, the present.

For Saussure, language is a system which means that all of it, grammar and lexicon, are interdependent on one another according to a set of rules. This system functions within a societal context, so that language is a social system. Saussure claimed that language is the most arbitrary social institution because the rules of the linguistic system depend only on itself and its own system.[53] The most characteristic aspects of a language are its primary feature of relating and combining words in different ways and in its continual transformation of itself through time.[54] These central aspects of a language, however, are social facts, so that while there is no inherent connection between d-o-g and the animal it signifies in the English language, those who use the English language at the present time agree that d-o-g points to a specific type of animal and not to other types of beings.

The relativists argue that because the relationship of a word to the datum in the outside world is arbitrary and a cultural artifact, we cannot get from the words, written or oral, to the historical datum itself. For that reason, all historical reconstructions are of equal value; none of them accurately point to anything "real" in the past. However,

---

[51] C. Sanders, *The Cambridge Companion to Saussure* (Cambridge, 2004), 1-6, 30-44; R. Engler, "The Making of the *Cours de linguistique générale*," in Sanders, *Cambridge Companion to Saussure*, 47-58.

[52] J.E. Joseph, "The Linguistic Sign," in Sanders, *Cambridge Companion to Saussure*, 60. See also C. Normand, "System, Arbitrariness, Value," in Sanders, *Cambridge Companion to Saussure*, 88-104.

[53] Normand, "System, Arbitrariness, Value," 90.

[54] Normand, "System, Arbitrariness, Value," 91. See the work of J. Scott, *Gender and the Politics of History* and *Only Paradoxes to Offer: French Feminists and the Rights of Man* as examples of an important contemporary historian who accepts much of this reading of Saussure's work.

Saussure does not deny that real things exist, or even that a society's language points to real things. He claims only that the signs we use to signify the "real things" derive from our minds and are agreed upon and function within a societal setting.[55] Far from concluding that language obscures or distorts reality, one could read Saussure as telling us that within any given society's linguistic system things in the real world are quite clear. Saussure's work, however, warns us as historians against interpreting past documents or realities or even lexical entities in our own terms. He keeps telling us to understand how the lexical elements functioned in a given society at a particular time. Language is a social phenomenon, so that it should not be employed or analyzed outside of the larger aspects of its social contexts. In order to comprehend the "meaning" of a document, one must have as clear an understanding as possible of the cultural milieu in which it was created and existed.

Saussure claimed that a culture has agreed about a set of signifiers for a set of individual entities, and that there is no inherent connection between the items and the signifier. A problem occurs when modern historians claim that there is a static, real entity, state of being, or concept which our culture and the rabbinic texts for 800 years consistently identified as woman, man, purity, salvation, and the like. The rabbinic corpus is replete with technical terms – legal, rhetorical, agricultural, social, theological, philosophical, liturgical, and the like. We must be sensitive to the fact that these terms can change, and probably have changed, meanings through time, just as Saussure claimed. We must be attentive to the time and place in which the term occurs, and we must interpret the term in light of its appropriate social context. This problem is further complicated by the fact that many of these technical terms have been explained by generations of exegetes, from the medieval to the modern periods. In addition, the terms may have parallels in the Roman, Greek, or Byzantine legal systems but not carry the same meaning in all of these contexts. Furthermore, technical theological and religious terms in Judaism may not carry the same meaning and weight within a Christian context. If we proceed carefully, we should be able to study the various complex entities that Judaism in late antiquity identified as "woman," "pure," "salvation," and the like. And, we should be able to understand how those cultural entities relate to the things our society signifies by these terms. By bringing

---

[55] On the challenge to those who claim that things exist only in human minds, see Appleby, Hunt, and Jacob, *Telling the Truth*, 249-250.

together more and more information about the various ways those data have been described within the Jewish contexts, or even within the Jewish contexts at a particular period, we can gain greater insight into the "real" datum to which these signifiers referred.[56]

A related issue derives from the postmodern interpretations of texts, documents, and literature. As historians of the ancient world, especially of Judaism in late antiquity, our knowledge rests almost solely on written texts,[57] documents, inscriptions, written references, and the like. We have few archaeological artifacts that supplement or challenge our written documents.[58] For these reasons, we must seriously consider the postmodern analyses of texts. The postmodernists begin by noting that written texts are not the only historical artifacts, and they suggest that limiting "text" to written documents alone is an error.[59] This insight should not be new to anyone involved in studying ancient history, or any history at all. Music, art, architecture, clothing, hair-styles, and the like have all been sources of information for historians, especially in the latter half of the twentieth century. Unfortunately, those of us who focus on Judaism in late antiquity do not have access to these sources of information. Those of us who concentrate on Jewish history or the history of Judaism in late antiquity remain tied to documents simply because they are often the only remnants of the period to which we have direct access. We crave more direct contact with all the other artifacts of the multiple cultural landscapes in which the documents were constructed. We may be tied to documents, but we know what we are missing, what we *wish* we could have. In one sense, what we can know about our period is limited, but unless we discover new sources of information that is a reality we have to accept.

The postmodern challenge can also affect the integrity of the individual as a "knower." Some postmodernists suggest that even the idea of "self" is an ideological construct, so that the idea that an independ-

---

[56] One can think of how the atom has been described over the last 50 years. The atom exists, but every subsequent experiment finds that it is not *only* what previous experiments discovered. It is possible, of course, that we may never totally *know* what constitutes an atom, but that does not mean that atoms do not exist.

[57] For a discussion of the oral nature of this literature see M.S. Jaffee, *Torah in the Mouth: Writing and Oral Tradition in Palestinian Judaism, 200BCE–400CE* (Oxford, 2001).

[58] For a brief and somewhat outdated discussion of these issues see E.M. Meyers and J.F. Strange, *Archaeology, the Rabbis and Early Christianity* (Nashville, 1981). See also R.A. Horsley, *Archaeology, History and Society in Galilee: The Social Context of Jesus and the Rabbis* (Harrisburg, 2004).

[59] Green and Troup, *The Houses of History*, 299.

ent "self" could gain knowledge of anything is absurd.[60] The "self" has no real ontological status; it is merely a cultural creation, so that its ability to amass and analyze data is a fallacy. We have seen above wthat historians understand about approaching their data as a representative of a particular cultural or personal point of view, so that we need not deal with this "theoretical" presupposition at this point.

Even if we reject the more radical view that the "self" has no real existence, we must face other issues the postmodernists have raised with regard to the texts we as historians study. The theory of language and literature often conflated with postmodernism is deconstructionism – one word which ties together an array of varying thoughts about and analyses of language, literature, and the human ability to employ either as a means of gaining access to the world and/or to knowledge. Taking Saussures' insights to another level, deconstructionism argues that any text can be read in multiple ways because there is no essential connection between the words in the texts and what they signify. Derrida maintained that when "deconstructed" many words are found to contain their binary opposite, so that texts are primarily self-referential, for the words can mean almost anything, and they gain their meaning from the text in which they appear.[61] The context in which the text was produced is irrelevant to our determining its meaning, which is constantly in flux, because what it means at one point or one time does not help us discover its meaning at another point in time or in another location. Additionally, Derrida argued that the author's intent is unimportant because in fact the "author as a real person" is a time-bound cultural artifact which will disappear with the passing of time.[62] The meaning of the text is created anew each time someone confronts it. The text means what it means independent of the person(s) who wrote it and the social/cultural context(s) in which it was composed because the text points only to itself. One can understand how this view of a written text could lead to the conclusion that we cannot gain any secure knowledge of the past, especially from written documents. But, because texts are cultural artifacts, they can be studied within the contexts of the cultures in which they were created and the meanings they had within those contexts.

The problem is complicated by the issues related to Foucault's thoughts about discourse and to the complicated notions of intertextu-

---

[60] Appleby, Hunt, and Jacob, *Telling the Truth*, 202, 212.
[61] Green and Troup, *The Houses of History*, 299.
[62] Appleby, Hunt, and Jacob, *Telling the Truth*, 215.

ality.[63] In discussing how one should understand a statement in a discursive analysis, Foucault argues that one has to "grasp the statement in the exact specificity of its occurrence" by examining a statement's "conditions of existence," "limits," "correlations with other statements that may be connected with it," and finally which other statements it "excludes." On the one hand, each statement "opens up to itself a residual existence in the field of memory, or in the materiality of manuscripts, books, or any other form of recording." On the other hand, every statement is unique and cannot be repeated, transformed, or reactivated. Finally, each statement is linked to the "situations that provoked it, and to the consequences that it gives rise to," and "in accordance with a quite different modality, to the statements that precede and follow it."[64] Foucault sees relationships among statements even if the author is unaware of the relationships, even if the statements come from different authors, or even if the statements come from quite different events.[65] Foucault writes that when one analyzes discourse, "one sees the loosening of the embrace, apparently so tight, of words and things, and the emergence of a group of rules proper to discursive practice. These rules define not the dumb existence of a reality, nor the canonical use of a vocabulary, but the ordering objects. Discourses are composed of signs; but what they do is more than use these to designate things."[66]

Foucault challenges each historian to see each text in a complex relationship to itself and to all other discursive events. However, if each discursive event is real in and of itself and if all of the relationships to all other discursive events are also real, some things are real. The historian must first unpack the discursive event of the documents she employs and deal with the relationship of that document to the other events that are relevant to her task. While this is complex, it is not impossible. Furthermore, this task does uncover some realities within each discourse, and if we follow Foucault's logic, even to realities outside of the discourse itself. One can agree with Derrida and Foucault that texts are open to multiple, even mutually-exclusive readings and that these readings often depend more on the "reader" than the au-

---

[63] For our purposes, the most important study of intertextuality and rabbinic literature is still D. Boyarin, *Intertextuality and the Reading of Midrash* (Bloomington, 1990). There are numerous reviews of this volume which one should also consult.

[64] M. Foucault, *The Archaeology of Knowledge and The Discourse on Language* (tr. A.M. Sheridan Smith; New York, 1972), 28.

[65] Foucault, *Archaeology of Knowledge*, 29.

[66] Foucault, *Archaeology of Knowledge*, 48.

thor. However, even Foucault's discussion of discourse recognizes that some discourses impose limits and boundaries on texts which limit the possibilities of its meaning. While these ideas warn the historian against assuming that she has the definitive reading of a text, they do *not* open up the possibility that *any and all* readings of text are possible.

In one sense, the rabbinic texts present themselves and have been presented by the traditional historians and commentators as interconnected. The Talmud is organized as a commentary to Mishnah in which it sought to connect Mishnah's teachings to the biblical texts. A passage may be connected to multiple verses, we may encounter an extended argument about the relationship to biblical texts, and we find the text concluding that no biblical warrant is possible. In the same manner, we find extended and complex arguments over legal issues, and even contradictory opinions attributed to rabbinic authorities. The midrashic collections often present several interpretations or comments on a given verse, word, or passage. However, none of these are limitless or random. The possible connections are always within the borders set by the rabbinic culture.[67] We may find many possible readings of any earlier text within a rabbinic collection, but this phenomenon is quite different from what Derrida is suggesting. The rabbis do not randomly construct their arguments, interpretations, or conflicting opinions. All of these fall within limited, culturally circumscribed boundaries. This does not mean, however, that the surface meaning or meaning ascribed to a passage by the traditional commentators is all to which the passage or saying might or could refer. Derrida and Foucault have opened our eyes to the necessity of "deep" readings, of finding the "markers" within a passage or saying which might point to "hidden connections" and realities which for some reason were intentionally placed below the surface of the text. For example, Boyarin's reading of the stories of Eliezer ben Hyrcanus possibly throws new light on the complex relationship between some of the early rabbis and emerging Christianity.[68] He takes the fact that when Eliezer was arrested for being a sectarian he did not denounce Jesus as an indication of the "rabbinic attraction to and repulsion from Christianity."[69] The complex ways in which Boyarin reads the Eliezer-corpus serve as an

---

[67] D. Stern, "Midrash and the Language of Exegesis: A Study of Vayikra Rabbah, Chapter 1," in G.H. Hartman and S. Budick, *Midrash and Literature* (New Haven and London, 1986), 105-124.

[68] D. Boyarin, *Dying for God: Martyrdom and the Making of Christianity and Judaism* (Stanford, 1999), 22-41.

[69] Boyarin, *Dying for God*, 27.

example of how one might read (or over-read) the rabbinic texts from the "new perspectives." Even if one does not accept all of Boyarin's conclusions, his analyses and arguments raise important and interesting issues with which anyone dealing with the Eliezer-corpus from this point forward must deal.

The severe limit of the available evidence for those of us who study Judaism in late antiquity precludes our ability to address all of the questions which the "new history" seeks to answer. However, we can address some of them in rather interesting ways. And some of the new approaches – post-colonialism, feminism, queer studies, gender studies, etc. – have raised new questions for the historian to ponder and perhaps find some tentative answers also.[70] The problem is not that historians of Judaism in late antiquity, especially those trained in America, disagree with the "new historians'" broader scope; the major obstacle is that we simply to do not have the artifacts to move easily into the new areas they are exploring.

The postmodernists' and deconstructionists' warnings do not negate the historians' tasks. They merely caution us more precisely about what we can and cannot actually accomplish as historians. Foucault's claim that discourse has many connections and meanings should warn every historian that he cannot argue that he has written the definitive interpretation of an artifact. Saussure's insight that our words reflect our mental concepts and not external realities should not mean that nothing exists outside the human mind or that we cannot have access to those things. Various "selves" within one culture or among different cultures may approach them differently, but with care and precision, we can communicate with one another within societies and across them. All of these issues merely advise us to be intellectually honest and extremely careful in our collecting and assessing of evidence. Once the historian has posed her question, she must seek out the relevant evidence as best she can. He then must examine that evidence with intellectual care and honesty, and finally, he must submit his conclusions and narrative to others to read, assess, and evaluate. As

---

[70] Women, gender, and sexuality have received the widest attention in the context of the rabbinic sources. A small sample of books which have been informed by many of the issues raised in this essay includes J. Neusner, *Androgynous Judaism: Masculine and Feminine in the Dual Torah* (Macon, 1993); J. Neusner, *How the Rabbis Liberated Women* (Atlanta, 1998); J. Hauptman, *Rereading the Rabbis: A Woman's Voice* (Boulder, 1998); D. Boyarin, *Carnel Israel: Reading Sex in Talmudic Culture* (Berkeley, Los Angeles, and London, 1993); J.R. Baskin, *Midrashic Women: Formations of the Feminine in Rabbinic Literature* (Hanover and London, 2002); M.B. Peskowitz, *Spinning Fantasies: Rabbis, Gender, and History* (Berkeley, Los Angeles, and London, 1997).

readers and critics, the community of scholars must evaluate others' works with the same care and honesty with which they were created. The objections we raise must be based on a critical assessment of the questions asked, the answers given, the evidence amassed, and the intellectual arguments constructed. Only in this way can we as a community of interested parties hope to gain any knowledge of past events. The various interpretative points of view which are available to us invariably produce different interpretations of an artifact which should often be piled on top of one another to produce a multilayered collection of interpretations which raise numerous possibilities of the artifact's meanings and what we can learn from it. Mutually exclusive interpretations do not mean that it is impossible to learn anything from an artifact. The different interpretations reflect different perspectives. If one historian interprets the rabbinic texts from a feminist perspective and another from a rabbinic point of view, the interpretations could be mutually exclusive, but the perspectives are not. If one reads the texts from the rabbis' point of view and one reads them from a feminist point of view, we have not negated the other's point of view; we have only complicated the interpretation of the documents.[71]

The issue is seldom a matter of right or wrong, although one can compose bad history, a careless study, a biased account. The problem occurs when historians believe that have written "the last word" or "the only word" on an artifact or set of data. The data or artifacts are always more complicated than one study or one perspective can elucidate. Good historians build on one another's work. They may disagree, they may argue, and they may re-interpret someone's data, but the constant give-and-take among historians always brings to light more information about the data at hand. Again, one can look at our growing information about the make-up of the atom. Previous investigations were not necessarily wrong; they merely failed to see everything they needed to see.

IV

Thus, the new historians have placed many obstacles before the traditional historians. When examined fully, the historian of Judaism in late antiquity can overcome the obstacles and produce creative, important, and interesting historical studies which offer us insights into the past.

---

[71] Appleby, Hunt, and Jacob, *Telling the Truth*, 256.

Jacob Neusner, who above was described as providing the "paradigmatic examples" of "traditional" historical studies, also produced the study which laid bare the dangers of employing the rabbinic collections as sources for "traditional" historical studies. The turning point occurred when he submitted to careful literary scrutiny the sources he had used to write his *Life of Rabban Yohanan ben Zakkai*. Neusner's *Development of Legend*[72] raised a profound challenge to anyone wishing to use the rabbinic texts as historical sources. This was followed by his work on the Pharisees[73] which extensively raised the issue of literary forms in rabbinic literature, so that the authenticity and accuracy of the material in the rabbinic collections was now open to serious question. From the early 1970s onward, those who wished to engage in writing "traditional" histories of Judaism/Jews in late antiquity had to face, or in many egregious cases simply ignore, Neusner's challenges.

The issue is not that *all or most* of the information in the rabbinic texts is inaccurate, fabricated, or worthless for use by the "traditional historian." The problem is that we currently have no way of separating the historically valid information from data which have been fabricated. The constraints of the literary forms which the editors/authors/compilers employed produced highly stylized passages within all of the rabbinic collections. Because it is impossible to penetrate the transmission histories or find the "original" version, if in fact the one before us now is not the original, means that in most cases all we have is what is before us. One simply does not know when the historical claims and reconstructions are based on reliable information or on data that have been intentionally or accidentally falsified. For that reason, it is impossible to know when the historian "has gotten it right."[74]

Neusner himself soon gave up the task of the "traditional" historian. In *Pharisees* he argued that in some cases the traditions attributed to the Ushans built upon and were later than the traditions assigned to the Yavneans, and he was able to show in many instances that versions of

---

[72] J. Neusner, *Development of a Legend: Studies in the Traditions Concerning Yohanan ben Zakkai* (Leiden, 1970).

[73] J. Neusner, *The Rabbinic Traditions about the Pharisees before 70* (3 vols.; Leiden, 1971).

[74] For a convenient attempt to set forth criteria by which one can decide what is "historically" valuable in the Babylonian Talmud see R. Kalmin, "Rabbinic Literature of Late Antiquity as a Source for Historical Study," in J. Neusner and A.J. Avery-Peck, *Judaism in Late Antiquity*, vol. II, part 3 (Boston, and Leiden, 2001), 187-199.

14. PORTON *Can We Write a History of Judaism in Late Antiquity?* 399

material in later collections built upon earlier sources. But this only confirmed the fact that in many cases later documents contained later version, and earlier documents contained earlier versions. These conclusions did not validate the accuracy or historical value of the earlier materials.[75] As it became to clear to him that the literary and formal issues of the documents had to be explicated before one could make even these basic chronological analyses of the traditions, Neusner turned to translating and analyzing the individual rabbinic documents to unpack what the sages were attempting to accomplish in the individual collections. His analysis of Mishnah still remains the classic example of this type of investigation.[76] After completing his work document by document, implying that one could unearth some "historical changes and development" by placing the documents in rough chronological order, Neusner became interested more in the continuities than the discontinuities among the documents. He has begun investigating rabbinic thought in its broadest theological, philosophical, historical and legal categories and contexts, showing how the various documents coalesce into a coherent theological statement.[77] One should note, however, that while he is dealing with the larger theological, philosophical, and legal categories of the rabbinic collections, he has not conflated everything into one amorphous whole. He has carefully placed the ideas in their various literary, textual, and discursive contexts.

An active debate continues over the possibility of employing the rabbinic documents as sources for the "traditional" historians.[78] Safrai explains how he and those like him go about their work and read the rabbinic texts as historical sources.[79] Stemberger[80] argues that while for Jewish history in Babylonia "we still have to rely almost exclusively on literary sources, [i]n Palestine . . . extensive archaeological excavations teach us to correct the picture offered by Rabbinic sources, or – more correctly – to revise our traditional reading of these sources."[81] Stem-

---

[75] J. Neusner, "Rabbinic Sources for Historical Study: A Debate with Ze'ev Safrai," in Neusner and Avery-Peck, *Judaism in Late Antiquity*, II:123-142.

[76] J. Neusner, *Judaism: The Evidence of the Mishnah* (Chicago and London, 1981).

[77] There are many examples of this type of work, and the project is ongoing at this time. For convenience, consult *The Halakhah: An Encyclopedia of the Law of Judaism* (5 vols.; Leiden, 2000).

[78] See Neusner and Avery-Peck, *Judaism in Late Antiquity*, I:141-230.

[79] Z. Safrai, "Rabbinic Sources as Historical: A Response to Professor Neusner," in Neusner and Avery-Peck, *Judaism in Late Antiquity*, I:143-167.

[80] G. Stemberger, "Rabbinic Sources for Historical Study," in Neusner and Avery-Peck, *Judaism in Late Antiquity*, II:169-186.

[81] Stemberger, "Rabbinic Sources," 173.

berger points to difficulties which arise when one attempts to employ the rabbinic materials for constructing the historical events within the Palestinian Jewish community. However, he argues that in some cases the archaeological evidence does support information found in the rabbinic materials, while in other cases the accuracy of the rabbinic materials cannot be maintained, and are even contradicted. Stemberger concludes:

> ... [W]e may accept [in the rabbinic texts] what can be confirmed by outside material. This does not enlarge our factual knowledge but teaches us how Rabbinic sources treat historical facts. The question we have to ask is whether we may transfer these criteria to the interior history of the Rabbinic movement where we have no external control . . . . There is no general procedure advisable: a certain measure of personal judgment remains in every historical reconstruction. But although it is no longer possible to use Rabbinic sources in a naïve way for reconstructing history, it is still extremely useful for historical questions. It would be the greatest damage to the history of Judaism if the Rabbinic texts were neglected altogether in the historical enterprise.[82]

Finally, David Kraemer[83] points to the problem of using oral traditions as a reliable source for reconstructing the rabbis' teachings. The difficulties are not lessened when we moved to written traditions because within the Talmud we find the same sayings in a variety of contexts, and we see that the "meaning" of the traditions have changed depending on the contexts in which they appear. Furthermore, Kraemer notes several difficulties for those who wish to use archaeological finds to explicate rabbinic materials or to date them. While Kraemer argues that one can set some material in the Babylonian Talmud in relative chronological order, moving from that point to reliable historical evidence is virtually impossible. Kraemer writes, ". . . [M]ost sorts of political, social, and religious histories cannot be constructed on the basis of Rabbinic testimony."[84]

These discussions have taken place within the environment of traditional historical enquiries. However, it should be clear that anyone who believes he has written the definitive traditional historical account of anything about Jews or Judaism in late antiquity will experience a rude awakening when his work reaches the public arena. Because of

---

[82] Stemberger, "Rabbinic Sources," 185-186.

[83] D. Kraemer, "Rabbinic Sources for Historical Study," in Neusner and Avery-Peck, *Judaism in Late Antiquity*, II:201-212.

[84] Kraemer, "Rabbinic Sources," 201.

the paucity of non-rabbinic and non-literary artifacts from late antiquity in Iraq, these problems are most acute for those interested in the Babylonian Jews who produced and appear in the Babylonian Talmud. Because we possess a good deal of non-rabbinic, even non-Jewish information about Jews in Syria-Palestine, and elsewhere in the "west,"[85] scholars are in a relatively better situation when discussing these Jews. But even here, we face a myriad of complex issues.[86]

V

We have seen that the historian faces certain dilemmas, some of which can be eliminated if we give up the impossible goal of total objectivity, accuracy, and finality in our individual studies. The past exists only in the artifacts which we have in the present.[87] However we imagine or construct the past or the mindset of those who produced the artifacts in which we are interested, we do so only because we accept at least three major assumptions about the past. We first assume that the past existed. Even though now it exists only in our minds, it did exist at one time independently of our current thinking about it. We further assume and that while the past is different from the present, it is also like the present in some ways.[88] This means that we can never know everything about the past. But, we can know some things about the past because we also assume that those who lived in the past are not radically dissimilar from us.[89] Finally, we assume that we can know some things about the past because the evidence we have points to one or another reality which existed outside of our thinking about it.

Each one of these assumptions is fraught with a multitude of philosophical and theoretical problems. However, the most philosophically and methodologically sophisticated historians find ways to wind their ways through the maze of discussions of these assumptions along with

---

[85] For example see L.V. Rutgers, *The Jews in Late Ancient Rome: Evidence of Cultural Interaction in the Roman Diaspora* (Leiden, Boston, Koln: 1994); Fergus Millar: *The Roman Near East: 31 B.C.–A.D. 337* (Cambridge, London: 1993); Hayim Lapin, *Religious and Ethnic Communities in Late Roman Palestine* (Bethesda: 1998); G.W. Bowersock, *Roman Arabia* (Cambridge, London: 1983).
[86] See Boyarin, *Dying for God*.
[87] Appleby, Hunt, and Jacob, 33; 255.
[88] Bunge, *Social Science under Debate*, 262.
[89] V.A. Harvey, *The Historian and the Believer: The Morality of Historical Knowledge and Christian Belief* (Urbana and Chicago, 1996), 14. At this point Harvey is explaining the three principles upon which Ernst Troeltsch claimed history rested. This is Troeltsch's principle of analogy.

those of us who are less concerned with the methodological issues underlying the writing of history. The best historians study the past, realizing that they do so in the present. They know the past is different from the present, but they assume that they similar enough that they can draw on their own experiences and their own knowledge to answers the questions they have posed, fully aware that their analogies are not perfect and that they can never know if all of their analogies are accurate or if the answers they have found for their questions are correct. Finally, they understand that historical knowledge, that is knowledge of the past, like all knowledge, is cumulative. The historian builds on the artifacts remaining from the past and previous interpretations of those artifacts. As new artifacts appear, they and their significance must be integrated into previous studies. Their emergence may supplement previous work or contradict prior solutions to problems. Whatever the case, they must be dealt with and the whole set of problems to which they are relevant must be tackled anew. Similarly, new methods for analyzing and interpreting data arise constantly. New insights into the complexities of nature or the workings of human societies and cultures may frequently necessitate reevaluating the evidence previously gathered or looking at it in new ways. New insights into literature, art, music, architecture, clothing, games, gender, etc. often provide us with fresh ways to understand previously studied artifacts. New methods of analysis may produce an original understanding of old artifacts or may even produce additional data which raise new questions. And, all new questions require new answers; new methods of analysis mandate a new investigation of the data.[90]

If each historian approaches the data from her own point of view, the only way we can move from total subjectivity to relative objectivity is, according to Appleby, Hunt, and Jacob, for each historian to be part of an open community of dialogue. Historians must make their work available for others to study, learn from, and criticize. By the same token, they must be an active participant in the community – reading the work of others, continually studying the artifacts of the past relevant to their concerns, remaining open to new ideas, new methods, new artifacts, new studies, and new perspectives. No historian ever solves a problem for all time; no historian ever closes her mind to the possibility that she has been wrong; no historian assumes that she has said all there is to say on any given topic. No historian

---

[90] Green and Troup, *The Houses of History*, vii; Bunge, *Social Science under Debate*, 264; Appleby, Hunt, and Jacob, *Telling the Truth*, 262.

14. PORTON *Can We Write a History of Judaism in Late Antiquity?* 403

who wishes to remain a historian can stop participating in the open discussion of the past. The point is that a collection of individual subjective studies placed side by side, or more appropriately one on top of the other, can produce the closest thing to objective information about the past that we can hope to achieve.

The need to be in constant conversation with other historians and to be open to revising one's work does not mean that all historical conversations are merely about equally valid personal opinions about the past. Each field of historical study requires a variety of expertise to discover, analyze, and communicate information about the data. In addition, there are informal and formal "rules" for using evidence, constructing arguments, supporting opinions. Not *everyone's* interpretation of the past needs to be accepted as equally valid in the conversation among historians. Some people simply lack the skills and knowledge required for participation.[91] Each work's use of evidence must be evaluated; each argument must be analyzed; each conclusion must be subjected to rigorous evaluation. Sloppy thinking, cavalier uses of evidence, weak arguments all must be rejected. Not everyone who attempts to construct a serious historical study succeeds.

Even though documents are open to many interpretations, those explanations are not random, nor are they unbounded. Words, discourses, texts, documents have meaning within their cultural milieu. The historian's task is to discover as much as possible about that society and the cultural setting which produced the document. Much of this work demands a careful analysis of the text itself. In addition, however, the text must be related to the other artifacts from that society which we possess. While we cannot help but read each text from our own point of view, we can also use that point of view as a lens into the past.

One should not conclude that because historians must engage in constant interchanges with one another that nothing about the past can ever be learned because nothing is ever settled. For the most part, historians tend to disagree about comparatively minor matters or specific details. As stated above, while historians may offer mutually exclusive interpretations of the data, the different perspectives from which they analyze the data are not mutually exclusive. If one historian interprets a text from the male perspective and another historian reads it from a female perspective, the latter historian has not negated the former historian's reading; she has merely complicated the task of inter-

[91] Appleby, Hunt, and Jacob, *Telling the Truth*, 261-263.

pretation. Furthermore, as Appleby, Hunt, and Jacob remind us, "perspective does not mean opinion; it refers to a point of view – literally, point from which something, an object outside the mind, is viewed."[92] Gaining knowledge about the past which is as accurate as possible takes time and the effort of many people, perhaps over an extended period of time. The trek may be arduous and time consuming, but the final view may be stunning.

---

[92] Appleby, Hunt, and Jacob, *Telling the Truth*, 256.

15

Different Ways of Looking at Truth

William Scott Green

On February 16, 2006, the *Los Angeles Times*[1] ran the following headline: "Bedrock of a Faith is Jolted: DNA tests contradict Mormon scripture. The church says the studies are being used to attack its beliefs." The story that followed, by William Lobdell, explained that scientific evidence appears directly to contradict important claims about the past made in the Book of Mormon, the church's scripture. According to the Book of Mormon, "a 175-year old transcription that the church regards as literal and without error," a tribe of Israelites sailed from Jerusalem to the New World in 600 BCE and divided into two contending factions: the God-fearing Nephites and the idolatrous Lamanites. The Lamanites, whom the church regards as the ancestors of native Americans and Polynesians, prevailed over the Nephites. The Book of Mormon asserts that "Native Americans were descended from a lost tribe of Israel that reached the New World more than 2,000 years ago."

According to the *Times*, DNA evidence shows that "the ancestors of American natives came from Asia, not the Middle East." Some figures in the church, "scholars who defend the faith" known as "apologists," have offered an "alternative interpretation" to the "traditional reading of the Book of Mormon – that the Hebrews were the first and the sole inhabitants of the New World and eventually populated the North and South American continents." The apologists argue that the "latest scholarship shows that the text should be interpreted differently. They say the events described in the Book of Mormon were confined to a small section of Central America, and that the Hebrew tribe was small enough that its DNA was swallowed up by the

---

[1] http://www.latimes.com/news/printedition/la-me-mormon16feb16,1,4709667.story?coll=la-news-comment-opinions&track=mostemailedlink

existing Native Americans." On this interpretation, the absence of the Israelite DNA is not surprising.

For some Mormons, the DNA evidence has undermined the credibility of church teachings and produced a sense of loss. Jose A. Loayza, a Salt Lake City attorney, describes the religious meaning and importance of the Book of Mormon's claims about the past: "We were taught all the blessings of that Hebrew lineage belonged to us and that we were special people. It not only made me feel special, but it gave me a sense of transcendental identity, an identity with God." Phil Ormsby, a Polynesian from Brisbane, Australia, reinforced the sense of identity that the claim of Israelite descent provides: "I visualized myself among the fighting Lamanites and lived out the fantasies [of the Book of Mormon] as I read it. It gave me great *mana* [prestige] to know that these were my true ancestors." For others, the DNA evidence has had little impact. The story cites Michael Otterson, a Mormon church official, "'The truth is, the Book of Mormon will never be proved or disproved by science.'" Professor Jan Shipps, Indiana University-Purdue University Indianapolis, an established scholar of Mormonism, assessed the data's impact on the religion: "'This may look like the crushing blow to Mormonism from the outside, but religion ultimately does not rest on scientific evidence, but on mystical experiences. There are different ways of looking at truth.'"

This account of the Book of Mormon and DNA – even if somewhat simplified – helps to make concrete the issues that animate this anthology. The story illustrates two different ways of knowing the past. One is represented by the Book of Mormon. As scripture, the Book of Mormon is the supernatural, normative warrant for a community, what Professor Mason calls a "charter narrative." The Book of Mormon describes what happened in the past and thus makes claims that are, *ipso facto*, historical. Jose Loayaza and Phil Ormsby show how such historical claims provide not only identity, but also prestige, purpose, meaning, and even transcendence. In this context, knowledge of the past is weighty and consequential. It anchors life – individual and collective. A second way of approaching the past is in the evidence of the DNA and the work of the Mormon "apologists." As a fact of nature – a datum our culture regards as both empirical and observable – the DNA evidence restricts what reasonably can be said about the Mormon past. The DNA is accidental and therefore neutral evidence. It is not the product of a text. It has no agenda and advocates no position. For the Mormon apologists, apparently, the empirical evidence of the DNA was a prod to reread, rethink, and re-understand at least one claim of their scripture. Their understanding of their text changed because of evidence that is immovable and unavoidable.

These two ways of appropriating the past – one based on a received and revealed text, the other on a neutral datum of nature – represent the "two kinds of historical knowledge" to which Professor Neusner refers in his Preface to this volume. They are roughly analogous to the categories "tradition" and "history" that Professor Mason develops. One kind of historical knowledge is present in the way a religious community knows itself to be a product of the past and uses the past, "to account for itself over time" and in the present. A second kind of historical knowledge is generated by critical, academic historians. Professor Porton demonstrates that academic history employs the critical attitudes and procedures of enlightenment, modern, and/or postmodern thought. The knowledge of the past it produces differs considerably in scope and epistemology from the knowledge produced by religious communities about their own past.

It is a virtual axiom of critical history that these two ways of knowing the past are fundamentally divergent and incompatible, that they share few, if any, common elements. It is conventional to assign the foundation of these two approaches to the Jews and the Greeks. Edmund B. Fryde[2] spells out the differences:

> The greatest and the most original achievement of the best Greek historians lay in their clear grasp of the need to distinguish truth from fiction and their conscious preoccupation with the methods of achieving this. This is admirably conveyed in a famous passage of Thucydides.
>
>> And with reference to the narrative of events, far from permitting myself to derive it from the source that came to hand, I did not even trust my own impressions, but it rests partly on what I saw myself, partly on what others saw for me, the accuracy of the report being always tried by the most severe and detailed tests possible. My conclusions have cost me some labour from the want of coincidence between accounts of the same occurrences by different eye-witnesses, arising sometimes from deficient memory, sometimes from deficient impartiality.
>
> The triumph of Christianity in the Roman Empire during the fourth century assured the predominance of a type of historiography radically different from the works of the pagan Greek and Roman historians. Its origins were Jewish. The Jews were the only people of antiquity who

---

[2] E.B. Fryde, "Historiography and Historical Method," *Encyclopedia Britannica* ([15]1978), VIII, 945-961: 947.

had the supreme religious duty of remembering the past because their traditional histories commemorated the working out of God's plan for his chosen people. By contrast, no Greek ever heard his gods ordering him to remember... The writers of these biblical books only gave an authoritative version of what everybody was supposed to know, and they were only concerned with the selection of such facts as seemed relevant in interpreting God's purpose.

In Fryde's description, historical knowledge in the Greek mode distinguishes "truth" from "fiction." By contrast, historical knowledge in the biblical mode consists of an "authoritative version" of the past marked by "the selection of such facts as seemed relevant in interpreting God's purpose." The "selection" of facts "relevant" to "God's purpose" apparently makes biblical historical knowledge "radically different" from that of the Greeks. The papers gathered here constitute a useful setting in which to explore and assess Fryde's distinction.[3]

In his review of recent developments in history writing, Professor Porton observes:

While discrete data may remain which are a result of past realities, one of the historian's tasks is to put that data together in order to discover from what/where they originated. The historians create the picture of the past from the data they encounter and the ways in which they assemble the data into a coherent account. Above all, this task is a mental process accomplished by individuals who have been nurtured in particular intellectual and cultural environments. Historical studies only answer the questions which the historians pose, and those questions are shaped by the historians' personalities, with all of their strengths and weaknesses, which reflect their cultural environments.

Theodore Hamerow's reflections on the changing nature of history supply additional illustrations of Professor Porton's point. Professor

---

[3] Professor Mason expresses a similar view: "First, the quest of Greek philosophers from the presocratics to Aristotle to know things by direct observation produced "the father of history," Herodotus of Halicarnassus – who first applied the Greek word-group for active "research" or "investigation" (*historie, historia;* verb *historiein*) to the study of the past – and the Athenian Thucydides, who advanced a rigorous program for cross-examining witnesses to the (recent) past. But the promise of that era, in history as in science, was never realized because of the prevailing social structures, discussed above. As long as knowledge remained in the hands of elite authorities, progress was severely limited in scope. And once that elite authority passed to religious leaders, in the fourth and fifth centuries CE, so that knowledge of history became the more tightly bound up with tradition and trust (or faith), it would take the combined force of the Renaissance, Reformation, Age of Reason, and European Enlightenment (16th to 18th centuries) to displace this intellectual juggernaut."

Hamerow explains that, before 1945, the leading historians accepted "the view that historical learning should focus on the bearers of authority and wielders of power."[4]

What historians wrote rested on underlying assumptions regarding the relative significance of the various kinds of data which the past presented for their consideration. They established a hierarchy of values in determining the importance of what had happened, a scale of priorities by which they decided which part of collective experience was worth preserving in historical memory.[5]

After 1945, Hamerow explains, the writing of history changed. What is known as the "new history was critical of the elites who had monopolized historical learning in the past. It found its heroes among the poor, oppressed, exploited, and ignored." The new history "changed the scale of values by which the significance of historical experience was determined."[6] Hamerow's description of history as in some central way a function of historians' "hierarchy of values" and "scale of priorities" reminds us that history is a value-driven activity.

The observations of Professors Porton and Hamerow implicitly acknowledge, and perhaps presuppose, what the philosopher of history Leon Goldstein referred to as the "epistemic impenetrability of the past."[7] Anticipating the general position of many contemporary historians, Professor Goldstein argued that, the "function of historical research is to constitute the historical past"[8] rather than to discover it. In his view, the "historical past is not the real past; it is the product of intellect and can never be known by acquaintance."[9] This is not an argument for intellectual relativism or the equivalence of all historical accounts. Rather, it is a recognition of the ineluctable perspectivalism that shapes knowledge of the past, even that produced by the academy. For the authors Professor Porton cites, the corrective to this appears to be incessant conversations among historians of different perspectives and comparisons of historical work. Useful and valuable as it is, even such exercise will fall short of achieving either objective or comprehensive knowledge of the past. As any group of academics knows from

---

[4] T.S. Hamerow, *Reflections on History and Historians* (The University of Wisconsin Press, 1987), 163.
[5] Hamerow, *Reflections*, 163.
[6] Hamerow, *Reflections*, 164-165.
[7] L.J. Goldstein, *Historical Knowing* (Austin, 1976), 9.
[8] Goldstein, *Historical Knowing*, xix.
[9] Goldstein, *Historical Knowing*, 38.

experience, consensus, even among professors, is no guarantee of objectivity or accuracy.

The chapters in this volume illustrate the diverse ways ancient and modern writers use perspective to constitute the past. The writings that draw or rely upon the materials in the Hebrew Bible graphically illustrate how a point of view can create the past. Professor Chilton's chapters display the varied interests that went into the composition of a range of biblical texts. His discussions of the multiple Israels in the Hebrew Bible and the varied Christian communities evident in early Christian writing show how focused and deliberate a group's appropriation of the biblical heritage could be. Professor Schiffman's chapter on the Dead Sea Scrolls and Professor Nickelsburg's on Jewish apocalyptic literature clearly show how these communities read and appropriated Israel's past in terms of themselves. In Professor Mason's description, Josephus' writing appears as the quintessential example of the historian's constitution of the past.

> The proposition I want to advance here is that Josephus is the creator of his compositions in much the same way that an artist (say, a painter or sculptor) is a creator, even if she uses a model and attempts realistic representation of it. The model is lost to us, and only the art remains. Or if you prefer, Josephus's writing process resembles the combined efforts of screenplay-writer and director in a contemporary film dealing with historical subjects (e.g., *Gladiator, Troy, Elizabeth,* or *The Passion of the Christ*). Although these films have an undeniable basis in "historical reality" – in events that really occurred and lives actually lived – and even though we know this as we watch the films, we realize that we are watching the invention, the *creation* from beginning to end, of a writer and director. Knowing *that* historical realities underlie the work does not immediately help us, in the absence of additional resources, to know *which* parts originated where... Josephus has created a master-work, a production combining intricate plot and colorful characters, based largely on real events and people but under his absolute authorial-directorial control.

Finally, Professor Neusner's treatment of the rabbinic view of history shows that the rabbis approached their scriptural past with paradigmatic thinking that shaped what they read and how they understood it. He explains:

> ... the only history the Rabbinic sages deem worth narrating – and not in sustained narrative even then – is the story of the Temple cult through days and months and years, and the history of the Temple and its priesthood and administration through time and into eternity. We now fully

understand that fact. It is because, to begin with, the very conception of paradigmatic thinking as against the historical kind took shape in deep reflection on the meaning of events: what happened before has happened again – to the Temple. Ways of telling time before give way, history's premises having lost plausibility here as much as elsewhere. Now Israel will tell time in nature's way, shaping history solely in response to what happens in the cult and to the Temple. There is no other history, because, to begin with, there is no history.

In the ancient world, Jews and Christians of varied religious orientations, locations, cultures, and political circumstance read the same scripture but found different stories in it, always about themselves. Israel's past was their past, and Israel's story was about them. Because Israel's scripture provided a cosmic and chronological framework that extended back to the beginning of space and time, it offered the longest of long perspectives, the biggest of big pictures. This temporal framework may help explain how all the biblically based texts and groups considered here – Israelite groups, apocalyptists, the sect at Qumran, early Christians, and rabbis – in different ways saw themselves as the product of a continual historical process that both stretched far back in time and reached forward to shape, determine, and account for their own lives. Perhaps it is not too much to ask if the nature of the biblical narrative itself encouraged those who relied on it to conceive the past in terms of enduring structures and purposive unbroken courses of time rather than episodic recent events.

According to Professor Dewald, the Greek approach was different. Herodotus and Thucydides, who – Dewald and Mason agree – devised the basic framework of critical historical investigation, wrote not about the distant but about the recent past: the Persian and Peloponnesian wars, respectively. Herodotus wanted to know why the Greeks defeated the Persians, and "he investigated by collecting and critiquing hundreds of stories from all over the Aegean basin." Herodotus's contribution to writing history, Professor Dewald explains, was in the novel and unprecedented range and management of his evidence.

> The meaning of the story, according to Herodotus, however, is not univocal, and it is not his own. It rather arises out of the patterns formed by the stories themselves. The only caveat he gives as an author is that one cannot listen selectively, only to the stories one likes, or that glorify people or causes one likes or that are convenient to one's own ideological purposes... History in Herodotus's hands was not propaganda for a particular point of view, religion, or race, not wish fulfillment or morality tale, but useful for its readers because it explored the process of change

over time, as a serious, critical record of the real doings and thoughts of many real people, ordinary and extraordinary from the lived human past.

Thucydides, as we saw above, "took Herodotus's method of careful collection and investigation of stories from the past and adapted it to tell, as his own account, a narrative that he felt was important, holding himself personally accountable to tell it as accurately as possible." What makes both historians credible, Professor Dewald suggests, is the multivocity of their accounts.

> Many real human voices go into the making of the narratives of our two historians, and that is ultimately why we trust both Herodotus's *Persian Wars* and Thucydides's *Peloponnesian War* as 'real' – that is, in some way credible – history, rather than fiction (as Hayden White and some other post-modern historiographers would have it). Herodotus's voices are the voices of the many stories from the past that he retells, while Thucydides's voices are those of the actors in events. But in each case, the historian is listening for the truth of a plot line that is not in its deepest sense his own. He is rather the critical, investigatory intelligence that finds the sources and determines if they are real and serious or not: but his goal is to find out what really happened, as best he can – not to impose his own favorite plot line on events.

But even the "critical, investigatory intelligence" Professor Dewald rightly attributes to the founders of history was not immune to the influence of perspective. Professor Mason reminds us that history writing was in some sense a matter of class and education and not agenda-free, and Dewald suggests how Thucydides's allegiance to the Periclean vision of democracy helped shape his account of the Peloponnesian War.

If it is the case that the past, and thus our knowledge of it, is constituted rather than discovered – or at least as constituted as it is discovered – then we can see the basic approaches to the knowing past represented by the Bible and the Greeks as on a continuum rather than in opposition to one another. At one fundamental level, each approach aims to understand the truth about the past. Neither assumes that it is engaged in the promulgation of falsehood. The kind of truth each approach seeks shapes the questions it brings to the past and the way it answers them. The Greeks juxtaposed and interrogated their sources of the recent past to account for a contemporary political situation. By most scholarly reckonings, the biblical writers merged and integrated sources to produce a single narrative that addressed basic questions of meaning, identity, and continuity. Each effort yielded a compelling picture of the past that addressed some interest in the present. If the historical past is constituted, then the work of history in some basic measure is not only a matter of finding out "what actually happened," but also of understanding how those who preceded us constituted their past to explain themselves.

This is not to suggest that historical knowledge is solely a matter of perspective. To the contrary, all accounts of the past are constrained in one way or another. In the case of the biblical constitution of the past, those constraints are partly, perhaps largely, theological. In the case of the more critical history that derives from the Greeks, the constraints are likely to be about argument and evidence. Herodotus and Thucydides had access to the testimonies of eyewitnesses, which they could compare and contrast. The problem for contemporary historians, Goldstein suggests, is how to "justify the claim that it is possible *now* to make warranted and responsible assertions about events in the human past which are forever beyond the scrutiny of the historian who makes them."[10] Critical history, in other words, is marked by a self-consciousness about evidence, method, and argument.

In this regard, the papers gathered here supply a valuable picture of the constraints on critical history of the ancient world. One component of that picture is the judgment that multiple sources are more useful as evidence than individual ones. Critical history does not and cannot begin with the assumption that all sources are reliable until proven otherwise. Rather, each must be assessed and evaluated. As in the case of Herodotus and Thucydides, multiple witnesses provide an excellent control. If there is only a single source, then a means must be found to make that source testify against itself. In biblical studies, the methods of literary criticism and form criticism are standard means to achieve that end. As Professor Mason rightly insists, in the absence of these controls, there may be no way for us to penetrate behind an ancient source. A second component of the picture is the centrality of language. The bulk of our sources are literary; they are species of writing. Writing is material and therefore empirical evidence. Close and careful attention to language provides a firm ground on which to identify choices in writing that authors made. A third element of critical history is the importance of discovered material evidence. In many cases, archaeological evidence, which is uncovered rather than transmitted, acts as the DNA evidence does in the case of the Book of Mormon. In an unavoidable way, it constrains what can be said. Professor Aviam's discussion of multiple material remains from ancient

---

[10] Goldstein, *Historical Knowing*, 143.

Galilee demonstrates how archaeology can help us understand who lived where in ancient Galilee and thereby shape and clarify our reading of ancient texts.

Once the empirical character and context of our sources have been identified, the next question for critical history is how to read them. In this regard, there is broad agreement among our authors that it is more difficult for us to derive social and political history from these texts than to study the history of ancient religion. To be sure, some political and social history emerges from the correspondence of elements of apocalyptic and Qumran texts to information present in other texts, but it is small in comparison to the material about the history of religion. For religion and history, Professor Chilton, whose work takes up a substantial portion of this book, has developed a comprehensive program. His approach builds on a clear recognition of the literary character of the primary evidence about Jesus, Paul, Mary Magdalene, and James. He brings to these texts what he calls a "generative question" or a "generative exegesis." He explains, using Jesus and James as examples:

> ... the Gospels (as well as other documents) refer back to Jesus as their point of generation, and we may infer what practices Jesus engaged in, what beliefs he adhered to, what teachings he promulgated, so as to produce the accounts concerning him in the communities of followers that produced the documents. The framing world of those practices and beliefs in the formative period of the New Testament (whether in the case of Jesus, James or their followers) was Judaism. Practices and beliefs are attested in the documents manifestly, whether or not their attribution to Jesus is accepted, and that is a suitable point of departure for the genuinely critical question of Jesus. That question cannot critically be formulated as, What did Jesus really say and really do? The critical issue is rather, What role did Jesus play in the evolution of practices and beliefs in his name?
>
> That generative question may be broadened, of course, to apply not only to Jesus and the Gospels, but also to primitive Christianity and the New Testament. In the present case, that involves specifying the practices and beliefs that attach to James within the sources, and seeking to understand his place within them. Not every practice, not every belief may be assumed to be correctly attributed to James, but the various streams of tradition the documents represent do come together to constitute stable associations of practices and beliefs with James. The nodal issues of practices and beliefs, not "facts," represent our point of departure.

With this approach, Professor Chilton seeks to apprehend the Jesus and James of history through the testimony about community belief and practice attested in the literary sources about them. By paying close attention to the language of those sources and seeking a context for that language in the literature and archaeology of Judaism and, in the case of Paul at least, the urban culture of the ancient Mediterranean, he identifies grounds for controlled inferences back to the figures of history. The strength and plausibility of this approach rest in the considerable degree to which it cleaves closely to the empirical evidence of the sources and produces efficient, rational explanations. The strategy of the "generative question" seeks to move behind a text to what produced it. In this regard, Professor Avery-Peck reminds us that the notion that events or deeds generate texts is but one explanation. Texts, reflection on them, and imagination about them also can generate writing, and this is a useful caveat for historians to keep in mind.

In the rich array of historical materials discussed in this book, we are the beneficiaries of both the Greeks and the Bible. From Herodotus and Thucydides, we have derived the questions and tools of critical history. For its part, the Bible has contributed the long perspective on time that reaches back to the beginning. When we write modern ancient history, we draw on both legacies. We constitute the past as the Greeks would have liked us to do, and we examine the extended and interconnected past that the Bible envisioned. Our intellectual efforts are richer for that mix.

Index of Authors

Adan Bayewitz, D. 197, 213
Akenson, D.H. 359
Alexander, P.S. 65
Allegro, J.M. 60
Allison, D.C. 239
Alon, G. 378
Amit, D. 117
Amitai A. 197, 213
Amoussine, J.D. 56
Anderson, R. 284
Appleby, J. 34, 51, 377, 386, 388,
    389, 391, 393, 397, 401,
    403, 404
Argall, R.A. 94, 99
Ariel, D.T. 204, 213
Auerbach, E. 31
Avery-Peck, A. 92, *175–195*,
    183, 221, 398, 399
Avi-Yonah, M. 378
Aviam, M. 133, *196–215*, 197,
    200, 203, 204, 206, 212,
    213, 214, 215, 385
Avshalom-Gorni, D. 200, 215

Bacher, W. 377
Bakker, E. 51
Bar Ilan, M. 282
Barber, M. 309
Baron, A. 382
Barr 151
Barrett, C.K. 274
Bartel, S.S. 222
Baskin, J.R. 385, 396
Bauckham, R. 278, 281, 284

Baumgarten, J.M. 67, 72, 222
Begg, C.T. 119
Ben Arieh, R. 205, 214
Bentley, M. 377, 384
Berchman, R.M. 221
Bergmeier, R. 135
Berkhofer, R. 52
Berlin, A. 91, 133, 197, 214
Bernheim, A. 278, 279
Berrin, S. 64
Betz, H.D. 316
Beyer, P. 380
Biale, D. 378, 384
Bieringer, R. 227
Biran, A. 205, 214
Black, M. 133
Blackman, D.R. 116
Bloch, M. 134
Bloom, H. 303, 324
Boccaccini, G. 100
Böcher, O. 238
Bockmuehl, M. 287, 301
Boertien, M. 292, 293, 294
Bokser, B.M. 385
Bond, H.K. 113
Borgen, P. 220
Bow, B.A. 94
Bowersock, G.W. 374, 401
Boyarin, D. 394, 395, 401
Boyle, A.J. 138
Braudel, F. 384
Breisach, E. 376
Brenon, A. 309
Brettler, M.Z. 91

Bright, J. 31
Brock, A.G. 311
Brockington, L.H. 103
Brooke, G.J. 56, 67, 74
Brooks, R. 191
Broshi, M. 62, 72, 133
Brown, P. 374
Brown, R.E. 251
Brownlee, W.H. 55
Broyles, C.C. 221
Büchler, A. 377
Bunge, M. 389, 401
Bunzl, M. 384
Burdajewicz, M. 205, 215
Burke, P. 376, 377

Callaway, P.R. 56
Carr, E.H. 386
Carroll, K.L. 288
Carson, D.A. 220
Chancey, M.A. 197, 200, 214
Charles, R.H. 103
Charlesworth, J.H. 56, 84, 221, 319
Chazon, E.G. 96, 239
Chico 191
Chilton, B.D. *1–31*, 31, *216–248*, 217, 218, 219, 220, 223, 226, 230, 231, 232, 233, 236, 238, 240, 241, 242, 243, 244, 245, 246, 247, *249–277*, 252, 265, 266, 267, 268, 269, 271, *278–301*, 279, 280, 282, 283, 284, 285, 287, 289, 290, 291, 297, 300, 301, *302–328*, 303, 305, 306, 307, 308, 313, 318, 324, 325, 326, 327, 328, *329–373*, 362, 368, 369, 372
Clarke, K.L. 120
Clifford, R. 87
Clines, D.J.A. 220
Cohen, S.D. 282, 330, 378, 379
Collingwood, R.G. 127, 134, 137

Collins, A.Y. 84
Collins, J.J. 56, 79, 81, 84, 87, 91, 99, 103
Connolly, R.H. 311
Connor, R. 35, 51, 52
Conzelmann, H. 372
Copan, P. 218
Cranfield, C.E.B. 371
Cribiore, R. 120
Cross, F.M. 56, 71, 190
Crossan, J.D. 217, 232, 318

Dailey, F.F. 86
Dalley, S. 235
Dan, J. 234
Dautenberg, G. 221
David, Jesus ben 245
Davies, P.R. 31, 74, 218
Davies, W.D. 31, 367, 383
de Jong, I. 51
de Jonge, M. 383
de Moor, J.C. 221
Degani, A. 197, 203, 204, 214
Delcor, M. 56
Derenbourg, J. 378
Dewald, C. 32–52, 37, 51, 52
Diamond, E. 284
Dimant, D. 55
Dominik, W.J. 138
Dupont-Sommer, A. 56
Durant, A. 382
Durant, W. 382

Edmondson, J. 138
Edwards, D.R. 232
Ehrman, B. 302
Eilberg-Schwartz, H. 186
Eisenberg, M. 205, 215
Eisenman, R.H. 278, 283
Engler, R. 390
Epp, E.J. 386
Eshel, E. 62, 64
Eshel, H. 56, 60, 64
Evans, C.A. 217, 218, 220, 221, 231, 279, 318, 369
Eyben, E. 135

Feldman, L.H. 119
Fiedler, P. 221
Finkelstein, L. 31, 383
Finley, M.I. 387
Fischer, M. 205, 214
Fitzmyer, J.A. 285
Fornberg, T. 101
Foucault, M. 394
Fowl, S.E. 220
Frankel, R. 197, 203, 204, 214
Freedman, D.N. 56, 317
Frerichs, E.S. 220
Friedland, E. 205, 214
Fryde, E.B. 407
Funk, R.W. 219
Funkenstein, A. 377, 387
Furnish, V.P. 236

Gafni, I. 378
Galchinsky, M. 384
Gardner, Z. 105
Gese, H. 275
Getzov, N. 197, 203, 204, 214
Gillman, F.M. 296
Goitein, S.D. 375
Golb, N. 56
Goldstein, J.A. 97
Goldstein, L.J. 409, 413
Goodblatt, D. 378, 385
Goodenough, E.R. 31
Goodman, M. 133, 134, 378, 379
Gottwald, N.K. 31
Gould, J. 51, 52
Grabar, O. 374
Grabbe, L.L. 132
Graetz, H. 382
Graf, D.F. 317
Grässer, E., Merk, O. 286
Green, A. 377, 384, 386, 392, 393, 402
Green, J.B. 218
Green, W.S. *196–215*, 215, 385, *405–415*
Greenfield, J.C. 56
Greenstein, E.L. 379
Grisbrooke, W.J. 311

Guthrie, H. 182
Gutman, S. 200, 214

Haases, W. 385
Hachlili, R. 317
Hadas, M. 382, 387
Haenchen, E. 284
Hagner, D.A. 220
Hamerow, T. 408, 409
Harrington, D.J. 285
Harvey, V.A. 401
Haskins, S. 304
Hauptman, J. 396
Havelaar, H.W. 221
Heinrich, C. 238
Hellholm, D. 101
Hengel, M. 275
Herbert, S.C. 197, 214
Herion, G.A. 317
Herman, S. 176, 179, 180, 188
Heschel, S. 384
Hirschfeld, Y. 117
Hodge, A.T. 116
Hoover, R.W. 219
Horgan, M. 55, 56
Hornblower, S. 51, 52
Horsley, R. 220
Horsley, R.A. 94, 208, 214, 232, 244, 392
Howard, I.H. 218
Hunt, L. 34, 51, 377, 386, 388, 389, 391, 393, 397, 401, 403, 404
Hurst, L.D. 287

Idel, M. 234
Ilan, T. 316
Immerwahr, H. 37, 52
Isaac, E. 271
Issac, B. 205, 214
Iwry, S. 74

Jacob, M. 34, 51, 377, 386, 388, 389, 391, 393, 397, 401, 403, 404
Jaffee, M. 191, 392

Jaros, K. 113
Jenkins, K. 52
Jervell, J. 274, 359
Johnson, L.T. 217
Joseph, J.E. 390
Jost, J.M. 378, 382
Juster, J. 378

Kalmin, R. 398
Keck, L.E. 217
Kee, H.C. 1, 31, 319
King, K.L. 312
Kittel, G. 298
Kitzberger, I.R. 316
Klijn, A.F.J. 103
Kloner, A. 214
Kloppenborg, J.S. 93
Knibb, M.A. 74
Knox, J. 251, 256
Kraemer, D. 400
Kraemer, R.S. 385
Kraft, R.A. 31, 386
Kugler, R. 222

Laato, A. 221
Lambert, M. 309
Lang 222
Lang, B. 235
Lapin, H. 218, 401
Lateiner, D. 51, 52
Leany, A.R.C. 31
Lebeau, P. 301
LeGoff, J. 145, 147
LeLoup, J-Y. 312
Lembi, G. 138
Lemche, N.P. 31
Lémonon, J.-P. 113
Leveau, P. 116
Levine, L.I. 375
Lightfoot, J.B. 282, 286
Lim, T.H. 56
Linder, A. 375
Livingstone, E.A. 218
Loayaza, J. 406
Lovering, E.H. 221

MacCulloch, J. 182
Maclean, N. 166, 167
MacRae, G.W. 386
Magen, Y. 214
Malherbe, A.J. 251, 290
Mandelbaum 191
Marincola, J. 51, 52
Martínez, F.G. 56, 96
Mason, S. *105–138*, 132, 138, 408
McCollough, C.T. 232
McGuire, A. 311
McKnight, S. 218, 363
McNamara, M. 31
Meeks, W. 290
Meier, J.P. 218, 281
Mendenhall, G.E. 31
Metzger, B.M. 103
Meyer, M. 377, 387
Meyers, E.M. 3, 197, 215, 392
Michel, O. 371
Milikowsky, C. 74
Millar, F. 133, 401
Mlynarczyk, J. 205, 215
Morgenstern, M. 316
Murphy-O'Connor, J. 255, 256, 257, 258, 264, 360

Nau, F. 311
Neusner, J. 31, 92, *139–174*, 161, 179, 191, 193, 194, 208, 217, 220, 221, 265, 279, 280, 282, 287, 290, *329–373*, 330, 360, 362, 363, 365, 368, 375, 383, 396, 398, 399
Newman 191
Newsom, C.A. 60
Nickelsburg, G.W.E. 31, *79–104*, 82, 83, 84, 85, 87, 88, 89, 91, 92, 93, 94, 95, 96, 97, 98, 99, 100, 101, 102, 103, 386
Nitzan, B. 55, 56
Noble, G. 284
Normand 390

North, R. 74
Noth, M. 31
Novakovic, L. 56

Oppenheimer, A. 182
Ormsby, P. 406
Ovadiah, A. 205, 214
Overman, A. 133, 205

Painter, J. 278
Pardee, D. 56
Parry, D. 56
Pasquier, A. 312
Patrich, J. 117
Pennington, A. 104
Perdue, L. 99
Peskowitz, M.B. 396
Pfann, S.J. 65
Pinnick, A. 378
Pleins, J.D. 317
Pollefeyt, D. 227
Popkes, W. 287
Porter, S.E. 220
Porton, G.G. *374-404*, 408
Pratscher, W. 278
Price, J.J. 134
Priest, J. 84, 103

Qimron, E. 66, 67, 71, 72

Rabin, C. 103
Rabinowitz, I. 73
Radding, C.M. 187, 188, 189, 190
Ramsay, W. 251
Ramsey, G.W. 143
Rapske, B. 359
Reed, J.L. 232, 363
Rendtorff, R. 222
Richards, K.H. 219
Rives, J. 138
Rodgers, Z. 132
Rogerson, J. 3
Roll, I. 205, 214
Rood, T. 51, 52
Rosenberg, D. 324

Roth, C. 236
Rubinkiewicz, R. 104
Ruck, C.A.P. 238
Ruether, R.R. 375
Rutgers, L.V. 401

Safrai, S. 383
Safrai, Z. 210, 215, 378, 399
Sanders, C. 390
Sarason, R. 182
Sarna, N.S. 220
Saussure 389
Sawicki, M. 282
Schaberg, J. 306, 318, 319
Schader, H.H. 298
Schiffman, L.H. 53-78, 55, 67, 71, 378
Schmithals, W. 288
Scholem, G. 234
Schuler, M. 205, 215
Schürer 133
Schwartz, D.R. 65, 71, 129, 130, 135, 378
Schwartz, S. 378
Scott, J.M. 221, 390
Segal, A. 205, 215
Shaked, I. 200, 215
Sherwin-White, A.N. 131
Shinn, H. 284
Shipps, J. 406
Sievers, J. 138
Simon, M. 375
Smith, D.E. 226
Spengler, O. 382
Spittler, R.P. 319
Staples, B.D. 238
Stauffer, E. 283, 287
Stegemann, H. 56
Stemberger, G. 375, 399, 400
Stern, D. 395
Stewart, A. 205, 215
Stone, M.E. 55, 85, 96, 103
Strack, H.L. 375
Strange, J.F. 392
Strikovsky, A. 204, 213
Strugnell, J. 66, 67, 71

Sussman, Y. 67
Sweet, J.P.M. 103
Syon, D. 133, 198, 199, 206, 214, 215

Tabor, J.D. 235
Talmon, S. 67
Tarn, W.W. 382
Taussig, H. 290
Taylor, J. 237
Temporini, H. 385
Tepper, Y. 214
Teugels, L. 221
Thomas, D.W. 10
Tov, E. 56
Toynbee, A.J. 382
Troup, K. 377, 384, 386, 392, 393, 402
Trubeck, J.M. 180
Tuckett, C.M. 220
Turner, J.D. 311

Ubieta, C.B. 316

van Aarde, A. 282
van Belle, G. 220
van den Broek, R. 309
van der Horst, P.W. 221
van der Woude, A.S. 56
van Segbroeck, F. 220
van Wees, H. 51
Vandecasteele-Vanneuville, F. 227
VanderKam, J.C. 88, 91, 103
Vaux-de-Cernay, P. des 310
Verheyden, J. 220
Vermes, G. 92, 217
Von Rad 190

Watson, A. 176
Weis, R. 309
Weiss, J.H. 378
Werline, R.A. 87, 94
Wieder, N. 74
Williams, R.J. 10
Williamson, G.A. 133

Williamson, H.G.M. 220
Wills, L.M. 96
Wilson, A.N. 253, 254, 255, 259, 260, 262, 264, 265
Wilson, R.M. 284
Wilson, R.R. 31
Wintermute, O. 103
Wise, M. 56
Wojciechowski, M. 301
Wright III, B.G. 96
Wright, N.T. 245, 261, 262, 263, 265

Yardeni, A. 64
Yerushalmi, Y.H. 377, 387

Index of Scripture and Ancient Writers

HEBREW BIBLE
/ OLD TESTAMENT

Genesis
1:1–24 186
1:2 239
2:4 186
2:4b–4 24
2:15 165
2:16 165
3:9 165
3:11 165
3:23 165
5:22 235
6:2 271
10:4 261
11 82
11:1–9 24
11:12 24
15 1, 25
15:1–21 10
17 1
17:1–14 10
22 1, 25
32–33 25
32:22–32 10
37–50 25

Exodus
1–4 25
1:8–10 10
2:15b–22 11
3:18 11
12:12 337
12:40 10
12:48 226, 289
18:13–26 11
19–20 25
20:2 11
20:4–6 115
22:18 316
22–26 11
24 25
24:1–11 11
24:1–8 240
24:9 240, 334
24:10 240
24:10–11 241
24:15 240
24:16 240
24:16b 240
24:17–18 240
27:20 165
32 25
33:30 241
34:29–35 240

Leviticus
3:1–17 12
11 12
11:5–8 59
11:34 297
16:2 373
16:13 373
16:14 373
16:15 373
16:16 373
16:17 373
16:18 373
16:20 373
17–19 27
21:8 336
21:12 336
23:17 352
24:2 165
25:29 208

Numbers
1:1 139
1:45 10
1:46 10
1:51 171
2:32–33 1
3:2–4 241
3:45 12
4:1–49 11
6:2 292
6:5 292
6:6–12 296
6:9–10 294
6:9 293
6:10 293
6:11 293
6:12 293
6:13 292
6:14–15 293
6:18 291
6:20 291
9:1–14 139
11 25
21:18 74

Index of Scripture and Ancient Writers

Deuteronomy
  12:3 351
  13:18 350, 351, 364
  14–18 25
  21:22–23 318
  26:1–15 182
  26:13 363
  28–32 95

Joshua
  1–8 23
  4:9 12
  4:20 12
  6 12, 13
  6:26 61
  7 12
  9–11 23
  15:61 76
  17:17 12
  17:18 12
  18 23
  20 23
  22:1–6 12
  24 23

Judges
  1:16–36 12
  1:16 13
  2–3 23
  4–5 23
  4:17–22 13
  6–9 23
  8:22–29:57 13
  11 13, 23
  12:1–6 13
  13–16 23
  17–18 23
  19–21 13, 23

Ruth
  3 28

1 Samuel
  1–15 23
  2:23f. 337
  2:23–25 337
  3:1–4:1 14
  4 14
  5 14
  7 14
  7:1 14
  7:2 14
  7:15–8:2 14
  8:4–22 14
  9:1 14
  9:2 14
  9:3–10:24 14
  13:8–15 14
  14:18–22 14
  14:31–35 14
  15 14
  15–31 24
  16:1–3 14
  18–20 14

2 Samuel
  1 24
  3 24
  6 14
  6:6–8 186
  6–7 24
  7:13 14
  7:18 159
  7:23 337
  9–1 Kgs 2 5
  11–20 24
  24 24

1 Kings
  2–3 24
  5:2 159
  5–11 24
  11 14
  11–12 25
  11:29–40 5
  14–16 25
  16:29–22:40 6
  17:1–2 Kgs 11 25

2 Kings
  2:11 241
  16 27
  16:1–20 6
  18:1–23 27
  21:1–23:37 27
  22:1–23:30 7
  24–25 27

2 Chronicles
  32:23 160
  33:10–11 160
  33:13 160
  34:1–35:27 7

Ezra
  3:10–13 15

Nehemiah
  8 28
  8–13 15

Esther
  7 28

Job
  19 28
  41–42 28

Psalms
  2:7 271
  6:2 159
  20:76:2 159
  29 28
  37:24 57
  37:32 58
  37:33 59
  47 28
  74 28
  93 28

Proverbs
  4–10 28

Ecclesiastes
  3–4 28

Song of Songs
  3–4 28

Isaiah
  2:2–4 223
  5:1 160
  6–8 27
  8:2 171
  11:4 161
  36–39 27
  37:3 160
  38:21 160
  40 27
  40–55 8
  40:3 76
  42–45 27
  47 27
  49:1–6 269
  53:5 160
  56 28
  58:6 243
  61:1 242
  61:2 242
  65–66 96

Jeremiah
  1:5 269
  2:7 165
  4 27
  7 27
  15:1 165
  17–20 27
  19:19 112
  23:1–8 8
  23:31 8
  26:18 171
  29–31 27

Lamentations
  1:1 165
  2:20 112
  4:10 112

  5:17–18 171

Ezekiel
  1 27
  4–5 27
  34–37 27
  36:22–27 238
  40 27
  40–48 8

Daniel
  7 86, 87, 89, 90, 101, 235, 283
  7:1–8 86
  7:1–2 86
  7:7–8 86
  7:9–12 86
  7–12 87, 95
  7:13–14 86
  7:17 86
  7:23–25 87
  7:24 86
  7:25 86
  7:26 86
  7:27 86
  8 86, 90, 101
  8:1–7 81
  8:2 86
  8:9–13 86, 87
  8:11–14 97
  8:13–14 86
  8:20–22 81
  8:22–25 87
  8:27 86
  9 86, 87
  9:11 165
  9:20–23 86
  9:24–27 86
  9:27 97
  10:1–12:13 80
  10:1 80
  10:2–21 80
  10:2–9 86
  10–12 81, 82, 86, 87, 90

  10:13 86
  10:20–21 86
  11:2–45 86
  11:2 81
  11:3 81
  11:5–45 81
  11:14 90
  11:15–20 81
  11:21–45 81
  11:31 97
  11:33 91
  11:45 81
  12 17
  12:1–3 81
  12:1 86
  12:3 91
  12:11 97
  12:11–12 86

Hosea
  1–2 25
  6:7 164
  8 25
  11:1 271

Joel
  2 28

Amos
  1–2 25
  5:26–27 74
  5:26 75
  5:27 75
  8 25
  9:11–12 286

Obadiah
  1 28

Jonah
  4 28

Micah
  3–4 25

Index of Scripture and Ancient Writers 425

Habakkuk
 1:13 57
 1:15 57
 2 28
 2:5–6 58
 2:17 58

Zechariah
 1:5–23 22
 3–5 27
 3–4 8
 8:4 171
 12:11 7
 14 8, 28, 224, 285
 14:2 160

Malachi
 1:7–8 98
 1:12 98

NEW TESTAMENT

Matthew
 2:4 22
 3:11 237
 3:13–17 239
 4:1–11 241
 4:1 241
 5:20 22
 7:29 22
 8:1–4 22
 8:2–4 242
 8:11 223
 8:19 22
 8:28–34 289, 299, 316
 9:3 22
 9:10–13 22
 9:14–17 22
 12:1–8 22
 12:9–14 22
 12:38 22
 12:43–45 297
 12:46–50 283
 13:52 22

 13:53–58 283
 13:55–56 280
 15:1–26 22
 15:1–20 289
 15:1 22, 23
 16:1–12 22
 16:21 22
 16:28–17:8 240
 17:1 240
 17:2 240
 17:10 22
 20:18 22
 21:12–13 224
 21:15 22
 21:23 22
 21–25 22
 21:45 22
 21:57 22
 22:15–22 22
 22:16 19
 22:23 20
 22:35 23
 22:42 244
 23:2 23
 23:13 23
 23:15 23, 363
 23:23 23
 23:25 23
 23:27 23
 23:29 23
 26:1–28:11 22
 26:1–27:2 22
 26:1–5 228
 26:3 22
 26:17–20 228, 289
 26:26 224
 26:28 224, 226, 228
 26:29 223
 27:41 22
 27:55–56 311

Mark
 1:8 237
 1:9–13 239
 1:11 271

 1:21–28 320
 1:22 22
 1:23–27 299
 1:23 298
 1:24 297
 1:25 298
 1:26 298
 1:34 298
 1:40–45 22, 242
 2:6 22
 2:15–17 22
 2:16 22
 2:18–22 22
 2:23–28 22
 3:1–6 22
 3:6 19
 3:21 281
 3:31–35 281, 283
 5:1–20 289, 316
 5:1–17 299, 325
 5:1–13 321
 5:14–17 300
 5:25–34 321
 6:1–6 283
 6:3 280
 6:13 308
 7:1–23 22, 289
 7:5 22
 7:31–37 321
 8:11–21 22
 8:22–26 317, 322
 8:31 22
 9:2–8 240
 9:2 240
 9:14–29 322, 325
 10:2–12 22
 10:33 22
 11–13 22
 11:15–17 224
 11:18 22
 11:27 22
 12:13–17 22
 12:13 19
 12:18 20
 12:25 304

12:32 22	8:2–3 308, 320	22:66 22
12:35 22, 244	8:2 297	23:10 22
12:38 22	8:3 307	
14:1–15:31 22	8:19–21 283	*John*
14:1–15:1 22	8:26–39 289, 316	1:19 22
14:1–2 225	8:26–37 299	2:13–17 224
14:1 22, 228	9:22 22	6:30–58 226
14:3–9 308, 323	9:27–36 240	6:60–71 227
14:9 308	10:25 23	7:2–10 283
14:12–17 228, 289	10:31 22	7:32 22
14:12–16 225	11:24–26 297	7:45 22
14:22 224	11:37–41 22	11:47 22
14:24 224, 226, 228	11:45 23	11:49 22
14:25 223	11:46 23	11:51 22
14:43 22	11:52 23	11:57 22
14:53 22	11:53 23	12:10 22
15:1 22	11:54 23	18:3–19:21 22
15:31 22	13:28 223	*Acts*
15:42–47 323	13:29 223	1:5 272
15:42–16:8 308	14:3 23	2:33 237
16:1–8 299, 323	15:1 22	2:42–47 225
16:3 305	15:2 22, 23	5:34 368
16:4 304, 305	15:11–32 281	6:9 263
16:5 306	17:14 22	7:58 263
16:9 316	19:28–21:38 22	9:2 273
	19:45–46 224	9:3–6 75
Luke	19:47 22	9:9 273
3:2 22	20:1–24:20 22	9:10–19 273
3:16 237	20:1 22	9:11 273
3:21–22 239	20:19 22	9:17–18 359
4:1–13 241	20:27 20	9:19 273
4:1 241	20:39 22	9:20–22 273
4:14 241	20:41 244	10:9–48 313
4:14–30 242	20:46 22	10:12–14 315
4:16–30 283	22:1–23:5 22	10:14 313
5:12–16 242	22:1 228	11:5–17 313
5:21 22	22:2 22, 228	11:19–26 265
5:29–32 22	22:7–14 228, 289	13:1–3 267
5:30 22	22:15–17 229	13:13–52 242
5:33–39 22	22:15 228	13:38–39 260
6:1–5 22	22:16 228	15:1–35 284
6:6–11 22	22:18 223	15:5 284
6:7 22, 23	22:19 228	15:7–11 313
7:30 23	22:19–20 223, 224	15:13 369
7:36–50 309	22:20 226, 228	15:15 286

15:16–17 286
15:16 281
15:19–24 268
15:22–33 229
18:2 268
18:12 268
18:18 291–94, 371
18:22 268
18:25 257
19:9 273
19:23 273
21:16–36 287
21:17 295
21:17–21 294
21:17–26 371
21:17–36 284
21:22–26 295
21:23–26 292, 294
21:24 294
21:26 294, 295
21:27–28:21 295
22:3 256, 329
22:4 273
22:12–16 273, 359
23:8 20
24:14 273
24:17–19 295
24:22 273
25–26 268
26:15 272

Romans
1:24 253
3:25 226, 372, 373
4 287
7:1–3 370
7:19 253
8:14–15 272
11:26 252
12:1 371
14:13–23 369
14:13 369
14:20 369
15:8 295
15:16 287, 295, 371,

372
15:17 295
15:25–29 295
15:25 295
15:26 372
15:30–33 295
15:31 295
16:1 295

1 Corinthians
4:12 370
5:1–13 369
5–6 287
5:11 369
6:1–11 369
6:15–20 370
6:19 370
7 370
7:7 257
7:8 257
7:14 370
7:16 371
7:17–24 371
7:29–31 369
8 370
8:1–13 369
8:4 369
9:5 257
9:6 257
9:19 370
9:22 274
9:26 274
10:1–4 226
10:14–22 370
10:16–18 370
10:16 223
10:19 370
10:21 370
11:23–33 236
11:23 226
11:24–25 224
11:24 228
11:25 228
12:1–13 370
12:12–31 370

12:17 370
14:1 262
15 315
15:7 283
16:1 372
16:2 372
16:8 372
16:19 268

2 Corinthians
3:12–18 359
11:7 370
11:32–33 267
12:1–4 236
12:2–4 267, 307

Galatians
1:11–12 359
1:12 236
1:14 262, 359
1:15–17 267, 269
1:16–17 359
1:16 272
1:17–18 274
1:17 272
1:18–2:21 284
1:18 228, 236
1:21–24 267
1:23 274
2 229, 265
2:1–10 267
2:8 267
2:11–21 268, 369
3–4 264
3:8 264
3:13 260
3:14 260
3:19 359
4:3–7 359
4:6 272
4:10 368
4:11 368
4:12–20 368
4:21–30 368
4:25 276

6:9 368

Philippians
3:5 262
3:6 262
3:7 275

1 Thessalonians
1:1 229
1:2 229
2:9 370
5:1–2 369

2 Thessalonians
1:1 229

1 Timothy
2:13–15 308

James
2:14–26 287
5:7–8 287
5:11 318
5:14 308

1 Peter
5:12 229

2 Peter
3:4 287
3:12 287
3:15–16 287

Revelation
16:16 7

APOCRYPHA

Baruch
4:1 100

2 Esdras (cf. 4 Ezra)
14 18

1 Maccabees
1:14 20
1:15 20
1:20–64 16
2:1–9:18 17
2:41 17
4:36–61 17
4:46 18
8 17
10:20 17

2 Maccabees
3:33 372

4 Maccabees
6:28 372
6:29 372
17:20–22 372

Sirach
24:23 99

OLD TESTAMENT
PSEUDEPIGRAPHA

Apocalypse of Abraham
25–27 99

2 Baruch
1–8 84
10:1 84
12:5 84
20:5 84
36–40 89
36–37 85
38:1 89
39:1 89
39–40 85
47:2 84
51:7 100
53 85
54–72 85
55:3 89
56–66 89
56–71 89

67 85
68 85
69–72 85
70–71 89
73 85, 89
76:4 84
77:13–16 100

1 Enoch
1–36 83
1–16 95
1–5 95
1:8 99
6–11 83, 101
9 97
10:18 99
12–36 83
12–16 98
14:8–12 271
17–19 95
20–36 95
26:1 98
36–37 96
37–71 83, 95
37–42 90
37:1–2 99
72–82 95
83–84 95
85–90 82, 85, 87, 91, 95
89:73–74 98
90:6–7 91
90:6 98
90:9b–16 82
91:11–17 83, 95
91:11 92, 98
91:13 98
92–105 83
92:1 99
93:1–10 83, 95
93:2 87
93:6 88, 98
93:7–8 88, 98
93:9 98
93:10 92, 99, 100

93:13 88
94–104 95
98:9 99
99:2 93
99:10 99
103 97
104:12–13 92
104:13 99

4 Ezra
3:1 84
11–12 85, 88, 89
12:10–11 85
12:11 88
12:19–24 85
13 88, 89
14:37–48 101

Psalms of Solomon
8:13 98

Testament of Job
46:1–51:4 319
52:8–12 318

Testament of Moses
2–4 84
5–9 84
5–6 97
5:2 93
6:6–7 84
6:6 84
8:5 97
8–9 84
23 88

DEAD SEA SCROLLS
AND RELATED
TEXTS

1QpHab
2:1–3 57
5:8–12 57
8:8–13 58
8:17–9:2 60

9:8–12 59
11:5–8 59
12:7–9 58

1QS
8:12–16 76

4Q379
fr. 22 col. 2 61

4QMMT
B1–3 66
C7–9 67
C9–11 67
C26–32 67

11Q64
11–13 318

CD
1:5–7 73
1:8–11 73
1:10 69
5:6–7 98
6:3–11 74
6:4–5 74
6:19 74
7:18–19 75
19:33–34 75
20:11–12 75

pPss A
1–10 III 15–16 57
1–10 IV 8–9 59

Prayer for King Jonathan
B1–9 64

Psalms of Joshua
B 22 II 7–4 61

QpNah
3–4 I 2–4 62
3–4 I 5–6 62
3–4 I 7–8 63

RABBINIC
LITERATURE

Bavli
Avodah Zarah
9a 73
Baba Mesia
85a 19
Baba Qamma
83a 363
Pesachim
57a 19
Semachoth
4:1 285
Yoma
35b 21

Mishnah
Abodah Zarah
3:4 350, 351, 364
3:7 351
5:2 351
Abot
1:1–18 18, 332
1:16 329
1:17 329, 367
1:18 329, 365
2:5 365
13–16 365
Arakhin
5:1 353
8:1 353
9:6 208
Baba Batra
9:7 351
Baba Mesia
7:1 351, 355, 366
8:8 351, 363
Bekhorot
4:4 352
5:3 352
6:6 352
6:9 352
Berakhot
1:1 339, 355, 367

2:1 346
2:5–7 346
2:5 340, 342,
    355, 358, 367
2:6 340, 342,
    355, 358, 366
2:7 340, 342,
    355, 358, 366
5:5 342
6:9 366
Besah
3:2 346, 348,
    355, 358, 364
3:8 348, 355
Eduyyot
5:7 351
7:7 350, 351,
    358, 361
Erubin
4:1–2 343, 347,
    355, 358
4:1 364
4:2 364
6:1–2 344, 347,
    358
6:2 355, 365
8:7 347
10:9 347
10:10 345, 348,
    358
Gittin
1:5 350, 365
4:7 350
6:6 350, 365
7:5 350, 366
Hallah
4:10–11 342
Kelim
5:4 353, 354
Keritot
1:7 19, 352, 353,
    366
Ketubot
1:10 349
7:10 349

Ma'aserot
2:8 346
Makhshirin
1:6 354
3:4 354
Menahoth
8:3–5 297
10:2 352
Miqvaot
4:5 354
Nazir
1:1 292
2:3 349
2:5 293, 294
3:6 293, 349
6:8 293
6:11 349
7:3 294
9:1 284
Nedarim
3:2 294
6:6 349, 355
Niddah
8:2 354
Ohalot
17:5 354
Para
4:3 222
Peah
2:5–6 341, 355,
    366
Pesahim
7:2 345, 348,
    355, 358, 366
Qiddushin
2:7 350
Rosh Hashanah
1:5–6 347, 348
1:7 348
2:7 333, 334
2:8–9 333, 343,
    348
3:8–9 338, 354
Sanhedrin
5:2 351

6:5–6 318
7:2 351
Shabbat
1:4 347
3:3–4 347
16:8 343, 347,
    355, 358, 364
24:5 347
Shebi'it
10:3 342
Sheqalim
3:3 366
Sotah
9:15 367
Sukkah
2:1 345, 355, 366
2:4–5 346, 348
2:5 355
2:7 348, 355
2:8 348, 355
3:8 338, 348
4:9 63, 64
Taanit
2:5 348
3:8–9 348
3:9–10 343, 348
4:6 168
4:7 169
Temurah
7:4 293
Yadayim
3:1 353–55, 358,
    366
Yebamot
16:4 349
16:6 349
16:7 349, 365
Yoma
6:3 348

Tosefta
Pesahim
1:27 367
Pisha
4:13ff. 357

4:14 357
Sanhedrin
  2:6 362
Shevi'it
  4:11 207, 208
Sotah
  13:3 240

Yerushalmi
Horayot
  2:6 336
  3:1 336
Sanhedrin
  7:13 316
Shabbat
  14:3 317
  14:4 317
Sotah
  1:4 317

MIDRASH AND
OTHER RABBINIC
WORKS

Exodus Rabbah
  17:4 319

Genesis Rabbah
  19:9.1–2 164

Lamentations Rabbah
  74.12 341

Pes. de Rab Kahanah
  7 319

Ruth Rabbah
  1:5 319

Parashah 5
  40.1.1 159

Sifre
  351 360

Sifre to Deuteronomy
  43.3.7 171

Sifre to Numbers
  64.1.1 139

CLASSICAL AND
EARLY CHRISTIAN
AUTHORS

Aelius Theon
Prog.
  60 121
  70 121

Cicero
Republic
  6.24 270

Epiphanius
Panarion
  1.29.3–4 281
  2.66.19 281
  3.78.7 281
  3.78.9 281
  3.78.13 281

Protoevangelium of
James
  9.2 281

Eusebius
History
  2.1.1–6 286
  2.23.1–18 284, 296

Herodotus
Histories
  1.5 41, 50
  1.8–14 36
  1.29–44 36
  1.34 49
  1.48 49
  1.85–92 36

1.95 37
1.108–130 37
1.110–113 37
2.139 39
2.172 37
3.27–38 37
3.39–43 38
3.64–66 37
3.80–88 37
3.120–125 38
7.12 49
7.14 49
7.45–52 40
7.57 49
7.101–104 40
7.140 49
7.209–210 40
7.220 49
8.36–39 49
8.104–106 37
8.109 49
9.16 41

Hippolytus
Didascalia of the
  Twelve Apostles
  9.26.6 311
  16.12.4 311

Homer
Iliad
  18.497–508 35
  23.483–87 35

Irenaeus
Against Heresies
  1.26.1–2 281
  2.29 315
  4.18 315
  5.7–16 315
  5.36 315

Josephus
Antiquities
  1–11 118

1 261	36 135	2.174 115
1.7 107	80 135	2.184–203 115
4.14–59 135	85–103 109	2.185 115
4.326 241	126–129 135	2.192–203 118
6.33–34 135	189–335 109	2.195 115
8.209 135	191f. 330	2.198 115
12–20 122	197 136	2.225 135
12.240 20	208–209 109	2.228–231 22
12.241 20	275–308 109	2.258–265 19
12.248–256 16	369–372 109	2.286 135
12.265 17	412 109	2.303 135
13.288–298 18	421 318	2.345–404 121
13.372–383 63	427 136	2.408–410 134
15.471 22		2.556 134
16.187 17	*War*	2.562 135
18.34–35 129	1–3 122	2.562–568 20
18.35–89 129	1.1–30 110, 119	2.564 19
18.35 20, 129	1.1–3 123, 134	2.565 19
18.36–38 129	1.2–3 115, 122	2.572–576 209
18.52 129	1.2 121	2.585 122
18.53–54 129	1.3 122	2.590–594 297
18.60 117	1.6 122	2.595 135
18.65–84 129	1.9 122	2.614–625 109
18.88–95 267	1.27 111	2.628 136
18.89 129, 137	1.31 108	2.648–651 135
18.90–95 19	1.31–40 108	3.35–40 209
18.95 20	1.31–35 16	4.128 135
18.109–119 267	1.33 16	4.133 135
18.170 130	1.70 17	4.137 111
19.293f. 294	1.96–114 18	4.224 19
20.6–14 19	1.109 135	4.225 19
20.9.1 284, 285	1.117 135	4.314–344 108
20.15 20	1.138 115	4.320–323 135
20.16 20	1.152–154 19	4.326–327 108
20.34–48 273	1.431–437 20	4.351 108
20.189 17	1.648–655 19	4.356 108
20.237 17	2–3 109, 119	5.194 22
20.246 17	2.49–50 108	5.362–419 121
20.247–251 20	2.117 130	5.392–393 112
	2.118 114	6.180–181 108
Life	2.119–161 131	6.200 111
5 136	2.123 296	6.202 111
11 236	2.165 20	6.205 111
12 135	2.169–177 113	6.206 111
27 109	2.172 115	6.214 111, 112

6.301–302 112
7.46–53 108
7.157 108
7.219–243 108
7.267 108
7.324–325 112
7.387 112
7.420–432 16
7.420–436 108
7.437–446 19

Justin
  1 Apology
    66.3 224

Origen
  Commentary on Matthew
    10:17 281

Philo of Alexandria
  Leg.
    299–305 113

Pliny
  Ep.
    7.17 121
    10.90 116

Pliny the Elder
  Natural Hist.
    5.73 131

Plutarch
  Precepts of Statecraft
    801a–804c 121
    813a–816a 121

pseudo–Clementine
  Recognitions
    11.35.3 286
    I.43–71 286

Suetonius
  Tib.
    41 130

Tacitus
  Ann.
    1.80 130
    2.85 129
    15.44 131

Thucydides
  History
    1.2–15 44
    1.20–22 42, 50
    1.22 50
    1.32–43 47
    2.3 49
    2.37 45
    2.47 48
    2.52 49
    2.60–64 45
    2.65 45
    3.37–40 47
    3.82–85 43
    4.78 ff. 44
    4.104–108 44
    5.26 44
    5.26.5 42, 44
    7.50 48

NEW TESTAMENT APOCRYPHA AND PSEUDEPIGRAPHA

Gospel According to Mary
  9.10 313
  9.19–20 313
  10.6–20 314
  17.9–19.1 315

www.ingramcontent.com/pod-product-compliance
Lightning Source LLC
Chambersburg PA
CBHW021350290426
44108CB00010B/185